HOW FRANCE
BUILT HER CATHEDRALS

HOW FRANCE BUILT HER CATHEDRALS

ELIZABETH BOYLE O'REILLY

ISBN: 978-93-89701-32-6

Published: -

LECTOR HOUSE LLP
E-MAIL: lectorpublishing@gmail.com

HOW FRANCE
BUILT HER CATHEDRALS

Soissons Cathedral. The Transept's Southern Arm (c. 1180)

HOW FRANCE
BUILT HER CATHEDRALS

A STUDY IN THE TWELFTH
AND THIRTEENTH CENTURIES

BY

ELIZABETH BOYLE O'REILLY

Honorary Member of the *Société Française d'Archéologie*
Author of "Heroic Spain" Etc.

ILLUSTRATED WITH DRAWINGS BY
A. PAUL DE LESLIE

CONTENTS

CHAPTER III

SOME OF THE PRIMARY GOTHIC CATHEDRALS: NOYON, SENLIS, SENS, LAON, SOISSONS

CHAPTER IV

NOTRE DAME OF PARIS AND OTHER CHURCHES OF THE CAPITAL

CHAPTER V

ERA OF THE GREAT CATHEDRALS, CHARTRES, RHEIMS, AMIENS

CHAPTER VI

SIX OF THE LESSER GREAT CATHEDRALS: BOURGES, BEAUVAIS, TROYES, TOURS, LYONS, LE MANS

CHAPTER VII

PLANTAGENET GOTHIC ARCHITECTURE

CHAPTER VIII

GOTHIC IN THE MIDI

CHAPTER IX

THE GOTHIC ART OF BURGUNDY

CHAPTER X

GOTHIC ART IN NORMANDY

Monastic architecture best expression of Norman character—Nor-mandy, like Burgundy, was a land of monasteries—Bernay's ab-bey church an ancestress of Norman Romanesque (note)—Bec Abbey, the Cluny of Normandy—Lanfranc made the school of Bec world-noted—At Bec, St. Anselm began the philosophical movement of the Middle Ages—William of Volpiano pioneer in the rebirth of architecture in the duchy—Jumièges, the first Nor-man church of architectural pretension, begun 1040—Only ves-

LIST OF ILLUSTRATIONS

HOW FRANCE
BUILT HER CATHEDRALS

INTRODUCTION

" E may live without architecture, and worship without her, but we cannot remember without her. How cold is all history, how lifeless all imagery, compared to that which the living nation writes and the uncorrupted marble bears. There are but two strong conquerors of the forgetfulness of men, Poetry and Architecture, and the latter in some sort includes the former, and is mightier in its reality; it is well to have, not only what men have thought and felt, but what their hands have handled and their strength wrought and their eyes beheld, all the days of their life."[1]

So wrote John Ruskin in one of his flashes of genius, and never was word truer. Architecture is the living voice of the past. Architecture is history. By architecture the forefathers from whom we come relate to us their progress in knowledge, their prowess in handicrafts, their economic conditions, their sorrows, their rejoicings, their aspirations. They wrote it down, those men and women whose blood is our blood, on great stone pages of perennial beauty for us to read — *if only we would*. By architecture we are linked in a grand solidarity with all that has gone before, with the proud periods of history that thrill us as we read, and with the tragic outbreaks of the oppressed that sadden our spirit.

Whenever men have set themselves to forget this solidarity, their first act has been to fling themselves in frenzy on cathedral and city hall. In 1914 they forgot it, and mighty Rheims fell. They forgot that Bamburg had learned its imagery from Rheims, that German Norbert, revered of St. Bernard, had helped France in the days when Gothic art was in formation, that he died bishop of Magdeburg, and Magdeburg is a Primary Gothic cathedral in the land which frankly called the new architecture *opus francigenum*. Would the civic halls of Noyon, Arras, St. Quentin, and Ypres lie in ruins if Frankfort and Lübeck had remembered?

In 1793, man again thought to set up a barrier between himself and his past, and he shattered the art treasures of a thousand years and tore down the cathedrals of Cambrai, Arras, and Avranches; he tore down Cluny, the greatest Romanesque church in the world, Cluny the civilizer, that had removed from agriculture

---

[1] Ruskin, *The Seven Lamps of Architecture*.

its stigma as serfs' work. Man fancied that to shatter and demolish was to build.

Again in 1562, a date most tragic in the annals of Gothic architecture, men tried again to rear a wall of hate between themselves and the generations gone before, and the cathedral of Orléans met the fate of Cluny and Cambrai, and from end to end of France images were decapitated, and ancestors' tombs wrecked impiously—even the tombs of spiritual ancestors who with painful journeyings afoot had brought the gospel light. Whether you go to chapel or to temple to-day, to meetinghouse or to cathedral, whether you worship under the open sky, be you a reader of Marx or of Aquinas, you were robbed most piteously of your patrimony in 1562, in 1793, in 1914.

How is it to be prevented again? By trying to make the monuments of the past loved, by relating the tale of their building, by telling the life story of the builders. If we know them we must surely revere them, and when we have learned to know and to love, we have learned to be liberal. Archæology is *to teach us to remember*. Those who have gone before have passed on to us cathedral and town hall; it is our obligation to transmit them intact to those who come after. They are not ours to destroy. Art is the high-water mark reached by civilization; art does not speak in English, or in German, or in the Latin tongue, but in a language understood of all peoples and all times. To destroy a great monument of the past is to betray civilization. It was proved in 1914 that erudition is not safeguard enough, nor is enthusiasm, sighs 1793, nor purpose to reform, admits 1562. We must comprehend intelligently our own personal solidarity with the past. We must never look at a noble building without proudly realizing that we had a hand in its making. Battles then can rage around cathedrals without danger of their destruction. As in golden amber, the past will preserve them, the past which is yours and mine and everyone's heritage.

It is a right instinct which makes a man treasure the home he has had transmitted to him through several generations. How much more—when loyalty is roused by an XVIII-century or a XVII-century habitation—should emotion be felt for what was reared from 1140 to 1270 by the very generations who began for us of to-day most of the big things we value: our universities, our literature, our political freedom, our prosperous trade.

Now in the making of these infinitely precious things, France played the leading role. Put partisan feeling aside and acknowledge it honestly. "I believe," said Ruskin, in a lecture at Edinburgh, in 1853, even before the new science of mediæval archæology was formulated, "that the French nation in the XII and XIII centuries was the greatest nation in the world, and that the French not only invented Gothic architecture, but carried it to its noblest developments."

French Gothic churches are a fountainhead, and should rank first. Because of them we have Westminster, Ely, and Lincoln, we had Tintern, Melrose, Mellifont, Holycross. They built the Burgos, Toledo, León, Seville, and Belem, which have given wings to the soul of the Peninsula. Because of the French cathedrals we have Cologne, Magdeburg, and Halberstadt, Vienna, Prague, Upsala, Siena, Florence, and Milan.

By her lyrics, her epics, and her architecture, France was the inspiration of Europe in the XII and XIII centuries. With his sword, the crusader carried compass and rule. Those indefatigable wanderers, Cluny, Cîteaux, and the men of Prémontré and Chartreuse carried with them the chisel and the Book. Then as now the commercial traveler was a valiant propagandist; in 1181 a cloth merchant of Assisi, returned from trading in France, where he had seen the cathedral of Lyons rising, or perhaps that of Paris, or that of Poitiers, and he had passed under wonderful new-imaged portals in the Midi and in Burgundy; so, in memory of beautiful things, he chose to call the son born to him, Francis, and the boy grew up to love and to chant the lyrics of France and named himself "God's little troubadour."

Backward and forward has moved the ebb and flow of races and their arts. When Celts from conquered Britain passed over to Armorica they carried with them the Arthurian cycle; Teutonic tribes, strong in bone and tissue, poured into Gaul a very avalanche; masterful Norsemen populated the seacoasts; and before the recording of time the Oriental and the Latin had made their home in the land between the northern seas and the big inland water of commerce. Does such history seem too remote to be of emotional value? Are personalities lacking? Not so in the missionary days of Columbanus and Benedict, first hewers of the cathedrals' foundation blocks, for never came a great movement of building activity that did not tread in the steps of spiritual regeneration. Your forefathers and my forefathers came into France to help her, to bring her art and letters in her dark hour. They came to teach and they came to learn, to succor and to find refuge. They came in the persons of Celtic Columbanus, Brieuc, Malo, Fiacre, Malachy, and holy Laurence buried at Eu, as English Alcuin, Stephen Harding, John of Salisbury, and Saint Edmund Rich buried at Pontigny. They came as German Radegund and the saintly Bruno and Norbert, as Italian Benedict, Fortunatus, Hildebrand, William of Volpiano, Lanfranc, Anselm, Aquinas, and Bonaventure, as Spanish Dominic, and Portuguese Anthony. They came from Egypt with Maurice and his Thebans, from the Levant with Irenæus and Giles, from Hungary with Martin the soldier. And the story of each one of them is recorded in the churches that stand in France to-day. Without architecture we would have forgotten them.

With the ebbing and flowing of the tide in the affairs of men, a day arrived when the big people and the little people of Normandy, Poitou, Anjou, and Flanders passed in large numbers into Great Britain and Ireland in the wake of the Conqueror and of Henry Plantagenet, so that the very names we bear are those of the cathedral builders.

Who has not watched the widening ripples of water spread from a center? Even so is each one of us a center whence in ever-widening circles stretch out our progenitors, embracing more and more men, more and more women, rippling over the pitiful barricades of 1793, sweeping over the factions of 1562, till by the time the widening ripple has reached the age of St. Louis, the age of Suger, it is scientifically impossible that we, in our very own forefathers, were not building some of the eighty cathedrals and three hundred great minsters with which France was then clothing herself as with a white mantle of churches. We were chatelaine, and burgher's wife, we were villein's daughter and knight's son, and side by side we harnessed ourselves to carts and dragged in the blocks for the tower at Chartres and the belfry at Rouen, and the canticles we sang during our voluntary servitude passed into the stones and are still chanting there—*if only we would listen*. No visionary notion this, but science and history. By architecture we remember.

Of our kin was the bishop who sacrificed his revenue to rear God's house. Of our kin were the architects, masters of the living stone, who with inspiration conceived their shrines of Notre Dame and were trained soundly enough in mason craft to achieve their dreams; of our kin were the artisans who put up the serene images at cathedral doors for the edification of the people, and chiseled with warm, loving touches the running bramble of the roadside. Even botany is to be learned in mediæval cathedrals. Not a leaf that grows in Champagne to-day but was carved on the walls of Rheims seven hundred years ago. Against the big capitals of Paris Cathedral they laid the broad plantain leaf of the marshy Oise, then, seeing around them that indigenous acanthus, the uncurling fern, they carved it, too, and as they grew adept with chisel they wrought ivy and vine leaf, parsley and holly, and in time, intoxicated with their skill, they undercut the rich foliage and serrated the lobes and curled the leaf edges, till summer ran riot in stone and the architectural line was well-nigh lost sight of in sheer joy of nature's glad livery.

The cathedrals of France are an enduring appeal to man's high faculty of imagination. In them we go crusading again. We scale the walls of Constantinople with doughty Bishop Nivelon, builder of Soissons Cathedral, we are ransomed from Saracen captivity with Bishop Albéric, builder of Rheims. We repent of our black feudal deeds with Fulk Nerra, and when we have finished our footsore penances in Holy Land, we punish ourselves in our purses, raising costly abbeys in Anjou and Touraine. On our Eastern pilgrimage we have seen visions of Oriental color, and, remembering them, we lighten our sober churches of the north with translucent mosaic tapestries. We dot our Western land with circular Holy Sepulcher temples. It is said that Suger, builder of the first great Gothic church in the world, maker of jeweled windows over which science sighs in despair of emulation, used eagerly to inquire of travelers returned from the East had they seen aught, even in St. Sophia itself, to surpass his St. Denis'. We are rightly sure that our new art surpasses all others. We may borrow, but our borrowings are creations.

By architecture in happy promiscuity we crowd to the international fairs of Champagne. We elbow and we jostle to see what our diligent brothers, the art-loving Flemish burghers, have brought for exchange, or what things beautiful the merchants from south of the Alps have to barter. To-day, at Troyes, we are astounded by the gathering of art treasures in that lesser-known city, and we wonder at the mighty rampart walls at Provins. *Then we remember*. It is architecture that will not let us forget what efficient traders we were in the XIII century.

By architecture we are Benedictines at Cluny, white monks at Fontenay, of Prémontré at Braine. Again we pace in meditative cloisters, we tuck up our robes to delve in mother earth to make the desert bloom, we illumine parchment pages, we teach the plain-chant to children, we cast bells, each with its own entity, each a living voice for the people, named with its own name.

By architecture we are one of the thousands athirst for knowledge, who gather at the feet of abstruse debaters in the schools of Bec, Auxerre, Rheims, Orléans, Laon, Chartres and Paris, king's son seated on the rush-strewn pavements next to peasant's son, both equally convinced that the most thrilling of all sciences are philosophy and theology. Books are scarce; as yet no printing press; we must wander far to gather crumbs of learning; our strong young brains are intact, prepared for service by long ages of active bone and muscle; with avidity we seize on problems so knotty that the learned ones of 1920 fear to touch them. "The time of big theories is the time of big results." It is we, in the person of the Scholastics who built Paris Cathedral, and Laon, the intellectual,—churches disciplined, sober and strong. It is we the multitudinous scholars of the Middle Ages who built Chartres, the wise mystic, and opalescent Auxerre, and Châlons on the Marne of Victory. And lest the hungry generations tread us down, we inscribed our loved subtleties on their walls, and at their portals placed images of the Liberal Arts.

By architecture we join one side or the other in the eternal struggle of Might and Right. Sometimes in atonement we spend the revenues secured by heedless Might on minster or cathedral. By pain and struggle we have won our city charter, and we are proud to record in God's sight and man's what thrifty burgesses we are, what trained journeymen. To work is to pray, say the cathedral windows set up by furriers, butchers, vintagers, and farm laborers. To work is as fine a thing as to fight at Roncevaux and Mansurah, as did our next-door donor neighbor here. The little people of the Lord are as grateful in his sight as the noble *prud'hommes*. *Le bon Dieu* likes to be shown how a tailor cuts his cloth and a baker bakes his bread just as well as to be entertained with pilgrimage adventures or the story of a canonized saint. Are we not saints in the making if only we can get the better of that prowling felon, the devil, whom we have set up over our church door with pitchfork and caldron as a warning to the unwary?

"O men and women of to-day"—appeal the windows at Chartres and Bourges and Tours—"you whose blood is our blood, who without our struggle would have no ordered government, no self-ruling cities, no trade to bind land with land in the sanity of peace, no arts and crafts, why not learn to read our story? There are those unable to decipher a line of our illumined pages who will assure you that we were sunk in gross superstition, that our sole religion was the worship of bits of cloth and bone. Yes, even from the halls founded by good Robert de Sorbon (in order that youth with its lean purse might get a free education) the erudites marshal against us every human frailty of our hardy, enterprising times. And yet, in unparalleled marvels of stone and glass we have recorded the deepest sentiments of mankind. But having eyes, they see not. Come then, you, and interpret us. Come, and through us, *remember*."

Each great cathedral is pleading to us by the alluring half-smile of its angels, by the dignified images of reverent personages at its entrances, by each gargoyle, each faithful guardian that has craned his neck for ages to keep rain water from the precious walls. Cease to be so superior to the legends and dreams we set forth, they seem to be saying. We know just as well as you that the apostle St. Thomas did not have all the adventures raising fairy palaces in India which we put to his credit in our windows and tympanums, even though good Bishop James of Voragine, in his cycle of church feasts, our iconographic chart—*Legenda Aurea*—relates it. The holy Jerome, close to the desert and the origin of things, real and apocryphal, warned us not to be too credulous. But symbols and legends are the breath of art, as art alone realizes through expression, the supersensual visions of mankind. Are there not millions of good Christian folk in India to-day? Her first evangelist builded better than ever we can relate by our imagery.

We are not at all dull, plead the waiting cathedrals. Encyclopædias they call us. Yes, we had our little weakness for symmetry, for the mystic beauty of numbers, for gathering into "Mirrors" all the knowledge of the world. But how admirable is our Mirror of Morals, with virtues and vices contrasted; how interesting our Mirrors of Nature and of History that tell the story from Genesis to Revelations, and that set the marvels of the skies and man's dumb fellow creatures, the beasts, side by side on the walls of the house of worship, with David and Isaias, St. Peter and St. Paul, Charlemagne and Louis. And our Mirror of Knowledge—how profound it is: not as enemies but as allies would it show forth science and religion. We are no more dull than the Bible is dull, than the *Divina Commedia* is dull. We satisfy the subtlest intellects; alike the lettered and the unlettered enjoy us.

Each French cathedral and each minster makes its own special plea. Lyons reminds us, in windows of apocalyptic radiance, that her first bishops came from John the Apostle, that Christian blood flowed in her forum as generously as in Rome's Coliseum. Of the very stones of the Amphitheater, hallowed by her martyrs, is her cathedral built, and the architectural methods of the north and the south are welded here in the ancient central city of Gaul whence rayed out the linking highroads of Rome.

At Tours, the charity of Martin to a beggar is recorded many a time, for it civilized middle Europe. Slow, steady, and deep were the accumulations of culture by the Loire of measured horizons and classic restraint. A tower named of Charlemagne recalls that Saxon Alcuin filled the schoolrooms of St. Martin's Abbey. A chiseled tomb reminds us that here worked the last sculptor of the Middle Ages (loyal to its humble and profound Christian traditions), as well as the first artists of the imported pagan Renaissance.

At Le Mans and Angers, at Fontevrault, with its tomb of Henry Plantagenet, who gave us our jury system, speak those fighting progressives, the Angevin rulers; and all their love of the arts and of adventure endures in the exotically beautiful development which we call Plantagenet Gothic. An unlettered king is an uncrowned ass, said a X-century count of Anjou.

At Poitiers, city of St. Hilaire who fought the Arians, is the most glorious window in the world—Christ triumphant on the Cross, and again we walk in procession to the strain of Bishop Fortunatus' hymn, and we read the Church Fathers in Greek and Hebrew in Queen Radegund's cloister. Aquitaine's line of troubadour dukes, passionate sinners, and prodigious repenters lives in every church in the old hill city, from the cathedral wherein Aliénor blended the indigenous art of her own Poitou with the Plantagenet suppleness of her Angevin husband, to the cupola-covered abbatial of St. Hilaire, where her son, Richard the Lion-hearted, was installed as duke.

At Caen we live with the Conqueror and Matilda in their penitential abbey-churches, full of thought and purpose, the architecture of hieratic pre-eminence which Normandy passed on to England. At Coutances, the cathedral walls record the Tancreds, so the people say; close by was the eyrie of that eagle brood who set up kingdoms in Italy and the Orient. At Rouen we mutter with the crowd in the market place that a grievous shame it is to burn a saint as a witch, and in reaction, soon we are to rear monuments whose every line is jubilant freedom. At Rheims we are crowned kings in a cathedral so sumptuous that on coronation days it needed no tapestries to adorn its walls. At Clermont and at Vézelay we don the crusaders' insignia with cries of enthusiasm. The lavish art of Bourges tells of Jacques Cœur's largess, the princely merchant who financed the army that rid France of her invaders, just as clearly as the ducal tombs and imagery at Dijon relate the pageantry of the XV-century Burgundian life. The stones of Pontigny tell of Becket the martyr, whose cause impassioned all Christendom, as many a sculptured group and storied window in France relate, and of another great Englishman, Stephen Langton, who passed from this cloistral peace—dividing the Bible into chapters for us—to the Magna Charta struggle in England. *By architecture we remember.*

Until we have seen Albi's aggressive fortress-church what do we really know of the Albigensian heresy, of the disease un-European, antichristian, antisocial, that bred in the precocious civilization of Languedoc? What do we know of that terrible struggle called a crusade, when the greedy barons of the north descended on the Midi (ever brutal and refined), thinking to cure its soul by the sword and with the same blows to carve out for themselves rich principalities? Forever is the story told in the Jacobins' church at Toulouse, in the red cathedral fortress above the Tarn.

All the isolating pride of feudalism is resumed in the ramparts of Carcassonne and Aigues-Mortes, all the frustrated destiny of Narbonne in its vast fragment of a cathedral, all the unbroken links with the Latin are in the sculpture at Arles and St. Gilles, all the immemorial story of *la grande bleu* in Maguelonne's solitary church. *By architecture we remember.*

The Celtic remnant, that in the volcanic-torn uplands of middle France inflicted on Cæsar his sole defeat, lives always in the churches of Auvergne, so stubbornly indigenous, planted so sturdily, contriving decorative beauty from the regional varicolored lava stones. In the granite churches of Brittany endures all the aloof individuality, the sensitive independence, the tenacious traditionalism of the dwellers by the sea in the far-north outpost of France. We have our souls to keep, say the lowly Breton shrines, we have always been too busy doing that to find time to erect great churches. But once our neighbors, the Normans, taught us tower-building, our Celtic imagination leaped *au delà* by their spires, so we raised our royal Kreisker which far out to sea welcomes home our Breton sailors.

Architecture is history. Architecture is what the old Greeks said of history, "philosophy teaching by examples." The cathedrals of France prove that there is no supreme architecture where there is not liberty or the will to attain it. In 1109 the bishop-baron of Noyon granted his city a charter, the first communal written laws on record. In 1145 Noyon began to build the first Gothic cathedral of France. In the Ile-de-France, where from the nation's birth were lived its intensest hours, sprang up the churches which are the most national, the most racially French in character, Noyon, Senlis, Soissons, Laon, Paris.

The history of architecture proves that without a right-minded national pride, ready to make sacrifices in order that it may transmit its high deeds to the future, no mighty monuments rise. In 1214 Bouvines' victory was won and French unity demonstrated. In 1220, not far away, was laid the foundation stone of Amiens Cathedral, the crowning achievement of the national art. A hazard, such juxtaposition? Ah, no. Nothing happens by chance in this science of the builder whose basic forces are long at work in silence. Architecture is the truthteller of history.

The history of France, which in the XII and XIII centuries meant universal history, is written on the walls of the cathedrals built under Philippe-Auguste and his grandson St. Louis, during the full flowering of the new national art. And in the days when France was neither happy nor good nor great, when faith flagged, when a minority's blind greed of gold ended the international fairs, drove out the Jews, overtaxed the clerical church builders, when the crusading enthusiasm ended in a Templars' process, then the structural logic of Gothic architecture turned to pitiless geometry. So proclaim the cold, uninspired XIV-century churches, and few of them ever were built. It seemed almost as if the Gothic cycle had run its course. The XII century had seen its rise; the XIII century its apotheosis; the XIV century its decline. Was the last word said? Churches are not built by generations that live in ceaseless war, in misrule, or under a foreign yoke.

There was to be another chapter for the Gothic tale. Aspiration was born again, national pride lifted its head and art flowered. Not from beyond the mountains or the sea came the needed missionary this time, nor from a Carolingian palace, nor out of Norman and Burgundian cloister. No saint-king was to lead now, but only a young girl from a peasant hamlet.

When Jeanne d'Arc broke the spell of foreign invasion, when she gave France a new soul, then all over the land rose that pæan of rejoicing which we call Flamboyant Gothic art, for verily it flamed up with joy. Never will you see an arch of double curvature, accoladed, soaring to its triumphal finial, never will you gaze at radiant belfries rising richer and richer with each story, never will you pray beneath a late-Gothic pageantry picture window with its mullions swaying in exaltation, but the thought of the Maid of Orleans and her mission will come to you. This Flamboyant art may run riot in details like any modern, but it remains true in its essentials to the Middle Ages. Forever will it tell of the freeing of France from foreign rule, even as the academic Rayonnant phase sets forth the lowered ideals of Philippe le Bel, or the ampleness of XIII-century Gothic, the creative age of Louis IX and his augmenting grandfather. No regional schools were there in the last manifestations of the national art; they built the same at Albi as at Rouen, at Bordeaux as at Lyons, for an entire people shared the same feeling of recovered self-respect.

You can learn to read it by yourself, learn to *remember*, if only you are not repelled by that stiff word "archæology." Just what generation made Dijon's crypt and Morienval's ambulatory, put the masonry roofs on the Caen abbatials, chiseled the column statues at the doors of Angers, Le Mans, and Chartres, made of Bourges' procession path a heavenly way of ruby, sapphire, emerald, and topaz, raised the tower at Senlis, paid tribute to St. Cecilia's gentleness in the white imagery of Albi's grim fortress—that is archæology. Archæology tells how Cluny lifted up a prostrate Christendom, how the Normans conquered England, how Abbot Suger reformed himself, how Bernard of Clairvaux exhorted Europe, how the Lion-hearted went crusading as had his fascinating mother before him, how Simon de Montfort won the Midi, how the wily Philippe-Auguste enlarged his domain, province by province—and all the while most of the Gothic cathedrals of France laid their foundations—and how the *bon-saint-homme-roy*, truest lover of the builders' art, sat under an oak tree, dispensing justice at first hand, with his loyal Joinville seated close beside him. That is archæology. It is written down clearly on great stone pages of perennial beauty for us to read—*if only we will*. A little knowledge of construction's laws is needed to show us how to see. A little more of history to guide us when to feel. If to love we must know, to know we must set ourselves to learn. Even in these days of easy motor travel one cannot go about book-laden. But there are open libraries in French cities where an inquirer is courteously lent the monographs on the town's monuments, or the big folios that picture the storied windows. It has, therefore, appeared advisable to give, with each cathedral, a list of its biographies, for they may be of use some rainy afternoon in France.

It seems almost unnecessary to remind ourselves that in the XII and XIII centuries the Church of Europe—barring the Greek schism—was one and united, save for the quarrels inseparable from all manifestations of mankind's history, and that the Protestant of to-day descends from the same mediæval forefathers as does the Catholic, from the same builders of cathedrals, crusaders, feudal proprietors, and commune winners. To refuse sympathy to the two best centuries of the Middle Ages because, three hundred years later, occurred a break in western Christendom is as illogical as the attitude of those historians who would liken the religious movement of the XVI century to the antisocial outcrop of Oriental dualism called the Albigensian heresy.

Let us then, with open minds, turn to this art of the builder, "the strongest, proudest, most orderly, most enduring of the arts of men that if once well done will stand more strongly than the unbalanced rocks, more prevalently than the crumbling hills; the art which is associated with all civic pride and sacred principle; with which men record their power, satisfy their enthusiasm, make sure their defense, define and make dear their habitation."[2]

---

[2] Ruskin, *Sesame and Lilies.*

CHAPTER I

WHAT IS GOTHIC ARCHITECTURE?[3]

Gothic architecture the logical fulfillment of Romanesque—Origin
of Romanesque architecture—Romanesque basilicas modified
by the liturgy—Horrors of the IX and X centuries in France—
Rebirth of the builders' energy after the year 1000—Cluny, the
civilizing force of the X and XI centuries—Various regional Romanesque schools of France—Normandy, Burgundy, Auvergne,
Poitou, Languedoc, Provence, and the Franco-Picard school—
Birth of Gothic art—An undecided question where the first diagonal-crossing ribs were used—Germany's and Italy's claims—
Claim of England—The Ile-de-France Picard region, the classic
land of Gothic—Gothic architecture not a layman's revolt against
monkish Romanesque—The architects of the Gothic cathedrals—
No heretical tendencies in Gothic sculpture—Origin of the term
Gothic—XVII- and XVIII-century scorn for Gothic architecture—
Modern French school of mediæval archæology.

Le temps
Où tous nos monuments, et toutes nos croyances
Portaient le manteau blanc de leur virginité
Où sous la main de Christ, tout venait de renaître.

—ALFRED DE MUSSET.

---

[3] Louis Gonse, *L'art gothique* (Paris, Quantin, 1891); Camille Enlart, *Manuel d'archéologie française* (Paris, A. Picard et Fils, 1902), 2 vols., 8vo; *ibid., Monuments religieux de l'architecture romane et de la transition dans la région picarde* (Paris, A. Picard et Fils, 1895), folio; E.
Lefèvre-Pontalis, *L'architecture religieuse dans l'ancien diocèse de Soissons au XIe et au XIIe siècle*
(Paris, Plon, 1894-97), 2 vols., folio; Arthur Kingsley Porter, *Medieval Architecture, Its Origins
and Development* (New York and London, 1909), 2 vols.; C. H. Moore, *Development and Character of Gothic Architecture* (New York, Macmillan, 1904); Anthyme Saint-Paul, "La transition," in *Revue de l'art chrétien*, 1895-96, vols. 44, 45, and 1912-13, pp. 206, 263; R. de Lasteyrie,
L'architecture religieux en France à l'époque romane (Paris, 1912), chap. x; *ibid.*, in *Revue de l'art
chrétien*, 1902, vol. 45, p. 213, his answer to Mr. Bilson, and Mr. Bilson's reply; Louis Régnier,
"Les origines de l'architecture gothique," in *Mém. de la Soc. hist. et archéol. de Pontoise*, vol. 16;
John Bilson, "The Beginnings of Gothic Architecture," in *Journal of the Royal Institute of British Architects*, 3d series, 1898-99, vol. 6, pp. 289, 322, 345; p. 259 (answer to M. de Lasteyrie);
vol. 9, p. 350; Mr. Bilson's papers were given in part in *Revue de l'art chrétien*, 1901, vol. 44,
pp. 369, 462; F. M. Simpson, *A History of Architectural Development* (London, 1909).

BOUT the year 1000 a new spirit animated the art of the builder in France. That rebirth, to which has been given the name Romanesque, held sway for a hundred and fifty years, and had reached its apogee when, in mid-XII century, it was superseded by the architecture we call Gothic. Gothic architecture did not spring up like a mushroom. Like all manifestations of art, it was the logical fulfillment of its predecessor. Romanesque and Gothic were phases of the same art. The dethronement of Romanesque was a voluntary abdication in favor of younger, more efficient leadership: "What is called the birth of Gothic is but the coming of age of Romanesque."

The XI-century monks who built monastic churches cleared the path for the laymen builders of the Gothic cathedrals. With persistency, with courage, the monk architects went forward, seeking a way. And the way sought, the problem on which they concentrated their energies, was how to protect their churches by masonry vaulting without sacrificing amplitude or lighting.[4]

Out of their trials to solve that problem there emerged a new principle of construction, and Gothic architecture was then born. Thrust and counterthrust was the law of its being. Instead of the Romanesque idea of equilibrium by dead load, by sheer mass, which may be called a continuous counterbutting of the vault's thrust, there now was substituted equilibrium by intermittent abutment. By means of diagonal-crossing ribs the vertical and lateral thrusts of the stone roof were collected at fixed points, which points alone had to be counterbutted. Thick walls were a necessity in a Romanesque edifice, if it were to be stable, but in a Gothic building the walls could be made a mere shell, since all the work was done by an active skeleton, a bone structure of stone, consisting of piers, arches, and buttresses.

To define shortly, Gothic architecture is the art of erecting buildings with vaults whose ribs intersect (concentration of load) and whose thrusts are stopped by buttresses (the grounding of the thrusts). The never-ceasing downward and outward thrust of the vaulting is met by an equivalent resistance in pier and buttress and solid earth. Equilibrium results from that well-adjusted opposition of forces.

Since the starting point in the development of Gothic was the vaulting, and how to substitute a stone vault for a wooden roof was the germinal idea of the Romanesque builder, it is no digression to turn to the earlier school, the chrysalis of Gothic. The name "Romanesque" is an affair of yesterday, employed by a French archæologist about 1825. Various local designations had hitherto been used, such as Lombard, or Norman, or Romano-Byzantine, but the term Romanesque for this architecture is as suitable as the name Romance is for the popular languages which, in that same period, were forming out of the corruption of Latin. A definition given by M. Camille Enlart is excellent: "Romanesque art was a product of

---

[4] "Gothic architecture did not arise from a reaction against the principles of Romanesque: on the contrary, it is the natural development of those principles, the logical consequence of the germ idea of the Romanesque builders, which was to protect the naves of their churches by vaults of stone." —R. DE LASTEYRIE.

Rome, animated by a new spirit, and combined with a certain number of elements of barbarian or Oriental origin."

Rome gave the basilica plan to western Europe, which for centuries continued to build its churches as oblong halls with a small apse at one end. The hall, or nave, consisted of a central vessel with side aisles that were divided from it by piers. In the treatment of vaulting and the method of stone laying Romanesque architecture also derived from Rome. Byzantine influences certainly were important, but they affected the decoration more than the plan or the structure; the use of the Byzantine cupola was merely occasional. The Romanesque masters copied the ivories and miniatures of the Eastern Greeks till, in time, they turned to nature for their models, and then their work took on new life and evolved into the glory which is Gothic sculpture.

While some have laid stress on the Oriental influences, rather than those of Rome, in the formation of Romanesque art, others have overemphasized the personality and fantasy introduced into French architecture by the Barbarian invasions. No doubt the influx of new blood added new elements, but since knowledge of the invaders' art is fragmentary, there can be no scientific base for the theory. Composite, certainly, were the causes for the new spirit which animated architecture after the Carolingian day, but it is safe to say that the influence of Rome predominated.

In the course of the centuries the Roman basilica was modified by the Catholic liturgy. For catechumens, or penitents, was made the porch, or narthex, before the western end. Tribunes were built over the side aisles.[5] Increased church ceremonial brought about a development of the choir. The custom of burying the dead in crypts under the main altar originated the raised chancel. Between the choir and the nave the builders began to insert a transverse nave called a transept.[6] Such an enlargement enabled the congregation to approach closer to the altar ceremonies; only the bigger churches built transepts in the XI century. Then the liturgical writers saw in a transept the extended arms of the Cross, and it was in that spirit the XIII-century transepts were made—their symbolism was posterior. The first ambulatories were no doubt built in churches which possessed some revered relic, to facilitate the passage of the pilgrim crowd. (The term ambulatory will be used to designate the continuation of the choir aisle round the apse.) Before long that curving processional path, with radiating apsidal chapels opening from it, was taken to represent the crown of thorns about the Sacred Head. "All things as pertain to offices and matters ecclesiastical be full of divine signification and mysteries, and overflow with a celestial sweetness: if so be that a man be diligent in his study of them, and know how to draw honey from the rock and oil from the hardest stone." So wrote William Durandus, the XIII-century French bishop whose *Rationale*, or treatise on church symbolism, was an inspiration for centuries and, next to the

---

[5] Any raised balcony, or gallery, in a church is called a tribune. The term will be used here mainly for the deep gallery over side aisles. The making of tribunes was brought about by the custom, in early Christendom, of separating the ages and sexes; in primitive days the kiss of peace used to be given among the congregation.

[6] Transept, or across inclosure, from *trans*, across, and *sepire*, to inclose.

Bible, the most frequently printed book of the older times.[7]

Despite a host of additions to the basilica of Rome—transept, ambulatory, a long choir, apse chapels, towers—despite the discarding of the classic orders and of antiquity's use of a veneer of finer stone (the Romanesque builder used the unadorned stone of his own region) the church of western Europe remained, in general plan, a Roman basilica. Like Rome, they covered their main vessel by a flat wooden roof, although they knew how to build barrel and groin vaulting.[8]

Now a wooden roof is an easy prey for fire. Such roofs, a succession of long-continued invasions, and the faulty construction of Merovingian and Carolingian churches are accountable for the fact that in France to-day is no church that predates the year 1000. Some portions of ancient wall are embedded in later work, and some few early crypts are intact. But to speak with certainty of Merovingian and Carolingian architecture is impossible, though they formed the incubating phase of Romanesque art.

In France the IX and X centuries were periods of overwhelming disaster. In the Midi were Saracen incursions. In northern and central France Norman pirates wiped out Charlemagne's revival of art. As far as Poitiers and Clermont the Northmen's path of destruction extended. "Look where you will," wrote Flodoard, the chronicler, "the sky is red with fires." To the litany was added a new invocation—*A furore Normannorum, libera nos, Domine*.

The falling to pieces of Charlemagne's civilization and the general return of social disorders have led to an overdramatic contrasting of the year 1000, when mankind, in terror, anticipated the ending of the world, with the rebirth of hope and of building energy, when the dread day had passed. Whenever the gaunt horses—famine, pest, war, and death—are afoot, humanity is prone to look for the fulfillment of the apocalyptic prophecy. Previous to the X century the final day had been awaited, and the same superstition was to seize on the world's imagination in following centuries.

The X century was certainly a desperate age. Fifty years of it were famine, and on the highroads people were killed for food. But the evils did not cease precisely with the year 1000; also it should be noted that a certain number of churches were begun before the XI century opened. However, to mark the start of a new art life the year 1000 is a convenient date if we bear in mind that it was not a sharp division between Carolingian and Romanesque architecture, since a gradual evolution took place. All through the XI century the vital renewal of architecture went on, and churches were built which, to this day, are unrivaled for their profound religious spirit. They exist to tell us that in the harsh life whence they emerged there were enlightened cases. They vindicate, by their grand simplicity and detachment of soul, the men who built them. Never was an art less one of routine than this of the so-called hidebound monks, an art of a people reborn, full of youth's daring,

[7] Guillaume Durandus, *Rationale Divinorum Officiorum*, translated as *The Symbolism of Churches and Church Ornaments* by Neale and Webb of the Camden Society (Leeds, T. W. Green, 1843).

[8] The barrel vault (a half cylinder) was known to the Egyptians and Assyrians. Rome used it extensively, also the groin vault (made of two intersecting half cylinders).

an art that was never to have an old age, eager, untiring, experimental, an art that fitly generated the most scientifically sound of architectures—Gothic.

The heterogeneous races, Celtic and Gallo-Roman, Germanic, and Norse, whose conflicts long had held France in anarchy, were at last welding into one people. The advent of a vigorous third dynasty, under whose leadership social conditions improved, was another cause of art's rebirth. Not long after 1000 the bishops formulated the *Trève de Dieu*, by which peace was enforced on the turbulent lords from Wednesday night to Monday morning. With interval of peace came commerce and wealth and the security necessary for works of the imagination. The rebuilding of churches was inevitable.

Invasions and wholesale conflagrations had impressed on the mediæval mind the necessity of a church roof more durable than wood, but a masonry vault over a wide space was a constructive feat too difficult to be achieved immediately. In fact, up to the very end of the XI century, though the builders had succeeded in vaulting with stone the crypt, the apse, and the side aisles, they continued generally to cover the wide central vessel in wood. However, the fecund idea was at work. From the time that it took possession of their imagination, to the day when Gothic, its fulfillment, was clearly enunciated, there was over a century of continuous effort—roughly speaking, from the year 1000 to the memorable day in 1144 when was dedicated the first truly Gothic monument of considerable size—the abbey church of St. Denis. Within that energetic span of years is embraced the Romanesque architecture of France.[9]

The monk, Raoul Glaber, wrote an account of the rebirth of architecture after the year 1000. It has been quoted to weariness, but is none the less a valuable contemporary record. The whole earth, he says, as of one accord seemed to throw off its tatters of old age and to reclothe itself in a white mantle of churches. The monastery in which lived monk Raoul, St. Bénigne, at Dijon, was one of the first to inaugurate the new century, and its present crypt dates from the year 1001. Soon after 1017 the monks of Mont-Saint-Michel, in the far corner of Normandy, began a new church, to which belonged part of the present nave. At Chartres, Bishop Fulbert undertook to rebuild his cathedral after the fire of 1020, and the vast crypt which to-day astonishes every beholder was his work.

The chronicler, Raoul Glaber, lived under the rule of the most powerful monastic brotherhood ever organized, Benedictine Cluny, embracing several thousand houses scattered over Europe. Founded in 910, during the darkest years of the Middle Ages, Cluny kept alive the light of learning and art, "the solitary torchbearer that passed on the flame from the spent glow of Charlemagne to the Gothic rekindling." Her monks were the pioneers of civilization. Cluny beat back barbarism with a pertinacity that should make hers an honored name in history.

---

[9] "There are few things more interesting, more instructive, or more beautiful in human history than the spectacle of those early cowled builders struggling against all difficulties and disadvantages, and laying the foundations of a new art which was, in the stronger hands of their lay successors, to culminate in the marvels of Chartres and Amiens."—CHARLES HERBERT MOORE, *Development and Character of Gothic Architecture* (New York, Macmillan, 1904).

So established was her reputation as a civilizer that William the Conqueror wrote to the great Abbot Hugues, to beg from him Cluny monks for England, saying that he would pay their weight in bullion.

Cluny formed the savants who made the XII century memorable. Her fertile seed provided Europe with doctors, ambassadors, bishops, and popes. Gregory VII had passed through her discipline, and in his giant task of reform, it was from Abbot Hugues that he solicited monks of Cluny. Urban II, who set in motion the First Crusade, had been a monk in the great Burgundian house. It is interesting to note that a generation of reforming pontiffs accompanied the expansion of the Romanesque movement. This would seem to contradict the notion, which many hold, that the clergy profits by keeping the people in superstitious ignorance. It is when religion is purified of its dross that man's respiritualized faith out-flows in generous donations to the Church.

St. Benedict had taught his sons that work as well as prayer was a part of salvation. The monks of Cluny fostered agriculture, thus taking away its stigma as serf's work. Thierry speaks of the mediæval monastery as a model farm. In Cluny craftsmen of every kind were trained; its school of music was noted, and along the roads, as they traveled, the monks from Burgundy sang canticles. But the art of arts for Cluny was that of the builder, the supreme art that takes into its service all the others, to lead them to the glorification of God's house. When, in bands of twelve, the monks of Cluny set out to colonize in Spain, in Germany, in Italy, in Poland, everywhere they carried with them the tool as well as the Book. As a rule they conformed in each province to the local building traditions. There was never a distinct Cluny school of Romanesque architecture.

By the end of the XI century the main provincial centers of France had each evolved its own special building characteristics. French Romanesque architecture has been divided into some six or seven regional schools—those of Normandy, Burgundy, Auvergne, Poitou, Languedoc, Provence, and a minor school, the Franco-Picard.[10]

[10] Let us run briefly over the French Romanesque schools to gain an idea of the monk builder's activities.

Normandy displayed a powerful regional genius, and carried through her Romanesque churches with native thoroughness. Her school was formulated early. By 1040 Jumièges abbey church was begun, and within thirty years the two abbeys of Caen were building. Norman Romanesque used the alternate system of piers, a central lantern tower, cubic capitals, and a geometric sculpture. Their architects were inclined to be overcautious; up to the advent of Gothic they often covered the middle nave with a timber roof, though they vaulted the side aisles with stone.

Burgundy's Romanesque school was bolder. Groin and barrel vaultings covered side aisles and central vessel; and the transverse arches which braced the vaulting were often pointed, since it was found that such an arch exerted less side thrust. Some of Burgundy's monastic churches were as lofty and spacious as the coming Gothic cathedrals. However, to obtain proper lighting by clearstory windows she sacrificed stability, and years later the Gothic builders had to add flying buttresses to prevent the collapse of the Romanesque churches. In this region where Gallo-Roman art had flourished, channeled pilasters were used. As was to be expected of the province where Cluny's arts and crafts were centered,

In their efforts to protect their churches by masonry roofs, these various regional schools made use of the barrel vault or the groin vault. The latter was found too insecure to span a wide space. Now, the thrust of a barrel vault was exerted along the whole length of the wall, which necessitated a continuous abutment—in other words, an enormously thick wall. Only small windows could be opened. Since the Romanesque architect had the ambition to light his church well, and not to encumber his floor surface by clumsy piers, a barrel vaulting could be but a temporary solution of the main problem.

Burgundy was a leader in monumental sculpture, and such portals as Avallon, Autun, and Vézelay attest her skill.

Auvergne produced a distinctive Romanesque school. Her art sprang direct from the ancient Roman traditions in the province. More cautious than her neighbor Burgundy, she soon gave up trying to light her upper nave by clearstory windows, but obtained light indirectly from side aisles and from a central tower. A precocious use of the ambulatory and of apse chapels appeared in the region. The two most striking features of her churches were the octagonal central tower set on a barlong base, and the apse whose exterior walls were decorated by the volcanic polychrome stones of the district.

Poitou's Romanesque school also developed early, and it, too, sacrificed spaciousness to solidity. The side aisles were made of almost equal height as the central vessel, and one roof covered all. The church interiors were often somber and cramped. The apse exterior was ornamented, and the boast of the region is its richly sculptured façades of which that of Notre-Dame-la-Grande at Poitiers is one of the best examples.

Languedoc built Romanesque churches of the first rank, such as St. Sernin at Toulouse, but the school had no definite uniformity. Sometimes it combined with the Romanesque of Poitou, sometimes with that of Auvergne, or of Burgundy. Because of Cluny affiliations, the Midi school was strong in sculpture—witness Beaulieu, Cahors, Moissac, and Toulouse.

Provence Romanesque covered a more limited area. Usually the churches were aisleless, with a simple apse. A flat stone roof was laid directly on the barrel vaulting, which had pointed transverse ribs like those of Burgundy. Provence also used the fluted pilasters of antiquity. The many remains of Gallo-Roman sculpture in the region served as models for the notable imaged portals at St. Gilles and Arles.

The Franco-Picard school had scarcely developed when it was supplanted by the nascent Gothic art. Besides these regional schools, two unique experiments in vaulting were essayed, though neither spread far afield. At Tournus, in the abbey church of St. Philibert was built a series of barrel vaults (carried on lintels) placed side by side transversely over the central vessel. And in Aquitaine, in the region of Périgueux and Angoulême, spreading in a line, north and south, arose a number of churches, each bay of which was covered by a cupola. Both these experiments were but partial solutions. While mediæval archæology was obscure, the pointed arch was looked on as the *sine qua non* of Gothic, and it was puzzling to find it in certain Romanesque churches, like those in Burgundy and Provence. The pointed arch was in use in Persia, in the VI century, and the Arabs early brought the form to Egypt, Sicily, and Spain. From the XI century it had appeared sporadically in Christian Europe. Such arches were not the first step in a new architecture, but were used either as a decorative feature or as an expedient to lessen the side thrust of a vault. From outside of France two schools of Romanesque art, the Lombard and the Rhenish, exerted considerable influences on their neighbor, but the forces paramount in each of the local French schools were the pre-Lombardic pre-Rhenish inheritances from Rome, blended with indigenous traditions.

The struggle for a satisfactory stone roof was pursued tenaciously. Many a clearstory wall was thrust apart by the vaulting's pressure. Thus the abbey church of Bec, finished in the 'forties of the XI century, was reconstructed in the 'fifties, and three times, again, had to be rebuilt. No failure could daunt the courage of those old monastic builders. Already inherent in the newly amalgamated race was the creative genius of France. Perseverance and courage were to have their reward.

The theory long taught in the École des Chartes was that in the first part of the XI century, among a number of rural churches in the royal domain, there gradually came into use the member which was to revolutionize the science of building. The idea did not spring from one brain; it was a collective, not an individual, triumph. When, under some groin vault, no doubt at first to reinforce it, some obscure mason constructed the earliest intersecting stone ribs, the first step in Gothic architecture had been taken.[11]

From that essential organ, the other characteristics of Gothic art were deduced: flying buttress, slender piers, expanse of windows. In a Gothic vault the infilling, or web, rested elastically on the diagonal ribs. As the load of the stone roof was thus concentrated at fixed junctures, it was necessary to reinforce only those given points. Buttresses became intermittent. All the disintegrating force of the heavy vaulting was gathered on the diagonally crossing arches. An arch never sleeps, said the old Arab proverb. Let us then, said the mediæval architect, set a guard on it that also never sleeps; and from that idea he proceeded to develop the greatest architecture of all times. The force of expansion was counteracted by a proportionate force of compression. By means of a framework made up of vault ribs, of piers, of buttresses, and flying buttresses, the edifice became a living skeleton. The walls between the active members, when relieved of their load, served merely as screen inclosures and could be carved into fragile beauty and hung with transparent tapestries of colored glass. Because the flying buttress transmitted a large part of the vault's pressure to the exterior buttress piles, the piers within the church could be lessened in diameter, and greater capacity be given to the interior.

Each new trial was a lesson learned. It was only with time that they adjusted precisely the sufficient counterpoise to the thrust of the vaults; it was only by degrees that the pier's diameter was lessened, only with practice that was learned the placing of flying buttresses neither too high nor too low. At first many a flying buttress was made needlessly heavy. The solid wall in between the buttresses was not discarded all at once. In the first Gothic churches windows continued to be single lights, then two or three lancets were placed side by side, subsequently each light was subdivided by mullions, and gradually an elaborate fenestration developed. For a time, too, the round arch continued in use, and the earliest vault ribs were semicircular. With the fusion of the equilateral arch and the counterbutted intersecting ribs, the essence of Gothic architecture was achieved.

Lesser consequences of the new form of vaulting followed in logical succession. Obeying the law that it is the thing borne which commands the form of the

[11] Rome had used some brick lines under the surface of certain of her groin vaults. They performed no separate function, but were embedded in the vaults' concrete. The true Gothic vault has the ribs independent of the infilling. In their elasticity is their strength.

thing that bears, the ribs may be said to have drawn out of the sturdy pier of Romanesque art the clustered columns of Gothic gracefulness.

Not a single beauty in a Gothic church but has a structural explanation. The soaring pinnacles that crown the buttresses are apparently mere ornaments, but in reality those gallant little bits of decoration are of sound engineering usefulness. By weighting the buttresses, they hasten to channel the transmitted lateral thrust of the vaulting into a vertical pressure, and they increase, too, the counterthrust of the flying buttress against the side walls.

A clear comprehension of Gothic is impossible unless the fact be grasped that architecture is nothing if not structural, and that no decoration can veil a faulty skeleton. Ornamentation is the spontaneous blossoming of the structure, else it is meaningless—a principle many a modern architect might well digest. Too long has the most scientifically exact of architectures been judged by its embellishments, which often enough, in the hands of the copyist, do become a florid veneer without reason.

The Gothic master-of-works was right when he said that nothing which was inherently needed could be ugly. No longer were flying buttresses hidden under the cover of wooden roofs. Proudly ranged about the church, those essential practical members became one of the distinctive beauties of the new science of building. Renan, with his treacherous half praise, has called the flying buttress a crutch needed by an architecture which, from its start, nourished the seeds of decay, since it was based on no sound constructive formula. Its success was a prestidigitator's trick, he said. Such criticism misunderstands the A B C of Gothic lore. Can a living limb be called a crutch? it has been aptly asked. The Gothic cathedral is not only the most complicated, but is also the most complete, organism ever conceived by man.

Where the first diagonal-crossing ribs are to be found will probably never be known. Various have been the claimants. The Rhenish claim is no longer taken seriously. Gothic made its first appearance in Germany as a fully developed French art, and its XIII-century name, there, was *opus francigenum*. In his Gothic work the Teuton showed a fondness for the *tour-de-force* and his manual dexterity surprises more than it satisfies. The best German works in architecture are the sober Romanesque churches. Germany's school was developed a century before the Romanesque of France; across the Rhine occurred no Norman invasion to sever art traditions from Charlemagne's renaissance. The pre-Gothic art suited her ethnical temperament, and was long adhered to. While France was building Gothic, Germany was still erecting Romanesque cathedrals. Not till the end of the XII century were churches along that "*rue des moines*," the Rhine, vaulted in the new manner.

The claim of Italy to be the first to use the diagonal ribs is denied by most French archæologists, but is put forward by the Italian scholar Rivoira and by Mr. Arthur Kingsley Porter.[12] The latter cites the church of Sannazzaro Sesia as

[12] G. T. Rivoira, *Lombardic Architecture* (London, Heinemann, 1910). Translated from *Le origini dell' architettura lombarda* (Milano, 1908); Arthur Kingsley Porter, *Lombard Architecture* (New Haven, Yale University Press, 1917), 3 vols. and Atlas; *ibid., The Construction of Lombard and Gothic Vaults* (New Haven, Yale University Press, 1911).

showing proofs that its high nave was Gothic vaulted by 1040. For a century, he says, the Lombard churches used diagonals, especially in Milan, where wood was scarce and it was easier to build permanent brick ribs under the groin vault than to mold the groin on a temporary substructure. Diagonal ribs were invented, he thinks, as a device to economize wood. That may be true of the Lombard churches, of which he has made an elaborate study. And it may be true that the use of such diagonals filtered into Provence and Languedoc, where appeared some early Gothic vaults sporadically before 1150, at Fréjus, Marseilles, Maguelonne, and Moissac, all with the rectangular profile of the Lombard type. The theory he advocates does not prove why the Ile-de-France masons could not themselves, without hint from Lombardy, have stumbled on the new feature which was to revolutionize the builder's art. Why should we prefer his explanation for the first use of diagonals—the desire to economize wood—to that advanced by the French scholars—the effort to brace a falling groin vault?

Mr. Porter acknowledges that not a single Lombard church was rib-vaulted throughout, that the Lombard architects never counterbutted their diagonals properly, that their vaults proved unsatisfactory, so that after 1120 they returned to their groin and barrel vaulting, or used timber roofs, in those regions where wood abounded. The destruction of Milan through the German invasion, in 1162, was a fatal blow to Lombard architecture. We can only conjecture how northern Italy might have worked out the problem of stone roofs. The best definition of Gothic, thinks Mr. Porter, is Professor Moore's, which concludes thus: "Wherever is wanting a framework maintained on the principle of thrust and counterthrust, there we have not Gothic." The Lombard churches never met the vault thrust with counterthrust of buttress. Surely not in Lombardy was conceived the new system of construction?

S. Ambrogio at Milan was cited as l'œuvre initiale, till it was proved that it was built not in the IX century, but after 1067; and as later disasters necessitated reconstructions, none of the present diagonals was extant before 1198. S. Abondio at Como, consecrated by Urban II, in 1095, has some very early intersecting ribs, but they are more a step toward the new system than a true Gothic vault, since the ribs merely reinforce and do not carry the cells.

M. Camille Enlart contends that the systematic use of Gothic in Italy was not earlier than the second quarter of the XIII century, and was brought across the Alps by French Cistercian monks. Though for centuries Italy used it, she apprehended its constructive principle imperfectly. Because she possessed a Niccola Pisano, a Giotto, a family of Cosmati to veil the poverty of her Gothic skeleton with details of consummate beauty, criticism is silenced. Her best Gothic monument, the cathedral of Siena, was insecure because of technical errors. Always was Italy adverse to showing the mechanism by which an edifice stood; few flying buttresses were ever built south of the Alps. She preferred the classic wide spacing of piers, an unencumbered interior, and small windows against her hot sun. Who remembers that he is in a Gothic church when in the somber cathedral of Florence? Its long nave is divided into four bays where a northern church would have used eight. For Italy the Renaissance was a whole-hearted return to a national art which she could fully understand.

No people outside of France better understood and developed Gothic art than the English. Their claim to priority is based on the date of the cathedral of Durham, whose choir-aisle diagonals Mr. John Bilson says are as early as 1093. Since those diagonals show no hesitation, they must have been preceded by others. Where in England are there to be found the earlier trials? The English claim is practically a Norman one, and Normandy's experimental work in Gothic vaultings remains to be traced. Rivoira claims that Lombard influences predominated in the formation of Normandy's Romanesque school. Can the Norman be said to have discerned in diagonals their immense possibilities any clearer than had the Lombard?

Those among the French archæologists who have disputed the Norman claim to priority say that the principal span of Norman and English churches was covered with timber roofs far into the XII century. We know that the Gothic vaulting of the two abbey churches of Caen were XII-century additions, and M. de Lasteyrie thought the same was true of Durham, though Mr. Bilson has convinced MM. Enlart and Lefèvre-Pontalis that Durham's choir-aisle vaults are an original part of the cathedral begun in 1093. Not till 1174, when Guillaume de Sens began Canterbury Cathedral, did French Gothic architecture, in its plenitude, appear in England.

The question of priority remains an open one. It might almost be said that vaulting with intersecting ribs began to appear here and there simultaneously, that if it had not cropped out in the Ile-de-France, it would have appeared in Normandy, or vice versa. And not long after them, the builders in Burgundy and Anjou began to use it. Before 1150, isolated samples of the Gothic rib vault appeared at Vézelay, Poitiers, Bordeaux, Quimperlé, Moissac, St. Gilles, Marseilles. The hour was ripe for the solution. Gothic architecture was the spontaneous invention of French builders at the dawn of the XII century, at a time when the poetry of France was imposing itself on the whole of Europe.

L'œuvre initiale will never be known. However, there was a region where the early use of the ogival vault was not accidental, but systematic, one spot in the heart of France where it immediately made a school, since there it found no strong earlier traditions to overcome, where it became a living organism and went through a succession of logical developments until it had taken on the main characteristics of the new art. There is one center from which Gothic architecture spread out with slow, sure march into the neighboring regions. In the Ile-de-France, all the trials were summed up and developed by Abbot Suger at St. Denis. From 1140 to 1144 he wedded definitely the pointed arch with the diagonal rib.

The French masters, who have contended that the Ile-de-France is the cradle of Gothic architecture, have had lesser controversies among themselves as to which special portion of the royal domain led in the evolution. M. Woillez, a pioneer, considered the environs of Beauvais the favored spot; M. Saint-Paul looked to the districts between Normandy and Paris; M. Enlart sought the nucleus in Amiens diocese in Picardy; and M. Lefèvre-Pontalis chose the classic diocese of Soissons. The two latter masters have modified their views since studying Durham's vaults, and they may modify them further in regard to Lombardy's early use of diagonals. The controversy is not closed.

The France of that day was more a feudal confederation than a united kingdom, and some of the king's vassals ruled territories larger than his own. If the feeling of nationality is created as much by great achievements in common, as by political boundaries and the ties of blood, if, as all now agree, the enthusiasm of the Crusades, those holy wars against a common foe, helped to weld the rival sections of France into one nation, surely that other enthusiasm of the day, those other *Gesta Dei* per Francos, the building of the Gothic cathedrals, played an important part in forming the national soul. From end to end of France they were building when at the battle of Bouvines a French king united with the jealous barons, with clergy and with burgess and with villein in a common defense of their native land. King, clergy, lords, and people fought at Bouvines, and king, clergy, lords, and people built the big national churches. All the energies of the times went to their making, all the primitive strong purposes, all the newly stirred intellect of the schools. Science was as needed for them as inspiration, for without the long manual training of the guilds, the mystic glow had not sufficed.

There has crept into various architectural manuals, since first M. Viollet-le-Duc voiced it, a theory which scarcely needs refuting, so disproved is it by modern research.[13] Gothic art is considered as the layman's expression of revolt against the Romanesque art of the monks, an idea that denies the structural sequence of the two phases of the same art, and would present Gothic as a reaction against its predecessor, instead of its supreme development.

We read that a cathedral was built as a sort of assembly hall for the rising communes, and not *pour loger le bon Dieu*. Now in every known case it was the bishop who started the rebuilding of each cathedral, and the works usually began with the choir, the part of a church suitable only for the cult. Even when a bishop, in his character of proprietor of a city (as in the case of Rheims and Laon), opposed the communal claims, he and the people went on building their cathedral together. We have precious documents to assure us in what spirit of piety the work was done. All classes and all ages, women as well as men, gave their voluntary labor to the new works, after having confessed and communicated in pious confraternities; sometimes it was for an abbot that they dragged in the stones from the quarry, as at St. Denis and St. Pierre-sur-Dives; sometimes it was to aid a bishop, as at Chartres and Rouen. To offset such irrefutable evidence there is not one contemporary reference to a laic, or communal purpose.

Also, when it is asserted that the bishop helped the cathedrals because they were jealous of the monastic orders, there is not one historical record to confront a host of documents which disprove the idea. Large numbers of the bishop-builders

----

[13] E. Viollet-le-Duc, *Dictionnaire raisonné de l'architecture française du XIe au XVIe siècle* (Paris, 1875), 11 vols.; Anthyme Saint-Paul, *Viollet-le-Duc et son système archéologique* (Tours, 1881). The masterly technical knowledge of M. Viollet-le-Duc did much to remove the stigma of caprice and extravagance which the neo-classic age had fixed on Gothic art. It is a pity that the pioneer who struck good blows for the rehabilitation of Gothic should have jeopardized the permanence of his work by giving free rein to his personal prejudices.

issued from monasteries, founded monasteries, and returned to monasteries to die. While Maurice de Sully was erecting Notre Dame, at Paris, he built four monasteries, in one of which he requested to be buried. The bishop who began Auxerre Cathedral chose Cistercian Pontigny for his tomb. The bishop-builders of Noyon, Laon, Senlis, Soissons, Rheims, Bourges, and Rouen were buried among the monks. That there should occasionally be friction between a bishop and an abbot over legal privileges is only characteristic of human nature in all times. As a class the bishops were not opposed to the monks, nor the Orders to the secular clergy. The monks of St. Remi honored the archbishop of Rheims in their choir windows.

The cloister welcomed the new architecture. Transition Gothic churches were built by the monks of St. Germain-des-Prés and St. Martin-des-Champs at Paris, and one could prolong the list into pages. Where in Burgundy is found the earliest Gothic? In the Cistercian church of Pontigny, and in Benedictine Vézelay. Where in Champagne?—the abbatials of Notre Dame at Châlons-sur-Marne and St. Remi at Rheims. In Normandy? In the Midi?—again the answer is, in abbey churches. Indeed, monastic building energy seemed inexhaustible, for where the prime of Gothic arrived, it was still the monks who produced that masterpiece of the new art, the Merveille of Mont-Saint-Michel.

In the XII century the spread of monastic life took on a phenomenal aspect. Benedictine houses and those of the newly founded Orders of Cîteaux and Prémontré increased, not by hundreds, but by thousands. The monks were in absolute accord with the spirit of their time. Sons of the cloister had inspired the entire XI century: Gregory VII, Abbot William of Dijon, St. Anselm, Lanfranc, St. Hugues of Cluny. A bevy of remarkable men of the cloister led the XII century, the chief being Suger of St. Denis, protector of the serfs, the man of genius who stimulated the bishops of France to remake their cathedrals in emulation of his Gothic abbey church, and St. Bernard of Clairvaux, on whose words all Europe hung.

Architecture passed to laic control when the protection of monastic life was no longer needed for artists, and when the science of building required the specialist, the man occupied with it alone. The schools of Cluny had trained the first guildsmen, and many of the names of Gothic architects—Orbais, Honnecourt, Corbic—indicate that they were born in places where monastic building industries flourished. It was in the natural course of events that the art should pass out of the possession of the few into the general national life.

Another natural happening has been distorted by partisans. The burning of monastery archives during the XVI-century religious wars and by the Revolution is accountable for the few names of architects that have come down to us. The scarcity of such names has been cited as an instance of the jealous suppression of the laymen by the clergy forced to employ them. Now precisely the contrary is the truth. What modern architect was ever accorded such prominence as was allowed by the bishops of Amiens and Rheims to their masters-of-works when they inscribe those laymen names in the labyrinth designs of the cathedral pavements? The monks of Marmoutier and of St. Germain-des-Prés were proud to bury in their abbey-churches their architects Étienne de Mortagne and Pierre de Montereau. In Rheims, the architects Hugues Libergier and Robert de Coucy were likewise honored.

By digging in old archives, the modern student is ever adding new names to the nation's honor roll. Many a gap still remains, but the very anonymousness of such masters of the living stone is stuff for the imagination. One likes to picture the old-time craftsman-artist rejoicing in his insignificance as he chiseled his leaf and vine just as he saw them by the roadside. He served a Master who gave like wages to all who worked in spirit and in truth, to him who, in the hidden corners where no human eye could penetrate, carved his leaf and flower with the same love as did the greater artist working on the stately imaged portals.

The "heretical Gothic-sculpture bogey" has led certain imaginations astray. There are those who find latent heresy in the old carvers' work; they point, with suggestive smile, to the bishop and monk placed among the damned in the Last Judgments at the cathedral doors. Let them turn to the sermons of the day and they will find precisely the same Christian doctrine of the equality of all men before sin and punishment, preached from the pulpit within the church. Not in all the myriad scenes from Old and New Testaments is a single doctrinal error to be found, says M. Émile Mâle, who is master of the iconography of French churches. The sculptor layman merely carried out the scheme of the trained theologian.

Many a sharp word does M. Viollet-le-Duc give as critic to those who enjoy in a cathedral the superficial beauties of decoration, but are blind to the efficient structure, to the scientific upholding skeleton. Surely it is a still more radical ignorance which perceives in a Gothic church its mechanical perfection, but denies the aspiration to immortality which was its inceptive spirit. To ascribe the origin of cathedrals to the need by the nascent commune of a town hall is to make of those soaring monuments veritable follies of human pride. Restore to them their religious soul, have eyes to see what may be called their spiritual framework, and as up-leaps toward the infinite they are sublimities. Can churches be the creation of rebellion and hate when into their very stones passed the clamorous vibrant faith of those crusading generations? Like hovering prayers their vaults seem to shut one in. The heart, weary of modern sophistry, draws strength from their eternal affirmation. He must have little music in his soul who is deaf to such a *Credo*. When men built Gothic cathedrals they knelt on both knees to pray, and never have they soared more supremely above themselves. "Deeds of God through the French" are these temples.

A word in regard to the term "Gothic." It is as unreasonable a misnomer as could have been chosen, but since usage has sanctioned it, it must pass. Primarily put into currency by the Italians of the Renaissance, in the injurious sense of barbarous, the term was adopted by the French neo-classics of the XVII century. Molière's scathing line on Gothic sculpture is well known—"*Ces monstres odieux des siècles ignorants.*" He complained that Gothic art "*fit à la politesse une mortelle guerre.*" When Racine spoke of Chartres Cathedral he made use of the term *barbare*; even to the churchman Fénelon the cathedrals of the Middle Ages appeared unreasoned and faulty.

The opprobrious term was fixed by the Encyclopædists of the next century, when prejudice against the Middle Ages became militant and organized. With exclusive pedantism they dismissed the most national and civilized of arts as worthy of those rough invaders, the Goths. Voltaire, who, says Guizot, garnered only what was mean and criminal in the Middle Ages, saw in the study of Gothic architecture "a coarse curiosity, lacking good taste." As late as 1800, a project was abroad to disencumber the soil of France of "these overcharged façades with their multitude of indecent and ridiculous figures." And still later, the students in the national school of architecture were taught to despise the most reasoned, the most robust, the most logical of arts as a style of confusion and caprice.

The rehabilitation of Gothic architecture in France, if tardy, has been ample. No branch of modern science presents a more able corps of workers. While true to the Latin genius, which unites clarity of style with an exact erudition, they have obeyed a yet deeper race instinct which knows that matter must be vivified by spirit, else learning sinks to a dry-as-dust recording, incapable of its highest flight. The telling of the monumental story of France has been touched by the sacred flame of patriotism. Like paladins, these modern knights are abroad on all the by-paths eager to rescue some hidden treasure of the national art. Future scholarship will look back at the brilliant achievements of the French archæologists of to-day with the same pride that is felt for the Benedictine savants of the XVII century.

The aim of archæology is to date a monument correctly. How to do this by scientific method has been taught the last two generations at the École des Chartes, the national school par excellence, so M. de Vögué called it. Archives are pored over to trace each link with history, and those monuments which have no authenticated pedigree are compared with those of certain date. Each manuscript date is verified by the analysis of the edifice itself, whose successive campaigns of building are deciphered, since few and far between are the homogeneous churches. Each restoration also is verified. One of the solid bases for archæological exactness is the knowledge of profiles, which are called by the English textbook rib molds, arch molds, pier molds, or base molds. By a comparative analysis of profiles, a monument can now be accurately dated. As keystones were of different types in the various earlier decades of Gothic, they too help to substantiate an edifice.[14]

Churches of one region are contrasted with those of another. The material employed is considered, since the stone of a province causes richness or poverty of sculpture: thus, Brittany's granite and Auvergne's lava mean an undeveloped sculpture compared with the fine white limestone districts of the Oise, or in Normandy and Poitou. When practicable, excavations under an edifice can give data concerning previous churches on the site.

M. Jules Quicherat was the first to teach that the history of the Middle Ages architecture was the history of the architect's fight against the weight and push of the vaulting.[15] Once the right path was blazed, many an able pioneer helped clear the

[14] E. Lefèvre-Pontalis, "Le plan d'une monographie *d'église et le vocabulaire archéologique*," in *Revue de l'art chrétien*, 1910, p. 379. He has written on the same subject in *Bulletin Monumental*, 1906, vol. 70, p. 453, and 1907, vol. 71, pp. 136, 351, 535.

[15] Jules Quicherat, "La croisée d'ogives et son origine," in *Mélanges d'archéologie et d'histoire* (1850), vol. 2, p. 497.

new road—such students as Viollet-le-Duc, de Caumont, Woillez, Prosper Merimée, de Dion, Coutan, de Beaurepaire, Grandmaison, Révoil, Rupricht-Robert,
Félix de Verneilh, Anthyme Saint-Paul, Louis Courajod, Buhot de Kersers. At the
École des Chartes, Robert de Lasteyrie occupied with distinction the chair held by
Quicherat for thirty years, and his pupils, Camille Enlart and Eugène Lefèvre-Pontalis, in their turn, are passing on the high tradition to a younger school. M. Enlart, the director of the museum of comparative sculpture at the Trocadéro, is an
authority on Romanesque architecture, and has initiated the study of the spread
of Gothic architecture in mediæval Italy, Spain, the North, and the Levant.[16] M.
Lefèvre-Pontalis has written a host of erudite monographs; one learns to accept his
decisions as final, in so far as the ever-expanding realm of knowledge can be final.
He directs the invaluable publications called the *Congrès Archéologique de France*
and the *Bulletin Monumental*, and he edits those excellent short studies known as
the *Petites Monographies des grands édifices de la France*, which are convenient pocket
guides for the serious tourist.[17]

Each year is producing final monographs on the chief churches of France. M.
Georges Durand has rendered fitting tribute to Amiens. M. de Farcy has identified
himself with Angers, René Merlet with Chartres, Lucien Broche with Laon, and
Lucien Bégule with Lyons. MM. Brutails has specialized on Gascony, the Thollier
and H. du Ranquet on Auvergne, Labande on Provence, Berthelé on Plantagen-
et Gothic, André Rhein on Poitou and Anjou, Émile Bonnet on Hérault, Charles
Porée on Burgundy, and Louis Demaison on Champagne. Other able students are
MM. Bouet, Louis Serbat, Marcel Aubert, Ernest Rupin, Jules de Lahondès, René
Fage, Amédée Boinet, Jean Virey, Robert Triger, and Louis Régnier.

Precious texts have been unearthed from the archives by Victor Mortet, Henri Stein, and Eugène Müntz. The sculpture of France has been studied by MM.
Robert de Lasteyrie, Émile Lambin, Léon Palustre, Eugène Müntz, Gabriel Fleury,
Raymond Koechlin, J. M. de Vasselot, Paul Vitry, Gaston Brière, André Michel,
Louis Gonse, and Émile Mâle. The latter three have brought out monumental general works. *L'art gothique* of Gonse gives the most exact and extended account of
the beginning of Gothic, says Anthyme Saint-Paul, who is himself one of the most
inspiring masters of mediæval archæology. M. Michel, who is conservator of the
national museums, has edited the superb *Histoire de l'art*, to which leading French
scholars have contributed.[18] And the iconography of French cathedrals has re-

---

[16] Camille Enlart, *Origines françaises de l'architecture gothique en Italie* (Paris, 1893);
ibid., *Les origines de l'architecture gothique en Espagne et en Portugal* (Paris, 1894); *ibid.*, *Notes
archéologiques sur les abbayes cisterciennes de Scandinavie* (Paris, 1894); *ibid.*, *Villard de Honnecourt et les Cisterciens* (Paris, 1895); *ibid.*, *L'art gothique et de la Renaissance en Chypre* (Paris,
Leroux, 1899), 2 vols.; Émile Bertaud, *L'art dans l'Italie méridionale* (Paris, Fontemoing, 1904).

[17] Other publications of value to the student are the *Revue de l'art chrétien*, *Gazette des
Beaux-Arts*, *Moyen-Âge*, *l'Archéologie*, *Bibliothèque de l'École des Chartes*, *Revue archéologique*,
and the Didron's *Annales archéologique*. There are H. Havard's *La France artistique et monumental*, Viollet-le-Duc's *Dictionnaire de l'architecture française*, Joanne's *Dictionnaire de la
France*. The regional and local monographs will be given here with each school of Gothic
and each cathedral as it is described.

[18] André Michel (Publiée sous la direction de), *Histoire de l'art depuis les premiers temps*

ceived no more magistral treatment than from M. Mâle, to whom is due the credit of establishing the scholastic character of Gothic imagery.[19] His path was cleared by pioneers such as Didron, Crosnier, Martin, and Duchesne.

Happily for the local schools, a bevy of intelligent churchmen have devoted themselves to their regional monuments. I hope I may be pardoned if I do not name each with his ecclesiastical designation, but cite them here simply as savants: the Abbés Eugène Müller (Senlis); Bourassé and Bosseboeuf (Touraine); Ledru (Le Mans); Auber, De la Croix, and Mgr. Barbier de Montault (Poitiers); Chomton (Dijon); Bulteau (Chartres); Abgrall (Brittany); Maurin (Aix-en-Provence); Bouvier (Sens); Cerf (Rheims); Bouxin (Laon); and for the Norman churches, the Abbés Fossey, Porée, Loisel, and Pigéon.

The list might be greatly extended. One can cite only a few. From the pages of such students have been written these chapters, by one who has felt that there must be many travelers who love the old cathedrals of Europe and have wandered among them puzzled by half-understood things, longing to know with exactitude how and when they were built. So it has not seemed a useless task to gather into these ten chapters what the French scholars are relating of their churches. So swiftly do archæological discoveries follow one another to-day, that statements accepted now may be obsolete to-morrow. The makers of history and art books can hope to serve only their hour.

The new school of Christian archæology is redeeming the misrepresented centuries after the year 1000. It is undoing the systematic falsification of history, and is teaching us to read the past other than by the printed page. Not hate, but love, opens new windows in the soul. The study of the churches of France adds flesh and blood to many a mere name in history. One gains a very special liking for little Abbot Suger, most dependable of men, whose life was a succession of big undertakings. One feels reverent affection for that sentinel of the Church and its guide, Bernard of Clairvaux, who said some harsh things of fine churches, all the while that he was feeding the mystic life that made them inevitable. And very real become the bishop builders when one knows their cathedrals. One pores over the old volumes of the *Histoire Littéraire de la France*, begun by XVII-century Benedictines, and still being continued by the Institute of France, to gather details of good Bishop Fulbert and doughty St. Ives, who built at Chartres; of that distinguished literary man, Bishop Hildebert de Lavardin, who worked at Le Mans; of the well-poised Bishop Maurice de Sully, who raised Notre Dame at Paris; of crusading prelates such as Albéric de Humbert, who began Rheims; and of Nivelon de Chérisy, who built Soissons, and who, on the Fourth Crusade, played a foremost role. One grows to love, above all, the saint-king, Louis, truest hero of *la douce France*, who illuminated his kingdom with fair churches. And no one can admire St. Louis and not keep a warm corner in his heart for Joinville, his comrade-in-arms, the irresistible seneschal of Champagne.

Crusades and chivalry and all the multicolored aspects of the XII and XIII cen-

chrétiens (Paris, A. Colin, 1906), 10 vols.

[19] Émile Mâle, *L'art religieux du XIIIe siècle en France* (Paris, Colin, 1908), 4to; *ibid., L'art religieux de la fin du moyen âge en France* (Paris, Colin, 1910), 4to.

turies become clearer to the imagination as one traces the story of the cathedrals of France; scholasticism and the early days of the schools, when Abélard sparred with Guillaume de Champeaux. Very real they all become: Peter the Venerable, good Stephen Harding, St. Thomas Becket, John of Salisbury, St. Edmund Rich, Stephen Langton, St. Dominic, St. Malachy O'Morgair, Innocent III, St. Bonaventure, and St. Thomas Aquinas. France welcomed them all during the two vital centuries when she imposed her literature as well as her architecture on western Europe, when the Paris schools were the intellectual center of the world.

To paint a rose-colored picture of the two best centuries of the Middle Ages would be absurd. They were full of very evil things. There were horrifying episodes in them. "Barbarism tempered by religion; religion disfigured by barbarism," is the definition of Balmes, the theologian. The inconsistencies were gigantic. The same men who sacked Constantinople in 1204, dealing art a staggering blow, were the very men who in western Europe were building cathedrals. Then, as now, there were many for whom religion served as a convenient cloak for the lower instincts; then, as now, there were many who never lost sight of the higher ideals. Side by side with the evil and the self-seeking should be set the sublime impulses which checked those untutored generations. Do not hide the merciless laying waste of Languedoc by the north, but do not forget that, in the same hour, men had reached an abnegation of self that led them to the African coast as voluntary substitutes for their brother Christians in bondage there.

In the midst of its human infirmities it was an age that aspired: its poets sang of the Holy Grail, its kings and its serfs were saints, there were saint scholars and barons and merchants, there was even a saint lawyer.

It is precisely the restored balance between good and evil which the study of Gothic art is bringing about. The partisan may go on compiling a police gazette and call it history.[20] While the towers of Gothic churches point upward, he is refuted. The modern mind has once for all grasped that it is psychologically impossible for an age to have been sunk in blind superstition when it could build, not merely one or two, but hundreds of churches whose every line is an aspiration toward sanctity. The cathedrals are the true apologetics of the Middle Ages. Archæology is again proving its claim to be the soul of history.

---

[20] "Il en est parmi nous qui préfèrent la victoire de leur parti à la victoire de la patrie. Écrire l'histoire de France était une façon de travailler pour un parti et de combattre un adversaire. Pour beaucoup de Français être patriote, c'est être ennemi de l'ancienne France. Cette sorte de patriotisme au lieu de nous unir contre l'étranger nous pousse tout droit à la guerre civile." —FUSTEL DE COULANGES.

CHAPTER II

ABBOT SUGER AND ST. DENIS-EN-FRANCE

Evolution from Romanesque to Gothic—St. Denis' abbatial, the first important Gothic monument—Some early-Gothic churches in the Ile-de-France—Morienval, the first Gothic-vaulted ambulatory extant (c. 1122)—Church of St. Étienne, at Beauvais (c. 1120)—St. Germer-en-Flay built from 1150 to 1175, yet less advanced than St. Denis—Poissy's church of St. Louis (c. 1135)—How Abbot Suger built his abbey church at St. Denis—St. Denis' school of glassmaking, the leader for fifty years—Dedication of St. Denis on June 11, 1144, consecrated the national art—Who Suger was and how St. Bernard converted him—What is left of the abbey church which Suger built—Reconstruction of St. Denis by St. Louis, 1231 to 1280—Pierre de Montereau, its architect—Tombs in St. Denis' abbatial—Deviation of the axis not symbolic—Some happenings in St. Denis during the XII and XIII centuries—Charles Péguy's verses, linking St. Denis, St. Geneviève, and Jeanne d'Arc.

Under the impulse of this monk, truly great in all things, Gothic architecture was born.

—Félix de Verneilh (of Abbot Suger).

HE churches built during the evolution from Romanesque to Gothic have been called transitional, a classification which would be most convenient for the amateur, had not archæologists decided it was an equivocal term. They say that, during the short period when "Romanesque and Gothic inhabited under the same roof," the Romanesque parts of the edifice were placed side by side with the simultaneously built Gothic parts, that there was juxtaposition, but no fusion. Vaults were either barrel, groin, or of the diagonal-rib type; there was no such thing as a transition form of vault. Arches were either round or pointed; there was no such thing as a transition or intermediary form of arch. And since the radical distinction between Romanesque and Gothic is caused by the vaulting, it is correct to call that part of a church where was groin or barrel vault Romanesque, and that part where were used the intersecting ribs Gothic.

The sequence of the passing from Romanesque to Gothic is obscure, because there is a lack of definite dates. From 1110 to 1140, while the intersecting ribs were coming into use in northern France, such a vault was practically the only sign in an edifice of the new movement. The walls still were massive, the windows still were small and round-arched, the sculpture still was coarse and heavy. Then, as the transition advanced, the supports grew lighter, the profiles (those cross-section outlines of ribs, arches, capitals, and bases) grew purer, and the sculpture discarded Byzantine traditions and took nature as its model.

French archæologists have thought that the use of diagonals came about first through the desire to hold up some groin vault, on the point of collapsing, which would seem a very sensible explanation, since the creative genius of the Ile-de-France seems dimly to have apprehended even in the first hour the stupendous possibility to be drawn from a member whose purpose was to concentrate force in order that other parts of the edifice might be relieved. From the initial hour began the evolution of the cardinal organ in the Ile-de-France. Whereas the Lombard architects looked on the diagonals as a mere contrivance, stubbornly keeping their eyes shut to the structural possibilities latent therein. The masons of the Ile-de-France at once began to profile their diagonals graciously, and even before the genius of Suger had coordinated, at St. Denis, all the foregoing progress of the nascent art, craftsmen had occasionally symbolized, as it were, the importance of the intersecting ribs by carving little caryatids for them to rest upon above the capitals; such figurines are to be seen in the Oise region at Bury and at Cambronne.[21]

Mr. Arthur Kingsley Porter's idea is that the transitional period resolves itself into a series of experiments on the part of the builders to erect a vault with a minimum of centering, and he cites the hollow spires at Loches as an experiment to put up a stone roof without the use of any temporary substructure of wood, which apparently was costly.[22] He thinks that the earlier Gothic vaults were *bombé* because that form facilitated construction without centering, and that the Lombards dropped their precocious diagonals after 1120, as soon as they had learned how to build domed groin vaults which required no temporary wooden substructures. What is of value in Mr. Porter's thesis is sure, in time, to pass into French currency; until a majority of French archæologists find his explanation better than their own it is permissible for us to agree with those who are telling the tale of their own national art.

Probably the earliest extant Gothic vaults in the Ile-de-France are those at Acy-en-Multien (Oise) and at Crouy-sur-Ourcq (Seine-et-Marne). Their outline is rectangular. Some intersecting ribs at Rhuis (Oise) are cited by M. Lefèvre-Pontalis as the oldest in the Soissonnais. Diagonals were put up, about 1115, at St. Vaast-de-Longmont (Oise), Orgeval (Seine-et-Oise), Viffort (Aisne), Airaines (Somme), and in other rural churches. The famous ambulatory vaults at Morienval were probably built about 1122. A year or two earlier, perhaps, are the side-aisle vaults of St. Étienne at Beauvais.

Bury (Oise) shows the first extant half dome with ribs. Of the same time, about 1125, are the diagonals at Marolles, St. Vaast-les-Mello, Béthisy-St.-Pierre,

[21] *Congrès Archéologique*, 1905, p. 39, on Bury (Oise), and p. 43, on Cambronne (Oise).

[22] Arthur Kingsley Porter, *The Construction of Lombard and Gothic Vaults* (New Haven, Yale University Press, 1911).

Bonneuil-en-Valois, and Bellefontaine, all in the Oise department. Bellefontaine, whose date of 1125 is certain, has helped to place other churches of the transition by comparing their diagonals with its pointed intersecting ribs. Bruyères (Aisne) is about 1130, Poissy (Seine-et-Oise) and Villetertre (Oise) are about 1135, and so are the ribs of St. Martin-des-Champs at Paris. In the Aisne region are Berzy-le-Sec and Laffaux (c. 1140) and in the Oise region is Chelles, building at the hour when Suger undertook St. Denis (Seine), 1140 to 1144. Cambronne (Oise) and Foy-St.-Quentin (Somme) are about 1145. Such churches as Glennes (Aisne), St. Leu d'Esserent (Oise), and, close to the latter, Creuil's church of St. Évremont were building in 1150; so were Chars (Seine-et-Oise) and, near it, Pontoise,[23] whose ambulatory vaults some claim are prior to those of the procession path of St. Denis, and therefore a link between Morienval and Suger's abbatial. The big church at St. Germer (Oise) was begun about 1150, though certain of its features are more archaic than St. Denis, built before it. Some of these churches, called transitional, used wall ribs for their diagonals, others omitted them; in some the intersecting ribs were pointed, in others, semicircular.

Mr. John Bilson, who contends that diagonals were used in Normandy some twenty-five years earlier than in the Ile-de-France, considers the early dates for these rural churches improbable, that scarcely any were anterior to St. Denis, that it was a case of little churches following the great churches, not vice versa. The earliest, he thinks, was St. Étienne at Beauvais (c. 1120), significantly close to Normandy. But Normandy did not suspect the value and fecundity of diagonals. That feat of creative genius none can deny to the Ile-de-France.

The traveler can do nothing more enlightening and delightful as a prelude to his journey among French cathedrals than to spend some early spring days exploring the rural churches of the privileged land of the national art which the old geographers chose to picture as an island inclosed by the Seine, the Marne, the Aisne, and the Oise. Numerous churches of the transition lie between Soissons, Senlis, and Beauvais, and once, around Amiens was another such center, but few of the monuments there have survived.[24] Go to Creuil and see, in the ruins of St. Évremont, a rudimentary flying buttress—a quarter arch once hidden under the lean-to roof. No doubt the architect built it with the intention of bracing the upper walls, but since he omitted to brace the flying buttress itself it failed of its purpose. Four miles away, at St. Leu d'Esserent, is an awkward early trial of a Gothic vault in the tribune above the porch, but as the ribs are embedded in the cells, no proper elasticity is achieved. Go to Morienval and study its remarkable essay in spanning

[23] In each vault section of the ambulatory of St. Maclou, Pontoise, was inserted a fifth rib, which sprang from the keystone to the middle of each apse chapel's rear wall, and which consolidated both chapel and procession path. The diagonals do not curve, as do those of Morienval. St. Maclou was entirely finished in the XII century, but it was reconstructed radically in the XV century: the present façade is 1450-70. Again in the XVI century the church was partly rebuilt, so that the double-aisled nave of to-day appears a beautiful example of Renaissance art. It was at Pontoise that St. Louis, in 1244, took the vow to go crusading. (See, Lefèvre-Pontalis, *Monographie de l'église St. Maclou de Pontoise*.)

[24] Arthur Kingsley Porter, *Medieval Architecture* (New York and London, 1909). In vol. 2, pp. 193-251, is a full list of monuments of the transition.

a curving section with diagonals. Trace these early steps of the national art, and the meaning of the Gothic bone structure grows plainer.

MORIENVAL[25]

> I approve the life of those for whom the city is a prison, who find paradise in solitude, who live by the works of their hands, or who seek to remake their spirit by the sweetness of their contemplative life, who drink of the fountain of life by the lips of their heart, and forget what is behind them to regard only what lies ahead. But neither the most hidden forest nor the highest mountains will give happiness to man, if he has not in himself solitude of the spirit, peace of conscience, upliftings of the heart to God.

—Letter of St. Ives, Bishop of Chartres, 1091-1115.

Of the experimental steps which led to Gothic art, the most appealing is the nunnery church of Morienval, a humble forerunner of Amiens Cathedral that has made as much stir in archæological controversy as Périgueux's cathedral of St. Front itself. Morienval may not be the passionately sought *œuvre-initiale*, since its vaults, while they betray inexperience, certainly were preceded by still cruder attempts, but it can boast that it is the first Gothic ambulatory extant, and as the curving aisle around the chancel is the most exquisite feature of the great cathedrals, Morienval's humble first essay of it merits a pilgrimage.

As one approaches the abbey church it does not appear till one is directly over it, so snugly hidden away is the village in a fold of the rolling country that skirts the forest of Compiègne. Perhaps the IX-century nuns who chose the site may have hoped that the marauders of that troublous time might ride by, unconscious of booty so close at hand. With gratitude one learns that the invasion of 1914 has left Morienval unscathed, as well as those other memorials of tentative Gothic, Acy-en-Multien and Crouy-sur-Ourcq.

Because of excellent proportions, the church appears larger than in reality. The exterior is Romanesque. Two time-stained towers of the XI century mark the angles between transept and choir, an arrangement derived from Rhenish churches. At the west façade is a beautiful XII-century tower. It was building while the nuns were proceeding to tear down a decrepit apse in order to erect the present east end of the church. In that new apse appeared the much-discussed early ribs.

A record tells that relics were installed in the church in 1122, and it was prob-

[25] *Congrès Archéologique*, 1905, p. 154, on Morienval; *ibid.*, 1908, vol. 2, pp. 128, 476, on Morienval, E. Lefèvre-Pontalis, Brutails, and John Bilson; E. Lefèvre-Pontalis, *L'architecture religieuse dans l'ancien diocèse de Soissons au XIe et au XIIe siècle* (Paris, Plon, 1894-97), 2 vols., folio. Also, his discussion on the vaults of Morienval in *Bulletin Monumental*, vol. 71, pp. 160, 335; 1908, vol. 72, p. 477; and in *Correspondance historique et archéologique*, 1897, pp. 193, 197; Anthyme Saint-Paul, "La transition," in *Revue de l'art chrétien*, 1895, p. 13. Also, his studies of Morienval in *Mémoires de la Soc. archéol. de Pontoise ...*, 1894, vol. 16; *Mémoires du Comité archéol. de Senlis*, 1892, vol. 7; *Correspondance historique et archéologique*, 1897, pp. 129, 161; John Bilson, on Morienval, in *Bulletin Monumental*, 1908, vol. 72, p. 498; and *Congrès Archéologique*, 1905; L. Régnier, in *Mémoires de la Soc. archéol. de Pontoise ...*, 1895, p. 124.

ably then that the new works were finished. Ambulatories had come into favor during the first third of the XII century, when need was felt for a suitable corridor for pilgrims to encircle the altar whereon relics were exposed. Now to vault a curving aisle was no easy task, owing to the trapeze shape of each section. Morienval's ambulatory must have been designed to hold extra altars, since entrance to the aisle is blocked at both ends by the towers, and the passage is so narrow that only one at a time can walk in it. There are no apse chapels. The sculpture is archaic. Some of the capitals show interlacings, and some are of the pleated type popular in Normandy. The diminutive corridor has four small bays whose clumsy intersecting vault ribs are of the size of the average stovepipe. They curve strangely, and two of the keystones are not in the axis of the passageway, nor has elasticity yet been wholly achieved, since the ends of the ribs plunge into the web of the vault.

Over the choir, consisting of one large bay, are intersecting ribs that appear to be posterior to those of the ambulatory. They, too, are rude and large, but are wholly detached from the cells. M. Lefèvre-Pontalis thinks that the ambulatory diagonals are contemporary, and owe their more archaic character to the difficulty of vaulting a curved passage. So swiftly did the early architects acquire skill in the new system of building, that when a chapel was erected on the northern arm of Morienval's transept, at the end of the XII century, each diagonal had become a single slender torus, virile and graceful.

Of less architectural importance is the Romanesque nave of Morienval, whose meager vault ribs are of the XVII century. The western tower was the prototype of the Romanesque belfries of the region and should be preserved. It is in a deplorable state, propped by beams, which are gayly scaled by the lads who ring the Angelus. Little Morienval has the human touch which the traveler craves. Set in the wall above the XIII-century lord of Viri's tomb are tablets that commemorate two pastors of this isolated Valois village who were heroes as valiant as any crusader. Their combined ministry covered a hundred and one years. The first died in 1840, after fifty-seven years of service here, "faithful to his duty in times most difficult," and difficult indeed was a priest's life during the Revolution. "Pray for his soul," begs his grateful commune, to which he had bequeathed the presbytery and all his savings.

His successor came to Morienval in his 'twenties, fresh from Paris, his birthplace, and on this dwindling village he expended his energies for forty-five years. Abbé Riaux loved his parishioners like a father, and was, says the memorial tablet, "physician for body as well as soul." During the cholera of 1849 his self-denial elicited a gold medal from Morienval and the village of Bonneuil, where is another primitive essay of a Gothic vault. "The state of decay of his beautiful church made him suffer," runs the inscription, so he willed his modest fortune toward its restoration. Happily, he lived long enough to see the church he loved become a savant's shrine. It was in 1880 that M. Robert de Lasteyrie first drew attention to Morienval as an early step in the tardily understood national art, and MM. Anthyme Saint-Paul, Eugène Lefèvre-Pontalis, and Camille Enlart joined in the debate. The archæologists' war horse they have called our little Morienval. Such widespread discussion and the good priest's bequest fortunately brought about a thorough restoration of the choir.

ST. ÉTIENNE AT BEAUVAIS, AND ST. GERMER[26]

> Sous le porche de l'église, chacun laisse le fardeau que la vie lui impose. Ici le plus pauvre homme s'élève au rang des grands intellectuels, des poètes, que dis-je? au rang des esprits: il s'installe dans le domaine de la pensée pure et du rêve. Le gémissement d'une vieille femme agenouillée dans l'église de son village est du même accent, traduit la même ignorance, le mêmepressentiment que la méditation du savant.... De ces parties profondes de l'être, de ce domaine obscur surgissent toutes les puissances créatrices de l'homme.

—Maurice Barrès.[27]

Close in date to Morienval are the aisle vaults of St. Étienne's nave at Beauvais, the old city that lies on a tributary of the Oise. The intersecting ribs are not quite so stout as those of Morienval, but their ends still plunge into the massive, and they, too, are round-arched; their date is approximately 1120. That they planned at the same time to throw similar diagonals over the principal span is proved by the existent lower structures, but the actual vaults there were not erected till after a fire in 1180. The transverse arches of the aisles are noticeably stilted. This device was to lead to a solution of the problem how to raise the arches framing each vault section to the level of the diagonals' crown, and thus avoid the excessive doming which is found in the earlier Gothic vaults.

In the XII-century north façade of the transept is an oculus big enough to be called the first rose window; a wheel of fortune it is called, because the images around its circle are an allegory of the fleet passing of man's greatness. This is one of the very early approaches to pure sculpture. The nave's two westernmost bays and its façade are of the XI century. Had the original choir of St. Étienne survived, it is thought that its ambulatory would be one of the missing steps connecting the cramped corridor of Morienval with the double procession path of St. Denis. The present choir, a Flamboyant Gothic structure, is famous for its gloriously colored windows, some of which were made by that notable family of local artists who designed the big rose windows of Beauvais Cathedral, Engrand Le Prince and his sons Jean and Nicolas, and his son-in-law Nicolas Le Pot. The latter carved the

[26] *Congrès Archéologique*, 1905, "St. Étienne, at Beauvais," pp. 15, 530; Viollet-le-Duc, *Dictionnaire*, vol. 3, pp. 254, 263; vol. 4, p. 289; vol. 7, p. 133; Stanislas de Saint-Germain, *Notice historique et descriptive de l'église St. Étienne de Beauvais*; Victor Lhuillier, *St. Étienne de Beauvais*; P. C. Barraud, "Les vitraux de St. Étienne de Beauvais," in *Soc. Académique d'archéologie, department de l'Oise*, vol. 2, p. 507; *Congrès Archéologique*, 1905, p. 81, "St. Germer," L. Régnier; and p. 406, "St. Germer," A. Besnard; E. Lefèvre-Pontalis, "L'église de St. Germer," in *l'Annuaire Normand*, 1903, p. 134; and *Bibliothèque de l'École des chartes*, 1885 and 1889; also *Bulletin Monumental*, 1886; A. Besnard, *L'église de St. Germer de Fly (Oise)*, (Paris, E. Lechavalier, 1913); Paul des Forts, "Une excursion en Beauvaisis," in *Bulletin de la Société d'émulation d'Abbeville*, 1903; Eugène Woillez, *Archéologie des monuments religieux de l'ancien Beauvoisis*.

[27] Maurice Barrès, *La grande pitié des églises de France* (Paris, Émile-Paul, frères, 1914).

cathedral's wooden doors, for versatility was characteristic of the artisan-artists of those days.

Ten miles from Beauvais, a crawling train sets one down in a field whence a two-mile walk leads to the sleepy bourg of St. Germer-en-Flay. The abbey was founded in 655 by Germer, a noble of Dagobert's court, nephew of St. Ouen the great bishop of Normandy's capital. To St. Germer's abbey came William the Conqueror to beg the French king to join him in his proposed descent on England. But Philip I gathered his counselors, and it was decided not to support the Norman duke, since, if he gained England, he would be richer than his own suzerain, the king of France, and if he failed, France would have antagonized the English.

The large abbatial church of St. Germer, if not beautiful, is of archæological interest. Formerly it was thought to be a monument of 1130, but closer study has shown that it was erected during one bout of work from 1150 to 1180. Hard though it was to believe it the contemporary of the cathedrals at Senlis and Noyon, its sculpture is too excellent to have been done earlier. The crocketed capitals of its westernmost bays were never made earlier than 1175. That the church was continued without pause from apse to façade is proved by the unity of profiles and details. Its anachronisms are to be explained because it derived from a side current of Gothic art, out of touch with the swift-moving main stream, which was channeled by Abbot Suger.

The architect of St. Germer showed in the main parts of his church a thorough understanding of the new Gothic vaulting, and at the same time he covered his tribune gallery with Romanesque groins. He made heavy Romanesque piers, and simultaneously he essayed to disencumber the pavement by employing the corbel, or side bracket. The Norman zigzag or chevron design decorates the heavy molding of the pier arches. Over the sanctuary he attempted the inartistic experiment of having his ribs converge, not on a keystone, but directly on a transverse rib. The ribs of the upper vaulting are heavy and ornamented. The pointed arches of the pier arcade are surmounted by round arches, in the tribunes. And between tribune and clearstory are square apertures neither Romanesque nor Gothic.

To meet the thrust of the upper vaulting, some rudimentary flying buttresses were built under the lean-to roof of the tribune galleries, but as they themselves were not braced, they remained ineffectual. The collapse of some of the high vaults caused the addition, later, of the present flying buttresses. The exterior of the church is gaunt, with windows that are small and round-arched. The west façade was wrecked during the Hundred Years' War, and never restored. Walled-up arches mar the spacious interior. Thick coats of whitewash cover it, and when dust gathers on that make-shift of cleanliness the effect is tawdry. Directly behind the apse of the big abbatial stands a masterpiece of Rayonnant Gothic, a diminutive church whose west façade faces, with awkward closeness, the back of the larger church. As it is connected with the latter's ambulatory by a glazed passage, it may be regarded as a sort of Lady chapel. Many such imitations of the Sainte-Chapelle of Paris arose, after St. Louis had made his shrine for the crown of thorns. The abbot who put up St. Germer's glass reliquary was Pierre Wesencourt, who ruled from 1254 to 1272, and it is thought that the king's own architect designed it.

That Louis IX contributed toward it is shown by the fleur-de-lis and the donjons of Castile in the storied windows. Over the altar once stood the alabaster retablo, depicting St. Germain's life, now in the Musée Cluny, at Paris.

POISSY[28]

Christianity is still for 400,000,000 of human beings the great pair of wings that are indispensable if man is to rise above himself, above humdrum living and shut-in horizons, it is still the spiritual guide to lead him by patience, resignation, and hope to serenity, to lift him by purity, temperance, and goodness to the heights of devotion and self-sacrifice. Always and everywhere for nineteen hundred years as soon as these wings flag or break, public and private manners degenerate. Neither philosophy, reason, nor artistic and literary culture, nor even feudal honor, military and chivalrous, no code, no administration, no government can serve as substitute for it.

—H. TAINE (1892).

The church of St. Louis, at Poissy, is a link in the normal development of Gothic, and not like St. Germain, a disconcerting anachronism. About 1135 both systems of vaults were here built at one and the same time.

Poissy lies on the Seine slightly above its junction with the classic Oise. A pleasant way to approach it is to walk from St. Germain-en-Laye through the forest, when it is carpeted with anemones. St. Germain's palace chapel is thought to be the work of Pierre de Montereau. One goes to Poissy in a spirit of pilgrimage, for at its font, in 1215, St. Louis of France was baptized.[29] He held the gift of Christian citizenship he here received above all that the world could bestow. To his intimates he often signed himself Louis of Poissy. His grandfather, Philippe-Auguste, had given the manor of Poissy to his son, on his marriage to Blanche of Castile. Living then in retirement at Poissy was the gentle Agnes of Méran, that aunt of St. Elizabeth of Hungary whom Philippe-Auguste had been forced by Rome's decree to set aside. When St. Louis was born, on St. Mark's Day of 1215, in order to spare the young mother, the church bells were silent. The Spanish princess asked the cause, and ordered—gallant woman that she was—that every bell in the town should ring out a joyous carillon because God had given her *un beau fils*. Shakespeare would inevitably admire Blanche; she was a Shakespearian character:

---

[28] Anthyme Saint-Paul, "Poissy et Morienval," in *Mémoires de la Société archéol. de Pontoise et du Vexin*, 1894, vol. 16; E. Lefèvre-Pontalis, *L'Architecture religieuse dans l'ancien diocèse de Soissons au XIᵉ et au XIIᵉ siècle* (Paris, Plon, 1894), 2 vols., folio; F. de Verneilh, *Le premier des monuments gothic* (Paris, 1864).

[29] Some naïve XVI-century lines are under the window of St. Louis' chapel:

"Saint Louis fut un enfant de Poissy,
Et baptisé en la présente église;
Les fonts en sont gardés encore ici,
Et honorés comme rélique exquise."

That daughter there of Spain, the hardy Blanche,
Is near to England; look upon the years
Of Louis the Dauphin and that lovely maid.
If lusty love should go in search of beauty,
Where shall he find it fairer than in Blanche?
If jealous love should go in search of virtue,
Where shall he find it purer than in Blanche?
If love ambitious sought a match of birth,

Whose veins bound richer blood than Lady Blanche?[30]

The wide ambulatory of Poissy is groin-vaulted, but diagonals cover the two oriented apsidioles that open on a false transept, which arrangement of pseudo-transept with chapels was copied soon after at Sens. The three easternmost bays of the nave have retained their primitive intersecting ribs, which are round-arched, decorated, and very broad, as are the transverse arches that separate the vault into sections. Poissy's sculpture is of an advanced type. Owing to later changes, there is much patchwork in the church.

ST. DENIS-EN-FRANCE[31]

Give all thou canst: high Heaven rejects the lore
Of nicely calculated less or more:
So deemed the man who fashioned for the sense
These lofty pillars, spread this branching roof
Self-poised.

—WORDSWORTH.

---

[30] "King John," Act II.

[31] Vitry et Brière, *L'église abbatiale de St. Denis et ses tombeaux* (Paris, Longuet, 1908); *ibid., Documents de sculpture française* (Paris, 1913); Anthyme Saint-Paul. "Suger. L'église de St. Denis, et St. Bernard," *Mémoire lu à la* Sorbonne, inséré au *Bulletin archéologique*, et tiré à part, 1890; F. de Verneilh, *Le premier des monuments gothiques* (Paris, 1864); Abbé Crosnier, "Vitrail de l'abbaye de St. Denis expliqué," in *Revue archéologique*, 1847, vol. 7, p. 377; Félicie d'Ayzac, *Histoire de l'abbaye de Saint Denis-en-France* (Paris, 1861), 2 vols.; Ferdinand de Lasteyrie, *Histoire de la peinture sur verre* (Paris, Didot, 1852), 2 vols.; Bushnell, *Storied Windows* (New York, Macmillan, 1914); Émile Mâle, *L'art religieux de la fin du moyen âge en France* (Paris, A. Colin, 1910); *ibid.*, "La part de Suger dans la création de l'iconographie," in *Revue de l'art ancien et moderne*, 1914; L. Levillain, "L'église carolingienne de St. Denis," in *Bulletin Monumental*, 1907, vol. 71, p. 211; L. Levillain et L. Maitre, "Crypt de St. Denis," in *Congrès Archéologique*, 1903, p. 136; Suger, *Œuvres complètes*, éd. Lecoy de la Marche (Paris, Renouard, 1867); *Histoire littéraire de la France.* (Begun by the XVII-century Benedictines and continued by the Institute of France.) Vol. 12, p. 361, on Suger, published in 1764.

Poissy. An Early Example of Gothic Vaulting (c. 1135)

Finally came the hour of the new architecture's clear achievement. After all the trial efforts, there now was built, midway in the XII century, a monument which was to wield momentous influence. With the erection of St. Denis, the center of Gothic art may be said to have shifted slightly south, to Paris. From the capital the new movement spread out in systematic progression—each church comprehending better than had its predecessor the principle of thrust and counterthrust, each drawing from it further consequences.

St. Denis did not put a stop abruptly to the coexistence in the same edifice of both systems of vaulting any more than it began immediately the usage of all the consequences of diagonals. Yet none the less the Royal Abbey is rightly called the first Gothic monument, since here first was demonstrated stout-heartedly the advantages of the new system. Abbot Suger was the first to employ the generating member with the full intelligence of its results. "From the moment of St. Denis' conception, Amiens had become inevitable."

It was Suger who wedded definitely the pointed arch and the intersecting ribs. He dared to make piers so slender that the beholders were astonished they could carry the weight of a stone roof; he dared to open his walls by windows so large that his choir was called by the people the lantern of St. Denis. The mastery by Suger's craftsmen of the art of stained glass was to have profound consequences in Gothic structure, since it hastened the suppression of the wall screen between the active members: "Behold I will lay thy stones with fair colors, and thy foundations with sapphires; and I will make thy windows of agates, and thy gates of carbuncles, and all thy borders of pleasant stones."

Suger has himself told us how the house of God, many-colored as the radiance of precious stones, lifted his soul from the cares of this world to divine meditation, for this Gothic art, whose spiritual appeal he had apprehended as profoundly as he had its structural laws, was most aptly fashioned to be a foretaste of the Beyond, neither touching the baseness of earth nor wholly the serenity of heaven.

Doubtless Suger understood the importance of the dedication day in 1144. He made of it a national ceremony. He started the Gothic movement intrepidly. Before a historic gathering of bishops and barons he demonstrated that a Gothic vault was lighter, more easily built, more economical, and more enduring than any other, and the important men of France went back to their own cities to spread far and wide the lesson they had learned.

In the course of the story of French architecture, fate has most graciously allied certain monuments of prime archæological interest with people or events of historic importance.

Gothic art made its debut in a unique setting. St. Denis was the patron of France, the missionary who first preached Christianity by the Seine, and who there had been martyred in the III century. On Montmartre is the crypt said to have been the burial place of the first Christian martyrs of Paris. In time there rose on the road outside the city a monastery dedicated to St. Denis, and thither were his relics transferred. Each of the three royal lines that have ruled France, Merovingian, Carolingian, and Capetian, chose the abbey of St. Denis as their final resting place and loaded it with favors. The first milestone on the highroad of Gothic art was the famous center of the nation's life, and the initiator of the new system of building was the maker of the nation's unity, Abbot Suger.

To Suger may be applied the mediæval term for an architect, Master of Works, *maître de l'œuvre*. He wrote an account of how he reconstructed his abbey, building it, he says, with the aid of his companions in the community and his brothers in the cloister. The people gave voluntarily of their labor. When a quarry with suitable stone was discovered at Pontoise, the whole countryside—men, women, and children being harnessed to the carts—dragged the blocks in pious enthusiasm to St. Denis.

The tomb of the martyred patron of Paris was a pilgrim shrine from earliest days. The same trait in human nature that, in 1915, sent Americans to gaze reverently at a relic of their national history, the Liberty Bell, when on a two weeks' journey from the San Francisco Fair to Philadelphia, it was exhibited in different cities, made the early Christians of Gaul flock to revere the relics of the holy man who had brought them the light and liberty of the gospel. Religion then and all through the Middle Ages was fraught with patriotism.

For St. Denis' abbey a Merovingian church had been built by Dagobert. Pépin and Charlemagne replaced it by a Carolingian church. By the XII century the abbatial had become inadequate for the pilgrim crowds; people were crushed to death on festival days, and Abbot Suger decided to rebuild. He began by demolishing a heavy vestibule which Charlemagne had put up as a kind of tomb over his father's grave, for Pépin had begged to be buried face downward in penance, before the abbey church. Suger replaced that encumbering porch by what is to-day a narthex, or forechurch, formed by the two westernmost bays of the edifice. In the thirties of the XI century he started the new works. Romanesque feeling lingered in the sculpture, and the stout vault ribs crossed each other in round arches. By 1140 the west façade was finished and ceremoniously consecrated.

A month later, a still greater gathering met at St. Denis for the laying of the corner stone of the choir. To the sound of trumpets, Louis VII descended into the trench prepared for the foundation, and placed the first stone, and as the choir chanted of the jeweled walls of the heavenly city, *Lapides pretiosi omnes muri tui*, the king, profoundly moved, took from his finger a costly ring and threw it into the mortar, which had been mixed with holy water. Each baron and bishop, as he laid down a stone, did the same. Their vehement faith would turn to literal meaning the Psalmist's dream of the celestial city.

In his choir, Suger united definitely the pointed arch with the intersecting ribs, and the ribs, now, were not the heavy ones used in his forechurch. All the arches at their crown were brought to the same height by a combination of stilting, pointing, or depressing them. In the outer aisle of his ambulatory, Suger introduced a fifth rib in each vault section, which welded the apse chapels with the procession path. For his inner aisle he employed what is called the broken-rib vault. First, the keystone was planted in the center and from it branched the four ribs, each regardless of making a straight diagonal. This became the generally accepted method for vaulting an ambulatory. Every part of his edifice Suger supervised with untiring energy. Owing to the waste of forest trees for machines of war, none of sufficient girth could be found for the outer roof covering. Suger lay brooding over this one night, then started up impetuously before dawn, took the measurements of the beams needed, and himself went into the dense forest. Before nine that morning he had found a giant tree; by noon ten others, and the timber was hauled in triumph to the abbey.

All France was talking of the new works at St. Denis. Never before had been such a gathering of skilled masons and sculptors, of goldsmiths and glassmakers. St. Denis' school was to direct the glassmakers' art through the second half of the XII century. Little is known of the origin of that art; the early basilicas of Christian Gaul had made use of pieces of colored glass framed together, and in the X century figures were represented. No work, however, previous to the XII century has survived. For the earlier fenestration the term "painted glass" is a misnomer, since each piece was colored in the mass, and only a few black lines were applied to denote the features, or the folds of the draperies. The artists of St. Denis obtained their relief effects by a skilled juxtaposition of tones; intensity of hue was increased by the employment of thick rough leaves of glass. Scarcely any white was used; in the ancient windows no spots spring out unpleasantly.

To St. Denis' school succeeded that of Chartres, which predominated during the first part of the XIII century, while its second half was ruled by the school of Paris, when windows of the Sainte-Chapelle type were the rule. Gradually the craftsmen gave up their sound tradition that a window should be a transparent mosaic, subordinate to its architectural setting. They began to treat a window as an isolated picture and the art declined.

Abbot Suger's school of glassmakers carried their art to its zenith. Not all the wonders of XIII-century fenestration equaled the unfathomable vibrant blue in the background of XII-century windows—a fugitive mystery whose secret has been entirely lost. The popular fancy was that Suger ground down sapphires to obtain his magic color.

All over the land the church builders desired windows like those of St. Denis. Suger's own craftsmen went to Chartres to make the three big lancets in that cathedral's western front. The St. Denis school influenced the superb Crucifixion window in Poitiers Cathedral, and others in the cathedrals of Angers and Le Mans and in the Trinité at Vendôme, also the Tree of Jesse window in York Cathedral. And, had the choir glass of Notre Dame at Paris survived, it would have been of the school of St. Denis.

Suger wrote inscriptions for his abbey windows to make their symbolism clearer. Owing to the vicissitudes of seven hundred years, few of the St. Denis lights have survived. Four are now reset in the central apse chapel and in that to its north. In a medallion at the base of one of these windows Suger himself is represented holding a scroll bearing his name. The medallion figures are of the hieratic Byzantine type. Every window has a closely woven pattern; each losenge has its own border, and a rich jeweled border surrounds the whole lancet. Bracing bars of iron run straight across the pictured story. Slowly, with infinite patience, worked those old XII-century artists, and never has their handicraft been surpassed as sheer splendor of ornamentation.

After three years and three months of passionate work, the choir of St. Denis was finished, and on June 11, 1144, the dedication day, the relics were installed. That date, forever memorable in the annals of architecture, may be called the consecration of the national art. At the ceremony assisted Louis VII with his queen,

Aliénor of Aquitaine, whose strange destiny was to make her patroness of that entirely different phase of Gothic called the Plantagenet school. The chief barons were present at the dedication, as well as five archbishops and some fourteen bishops. They looked and wondered, and not a few of them returned home to imitate. The bishops of Noyon and Senlis hastened to rebuild their cathedrals in the new way, and some of Suger's masons passed into the service of the former prelate. Bishop Geoffrey de Lèves went back to Chartres to build the most beautiful tower in the world, and the sculptors who had made Suger's western portals (now no longer extant) worked on the three west doors of Chartres.

On the day of St. Denis' dedication, Abbot Suger, small and frail in person, but towering in personality, was honored on every side. When the abbot of great Cluny, Peter the Venerable, passed from the marvels of the new church to Suger's narrow cell, he cried out in honest distress: "This man condemns us all. He builds, not for himself, but for God alone!"

Though the last half of Suger's life was an example of monastic simplicity, not always had he been content with a monk's cell. Perhaps because of his conversion midway in life, he appeals to us in a more human way. Not that he was converted from evil doings; his purpose always was high. But in his position as St. Denis' abbot, as a powerful feudal lord, he lived sumptuously, according to the accepted standards of the time. He mixed freely in the world; he directed state affairs for the king to whom he was devoted; he went on embassies; he even led armies. In 1124, when an irate German emperor was marching on Rheims, which he had vowed to destroy, Suger in person led against him some ten thousand of his abbey's retainers. That was the first time the oriflamme of St. Denis was carried as the national emblem.[32] Suger had grown up in the secular atmosphere of the Royal Abbey, and took its worldliness as a matter of course.

Of peasant parentage himself, he had been brought, a child of ten, to live with the monks, because he already showed exceptional qualities. Among his fellow students in the abbey school was the king's son, the future Louis VI, and an intimacy began between the two lads destined to continue till death. When Suger became a monk he was sent on notable missions, for he was gifted with tact and good manners, vivacity and charm. Sweetness of disposition, mental energy, courage, and absolute integrity won for him general esteem. Early and often this born lover of things beautiful made the journey into Italy. It was while returning from one of his missions there, in 1122, that he learned of his election as abbot by his fellow monks in St. Denis. Louis VI had come to the throne; henceforth Suger was to lead in all state affairs.

The genius of this son of field workers had pierced to the vital need of the age—unity of government. Only a strong, central administration could cope with the disintegration which was feudalism. For its very existence the feudal system depended on the absence of well-enforced general laws. It was Suger's strong hand that guided the early steps toward national unity, and king and people worked for it together. Under the king whom Suger served France began her great role of redresser of wrongs. Louis VI was the first to use the title, king of France, not

[32] Marius Sepet, *Le Drapeau de la France.*

king of the Franks. The ideal of this XII-century statesman was a strong central monarchy, coexistent with a national assembly. His high conception of solidarity was to fructify, within a hundred years, under Philippe-Auguste, the grandson of Suger's master.

Suger was one of the first in Europe to understand political economy. He laid the base of a sound financial administration. His confirmation of a charter for the townsmen of St. Denis gave security to trade; he relieved the abbey serfs of *main-morte*, built a Villeneuve for homeless nomads, and found time to study agriculture scientifically. In his writings we feel the first breath of a national patriotism. A new note in that age of unfettered personal impulse when might meant right, was Suger's constant reference to "the poor weighed down with taxations," to "that which has been too long neglected, the care of the surety of laborers, of artisans, and of the poor." Many a modern politician could well ponder Suger's censure of the spoils system. "The officers dismissed carry off what they can lay their hands on," he said, "and those who replace them, fearing to be likewise treated, hasten to steal, to secure their fortune."

Suger's pre-eminence in public affairs continued during two reigns. Louis VII, after stumbling some years without guidance, turned to his father's counselor and, during his absence on the Second Crusade, appointed him regent of France. So masterly was the abbot's rule that king and people publicly proclaimed him *Père de la Patrie*. Suger studied the causes of the crusade's lamentable failure; he felt that forethought and prudence might win success, and, though he was seventy years of age, he began preparations to carry out a crusade at his own expense. Time was not given him again to prove his genius for leadership. When news of his death (1151) reached the court, the king and the Grand Master of the Templars, who was with him, burst into tears. On his grave in the abbey church which he had built they cut the simple inscription, "Here lies Abbot Suger." No need of panegyric. "The single names are the noblest epitaphs."

The commanding place held by this monk in the estimation of Europe is vouched for by letters from pope, kings, and many a dignitary. The king of Sicily wrote to beg a line from him; the king of Scotland sent gifts; the bishop of Salisbury made the journey to France expressly to know Suger. By one clear stroke after another—and above all by his own writings—every line of which is of historical value—the picture is filled in of this admirable churchman who was as soundly honest and forceful as the architecture he fostered, and whose delicate, ardent soul accomplished remarkable things with the reasoned orderliness of the art he loved.

Suger's sudden but thorough conversion is attributed to St. Bernard. Up to middle life he had been a type of those who soar as high as human abilities can reach without super natural aid. Entangled in the mesh of various employments, his soul could not rise to heavenly things. Then the trumpet of Bernard's reform sounded in Europe. Men's hearts were set on fire with repentance and aspiration toward the highest. Bernard's clear eyes read beneath the outer circumstance of Abbot Suger's life. He saw that here was a good man, capable of becoming a holy one. He wrote fearless words of disapproval. "One would think it was a governor of a province, not of souls," he wrote, when he saw the abbot of St. Denis ride by with sixty horsemen.

Suger began to scrutinize his manner of life. Grace touched his soul, pomp was laid aside, and he set about his conversion with the same thoroughness that he displayed in all his acts. Before reforming his monastery, he completely reformed himself. With St. Bernard, who was ten years his junior, he was linked in ennobling friendship to the end. "I know profoundly this man," Bernard wrote of Suger to the pope, "and I know that he is faithful and prudent in temporal things, that he is fervent and humble in things spiritual. If there is any precious vase adorning the palace of the King of Kings, it is the soul of the venerable Suger." When Suger lay dying, he wrote to St. Bernard: "Could I but see your angelic face before I die, I should go with more confidence." And Bernard, who was to follow in a year, begged that when Suger reached Paradise he would "think of him before God."

Yet, if the overwhelming saint could change the whole tenor of Suger's life, the cultivated little abbot of St. Denis offered a gentle, stubborn opposition to the puritanic ideas of Bernard in the domain of art. "Vanity of vanities," cried the ascetic, in the well-known open letter in which he denounced the new luxury in church building. Churches were made too long, he complained, too high, and needlessly wide; the capitals were carved with monsters more apt to distract than to lead to pious recollection.

The art lover in St. Denis' abbey smiled at such iconoclastic vehemence. Suger thought that nothing was too precious for the house of God. He proceeded to erect an abbey church as imposing as a cathedral, and to enrich its treasury with goldsmith work. Over the three gilt-bronze entrance doors of his church he inscribed, "The soul on its earthly pilgrimage rises by material things to contemplate the Divine." To this day both men have vigorous partisans, and those who set out on a cathedral tour in France are more likely to be on Suger's side in the controversy.

Suger's subtle mind reached beyond the ascetic's maxim. Well he knew that both saint and art patron were needed, well he knew that Bernard of Clairvaux was as instrumental as himself in the formation of the cathedral builders. A living example of Christian perfection, Bernard fortified the faith of all Europe. He might advocate church simplicity, but it was not without cause that his apostolate preceded the most fecund creative period of mankind's art. His impassioned love of God warmed the imaginations of the men who began the big Gothic churches.

What remains to-day of the XII-century abbatial built by Suger of St. Denis? Comparatively little. The lower parts of the west façade and the two first bays of the nave which form a narthex, or vestibule, are his work. In the choir, his beautiful ambulatory begins at the third bay of the double aisles. There are nine bays of Suger's processional path, and from them radiate seven apse chapels. The pillars that divide the lovely curving double passage are the very ones which the generous enthusiasm of the people dragged from Pontoise, and, in memory of the little abbot, some will touch those slender columns with reverential gesture. It was Suger who created the disposition of the *rond point* found in its perfection at St. Denis and copied in the great cathedrals. The crypt also is his work, though its nucleus belonged to an underground shrine built by Abbot Hilduin in the XI century. When Abbot Suger had finished his choir, he proceeded to make a new Gothic transept and nave; but of them scarcely a vestige remains. Some sculpture at the north door of the transept is of the XII century. Whether the construction was faulty, or whether the monks desired a more ample church, there was a total reconstruction of St. Denis' abbatial, a hundred years after Suger's day.

THE ST. DENIS OF ST. LOUIS

Tax not the royal Saint with vain expense,
With ill-matched aims, the architect who planned
(Albeit laboring for a scanty band
Of white-robbed scholars only) this immense
And glorious work of fine intelligence.

—WORDSWORTH.

From 1231 to 1280, at St. Louis' own expense, the present nave and transept of St. Denis were built, and the first bay of the choir as well as the upper parts of the chevet were reconstructed. Inasmuch as the new nave was wider than the choir, a canted bay of the latter joined it to the transept.

St. Denis, as it now appears, presents the noble elegance of Gothic art in its golden hour. The new transept was made of exceptional width; its aisles and stately piers compose picturesque vistas. The triforium of the reconstructed church was glazed, one of the first essays of a feature which was to be in general use in the XIV century. To unite triforium and clearstory in a brilliant sparkle of color added to the magnificence of a church, but it marked a decline in the sound structural laws of Gothic. The purpose of a triforium arcade was to beautify the plain wall surface necessitated by the lean-to roof over the side aisles. When that blind arcade was opened, the lean-to roof of the aisles had to be changed to a conical one, which signified an inner channel for rain water and the ultimate deterioration of the masonry. Suger's St. Denis had started the delight in stained glass, and the St. Denis of St. Louis merely carried out its consequences—the suppression of wall inclosures. The present upper windows of the abbatial are poor examples of Louis-Philippe's day.

The architect of Louis IX, Pierre de Montereau, designed St. Denis as we have it to-day, so says a record recently unearthed by M. Henri Stein.[33] He was an innovator who here first accentuated the upward sweep of Gothic lines. To that XIII-century master they attributed for a time the Sainte-Chapelle of the king's palace in the Cité, but now that it is certain that he planned St. Denis, it is doubted if he made the Sainte-Chapelle, as there is little kinship between the two. There is a decided likeness between St. Denis and the chapel of the palace at St. Germain-en-Laye, and also with the Lady chapel of St. Germer-en-Flay. Pierre de Montereau was buried in 1267 in a now-destroyed Sainte-Chapelle which he had erected within the monastery inclosure of St. Germain-des-Prés, at Paris.

Both Montereau and Montreuil claim this distinguished master. Probably he

[33] Henri Stein, *Les architectes des cathédrales gothiques* (Paris, H. Laurens, 1908); ibid., "Pierre de Montereau," in *Mémoires de la Société des antiquaires de France*, 1900, vol. 61.

was born in the former town on the border of Champagne, as his church at St. Denis shows a trait of that region, the gallery of circulation under the windows of the side aisles. Moreover, two of his abbot patrons came from Montereau. The architect Eudes de Montreuil, whom St. Louis took with him on his first crusade, and who worked on the fortresses of Aigues-Mortes and Jaffa, was a son of Pierre de Montereau, it is supposed, and his name should be spelled in the same way.

No tomb in St. Denis' abbey church predates the XIII century. To honor King Dagobert, founder of the abbey, St. Louis put up an elaborate monument and ordered the effigies that distinguish his royal predecessors' graves. With the tombstone of St. Louis' son, Philip the Bold, began portrait work. An exact likeness of Charles V, the good Valois king, was made by his Flemish sculptor, André Beauneveu, and of almost too great realism is that of his general Bertran Duguesclin, whom King Charles ordered buried with royal honors in the national necropolis.

It was the XVI century that added to St. Denis' the three tombs of most architectural pretensions, those of Louis XII, Francis I, and Henry II. The monument of Louis XII and Anne of Brittany was undertaken (1516-32) by Jean Juste, who with his brothers had come north from Florence, being among the first to bring into France the ideals of the Renaissance.[34] It has been suggested that the king's and queen's kneeling images are from the studio at Tours of Guillaume Regnault, who for forty years was co-worker with Michel Colombe, last of the great Gothic artists. The priants are still quite French in treatment. Jean Juste made the gisants and his brother and nephew aided with the lesser sculpture. It was Louis XII who ordered artists at Genoa to make, in 1502, the Carrara marble tomb of his father, the poet-duke, Charles d'Orléans, and of his grandfather, the murdered duke of Orléans, builder of Pierrefonds Castle, and son of the art-loving Valois king, Charles V.

The tomb of Francis I (1549-59) was designed by Philibert de Lorme. Pierre Bontemps fashioned the bas-reliefs that celebrate the wars in Italy; he and other masters made the *priants* and *gisants*. The tomb of Henry II and Catherine de Medici (1570) of less artistic value, has a complicated history. The Italian, Primatici, directed the works; Domenico Florentino made the king's kneeling figure, and Germain Pilon his *gisant*; Jerome della Robbia chiseled the queen's death image.

To sum up: there are in St. Denis' abbatial three totally different parts, built in different periods. There is Suger's forechurch, in which linger Romanesque echoes; there is the ambulatory of purest Primary Gothic built a little later by the same great abbot; and finally there are nave, transept, and the main parts of the choir erected during the reign of St. Louis in the zenith of Gothic art.

As one stands in the center of the church, gazing along its vaulting, it is easy to perceive that the axis is broken three times, and each divergence from the straight line conforms to one of the different stages of work. The deviation of the axis line once was called poetically *inclinato capite* (*et inclinato capite, emisit spiritum*—St. John xix:30). It was thought to symbolize the inclining of Christ's head on the

[34] A. de Montaiglon, "La famille des Juste en France," in *Bulletin Monumental*, 1876, vol. 42, pp. 76, 768. Details of the tombs of St. Denis are to be found in Palustre, *La Renaissance en France* (1888); Gonse, *La Sculpture française depuis le XIVe siècle* (1895); Vitry, *Michel Colombe et la sculpture française* (1901); and in writings by A. Saint-Paul and Louis Courajod.

Cross. When M. Robert de Lasteyrie proved that a constructive miscalculation was the cause of the irregular line, the beautiful idea had to be renounced.[35] In each successive addition to a church it was difficult for the architect to start the new part exactly on the same axis as the old, since usually a temporary wall shut off the portion of the church already finished and in use. The slightest miscalculation at the start led to a very apparent deflection of alignment. Those churches which show irregular alignment are known to have been built in successive stages. A number of church choirs slant to the south, whereas were the figure on the crucifix taken as model they would deviate to the north. In churches without a transept, or, in other words, churches that lack the extended arms of the cross, is sometimes found a decided slant to the north. Moreover, the crucifix of that epoch represented a triumphant Christ with erect head, for the art of the XIII century was serene; the pathetic in religious iconography was a later development. No writer of the period mentions a symbolic interpretation of the deviated axis, not even Bishop Guillaume Durandus, in his noted *Rationale*, or *Signification of the Divine Offices*. There is, instead, a text of the XIV century which says that a certain architect was so chagrined at having built a tortuous axial line that he never returned to be paid by the cathedral chapter. Mr. Arthur Kingsley Porter thinks that the deviation of the axis was intentionally done, in order to overcome that tendency of perspective which lessens the apparent length of a church by foreshortening its far bays. By slanting the east end, the distant bays could be brought into view, and thus the edifice would seem longer.

[35] R. de Lasteyrie, "La déviation de l'axe des églises est-elle symbolique?" in *Bulletin Monumental*, 1905, vol. 69, p. 422, also published separately; A. Saint-Paul, "Les irrégularités de plan des églises," in *Bulletin Monumental*, 1906, vol. 70, p. 129; John Bilson, "Deviation of Axis in Medieval Churches," in *Journal of the Royal Institute of British Architects*, December 25, 1905; W. H. Goodyear, "Architectural Refinements in French Cathedrals," in *Architectural Record*, vols. 16, 17, 1904-05, and *Journal of the Royal Institute of British Architects*, 3d series, 1907, vol. 15, p. 17.

St. Denis-en-France and Its Royal Mausoleums

The Royal Abbey of St. Denis suffered during the Hundred Years' War, from which period dates the crenelated wall at the birth of the towers. In those checkered times the silver tombs of St. Louis, of his father Louis VIII, and of his grandfather Philippe-Auguste, disappeared. In the XVI-century religious wars the abbey was pillaged, and its library, a national treasure, was burned. The Calvinists carried off Suger's altar vessels of silver and gold, on which the learned little abbot had inscribed Latin verses. The Revolution completed the havoc; of the monks' quarters nothing remains to-day. The Committee of Public Safety voted to destroy the tombs of "our ancient tyrants" on the first anniversary of the August 10th that had unseated the monarchy. So the mob sallied forth to St. Denis and scattered the dust of the patriot Suger, whose life work had been the public weal, and the dust of St. Louis, the most conscientious man who ever ruled a nation and the first to give France her written laws. The gruesome account of the wrecking of the royal tombs was written by an eyewitness.[36]

In the opening years of the XVIII century, the abbey church was described by Chateaubriand as in a ruinous state, with the rain falling through its roof and grass growing on the broken altars: "The birds use its nave as a passageway; little children play with the bones of mighty monarchs. St. Denis is a desert." Napoleon began its restoration, and many of the scattered tombs were brought back. During the first half of the XIX century some deplorably bad work was carried on, and the robust primitive profiles were chiseled away. No sooner was the spire on the north tower finished than cracks showed, and the tower was dismantled to the level of the roof. Later changes have repaired some of the stupidity of those tasteless renovators.

The very history which had been enacted within the walls of the great abbatial would suffice to make it a national relic. To the Primary-Gothic church which Suger was building came Louis VII for the oriflamme, the banner carried before the army in momentous wars. He shared bed and board with the monks the night before he set forth on the Second Crusade. To the same early-Gothic church, in 1190, came his son Philippe-Auguste, to receive the oriflamme for the Third Crusade. The flame-colored abbey gonfalon on its gold lance flouted the German emperor when Bouvines' great victory was won in 1214. At the funeral of Philippe-Auguste, in 1223, a little lad of eight marched to St. Denis' behind his grandfather's bier. It was the first time that the populace had beheld their future saint-king, and an old record tells how his noble bearing gladdened their hearts. At his side walked Jean de Brienne, king of Jerusalem, leader of the recent Fifth Crusade. When St. Louis came to St. Denis for the oriflamme in 1247, it was to find a totally reconstructed church, for Pierre de Montereau had been many years at work. Joinville in his memoirs described the landing in Egypt of the Royal Abbey's banner, how for miles the sea was dotted with the gleaming ships of the crusaders, how the king, standing head and shoulders above the rest, on perceiving that the leading vessel which bore the oriflamme had touched shore, leaped into the sea, sword in hand, with the cry, "Montjoye St. Denis!" And uttering the same battle cry of France, princes and knights followed. Five years later, tested by defeat and imprisonment, as fine gold is by fire, Louis IX brought back the oriflamme to St. Denis. Again he returned for it in 1270 for his last crusade. Within a year, the whole nation, in

[36] During three days in August, 1793, and again in October of the same year, the tombs at St. Denis were violated. Robespierre stood long studying the chivalrous head of Henry IV, then plucked some hairs from the king's white beard and put them in his portfolio; Henry IV had abjured Calvinism in this very church of St. Denis in 1593. The corpse of Louis XIV presented an air of serene majesty. When the coffin of Louis XV was opened the air was infected insupportably. On that same day in October, 1793, Marie Antoinette mounted the scaffold. Her remains and those of Louis XVI are to-day laid in the inner core of St. Denis' crypt.

mourning, came out to the abbey. In a reliquary, the king's bones, embalmed with fragrant spices, had been brought from Tunis, and the new king bore the *châsse* solemnly, and wherever he paused, on the way from Notre Dame to St. Denis, a memorial cross was erected. But, to give the annals of the abbey church would be to tell the history of the French monarchy.

The first time that the gonfalon of St. Denis was carried against Frenchmen was in 1413, two years before the defeat at Agincourt, in the black days of the Hundred Years' War, days as fatal to the builders' art as to the civic life of France. What those dire times were that rent France to shreds, and how *la fille de Lorraine à nulle autre pareille* came to the rescue, have been sung by a poet whose high destiny it was to fall in recent battle. Charles Péguy, in his poem, linked the momentous epochs of the capital: St. Denis, who brought the Light; Ste. Geneviève, the sentinel patroness of Paris, who guarded it, and Jeanne d'Arc, who lifted up the torch from the mire—the torch which the fallen heroes of the World War have passed on refulgent.

In the V century it was at Geneviève's instigation that a basilica was raised to honor St. Denis. In the XV century Jeanne d'Arc paid tribute to the first martyr of Paris. Her troops lodged in the town of St. Denis, then moved in closer to Paris, and in a shrine dedicated to St. Denis, in the village of La Chapelle, Jeanne heard Mass, the morning that she led the assault on the walls of Paris, September 8, 1429. When wounded she was carried back to La Chapelle (to-day a dense industrial faubourg of the city), and on St. Denis' altar she offered tribute. During her trial at Rouen they asked her what arms she had offered to St. Denis.[37]

"A complete knight's outfit in white, with a sword that I had won before Paris," was Jeanne's reply. "And why did you make that offering?" asked the judge, bent on twisting her every act to sorcery. Jeanne answered hardily: "For devotion, and because it is the custom for all men-of-arms when they are merely wounded thus to give thanks. Having been wounded before Paris, I offered my arms to St. Denis because his is the cry of France."

But let Charles Péguy speak, he who fell between Belgium and Paris in August, 1914:[38]

> Comme Dieu ne fait rien que par miséricordes,
> Il fallut qu'elle [Ste. Geneviève] vît le royaume en lambeaux,
> Et sa filleule ville embrasée aux flambeaux,
> Et ravagée aux mains des plus sinistres hordes;
>
> Et les cœurs dévorés des plus basses discordes,
> Et les morts poursuivis jusque dans les tombeaux,
> Et cent mille innocents exposés aux corbeaux, ·
> Et les pendus tiront la langue au bout des cordes;
>
> Pour qu'elle vît fleurir la plus grande merveille

[37] E. O'Reilly, *Les deux procès de condamnation ... de Jeanne d'Arc*, vol. 2, p. 134, the eighth interrogation, March 17, 1431 (Paris, Plon, 1868), 2 vols.

[38] Charles Péguy, *Œuvres de*, "La tapisserie de Sainte-Geneviève et de Jeanne d'Arc," vol. 6 (Paris, édition de la Nouvelle Revue française, 1916-18).

Que jamais Dieu le père en sa simplicité
Aux jardins de sa grâce et de sa volonté
Ait fait jaillir par force et par necessité;

Après neuf cent vingt ans de prière et de veille,
Quand elle vit venir vers l'antique cité ...
La fille de Lorraine à nulle autre pareille ...
Gardant son cœur intact en pleine adversité,
Masquant sous sa visière une efficacité,
Tenant tout un royaume en sa ténacité,
Vivant en pleine mystère avec sagacité,
Mourant en plein martyre avec vivacité ...

Jetânt toute une armée aux pieds de la prière.[39]

---

[39] The following is a free rendering of Péguy's verses:

Since God but acts for pity of us here,
So Geneviève must see her France in shreds,
And Paris, her own godchild, swept by flames,
And ravaged by the most sinister hordes.

And hearts devoured by blackest base discords,
And even in their graves the dead pursued,
On gibbets many an innocent hung high
With tongue protruding, pecked by raven birds.

France all despair. Then saw she come the Sign,
A greater marvel never God had willed
In His Serenity and Grace and Force,
After nine hundred-twenty vigil years
Geneviève saw approach her ancient city
Her of Lorraine, emblem of God's pure pity—
Jeanne the Maid!—

Guarding her heart intact in dire adversity,
Masking beneath her visor her efficacity,
Living in deep mystery with sweet sagacity,
Dying in drear martyrdom with brave vivacity
Sweeping all an army to the feet of Prayer.

CHAPTER III

SOME OF THE PRIMARY GOTHIC CATHEDRALS: NOYON, SENLIS, SENS, LAON, SOISSONS

Great Cathedrals—Individual plan of its choir-chapels—St. Leu d'Esserent, on the Oise, the best type of the small churches in the classic Ile-de-France—Its forechurch shows transition work (c. 1150)—Primary Gothic work to be found at Étampes, Vendôme, Fécamp, Rouen, Lisieux, Angers, Mantes, Paris.

C'est vers le Moyen Âge énorme et délicat,
Qu'il faudrait que mon cœur en panne naviguât.
... Roi, politicien, moine, artisan, chimiste,
Architecte, soldat, médecin, avocat,
Quel temps! Oui, que mon cœur naufragé rembarquât.
Pour toute cette force ardente, souple, artiste!...
Guidé par la folie unique de la Croix
Sur tes ailes de pierre, ô folle Cathédrale!

—PAUL VERLAINE, *Sagesse, IV.*[40]

ST. DENIS' abbatial was an object lesson in the new art, and the bishops returned to their dioceses to emulate it. Two of Suger's personal friends, the bishops of Noyon and Senlis, were the first to rebuild their cathedrals. Already during the Romanesque stage the cathedral of Sens had been initiated; it now was to be carried on according to the new system of building. At Laon was begun a splendid Gothic edifice. At Soissons, a new cathedral was started by that masterpiece of Primary Gothic, the transept's southern arm. And many a lesser church now rose: the collegiate at Braine, the abbey church of St. Leu d'Esserent, and two abbatials in Champagne as imposing as cathedrals, St. Remi at Rheims, and Notre Dame at Châlons-sur-Marne. Also in Champagne is the Primary Gothic church of St. Quiriace at Provins.

The cathedral of Paris was also begun in the primary stage of the national art. But Notre Dame of Paris must have a chapter to itself. Before its main parts were completed, Gothic architecture had reached its culminating point. With it ended the primary group and opened what we shall call the Era of the Great Cathedrals, though let it be remembered that all such divisions are arbitrary and made use of merely for clearness. From its first assured steps to its apogee, from the middle of the XII century to the middle of the XIII, the sequence of Gothic architecture is welded too logically to be defined by cut-and-dried nomenclature.

During the XII century, the Gothic cathedrals retained Romanesque features, such as deep tribunes over the side aisles, which gave them a wall elevation in four stories—pier arcade, tribune, triforium (to veil the lean-to roof over the tribune), and clearstory. At first it was common usage to encircle the clustered shafts at intervals with stone rings, but by the XIII century the desire for an unbroken ascending line had grown stronger, and the employment of such horizontal bands died out. The simultaneous use of both round and pointed arch is found in all five of these Primary cathedrals; but after the opening of the XIII century, semicircular

[40] Paul Verlaine, *Choix de Poésies* (Paris, Charpentier, 1912).

and equilateral arches rarely were used at the same time in a church. Slowly, as if with reluctance, the new architecture dropped favorite traits of the old school. Sculpture continued longest faithful to Romanesque traditions.

Noyon, Senlis, Sens, Laon, and Soissons—it seems rash to treat of such a bevy of churches in one chapter, when students have made a single cathedral their life work. The passing traveler is encouraged by one fact: each big French church, once seen, remains a clear-cut memory, for each possesses a distinct personality. To confuse one cathedral with another is impossible.

It is an instinct deeper than mere fancy to choose a season æsthetically right for a first visit to such sanctuaries. For these Primary cathedrals the fitting occasion is that fugitive hour when the leaves are multiple yet half transparent still, only partly veiling the virile framework of the tree. In them is the evanescence of spring, the slenderness of adolescence and its virginal restraint, that something of youth's severity, that something of youth's radiance which is joy, but not abandonment to joy.

There is something sacred in the modest sobriety of the earlier Gothic churches.... But what words can express their unimaginable charm! If all true art is but a symbol, a prefiguring of the mystery, these churches veil and reveal the coming harmonies of the Beyond as it never before was revealed and veiled. We speak of Chartres as a recollected holiness; the stones of Rheims were made majestic for royal pageants; Amiens is a *sursum corda*. And yet there is something in the first fugitive hour when Romanesque and Gothic met that makes a deeper appeal to the soul. No Greek, in portico or sepulchral tablet, conceived beauty of lovelier proportion, of more heart-piercing simplicity, than some of the earlier churches of the national genius.

When in the French towns the word passed from mouth to mouth, on a tragic day of September, 1914, that Rheims Cathedral was in flames, there were many who asked breathlessly: "And St. Remi? What of St. Remi?" And when the invaders burst upon Senlis, many who knew the lovely springtime Gothic church of St. Leu d'Esserent trembled for its fate. Over the birthplace of the nation's unity of language and architecture has poured a pitiless rain of iron and fire, a destruction akin to desecration.[41] Cradle and necropolis!

The iron grip has held cloistral Noyon that was only too content to be forgotten in its distinguished retirement. The proudest mediæval thing in France, Laon set with feudal arrogance on its high hill, has been long years in chained captivity. For seven centuries the faithful bulls on Laon's towers have looked out, like sentinels, over the city. With dread forebodings they stood in their captivity, aware that the angel guard set about Rheims Cathedral had pleaded in vain, that the tower of Senlis, pride of all the Valois country, had been selected as a target by the invaders' guns. And Bamburg and Limburg, Halberstadt and Magdeburg, had copied Laon Cathedral in the old days when the *opus francigenum* aroused emulation, not hate,

---

[41] "The privileged land where the Seine, the Oise, and the Marne approach their waters gave France its laws and political unity, its literary language with its incomparable clarity, and its Gothic art."—ERNEST LAVISSE, *Histoire de France.*

across the Rhine.

Month after month, year after year, the shells rained on Soissons; town and cathedral lie in ruins. The fair cities of this inmost heart of France have been desolated, the loyal places that hastened to open their gates to Jeanne d'Arc when she rode by with her king from the coronation in Rheims—Senlis and Laon, Soissons and Compiègne,[42] and Crespy-en-Valois, the countryside that greeted her with such love that she said she hoped to be buried among such good folk, among these *chiers et bons amis les loyaulx Franxois habitons les bonnes villes*.[43] Always in the vanguard of battle were these ancient cities of France, always the boulevard of the capital, yet the wars of centuries had respected their churches. Future ages will read of the glorification of brute force by the invaders who refused to take pity on Soissons, Noyon, and Rheims, when they stand before the giant amorphous 1913 memorial at Leipzig. Therein speaks the Prussian purpose as distinctly as, in Gothic cathedrals, speaks the idealism that sent the old and young crusading, and spurred man on to "the bravest effort he ever made to save his soul."

Tragic irreparable early churches of France! Like martyrs in the arena, you have been laid low, one after the other.... But martyrs leave undying memories. If loved before with an almost unfair preference, you are sacred now. Rheims, Soissons, Noyon, and Senlis—your names have become sacramental.

NOYON CATHEDRAL[44]

Vous entendrez rugir une de ces batailles
Où les peuples entiers se mordent aux entrailles,
Un combat formidable aux cris désespérés,
Dont parleront longtemps les hommes effarés;
Car nous saurons de moins, si notre France expire,
Lui creuser un tombeau plus large qu'un empire.

—Louis Bouilhet.

Most of the cathedrals of France have an early history following the same general lines. Each may be said to have passed through a Merovingian stage, and

[42] *Congrès Archéologique*, 1905, p. 131, "Compiègne."

[43] The people of the Valois country cried "Noël!" as Jeanne passed. And as she rode between the great Dunois and the archbishop of Rheims she exclaimed, with emotion: "Here is a good people! Happy would I be, when I come to die, to be laid here to rest." "Know you when you will die, Jeanne?" said the archbishop. "I know not. I am in the hands of God," she made answer. "I would it pleased God, my creator, that I could go back now to serve under my father and my mother, and to keep their sheep with my brothers, who would be right glad to see me home."—From the testimony of the Comte de Dunois, in 1455, Jeanne's companion-in-arms in 1429.

[44] *Congrès Archéologique*, 1905, p. 170; E. Lefèvre-Pontalis, *Histoire de la cathédrale de Noyon*, (1901); Vitet et Ramée, *Monographie de l'église Notre Dame de Noyon* (Paris, 1845), 2 vols., 4to and folio; *Brière, Précis descriptive et historique de la cathédrale de Noyon* (1899); Camille Enlart, *Hôtels de Villes et beffrois du nord de la France* (Paris, H. Laurens, 1919); Marcel Aubert, *Noyon et ses environs* (Paris, Longuet, 1919).

to have rebuilt itself larger and finer in Carolingian times.[45] The inroads of the Northmen pirates and the conflagration of timber roofs wrecked most of the cathedrals, so that a third and often a fourth reconstruction went on during the Romanesque era — the century and a half that followed the year 1000. When the evolution of Gothic art was accomplished, there were few churches that were not renewed. It has been said that never before had such a noble frenzy of building seized on mankind.

In the short biography traced here of each cathedral, seldom will an account be given of former edifices, but rather the story of each church as it now stands. While some portion may be Romanesque, it is uncommon to find any Carolingian vestige remaining.

The bishop of Noyon took the initiative set by Abbot Suger at St. Denis. He was the first to start a cathedral in the new way just as Noyon can boast that hers was the first communal charter of which there is record. In 1109 the liberal Bishop Baudry granted the town its franchise, without the turbulent scenes by which other cities were to wrench theirs from their feudal proprietors. "Know then, all Christians, present and future, that by advice of priests, knights, and townsman I have established a commune in Noyon," begins the bishop's parchment. Many a neighboring city modeled its charter on that of Noyon.

The quiet towns on the Oise played a precocious part in what Gratry calls "the big historic effort at justice which occurred in the XII century, the strong will to get out of barbaric chaos which began our era, and which, eight hundred years ago, started the impulses of modern progress." From city to city the communal movement quickened. France began to be covered by associations for mutual aid, and the winning of city charters and the creation of guilds went hand in hand with the intellectual ferment in the schools and the creation of a national architecture.

A second Carolingian cathedral of Noyon was replaced in the XI century by a Romanesque one which was burned in 1131, when the city was laid in ashes. At that time, Pope Innocent II was visiting a lord of the region, a cousin of Louis VII, and the brother of the bishop of Noyon, Simon de Vermandois. The pope wrote to various French prelates enjoining on them to help Noyon in its disaster. Bishop Simon must have built part of the walls of the present choir, but as he accompanied Louis VII on the Second Crusade, and died in the East, it was his successor, Bishop Baudouin II (1148-67), friend of Suger, friend, too, of St. Bernard, who really inaugurated the present cathedral about 1150. He sacrificed in large part what was already done of Bishop Simon's choir in order to put it into character with the newly expounded principles of architecture. The choir of St. Denis was his direct

---

[45] Noyon was made a bishopric in the VI century, when St. Médard translated the see from St. Quentin, before the advance of the Huns and the Vandals. St. Médard gave the veil to Queen Radegund in the Merovingian cathedral of Noyon. Two Carolingian cathedrals stood in succession on the site: in the first, Charlemagne was consecrated king, 768, Noyon being his residence before Aix-la-Chapelle; in the second church, which rose after a Norman sacking, Hugues Capet was elected king shortly before 1000 — the first monarch of the House of Capet, which was to rule over France during seven hundred years. Since the Revolution the sees of Noyon, Senlis, and Laon have been suppressed.

model, and he obtained from Abbot Suger some of his masons; the profiles and ornamentation at Noyon are identical with those of St. Denis.

In 1157, the relics of St. Eloi, Noyon's noted VII-century bishop, a skilled goldsmith and prime minister for King Dagobert, were transferred to the new sanctuary, probably because it was then completed. In the time of Bishop Baudouin III, who died in 1174, the transept was finished, as well as the bays of the nave near it. Noyon's western limb rose during three campaigns of work, as is indicated by differences in its details, but in main part the nave is a work of the final quarter of the XII century.

The cathedral was finished by the westernmost bay of its nave, its capacious porch, and the southwest tower, under Bishop Étienne de Nemours (1188-1222), who had three brothers, also bishops and builders, at Paris, at Meaux, and at Châlons, the sons, all four of them, of a lord chancellor of France. In Noyon, Bishop Étienne was a sound administrator; he was favorable to the municipality, regulated the town's moneys, and built a hospital. Philippe-Auguste sent him to Denmark to escort to France the unfortunate Princess Ingeborg, who was to be his second wife. The bishop was buried as a benefactor in the abbey of Ourscamp, four miles from Noyon, farther down the Oise, which house was a foundation of Bishop Simon de Vermandois, though only vestiges of its XII-century parts remain.[46]

During the last decade of the XIII century a terrible fire raged for two days in Noyon Cathedral. The vaulting throughout the church, save in the choir aisle, had to be reconstructed. For the sexpartite system, which embraces two bays, and has six branches from the keystone of each vault section, was now substituted the barlong plan, where diagonals cover one bay. The early-Gothic architects took up with enthusiasm the Normans' sexpartite plan, but after using it for half a century they most sensibly returned to the quadripartite system as better suited to their needs. The sexpartite vault calls for piers of alternating strength, since on the heavier pier fall diagonals and transverse arch, and only a transverse arch on the intermediate pier.

Noyon Cathedral had from its start planned for a sexpartite vault by building its ground supports of alternating strength. Its piers, therefore, became illogical when a barlong vaulting was erected after the fire of 1193. And one regrets that it has not its original stone roof, since the correlations in this hardy first cathedral are elsewhere very perfect. Throughout the church are details of subtle charm. There is a slight bending out, like a horseshoe, of the archivolts of the pier arcade, which archivolts are severely plain. Usually from the abacus of a main pier rise five clustered shafts to the level of the vault-springing, two to catch the diagonals, two for the longitudinal or wall arches, and one for the transverse arch. Noyon showed

---

[46] The abbey church of Ourscamp is a ruin, but with the choir and ambulatory of the end of the XIII century partly standing. Where once were the piers of the nave have been planted two rows of poplars. Like Longpont and Royaumont, it was a Cistercian church that paid no heed to St. Bernard's strictures on lavish architecture. The former infirmary of the monastery, now used as a factory, is one of the most graceful civic halls of the age (c. 1240); Peigné-Delacour, *Histoire de l'abbaye de Notre Dame d'Ourscamp* (1876), in 4to; *Congrés Archéologique*, 1905, p. 165, on Ourscamp.

constructive agility in concentrating its wall ribs and diagonals on a single shaft, which meant only three clustered colonnettes from main piers to vault-springing.

Each cathedral in France possesses a few traits peculiar to itself. Noyon is unique in having both ends of its transept terminate in hemicycles, like a Rhenish church.[47] The Romanesque school of the Rhine had derived the feature from the early chapels of Rome. Probably Noyon's transept apses came from retaining the foundations of the previous cathedral. A church which was long in the jurisdiction of Noyon—the cathedral at Tournai—still possesses its Romanesque transept with semicircular ends. Cambrai Cathedral, destroyed by the Revolution, once had a similar pre-Gothic transept; its choir, built from 1220 to 1237 in the golden day of the national art, was an irreparable loss. Noyon Cathedral showed another Germanic trait in what may be called a western transept, made by the lower stories of the façade towers and the middle section of the first bay.

The nave of Noyon is a noble vessel, with an interior four-story elevation of happier proportions than was achieved in the transept. No longer do annulets bind the clustered shafts, thus breaking the ascending line as in the choir. Throughout the church is to be found the simultaneous use of round and pointed arches, and, curiously enough, it is the lower stories, pier arcade, and tribune, that used the pointed arch; in the triforium and clearstory the arches are semicircular. Everywhere the sculptured capitals are of rare beauty. The Romanesque acanthus leaf is found in juxtaposition with the Gothic crocket.

Noyon is exceptional in having retained its annexes: the treasure hall built by Bishop Baudouin II, the chapel of the episcopal palace, a half-timber library, and a beautiful chapter house (c. 1240). This latter, opening on a fragment of the cathedral cloister, is a hall divided into two aisles by a row of slender pillars, the type preferred by the French, whereas in England the circular hall whose vault ribs were gathered on a central pier was more popular. Noyon's chapter house was built by Bishop Pierre Chalot, who died at sea, off Cyprus, on St. Louis' crusade of 1248.

When in late-Gothic times Noyon was adding chapels and side aisles, her master-of-works was Jean Turpin, who at Péronne—pitiful Péronne la Pucelle entirely a ruin to-day—erected a Flamboyant Gothic church which was a veritable gem.

The battle of giants, foreseen in the poet's dream, twice engulfed Noyon during the World War. From the first occupation by the enemy the city escaped without serious injury. Then in March, 1918, began the Germans' desperate advance on Paris. At the end of the month the mayor of Noyon quitted the city, the last to leave. And in September he was the first to re-enter Noyon after the second battle of the Marne had driven back the invaders. He found his town a ruin. Not a single building had escaped injury, and only ten days earlier a photograph taken from a French airship had shown that the Renaissance Town Hall and Noyon's chief square were intact; few monuments had suffered from the occasional bombardments by the Allies. The Hôtel de Ville had been built in the dawn of the clas-

---

[47] Camille Enlart, *De l'influence germanique dans les premiers monuments gothiques de la France*, 1902.

sic Renaissance, and its fine façades retained much of the Gothic spirit. Before their departure the invaders blew up the town; not even Calvin's birthplace was spared. Hardly 10 per cent of the houses of this amiable little city that asked only to be left unmolested by the fever and fret of new things are to-day worth reconstruction.

Noyon's Chapter House (1240-1250)

As if by a miracle, the cathedral and a side street named for the old goldsmith bishop, St. Eloi, were preserved. The cathedral roof is pierced by shells in a dozen places and the northern tower and the porch between the towers are smashed, but the interior is but slightly damaged. In one of the side chapels a vandal fired his pistol many times at a picture of the Saviour. Perhaps it was the memory that Noyon's rounded transept ends and forechurch were Germanic which saved the cathedral. Better is it to remember by a Radegund, by a Charlemagne, than by Odin and Thor.

THE CATHEDRAL OF SENLIS[48]

To-day analysis has seized on all things, and it is leading us
to death. Man, we must not forget, lives intellectually by synthe-
sis.... If archæology is to make known the monuments of the past,

[48] Marcel Aubert, *Monographie de la cathédrale de Senlis* (1907). He has also described Senlis in the collection, *Petites monographies* (1910); *Congrès Archéologique*, 1905, p. 89, E. Lefèvre-Pontalis; *passim*, 1877, vol. 44, "L'architecture dans le Valois," Anthyme Saint-Paul; E. Lefèvre-Pontalis, *À travers le Beauvaisis et le Valois* (1907); Émile Lambin, "La Cathédrale de Senlis," in *Revue de l'art chrétien*, 1898, vol. 47; Abbé Eugène Müller, *Senlis et ses environs* (1897); André Hallays, *En flanant à travers la France. Autour de Paris* (Paris, 1910); G. Fleury, *Études sur les portails imagés du XII siècle* (Mamers, Fleury et Dangin, 1904); *Histoire littéraire de la France* (Paris, 1835), vol. 18, p. 33, "Guérin, évêque de Senlis."

it ought, before all else, to try to make them loved, for, given the uncertitude of the future, it is in that love that they will find their only chance of safety.

—ÉMILE LAMBIN.[49]

Senlis was the second begun of the Gothic cathedrals. The most fecund region for early essays in the nascent national art lay between Senlis and Noyon. Thibaut, bishop of Senlis, was present at Abbot Suger's deathbed in 1151. Filled with the ambition to replace his half-ruined church by a Gothic one, he began, about 1152, the new works, and once more the abbey church of St. Denis was the model. Some of Senlis' original vaults remain over side aisles, tribune, and apse chapels. Their intersecting ribs show a certain inexperience, and in places semicircular diagonals still are used. The framing arches of each section are lower than the keystone of the diagonals, which imparts a *bombé* shape to the vault. As the masons acquired skill in the making of Gothic stone roofs, this domical form died out; by stilting, by depressing, and by pointing the arches was the difficulty solved. Like Noyon, Senlis played a part in the early history of France. The Merovingian and Carolingian kings and those of the House of Capet frequented the little city in order to hunt in the forests of the Oise. Louis VII made Senlis his favorite residence, and when the new cathedral was undertaken he allowed donations to be collected over the entire kingdom.

When Bishop Thibaut died, the succeeding prelates, Henri and Geoffrey, continued to give largely of their revenues to the new works, but the progress was slow. Senlis was a small diocese for so big a monument. About the time that the choir was finished, 1180, the sculpture of the central-western portal was set up, a gem of Primary Gothic, though sadly damaged by time. It marks a date in French mediæval sculpture. On the lintel is related the Death of the Virgin and her Assumption, in the tympanum her Coronation. Senlis was the first to use this ordinance which the XIII century frequently repeated; we find it at Chartres' north portal, and at the entrance under the northwest tower of Notre Dame at Paris.

M. Émile Mâle with his usual happy phrasing speaks of the lyric beauty of the lintel stone at Senlis.[50] It was partly inspired by the *Golden Legend* of the good Bishop James of Genoa, which in its turn had used the apocryphal gospels freely.[51] The legend relates that at the deathbed of Our Lady, the Apostles gathered, and St. John cautioned them: "Be careful when she is dead that no one weeps, lest the people, seeing our tears, be troubled, and say, 'They fear death, who preach the Resurrection.'" For three days Our Lady rested in her tomb in the valley of Jehoshaphat, then came her Divine Son, with angels, singing the Canticle of Canticles, to escort her to Paradise. The old sculptor of Senlis has depicted the touching reverence with which the angels bend, to lift from the tomb their future Queen of

[49] Emile Lambin, *La Flore des grandes cathédrales* (Paris, 1897).

[50] Émile Mâle, *L'art religieux en France au XIIIe siècle* (Paris, A. Colin, 1908).

[51] Jacobus de Voragine, *The Golden Legend.* Translated into English by Caxton and reprinted by William Morris, Kelmscott Press, 1872, 3 vols. Translated also in Temple Classics. One of the best recent French editions is that of Théodor de Wyzewa (Paris, Perrie et Cie, 1909).

Heaven. Their gesture of eager love is one of the exquisitely delicate conceptions of mediæval sculpture.

While they were carving the west portal there came to Senlis a touching figure, the young mother of the future Louis VIII, Isabelle, daughter of Baudouin V of Flanders, who claimed direct descent from Charlemagne; through her the blood of the Carolingian line passed into the third dynasty of France. She was to die, at nineteen, almost repudiated by Philippe-Auguste, because her people declined to support one of his projects. In Senlis Cathedral this gentle grandmother of St. Louis walked barefooted, candle in hand, beseeching assistance from the Mother of God with such humility that the beholders wept. She founded a chapel in the cathedral.

A few years later, in 1191, the cathedral of Senlis was consecrated by that arch-bishop of Sens who was Philippe-Auguste's uncle, Guillaume of Champagne, William of the White Hands, the prelate who had completed the cathedral at Sens. And there came to the dedication Bishop Nivelon de Chérisy, just starting Soissons' Cathedral; Bishop Étienne de Nemours, at work on Noyon's; the prelate of Meaux, who was raising that cathedral; and many another expert in the new art. Sometime later, Bishop Geoffrey resigned his see, and in his place was elected Pierre Guérin, chancellor of France under three kings, a figure worthy to stand beside those Gallo-Roman bishops who remained as bulwarks of society when the Roman Empire fell in pieces around them.

Bishop Guérin was a man possessed by a passion for the public weal. His prudence and firmness caused Philippe-Auguste and Louis VIII to name him executor of their testaments. One of his enterprises was the organizing of the royal archives. It was he who came to Blanche of Castile to break the news of her husband's death as she rode out from Paris to meet Louis VIII returning from the southern war. For Louis IX during his minority he showed a father's affection. "He governed marvelously well the kingdom's needs," says the old chronicler, and when he died, on his grave they inscribed, "Here lies Guérin, whose life was an untiring work."

In early life Guérin had, in Palestine, become a Knight Hospitalier of St. John of Jerusalem, and, as bishop, continued to wear the white habit of that military order. At the battle of Bouvines, though not an actual combatant, he exhorted the troops and directed maneuvers, for he was skilled in the strategy of war. A survey of the enemy's position made him urge Philippe-Auguste to attack at once, and the king, who knew Guérin to be *sages homs et de parfont conseil*, obeyed, thus winning the greatest victory of the century. "On that day French unity received its baptism."

The king had vowed, were his arms successful, to endow an abbey. Bishop Guérin laid for him the first stone of the Abbaye de la Victoire, near his episcopal city.[52] Before this greatest of the bishops of Senlis died, his cathedral had begun

[52] The Church of the Victory, consecrated by the warrior-bishop in 1225, was ruined during the Hundred Years' War by the Duke of Bedford's troops, who day after day were pricked on by Jeanne d'Arc's army to a battle. In Flamboyant Gothic times the abbatial was rebuilt, but again it was wrecked in the XVIII century. Only a few late-Gothic bays now stand on the lawn before the country house of the Comte Boula de Coulomier. Bishop Guérin also consecrated the church of Chaalis abbey, where he was buried in 1228. Chaalis

to crown its southwest tower by the octagon and spire which are the boast of all the Valois country. St. Louis must have contributed to Senlis' famous tower, which places in foremost rank, this, the smallest cathedral in France. The unknown architect gathered features from many a beacon to unite them here in a masterpiece. He may be said to have created a new type, since his belfry at Senlis made a school in the region.[53]

The graduation of the upright shaft into the inclined plane, which in every tower is the crucial point, has here been accomplished with such address, such rhythm, that precisely at what instant the fusion takes place is not to be determined. It has been said that the shaft of the tower is too high in proportion to its spire; at a distance perhaps the criticism may seem justified, but not on closer view. Some have thought that Senlis' belfry was a trifle too conscious of its charms, that it had not the calm poise of Chartres' tower. So it may be; there is more of the woman than the archangel in it. Its personal graciousness has become so wedded with the lives of Senlis' townspeople that they wish it good morning as they pass. The voyager will not find himself many hours in Senlis without pausing at every coign of vantage to gain some new silhouette effect of the slender beacon. It is charming when viewed in the same group as the Gallo-Roman ramparts. And from the open door of the church of St. Frambourg,[54] it can be studied at leisure.

In the original plan of Senlis' Cathedral there was only an indication of a transept—two small lateral chapels that open, to-day, from the choir aisle. When, about 1240, the radiant tower was finished they undertook to make a real transept. To insert one they had to do away with four bays of the nave; some ancient columns in the west piers of the transept witness to this change. In its present form the transept of Senlis belongs to the XIII century only in its lower walls.

In 1504 a conflagration lasting several days destroyed the cathedral's upper vaulting and necessitated the total reconstruction of the clearstory. In consequence, the exterior appearance of this very early Gothic church is most decidedly Flamboyant. Only the apse and the west façade have retained their Primary Gothic aspect. Chapels with complicated pendant vaults were built, aisles were added, and balustrades put before the tribune opening. Thick coats of whitewash coarsened the lines; in fact, restorations have been so radical, and many of them so

is now a picturesque ruin.

[53] E. Lefèvre-Pontalis, "Les clochers du XIIIe et du XVIe siècle dans le Beauvaisis et la Valois," in *Congrès Archéologique*, 1905, p. 592.

[54] The corner stone of St. Frambourg was laid in 1177 by Louis VII. It is a sort of forerunner of the Sainte-Chapelle type of edifice, without aisles or transept. Its sober, pure lines show faultless constructive skill, and a grievous pity is its present abandonment. Behind the cathedral is the church of St. Pierre, built in six different epochs: the lower stories of the tower, XI century; the choir and transept, 1260; the piers of the nave and the north tower's top story, XV century; the rich façade, XVI century, a work of Pierre Chambiges; and the heavy, cold south tower, of the XVII century. In Senlis are St. Vincent's church with a choir built after 1136, a XII-century tower, contemporary of the cathedral, and a groin roof of the XVIII century. St. Aignan's belfry is of the end of the XI century, and served as model for the towers of St. Vincent and St. Pierre, just as all three of them contributed toward the inspiration of that sovereign thing of Senlis, the cathedral tower.

over-ornate, that this cathedral has been called the Gothic of bad taste. An extreme criticism, for if some of the changes are distressing, Senlis' transept façades, which also are later additions, are to be reckoned among the best work of the final phase of the national art.

After the fire of 1504 the cathedral chapter sought assistance from the king: *"Plaise au Roy d'avoir pitié et compassion de la paoure église de Senlis ... laquelle, par fortune et inconvénient de feu a été bruslée, les cloches fondues, et le clocher qui est grant, magnifique et l'un des singuliers du royaume, au moyen du dit feu tellement endommagé qu'il est en danger de tomber."* Royalty responded generously as the sculpture shows; at the transept's portals are to be seen the porcupine of Louis XII, the ermine of Anne of Brittany, and the salamander of Francis I.

Under the learned Bishop Guillaume Parvi, confessor to Francis I, was laid the first stone of the transept's elaborate south façade in 1521. On it worked Pierre de Chambiges, son of the noted maker of late-Gothic frontispieces, and Jean Dixieult. And when it was nearing completion in 1560 the north façade was begun, and finished by the latter master.

Effective, vivid, alertly handsome are Senlis' transept fronts. The wise traveler, even if he infinitely prefers the purer lines of early Gothic, will learn to value this florid final expansion of the national art. The renewal of builders' energy in the XV and XVI centuries was a sumptuous phase worthy of admiration. Those who are partial to English Gothic do not need to be warned against depreciating French Flamboyant work. The advice to be eclectic in travel, so as not to lose any source of artistic pleasure, is for those whose ideal of the builders' art is that of the Ile-de-France, comprised between 1150 and 1250. For such the chief interest of Senlis will be the cathedral's apse, its main façade, and the splendid tower. Let them widen their sympathies and take in the effective transept-fronts of the Flamboyant rebirth.

Senlis of the towers, of the silent squares, of the quaint names—rue des Fromages, rue du Puits-Tiphane, rue des Pigeons Blancs—a charming aristocratic little city, set in an undulating Corot-like landscape, dotted with country houses, was the very epitome of well-conditioned provincial life. Before the summer of 1914 no spot on earth seemed farther removed from violence and crime. Then came the invading hordes over the Valois land. On September 2, 1914, the Germans surrounded Senlis, which, *ville ouverte* though it was, they proceeded to bombard. One third of the obus that fell hit the cathedral. That the guns, three miles away, were pointed on the famous tower would seem to be proved by the fact that only those houses were damaged which lay in the direct line between the German battery and Notre Dame.

When the enemy entered the city the mayor (shot later in reprisal) met them at the Hôtel de Ville. He had scarcely assured them that no troops remained in Senlis when shots rang out: by ill luck some colonial colored troops, on retiring, fired a salute. Thereupon followed the usual accusation that civilians were the combatants, and the usual tragic scenes of reprisal. Down the main street of the little city passed the trained wreckers of peaceful homes, prying open the doors to throw in incendiary bombs. Before night a whole section of Senlis lay an unsightly blackened ruin.... Then came the victory of the Marne and the invaders retreated. The havoc done to the cathedral can be repaired, though, in the process, must be lost the exquisite golden lichen stain which long ages had achieved. The preservation of Senlis' tower was due to a curé of the cathedral who fearlessly pleaded for his church before the German commandant.

THE CATHEDRAL OF SENS[55]

What were Rheims and Soissons before their martyrdom but the transfiguring of stone and metal and wood; dead matter delved from the ground or hewn out of the forest, through the labor of man exalted into forms of absolute beauty, and, because of this loving labor, transformed ... into a mysterious creation that, in the words of Suger of St. Denis, was neither wholly of earth nor wholly of Heaven, but a mysterious blending of both.

—RALPH ADAMS CRAM.[56]

---

[55] *Congrès Archéologique*, 1907, p. 205, Charles Porée; E. Chartraire, *La cathédrale de Sens* (Petites Monographies), (Paris, H. Laurens, 1920); E. Bérard, "La cathédrale de Sens," in *L'Architecture*, 1902; E. Vaudin-Bataille, *La cathédrale de Sens* (Paris, 1899); Bouvier, *Histoire de l'église de l'ancien archdiocèse de Sens* (Paris, 1906); A. de Montaiglon, *Antiquités de Sens* (Paris, 1881); A. J. de H. Bushnell, *Storied Windows* (New York, Macmillan, 1914); A. F. Didot, "Jean Cousin, peintre verrier," in *Bulletin Monumental*, 1873, vol. 39, p. 75; Marius Vachon, *Une famille parisienne d'architectes maistre-maçons: les Chambiges*; Crosnier, in *Congrès Archéologique*, 1847, "Iconographie des portails de Sens"; Viollet-le-Duc, *Dictionnaire*, vol. 9, pp. 222, 506; vol. 8, p. 74 (on the synodal hall); *Histoire littéraire de la France*, vol. 15, p. 324, "Michel de Corbeil, archévêque de Sens"; p. 524, "Guillaume de Champagne, cardinal, archevêque de Rheims" (Paris, 1820); vol. 17, p. 223, "Pierre de Corbeil" (Paris, 1832); vol. 18, p. 270, "Gautier de Cornut, archévêque de Sens" (Paris, 1835).

[56] Ralph Adams Cram, *Gold, Frankincense, and Myrrh* (Boston, Marshall Jones Company, 1919).

Senlis' Tower (c. 1230-1250)

Sens was a chief Celtic city at the intersecting of the Roman roads from Lyons to Paris, from Orléans to Troyes. Long did it dispute the title of primate of Gaul with Lyons and Rheims; even down to the XVI century Paris was within its jurisdiction. To-day as the express trains rush by from Paris to Marseilles, many a traveler looks out on a cathedral that seems to over-tower and overpower a flat, sleepy little town whose name he scarcely knows. When the cathedral was building in the XII century Sens was a center of the nation's life, and under a succession of noteworthy archbishops reached its zenith.

Here at the Council of Sens, in 1140, was scheduled to take place a final contest between St. Bernard and Abélard, and in that hour of enthusiasm over abstract controversy, the king with his court and people of every degree flocked to Sens for the schoolmen's debate on the Trinity. At the last moment Abélard, the inexhaustible arguer who had himself called for the test, quitted the combat. Some twenty years later Pope Alexander III spent a year and a half in Sens, and hither came Thomas Becket to seek papal indorsement for his opposition to Henry II's interference in church affairs. Between these two events, 1140 to 1164, lies the building of Sens Cathedral. At the time of Abélard's and St. Bernard's visit the present edifice had been started. During the residence here of Alexander III and the archbishop of Canterbury it was nearing completion. The pope is recorded as dedicating an altar.

For a time Sens usurped the claim to be the oldest of the Gothic cathedrals. Its choir was started as Romanesque, but the walls rose slowly, and before a stone roof crowned the ambulatory the new system of building had conquered public opinion. The choir-aisle walls, intended to carry a groin vault, were rearranged to bear one with diagonals. On the outer wall the diagonals were caught on corbels placed above the capitals, and though such an arrangement shows maladroitness, the ribs themselves were made by no novice hand. Sens was a pioneer in the use of the broken rib to avoid the curving of diagonals: from each keystone, set precisely in the center of each section, branched the four ribs.

The walls of the procession path and an apsidal chapel opening on the transept's north arm, are the oldest parts of Sens Cathedral. It is true that they antedate the dedication of St. Denis, but not by a few Romanesque vestiges can Sens substantiate its claim to be the first built of Gothic cathedrals. In its main parts it belongs to the third quarter of the XII century. It was a distinct advance on Noyon and Senlis, because it eliminated the deep tribunes over the side aisles. One of the striking characteristics of Sens is the way that light floods it from the aisle windows, which are on a noble scale. Because the church was built during a tentative hour its deficiency lies in the height of the central nave. For right proportion, when flanked by such lofty aisles, the nave should have been made considerably higher.

Sens Cathedral was begun by Archbishop Henri-le-Sanglier (1122-43) to replace a church dedicated at the end of the X century. Such strides has mediæval archaeology taken in France during the last generations, it is hard to believe that serious students, during the Congrès Archéologique held at Sens in 1840, could have considered the present edifice to be the one dedicated before 1000.

Henri-le-Sanglier had been appointed by Louis VI to the see of Sens before he had received holy orders, and in the lax spiritual standards of the day, he saw no harm in living like the feudal lord he was by birth. He had not Thomas of Canterbury's unbending consistency. When his worldliness was censured by St. Bernard he changed his way of life, and ultimately proved himself a loyal and humane pastor.

Of the six archbishops who were to follow him as builders of Sens' metropolitan church, all of them were national figures. Under the long rule of Hugues de

Toucy (1143-68) the church was mainly erected. He was the friend of Abbot Suger the pioneer, the friend, too, of Bernard the regenerator, who came as his guest to Sens, after preaching the Second Crusade at Vézelay. The same hospitable bishop welcomed on two occasions the exiled archbishop of Canterbury. The second visit of St. Thomas Becket was when he had been forced to quit the abbey of Pontigny, situated close by over the Burgundian border, because Henry Plantagenet swore to close every Cistercian house in his English and French domains if further refuge were offered the prelate. Moved by the welcome given him in his distress by the archbishop of Sens, the famous Englishman cried out—so his secretary, Herbert of Bosham, records: "Ah, we have proved the truth of the old saying—'*douce France! ô douce encore, ô très douce France! Oui, elle est douce, vraiment douce, la France!*'"

By a series of logical inferences the name of the architect of this Primary Gothic cathedral has been added to the roll call of honor. It is known that Guillaume de Sens, a French master, was chosen in 1174 by the chapter of Canterbury to rebuild their cathedral, destroyed by fire. He drew the plan of Canterbury and had put up its apse, its Lady chapel, and two bays of the choir, when one day he fell fifty feet from a scaffold, and returned, in 1180, to his native land to die. An English architect, also named William, continued the works at Canterbury, always on the plan of French William.

Now the chevet of Canterbury has strong analogies with that of Sens. There is the same single chapel in its axis; at Sens other apse chapels were added in the XVI and XVIII centuries. The profiles were alike in both cathedrals, and so were the sexpartite vaulting and the embryo transept. In both Canterbury and Sens is an exceptional feature, of Champagne origin, which could hardly have been used accidentally by two men in the same generation. Each alternate pier, at Sens, consists of twin columns, placed side by side according to the width, not the length, of the church. At Canterbury, despite subsequent rebuildings, the same arrangement is still to be found in the bay before the sanctuary.

Guillaume de Sens was too prominent to have copied another man's work, and since it is certain that the plan of Canterbury is his, it is now accepted that he built the cathedral of his native town before he proceeded to England. The homogeneous choir and nave of Sens show that they are the work of the years preceding 1175. And Guillaume's claim to be Sens' architect is further strengthened by a historic link. Not only did Thomas Becket spend three weeks with Archbishop Hugues de Toucy on his first arrival in the city during the pope's stay there, but, after quitting Pontigny, he passed some years in St. Colombe monastery by the town. Without a doubt he knew the master-of-works who was erecting the cathedral, and it may have been he who, on his return to his own see, made the French architect's skill known to his cathedral chapter. Guillaume was not called to Canterbury, however, till after the martyrdom of its great archbishop.

Sens Cathedral was completed by a prince of the reigning house of Champagne, a son of Thibaut the Great, Archbishop Guillaume-of-the-White-Hands (1168-76). He, too, was Becket's stanch supporter, and denounced his murder to the pope, though by blood he was Henry II's cousin. In 1178 he crossed to England to pray by the tomb of the newly canonized saint—one of the first of the

Canterbury Pilgrims who for over three hundred years were to wend their way to the shrine in Kent. Through his influence, Becket's friend and adviser, John of Salisbury, the ablest scholar of his generation, was raised to the see of Chartres. Both William of Champagne and John of Salisbury received episcopal consecration from the hands of good Maurice de Sully, the builder of Paris Cathedral. In his later life Archbishop Guillaume was transferred to the see of Rheims, and in that cathedral he anointed as king his own nephew, Philippe-Auguste, whose prime minister he was; when Philippe II went on the Third Crusade he left as regents his uncle and his mother, Alix of Champagne. The archbishop's affection for his nephew led him to sanction the king's divorce from Ingeborg of Denmark and his marriage to Agnes of Méran, which drew on France the papal interdict, and on William of Champagne the censures of Innocent III.

The house occupied by Thomas Becket, in the cloister of Sens Cathedral, was decorated by a statue of him, which disappeared during the Revolution. During excavations in the cloister, in 1899, they came upon an image representing a bishop, and marked with the seal of Archbishop Guillaume-of-the-White-Hands. The statue is now set up in the choir aisle on the site where once stood an altar dedicated to St. Thomas of Canterbury.

The tutelary of Sens Cathedral is St. Stephen, the first martyr. A XII-century statue at the trumeau, or central shaft, of the west door presents him as the beautiful youthful servant of the Lord. Gazing at it one thinks of St. Augustine's words: "The Church would never have had St. Paul but for St. Stephen's prayer." Paul, holding the robes of those who stoned Stephen, heard the martyr pray for his executioners. The trumeau statue of St. Etienne with its parallel feet marks the transition from the column image, such as those at Chartres' western portal, to the XIII-century type of saintly personages at the doors of Rheims and Amiens. It escaped mutilation during the Revolution because some one had the wit to write on the stone tablet in the saint's hand, *The Book of the Law*. The foliage relief on the shaft is exquisite.

As the XII century closed the archbishop of Sens was Michel de Corbeil (1194-99), a well-known scholastic writer. Under him and Pierre de Corbeil (d. 1222), his successor and also a learned teacher from the Paris schools, the axis chapel at Sens was rebuilt, and the upper vaulting of choir and nave reconstructed in order to enlarge the windows. As the longitudinal or wall arches were now raised to the level of the keystone, the bombé shape of the vault disappeared; in the chevet the wall ribs show as many as three sets of capitals. The vault sections of the side aisles, however, remained domical, as originally built.

Two other distinguished brothers, men of great lineage and intellectual attainment, ruled the see of Sens during many years, Gautier de Cornut from 1222 to 1241 and Gilles de Cornut, who died in 1254; and they had a brother who busied himself with the new cathedral at Beauvais. Gautier de Cornut, who while doctor of law in Paris University served as chaplain to Philippe-Auguste and Louis VIII, was the envoy sent in 1234 to fetch Marguerite of Provence to be married to Louis IX in Sens Cathedral, the king then being in his twentieth year. The young princess of the art-loving Midi came north accompanied by a troop of minstrels. Again in

1239 St. Louis returned to Sens for the Crown of Thorns, on its transit from Venice to Paris, and he walked out some miles from the city to meet it. Barefooted, he and his brother, Robert of Artois, bore back the previous relics to the cathedral, through streets hung with tapestries and lighted by candles. The relic rested in St. Étienne's church all night and then in a solemn, eight-day procession was carried to Paris. The king had the archbishop write the formal account of it all. Gautier de Cornut erected the synodal hall which touches the cathedral's façade, and his own statue and that of the young king decorated its buttresses. The best civic monument of St. Louis' reign many think it to be, and as perfect in its own way as the hospital hall at Ourscamp, its contemporary.

In 1267 the cathedral's southwest tower fell; it may have been one built in Carolingian times from the proceeds of a gold retable, or it may have been a XII-century tower of Archbishop Hugues de Toucy's time, as are the two lower stories of the present northwest tower. Its fall necessitated the remaking of the last two bays of the nave and of the damaged western doors during the early XIV century. The side chapels were built then, too, but they have been rehandled in the present day, and are now dissimulated behind an arcaded wall. A record of 1319 speaks of the able Nicholas de Chaumes as architect here before he proceeded to Meaux Cathedral. He demolished the ancient chapel on the transept's southern arm, but its corresponding chapel, on the transept's northern arm, still exists and is, with the ambulatory walls, the oldest part of the church. Not till after the Hundred Years' War, however, was the plan to erect a new transept carried through.

Sens then possessed as its archbishop, during forty years, the energetic Tristan de Salazar (d. 1519) who had fought, sword in hand, with Louis XII in the Italian wars. Like Bishop Jacques d'Amboise, who was then finishing at Paris the present Musée Cluny as town house for his abbey of Cluny, Archbishop de Salazar built the Hôtel Sens in Paris for his diocesan house. To his own cathedral he added the southwest tower's upper story (to which later a Renaissance lantern was attached) and he connected the synodal hall with the episcopal palace by a rich gallery. Some sculptured panels now attached to a pier in the nave of Sens Cathedral originally formed part of a tomb he had made for his parents. It was this munificent art patron who began the late-Gothic transept. In 1490 the most notable architect of the day, Martin Chambiges, was invited to direct the work, and for four years he gave it his personal supervision until called to Troyes to make the Flamboyant Gothic façade of that cathedral.

Sens Cathedral contains some ancient windows, four of which are among the best in France and allied with Suger's school, though probably executed as the XIII century opened, since the saddle bars follow the outline of the medallion pictures. Those four exceptional windows of the choir aisle sparkle with the jeweled intensity of the golden age of the vitrine art. In one of them is told the story of St. Eustace, often to be met with in French iconography, since he figured in the *Golden Legend*. Another describes the return to England of Thomas Becket and his immediate martyrdom. Originally next to it hung a companion lancet, giving Becket's early life, but this was done away with to make room for a chapel. The other two lancets are of the *Biblia Pauperum* type. In one, the parable of the Prodigal Son is given. In the other is the story of the Good Samaritan, and the half medallions on either side of each central scene interpret it symbolically. Such correlation of the Old and the New Testament was most popular in the Middle Ages. Beside a medallion which shows the traveler fallen among thieves stands the expulsion of Adam and Eve from the Garden of Eden; and the scene of the charitable Samaritan is accompanied by pictures of the Saviour's death and resurrection. They might not be able to write and read, the ordinary men and women of that day, they had no daily journal to crowd their minds with half-digested facts, but their souls were fed by sound ethical truths set forth clearly in their one great book, the cathedral. The artisan donors of such windows we may be sure knew the symbolic meaning of every panel.

In the clearstory windows at the curve of Sens' choir is more XIII-century glass, but it is later work, lacking the marvelous glow of the choir-aisle lancets. The two big roses of the transept are splendid. A celestial concert was then a favorite theme. The south rose (1500) was made by the same Champagne artists, Lyénin, Varin, Verrat, and Godon who filled the nave of Troyes Cathedral with its high-colored translucent woodcuts. The north rose of the transept finished in 1504, was the work of native masters, influenced by the noted school of Troyes. The side windows in Sens' Flamboyant transept are equally good.[57]

Jean Cousin, born in Sens, 1501, made two of the cathedral's windows, the rich one of St. Eutropius, in the nave, and the Tiburtine sibyl of amplest design, in the shrine to the south of the axis chapel. Nothing could be more resplendent as picture windows, but Gothic-Renaissance work, whose tendency was to treat each light as an isolated picture, is not equal to the close-woven patterns of XII-and XIII-century mosaic glass, which kept itself in subordination to its architectural setting. The immense superiority of the earlier windows is demonstrated in Sens Cathedral, which offers us both types at their best.

---

[57] At St.-Julien-du-Sault, fourteen miles from Sens, are over a dozen good XIII-century windows, and some four of the XVI century. St. Louis was a donor. In the window devoted to Ste. Geneviève are interesting XVI-century costumes.

The Interior of Laon Cathedral (XII Century). View from the Tribune Gallery

THE CATHEDRAL OF LAON[58]

And I saw the holy city, the new Jerusalem, coming down
out of heaven from God, prepared as a bride adorned for her husband.

—Apoc. xxi:2, used in the office for the dedication of a church.

While Sens, Noyon, and Senlis were building, the splendid cathedral of Laon
was begun, about 1160. The usual transition features of Primary Gothic showed
in its retention of tribunes over the side aisles, in the simultaneous use of round
and pointed arches, the beringed colonnettes, and the salient transept arms. The
chapel, in two stories, that opened on each arm of the transept, was another Romanesque tradition.

The interior of Laon, "the cathedral of Purity, Silence, and Power," is indeed
most impressive. One bay follows another with a regularity that is accentuated by
the interior elevation being in four stories—pier arcade, tribune arches, triforium
wall arcade, and clearstory. It is not a lofty church, but, like English cathedrals,
what it lacks in height is compensated for in length. There are eleven bays in the
nave, and ten in the choir. Moreover, because it was comparatively low it could
build a square transept-crossing tower, and the average French cathedral was too
high for such a tower to be artistic. Laon and Braine were exceptions among Ile-
de-France churches in having central lanterns; they were derived from Normandy,
since the Rhenish lantern usually was octagonal. Strange as it may seem to say
of the most prominent, most open, and best-lighted part of a church, there is a
blessed seclusion beneath the wide white tower of Laon that "shuts the heart up
in tranquillity."

Down the long church, the stout monolithic piers make two virile lines. Only
during a short period were such sturdy cylinders used, here and in Notre Dame at
Paris are the chief examples, and both cathedrals were artistically right in prefer-
ring their uniform columns, even though both of them used the sexpartite vaulting
that called for alternating ground supports. The coming cathedrals were to adopt
once for all the barlong system of vaulting, where the concentration of loads fell
equally on every bay, and to evolve a classic type of pier, consisting of a central
cylinder flanked by four semi-attached columns. At Laon a few piers in the nave
experimented with free-standing colonnettes, three of which were placed in front

[58] *Congrès Archéologique*, 1911, Lucien Broche, p. 158, the cathedral; p. 225, St. Martin's church; p. 239, the Templar's church; Chanoine A. Bouxin, *La cathédrale Notre Dame de
Laon. Histoire et description* (Laon, 1902); Jules Quicherat, "L'âge de la cathédrale de Laon"
in *Bibliothèque de l'École des chartes*, 1874, vol. 35, p. 249; Lucien Broche, *Laon et ses environs*
(Caen, 1913); *ibid.*, "L'évêche de Laon," in *Bulletin Monumental*, 1902, vol. 66; De Florival et
Midoux, *Les vitraux de la cathédrale de Laon* (Paris, Didron, 1882), folio; E. Fleury, *Antiquités
et monuments du département de l'Aisne*, (1879), vol. 3, p. 153; Émile Lambin, *Les églises de l'Ile-
de-France* (Paris, 1906). His description of Laon is also in the *Revue de l'art chrétien*, 1901-02,
vols. 14, 15; E. Lefèvre-Pontalis, "Les influences normandes au XIe et au XIIe siècle dans le
nord de la France," in *Bulletin Monumental*, 1906, vol. 70; *Histoire littéraire de la France*, vol. 10,
p. 171, "Anselm de Laon" (Paris, 1756); vol. 11, p. 243, "St. Norbert" (Paris, 1759); vol. 13, p.
511, "Gautier de Mortagne, évêque de Laon" (Paris 1814); H. Havard, éd *La France artistique
et monumentale*, vol. 4, p. 81, Mgr. Dehaisnes, on Laon.

of the pillar to enlarge, there, the abacus of the capital on which stood the shafts that mounted to the vault-springing. The elliptical piers of Beauvais, longer from north to south, were to be the most perfect solution of the problem of ground supports.

There is no denying that Laon's interior is to-day too white, but we must remember that originally color was used on the stones, so that any effect of a hall would have been impossible in the olden times. Viollet-le-Duc called Laon the laic cathedral *par excellence*. He considered it a great civic hall wherein the populace "could unite and enjoy spectacles more or less profane." And even in the flat eastern wall he found something occultly heretical. The towers, he said, were more those of a château than a church. He shut his mind to the fact that Laon was erected largely by its bishops, that it was begun by the choir end, which is suitable only for divine service, and that if its seven towers had been crowned with the sky-pointing spires of the architect's plan, and if its sky-dreaming windows were still intact, there would be little of the aspect of a town hall about this stately church. Critics like Huysmans have exaggerated its present iciness: no one can pray in Laon, he exclaimed; its soul is fled forever. But what would be Chartres, his spot of election for prayer, were it unsoftened by its "storied windows richly dight"?

Only a slight amount of ancient glass has survived in Laon. The north rose of the transept shows pictures of the sciences. Beneath the rose window in the flat eastern wall are three handsome lancets made by the school of Chartres early in the XIII century. They show the passing away of the hieratic Byzantine gesture: in the Annunciation and Visitation medallions the robes float naturally; in the Nativity scene the natural gesture of a woman who tests the warmth of the water before bathing the Holy Child has been well rendered.

If a lack of accessories makes the interior of Laon Cathedral seem to-day more philosophic than religious, there are certain lovable individual touches in it that warm both heart and imagination. In the first place it is a church fairly garlanded with springtime foliage. The wonder of eternal youth is in its half-curled leaves which the sculptors conventionalized just enough to make them architectural. Not one sprig, not one leaf is like another. Never was nature more profoundly loved or more convincingly interpreted.

Then there are the stone bulls of Laon. They stand high on the western towers, those sixteen massive oxen, stretching their necks, as if watching the people climb the steep hill below. Each stands under a columned canopy. The popular fancy is that they commemorate the patient beasts who dragged the stones for the cathedral up Laon's precipitous crags, and there is nothing improbable in the idea. It was a day when St. Francis was telling man to love his dumb fellow creatures. The towers of Laon Cathedral are worthy of the magistral setting of the church on the edge of the abrupt hill where had grown the ancient city. For miles Laon's towers command the plain, "an assembly without rival among Gothic monuments." Incomplete though they are, Laon's five towers come nearer to the ideal plan of seven spires than does any other cathedral. The corner tourelles pass from one form to another, as they rise, converting themselves into octagons. "Ponder it well," wrote the XIII-century architect, Villard de Honnecourt, in his famous sketchbook.

"I have been in many lands, as you can see by this book, but never in any place is to be found a tower equal to Laon."

Four of the towers are alike, each with the same long lancet openings, the same free-standing pillars at the corners. Rows of crockets mark the main lines, for the old-time masters were adepts in every device whereby to fix the eye on the essential. There are aspects when the fretwork designs made by Laon's towers against the sky are superb.

The date of the cathedral long gave rise to discussion in the days when mediæval archaeology was still hazy. No one now contends that the present Notre Dame is the church which was patched up hastily by Bishop Bartholomew de Vir after the fire of 1112. That conflagration was a semi-lawless act. Laon's bishop was also its feudal proprietor, hence a greedy baronage contended to hold the see. One Gaudry, a knight adventurer who had served under William the Conqueror in England and there grown rich, obtained the bishopric of Laon by simony. All his talk was of hawks, hounds, and hunting. During one of his absences in England the townspeople set up a commune, and Gaudry bent his energies to frustrate it. In an uprising in 1112 the infuriated populace murdered him. The fire, started during the riots, spread to the cathedral, which was practically consumed. The burghers, being unskilled in arms, were forced to call to their aid a fierce robber-baron of the house of Coucy, Thomas of Marle, who, according as he found it profitable, fought, now against, now for, the communes.[59] It took the king of France half a lifetime to destroy that "raging wolf," as Abbot Suger called him.

Guizot has brought out that the XII-century uprisings against feudal exactions on the part of the burgesses were often favored by king and clergy. Such was the unformed state of society that no liberal general views could be adhered to; the king is to be found granting charters to some towns and marching against the rebellious citizens in others. The bishops of Noyon, Beauvais, and Soissons favored the people's claims. The prelates of Rheims and Laon opposed them. Such feudalism as that of Thomas of Marle meant permanent anarchy; for the royal power to centralize authority then meant law and order.

It is sad to relate that no sooner did the burgess gain his civic rights than he began to oppress the peasantry. Before the XIII century closed there were outbreaks of the peasants against the prosperous townspeople. In our own day has the cry of the underman, voiced by the old Norman poet, been silenced? "We are men as they. The same in stature, the same in limb, and the same in strength—*for suffering*. Are we not men even as they?"

---

[59] For Coucy-le-Château (between Soissons and Laon) see M. Lefèvre-Pontalis' study (1909) in the *Petites Monographies* series; or the *Congrès Archéologique*, 1911, p. 239. The XI-II-century donjon was the most massive conception of the Middle Ages. Coucy's lord ruled a hundred towns and was one of the big figures in feudal France. His proud device read: "*Roi ne suis, ne prince, ne duc, ne comte aussi—Je suis le sire de Coucy.*" The superb pile has been demolished in the World War. Madame Yvonne Sarcey visited Coucy in April, 1917. Of the imposing mediæval castle, hanging like a bourg to the flank of the hill, there remain two gaping porticos. "*C'est tout!... C'est tout!*" she lamented. "*Ce paysage adorable de l'Ile-de-France portera sa croix.*" The Germans blew up the castle before their strategic retirement, in 1917.

At Laon the antagonism between bishop and citizens continued for a century; several times the charter was won, only to be abrogated later. There is food for thought that all through the embittered struggle the building of the cathedral was carried forward, and it was an enterprise that required the collaboration of bishop and people. The people might fight their baron bishop to wrench from him certain civic rights, but they were aware of the difference between his temporal claims and his spiritual authority. Their robust faith was not disconcerted by a discrepancy between "Peter's key" and "Peter's sword." To the end of time Peter will show his weak human side. Had he not denied thrice? Had not another of the selected twelve betrayed for paltry lucre? Had not everyone of them run away in the hour of need?

While Bishop Gaudri's ill-gotten gains were buying him a bishopric there was in Laon's cathedral chapter a famous scholar who had stoutly opposed his election. Anselm of Laon, son of a laborer, "the grave, the sweet, the prudent," was a pupil of St. Anselm of Bec and Canterbury. For over forty years he taught in Paris and in Laon, and from the nucleus of his pupils, among whom were Guillaume de Champeaux and Abélard, was to emerge Paris University, which was not, however, to appear by name in history till 1215. Anselm of Laon (d. 1117), like his greater namesake, was a pioneer in scholasticism, which brought to the study of Christian doctrine not only the aid of tradition, the Old and New Testaments and the Church Fathers, but also the use of metaphysics and dialectics. The school of this master at Laon became a veritable university to which flocked students from Italy, Spain, Germany, and England.

Laon Cathedral is justly entitled to carve the Liberal Arts on its façade. A score of the coming notable men of the XII century were Anselm's pupils; one of them was that bishop who began the Primary Gothic tower of the cathedral at Rouen. Anselm and his brother trained the youths who, having heard St. Norbert of Cologne preach in Laon Cathedral, in 1120, followed him to Prémontré, in the forest of Coucy, which estate gave its name to the new order Norbert there founded. Like the Cistercians, so swift an increase had the white canons of Prémontré that they soon counted a thousand houses over Europe and were an evangelizing force for their century even as Cluny had been earlier and as the Franciscans and Dominicans were to be in the XIII century. The citizens of Laon clamored for Anselm as their bishop when the miserable Gaudri was killed in 1112, but he declined the honor and directed the choice to the worthy Bartholomew de Vir, who restored temporarily the cathedral.

It is not known exactly when was laid the foundation stone of Laon's Gothic cathedral. By its sculpture, the profiles, and the noticeable keystones, the archæologists say that it belongs to the last third of the XII century and that it kept to its original plans, though its building continued into the first third of the XIII century. The bishop-founder was a pupil of Anselm's and himself had taught rhetoric in Paris. Gautier de Mortagne (1155-71) gave generously of his own revenues to the new works. The choir he built ended in a semicircle and consisted of the present three bays next the transept. There, and in the west wall of the transept, the profiles are different from those elsewhere in the church.

In a second spell of work they finished the transept, the nave, the towers, and the west façade just before 1200. Laon's façade ranks among the great western frontispieces of Gothic architecture, a model for that of Rheims. What chiefly characterizes it are the profound shadows made by cavernous porches, projecting gables, and other varied surfaces. It has been called a supreme composition in light and shade. In accentuating the upward surge of lines it was a pioneer. When the façade was finished the choir was lengthened by seven bays, and now was terminated by a flat wall whose prototype is to be found in Laon town in the church of St. Martin, an early-Gothic edifice, building about 1165. Various regional churches used the square chevet. As the custom died out in France, it struck root in England, where the Cistercians made it popular. Those accustomed to the rectagonal chevet of the English cathedral may prefer that type, but to a lover of the apse of the French cathedral, of the curving procession path with its radiating chapels that mystically suggests the thorn crown around the Sacred Head, it will ever seem a dull way to end a sanctuary precisely like a transept arm.

The cathedral of Laon was consecrated in 1237. That same century built the treasure hall and the large chapel beside the west façade. The XIV century added side chapels between the buttresses, and in those chapels at Laon appears the academic precision of that skilled but dry period. About the same time was made a new southern portal for the transept, and the wheel window over it was replaced by a big Rayonnant Gothic light.

The hill citadel called by Charlemagne in the *Chanson de Roland* "my good town of Laon" was held by the invader from August, 1914, to October, 1918. Though the city was shelled by the French, not a piece of glass in the cathedral was broken. St. Martin's abbatial, too, is intact, and the XII-century Templar's church, the only well-preserved monument in France built by the great military Order. The Prussians' horses were stabled at first in the cathedral till a general public protest stopped such a desecration. When the Allies, under General Foch, drove back the German lines in the final weeks of the war, the retreat was too swift for much havoc to be wrought. On October 13, 1918, General Mangin made his triumphal entry into Laon, whose much-enduring citizens flocked around him in the cathedral to chant a solemn *Te Deum*.

THE CATHEDRAL OF SOISSONS[60]

The other evening before the ruins of a Cistercian abbey,
that once harbored St. Louis and his mother, Blanche of Castile,
a group of Alpine chasseurs and Zouaves fell to recounting their

[60] *Congrès Archéologique*, 1911, E. Lefèvre-Pontalis, p. 315, the cathedral; p. 337, St. Médard; p. 343, St. Léger; p. 348, St. Jean-des-Vignes; Étienne Moreau-Nélaton, "Soissons avant la guerre," in *Les cités ravagées* (Collection, Images historiques), (Paris, H. Laurens, 1919); *ibid., Les églises de chez nous: Soissons* (Paris, H. Laurens); Abbé Poquet, *Notice historique et archéologique de la cathédrale de Soissons* (Soissons, 1848); Émile Lambin, "La cathédrale de Soissons" in *Revue de l'art chrétien*, 1898, vol. 47; Émile Mâle, *L'art allemand et l'art français du moyen âge* (Paris, 1917); Bouet, "Excursion à Noyon, à Laon et à Soissons," in *Bulletin Monumental*, 1868, vol. 34, p. 430; E. Lefèvre-Pontalis, *L'architecture religieuse dans l'ancien diocèse de Soissons au XIe et au XIIe, siècle* (Paris, Plon, 1894-98), 2 vols., folio.

daily feats of heroism just as in the times of chivalry the strong, swift strophes of the *chanson de geste* celebrated knightly prowess. To the north, the cannon thundered.... And the next morning, a Sunday, I assisted at Mass in a Gothic-vaulted hall that had served as *promenoir* for the monks of Cîteaux. Soldiers filled all the wooden seats, others thronged the threshold, bareheaded in the shadow of the ruins.... Then when the sacrifice of the body and blood of our Lord was celebrated, a song rose in the dawn: *"Kyrie Eleison! God be praised!"* And the soldiers within the chapel and without sang before returning to battle as in the ancient *Chanson de Saucourt: "Kyrie Eleison!"* Even those harnessing the great cart horses, those saddling their own restive mounts, those extinguishing the fires of the night's bivouac, and those charging the six-wheeled camions, all took up the canticle: *"God be praised! Kyrie Eleison!"* .... And the implacable cannonading to the north echoed in the deep quarries, whence had come the stones builded here for God's glory.

> —A war picture of Longpont abbey,[61] by GABRIELE D'ANNUNZIO, who visited the battle-front in 1914.

---

[61] *Congrès Archéologique*, 1911, p. 410, Longpont abbatial; Abbé Poquet, *Monographie de l'abbaye de Longpont* (1869). Longpont, where the bishops of Soissons were buried, was founded by Gerard de Chérisy, who had married Lady Agnes of Longpont. St. Bernard sent twelve Cistercian monks to start the new house in 1131. The splendid Gothic church, which departed from Cîteaux's rule of church simplicity, was consecrated in 1227 before the queen regent and Louis IX, by the bishop of Soissons, Jacques de Bazoches, who had just anointed Louis as king, at Rheims. Longpont was sacked by the Huguenots in 1567, and wrecked by the Revolution. The picturesque ruins were acquired by the de Montesquieu family in 1850.

The Oxen on Laon's Towers

To-day the fair white city of Soissons lies a scene of desolation, only to be likened to a wrecked town of old-time barbarism. They say that Soissons Cathedral is more damaged than if a geological convulsion had wrecked it. Deliberately was it taken as a target, though, as French troops held the highlands round the flat town, there can be no excuse that the towers were used as posts of observation. The westernmost bays are ruined; the north side of the big church has been riddled with projectiles; flying buttresses have been cut off; great rents show in roof and sides; the vaulting hangs in air; a pier lies prone, its stones scattered like a pack of cards; the aisles are dismantled, and the windows, some of which Blanche of Castile gave in 1225, have been reduced to powdered dust. In one week of January, 1916, over three hundred projectiles fell on the church, said the old priest, who lived in the midst of the wreckage, to a visitor to whom he spoke gently of God's mercy. In the once "sweet and tranquil provincial city, whose soul was the daughter of honorable simplicity, grass grows in the street. Soissons is a dead city. Its casementless windows fix you like the eye of the blind." Always has it lain in the path of war, this ancient capital of Clovis that has ever been part of the very heart of France, but never war such as this!

Here, in 486, Clovis won the battle of Soissons that annihilated the last remnant of Rome's empire in Gaul, and conquered the land to the Loire. In the evil days of the Hundred Years' War, Soissons suffered. So depopulated was it by the XVI-century religious wars that it took over a century to recover. Nor did the Revolution spare the seat of the ancient monarchies of France. In 1814 occurred an explosion of gunpowder that wrecked precious windows in the cathedral, some of them the gifts of Philippe-Auguste. In 1870 the Prussian bombardment of Soissons devastated what remained of the abbey church of St. Jean-des-Vignes, whose Flamboyant Gothic spires have been mutilated again in the World War.[62]

Under the southern flank of the shattered cathedral nestles the diamond of Primary Gothic art in France, the transept arm built by the crusading bishop, Nivelon de Chérisy. As by a miracle it has escaped. The most exquisite thing in France, many of us hold it to be. It has drawn its devotees back to Soissons time and time again, this perfect thing so little heralded. They would test a second and a third time the overpowering first impression it had made. Perhaps it had been some happy mood, some subtle lingering shadows of the late afternoon, that had touched it momentarily to an ethereal grace. And then standing face to face again with its small and stately beauty, those who love this early-Gothic monument of France know that its power is not a chance or borrowed comeliness.

Sit before it for hours; study the mystery and play of its lights and shadows; try to seize in what lies its young poesy of grace, its maturity of dignity, "its invincible impression of virginity." In vain to analyze it. Can that intangible quality which is sheer inevitable beauty be dissected? Those who fall under the spell of

---

[62] The monastery church of St. Jean-des-Vignes was in size a cathedral, and the maker of the great façade at Rheims, Bernard de Soissons, is said to have designed it. The cloisters, once the most sumptuous in the kingdom, were begun by an abbot who died in 1224, after he had built an aqueduct for the city which still is in use. St. Jean's big west rose had been, since 1870, an empty circle. Little more than its façade and western towers stood before 1914. Sacked by the Revolution, its real demolition was under the Empire, when to repair the cathedral the deserted monastery was sold for a paltry sum, and stone by stone removed. The congregation of good men in this abbey did parish work for many centuries. In such good repute with the citizens were they that, when the Revolution suppressed the house, Soissons' municipality protested, saying that the abbey had "always claimed with zeal its share of public duties." Taine in his *L'Ancien Régime* quotes the protest: "In calamities this abbey opens its doors to the destitute citizens and feeds them. It alone has borne the expense of the citizens' meetings, preparatory to the election of deputies for the National Assembly. It now is lodging a company of soldiers. Always when there are sacrifices to be made it is on hand." However, the revolutionary authorities paid no heed to the citizens' desire to retain their historic house.

its supernal loveliness lose all false shame that would prune adjectives, lest their praise be excessive. No glow of words can convey the something celestial here. The nave and the choir of Soissons Cathedral are XIII-century Gothic at its prime, and yet they seem merely to be the setting for a jewel, for the small apse preceded by one bay, which is the transept's southern arm. That apse and bay are the culmination of the Romanesque ideals, and at the same time, indissolubly part of the new and richer art, they crown the Primary Gothic hour.

Soissons' chief church is better documented than Laon's. Bishop Nivelon I de Chérisy (a Chérisy fell on the field of honor in 1914) occupied the see from 1176 to 1207. The Romanesque cathedral which he inherited had become inadequate, so the bishop gave land from his episcopal garden, and about 1180 the foundation of the south arm of the transept was laid. Like Noyon's transept, it terminated in a hemicycle, and its interior elevation was also in four stories, but here was attained a consummate symmetry not achieved at Noyon. Soissons' curving transept arm is exceptional in having an ambulatory. The apsidal chapel which opens in its eastern wall has over it a similar chapel that gives on the tribune gallery. Slender columns with stilted arches are planted at the entrance of each of these chapels in the gracious fashion originated by the Champagne school of Gothic. It was born of a necessity, in order that a more regular vaulting might be built over the curving aisle. St. Remi at Rheims had used the same arrangement. So many are the points of resemblance between Soissons' transept arm and the choir of St. Remi's abbey church that it is thought the architect of the Champagne abbatial proceeded to Soissons later; there are the same profiles, the same plan, the same encircling frieze of sculpture. At Soissons, the architect had grown bolder and dared to diminish his supports. To have made Soissons' curving wall of arches and colonnettes proves him to have been, not only well practiced in mason-craft, but a man of genius who had visions. He here created a thing apart. The exterior of the transept's arm is unimpressive and plain; the lower windows are round-arched. Inside, the pointed arch reigns, however. "The king's daughter is all glorious within."

The prelate who built Soissons Cathedral was a remarkable personage and played a foremost part on the Fourth Crusade. Villehardouin tells us that it was Bishop Nivelon de Chérisy who was sent as an envoy to Innocent III, when against papal commands the Crusaders had turned aside to capture the Christian city of Zara on the Dalmatian coast. The bishop-ambassador found the pope at Viterbo and obtained from him the raising of the excommunication on condition that the knights should proceed direct to Palestine. We all know how, a second time, they went filibustering. Among the first to scale the walls of Constantinople was Nivelon de Chérisy; with him was the bishop of Troyes. When the chief barons met to elect the first Latin emperor of Constantinople, it was Bishop Nivelon who passed out to the waiting crowd to announce that Baldwin of Flanders had been chosen—Baldwin who began the Cloth Hall at Ypres—and it was he who crowned Baldwin in St. Sophia. When that new emperor was captured by the Bulgars the bishop of Soissons returned to Europe for aid.

All the time that he was absent in the Holy Land Nivelon had devoted the revenues of his see toward the renewal of the cathedral. Strangely enough, it was this same prelate who also built Soissons' choir, which in scale and plan differs so radically from the transept arm. The fleeting hour of Primary Gothic was over. The new art was moving forward swiftly; irresistible the development of its principles and impossible at such a time that the work of one decade could be similar to the decade preceding it unless, as at Laon, the primitive plan was insistently adhered to. Whoever the master that designed Soissons' choir and nave, he incorporated the perfect transept into his bigger church with reverence. Not to dwarf it was his main care, for he bowed before the touch of perfection in his predecessor's work, and sought to give to his own monument, different though it was, a like clarity and noble simplicity. Examine the skill with which choir and nave are joined to the small transept arm. It is lower than they, it has four vertical stories to their three, and yet no discrepancy is felt. It was as if the new builder said: "Here is a miracle of force and grace, done in a fugitive hour never to be recaptured. Let us enshrine it fittingly."

In 1212 services were held in the finished choir. The nave proceeded without interruption and was in use in the first years of St. Louis' reign. Probably the final touches were given to it by that bishop of Soissons of whom Joinville tells, Mgr. Jacques de Castel, *fort et vaillant homme*, who started with the king on the crusade of 1248. After Mansourah's battle and the disastrous retreat toward Damietta good Bishop Jacques felt such a desire "to go to God" that he rushed alone to attack the infidels, whose swords soon "dispatched him to God's company with the martyrs."

Singular good taste has at all times guided the builders of Soissons. The XIV century decided to make a northern arm to the transept; and as if to avoid all hint of rivalry with its peerless neighbor, the new structure was finished by a flat end wall without a portal.

The cylinder piers of Soissons choir and nave are a distinguishing trait of the church interior, neither too high nor too short. Before each is engaged a slender shaft which rises to the level of the springing and causes the edifice to appear more lofty than its reality. Everywhere, in the church, the fitting of the stones was done with peculiar nicety, though the picking out of the mortar lines in black, a recent innovation, was a sad mistake. In the choir and nave the clearstory windows were an advance on those of Chartres, their model, for the lights were made longer, and the oculus, above the twin lancets, smaller, which gave greater compactness to the whole composition. St. Gereon at Cologne copied these windows. Marburg's church also was aided by Soissons.

The talc of this desolate city during the World War is heartrending. The Germans first entered Soissons on September 1, 1914. The mayor had fled. But an admirable woman, Madame Macherez, the widow of a senator, went to the *état-major* of the Prussians and assumed the responsibility to keep order among the civilians: *"Le maire c'est moi."* Already the poets of France have enshrined the memory of this heroine of sixty winters who saved her city from pillage:

> Le regard bleu comme strié de lave
> De Jeanne Macherez qui nous sauva Soissons.

Ah! la vieille brave!

For ten days the Germans occupied the town. The first battle of the Marne caused their departure on September 12th. Then a French reverse in January, 1915, let them draw near enough to the city to bring it within the range of fire, and such was its tragic fate till the Germans' strategic retreat in the spring of 1917. The enemy had intrenched himself solidly in the vast quarries on the left bank of the Aisne, and month after month poured his fire on desolated Soissons. Then came the final grand act of the war. Rolling forward in overwhelming numbers in March, 1918, the invaders drove the French troops from Soissons after a desperate resistance in the streets. There they encamped until the first days of the following August, when the French army re-entered the smoking ruins of a dead city over which stood a phantom cathedral.

Noyon, Senlis, Sens, Laon, and Soisson, are with Notre Dame of Paris the first cathedrals of the national art. They are far from being the complete list of Primary Gothic monuments, which includes such churches as the Trinité at Vendôme, two churches at Étampes,[63] the collegiate of Notre Dame at Mantes, the Trinité at Fécamp, and Lisieux Cathedral. There are the two towers built in an hour of religious enthusiasm: the *clocher vieux* at Chartres and the belfry of St. Romain at Rouen. The nave of Angers Cathedral is the Primary Gothic of the Plantagenet school.

The Attica of Gothic art is the Ile-de-France, and where Picardy touches it on the north, and Champagne on the south. In that land filled with never-to-be-forgotten churches speaks the clarity of French genius in its classic simplicity. The beauty of such churches comes from their rightness of proportion, that quality which gives the most enduring joy in architecture, beyond all richness of detail or startling effect. From such churches one learns the difference between the architect born and the architect made. The supreme quality of proportion must be innate; it is never acquired. The artist blessed with it may only produce a small masterpiece, such a church as that of St. Yved of Braine or a St. Leu-d'Esserent, but one is sure that he would not exchange the glow which his work gave him for the fame of building even a Strasbourg.

It is in the early-Gothic churches of the Ile-de-France that the taste is best purified and trained. There the sense of beauty is spiritualized. In them art gives an entity to what is ethereal, art seems to make tangible what is impalpable. In them the heart feels the loveliness of the space inclosed as the eye rejoices in the inclosing walls. There is something of poignancy in such churches. Standing in all

[63] For the churches of Notre Dame and St. Martins, at Étampes, see *Bulletin Monumental*, 1905, vol. 69, and *Annales de la Société hist. et archéol. du gatinais*, 1907, Lefèvre-Pontalis; also the *Congrès Archéologique*, 1901, p. 71. Notre Dame was begun about 1160. Its strongly Romanesque south portal is of the same type as Chartres' western doors. The crypt and piers of the nave are XI century, and the transept and choir were rebuilt about 1170 as early Gothic. The Romanesque tower is one of the best of its epoch; its base is approximately 1050; the next two stories about 1075; the fourth story, 1125; and the spire, 1130. The church is full of irregularities from rebuildings. St. Martin's church is XII and XIII century; its much discussed ambulatory of the Champagne type is about 1165. The number of supports for the vault was doubled in the outer wall, thus making the space to be covered a series of square compartments alternating with triangles.

the promise of their youth, of the youth of the greatest architecture the world ever produced, they gravely admonish us that beauty even as theirs is but a momentary lifting of the veil. To such churches the memory returns with nostalgic regret amid the magnificence of the Gothic expansion, when the leaves opened wide to show the golden pollen. But the sadness which the early-Gothic churches of France rouse in the soul, is it not the stumbling name we give to an eternal Hope? "There are no hours in this cathedral," wrote Rodin of Soissons; "there is Eternity."[64]

THE ABBATIALS OF ST. REMI AT RHEIMS, AND NOTRE DAME AT CHÂLONS-SUR-MARNE[65]

There are two things for which all the Faithful ought to resist
unto blood, Justice and Liberty.

—PIERRE DE CELLE, Abbot of St. Remi (1162-81).

Before closing our crowded chapter on Primary Gothic cathedrals, let us add a few notes on a few early-Gothic churches. Those of chief interest, in the story of the national art, are the big abbey churches at Rheims and at Châlons, sister monuments, equal in size to cathedrals. So closely do they resemble each other in plan and ornamentation that it is thought one architect planned both. They are the earliest Gothic edifices in Champagne.

Notre Dame at Châlons-sur-Marne was reconstructed soon after 1157. Three periods of work appear in it. The transept and the four towers—which give an imposing air to the church—belong to the Romanesque rebuilding of 1130. The towers which stand between choir and transept are not set symmetrically, since, in that to the south, use was made of the foundations of an earlier tower, a boundary mark between the lands of the big abbey and those of the bishop of Châlons.

In 1157, the Romanesque choir of Notre Dame collapsed, and when rebuilt the citizens of the ancient city on the Marne displayed the same pious enthusiasm as had the men and the women of Chartres in 1145. In 1165, Guy de Bazoches, then a canon of Châlons Cathedral, wrote to his sister to describe how all ages and conditions brought material to the new church of Notre Dame-en-Vaux, and how the people, harnessed to carts, sang canticles as they labored. When the new Gothic choir was under way the nave of 1130 was remodeled. The pier arches and the tribune arches were made pointed, and the upper walls were raised in order that a Gothic vaulting might be added.

[64] Auguste Rodin, *Les cathédrales de France* (Paris, A. Colin, 1914), 4to.

[65] *Congrès Archéologique*, 1911, St. Remi (Rheims), p. 57, and Notre Dame (Châlons), p. 473, Louis Demaison; Louis Demaison, *Les églises de Châlons-sur-Marne* (Caen, 1913); E. M. de Barthélemy, "Notre Dame-en-Vaux à Châlons-sur-Marne," in *Revue de l'art chrétien*, vol. 15, p. 97; A. de Dion, "Notre Dame-en-Vaux à Châlons-sur-Marne," in *Bulletin Monumental*, 1886, vol. 52, p. 547, and 1887, vol. 53, p. 439, Louis Grignon; L. Grignon, *Description et l'histoire de Notre Dame de Châlons-sur-Marne* (Châlons-sur-Marne, 1884), 2 vols.; Abbé Poussin, *Monographie de l'abbaye et de l'église de St. Remi de Rheims* (Rheims, 1857); Alfonse Gosset, *La basilique de St. Remi à Rheims* (Paris, 1900); L. Barbat, *Histoire de la ville de Châlons-sur-Marne*; R. de Lasteyrie, *L'architecture religieuse en France à l'époque romane* (Paris, 1912), p. 158, St. Remi.

Notre Dame's choir is very beautiful. Its three apse chapels open on the ambulatory, by columns and stilted arches, perhaps the first time this disposition of Champagne Gothic was used. Soon it was repeated in St. Remi at Rheims. Auxerre and St. Quentin also used it, and it reached its apotheosis in the ethereal charm of Soissons' transept. Notre Dame at Châlons was in other ways a precursor; here first were set in each bay of the clearstory three windows side by side, a triplet of lancets that started the complex fenestration of the new art. In its first plan were no flying buttresses, but they were soon added when it was found that the thrust of the upper vaulting was not sufficiently counterbutted. In the XV century the Flamboyant south porch was built. Of the XVI century are some rich windows of the school of Troyes, now set in the nave's aisles. One of them represents the victory of Spain's crusaders over Islam at Las Navas de Tolosa in 1212, and is the best battle scene depicted in colored glass. With its beautiful Gothic cathedral, its immense abbatial, and all of its churches rich with storied windows, one is profoundly grateful that Châlons-sur-Marne only for a short hour early in the World War formed part of that *"ligne doulereuse et triomphale, ce ruban de pourpre et de lumière qui s'étend de Belfort au rivage des Flandres, la Voie Sacrée."*

Tragic the fate of its sister abbatial, St. Remi, in martyred Rheims. That grand ancestral church lies well-nigh mortally wounded on the field of honor. It stood up above the city as prominently as the cathedral itself, and has been mercilessly wrecked. The vaulting has fallen, and great rents have been torn in the walls of the precious Primary Gothic choir. A recent traveler found that its devastated nave recalled gaunt Jumièges.

Some ten years after the reconstruction of Notre Dame at Châlons, the monks of St. Remi began to make over their abbey church under the inspiration of Abbot Pierre de Celle, of the same lineage as the heiress of Braine who, with her husband, a brother of Louis VII, built the church of St. Yved. While John of Salisbury was a young student in France, Pierre de Celle entered into a friendship with him which continued to deepen till their death, both of them being men of the highest culture, strong literary abilities, and solid character. Pierre de Celle succeeded the English scholar as bishop of Chartres in 1181; *summi et incomparabilis viri,* so his epitaph sums him up.

It was this distinguished churchman who built, about 1170, the superb choir of St. Remi, and who remodeled as Gothic the ancient Romanesque nave. The choir had five radiating chapels, each of which opened on the ambulatory in the beautiful Champagne way, by slender columns bearing stilted arches. As tribunes were built over the aisles, the wall elevation was in four stories, and below two of them ran friezes of sculptured foliage. As if the architect felt that he had thus over-accentuated the horizontal line, he bound his triforium and clearstory into one composition by continuous moldings, a precocious first step toward the glazed triforia of Rayonnant Gothic. Originally no flying buttresses braced this early-Gothic choir; those that were added, about 1180, are probably the first ever made. Nothing could better show the swift development of Gothic structure than to compare the plain old flying buttresses of St. Remi with the luxuriant counterbutting members of Rheims Cathedral built fifty years later.

Between St. Remi's choir and the hemicycle transept of Soissons Cathedral there is such similitude of profile, detail, and plan that it is thought the same architect designed both. The able Pierre de Celle built the two westernmost bays of St. Remi's nave, and opened the tribune on the middle vessel with Gothic arches. He also built the west façade, which to-day is ancient only in its lower stories, as it was reconstructed in 1840. The north tower was re-done in the XII century; the south one is of the XI century, Abbot Herimar's time.

With book in hand should be read the complicated story of St. Remi's nave and transept, the ancient Romanesque edifice re-dressed as Gothic in 1170. Nothing remains of the church built in the IX century under Bishop Hincmar of Rheims. The oldest parts extant are the piers of the nave, which belonged to the reconstruction of the abbatial by Abbot Airard (1005-33). His successor, Thierry (d. 1041), decided that the works then under way were on too elaborate a scale to be within his means, so he simplified the plan. The outer side aisles were suppressed, the archivolts were doubled, the bays widened, and the old columns replaced by compound piers. In the transept his work still exists in the west wall (north arm) where are two stories of arcades supported by thick, short, cylinder piers whose capitals are coarsely carved acanthus leaves.

The rest of the transept (save what was added in 1170 to connect it with the Gothic choir and the re-dressed nave) is the work of Abbot Herimar who raised the west towers. Under him occurred the notable dedication of St. Remi's new Romanesque church, in 1049, by Leo IX, the reformer, with whom the Benedictine Order took possession of the papacy for some vital years of needed regeneration.

St. Bruno of Cologne, the future founder of the Carthusian Order, was a student in the episcopal school of Rheims while Romanesque St. Remi was building. And later he returned from Germany to direct the school from 1057 to 1075 with great prestige. His most notable pupil, Eudes de Châtillon, became the pope of the First Crusade, Urban II. Feeling the call for a life of prayer and retirement, Bruno thought of joining the group of earnest men about to commence the Cistercian Order, but his destiny led him to Grenoble, near which in the mountains he began the Grande Chartreuse (1084) where they say reform never was needed.[66]

In St. Remi's abbatial the last phase of Gothic art was to be represented. The transept's south façade is Flamboyant, and over its sculptured portal is a highly colored XV-century window. The façade was finished by Abbot Robert de Lenoncourt (d. 1531), who later became archbishop of Rheims. To his abbey church he presented ten rich tapestries relating the life of the first bishop of the city, St. Remigius, who baptized Clovis in 496, and whose rule of seventy years is the longest spiritual reign on record. Clovis and Clotilda founded the abbey. At its church altar St. Louis was knighted. On the day of Charles VII's coronation the barons rode

[66] "Il est digne de remarque, que de toutes ces règles monastiques les plus rigides ont été les mieux observées: les Chartreux ont donné au monde l'unique exemple d'une congrégation qui a existé sept cents ans sans avoir besoin de réforme."—CHATEAUBRIAND, *Génie du Christianisme.*

In April, 1903, two squadrons of dragoons expelled the last monks from La Grande Chartreuse. An economic loss for the entire region has resulted.

their steeds into the basilica, dismounting at the sanctuary to ask for the sacred ampulla needed for the king's anointing in the cathedral.

In the clearstory windows of St. Remi's choir were thirty-three lancets in which were portrayed the archbishops of Rheims from holy Remigius to Robert of France, brother of Louis VII, who was ruling here from 1162 to 1175, while Abbot Pierre was building his choir. The windows were probably set up in the time of Archbishop Robert's successor, Archbishop Guillaume of Champagne, who had finished the cathedral at Sens. They were memorable for their lovely browns and greens, and were allied, undoubtedly, with St. Denis' glass, though executed by local workers. Deep borders surrounded each lancet. Similar ornate borders and a magnificent deep blue color distinguished still older XII-century windows in the tribune gallery. The central lancet was an extraordinary Crucifixion, somewhat like that at Poitiers. An irreparable loss to art is the destruction of St. Remi's windows, though it is said that some of them were dismounted in time and carried to a place of safety.

ST. QUIRIACE CHURCH[67] AT PROVINS

Provins, une des plus charmantes villes de France, rivalise avec la vallée de Cachemire.... Des croisés rapportèrent les roses de Jéricho dans cette délicieuse vallée, où, par hasard, elles prirent des qualités nouvelles, sans rien perdre de leur couleurs.

—BALZAC, *Pierrette* (whose scene is Provins).

Another Primary Gothic church in Champagne is St. Quiriace at Provins, which one goes out of one's way to see because Provins is one of the most individual little towns in France, still in part surrounded by massive XII-and XIII-century ramparts. Thibaut IV the Singer added to the great walls of the lower town about 1230. They say that when crusaders drew near to Jerusalem on its hill encircled by its walls and towers they often cried out, "Provins!" Once the population of this shrunken little city rivaled that of Paris. Here were held annual fairs to which flocked the merchants of Europe, and the sensible counts of Champagne encouraged their visitors by wise regulations and strictest justice. The money of Provins was accepted in Florence and Rome.

The valley of roses was the favorite residence of the reigning counts. Here Thibaut IV, the most celebrated lyric poet of the Middle Ages, wrote his songs that wedded the art of the Midi troubadour with the salt of the northern trouvère. His son, Thibaut V, married the daughter of St. Louis and brought her in state to Provins, *"où ils firent leur entrée accompagnés d'une grande foison de barons,"* wrote Joinville, who had helped to arrange the match. Thibaut V's heart is contained in a XIII-century monument now in the chapel of the Hôtel Dieu, which hospital was originally the ancient palace of the countesses of Champagne. Thibaut V and his wife died returning from the tragic last crusade of Louis IX. Their niece Jeanne

[67] *Congrès Archéologique*, 1902; Morel-Payen, *Troyes et Provins* (Collection, Villes d'art célèbres), (Paris, H. Laurens, 1910); Félix Bourquelot, *Histoire de Provins* (Paris, Techener, 1840), 2 vols.; Gabriel Fleury, "Le portail de St. Ayoul de Provins," in *Congrès Archéologique*, 1902, p. 458, or in *Études sur les portails imagés du XIIe siècle* (Mamers, Fleury et Dangin, 1904).

married the king of France, and the prosperous days of Champagne ended when it merged its independence in the royal domain, for new regulations soon impaired the popularity of its famous fairs. It was Countess Jeanne of Navarre who persuaded her seneschal, Joinville, to write his reminiscences.

In the days when Provins was a world center St. Quiriace church was begun about 1160 by Henry the Liberal, the reigning count who was warmest patron of John of Salisbury when the latter, forced to quit England, lived in Provins. Little more than the choir of St. Quiriace now remains. In the tympanum of a late-Gothic portal is a XIII-century image of Christ. The semicircular chevet is boxed in a square ambulatory on which open square eastern chapels. The shafts are banded with annulets. There is Romanesque feeling in the zigzag ornamentation on the heavy ribs; the round arch reigns in the triforium, although the pier arcades below are pointed. The choir shows a curious experiment in vaulting hardly to be called successful: three bays are embraced by the vault section of eight branches.

St. Quiriace crowns the hilltop; in the lower town is St. Ayoul, whose portal sculpture (c. 1160) is of the same type as the three western doors at Chartres, as is the portal of St. Loup-de-Naud (Seine-et-Marne), close by.[68] Those who have fallen under the spell of Chartres' fascinating column statues will always study their sister images with interest.

Epitaphs on the walls of St. Quiriace recall two true shepherds of this church, one, who went daily into the hills to teach children and to tend on the sick poor in their homes, and the other, who opened up the forgotten crypt and left a school and presbytery to his parish. There is a quaintly worded tablet of the XVI century telling of the *haute et puissante dame*, the Marquise de Chenoise, who had "for God a tender solid piety; for her husband a submissive, respectful love; for her children a Christian and reasonable tenderness; for her friends a sincere and generous affection; for the poor charity without limit; and for the rest of the world *une bonté, une douceur, une honestété charmante*." One would not mind being the rest of the world for this gracious person. Both her sons were killed in one week, fighting under Turenne, so she passed the last years of her life in a retirement, which "she sanctified by prayer, and her prayer she nourished and sustained by good works." The robust piety of Bossuet's preaching breathes in such records. In St. Remi's abbatial at Rheims is the eulogy of another good lady of Champagne who was "Rachel in beauty, Rebecca in fidelity, Suzanna in purity, Tabitha in piety of heart, Ruth in sentiment, and Anna by good works." Paragons those old-time ladies seemed to be!

---

[68] The transept of St. Ayoul is good Romanesque. After a fire in 1160 the nave was rebuilt as XIII-century Gothic; the choir is XVI century. At St. Loup-de-Naud there is a central lantern on squinches (XII century).

ST. YVED AT BRAINE[69]

> I am just back from the battle line in that Royal Domain of
> Soissons, where the soul of ancient France seems more itself
> than in any other region, country of martyrs, and of kings, of
> Merovingian crypts, of the donjon of Coucy, of the five apses of
> St. Yved—realm of the first race of rulers bearing vestiges of the
> greatest history of France.
>
> —GABRIELE D'ANNUNZIO, 1914.

Strictly speaking, St. Yved at Braine is not so much a Primary Gothic monument as it is a link between that first tentative hour and the fuller development of the national art represented by Rheims and Amiens. In the same group as Braine, between Primary Gothic and the Era of the Great Cathedrals, are St. Leu d'Esserent, Montréal, Vézelay's choir, and the church of St. Laumer at Blois.

Braine, on the ancient Roman highroad between Rheims and Soissons, had been a farm of the Frankish kings. In the VII century it belonged to the father of St. Ouen, and it was here that the future bishop of Rouen, as a child, was blessed by a passing guest, the Irish missionary St. Columbanus, whose Celtic rule of Luxeuil dominated, in Gaul, the century called of saints.

Lady Agnes of Braine espoused a son of Louis VI, the turbulent Count of Dreux (d. 1188), and, from them came the funds for St. Yved, the second foundation of the new Order of Prémontré. The recorded date of the enterprise is from 1180 to 1216, but as the church is perfectly homogeneous, it must have been built in one campaign, probably in main part before the dedication of 1216.

As a composition, the plan of the collegiate is original. The apse chapels on each side of the choir chapel are placed on the bias so that the sanctuary opens out like a fan, with five altars visible at the same time. The arrangement was copied in far-off Hungary in St. Martin's church at Kassovie, built for the king by the wandering Picard artist Villard de Honnecourt. In Cologne the church of St. Gereon, and in Marburg that of St. Elizabeth, show the influence of Braine. St. Léger's abbatial at Soissons copied it. St. Yved has a square transept-crossing tower that opens still farther the central part of the edifice. Carved about the interior is a cordon of free springtime foliage. There is youth in every line of this beautiful white church. The superb monocylindrical columns and their capitals are robust virility itself. Everywhere is firmness of touch, and never has the unity been marred by patchwork reconstructions. Like its neighbor, Soissons, the same nicety of stonework is shown.

Before the Revolution the collegiate at Braine harbored an unparalleled collection of tombs, since here for centuries were laid to rest the barons and bishops of the proud family of Dreux, warriors at Bouvines, crusaders, and donors of storied windows at Chartres and Rheims. The four west bays of the church of Braine were stupidly demolished after the Revolution, because funds for repairs were at that

---

[69] *Congrès Archéologique*, 1911, p. 428, E. Lefèvre-Pontalis; S. Prioux, *Monographie de l'ancienne abbaye royale St. Yved de Braine* (1859), folio; *Bulletin Monumental*, 1908, vol. 72, p. 455, A. Boinet.

time lacking. From the destroyed portal were saved the two statues now set in the choir's wall. They represent the Coronation of Our Lady; the robes flow easily and there is scarcely a touch of Byzantine rigidity left in them.

Twice during the late World War was Braine's collegiate in the direct path of invasion. The first battle of the Marne freed it, but in May, 1918, the Germans again entered the little town. Then swept forward the second battle of the Marne, and Braine was liberated in September. One can only pray that, in such hasty retreats, St. Yved escaped mutilation.

ST. LEU D'ESSERENT[70]

> I think that that style which is called Gothic is endowed with a profound and a commanding beauty, such as no other style possesses ... and which probably the Church will not see surpassed till it attain to the Celestial City.... The Gothic style is as harmonious and as intellectual as it is graceful.
>
> —CARDINAL NEWMAN.

St. Leu d'Esserent is one of the small but perfect churches of the classic Ile-de-France that satisfy both eye and soul by the exquisite justness of their proportions. Its serene white charm is unobtrusive. Only a master of the inmost heart of France could have produced the assured rightness of its proportions. Unforgettable are the moments spent in this Benedictine abbatial on the Oise; sometimes up and down its lovely white avenue flits some happy lost bird, rejoicing in the paradise of quietude he has found.

The quarries round St. Leu d'Esserent were noted, and many a church of France has been made of their firm white stones. The origin of Gothic art is comprised, thinks M. Lefèvre-Pontalis, in this region where good quarries abounded, with Senlis taken as a center. A line from Senlis to Laon, if carried round, would pass through Rheims, Provins, Montereau, Étampes, Vernon, Amiens, Péronne, St. Quentin. Well within that circumference lies St. Leu d'Esserent.

The Benedictine church stands on prominent foundations overlooking the river loved of Corot and Daubigny. The priory was founded and presented to great Cluny by a knight of Esserent as thank-offering for his ransom from the Saracens by monks of St. Benedict. Of the church built in that XI century, there remain only the two stout columns, with archaic capitals, which now are embedded in the westernmost bay of the nave.

About 1150 the present church was begun, and for a century continued building, in three distinct bouts of work. First was made the west façade, only one of whose Romanesque towers was ever finished with a spire, the octagonal faces of which were relieved by curious lancelike ridges not repeated elsewhere. In the narthex, or porch between the towers, was tried an experiment to eliminate the so-

[70] *Congrès Archéologique,* 1905, p. 121, E. Lefèvre-Pontalis; E. Lefèvre-Pontalis, *À travers le Beauvaisis et le Valois* (Paris, 1907); Émile Lambin, "L'eglise de St. Leu d'Esserent," in *Gazette des beaux-arts,* 1901, tome 25, p. 305; Viollet-le-Duc, *Dictionnaire,* vol. 2, p. 504; vol. 4, pp. 83, 230; vol. 7, p. 384; vol. 9, p. 280; Abbé Eugène Müller, *Senlis et ses environs* (1897).

called domical shape of the first Gothic vaults. The transverse arches were loaded with masonry to raise them to the vault's apex. Experimental also are the ungainly diagonals, in part ornamented with Norman chevrons, that span the tribune over the forechurch (c. 1150). The ribs are not free of the vault web, so elasticity is missing.

During the last quarter of the XII century, the chevet was built, as were the two towers placed beside the apse, an arrangement derived from Rhenish churches. Of that time, too (c. 1180), is the double bay, surmounted by a sexpartite vault which precedes the apse. There is no transept. The recently finished choir of Senlis Cathedral influenced the ambulatory and apse chapels of St. Leu. At Senlis and here occur the earliest examples of double flying buttresses. The six bays of the nave were added about 1220, after a pause in the works. Previously, each bay of the church had been lighted by a single lancet; now two lancets surmounted by an oculus were used, which added much dignity to the exterior aspect of the edifice. Over the axis chapel was built a second story. The unvaulted tribunes, above the side aisles, were transformed into a sort of triforium by building a wall slightly behind their arcaded openings. As that wall was pierced by some odd little square windows, this may be regarded as one of the first essays of a glazed triforium, the feature which was soon to develop into the decorative richness of St. Denis, Troyes, Le Mans, Tours, and Beauvais.

CHAPTER IV

NOTRE DAME OF PARIS AND OTHER CHURCHES OF THE CAPITAL[71]

Notre Dame, begun in 1163—Its exterior unsurpassed, the west façade a classic—Scholastic training of its bishop-builders—Summa of the supreme scholastic, Aquinas, like a Gothic cathedral—Thirty thousand students then in Paris University—Bishop Maurice de Sully (1160-96) built Notre Dame—Bishop Eudes de Sully made the portals of the west façade—Bishop Pierre de Nemours died a crusader, before Damietta, 1219—Bishop Guillaume d'Auvergne finished the north tower (1228-49)—All the prelates building Paris Cathedral good and able men—Their sincerity lives in its stones—First architect unknown—Jean and Pierre de Chelles made the transept and apse chapels—Sculpture of Notre Dame masterly—Sainte-Chapelle built by St. Louis, 1246 to 1248—St. Julien-le-Pauvre a contemporary of Notre Dame's choir (c. 1180)—Same noble sculptured capitals—Three Benedictine abbey churches of Paris show early trials of Gothic vaulting—St. Germain-des-Prés, St. Martin-des-Champs, St. Pierre-de-Montmartre—St. Louis and his friend, Joinville—Louis IX illuminated his kingdom with fair churches—On his first crusade spent five years in the East, 1248

[71] Marcel Aubert, *La cathédrale de Notre Dame de Paris* (Paris, Longuet, 1909); Lassus et Viollet-le-Duc, *Monographie de Notre Dame de Paris* (Paris), folio; V. Mortet, *Étude historique et archéologique sur la cathédrale et le palais épiscopal de Paris* (Paris, 1888); Queyron, *Histoire et description de l'église de Notre Dame* (Paris, Plon, Nourret et Cie); De Guilhermy, *Description de Notre Dame de Paris* (1856); *ibid., Itinéraire archéologique de Paris* (1855); S. François, *La façade de Notre Dame de Paris* (Brussels, Imprimerie Goosens, 1907), 4to; E. Lefèvre-Pontalis, "Les origines des gables," in *Bulletin Monumental*, 1907, vol. 71, p. 92; Camille Enlart, *Le musée de sculpture comparée du Trocadéro* (Collection, Les grandes institutions de France), (Paris, H. Laurens, 1911); H. Bazin, *Les monuments de Paris* (Paris, 1904); G. Riat, *Paris* (Collection, Villes d'art célèbres), (Paris, H. Laurens); Amédée Boinet and Jean Bayet, *Les édifices religieux de Paris* (Collection, Les richesses d'art de la ville de Paris), (Paris, H. Laurens), 3 vols.; L. Barron, *La Seine* (Collection, Fleuves de France), (Paris, H. Laurens); Émile Lambin, *La flore des grandes cathédrales de France,* (Paris, 1897); *ibid., Les églises des environs de Paris étudiées au point de vue de la flore ornamentale* (Paris, 1896), folio; *ibid., Les églises de l'Ile-de-France* (Paris, 1906); Anthyme Saint-Paul, "Notices sur les églises des environs de Paris," in *Bulletin Monumental*, vol. 34, p. 861, and vol. 35, p. 709; Alexis Martin, *Excursions dans les environs de Paris* (Paris, 1900); Henri Stein, *Les architectes des cathédrales gothiques* (Paris, 1908); Émile Mâle, *L'art religieux du XIIIe siècle en France* (Paris, Colin, 1908), 4to.

to 1259—From 1254 to 1270 worked for his people—Death of St. Louis on the crusade of 1270—His characteristics: justice, pity, other-worldliness—Inimitable charm of Joinville's Histoire de St. Louis—Describes his friendship with the king in Palestine—Joinville's old age and death in 1319.

Mantes' collegiate of Notre Dame is Primary Gothic—A contemporary of Paris Cathedral—Perhaps by the same architect—Its chapel of Navarre one of the best works of Rayonnant Gothic.

Meaux Cathedral, a difficult architectural page to decipher, owing to reconstruction—Begun in 1170, but rebuilt radically after 1270—Bossuet, its greatest bishop (1681 to 1704)—Meaux, the cathedral for the Te Deum of victory—Battle of the Marne, 1914, waged at the city gates.

It is important to meditate often and with ardor and respect on the documents which the ancestors have left us.

—St. Thomas Aquinas.

HE Era of the Great Cathedrals was inaugurated by Notre Dame of Paris, the most imposing Gothic church hitherto attempted. The popular voice has chosen to group it among the chief four, with Chartres, Rheims, and Amiens—all four of them dedicated to Our Lady, though in a special way Notre Dame of the capital seems to have appropriated the name.

Of the four, the cathedral of Paris was the first built, and traits of the Romanesque epoch lingered in it, such as the tribune galleries over the side aisles, the division of its interior wall into four vertical stories, and the Byzantine feeling of its earlier sculpture. The piers were massive single columns of true majesty. In the sixth pier of the nave, counting from the east, an experiment was tried when an engaged shaft was added to its front. The seventh pier (c. 1192) marks a date in the development of Gothic structure since with it was made the type of ground support which was to predominate in the XIII century—four engaged shafts around a central pillar. When the middle core was made elliptical, as at Beauvais, the type pier was achieved.

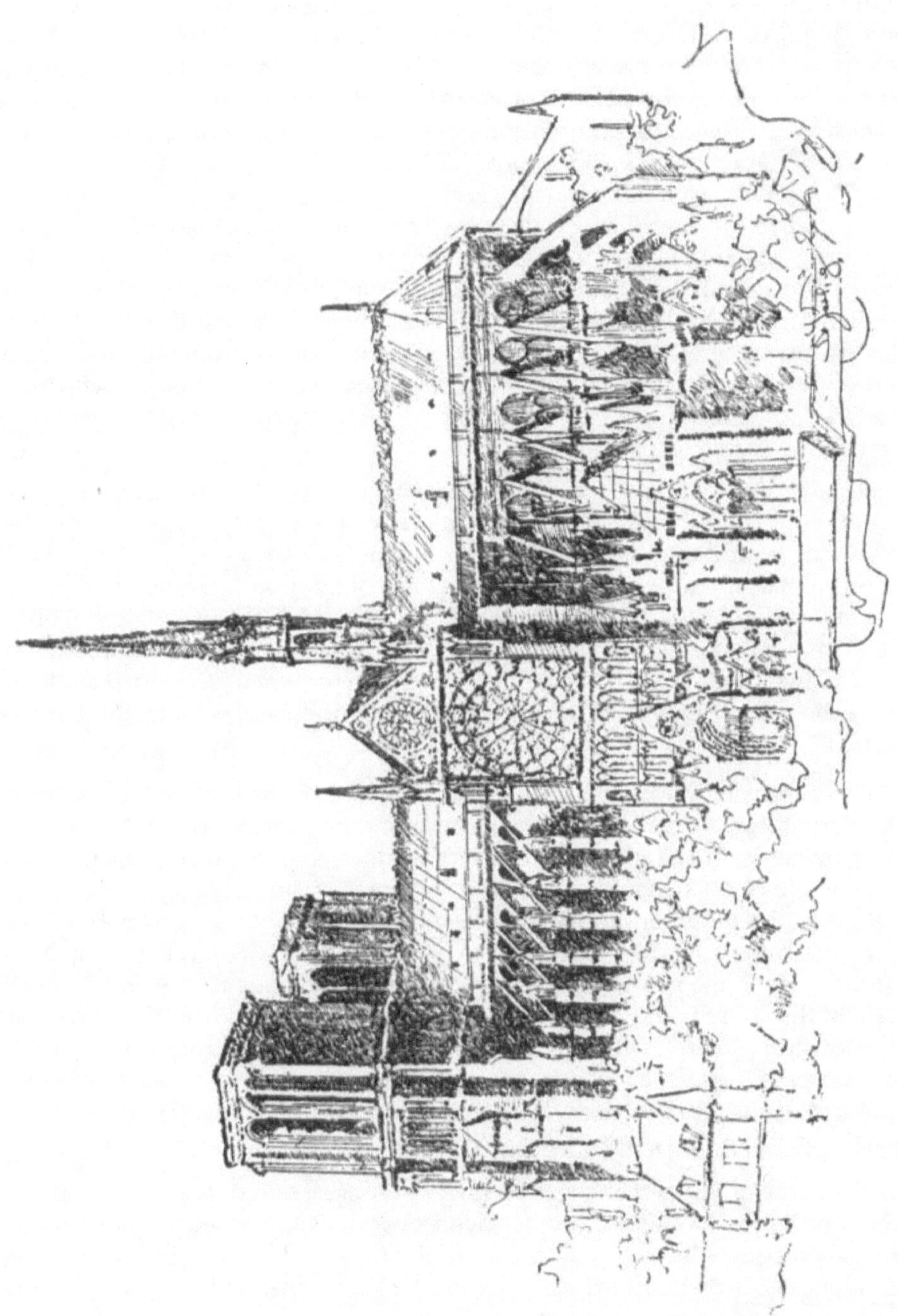

Notre Dame of Paris. View from the South

Notre Dame of Paris used the sexpartite system which calls for alternating ground supports. Either the uniform piers here were laid before a sexpartite vault was thought of, or else the architect preferred them for æsthetic reasons, and in this case he certainly was right. Double aisles about both nave and choir differentiate the interior of Notre Dame of Paris from that of the average cathedral. The far-stretching aisles of this church compose vistas of unsurpassed picturesqueness and variety of perspective. Some have said that the central nave is not sufficiently wide for such a stretch of lateral aisles, and have found a certain monotony in the clearstory, tribune, and pier arcade being of equal height. Originally, beneath the clearstory were small circular unglassed apertures giving on the rafters over the tribune. Those oculi were done away with during the XIII century, when the clearstory windows were lengthened for the better lighting of the church. During his able restoration of Notre Dame, M. Viollet-le-Duc found hidden under the pavement some of the discarded window frames, and he took the liberty (which many regret) of replacing a few in the bays near the transept, thus marring the uniformity of the interior.

Despite the enlargement of the upper windows and the changes made to give more light to the tribunes, none can deny that, in gloomy weather, Notre Dame can be somber and even cavernous. Yet who, of its devotees, would have it different? Supreme cathedral it is for that supremest of hymns, the *Dies Iræ*—sound and sense and vision welded. To exchange its severe majesty for an expanse of brilliant glass—save Suger's glass—is unthinkable. In Notre Dame you comprehend the spectacular repentances of the Middle Ages. Here, when pestilence stalked the city or the enemy was at the gate, have echoed the *Miserere* and the *Libera nos, Domine.*[72]

There is an individuality in the cathedral of Paris that overrides every criticism. Perpetually does the worshiper find in it new aspects, in the dim, low aisles full of mystery, in the gleam of transept windows as seen through the tribune arches while one listens, perhaps, to a lenten friar preacher discoursing of sin, justice, and the judgment to come; here on the very spot where Dominic himself taught the same sobering lessons; here where, six hundred years later, his son, Lacordaire, held the manhood of Paris spellbound. Or, again, one gazes down the length of the church, with its incomparable perspective, while around one rise the voices of strong men fresh from the battle of Verdun, fresh from their firm "They shall not pass," and their *Magnificat* of thanksgiving to Notre Dame swells in a volume of sound like the eternal sea. The crusaders of St. Louis' time prayed, too, for strength in Notre Dame of Paris.[73]

The curve of the sanctuary as seen from the west end of the nave is one of the splendors of the monument, and no chevet ever built surpassed it. The cause of the magic is practical—a structural problem solved, as is the case with the best aspects of Gothic art. At that eastern curve extra piers were inserted between the double

[72] "Les ardentes prières, les sanglots désespérés du moyen âge avaient à jamais imprégné ces piliers et tanné ces murs."—J. K. Huysmans.

[73] "Il me sembla que tout le passé de mon pays se dressait devant moi. Tout ce qu'elles ont vu, ces pierres!... Tout ce qu'elles ont entendu, ces voûtes!"

—Pierre l'Ermite (Abbé Loutil)

aisles in order to obviate the difficulty of vaulting such irregular trapeze-shaped sections.

The enthusiast maintains that the exterior of Notre Dame surpasses that of all other cathedrals. Certainly better transept façades were never made nor was apse more romantic than that of the chief church of Paris, as it rises in three grandiose steps, with flying buttresses of wide span leaping with an audacity that fairly catches the breath; and again the success is a case of sound science solving a problem.

The west façade is an accepted classic, "an architectural glory of France," irreproachable. Once the intelligence has grasped its pre-eminence, allegiance to it will never waver. The frontispieces of Rheims and of Rouen are richer and may appeal more to the imagination. It is possible that the severe dignity of Paris may even chill at first. But what clarity of plan! Four strong buttresses accentuate the big square parallelogram. Excess of ornamentation has been avoided in order that the whole may stand forth. Lest the two towers might appear to rise abruptly from the massive, some master hand made there the graceful open colonnade.[74]

The façade of Notre Dame is true to its epoch in its appeal to the intellect rather than to the emotions. It was built in the golden age of scholasticism, when religion and philosophy went hand in hand, when the teachers in the schools of Paris, the *cité lettré*, the *œil du monde*, thought that Faith and Reason could give mutual aid one to the other, that the truths of Revelations could coincide with the natural judgment.

Scholasticism has been belittled by the modern sophists from the time of the XVIII-century Encyclopædist to the XIX-century superman. Yet scholasticism was an important factor in the formation of the French intellect, which, in its virile youth, it put through a course of useful mental gymnastics. Precisely the race, whose ancestors sharpened their wits in the *Sic-et-Non* debates of the mediæval schools of Paris, is to-day pre-eminent in precision of language and freedom from fogginess of thought. Easy enough for the modern mind to ridicule the quarrel of generations over nominalism and realism, pursued with the personal heat of a modern political campaign.[75] Certainly the abuse of the scholastic system led to hair-splitting disputes, for the deductive method, when carried to excess, ends in thin subtlety. But why judge a system by its extremes? Because XIV-century architecture grew rigid with set formulas and the abuse of its own laws, does that discredit the virile period to which it succeeded?

The bishops who built Notre Dame were notable scholastics. The generations who built cathedrals were impregnated with the certainty that what was Christian

[74] "The first of the great Gothic façades in point of dignity is undoubtedly that of Paris, a design of which no words can express the exalted beauty. Grandeur of composition, nobility of silhouette, perfection of proportion, wealth of detail, infinitely varied play of light and shade combine to raise this composition, so majestic, so serene, to the place it has ever occupied in the heart of everyone endowed with the slightest feeling for the beautiful."—ARTHUR KINGSLEY PORTER.

[75] The problem of Universals remains still a real one for the thinker—how our intellectual concepts correspond to things existing outside our intellect.

was rational. Scholasticism produced St. Thomas Aquinas, whose philosophy has outlived a dozen systems, whose *Summa* was placed on the assembly table of the Council of Trent, the sole companion of the Scriptures, Aquinas, whose sanity of ethics and doctrine was held up by Leo XIII as the best guide amid current errors.

With Aquinas, who taught the inextricable union of Faith and Reason, Christian philosophy reached its zenith.[76] Too long has it been the fashion to look on orthodoxy as a sign of mental inferiority. Professors still dismiss the *Summa* with a scathing line. They have never opened its pages, perhaps, but second-hand knowledge to vast regions of human thought is no impediment to a chair in the modern university. "Abstractions as repulsive as they are frivolous," is the dictum of a group of present-day French scholars who seem to think that to belittle things mediæval is proof of patriotism.

We have looked on at the rehabilitation of certain mediæval saints. It was not so long ago that the poor man of Assisi was patronized as an ignorant fanatic. The appeal of St. Francis is to the emotions, while that of St. Thomas Aquinas is to the intellect, so, perhaps, it is expecting too much to hope that some day the average man may appreciate this thinker who set sane boundaries round the human mind. Too long have the prime sanities of reason been flouted by hazy abstract thinking in the void; too long has man shut his eyes to the fact that a crime of the intellect is of more consequence to mankind than a crime against the civil law; too long has applause been given to philosophers who obliterated the distinctions between right and wrong—like Hegel, teaching the identity of Being and non-Being—so that the very soul of the peoples grew perverted and appalling cataclysms threatened civilization.

What the older centuries thought of Aquinas, the painter as well as the poet tells us. In the Louvre hangs Benozzo Gozzoli's picture of the *doctor angelicus* sitting in luminous repose amid pope, doctors, saints, and the sages of antiquity, and the inscription runs: *"Vere hic est lumen ecclesiæ."* And in Milan hangs Piero della Francesca's profound study of the saint. "I place Plato high," wrote a sound French thinker, "but as I see Aquinas he is as superior to Plato, and even more, than is our knowledge of the physical world to that of the Greeks.... He embraces St. Augustine, Aristotle, and Plato."

Often has it been said that a Gothic cathedral is the *Summa* translated into

---

[76] In his *Summa totius theologiæ* St. Thomas held that the existence of God was to be known by reason. He took his stand on a palpable fact—the existence of creatures. He began with the fecund idea of motion, the stars in their orbits, man engendering man. If there is movement there must be a First Motor. If there ever had been an instant when nothing was, nothing ever would have been. Effects must have a cause. Either nothing is, which is an absurdity, or there must be One Being eternally immutable.

That the movement is ordered, such as night and day, season following season, shows a supreme power directing. That creatures are more or less perfect supposes a perfect being. One by one Aquinas laid his foundation stones till a solid lower wall was built, on which he reared his majestic structure. In the Roman Breviary, he is thus recorded: "Thou hast written well of me, Thomas, what recompense do you ask of me?" "None but yourself, Lord!" (*"Non aliam, Domine, nisi te ipsum!"*).

stone, logical, ordered, interlinked, leaving nothing to chance, a sound skeleton on a sound base, so securely balanced that great windows could be opened on the sky, like flashes of intuitive genius lifting the soul to the infinite. Many were the points by which St. Thomas touched Gothic art in its heyday. He was a student in Cologne when its mighty cathedral was begun. He was in Paris during the years when the transept of Notre Dame was building, and the Sainte-Chapelle and St. Denis' abbatial. By blood he was related to St. Louis, and often was his guest at table, where talk must have turned on that keen interest of the hour — the making of Gothic churches.[77] He was to die (1274) in Cistercian Fossanuova, the first Gothic monument of Italy. And his great work, like many a cathedral, was left unfinished.

Never was aspiration toward the infinite more passionate than in that scholastic disputing, commune-winning, cathedral-building, crusading age. The absorbing interest for old and young, for bishop and layman, for king and poor student, was to know God, to know their own souls, to learn how to make life more worthy of God. "In the entire length of France," wrote the archbishop of Sens to the pope, in 1140, "in towns and even in villages, in the schools and outside them, all, even simple people and children, are disputing on the Holy Trinity." Paris became the center of the seething new interest in theology and philosophy. In 1109 Guillaume de Champeaux opened a school of logic on the slopes of St. Geneviève's hill (where to this day reigns Paris University), and soon all Christendom frequented it.[78] His pupil, and later his opponent, was Abélard, brilliant, restless knight-errant of dialectics, whom the modern orthodox student finds to be a forerunner of the new method of biblical criticism rather than a rationalist.

---

[77] The father of St. Thomas was the Count of Aquin, nephew of the Emperor Frederick Barbarossa. His mother came of the line of the Norman rulers in Sicily; the same stocks produced that undisciplined, undecipherable genius of the XIII century, Frederick II.

[78] L. Liard, *L'Université de Paris* (Collection, Les grandes institutions de France), (Paris, H. Laurens); L. Maître, *Les écoles épiscopales et monastiques de l'occident depuis Charlemagne jusqu'à Philippe-Auguste* (Paris, 1866); Tarsot, *Les écoles et les écoliers à travers les âges* (Paris, H. Laurens); H. Rashdall, *The Universities of the Middle Ages* (Oxford, Clarendon Press, 1895), 2 vols.; Bonnard, *Histoire de l'abbaye royale de St. Victor de Paris* (1907); V. Cousin, éd., *Œuvres de Pierre Abélard* (Paris, 1849-59), 2 vols.; B. Hauréau, éd., *Les œuvres de Hugues de St. Victor* (Paris, 1887); B. Hauréau, *Histoire de la philosophie scholastique* (Paris, 1872), 3 vols.; A. Mignon, *Hugues de St. Victor* (Paris, 1895); Léon Gautier, éd., *Œuvres poétiques d'Adam de St. Victor* (Paris, 1858), 2 vols.; Léon Gautier, *Histoire de la poésie religieuse dans les cloîtres des Xe et XIe siècle* (Paris, 1887); Noël Valois, *Guillaume d'Auvergne* (Paris, 1880); E. Berger, *La Bible française au moyen âge* (Paris, 1884); Lecoy de la Marche, *La chaire française au moyen âge* (Paris, 1886); *Histoire littéraire de la France.* (Begun by the XVII-century Benedictines, continued by the Institute of France.) Vol. 9, p. 1, "L'État des lettres en France, XIIe siècle" (Paris, 1750); vol. 10, p. 309, "Guillaume de Champeaux" (Paris, 1759); vol. 12, p. 1, "Hugues de St. Victor"; p. 86, "Abélard"; p. 585, "Pierre Lombard"; p. 629, "Héloïse" (Paris, 1764); vol. 13, p. 472, "Richard de St. Victor" (Paris, 1814); vol. 15, p. 40, "Adam de St. Victor"; p. 149. "Maurice de Sully" (Paris, 1820); vol. 16, p. 1, "L'état des lettres en France au XIIIe siècle" p. 574, "Eudes de Sully" (Paris, 1824); vol. 18, p. 357, "Guillaume d'Auvergne" p. 449, "Vincent de Beauvais" (Paris, 1835); vol. 19, p. 38, "Hugues de Saint-Cher"; p. 143, "St. Louis"; p. 238, "St. Thomas d'Aquin"; p. 266, "St. Bonaventure"; p. 291, "Robert de Sorbon"; p. 621, "Les trouvères," (Paris, 1838).

In the abbey of St. Victor, whose free classes were founded by Guillaume de Champeaux when harried by Abélard, there gathered a group of mystic scholars and poets: Hugues de St. Victor, the Augustine of his day (d. 1141), whose work on the sacraments was an interlinked system of theology. Lucid in intellect, tender in sentiment, was this friend of St. Bernard, whom Dante places in Paradise with St. Anselm and St. Bonaventure (*Par.*, xii: 30); and Hugues' disciple, Richard de St. Victor (d. 1173), ranked in Paradise as the companion of the Venerable Bede and St. Isidore of Seville, "Richard, who in contemplation was more than man" (*Par.*, x: 132); and Adam de St. Victor, one of the best poets of the XII century, whose sequences and rimed proses fill the liturgy. Another pupil of the learned Hugues was Pierre Lombard, who died bishop of Paris in 1160; his *Book of Sentences* became a textbook in European universities for centuries to come.

From the cathedral school and the mount of St. Geneviève and St. Victor's cloister[79] evolved the University of Paris, "elder daughter of France," whose title first appears in 1215, the oldest university in Europe with that of Bologna—one the high priestess of theology, the other the leader in canon and civil law. In the XII-century schools of Paris, John of Salisbury met Thomas Becket and Nicholas Breakspear (the English pope, Adrian IV), and there the future Innocent III became the friend of Stephen Langton.

By the XIII century over thirty thousand students thronged the colleges in Paris. Aquinas taught in the Dominicans' branch of the university, in which same convent, called the Jacobins, lived the reader of Louis IX, Vincent de Beauvais, whose four *Mirrors* were depicted in the imagery of the great cathedrals. No age was ever more enamored of encyclopædias. To overclassify was a characteristic of the times which even the great Aquinas could not escape. They say that over five hundred monks, under the guidance of the Dominican cardinal, Hugues de Saint-Cher, were busy in the rue St. Jacques preparing the first concordance of Scriptures. The entire Bible was translated into French in the XIII century. In the Franciscans' branch of the University St. Bonaventure taught. The king's chaplain, Robert de Sorbon, founded a house where poor students could live in common. Canterbury's archbishop, St. Edmund Rich, was a pupil in Paris, then a teacher. Roger Bacon, first to grasp the importance of experimental science, studied there, and so did Robert Grosseteste, builder of Lincoln Cathedral, whom Bacon said excelled all other masters in his range of useful knowledge.

The smelting pot of modern society those fecund formative years of the XII and XIII centuries have been called. A life-time's study it would be to draw adequately the picture of the one city of Paris then, when Philippe-Auguste and his grandson, St. Louis, were busy raising their Louvre and their Cité palaces, their Notre Dame, and their Sainte-Chapelle, busy cleaning the city streets and the city laws; when one scholarly bishop succeeded another as slowly rose the capital's cathedral, when lovely Latin hymns poured from St. Victor's abbey, while in the street the students sang the new lays of trouvère and troubadour, telling of "love that is a thing so high," of Roland and the *gestes* of paladins, of the Celtic heroes,

---

[79] The last vestige of St. Victor's monastery, foyer of sanctity for the XII century, was wiped out by order of a stupid municipality of Paris, in 1842.

Tristan, Lancelot, and Percival; when all the newly awakened intellectual and art life was astir welding old blood and new, making Frenchmen, at last, of Celt and Latin and Frank, making a kind of commonwealth of the nations that met in universities whose common speech still was Latin.[80]

That there were black shadows in the picture, none deny. There were pillages and massacres. It was an agitated day full of tumults and heresies and terrible reprisals. One has only to read the censures of St. Bernard and of Innocent III to learn of the cupidity and the lust. Joinville has told of a sink of corruption lying within a stone's throw of the saint-king's crusading camp. But, above all the lawlessness, the men of those ages of faith aspired. Their acts might fall short; their principles remained sound. "No easy-going doctrines, then, to legitimize vice," says Ozanam. Man knew how to beat his breast in humble repentance. He lifted his eyes toward an ideal so far above himself that it was given his human weakness to build cathedrals such as Notre Dame of the capital. Not so does he build when as superman he sits on a self-raised altar.

The virtuous bishop, who had most to do with the erection of the cathedral of Paris, had been a student and later a teacher of scholasticism. Maurice de Sully was born of simple parentage in the village of Sully-sur-Loire, and he came as a poor scholar to the great city. His abilities and the integrity of his conduct won him recognition, and after teaching belles-lettres, he was elected to the see of Paris as the seventy-second successor of St. Denis. From 1160 to 1196 he directed his diocese, a true shepherd whose special care was the training of young priests. Crowds flocked to his sermons, wrote a contemporary. He took an active part on the side of Thomas Becket during the English archbishop's struggle with Henry II, and it was he who consecrated as bishop of Chartres Becket's friend, the intellectual John of Salisbury. To Bishop Maurice, who had baptized him, Philippe-Auguste left the care of the Royal Treasury when he went on the Third Crusade. So wisely did this churchman administer his revenues that he was able to build hospitals and abbeys, as well as erect, in larger part by his personal donations, his own cathedral.

The first stone of Notre Dame was laid in 1163, and tradition says that Alexander III officiated in the same month that he dedicated for the Benedictines the new choir of St. Germain-des-Prés; the exiled pontiff resided in France for four years. Though the name of the architect of Notre Dame has not survived, his design was adhered to during a century and a half. A transept was not in his plan; however, a short one was inserted before the nave was laid down. That nave was nearly finished when Bishop Maurice de Sully died, in 1196, leaving large sums, in his testament, for the completion of his beloved church. The two westernmost bays of the nave are not of the bishop-founder's time.

Notre Dame, because of interruptions in its construction, presents an irregular

[80] Petit de Julleville, éd., *Histoire de la langue et de la littérature française* (Paris, Colin, 1900), 8 vols. In vols. 1 and 2 the Middle Ages are treated by Gaston Paris, Léon Gautier, and Joseph Bédier; Gaston Paris, *La littérature du XIIe siècle* (Paris, Hachette, 1895). He places the classic epoch of the literature of the Middle Ages between 1108 (opening of Louis VI's reign) and 1223 (end of Philippe-Auguste's rule); Joseph Bédier, *Les légendes épiques* (Paris, H. Champion, 1908-13), 4 vols.; Remy de Gourmont, *Le Latin mystique*.

alignment, and it is easy to perceive, as one gazes along its vaulting, that its choir slopes toward the north. Archæologists have given up the poetic explanation that the slanting choir was symbolic of the droop of Christ's head on the cross. Nor can the symbol seeker now call the Porte Rouge (an extra door in the north wall of the choir) a souvenir of the spear wound of the Saviour, since if made with such intention it would have been placed below the extended arms of the transept.

Three campaigns of work built Notre Dame, and each time that the work was resumed the axis deviated slightly. First rose the choir and a short transept. Then was done the nave, save its westernmost bays. And finally, at the beginning of the XIII century, they undertook the west façade and the two bays behind it. The carving on the pier's capitals shows the gradual advance in sculpture: in the choir they cut the large leaves of water plants which were the first nature models copied when the conventional Byzantine models were discarded. Then, in the nave, the foliage grew richer, and oak and vine and curled-up ferns appeared. Capital by capital should be studied, for their sculpture is masterly. The capitals of the nave's triforium are said to mark the culmination of Gothic art in foliate design. While unity was kept throughout the entire arcade, there was unceasing variation in details.

When Bishop Maurice de Sully, the peasant, died, he was succeeded by Bishop Eudes de Sully, the feudal baron, descended from the reigning counts of Champagne, from Louis VII and Aliénor of Aquitaine, and in whose veins ran the blood of William the Conqueror through his daughter Adela. The ability to build was his by inheritance. He began the west façade, and probably at his death all three of the portals were in place. To him we owe that fairest of sculptured entrances, the Virgin's door, under the northwest tower, called "the most beautiful page of stone that the Middle Ages have left us." *Visibile palare* are Dante's words for such art as this. In the carved tympanum, "Gothic art reached the simple perfection of Phidias." The draperies flow easily; only in the abrupt turning up of the edges of the robes lingers an archaic touch. Below are represented kings and prophets, the ancestors of Mary. Above them is a moving version of the Assumption; and in the upper triangle is the Coronation of the Queen of Heaven by her Divine Son—she, the mortal, turned toward Him, the divinity, with a gesture of adoration. The Christ is the Nazarene, a noble Oriental.

No haziness then in their knowledge that the patroness in whose care they placed their cathedrals was a fellow creature. To the common sense of the Middle Ages, it would have seemed a muddle-headed way of thinking to have called Jesus, God, and at the same time to have refused homage to His Mother, the one whom God chose to honor above all mortals, "she who didst so ennoble human nature that its own Maker scorned not to become its making."[81] It was only logical, they thought, that the best advocate with the son should be the mother. "All of us who fear the wrath of the Judge, fly to the Judge's mother," wrote Abélard. "*Que Dieu nous l'octroie par la prière de sa douce mère,*" wrote the crusader Joinville. So, without worrying over future carpers who might murmur "Mariolatry," the Middle Ages chanted "*Laus Deo et Beatæ Mariæ laudum.*" And the cathedral of Paris

---

[81] *Paradiso*, xxxiii: 4-6.

dared to dedicate four of its six doors to the Queen of Heaven.

The door under the southwest tower commemorates St. Anne, the Blessed Virgin's mother. It is a composite work, carved in Bishop Maurice's time, between 1160 and 1170, but not set up here till Bishop Eudes de Sully had undertaken the façade; in its tympanum are representations both of Louis VII and of Maurice de Sully. St. Anne's door was a link between the still archaic western doors of Chartres and the clearly enunciated Gothic portal under the northwest tower of Paris Cathedral. In the multitudinous folds of the draperies is Byzantine feeling, and sacerdotal is the Madonna who gravely presents her son to be adored. By the middle of the XIII century, the Madonna had become a natural mother, and so she is sculptured at the north entrance to Notre Dame's transept.

Bishop Eudes de Sully, like his predecessor, had many a link with scholasticism and with other bishop-builders. He had been fellow student in Paris with the future Innocent III, and that expert in men when pope called on his aid to find capable occupants for the French sees. Eudes' own brother Henry was the archbishop of Bourges who initiated the new cathedral there; and when his brother died, Eudes assisted in placing in his see the saintly Guillaume, who built the chevet of Bourges. Through Eudes de Sully, the bishop-builder of Rheims Cathedral, Albéric de Humbert, was elected, and he also helped to elect Bishop Hervé, who began the cathedral of Troyes. Able men ever found a protector in the capable bishop of Paris, whose strict sense of duty was incorruptible. When Philippe-Auguste, his near kinsman, broke the marriage law, Bishop Eudes went into exile rather than sanction the scandal. To him Innocent III sent St. Jean de Matha, that the prelate might draw up a Rule for the new Order of Trinitarians, established to redeem captives from Islam. It was Eudes de Sully who founded, in 1204, the abbey of Port Royal, a name to become of note in French letters.

The bishop of Paris from 1208 to 1219 was Pierre de Nemours, one of four brothers who were bishop-builders, at Paris, at Noyon, at Châlons, and at Meaux. He died a crusader under the walls of Damietta. Scarcely a cathedral but has its crusade memory. The façade of Notre Dame had almost reached the crowning open arcade when the scholarly Guillaume de Seignelay was transferred to the see of Paris from Auxerre where he had begun the Gothic cathedral. The *galerie des rois*, whose date is about 1223, was no doubt his work. Such galleries are found only in cathedrals in the royal domain, and it is just as likely that they honor the kings of France as the kings of Judea as some maintain. The majority of the larger statues of Paris Cathedral are restitutions. Viollet-le-Duc had an English sculptor, George Frampton, make the gargoyles and grotesques of Notre Dame, since the Revolution wrecked most of the exterior sculpture.

Still another noted scholastic, Guillaume d'Auvergne (1228-29), was to rule the see of Paris while its chief church was building. He finished the northwest tower, which differed slightly in size and details from that to the south; across the face of the former are ten statues, whereas nine only are set before its companion tower. Perhaps a change of architects caused the disparity, or it may be that when the houses were cleared away for the erection of the north tower, more space was available. Bishop Guillaume d'Auvergne's writings show him to have been one of the most original thinkers in the XIII century, a theologian, a philosopher, a mathematician, and one versed in Arab and in Greek literature. He became for St. Louis a kind of prime minister in ecclesiastical business, and, like the king, he founded hospitals and houses of charity. There is a charming page in Joinville's reminiscences concerning this able man. A priest expressed his doubts to him on the Eucharist. Bishop Guillaume asked if he tried to resist the temptations, and he replied that he did so with all his force. "Now I," said the good bishop, "have not a single doubt about the Real Presence. I am like the fortress of Montleheri, safe in the heart of France, far from the danger line; but you, who fight unceasingly, are like the king's fortress of Rochelle in Poitou, on the frontier. Now, of us two, whom will the king most honor for guarding his fortresses?"

Peasant and prince, crusader and scholar, humanist and mathematician, men of exemplary lives, born rulers and guides, such were the builders of Notre Dame of Paris, and their ability and sincerity live eternally in their work.[82] They gave free wing to the soul in raising their great church, while they cheerfully accepted the human law of working within limits. No cathedral in France shows more clearly the relation between builders and building, more clearly vindicates the ideals of its age. The partisan historian may cite his instances to prove that the religion of that age was superstitious. While Notre Dame stands, such charges are refuted. It is a historical document as potent for the vindication of the truth as the *Divina Commedia* itself.

When Bishop Guillaume d'Auvergne had finished the towers of Notre Dame he caused to be made the open arcade from which they emerge, as from a royal peristyle. About the same time side chapels were inserted between the buttresses, and the line of small rose windows, which had hitherto marked the triforium story, was done away with, in order that the clearstory windows might be lengthened. Only step by step were the builders learning that they might open the entire space between the active members of a Gothic structure; the upper windows of Chartres had passed on the lesson to Paris.

The plan of the first architect was adhered to throughout, and since the later masters-of-works were likewise natives of the Ile-de-France and innate in them a classic restraint and a hardy daring (the hall-mark of the best Parisian art to this day), the cathedral of Paris was homogeneous. Midway in the XIII century Jean de Chelles, a precursor of Rayonnant Gothic, lengthened the transept arms by a bay and finished them with admirable façades. His name, and the date 1257, are cut on the foundation stone of the south façade. The sculpture of that southern entrance honors St. Stephen, since on the site had once stood a church dedicated to the first martyr; the tympanum of the door is another *chef-d'œuvre* of Notre Dame. Jean de Chelles was the first to use perforated gables. It is thought that on the north façade worked Pierre de Montereau, the architect of St. Denis. As the XIII century merged in the XIV Pierre de Chelles, probably a son of Jean, directed the making of the

---

[82] Some of the modern archbishops of Paris have added to the prestige of their see. Monseigneur Affre was shot on the barricades, in 1848, when he went forth bearing a message of peace. Monseigneur Darboy was shot in prison by the Commune of 1871. Both are commemorated in side chapels of the cathedral's choir.

apse chapels and the superb flying buttresses which leap unhesitatingly over chapels and aisle and tribune gallery. He added the big tribune windows with gables.

The classic restraint which is the leading quality of Notre Dame was never poverty. Sculpture was lavish where it should be. At the portals the Scriptures were set forth in detail and saints were held up for the edification of the people. The signs of the zodiac were carved, as well as the personification of the seasons and the months. Pinnacle and parapet were weighted with winged beast or demon, and the useful water spouts, or gargoyles, were chiseled as crabbed images. However, one should always remember, in climbing the towers of Notre Dame, that most of the present stone monsters are modern, and it is one of the weaknesses of the restorer to overemphasize the grotesque in the art of the Middle Ages.

A strange world of fabulous creatures dwell on the roof of Our Lady's church — conceptions that are half terrible and half fantastic, imaginations that are survivals of the old pagan superstitions which Christianity could not wholly extirpate. The XII and XIII centuries were not so far removed in time from the invasions of the northern Barbarians, and the Church made concessions to primitive inheritances. Artists were allowed to carve on roof or pinnacle the chimeras and vampires which through long centuries had haunted the imagination of their ancestors, provided that they expounded the truths of Christian doctrine in such principal places as portals, façades, and choir screens. Might not a mocking grotesque beside an angel be taken as emblem of the external antagonism of the animal and the spirit in man? The choir screen of Notre Dame of Paris is sculptured with the apparitions of the risen Lord, from Easter Day to the Ascension. "If Christ be not risen again, then is our preaching vain."[83]

The cathedral of Paris during the first centuries of its existence was the setting of many national scenes. Here the kings of France deposited their crown and renewed their vow to be just fathers of their people. Before its altar their newborn heir was blessed. In 1182 the main altar of Notre Dame was consecrated, and three years later the patriarch of Jerusalem preached from it the Third Crusade. On the eve of both his crusades St. Louis prayed here, and in 1270, when his remains were brought back from Tunis, they rested in Notre Dame for a solemn night of chanted mourning.

In Notre Dame the Duke of Bedford had his nephew, Henry VI of England, crowned as king of France. Factional hate and a foreign enemy in control caused a *Te Deum* of rejoicing to be sung in this, the most national of French cathedrals, when the news came that Jeanne the Maid had been taken prisoner before Compiègne, in 1429, but solemn reparation was made in 1456, when, in the presence of Jeanne's mother and brothers, the bishop of Paris (a Norman, and brother of the poet Alain Chartier) opened in Notre Dame the inquest that was to lead to the Rehabilitation of the heroine of Orleans.

To the hidden places over the vaults of Notre Dame fled the illustrious chan-

---

[83] G. Sanoner, "La Bible racontée par les artistes du moyen âge," in *Revue de l'art chrétien*, 1907-13; *ibid.*, "La vie de Jésus-Christ racontée par les imagiers du moyen âge sur les portes d'églises," in *Revue de l'art chrétien*, 1905-08.

cellor of Paris University, Gerson, to whom during two centuries was attributed the *Imitation of Christ*. In 1407 he had reprobated the murder of the Duke of Orléans (builder of Pierrefonds) by the Duke of Burgundy (of the regal Dijon tomb), and the mob rose and sacked his house. It is said that for months Gerson lay concealed in Notre Dame, alone with his books, and given over to prayer and meditation.

The present stained glass in Notre Dame is modern, save for the north, south, and west rose windows, the trilogy of light usually found in big cathedrals. The roses of the transept belong to the Paris school which led in the art of glassmaking during the second half of the XIII century. So large were the spaces then to be filled that the scrupulous patience of the St. Denis craftsmen was no longer possible. Backgrounds had to be made quickly by bold, simple trellis designs, and as the most frequent background was a red trellis on a blue field, and the juxtaposition of red and blue makes violet, in too many of the windows of that period prevails a melancholy purplish hue. Originally the choir of Notre Dame boasted some glass given by Abbot Suger himself to the preceding Romanesque cathedral. In the XVIII century, those over-confident *gens de goût*, the cathedral canons, whose taste admitted only the neo-classic, substituted uncolored glass for the ancient windows. They say that when the workmen were removing Suger's priceless glass, they were dumfounded by its deep, ineffable blue.[84]

[84] Once the Paris churches were filled with late-Gothic windows, though the troubled history of the city has left but few. Some XVI-century glass is still to be found in St. Merri and St. Germain-l'Auxerrois, for which churches see Huysman's *Trois églises et trois primitifs* (1908). St Étienne-du-Mont has in a chapel an Engrand Le Prince window, a symbolic wine press with portraits of Pope Paul II, Charles V, Francis I, and Henry VIII; and reset in the passage leading to the catechism chapel is the masterpiece of Pinaigrier, twelve panels that are veritable enameling on glass. In St. Gervais, where on Good Friday, 1918, a projectile from the long-distance German gun crashed through the masonry roof, killing many, are two windows, Solomon's judgment (1531), and St. Laurence (1551), said to be by Jean Cousin, also some Pinaigrier glass. To Jean Cousin are attributed the five splendid windows of the Apocalypse in the chapel at Vincennes, whose design derives from Dürer's woodcuts, published in 1498. They have deep shadows and are strong in color and plan. M. Mâle says that Dürer's German has here been translated into graceful Renaissance Italian. Vincennes' chapel had been begun by Charles V in 1378. Then came the pause of a century, and the works were finished by Henry II, still on the Gothic plan, however. Henry donated the windows and he had Diana of Poitiers pictured among the righteous souls in the fifth seal of the Apocalypse. Francis I is represented at the base of the second window. Excursions can be made from Paris to places within easy distance that posses Gothic-Renaissance glass. At Écouen, nine miles from Paris, in the church of St. Acceul, are sixteen windows due to De Montmorency patronage. Originally in Écouen's guard hall were the forty-four panels (made for the constable, Anne de Montmorency) now in the long gallery of Chantilly, the château bequeathed to the Institute of France in 1897 by the Duc d'Aumale. The story of Cupid and Psyche is told in that camaïeu glass so suited for domestic decoration, a species of iron-red grisaille, whose only other hue is yellow stain. Chantilly's panels were painted in the Raphaelesque style by the Flemish master, Coexyen, trained in Van Orley's school. At Montmorency, ten miles from Paris, in St. Martin's church, the history of France seems written in the windows, with the portraits of Francis I, Henry II, Adrian VI, and members of the houses of Montmorency, Pot, and Coligny. Three of the lights are by Engrand Le Prince. More portrait work appears in the many windows at Montfort l'Amaury, twenty-nine miles from Paris (1544-78), work not equal to the earlier XVI-century glass.

Many a treasure of Notre Dame was destroyed by the Revolution, and the church itself was put up for sale and escaped demolition by merest chance. It served as Temple of Reason, as warehouse, as fête hall. Again, during the Commune, in 1871, for the purpose of destroying it, chairs were piled high in the choir and set on fire, but brave men broke in the doors and extinguished the flames. Early in the World War, in 1914, a German airship dropped a bomb on Notre Dame which pierced the roof of the transept's northern arm.

THE SAINTE-CHAPELLE[85]

Li cuers doit estre semblans à l'encensier,
Tous clos envers la terre et overs vers le ciel.

—(Old song of the Middle Ages).

On the same isle in the Seine with Notre Dame stands the Sainte-Chapelle, the reliquary of stone and jeweled glass which the saint-king had made to enshrine the Crown of Thorns redeemed from Constantinople. To-day it is a body without a soul, as the revered crown is kept in the treasury of Notre Dame, and until a memorial service during the World War, Mass had not been said in the *reliquaire de souvenirs* for fifteen years.

The chapel, which was connected with the king's palace, was begun in 1246 and dedicated in 1248. "It was," said one who knew St. Louis well, "the king's citadel against the adverses of the world." He would rise at midnight to pass into the chapel for the singing of matins. "Into this shrine Louis IX put all the memories of his crusading ancestors, all the hues of the Orient. It was his vision of the Heavenly Jerusalem." The walls were rich with gold and color. The present polychromatic decorations of the walls are a deplorable modern experiment. Fifteen splendid windows told the Bible story in a thousand small medallions; ninety-one scenes related Genesis; one hundred and twenty-one gave Exodus. A window on the south side told the True Cross story, and the three central windows were devoted to the lives of the Saviour and John the Baptist. The western rose was added during the Flamboyant Gothic revival following the expulsion of the English invaders.

The making of the vast windows of the Sainte-Chapelle raised Paris to the leadership of the vitrine industry during the second half of the XIII century. Of that school are windows in the cathedrals of Angers and Clermont, and Soissons' western rose. Though of splendid effect, such windows do not equal those of the preceding hundred years, when Chartres and St. Denis led. The borders round each medallion had now become mere zigzags, since expedition was required for

H. Havard, éd., *La France artistique et monumentale*, vol. 4, Écouen; vol. 5, Chantilly, Vincennes, Pierrefonds; F. de Fossa, *Le château de Vincennes* (Collection, Petites Monographies), (Paris, H. Laurens); E. Macon, *Chantilly et le musée Condé* (Paris, H. Laurens).

[85] Henri Stein, *La Sainte-Chapelle de Paris* (Paris, 1912); F. de Guilhermy, *Description de la Sainte-Chapelle* (Paris, 1899), 12me; Troche, *Notice historique et descriptive sur la Sainte-Chapelle*; Morand, *Histoire de la Sainte-Chapelle* (Paris, 1790); Louis Courajod, *La polychromie dans le statuaire du moyen âge et de la Renaissance* (Paris, 1888); Abbé A. Bouillet, *Les églises paroissiales de Paris*, vol. 5, *La Sainte-Chapelle* (Paris, 1900); F. de Mély, "La sainte couronne d'épines," in *Revue de l'art chrétien*, 1899, vol. 42.

the glazing of enormous spaces.

The Sainte-Chapelle, as Gothic science, could be carried no farther without violating its own laws and becoming what an English critic said of the late-Gothic of France, "all muscle and glass." Everywhere was the ascending line accentuated; over the windows are some of the earliest gables extant. They break the horizontal band of the balustrade above, and serve structurally as weights on the longitudinal wall arches.

Perhaps it was because the architect felt he was overemphasizing the ascending line that he interrupted the soar of the columns marking the chapel walls, by placing against each shaft the amply draped statue of an apostle—the twelve pillars of the Church. To-day only the forth and fifth statues on the north side are originals; there are merely ancient fragments in the other images. For some time it was thought that the Sainte-Chapelle was the work of Pierre de Montereau, the king's own architect. A newly discovered record proves that he designed St. Denis' abbatial, which shows, however, no family likeness with the chapel of the Cité palace. Now, that chapel does display a certain likeness to the façades of Notre Dame's transept, and it has been suggested that Jean de Chelles, who designed the transept, was the architect of the Sainte-Chapelle.

ST. JULIEN-LE-PAUVRE[86]

La France est l'homme,
Paris est le cœur.

—HENRY IV.

Close to the Seine, under the hill of St. Geneviève, stands a small contemporary of the choir of Notre Dame, St. Julien-le-Pauvre, built by the Cistercians of Longpont, about 1180, and claiming as its patrons three saints of the same name, St. Julian, martyr, St. Julian, bishop of Le Mans, and a humble St. Julian who had founded a hospice for pilgrims by the Seine and used to help the poor across the river. It is said that a leper whom he was piloting over vanished in midstream, whereupon the people said it had been the Lord himself come to test the holy man's charity.

The western bays of St. Julien-le-Pauvre have been demolished and all that remains intact of the Primary Gothic church are the choir, with three apsidal chapels, the side aisles' vaulting, and the columns against the side walls. The same sculptor who worked at Notre Dame made the virile capitals of this little church.

St. Julien to-day is used by the Greek-Melchite rite of Roman Catholics. It long was the patron church of letters and science, and every year from its altar started the procession of the University of Paris to the fair at St. Denis called Lendit, for the solemn purchase of a twelve months' supply of parchment. The rector of the university led the throng, and so vast was the concourse of students that the head of the procession was in St. Denis' abbatial before the rear ranks had quitted St. Julien-le-Pauvre. For four hundred years Paris University elected its rector in this lit-

[86] Armand le Brun, *L'église St. Julien-le-Pauvre* (Paris, 1889); J. Viatte, *L'église de St. Julien-le-Pauvre de Paris* (Châteaudun, Prudhomme, 1899).

tle church, and tradition says that Dante prayed here when he crossed the Alps in 1304. In his imagination was then surging his mighty poem, and the men of France have pictured him pausing to muse over the images of Hell at their own cathedral doors. The great exile of Florence was himself the purest product of scholasticism, as impassioned as were the cathedral builders for theology and philosophy, for symmetry and rhythm and the mysterious beauty of numbers. The *Divina Commedia* was a poetic *Summa*.

ST. GERMAIN-DES-PRÉS, ST. MARTIN-DES-CHAMPS, AND ST. PIERRE-DE-MONTMARTRE[87]

Ces vénérables bénédictines dont la science n'était égalée que
par leur modestie

—F. Brunetière.

There are in Paris three abbey churches that show steps in the transition to Gothic art: St. Germain of the meadows, St. Martin in the fields, and St. Peter's church on the martyr's hill, names that keep alive early Christian traditions—the first bishop and martyr of Paris, St. Peter whom always "the eldest daughter of the Church" was glad to honor; St. Martin, first beloved of the apostles of Gaul, and Bishop Germain (d. 576) who founded outside the city walls the abbey called later by his name, and who helped to Christianize the new Frankish conquerors. So disinterested was he that, to feed the poor, he sold a horse given him by the king; whether riding or walking, the saint-bishop ever went in prayer.

The present church of St. Germain-des-Prés has a tower that in part predates the year 1000; it was erected by an abbot who ruled from 990 to 1014, and shows the small stones used at that period. The nave and transept, finished before the XI century closed, under a bishop of Paris who was uncle of Godfrey de Bouillon, comprise the only remaining Romanesque work in the capital. Twice in the XII century the choir was reconstructed by the monks, first about 1125, and at the same time the ancient tower's upper story was built; and again, after Suger, in 1144, had demonstrated the superiority of Gothic vaulting. St. Germain's abbot wrote, in 1163, that he had repaired his church in a new fashion. In the ambulatory the round and the pointed arch appeared side by side, and the groin vault was used simultaneously with the diagonals. The capitals were altogether Romanesque, since sculpture changed less swiftly than construction in those transitional

[87] Jules Quicherat, "St. Germain-des-Prés," in *Bibli. de l'École des chartes*, 1865, vol. I, p. 513; and *Mémoires de la Soc. des Antiquaires de France*, 1864, vol. 28, p. 156; Jacques Bouillart, *Histoire de l'abbaye royale de St. Germain-des-Prés* (Paris, 1724); Auger, *Les dépendances de St. Germain-des-Prés* (Paris, 1909), 3 vols.; E. Lefèvre-Pontalis, "Étude sur le chœur de l'église de St. Martin-des-Champs à Paris," in *Bibliothèque de l'École des chartes*, 1886, vol. 47; F. Deshoulières, *St. Pierre de Montmartre* (Caen, H. Delesque, 1913); also in *Bulletin Monumental*, 1913, vol. 77, p. 4; H. Havard, éd., *La France artistique et monumentale*, vol. 6, p. 66, "Le conservatoire des arts et métiers" (St. Martin-des-Champs); A. Lenoir, *Statistique monumentale de la ville de Paris* (Paris, Imprimerie Impériale, 1867), 3 vols., folio (valuable drawings of the Parisian abbeys); Em. de Broglie, *Mabillon et la société de l'abbaye de St. Germain-des-Prés* (Paris, 1881).

years. Perhaps the new choir of St. Germain was not wholly finished when Pope Alexander III dedicated it in 1163, the year that the foundation stone of Notre Dame was laid. The choir's triforium arches were cut off, later, to lengthen the clearstory windows, and the nave has been revaulted.

In the abbey inclosure a Sainte-Chapelle, a cloister, and a refectory were built by Pierre de Montereau; he and his wife, Agnes, were buried in the chapel. Fragments of his work have been collected in the small garden beneath the Carolingian tower of the abbatial, as well as in the gardens of the Musée Cluny.[88] The Revolution entirely wrecked the monk's quarters.

St. Germain-des-Prés, in popular speech, was *The Abbey*. Here gathered the learned men of Paris for mental stimulus. In its priceless library, destroyed by the Revolution, worked those famous scholars Dom Luc d'Achery (d. 1685), Dom Mabillon (d. 1707), and Dom Rivet (d. 1749), whose tireless patience and scrupulous respect for historical truth made the name Benedictine a synonym for "savant." Three monumental works were begun by the XVII-century reformers who renewed the love of letters in the leading monastic houses of France: the *Acta Sanctorum*; the annals of the Benedictine Order; and that pride of French letters, the *Histoire Littéraire de la France*, which to-day the Institute of France is continuing. "*Gros livres inutiles*," Voltaire glibly called the invaluable books which for the modern school of mediæval archæology have made flesh-and-blood men of the old prelate-builders of cathedrals.

The parts which have survived of that other notable Benedictine establishment in Paris, St. Martin-des-Champs, are now comprised in the *Arts et Métiers* establishment. Affiliated with great Cluny, St. Martin's priory was as like it, said Peter the Venerable, as seal is like signet. To-day in the ancient church is installed an exhibit of machinery. The beautiful hall, once the monks' refectory, and now a technical library, is thought to be the work of Pierre de Montereau. The slender pillars dividing it into two aisles, the well-carved capitals, the elaborate keystones, and the portal's foliage all belong to the golden hour of the national art.

For the student it is the choir of the church (c. 1135), built by the prior who surrounded the monastery lands with walls (1130-40), which is of chief interest, for in it were taken marked strides in the advance of Gothic structure. Here first was attempted a double ambulatory, an idea which Suger within a few years was to carry out in its fulfillment at St. Denis. The Lady chapel, a lobed half dome—the sacred trefoil—developed further the ribbed apse first found at Bury (c. 1125); here the ribs are structural, not merely decorative. Like other monuments of the tran-

---

[88] The Hôtel Cluny, which became a national museum in 1848, was built as the town house for the abbot of Burgundian Cluny, by those two art patrons, Jean de Bourbon (1456-81) and Jacques d'Amboise (1481-1514). It is one of the best works of Gothic civic architecture in France. It stands on the site of Roman baths, alleged to be those of Julian the Apostate, above which had later risen a residence of the Merovingian kings. In the time of the Carolings, Alcuin taught on this spot. The Palais des Termes was purchased for Cluny by Abbot Pierre de Chastellux (1322-43). H. Havard, éd., *La France artistique et monumentale*, vol. 1, p. 161, A. Darcel, on Musée Cluny; E. du Sommerard, *Le palais des thermes et l'Hôtel de Cluny*; Ch. Normand, *l'Hôtel de Cluny* (Paris, 1888).

sitional hour, St. Martin used simultaneously intersecting ribs and groins, round and pointed arches. Its XIII-century nave was never vaulted.

The third monument of the capital which shows other stumbling first steps of the national art is the little church of St. Pierre under the towering new basilica of the Sacred Heart on Montmartre.[89] Till the XII century there stood on the site of St. Pierre a church dedicated to St. Denis, for tradition said that the first martyr of Paris had here been interred until his relics were removed to the new abbey of St. Denis on the Roman road outside Paris. In the crypt, by St. Peter's, on Montmartre, it is said that the earliest Christians of the region held their rites. And to that hallowed spot has come many a soul to beseech enlightenment on the eve of some projected good work. Here, in 1534, St. Ignatius Loyola, St. Francis Xavier, and the first Jesuits passed a night in prayer and vowed themselves to God's service. Here came St. Francis de Sales before founding the Visitation Order, St. Vincent de Paul before founding the Lazarists, and M. Olier before he organized St. Sulpice. Ursulines and Carmelites also have memories with St. Pierre-de-Montmartre.

A Benedictine priory was installed here by Louis VI and his queen, Adelaide, niece of Pope Calixtus II of the Capetian house of Burgundy. They began the present church as Romanesque, but soon the new system of vaulting was employed. Slowly but consecutively throughout the XII century St. Peter's church was built. Its oldest Gothic vault is the one over the section of the choir preceding the apse; the stout ribs have profiles like those which Abbot Suger was making about that same time in the forechurch of his abbatial.

The solemn dedication of St. Pierre-de-Montmartre took place in 1147 with Pope Eugene III officiating and St. Bernard and Peter the Venerable acting as deacon and subdeacon. Since the rebuilding of the apse, at the end of the XII century, numerous reconstructions have gone on in order to preserve the revered church.[90]

[89] Paul Abadie, who over-restored the cathedrals of Angoulême and Périgieux, won the competition for the national memorial basilica of the Sacré-Cœur, and began his strange Romano-Byzantine monument in 1873. He united Auvergne's Romanesque ambulatory with the cupola church of Aquitaine. There is not sufficient contrast between his elongated dome and the tower. Nevertheless, the immense pile of white stone standing over the capital presents exotic and superb effects in sun and mist, and no one can deny that a profound religious spirit breathes in this new shrine of France, as if the prayers and sufferings of generations had already hallowed its walls. Below the basilica stands a statue of the young Chevalier de la Barre, a victim of the personal intrigue of a corrupt magistrate of Abbeville and the lax law courts of Louis XV's time, not in any way the object of clerical hate, as the inscription on his statue would indicate. His abbess aunt was his warm defender, as was the bishop of Amiens, and on the day of his execution he received the sacraments piously. See Cruppi, *Révue des Deux Mondes*, March, 1895. As this mythical hero meets one in many a French city, it were well to know his real story.

[90] Some of the later manifestations of Gothic art in the capital are the porch and façade of St. Germain l'Auxerrois (1431-39), one of the first signs of renewed energy after Jeanne d'Arc's mission; the tower of St. Jacques (1508-22), attributed to the late-Gothic master, Martin Chambiges, and formerly part of a Flamboyant church destroyed by the Revolution; and the church of St. Merri (1520-1612), still Gothic in spirit. Th e Renaissance appears in St. Étienne-du-Mont (1517-63), whose interior is alluringly graceful, though it cannot boast of purity of style. St. Eustache (1532-1642), begun slightly after St. Merri, has a Gothic

ST. LOUIS AND JOINVILLE[91]

Je dis que droit est mort et loyauté éteinte
Quand le bon roi est mort, la créature sainte,
A qui se pourront désormais les pauvres gens clamer
Quand le bon roy est mort qui tant les sut aimer?

—REGRES DU ROY LOEYS.

The greatest glory of the Middle Ages was the saint-king himself. He was essentially of his epoch both in his love of theology and his enthusiasm for building. Under his grandfather, Philippe-Auguste, most of the Gothic cathedrals of France were begun. The majority of them continued building under Louis IX. In his reign Beauvais Cathedral was started, that of Meaux rebuilt, as was also St. Denis' cathedral-like abbatial. There rose now a host of lesser Gothic edifices, such as the Sainte-Chapelle at Paris, the synodal hall at Sens, and the hospital hall at Ourscamp. "And as a writer who has made his book, illuminating it with gold and azure, so our king illuminated his kingdom with the beautiful abbeys he built," wrote his friend Joinville.

All too many of his abbatials have been swept away—Royaumont,[92] built with the proceeds from his father's jewels, where Louis IX had worked side by side with the masons, where he had passed his saddest hours, for in its church was laid to rest his promising eldest son, whose beautiful tomb now is harbored at St. Denis. Gone, too, is Maubuisson Abbey, where was buried his mother, Blanche of Castile. Her bronze tomb was melted up and made into cannon during the Revolution, but one knows that the something high and Spanish in Blanche (whom her contemporaries compared to stag and eagle) would have preferred a cannon to the copper pennies into which were transmuted all too many of the ancient tombs. The mother of St. Louis was a woman cast in a heroic mold, daughter of that Spanish king who at Las Navas de Toloso saved Europe from an avalanche of 400,000 Mussulmans and granddaughter of art-loving Aliénor of Aquitaine and Henry II, Plantagenet.

---

skeleton, "dressed in Renaissance robes sewed together like the pieces of a harlequin's garment, bizarre and contradictory, satisfactory to neither taste nor reason." The old church of St. Séverin used to be employed by M. Jules Quicherat as an object lesson for his pupils, since four different epochs are traceable in it; the three westernmost bays of the nave are early XIII century; and there is much Flamboyant Gothic with disappearing moldings. Abbé A. Bouillet, *Les églises paroissiales de Paris* (1903); H. Escoffier, *Les dernières églises gothiques au diocèse de Paris* (Thèse, École des chartes, 1900).

[91] Le Nain de Tillemont, *Vie de St. Louis* (Paris, 1848-51 éd., Gauble), 6 vols.; Sertillanges, *St. Louis* (Collection, L'art et les saints), (Paris, H. Laurens, 1918); H. Wallon, *St. Louis et son temps* (Tours, 1865), 2 vols.; A. Beugnot, *Essai sur les institutions de St. Louis* (Paris, 1821); Jean, sire de Joinville, texte original accompagné d'une traduction, Natalis de Wailly, éd., Paris, 1867. Translated into English, Bohn's Antiquarian Library, London; Gaston Paris, "Jean de Joinville," in *Hist. littéraire de la France*, 1848, vol. 32, p. 291; also Delaborde's biography; Lecoy de la Marche, *La France sous St. Louis et sous Philippe le Hardi* (Paris, 1894); A. Molinier, *Les sources de l'histoire de France* (Paris, 1901-06); U. Chevalier, Répertoire *des sources hist. du moyen âge* (Montbéliard, 1903).

[92] Philippe Lauer, "Royaumont," in *Congrès Archéologique*, 1908, vol. 2, p. 215.

The prudence of Blanche of Castile saved the kingdom for her son against the insurgent barons of France. She hastened to have him crowned at Rheims, in 1226, in the same year that St. Francis died, in Italy. It is said that the lad of twelve held up firmly the sword of the Emperor Charlemagne, whose blood ran in his veins. The barons tried to kidnap the young king from his mother, and when he escaped the snare and rode back to Paris all the countryside poured out to bless him. Years later he told Joinville it was from that hour he dedicated himself to the welfare of his people.

In 1234, at twenty, he was married in Sens Cathedral to a princess of the cultivated house of Provence; Dante has a line for the daughters of Raymond Berenger IV, patron of the troubadours: "Four daughters had he and each a queen."[93] Marguerite of Provence was somewhat overridden by the stronger personality of Blanche, her mother-in-law. For his valiant mother, Louis IX retained always a passionate admiration. On his first crusade he left his kingdom in her charge, which, however, he did not do for his queen, when he last went crusading. He had seen her sister, on the throne of England, tamper with that country's interests for the advancement of her own family, and he recognized in his Marguerite a strain of the same intriguing. She could rise to her lord's level, however, and was his faithful lifelong companion. A sublime word of hers has come down to us: they were sailing back to France after four years' sojourn in Palestine; off Cyprus the ship was well-nigh wrecked, and an attendant rushed to ask if he should awaken the royal children. "No," cried the queen, "let them go to God in their sleep."

That a king whose forebears had fought in all the crusades should, in his turn, strike a blow for Christendom, was inevitable. Jerusalem had fallen in 1244, and the instinct of Europe felt the menace of the Mongol advance from the East. Was not the fate of Spain close at hand to prove the possibility of Oriental invasion? So St. Louis took the crusader's vow, and with him went the turbulent lords whose departure gave France some needed years of peace. He had in vain tried to negotiate peace between Papacy and Empire, in whose protracted duel he remained neutral.

In Cyprus, in 1248, the crusaders paused before descending on Egypt, and there St. Louis and Joinville drew together. The hereditary seneschal of Champagne was a very great lord, his mother being of Burgundy's Capetian line, and his Joinville forebears notable crusaders.[94] The contingent which he provided for

[93] One sister of St. Louis' queen married Henry III of England, under whom was built Westminster Abbey (1217-54). The second was the wife of King Henry's brother, Richard of Cornwall, who was titular emperor of Germany. The youngest sister inherited Provence and wedded St. Louis' brother, Charles d'Anjou, king of the Two Sicilies. E. Boutarie, *Marguerite de Provence, femme de St. Louis* (Paris, 1869); E. Berger, *Blanche de Castille* (Paris, 1900).

[94] Joinville, in Syria, went to the Krak, the great Christian fortress beyond the Jordan, to obtain, as a relic for his church at Joinville, the shield of his crusading ancestor whom Richard Cœur-de-Lion had admired. His *"beau chastel"* on the Marne was wrecked by the Revolution. His line had ended in an heiress who married into the ruling house of Lorraine, so that the XVI-century Duke of Guise, whose personal charm made him the idol of the French people, was fifth, by female descent, from the irresistible seneschal. A brother of Joinville's, Geoffrey, married Mahaut de Lacy, heiress of Meath, and became Lord Chief

the holy wars consisted of nine knights and seven hundred men, but because of the long winter's halt in Cyprus he found himself in straits to meet their expenses. Louis IX, ten years his senior, came to his aid, although the ruler of Champagne and not the king of France was Joinville's suzerain. Side by side the two friends went through the disastrous campaign in Egypt—the delayed march on Cairo, which ended in Mansourah's defeat. Together they shared imprisonment, and the king's elevation of soul won the Mussulmans' respect. Then, their ransom paid, they sailed together for Palestine, and there, in the daily intimacy of years, the affection of these two loyal knights struck deep root. To Joinville the king intrusted his wife and children in the perilous overland journey in Syria, before they embarked for France.

When, in 1254, Louis IX came back from the East, he gave himself up for fifteen years to his country's welfare, "the most conscientious man who ever sat on a throne," touched to the core by that divine unrest which is man's highest faculty and does lasting work for God, revered by the "little people of the Lord" as their champion for justice and social progress. "*Il est en doulce France un bon roy Loeys,*" sang the minstrels then. Never did king love more *la doulce France* and prove it more conclusively. Justice was inherent in him. A most sensitive feeling of duty ruled his every act. Yet he knew how to mete out deserved punishment unflinchingly. From his shrewd and capable grandfather, so little of a saint, he had learned that no one could govern well who could not refuse as well as grant.

That Louis IX understood his age is shown in his dealings with the feudal system. He made no attempt to destroy it, which would then have been impossible, and, moreover, his respect for the rights of others always kept him from extreme measures; but he regulated its excesses, knowing that organized anarchy could be broken only by organized laws. One of the best laws he passed was that of the *quarantaine-le-roy*, which forbade any baron to wage war on his fellows without a notice of forty days. The king favored the written law to offset the law of custom, on which feudal abuses were based. During a generation he had his agents all over France collect old laws and customs—Roman law, canon law, feudal privileges, and from their composite mass was created the great code called the *Établissements de St. Louis*. He substituted jurisprudence by inquest, and witnesses for that by force, and he made a supreme court by instituting the right of appeal. Admirable were some of his treaties such as that which made the Pyrenees the natural boundary between Spain and France. His reform of the coinage was another link of unity for France.

In Paris he organized a police, protected commerce by regulations, put an end to the selling of magistratures, and he began, there, the library which to-day is the richest in Europe. In the garden of the Cité and under the oaks of Vincennes, the king held open courts of justice, and when his youngest brother, Charles d'Anjou,[95] tried to browbeat one of lesser rank, the king gave a legal councilor to the

---

Justice of Ireland in 1273. Under Henry III and Edward I he played a role, and went crusading in 1270. He left nine children. On his wife's death he entered the Dominican convent of Tuam, where he died in 1314.

[95] Often did Louis IX sigh over his youngest brother. "Charles d'Anjou! Charles

poor knight who won the case against the prince. Louis IX's very enemies chose him as arbiter. Little wonder that the people of France have sung of him:

> Ha! le bon Roy!
> Simples, ignorans supportait
> Pauvres, mendians confortait,
> Observant de Jhusys la foi,
> Redoutant Dieu —
> Ha! le bon Roy!

Joinville has drawn for all time the picture of the years between the saint-king's two crusades, a golden age, if ever there was one. The friendship begun during their years of Syrian comradeship continued, and the seneschal often came up to Paris. It was he who arranged the marriage of the king's daughter with his own suzerain, the son of Thibaut IV, the song maker, in whose court of Champagne Joinville had acquired his delightful mode of speech.

Then, again, came the call of the East. Jaffa and Antioch had fallen to Islam, and the condition of the Oriental Christians was heartrending. Louis IX could not resist their cry for aid. In 1270, twenty-two years after his first departure from Aigues-Mortes, the king sailed again from that half-finished fort by the dead waters. Joinville was not with him, for he was needed by his "little people," an excuse which his friend acknowledged.

The crusaders had scarcely landed on the coast of Africa when plague struck them down. First died Tristan, the son born to St. Louis in the sorrowful, earlier days in Egypt. Then the saint-king himself passed away; and on his lips was the prayer that his race might learn to despise the prosperity of this world and not to fear adversity, and that France might never deny the name of Christ. The night before he died they heard him singing, *"Nous irons en Jerusalem,"* the holy city he had never seen, the aspiration, the magic name that stirred those strong generations.[96] Before the century closed the Church canonized him. "House of France," announced the pope, "rejoice to have given the world so great a prince, and to heaven so great a saint. People of France, rejoice to have had so great a king."

"If ever the golden age of the good old times existed," wrote Sainte-Beuve, "it certainly was under St. Louis, and it is by the pen of Joinville that it exists for us. They believed then in their king, they believed above all in their God, as if

---

d'Anjou!" he would say, sadly. As king of the Two Sicilies, Charles won the title of the Merciless, and his harshness was punished by the Sicilian Vespers, 1282. Dante abominated the house of Anjou in Italy. Of Charles he wrote in the *Paradiso* (viii: 73-75), "His evil rule, which ever cuts into the heart of subject people, caused Palermo to shriek out: 'Die! Die!'" St. Louis loved especially his brother Robert d'Artois, whose overhardy courage caused the defeat of the crusaders at Mansourah. When word was brought to the king of his brother's death in that battle, tears warm and full fell from his eyes, though he said, "God must be thanked for all he sends." The other brother of Louis IX was Alphonse of Poitiers, who married the heiress of Toulouse and took guidance of the king in his administration of the Midi.

[96] In 1841 Louis-Philippe built a chapel on the site where St. Louis had died in Tunis, 1270. In the *Ville d'Art Célèbres* series (H. Laurens, Paris), see H. Saladin, *Tunis et Kairouan,* and R. Cagnat, *Carthage, Tingad, Tébessa.*

God were present in the smallest occurrences of daily life." In the *Histoire de St. Louis* by Jean, sire de Joinville, there is not a mawkish note, and considering what happens to too many saints in their biographies, it must be acknowledged that the seneschal accomplished a feat. As depicted by his contemporaries, Louis IX is so convincingly himself that later efforts to stereotype him as the sacristan's ideal of piety have failed. His "pleasant manner of speech seasoned with wit" had nothing of the prig in it. From his childhood to his deathbed of ashes in ancient Carthage (birthplace of his favorite Augustine), St. Louis possessed a direct personal touch with God. *"Beau Sire Dieu, garde-moi mes gens!"* he rose at night to petition with insistent outstretched arms when, in Egypt, the "Greek fire" was hurled into the Christian camp. And Joinville, who had a wholesome dread of the Saracens' projectiles, turned to rest, feeling secure while such prayers were beseeching Heaven.

Louis IX was a tireless student of the Bible and works of the Church Fathers. He had a passion for the liturgy. The number of hours which he spent in prayer has roused the sarcasm of our indifferent generation. His hours before the Tabernacle bore fruit in deeds. His temper was naturally quick, and he had a keen sense of irony, but his friend, the seneschal, was able to bear witness, at his canonization process, that in an intimacy of over twenty years never had he heard a word of disparagement of others fall from the king's lips. "There was something in the mere sight of him that found a way to the heart and affections," wrote one who knew him; "the eyes of a dove," said another. "He seemed pierced to the heart with pity for the unfortunate," wrote Queen Marguerite's chaplain who had daily intercourse with him. An observant Italian who saw the king on his way to his first crusade described the something of rare refinement and grace in his bearing.

Not a touch of self-consciousness was in Louis; barefooted, in a white tunic, he carried the Crown of Thorns through the streets of Paris. In his sublime other-worldliness, he bathed the feet of beggars, dressed the sores of lepers, and when he felt that his soul needed it he scourged himself. And at the same time he was a model of knightly prowess, who many a time had fought

> For Jesu Christ in glorious Christian field,
> Streaming the ensign of the Christian cross
> Against black pagans, Turks, and Saracens.[97]

At the battle of Mansourah, Joinville saw the king, "the most beautiful of men," to his eyes, fair, gallant, in stature head and shoulders above those around him, defend himself alone with great slashing sword cuts from the onslaught of six paynims. He was a true prud'homme, a name for which he had a weakness, for to be a prud'homme meant to be a knight, not only bodily, but in one's soul.

Side by side with his other-worldliness went a sound practical sense. When his son-in-law, Thibaut V of Champagne, gave overgenerously to a monastery in Provins, all the while that he was in debt, St. Louis asked him was it fair to bestow alms with other people's money. His personal tastes were unostentatious, but he held court sumptuously when the occasion required, and he advised his lords to dress well so that their wives would love them better. He was ever human; when

---

[97] Shakespeare, "Richard II." iv: 1.

word came to him in Palestine that the mother he adored had died in France, he shut himself away from sympathy for two days, then sent for the friend he loved best. As Joinville approached, the king opened his arms to him with the cry, "Ah, seneschal, I have lost my mother!"

Joinville has recounted a scene which took place between him and his friend, that is one of the fairest things in literature, slight episode though it is. In council, in Palestine, the barons urged the king to return to France. Almost alone, Joinville held out against such a course while their retainers were still unredeemed from captivity. For he remembered how a knight of his family had admonished him: "You are going beyond the seas. Be careful how you come back. For no knight, rich or poor, can return an honored man if he leaves in Saracen hands the humble folk of Our Lord with whom he started forth."

The king listened in silence at the council, and in silence sat through the banquet that followed, paying no heed to Joinville, who was placed by his side. The seneschal, saddened by what he thought to be his friend's displeasure, was standing alone, leaning against a casement, thinking that when the others returned to France, he would join the Prince of Antioch, his cousin, till another crusade came to deliver the "little people of the Lord" unransomed still in Egypt. As he leaned against the window bars he felt friendly arms laid about his shoulders: "Have done, Monseigneur," he cried, thinking it was one of the barons come to mock him, "leave me in peace." Then the loving hands slipped over his face and he recognized the emerald ring worn by the king. The dear words of mock reproach: "What you, the youngest, dare advise me against all the great and the wise men of France? Tell me, you think I would do wrong in leaving?" Then sturdy Joinville, who paints his friend, too, by the confession, "Never did I lie to him," made answer, "Yes, Sire, as God is my aid." "And if I stay, will you stay?" asked the king.

The bloom of the exquisite moment has come to us across the dividing centuries because Joinville was not thinking of making a book when he wrote his reminiscences. His object was to have others understand the gracious distinction, the tender familiarity with him of this king-crusader whom he loved and who loved him. Written artlessly, and in entire good faith, his book is full of that indefinable quality called charm. The seneschal's honest heart is in its infinitely precious pages.

In that other early monument of French prose, the grave Villehardouin rises to the historian's plane in depicting the Fourth Crusade. Joinville cannot be said to have taken in the Sixth Crusade as a whole; he muddles the battle scenes; he digresses to right and to left in idle details, then catches himself up with happy ease, as if saying, "Dear me! I forgot to mention," imparting to his chronicle an inimitable quality all its own. No one would have Joinville different. Amiable, jocund, unaffected, the soul of honor, candor itself, he does not fear to acknowledge that he could tremble with fright in battle despite his stalwart six feet and over. He beguiled his captivity by trying to convert a Mohammedan by highly colored descriptions of hell. He whiled away the long hours in Syria in composing a treatise of theology, a *Credo*, wherein he warns every *prud'homme* to hold on to God with both arms lest that felon, the devil, come between. And the two arms by which a man was to hold on to God were Faith and Good Works. "You must have both, if you wish to keep God: one without the other is worthless," warns the young seneschal. No quibbling then!

Joinville had also that quality which the French term *enjouement*, hard to translate, a playful, most lovable frankness, a mocking vivacity which was for St. Louis a source of relaxation. The king loved conversation; he thought there was no book so good as *quolibet*, or say what you please. Some Armenian pilgrims besought of the seneschal a glimpse of the saint-king. Joinville came merrily to tell his friend, warning him that he, the seneschal, was not yet prepared to kiss his bones. And the king laughed, too, but because he knew it would give the devout Armenians pleasure, he accorded them an interview. Stroke by stroke, Joinville filled in the picture of Louis IX, and all the while he unconsciously paints himself as well. He is so eager to make you love his hero that you learn to love himself. A tear is always close to the eye in reading Joinville, not that what he relates is sad, but because this story of a high soul, written by his loyal friend, touches things that lie deep in all true hearts.

Joinville was to survive his friend for half a century. He died in 1317. With a character ripened by six years of intimacy with the *bon saint-homme roy*, he came back from the East and set himself to work for his people's welfare, the "little people of the Lord" by whom he had stood in their hour of need. He was then but thirty. In his old age he was the accepted arbiter of good taste, admired as the last of a generation of courtesy. When over ninety, this vigorous old crusader rode into Flanders on a military expedition for the crown. He had seen the reigns of six French kings and the passing away of the crusader's spirit. He had seen his own Champagne become a part of the royal domain, when the heiress Jeanne was married to the grandson of St. Louis. And it was at the bidding of that queen of Philippe-le-Bel that Joinville wrote down his memories of Louis IX.

France has high advocates to plead for her before the Throne in hours of national peril. Jeanne d'Arc said that she saw St. Louis petitioning God in the dire hour of foreign invasion. "May they never deny Thy name," prayed the saint-king at Tunis, as he rendered "his pure soul unto his captain, Christ, under whose colors he had fought so long." And in the men of 1914-18, true *prud'hommes* after the heart of St. Louis and his dear friend Joinville, stirred the crusader blood of their ancestors.

THE COLLEGIATE OF MANTES[98]

The king was very well built, of easy bearing and smiling countenance, bald, high-colored, a great eater and drinker. Toward his friends he was most generous; toward those who displeased him he was very firm; in his designs he was foresighted and tenacious, very catholic in his beliefs, and he judged rapidly

---

[98] *Congrès Archéologique*, 1905; Léon Gautier, *La France sous Philippe-Auguste* (Tours, Mâme et fils, 1869); A. Luchaire, *La société française au temps de Philippe-Auguste* (Paris, Hachette, 1909); W. H. Hutton, *Philip-Augustus* (London and New York, Macmillan Company, 1896); Viollet-le-Duc, *Dictionnaire de l'architecture*; see articles on cathedral, rose, triforium.

and with great perspicacity. Easy to arouse, he was also easy to appease. Upon the great who disobeyed him he was hard, and he enjoyed sowing discord among them, and to make use of the little people in his purposes.

—Portrait of Philippe-Auguste by a canon of St. Martin, Tours.

Notre Dame of Mantes (1160-1200). The Contemporary of Paris Cathedral

From Paris can best be visited the cathedral-like collegiate at Mantes on the Seine to the east, and the cathedral of Meaux on the Marne to the west. Mantes-la-Jolie, the "well-beloved" city of Philippe-Auguste, and where he died in 1223, is set picturesquely above the Seine, in whose widened course are wooded islands. From the bridge crossing the river[99] may be had the best view of the town. The collegiate church of Notre Dame stands above the houses of the pleasant little city, in the high-shouldered way of many a French church. Happily, it has never been reconstructed. It has various traits in common with Notre Dame of Paris, and some think that the same architect planned both.

Mantes' Primary Gothic church was begun about 1160, at the same time as the cathedral in the capital, but, being on a lesser scale, it was finished sooner, and thus appears more archaic. Normandy's Romanesque zigzag ornamentation was still retained, and the cells of certain vault sections show the hesitating rough work of masons as yet unpracticed. While the transverse arches are pointed, those of the diagonal-crossing ribs are round. Too wide an expanse of plain wall space was left between tribune and clearstory, for it was to take half a century longer before architects dared fill their entire upper wall with windows. Like Notre Dame of Paris, the tribunes open on the middle church by wide, graceful arches. And this smaller Notre Dame also has western towers that are connected by an open colonnade. The collegiate has no transept, and one recalls that neither had Paris Cathedral in its first plan. The flying buttresses here are among the first ever made. A striking feature of the exterior of the church is the row of litt ble oculi that light the tribunes over the aisles, some of which have been changed to windows of Rayonnant tracery. The deep galleries once were entirely vaulted by transverse half cradles borne on low lintels, an experiment in masonry roofing first tried at Tournus, but which never became popular; at Caen the tribunes of the Abbaye-aux-Hommes had been vaulted by similar half cylinders whose axial lines were at right angles to that of the nave.

The first Gothic rose window of big dimensions adorns the west façade of Mantes collegiate. It is what they call plate tracery—that is, the pattern is formed of voids, the window being a group of variously shaped openings, and not, as in bar tracery, a single opening with the pattern made by solids, or stone mullions. The western rose at Laon stands halfway between plate and bar tracery. Mantes' rose was the prototype for that at Chartres.

Like most of the larger XII-century churches, the sexpartite system of vaulting was used. Mantes also followed Noyon and Senlis in having alternating piers and, like Noyon, it showed the Rhenish trait of a western transept, formed by the two lower stories of the towers and the westernmost bay of the middle vessel. Two of the portals are of the XII century, but the largest—the one under the south

---

[99] Two miles from Mantes, across the river, is Gassicourt (Seine-et-Oise), once a Cluniac priory. Its earliest diagonals were built about 1125. The nave and tower are XII century; the choir and transept are Rayonnant Gothic. Some of the windows donated by Blanche of Castile remain. Bossuet long held the living of Gassicourt. See Lefèvre-Pontalis, "Monographie des églises Gassicourt, Meulan," etc., in *Bul. de la Commission des antiquités et des arts de Seine-et-Oise*, 1885-88, vols. 5 to 8.

tower—was made by Raymond du Temple. And probably that same XIV-century architect of Charles V added the gracious chapel of Navarre which is among the best works of Rayonnant Gothic. In it are four charming statuettes of the donors, the princesses of Navarre, portrait work showing personal mannerisms. When the sister of the art-loving Valois king, Charles V, married Charles the Wicked (a scion of Capetian stock who was count in Évreux and king in Navarre) she brought the town of Mantes in her dowry, and it was probably her daughters who are sculptured in this chapel of Navarre—their gift to Mantes collegiate.

On the site of the present church once stood a Romanesque edifice built by funds donated by William the Conqueror on his deathbed, to atone for his having set fire to the ancient church (1087). Angered by a coarse joke of the French king's, he had sworn his usual oath, "by the splendor and resurrection of God," that he would light a hundred thousand candles when he went to his churching Mass; so he marched against his tormentor and set fire to Mantes that lay in his path. For, as Mr. Henry Adams has picturesquely expressed it, "Mantes barred the path of Norman conquest in arms, as in architecture." As the corpulent Conqueror rode around the place, his horse stumbled, and from the injury then received he died in Rouen in a few weeks. That burning of Mantes by the Duke of Normandy and King of England has been called the prelude to the Hundred Years' War between France and England, whose actual span was from 1337 to 1453. And in a way Waterloo was its epilogue. The shoulder-to-shoulder fight of the ancient rivals, from 1914 to 1918, let us hope, has put the seal on their pact of peace.

THE CATHEDRAL OF MEAUX[100]

Ah, see the fair chivalry come, the companions of Christ!
White Horsemen who ride on white horses, the Knights of God!
They, for their Lord and their Lover have sacrificed
All, save the sweetness of treading where He first trod!
These through the darkness of death, the dominion of night,
Swept, and they wake in white places at morningtide....
Now, whithersoever He goeth, with Him they go;
White Horsemen who ride on white horses, oh, fair to see!
They ride, where the Rivers of Paradise flash and flow,
White Horsemen, with Christ their Captain: forever He!

—LIONEL JOHNSON, *Te Martyrum Candidatus*.[101]

To decipher Meaux Cathedral has been a student's *tour-de-force*, so early and

---

[100] J. Formigé, *La cathédrale de Meaux* (Pontoise, 1917); Amédée Boinet, "La cathédrale de Meaux," in *Revue de l'art chrétien*, 1912; I. Taylor, *La cathédrale de Meaux* (Paris, Didot, 1858), folio; Emile Lambin, "La cathédrale de Meaux," in *Revue de l'art chrétien*, 1900; Henri Stein, *La cathédrale de Meaux et l'architecte Nicolas de Chaumes* (Arcis-sur-Aube, 1890); Du Carro, *Histoire de Meaux et du pays meldois* (Meaux, 1865); Monseigneur Allon, *Chronique des évêques de Meaux*; also his *Notice hist. et descript. de la cathédrale de Meaux* (1871); O. Join-Lambert, *Le diocèse de Meaux* (Thèse, École des chartes, 1894).

[101] Lionel Johnson, *Poetical Works* (New York and London, Macmillan Company), p. 252.

unceasing have been its rebuildings. With Troyes and Séez, it was the only Gothic cathedral that had a flaw in its structure. Begun with the choir, in the last decades of the XII century, it still retained the Romanesque idea of deep galleries over the side aisles. Whether poor foundations were laid or whether the tribune vaults were made too cumbersome, the edifice gave signals of insecurity from the start.

As the XIII century opened, the transept and that part of the nave near it were building with the tribunes still, although by that time such galleries had fallen into disuse. Repeated restorations delayed the works. Cracks continued to show until, about 1270, when the collapse of the whole church was threatened, a complete reconstruction was undertaken by Bishop Jean de Poincy.

Already, in 1220, the choir had been redone and two more chapels added, making five apsidioles in all. In 1270 they demolished throughout the church the tribunes over the side aisles, and thus the aisles became twice their intended height. In the first three bays of the choir were retained the arches of the tribune, so that now certain bays of the choir aisles open on the central vessel by pier arcades surmounted by false-tribune arches. Striking effect is made in the nave by some giant cylinder piers whose height is double what was originally planned and whose capitals are gems of interpretative sculpture, vine leaf and fern. Much mechanical dexterity was shown in the recutting of piers and the elimination of the tribunes, but even now a few of the shorter columns are to be found embedded in the newer parts, and a few sections of the triforium show their primitive plan.

By the time Meaux Cathedral was completed it was practically an edifice of the end of the XIII century. Its chief patroness was the queen of Philippe-le-Bel (St. Louis' grandson), the Jeanne of Champagne who brought that rich province to the Crown, as well as the kingdom of Navarre, the same princess who encouraged Joinville to write his reminiscences. The city of Meaux was in her dowry, and they say that her portrait was carved on a keystone of the choir. When she died, in 1305, she named the bishop of Meaux as her executor and donated a legacy to his church.

A well-known XIV-century architect, Nicolas de Chaumes, worked on the west façade, two of whose portals are of that period, and one of the XV century. Unfortunately, use was made of a soft stone which time has sadly eroded. Flamboyant Gothic sculpture, with foliage in gracious disorder, appears in the western bays: the undulating flora of the XIV century, and the nervous, deeply indented, pointed leaves of the XV century when such complicated forms as the curly cabbage were taken as models. Wiser were the earlier sculptors who had interpreted and arranged their leaves with architectural fitness. The south portal of Meaux's transept must have had in mind St. Stephen's door of the cathedral at Paris. At Meaux the sculptured figures show certain mannerisms, such as the throwing out of one hip, a trait soon to be exaggerated. The carvings throughout the church were mutilated by the Huguenots in 1562, and from that date no further work was done on the edifice. One tower of the façade remains painfully stunted.

The church of Meaux would stand well in the front rank of Gothic cathedrals were it not for certain flaws of proportion. Such exceptionally high side aisles call for a nave twice as long, and the clearstory appears dwarfed by the lofty pier arcades of the chevet. Yet though made piecemeal, and without uniformity of style in its main parts, Meaux possesses a unity of its own, and its effect as a whole is one of elegance and even radiance.

The tomb of its greatest bishop is an immense slab of marble in the pavement of the choir. Bossuet devoted himself to his diocese for over twenty years (1681-1704). Frequently he preached in the cathedral built by the generosity of Jeanne of Champagne, the founder of the College of Navarre, where he had studied in his youth. There is something akin in Meaux Cathedral to the high soul and courtliness of Bossuet. The two most religious and national epochs in French history were the XIII and XVII centuries.

Few churches in France present a better setting for a festival of solemn joy than the cathedral of Meaux. It is the church for *Noël*, for the white radiance of First Communion gatherings, for the *Te Deum* of victory. Fitting is it that the victory of the Marne should here have become a personal heritage. At the very gates of Meaux came the turning of the tide on September 5, 1914, when the thunderous advance on Paris was suddenly arrested. The password for that day of miracle was "Jeanne d'Arc." Near by, on the Oureq, Jeanne's troubadour, Péguy,[102] fell on that same September 5th, he who had chanted prophetically:

> *Heureux ceux qui sont mort pour une juste guerre ...*
> *Heureux les épis murs et les blés moissonnés,*
> *Heureux ceux qui sont mort dans les grandes batailles,*
> *Couchés dessus le sol à la face de Dieu.*

Close to Meaux the battle raged outside, and the wounded, in bewildering numbers, were carried into the desolated town which lacked a civic head. The bishop of Meaux, Monseigneur Marbeau, stepped forth as the accepted leader, as in the time of those earlier invasions when the bishops of Gaul saved Latin civilization.

Again, in 1918, the invader drew perilously near, and a second victory of the Marne swept back the avalanche. From the fields around the city forever will an invisible white army of martyrs swell this cathedral's *Te Deum*. In Meaux on the Marne, God will always be the omnipotent Lord God of Battles, the *Dominus Deus Sabaoth* of the great hymn of thanksgiving.[103]

---

[102] Péguy pierced to the very soul of the Maid in his *Mystère de la charité de Jeanne d'Arc*. Jeanne, in Domrémy, seeing the evil round her caused by war, says: "Je pourrais passer ma vie entière à la maudire, et les villes n'en seront pas moins efforcées, et les hommes d'armes n'en feront pas moins chevaucher leurs chevaux dans les blés vénérables ... blés sacrés, blés qui faites le pain ... sacrés blés qui devîntes le corps de Jésus-Christ."

[103] Another who fell in battle in that same summer of 1914, Ernest Psichari, divined this pregnant region: "Diocèse de Meaux, cryptes de Jouarre, cloches des petites communes ... l'harmonie délicate, la grâce parfaite, le bon goût de ces paysages modérés. Ici la race est d'accord avec le paysage, sérieuse comme lui, ardente sans frivolité, sans élégances inutiles. Certains soirs, on pense à Pascal, si français, quand il écrivait: 'Certitude.... Pleurs de joie.' " —*L'Appel des Armes* (Paris, G. Oudin et Cie, 1913).

The Cathedral of Meaux, Viewed from the Nave's Aisle

CHAPTER V

ERA OF THE GREAT CATHEDRALS, CHARTRES, RHEIMS, AMIENS

Cathedral of Chartres—Bishop Fulbert's Romanesque Notre Dame burned in 1194—His vast crypt, of 1020, still exists—Bishop Geoffrey de Lèves built the tower of Chartres, called the most beautiful in the world (1145)—Making of the three western portals (c. 1155)—Gothic cathedral begun after the fire of 1194—Primary Gothic west façade escaped the fire—Jehan de Beauce crowned the northwest tower, 1506 to 1513—Sculpture of the transept portals and porches, 1220 to 1260—Chartres excels all cathedrals in the wealth of its stained glass, chiefly of the XII and XIII centuries.

Cathedral of Rheims, begun by the crusader, Bishop Albéric de Humbert, 1211—Its architects recorded in the pavement labyrinth—Its west façade the culmination of Gothic art—Coronation of Charles VII in 1429, Jeanne d'Arc present—Astounding sculptural wealth of this "Cathedral of the Angels"—Martyrdom of Rheims in the World War.

Cathedral of Amiens, the Parthenon of Gothic art—Bishop Evrard de Fouilloy began it, 1220—Designed by Robert de Lusarches—Its sculpture the peer of Rheims and Chartres—Its portal of the Vierge Dorée (c. 1280).

I stood before the triple northern porch
Where dedicated shapes of saints and kings,
Stern faces bleared with immemorial watch,
Looked down benignly grave, and seemed to say:
"Ye come and go incessant, we remain
Safe in the hallowed quiets of the past.
Be reverent, ye who flit and are forgot
Of faith so nobly realized as this."

—JAMES RUSSELL LOWELL, *The Cathedral.*

OF the four master cathedrals of France, that of Paris was begun first. Thirty years later, in 1194, the cornerstone of Chartres was laid, that of Rheims in 1211, and that of Amiens in 1220. In the case of Chartres, Rheims, and Amiens, rebuilding was undertaken when fire had destroyed their Romanesque cathedrals. All four of these great churches have the same patroness, Our Lady, "the glorious mother of God, our advocate against our enemy of hell"—thus those generations spoke of her of whom Dante chanted: "Lady, thou art so great, and hast such worth that if there be who would have grace, yet betaketh not himself to thee, his longing seeketh to fly without wings."[104]

It is difficult for many a modern mind to understand the passion of spiritual chivalry felt by the generations that built cathedrals for her whom they called their sovereign lady, but unless some comprehension of that mystic ideal is grasped no complete sympathy for mediæval art is possible. Mr. George Santayana, who would renew our sense of the moral identity of all the ages, may see in the mediæval devotion to Our Lady a development of Platonic love, which he calls the transformation of the love of beauty into the worship of an ideal beauty, the transformation of the love of a creature into the love of God. All love is to lead to God. All true beauty leads to the idea of perfection, said Michael Angelo, who practiced Platonism, even as had Dante, who was of the very essence of the great scholastic century that built Chartres, Rheims, and Amiens.

THE CATHEDRAL OF CHARTRES[105]

Discipline is indispensable to art.

—GEORGE SANTAYANA.[106]

---

[104] *Paradiso*, xxxiii: 15-16.

[105] *Congrès Archéologique*, 1900; René Merlet, *La cathédrale de Chartres* (Collection, Petites Monographies), (Paris, H. Laurens, 1909); *ibid.*, "Les architectes de la cathédrale de Chartres et la construction de la chapelle Saint Piat au XIVᵉ siècle," in *Bulletin Monumental*, 1906, vol. 70, p. 218; E. Lefèvre-Pontalis, *Les architectes et la construction des cathédrales de Chartres* (Paris, 1905); *ibid.*, *Les façades successives de la cathédrale de Chartres au XIᵉ et au XIIᵉ siècle* (Caen, 1902); Abbé Bulteau, *Monographie de la cathédrale de Chartres* (1891), 3 vols.; E. Lefèvre-Pontalis, "Le portail sud de la cathédrale de Chartres," in *Revue de l'art chrétien*, 1907, p. 100; F. de Mély, *Études iconographiques sur les vitraux du XIIIᵉ siècle de la cathédrale de Chartres* (Lille, 1888), 4to; J. K. Huysmans, *La Cathédrale* (Paris, 1898; tr. London, Paul, Trench & Trübner); Henry Adams, *Mont Saint-Michel and Chartres* (Boston, Houghton Mifflin Company, 1913); De Lasteyrie, *Études sur la sculpture française au moyen âge* (Paris, 1902); Cherval, *Chartres, sa cathédrale, ses monuments* (Chartres, 1905); *ibid.*, *Les écoles de Chartres au moyen âge* (1895); Lucien Merlet, tr. *Lettres de St. Ives, évêque de Chartres* (Chartres, Petrot-Garnier, 1885); A. J. de H. Bushnell, *Storied Windows* (New York, Macmillan Company, 1914); Crosnier, *Iconographie chrétienne* (Tours, Mâme, 1876); Gabriel Fleury, *Études sur les portails imagés du XIIᵉ siècle* (Mamers, Fleury et Dangin, 1904); *Histoire littéraire de la France*, vol. 7, p. 1, "État des lettres en France, XIᵉ siècle"; p. 261, "St. Fulbert" (Paris, 1746); vol. 10, p. 102, "St. Ives" (Paris, 1756); vol. 13, p. 82, "Geofroi de Lèves" (Paris, 1814); vol. 14, p. 89, "Jean de Sarisbéry"; p. 236, "Pierre de Celle, évêque de Chartres" (Paris, 1817).

[106] George Santayana, *Interpretations of Poetry and Religion* (New York, Scribner's, 1905).

Chartres was Our Lady's shrine in a peculiar way, her "special chamber." A local tradition, so old that it reached back to the dimmest past, told of a prophecy concerning a virgin mother, pronounced by the Druids, a hundred years before the Christian era on the site where Chartres now stands, and in the cathedral first built on the revered spot the bishop retained a pagan well which from time immemorial had been honored by the populace. That Puits des Saints-Forts has been included in the crypt of each succeeding cathedral of Chartres. Finally some priggish XVII-century prelates looked with disfavor on the policy, advocated by the apostle of the gentiles, to make use of the ancient superstition for the spread of the true faith. So the pagan well was filled in, and trace of it was lost till M. René Merlet discovered it in 1900 and had it excavated.

That Chartres was a meeting place of the Druids, we know from Cæsar, and the XIII-century sons of the Gauls, as if in souvenir, carved the druidical oak leaf freely upon the present cathedral. Is it fanciful to feel that in the grave forest stillness of Chartres' interior lingers much of the theocratic nostalgia that forever haunts the Celt? In druidic times priest, teacher, and lawmaker were honored above brute force of arms. The present crypt of Chartres includes part of the Gallo-Roman walls. The V-century Merovingian cathedral abutted on the city ramparts. Then came wars which in part demolished the town walls, so that the reconstructed church was able to extend itself beyond the ramparts. It was doubtless after the Norman inroads that was built, in the IX century, the chapel of St. Lupus which forms the core of the present crypt. The Carolingian cathedral of Chartres was destroyed by a terrible fire in 1020.

Now, in 1020, the see of Chartres was occupied by one of the notable bishops of French history, Fulbert (1007-29), revered of the people, a scholar enamored of the life of study, though the events of that agitated age forced him to play an active part in the national life. Like Abbot Suger, he was of lowly extraction. He had studied in the cathedral school of Rheims, made notable by Archbishop Gerbert, who later became Sylvester II, the pope of the year 1000. Fulbert, too, like his master, was a versatile genius—doctor in medicine as well as theologian, and one of the first to take up the new musical system of the Benedictine Guy d'Arezzo. He made the cathedral school of Chartres a center of learning, and men who were to be the leaders of the age were his pupils. Like Socrates, he taught his disciples as they paced up and down the cathedral precincts. In his exhortations there was an appealing tenderness that had a singular power in moving men's hearts, and letters from his pupils still exist, complaining of the exile they felt when separated from him.[107]

---

[107] Bishop Fulbert was buried in 1029 in the church of St. Pierre-en-Vallée. St. Pierre's choir is Romanesque and early Gothic; its sanctuary is a gem of XIV-century Rayonnant; its nave is in larger part of the XIII century, but later than the cathedral of Chartres; its west tower is of the XI century. At present it possesses a treasure of enamel work, the plaques of the apostles, by Léonard Limosin, which Francis I had made in 1545, and which Henry II gave to Diana de Poitiers for the château of Anet. There is much grisaille glass in St. Pierre; each window of the nave is divided perpendicularly into three panels—a colored one in the center and grisailles on either side. In the choir is some XII-century glass; the brilliant apse windows are XIV century, as are a few in the nave. P. Lavedan, *Léonard Limosin el les émail-*

To rebuild his cathedral, Bishop Fulbert gave up his own revenues. Gifts poured in from the kings of England and Denmark, from the bishop's schoolmate of Rheims, the good and cultivated King Robert of France, from the Duke of Aquitaine, who donated the treasure accumulated in St. Hilary's abbatial at Poitiers. The work was pushed forward with such energy that after four years Bishop Fulbert was able to write that, by winter, his lower church would be vaulted.

The present magnificent crypt under Chartres Cathedral is the very one built by St. Fulbert. It is the most extensive crypt in France. Its soundly constructed groin vaults stood firm when, two hundred years later, the upper church was destroyed by fire. In times of public calamity the people have fled to Fulbert's subterranean passages, and the devotion of generations has hallowed his shrine. If you would know the soul of this mystic cathedral, gather at dawn with the silent worshipers who choose that hour to kneel daily in the secluded intimacy of Notre-Dame-sous-Terre. The true hour for Chartres is not at noontime, when the tourists flock to the empty church, but in the morning with the dawn.[108]

Fulbert's Romanesque cathedral was finished in the same XI century by St. Ives of Chartres, another born leader of the nation, who righted many abuses. He dared stand up against Philip I himself, because of the king's adulterous marriage with the beautiful Bertrada de Montfort, stolen from the Count of Anjou. The bishop wrote thus to the king, refusing to attend his wedding, "out of respect for my own conscience, which I wish to keep pure before God, and because I would retain the good repute by which a priest of Christ should honor himself before the faithful. I would rather be flung into the bottom of the sea, with a millstone round my neck, than be a stumbling block to the weak. Nor do I fail in the fidelity I owe you, in speaking thus to you, but rather I give you proof of it, for I believe that you are risking your immortal soul and are putting your crown in jeopardy." The king's answer was to throw him into prison and to pillage his church.

Bishop Ives, in 1095, attended the preaching of the First Crusade at Clermont, after which he accompanied Urban II to the Council of Tours. Scarcely a big event of his day or a leading personage that he was unassociated with, and the three hundred of his letters which are extant form a valuable contribution to history. Twice was the exiled St. Anselm of Canterbury his guest, and in 1107 Paschal II—the pope who built the upper church of S. Clemente at Rome—stopped with him in Chartres. Bishop Ives had been a pupil at Bec, of the celebrated Lanfranc, so he was fully competent to keep up the prestige of his cathedral school.

The Romanesque basilica, begun by Fulbert and finished by Bishop Ives, lasted for over two hundred years. The present northwest tower was started probably in 1134, when the nave's western bays had been damaged by fire. Following a pre-Romanesque tradition, the tower was placed a little distance before the church, apart from it, and so it remained for some ten years. Then, one day in June, 1144, the eloquent Bishop Geoffrey de Lèves, successor of St. Ives, was the guest of

leurs français (Collection, Les grands artistes), (Paris, H. Laurens); Alleaume et Duplessis, *Les douze apôtres; émaux de Léonard Limosin* (Paris, 1865).

[108] "Chartres est sage avec une passion intense.... Palais de la paix et du silence!... C'est du paix héroïque qu'il s'agit ici." —RODIN, *Les Cathédrales de France* (Paris, Colin, 1914).

the abbot of St. Denis during the dedication of Suger's abbatial, and what he there saw of the new system of building made him determined to reconstruct his own church of Chartres. Being an excellent administrator, he was able to start the new works immediately.

Within a year was begun the southwest tower of Chartres (1145), which many hold to be the most beautiful in the world. While it was building, the side aisles of Fulbert's basilica were lengthened to meet both western towers. That the one to the south never was intended to stand isolated is shown by the absence of windows on the two sides where it joins the church, whereas the tower to the north had windows on all four sides. While these works were in progress St. Bernard came to Chartres to preach the Second Crusade. He and Bishop Geoffrey had recently traveled together through Aquitaine, combating the Cartharist heresy.

It was Geoffrey de Lèves who accompanied the future Louis VII to Bordeaux for his marriage with Aliénor of Aquitaine, and when the death of the king suddenly called Louis away, he left his bride in the care of the bishop of Chartres. Geoffrey was long the sincere defender of Abélard, though finally he disapproved of what was overhardy in his doctrine; with Peter of Cluny he held that the errors of the brilliant schoolman were of the head rather than the heart.

Two often-quoted ancient records described the surge of religious fervor which raised the western end of Chartres Cathedral. In 1145 the archbishop of Rouen wrote to the bishop of Amiens to relate how the people of his diocese, knights and ladies, townspeople and peasants, went in a spirit of penitence to Chartres, there to help in the new work of Notre Dame. No one could join the pilgrimage who had not confessed, and renounced all enmities and revenges. As the quarries were some miles from the city, it was a heavy task to drag in the big stones. In that same 1145 Abbot Haimon of St. Pierre-sur-Dives in Normandy, wrote to some monks in England to picture the scenes at Chartres: "Whoever heard tell in times past of powerful princes brought up in honors and wealth, of noble men and women bending their proud necks to the harness of carts, and like beasts of burden dragging stones, cement, wood, to build the abode of Christ? And while men of all ranks drag these heavy loads—so great the weight that sometimes a thousand are attached to one wagon—they march in such silence that not a murmur is heard. When they halt by the roadside, only the confessing of sins, and prayer, humbly suppliant, ascend to God. If anyone is so hardened as to refuse to pardon his enemies, he is detached from the cart and refused companionship in that holy company. When they have reached the church they arrange the wagons about it like a spiritual camp, and during the whole night they celebrate the watch by hymns and canticles."

It was not long after this wave of enthusiasm that the Portal Royal was begun, probably about 1155, though some have placed those three western doors earlier and some later. As they resembled the doors of St. Denis (now destroyed), they were made, doubtlessly, within ten or fifteen years of Suger's work. By 1175 cracks appeared in the new west foundations, and the three doors were moved forward, stone by stone, and placed on a line with the towers. In their first position, set back between the advancing towers, they had shown to better advantage, but it is to the advance of Chartres' western façade that we owe the preservation of its priceless glass and sculpture.

At the time of these changes the bishop of Chartres was John of Salisbury (1176-80), perhaps the most learned man of his century, and certainly one of the wisest, sincerest, and most likable men who ever lived. In his works this humanist advocated a proper use of dialectics, as opposed to the sterile subtlety then increasing among scholars. His stand on the problem which agitated the thinkers then—how our ideas correspond to things existing outside our intellect—was one of moderate realism. Abélard had led up to such an outlook, and the scholastics of the XIII century, notably Aquinas, also classed themselves as moderate realists. John of Salisbury possessed what the French call *esprit*, and he poked some fun at the hair-splitting in the schools. Hebrew and Greek he knew, and his Latin was of good literary quality, which was rather an exception among scholastic writers.

When Thomas Becket was raised to the see of Canterbury, his friend, John of Salisbury, became his chief adviser, and though the latter held principles equally firm, he endeavored to curb the primate's excess of zeal. Through the years of Becket's exile, John lived in France, returned with his archbishop to England, and witnessed his martyrdom in Canterbury Cathedral. At Sens he, too, must have watched with interest that cathedral building, being himself an artist and modeler in clay. Sens' archbishop, Guillaume de Champagne, admired the balanced character and solid scholarship of the Englishman, and after the Canterbury tragedy proposed him for the see of Chartres. No one could have appreciated better than John of Salisbury the strange charm and beauty of the column statues which one by one were moved to a new position at his cathedral's west doors while he governed this see.

And no one was more fitted to comprehend the glory of the three XII-century windows, also dismounted and reset in those years, than John of Salisbury's successor at Chartres, his intimate of many years past, Pierre de Celle, who, while abbot of St. Remi at Rheims, had adorned the lovely Primary Gothic choir he built there with admirable colored lights. The south tower was crowned with its mighty spire in his day, and he paved the streets of Chartres and raised the town walls. Both these best types of scholastic authors were interested in maintaining the high repute of their cathedral school. As Pierre de Celle died in 1183, he was spared the sight of his cathedral's destruction.

On the night of June 10, 1194, a terrible conflagration wiped out Fulbert's Romanesque basilica. To its cavernous crypt the clerks bore the treasured relics, and after three days emerged, when the fire was spent. Only the crypt and the more recent west façade, with its two towers, escaped destruction; the north tower at the time still lacked its upper stories.

On the smoking ruins the pope's legate made an appeal to the people's generosity, and once again Chartres presented the devotional scenes of 1145. Bishop and canons gave up three years of their revenue, and pious confraternities dragged in the big stones. Those passionate rivals, Richard Cœur-de-Lion and Philippe-Auguste, were donors. Thus every part of Chartres Cathedral has been raised by the hands and hearts of faith, and surely the personality which builders impart to their work breathes here in a piety of the soul that not all the science of later times has ever been able to simulate. *Non est hic aliud nisi Domus Dei et porta coeli.*

The new cathedral went forward apace; early in the XIII century the big west rose was added to the much-transformed façade. By 1224 the upper vaulting was entirely closed in. The formal dedication was postponed till 1260, to allow for the completion of the two elaborate porches before the transept's doors. To that delayed consecration came St. Louis and his court.

The name of the architect of Chartres is unknown, but its unity of plan is proof that it emanated from the brain of one man. The choir had double aisles, the nave a single one. It is believed that to the absence of side chapels in the nave is due the exceptionally good acoustic properties of this church in which the preacher's voice carries to every part. Unknown, too, is the architect of the tower built in the dawn of Gothic art, two generations before the present cathedral. The veriest amateur as he gazes at it is conscious that he has before him one of the supreme things of France.

The more closely the *clocher vieux* is analyzed, the more it becomes a touchstone by which will be judged other towers. A miracle of just gradation, it sprang in one jet from the brain of a man of genius. With a pleasurable sense of harmony the eye travels from the base to the tip of the spire. Proportion, not ornament, is the secret of its transcendent influence. The width is right—and so many towers fail there—the division of the stories is right, and radiantly right is that crucial point, the transition from the vertical square shaft to the inclined octagonal spire, accomplished here by means of dormers and turrets. An innovator was the architect of Chartres' belfry when he placed open windows in the gables. To obviate any monotonous optical effect, he made a ridge down each inclined plane of the spire, which spire is a massive pyramid forming almost half of the tower's height. Its bare nobility surpasses the richer open stonework of the spire to the north.

The Cathedral of Chartres (1194-1240). The Southern Aspect

It is confusing that the north tower at Chartres façade should be called the *clocher neuf* because of its Flamboyant Gothic upper stories, for its lower Romanesque parts were built before the *clocher vieux*. When towers were rising in every part of France as the XVI century opened, the chapter of Chartres Cathedral invited a local architect, Jean de Texier, called Jean de Beauce,[109] to complete their

---

[109] "I am Beauceron, Chartres is my cathedral," said Charles Péguy, who walked in pilgrimage a hundred miles to pray in the cathedral when his little son lay dying with diphtheria. No one has celebrated it better than that XX-century maker of mystery plays, true artisan-artist of the *moyen âge*:

> "Voici le lourd pilier et la montante voûte;
> Et l'oubli pour hier, et l'oubli pour demain;
> Et l'inutilité de tout calcul humain;
> Et plus que le péché, la sagesse en déroute.
>
> "Voici le lieu du monde où tout devient facile,
> Le regret, le départ, même l'événement,
> Et l'adieu temporaire et le détournement,
> Le seul coin de la terre où tout devient docile....
>
> "Voici le lieu du monde où tout rentre et se tait,
> Et le silence et l'ombre et la charnelle absence.
> Et le commencement d'éternelle présence,
> Le seul réduit où l'âme est tout ce qu'elle était."

truncated northern tower, whose temporary top had just been consumed by fire. Jean de Beauce saw that the XIII-century rose window had crowded the south belfry. While the rose was making, a new story had been added to the north tower. To that tower he decided to add still another story before he topped it with an elaborate lacework spire. In consequence the *clocher neuf* is out of all proportion to its mate. Nor does it carry the eye smoothly from soil to tip; its renewals are abrupt. However, if it lacks subtlety, its crown is none the less a strikingly effective monument of the final phase of Gothic architecture. The spire is adjusted to the shaft by means of little flying buttresses which spring from the angle and face turrets, and help to unify the design.

Some human vanity the north tower of Chartres displays, but no arrogant pride, no Renaissance pretentiousness. And in the inscription commemorating its renewal still breathes the reverential, loving, personal note of the Middle Ages:

"I was once built of lead, till after the fire on the feast of St. Anne, six o'clock in the evening, 1506, Messires the Chapter ordered me rebuilt in stone. In my necessity good people helped me. May God be gracious to them."

Under his belfry tower, Jehan de Beauce built a pretty pavilion to regulate its chimes. Sculptor as well as architect, he designed the sumptuous screen about the choir, on whose exterior wall is portrayed the life of Our Lord in groups made during seven generations. The oldest and best scenes are those in the south aisle nearest the transept.

The mystery plays gave to the iconography of the late XV century its realistic character. In these sculpture panels at Chartres, not only were the costumes of the religious theater copied, but the stage settings. A group was represented in a room, whereas in earlier work the sacred personages "stood with a sort of spiritualized detachment, clad in the long tunic of no country, of no time, the very vestment itself for the life eternal."[110]

One of the earlier scenes of Chartres' choir screen presents Our Lady seated in the cosiest of interiors, like a XVI-century housewife, a reticule by her side and a chaplet, which last touch was a charming anachronism. She sews serenely while poor distracted St. Joseph dreams. A complete contrast to this human Virgin Mother is a XIII-century lancet across the aisle from it — the much-venerated Notre-Dame-de-la-belle-verrière, a mother of God, the austere symbolic Throne of Solomon, almost uncanny in her solemn passiveness. In some of the later groups sculptured on the outer walls of the choir screen appears the icy hand of the Renaissance, though the setting remained Gothic throughout.

The two decorative glories of Chartres Cathedral are its sculptured portals and its wealth of stained glass, "an assemblage unique in Europe, the thought of the Middle Ages made visible." Though over ten thousand personages are represented, decoration is kept subordinate to structure with an instinct for discipline

---

— "Prières dans la cathédrale de Chartres," Œuvres de Charles Péguy, vol. 6, p. 383, éd., Nouvelle Reçue française, 1916-18.

[110] Émile Mâle, *L'art religieux du XIIIe siècle en France* (Paris, A. Colin, 1908); *ibid., L'art religieux de la fin du moyen âge en France* (Paris, A. Colin, 1910).

inherent in the best Gothic art.

For the archæologist, the three western doors are of prime importance, last of the Romanesque, first of the Gothic portals, call them whichever you wish. To speak of a transition is to be metaphysical, employing words for what has no existence in reality, since there was no break in the sequence of sculpture from the first imaged portals of French Romanesque art, at Beaulieu, Moissac, Autun and Vézelay to those at Le Mans and Chartres, and to that masterpiece of Gothic sculpture, the portal of Our Lady under the northwest tower of Paris Cathedral.

For the making of his three western doors at Chartres, Bishop Geoffrey de Lèves must have obtained workers from his friend, Abbot Suger of St. Denis. Archaic enough seem these kings and queens with their strange, haunting faces, their slim, parallel feet, with their slender figures more architectural than sculptural as they stand against the pillars to which they conform, yet none the less they show freedom from the stereotyped Byzantine traditions. The attitudes are less rigid than in previous column statues, and personality is dawning in the faces. The Madonna is own sister of the Eastern empress of St. Anne's door at Paris, made about fifteen years later under Bishop Maurice de Sully.

The "celestial portal" of Chartres portrayed the life of Christ from his birth to his ascension. At the northern doors of the transept was set forth the Creation, to the coming of the Messiah, and Our Lady was especially honored. And the southern portal commemorated from the coming of the Lord to his second advent at the Last Judgment. It was the custom to represent this last scene at the west façade, where it might be illumined by the setting sun of the world's final day, the *dies iræ* long dreaded. But since the west portal of Chartres had followed a Romanesque tradition by carving in its place of honor a Christ in the elliptical aureole of eternity, accompanied by the symbols of the four evangelists, the Last Judgment was relegated to the transept's south entrance.

Between the two lateral portals of Chartres there is little choice. In them Gothic sculpture appears in full bloom. Each is a national heritage. In the first plan of the transept the entrances lacked their magnificent porches begun as afterthoughts (about 1240), but so well adjusted to the doors that they appear to be of the same date. Among the seven hundred statues at the northern entrance, some show that they were portrait studies, but it is mere hypothesis to give names to them. Not a statue was placed haphazard. A prearranged dogmatic scheme was consistently followed, since to the mediæval mind art was before all else a teacher. Our Lady stands at the central door, accompanied by ten big figures representing Melchisedek, Abraham, Moses, Samuel, and David on her right, and Isaac, Jeremiah, Simeon, John the Baptist, and St. Peter on her left. They are the patriarchs who prefigured her Son and the prophets who foretold Him, and the two who witnessed His coming, one as foreteller, the other to be His symbol in the future. Each personified a period of history: "Fathers of the people, pillars of humanity, contemporaries of the first days of the world, they seem to belong to another humanity than ours. They are to be counted among the most extraordinary images of the Middle Ages." It is inevitable that M. Mâle be quoted on all points of mediæval iconography.

Usually under each large statue was carved a pedestal scene having some connection with it. Thus beneath the Queen of Sheba is a negro; beneath Balaam, his ass. At the south porch, under St. Jerome, translator of the Bible, is the Synagogue with bandaged eyes, and under St. Gregory the Great is a crouching scribe, who cranes his neck to see the saint, for the legend was that one day as the pope dictated to his secretary, a long pause came, and the scribe peeped through the curtain that hung between them and saw a dove perched on the saint's shoulder, symbolic of the Holy Spirit directing him. St. George and St. Theodore garbed as crusaders are the only youthful images at the south porch, and must have been studied from some of St. Louis' knights.

At her entranceways Chartres set forth the calendar of months in small medallioned allegories, and here and at Amiens, Paris, and Rheims was given a complete system of moral philosophy through the contrast of virtues with vices. On the north façade of Chartres is carved "Libertas" under the image of a virtue. Bishop John of Salisbury would have approved this: "For there is nothing more glorious than freedom," he wrote, "save virtue, if indeed freedom may be rightly severed from virtue, for all who know anything know that true freedom has no other source."

In structural technique the fenestration of Chartres was a stride forward, and both the cathedrals of Paris and Soissons learned immediately from its clearstory arrangement—the first attempt to fill with colored glass the entire space between the active wall shafts. "In certain parts of the cathedral of Chartres," says M. Mâle, "is a magnificent amplitude, a superabundance of power. Each of the nave's windows is surmounted by an immense rose as wide as the bay, a conception as proud as ever an architect realized. It is one of those flashes of genius such as came to Michael Angelo. Those great orbs of light, those wheels of fire that dart sparkling rays are one of the beauties of the cathedral."[111]

Notre Dame has preserved over two hundred of the ancient, imaged windows. The oldest and the best are three large lancets under the western rose which, like the Royal Portal beneath them, are the work of Suger's craftsmen who came here from St. Denis. One of these noted windows relates the childhood of Christ, another His Passion and Resurrection, and the third is a tree of Jesse, similar to one in St. Denis.[112] The iron bars supporting the sheet of glass do not conform to the outline of the medallions, hence it is somewhat more difficult to decipher the scenes than in XIII-century work. None the less, these, the oldest windows of the cathedral, are the peer of any colored glass ever made, because of their inherent

[111] Émile Mâle, *L'Art allemand et l'art français du moyen âge* (Paris, A. Colin, 1917).

[112] "Lovelier color the hand of man has not produced. There are times when human art seems to be something more than mortal; when it rises to heights infinitely above the ordinary achievements of men. French glass of the XII century is such an art. It is impossible to stand in the presence of these translucent mosaics without experiencing a depth of æsthetic emotion that at once disarms the critical faculty. Such sensuous beauty of tone, such richness of color, has been equaled by no painter of the Renaissance, by no Byzantine worker in mosaics. Yet it is not only for their absolute beauty, but also for their perfectly architectural character that these windows claim unqualified admiration."—ARTHUR KINGSLEY PORTER, *Medieval Architecture* (New York and London, 1907), vol. 2, p. 108.

genius for decorative effect and their conscientious workmanship. Many a pen has tried—in vain—to describe the marvelous deep blue which blends together the other colors—the streaky ruby, the emerald green, the sea-green white, the brownish purple and pink, the yellow pot metal.

Even after the opening of the XIII century the St. Denis school exerted influence, as is shown by the Charlemagne-Roland windows in Chartres' ambulatory, whose outline was taken from a crusader window of Suger's abbey. The majority of Chartres' windows belong to the early XIII century, when the city was mistress of the vitrine art and supplied the cathedrals of Bourges, Rouen, Sens, Laon, Auxerre, Tours, Le Mans, Poitiers, and even Canterbury. In the nave's north aisle, the St. Eustace window (the third) is held to be of faultless artistry. The large lancets which light the aisles scintillate as with precious jewels. Only some five or six have floral scrolls filling the spaces between the medallions and the deep border that surrounds each window; in France a geometric pattern for such interstices was more frequent.

At the base of each window is what is called its signature—a medallion which usually represents the avocation of the donors, whether kings, knights, priests, butchers, shoemakers, furriers, or water carriers. Thus below the Charlemagne-Roland windows tradesmen display rich fur mantles, and we know that the *pelletiers* were the donors. Splendid were the gifts of the old artisan guilds. The tanners presented an apse-chapel window in honor of St. Thomas Becket, the vintners one that related the story of Noe, planter of vines. An overpowering sensation it must have been for those mediæval workmen to worship beneath the vaults they themselves had helped to build, under the windows they had contributed. Kings and knights were their fellow donors, but in the cathedrals of France the gifts of the lowly were the most plentiful, a Christian quality which endured till the XVI-century disunion.

To Chartres St. Louis gave a window in honor of St. Denis, patron of his kingdom. The splendid red northern rose, "The Rose of France," is a glorification of Our Lady. The donjons of Castile adorn it in honor of the queen regent. Directly opposite is the big south rose presented by Blanche's enemy, Pierre Mauclerc, who tried to kidnap Louis IX from his mother, but who was to die fighting the infidels under his cousin the king, as did Pierre de Courtenay, another donor of a window at Chartres. Pierre de Dreux, it is said, began the porch before the southern entrance to commemorate his marriage with the heiress of Brittany, a granddaughter of Henry II, Plantagenet. Like every door of this church of the resplendent entranceways, it is a mass of sculpture. Mauclerc was grandson of the builder of St. Yved at Braine, and brother of Archbishop Henri de Dreux, who donated windows to his cathedral at Rheims. Below the Dreux rose at Chartres, four of the Prophets are borne on the shoulders of the four Evangelists, for never could those generations, enamored of symmetry, resist the opportunity to weave together the Old and New Testaments.

A first cousin of St. Louis, Ferdinand III, the saint-conqueror of Seville and Cordova, donated to Chartres a window commemorating the patron of Spain. Three times was St. James honored here, so popular was the Santiago Compostela pilgrimage. St. Martin and St. Nicolas of Bari are also commemorated, the former some seven times, for it pleased the voyagers to noted shrines to record their travels. By pilgrimages French art and song spread in Italy and Spain.

Single monumental figures of prophet or saint were used in the clearstory windows instead of small medallions, which would be indistinct when viewed at such a height. Although most of the windows in the cathedral belong to the XIII century, the XV century is represented in the Vendôme chapel, begun in 1417 by Louis de Bourbon, an ancestor of Henry IV. Much white was then employed for the better lighting of the church, and the straight saddle-bars of Suger's time were again made use of.

No attempt was made for perspective in the earlier glass, which was treated like a translucent mosaic: relief was obtained by the skilled juxtaposition of tones. The old workers had taught themselves many of the secrets of optics. They knew that designs on a background of blue—an expansive color—should be larger than those on red—an absorbent. They knew that blue was a sedative, that red excited the vision, and that yellow stopped contours, hence it was to be employed in borders.

It is not of technique that one thinks when standing face to face with the windows of Chartres. "Create in me a new heart, O God!" one murmurs when gazing at them. When at noon the sun renders the colors dazzling and bewildering, the cathedral seems to be chanting *"Sanctus! Sanctus! Sanctus!"* with the seraphim proclaiming that the whole earth is full of the glory of the Lord. Live coals from heaven's high altar are the windows of Chartres, then, cleansing us of our iniquities; and seeing with our eyes we see, and hearing with our ears we hear, and understanding with our heart we comprehend the vision and are converted and healed.

When evening blots out the rest of the church, and in luminous obscurity the windows hang ethereally in space, they are psalms of intercession and penitence. To gaze at such windows is to pray, think the Levites who serve in this temple. At sunset it is no unusual sight to see a young student of theology seated with his back to the choir, his forgotten breviary open on his knee, gazing spellbound at the western lancets, in his face a rapt reverence, indicating that his soul is in prayer. Each evening the windows of Abbot Suger's craftsmen hymn the suave and lovely *Te Lucis ante* which ushers in night's purity. A mediæval cathedral was designed for the Real Presence, and without that soul of all ritual it stands bereft. Windows such as Chartres' proclaim the miracle of the Tabernacle as symbolically as do those pillars of humanity sculptured by the northern doors, Melchisedek and Peter, types of the Christ, each holding a chalice, or as do the transept's outspread arms that recall the sacrifice on Calvary, renewed daily in the sacrifice of the Mass.

That Chartres Cathedral has preserved its wealth of colored glass is proof that it came gently through the ages; moreover, it was constructed solidly, being a pioneer in the use of flying buttresses with double arches united by an arcature. Its lower walls never were weakened by the insertion of side chapels, those customary XIV-century additions. That academic period built at Chartres merely the semi-detached chapel of St. Piat, to which a stair ascends from the ambulatory. In the XVIII century some well-intentioned but misguided canons of the cathedral lined their sanctuary with neo-classic marbles and stucco, and cluttered the plain wall spaces over the pier arches with needless ornament.

In the time of the Revolution, the entire demolition of the big church was proposed, but happily the embarrassment of how to dispose of such a mountain of stone prevented the vandalism. Lead was stripped from the roof to make bullets and pennies. In the XIX century the vast timber covering of the masonry vaults, called *la forêt*, was burned, but the new steep-pitched roof covered with lead has taken on a greenish hue that blends well with the ancient gray stones.

The easy hill of the town serves as pedestal for Chartres Cathedral. Walk through the little city, whose air of cold propriety is very typical of French provincial life, pass through the Porte Guillaume, and from the boulevard beside the stream study the chief edifice of this Beauce which is "the granary of France." Observe how salient are the transept arms. Another Romanesque trait is the placing of two towers—unfinished here—between choir and transept. What Huysmans called the *maigreur distinguée* of youth is a characteristic of this church. In Rheims, the next begun of the big Gothic cathedrals, is no trace of youth's structural plainness.

As you sit by the stream watching Notre Dame of Chartres, its Flamboyant Gothic tower, perfect of its kind, seems to ride imperiously over the nave; none the less it will be the weather-beaten southwest tower on which the eye will linger longest. Though it was designed to accompany a church of lesser proportions, though it labors under the disadvantage of being overtopped by its sister beacon, nothing can diminish its unparalleled unity. Virile, virginal, aërial, majestic, venerable in youth and youthful in its venerable age, the *clocher vieux* of Chartres is one of the supreme things of the national art, "full of sweet dreams and health and quiet breathing."

THE CATHEDRAL OF RHEIMS[113]

The nation that made a compact with God at the baptismal
font of Rheims will be converted and will return to her first vo-

[113] *Congrès Archéologique*, 1911, Rheims, p. 19, the cathedral; p. 57, St. Remi, L. Demaison; Louis Demaison, *Album de la cathédrale de Rheims* (Paris, 1902), 2 vols., folio; *ibid.*, *La cathédrale de Rheims* (Collection, Petites Monographies), (Paris, H. Laurens, 1910); Abbé Cerf, *Histoire et description de Notre Dame de Rheims* (Rheims, Dubois, 1861), 2 vols., 8vo; Alphonse Gosset, *La cathédrale de Rheims* (Paris and Rheims, 1894), folio; *ibid.*, *Rheims monumental* (Rheims, 1880), 12mo; Anthyme Saint-Paul, "La cathédrale de Rheims, au XIIIe siècle," in *Bulletin Monumental*, 1906, vol. 70, p. 288; E. Moreau-Nélaton, *La cathédrale de Rheims* (Paris, 1915); Monseigneur Landrieux, *La cathédrale de Rheims* (Paris, H. Laurens, 1917); Louis Bréhier, *La cathédrale de Rheims* (Paris, H. Laurens, 1919); Max Sainsaulieu, *Rheims avant la guerre* (Paris, H. Laurens); Vitry, *La cathédrale de Rheims, architecture et sculpture* (Paris, Longuet, 1913); Ch. Loriquet, *Les tapisseries de Notre Dame de Rheims*; H. Bazin, *Une vieille cité de France, Rheims; monuments et histoire* (Rheims, Michaud, 1900), 4to; Louise Pillion, *Les sculpteurs français du XIIIe siècle* (Collection, Les maîtres de l'art), (Paris); Émile Lambin, *Flore des grandes cathédrales* (Paris, 1897); Vitry et Brière, *Documents de sculpture française au moyen âge* (Paris, Longuet, 1900).

cation. Her errors may not go unpunished, but the child of such virtues, of so many sighs, of so many tears, will not perish. A day will come, and we hope it may not long tarry, when France, like Saul on the road to Damascus, will be enveloped in a supernal light whence will proceed a voice, asking: "Why persecutest thou me? Rise up and wash the stains that disfigure thee. Go, first-born of the Church, predestined nation, race of election, go carry as in the past my name before all the peoples and before all the kings of the earth."

—Address of Pope Pius X, in 1912, to the visiting French cardinals.

The other two of the four great cathedrals have no setting equal to the hill pedestal of Chartres or to the river island of Notre Dame of Paris. Seldom is a French cathedral surrounded by the pleasant precincts and cloisters preserved by the English minsters, and Rheims Cathedral is no exception in its abrupt rise from flat city streets. Its druidical massiveness can easily dispense with a pedestal. Rheims imposes itself. Even in the night its prodigy of magnificence endures. "The huge bas-relief is always there in the darkness," wrote Rodin. "I cannot distinguish it, but I feel it. Its beauty persists. It triumphs over shadows and forces me to admire its powerful black harmony. It fills my window, it almost hides the sky. How explain why, even when enveloped in night, this cathedral loses nothing of its beauty? Does the power of that beauty transcend the senses, that the eye sees what it sees not?... *O Nuit! tu es plus grande ici que partout ailleurs!*"[114]

The "masters of the living stone" who built Rheims Cathedral are known to us to-day. Their names were commemorated in a labyrinth that once formed part of the nave's pavement, a drawing of which has been unearthed by M. Louis Demaison. The obliterated figure in the middle of the labyrinth no doubt represented the bishop who laid the foundation stone. He was Albéric de Humbert, formerly archdeacon of Notre Dame at Paris while the bishops Maurice and Eudes de Sully were raising that cathedral. Builder and crusader, Albéric was a true product of his age. He marched into Languedoc, in 1208, to chastise the Albigensian heretics; he attended Innocent III's great Council of the Lateran in 1214, and when he ventured again to the East to take part in the crusade of Jean de Brienne, he was captured by Saracens and ransomed by the Spanish knights of Calatrava. He died on the return journey, 1218.

For a man of such energy, it could have been with slight regret that he witnessed, in May, 1210, the destruction by fire of the decrepit church he had inherited, one of whose builders had been Archbishop Hincmar in the IX century. That early cathedral of Rheims had been redressed with a façade by Archbishop Sampson, a friend of Abbot Suger's, and among the prelates who attended the memorable dedication of St. Denis. His Primary Gothic work, wiped out in the conflagration of 1210, was a loss indeed for art.

Bishop Albéric de Humbert set vigorously to work, and within a year of the

---

[114] Auguste Rodin, *Les cathédrales de France* (Paris, Colin, 1914).

fire had laid the corner stone of the present cathedral (1211). By 1241 services were held in the finished choir. An archbishop of the Dreux line (1227-40) gave windows to the upper apse, and although he and the townsfolk were at bitter odds, the building of the great church by both prelate and people went on unabated. The imperious Henri de Dreux, like Pierre Mauclerc, the donor of Chartres' south rose, was a grandson of that brother of King Louis VII who built the beautiful church of St. Yved at Braine on the highway between Rheims and Soissons. While the cathedral of Rheims was building, another of its archbishops was a Joinville, and in 1270 its sixtieth ruler died on St. Louis' last crusade.

The plan of the cathedral was made by Jean d'Orbais, who had watched the erection of the abbatial (1180) in his native town of Orbais,[115] a church modeled on the choir of St. Remi which the celebrated schoolman Pierre de Celle had built from 1170 to 1180. Thus Orbais is the intermediary between the big abbey church of Rheims and Rheims Cathedral.

For twenty years Jean d'Orbais directed the works at Rheims, so stated the inscription in the labyrinth; and on his death Jean de Loup became directing architect for sixteen years (1231-47), during which the transept and its portals were constructed. The third architect, Gaucher de Rheims (1250-59), began the west portals and worked on the nave. In his precious notebook, Villard de Honnecourt sketched a bay of the nave before 1250. The fourth master-of-works at Rheims, whose name was inscribed in the labyrinth, was Bernard de Soissons. He worked here for thirty-five years; the inscription states that he made five bays of the nave—no doubt the westernmost ones—and that he opened the big O, the rose window of twelve mammoth petals that flowers in the west façade, and is one of the most beautiful designs of the age. By the end of the XIII century, therefore, Rheims Cathedral was completed in its main parts. Carried on with scarcely a pause, and always after the original plan of Jean d'Orbais, the great church kept its unity throughout. The first four architects who during a century had directed the works were succeeded by Robert de Coucy, to whom for a time was erroneously attributed the original plan, but who really continued to build the elaborate west façade.

That frontispiece of Rheims Cathedral, with its cloud of witnesses, is a culmination of Gothic art. Some have called it a work of the XIV century, but the labyrinth, set in the pavement before Robert de Coucy's day, distinctly attributed the placing of the big rose window to Bernard de Soissons, who was in the city till 1298. Also a text of 1299 refers to one of the west towers, and the armor worn in the David-Goliath group of the gable is of the 1280 type. All critics acknowledge that the big statues of the portals belong in main part to the golden period of Gothic sculpture, and were done between 1250 and 1260.[116] The images under the

[115] The Benedictines' church at Orbais (Marne), between Rheims and Châlons, contains some exceptionally good XII-century windows. Its nave has been destroyed, but the transept and the choir, with its radiating chapels (c. 1200), survive. The World War swept over Orbais, but the abbatial is unharmed. Héron de Villefosse, *Abbaye d'Orbais* (Paris, 1892).

[116] It has been suggested that about 1260 a façade then rising was dismounted and moved forward, to allow for the insertion of several more bays in the nave, but the idea remains a hypothesis.

southwest tower had been prepared about thirty years earlier, in the time of Jean d'Orbais. The façade of Rheims inspired many a later Gothic frontispiece—Meaux, Tours, Rouen, Troyes, and Abbeville.

The cathedral went on perfecting itself in detail, and was nearing a complete finish when, four months after the raising of the siege of Orléans, Jeanne d'Arc brought her king to be crowned in the city where two hundred years earlier St. Louis had been anointed. Three gentlemen of Anjou wrote a letter to the queen of Charles VII, Marie of Anjou, and to her mother, Jolande of Aragon, to describe the ceremonies at Rheims on that fifth day of August, 1429. As the crown was set on the king's head trumpets rang out, till it seemed that the vaults would crack, and every man cried *"Noël!"* and drew his sword. A fair sight it was to see the gallant bearing of Jeanne the Maid as she stood by the king, holding the banner she cherished more than the sword.

At her trial in Rouen even her standard was used against her. "Why," asked her judges, "was your banner carried into the church of Rheims to the consecration rather than those of the other captains?" And Jeanne made one of her ringing answers: "It had been in the fray, surely there was good reason it should be at the victory"—*à la peine ... à l'honneur*—her phrase was to become a proverb of France.[117] Jeanne liked fair play. In her army she would tolerate no pillage, nor eat of food which she thought had been so obtained. But then Jeanne had no *Kultur*. She was merely an unlettered peasant girl of the Middle Ages, who called it plain thieving to carry off household goods in an invaded country. For her good friends of Rheims *la bonne Lorraine* kept a warm place in her memory, as her letter to them showed: *"Mes chiers et bons amis les bons et loyaulx Franxois de la cité de Rains, Jehanne la Pucelle vous faict à savoir de ses nouvelles ... je vous promect et certiffy que je ne vous abandonneray poinct."*

Not many years after that national hour of rejoicing the cathedral of Rheims suffered a disaster which put a stop to further construction; henceforth only restorations went on. In 1481 some careless plumbers set on fire the timber overroof and the molten lead ran like a river into the streets. Many a citizen perished in the effort to check the flames. The stone roof of the cathedral stood firm, justifying those generations whose life struggle had been the problem how to cover their churches enduringly. Though all France contributed, the huge edifice was never to be crowned by the six spires of Jean d'Orbais' plan; yet even as it is, Rheims presents the ideal exterior of a Gothic cathedral.

The main façade was made most appropriately a thing of pomp and circumstance, regal and gorgeous for the royal coronations. No need to hang such walls with tapestries for the feast. The three deep portals were united as one by means of an unbroken line of thirty or more large images, deriving from similar arrays at Chartres and Amiens, but possessing a pronounced indigenous genius. In the groups of the Annunciation and the Presentation the Blessed Virgin is a figure of spotless purity, meek and infinitely touching in her little mantle that falls in

[117] E. O'Reilly, *Les deux procès de condamnation ... de Jeanne d'Arc*, eighth interrogation, March 17, 1431. "Il avait été à la peine, c'était bien raison qu'il fût à l'honneur." (Paris, Plon, 1868), 2 vols.

straight simplicity from her slender shoulders. "By humility the holy Virgin merited to become the mother of God," was the answer given by St. Isabelle of France, the only sister of St. Louis, when asked why she named her convent at Longchamp, L'Humilité-Notre-Dame. A very different Virgin is that in the Visitation group. She and St. Elizabeth are draped voluminously like stately Roman matrons. Those two statues (imitated by Bamburg Cathedral in 1280) must have been inspired by some work of antiquity, of which Rheims possessed a number. Classic influences in the imagery of northern France during the Middle Ages was transitory, however. First and last mediæval sculpture was a building-stone sculpture.

In the eyes and on the lips of a few of the entranceway statues hovered a half-smile, a fleeting, rare expression which, long centuries before, the Greek sculptors preceding Phidias had achieved. Again, at the Renaissance, Da Vinci was obsessed by the same expression, "born of a miracle, meant to gladden men's souls forever." To-day, the angel image La Sourire stands headless at the portal under the north tower.

Not only was the west frontispiece of Rheims unique, but its transept façades would have distinguished any cathedral. One of the three doors of the north façade is composed of fragments from a monument which had been in the Romanesque metropolitan burned in 1210. The middle door commemorates local saints, for cathedrals were historians and linked the generations with that continuance of tradition which makes the strength of a race. To honor their spiritual forefathers was held to be patriotism by those believing generations. At both west and north façades was an image of St. Nicaise, the eleventh bishop of Rheims, who had been martyred as he knelt by his cathedral door. Tradition relates that he was reciting the Psalmist's words, "My soul is bowed to earth," when the Vandals struck off his head, and that the severed head finished the verse: "Verify me, O Lord, according to thy word."[118]

The fifteenth bishop (459-533), St. Remigius, apostle of the Franks, is honored by a statue. In the cathedral of his day he baptized Clovis, and thus made France the first orthodox Christian kingdom of the West, since Gaul's other conquerors had fallen into the Arian heresy. Many an archbishop of Rheims played a foremost part in the life of the nation. The military prowess of Turpin, the twenty-seventh prelate here, is related in the *Chanson de Roland*.[119] The forty-first archbishop was

---

[118] During this summer of 1020 excavations made under Rheims Cathedral have brought to light vestiges of the cathedral of the Virgin, founded by St. Nicaise in 401. Three Roman arches in good condition support the venerable nave, in a corner of whose floor was found buried sacred images of ivory most beautifully carved. Evidently they had been hidden to save them from the invading Vandals.

[119] "Et les Français disent: Quel grand courage!
    Avec Turpin la croix est bien gardée!"

Roland addressed the dead archbishop on the field of Roncevaux:

"Eh! Chevalier de bonne aire, homme noble,
Nul ne sut mieux, depuis les saints apôtres
La foi garder et convertir les hommes:
Du paradis lui soit la porte ouverte!"

the learned Gerbert, who died Pope Sylvester II (1003). He made the cathedral school famous, among his pupils being the king's son and Bishop Fulbert of Chartres.

One of the students in Rheims in that age was St. Bruno of Cologne, founder of the Carthusian Order. For long years he directed the cathedral school, guiding the people during the misrule of a scandalous archbishop. A pupil of his at Rheims became Urban II, who instigated the First Crusade. And a century later one of his ablest and holiest sons, St. Hugh of Avalon, built the cathedral choir of Lincoln, as well as its small transept, and part of the big transept—the oldest examples of Early-English Gothic. In 1180, the archbishop of Rheims, Guillaume de Champagne, crowned as king his nephew, Philippe-Auguste. Only those shepherds of the flock who attained to canonized sainthood were honored by statues at the church entrances.

The Beau Dieu of Rheims of most benign majesty is the central image of the transept's northern façade. Surmounting it is a Last Judgment that speaks well for the honesty of the clerics whose pupils were the sculptors. Here at the king's own basilica, whither he came for the most brilliant hour of his life, was sculptured a crowned monarch, as the front figure, marching to hell, and behind him walked a bishop. No pharisees were the men of the XIII century. Sin was sin, and all men were equal before sin's punishment.

There are statues on the towers of that same north frontispiece to which names have been given. One has been called Philippe-Auguste, and it certainly was a portrait study, whether or not it represented the most able monarch of the feudal ages, the victor of Bouvines, who tripled the area of France and under whom was begun almost every Gothic cathedral in the land. The name of his grandson, St. Louis, has been given to another image. In a niche of the façade stands a charming Eve holding a very mediæval serpent.

One can merely indicate, in passing, the astounding wealth of Rheims—five thousand images whose verve and fecundity are marvelous. "If your heart is right, all creatures will be for you a book of holy doctrine," so they dared to carve clown, dog, cat, or sheep on pinnacle, or in hidden nook, and their flora was as generous as their fauna. A local botanist has found that every leaf growing to-day by the roadsides was reproduced in the cathedral. It was only natural that in Champagne the vine leaf should be popular; on one of the capitals of the nave a pleasant vintage scene is represented.

If the gorgeous west approaches of the Cathedral-Royal were suited for earthly pageantry, its eastern end paid homage, in holier simplicity, to the Spiritual King. Around the exterior wall of the apse was set a guard of angels, each carrying an emblem of the Passion, or of its symbol, the Mass—chalice, censer, missal, spear—and the procession met at the Christ image placed in the center of the curving wall. The ordinance was derived from Byzantine art. Many an artist has said of the apse sculpture of Rheims that the Greeks can show no lovelier work. A few years later, more angelic thrones, dominations, and powers were set around this,

—La Chanson de Roland (Edition, A. d'Avril).

the Cathedral of the Angels. A seraphic sentry adorned each buttress and at the same time increased its counterbutting force, and were agents toward the swifter grounding of the load.

And now, having touched superficially on the exterior of this inexhaustible church, let us step inside its imaged doors. On the inner wall of the three western portals is an elaborate decoration found nowhere else. Tier upon tier of statues shrined in foliage-covered niches rise to the level of the triforium. Never has a wall been more glorified both within and without. Lavish leaf ornamentation forms the capitals of the piers. Each pier consists of a circular shaft cantoned by four lesser columns; the capitals of the latter are divided into two stories because their diameter is less—a skillful contrivance that solves the difficulty of grouping pillars of different sizes.

The Angel Apse of Rheims (c. 1220)

The nave of Rheims was never weakened by the addition of side chapels, which always diminishes the integrity of an edifice. In fact, the lower walls[120] as

[120] Along the lower walls of the side aisles of Rheims hung splendid tapestries, "color of incense, silver-gray dashed with blue, with red." They related Our Lady's life and were

well as the piers were made oversolid for what they bear, since it had not yet been learned how to apply exactly the right counterforce to the pressure of the vaulting. Amiens was to be the first to achieve that perfect equilibrium.

The interior proportions of Rheims are harmonious; the side aisles are relatively right with the central vessel, and the nave leads up well to the sanctuary, which, inside and out, is beyond criticism. As a whole, however, the interior of this cathedral has not the slender upwardness of Amiens nor the ascetic holiness of Chartres. It stands more than it soars. It praises the deity in another fashion than does the mystic cathedral. The keynote here is a right-minded human splendor. Robust and majestic, this is the church for state pageants, the regal temple for national festivals.

Alas! poor battle-worn Rheims! Alas for the *bons et loyaulx Franxois de la cité de Rains!* Has Jehanne la Purcelle forgotten her promise never to abandon you?

> Mourant en plein martyre avec vivacité ...
> Masquant sous sa visière une efficacité ...
> Jetant toute une armée aux pieds de la prière....

So wrote the poet who fell on the field of honor, in September, 1914, of St. Jeanne, whose martyrdom was a victory; so he might have written of Rheims Cathedral. Again a sublime holocaust was needed for the saving of the soul of France.

RHEIMS SINCE 1914

> How doth the city sit solitary that was full of people. How is she become a widow, she that was great among the nations.
>
> —Jerimiah: *Lamentations.*

Designer infinite!
Ah! must Thou char the wood e'er Thou canst limn with it?

> —Francis Thompson, *The Hound of Heaven.*

In the first days of September, 1914, after the battle of the Marne, the Germans evacuated Rheims, which they had occupied for little over a week. Before they quitted the city, some cans of inflammable liquids, with bundles of straw, were set on the roof of the cathedral, and there they were found and made note of officially by Frenchmen who ascended the towers to hang out the Red Cross flag. The destruction of Rheims Cathedral was planned deliberately and in cold blood it was carried out. No military excuse for the crime is possible, since General Joffre made a formal statement that at no time were the church towers used as posts of observation.

From the heights a few miles away the enemy opened fire on the city. It is said

---

given in 1530 by the saintly archbishop, Robert de Lenoncourt, the same who presented to St. Remi's monastery church other sumptuous embroideries, and who remade as Flamboyant Gothic St. Remi's south façade. The tapestries of Rheims were saved from the wrecked city and exhibited in Paris during the World War for the benefit of the refugees. It is said that a certain number of the stained-glass windows of the cathedral were dismounted in time to escape annihilation.

that Baron von Plattenburg ordered the bombardment. General von Haeringen is also cited as an executioner of Rheims Cathedral. On September 17th and 18th the church was riddled with projectiles. Between dawn and sunset, on September 19th, over five hundred of them struck the mammoth church. About four o'clock on that fateful day, Saturday, September 19, 1914, the timber roof caught fire from an inflammable bomb. In less than an hour flames were devouring the wooden scaffolding which, by ill luck, because of repairs in progress, framed part of the edifice. Fire lapped and calcined the outer walls, obliterating the kings and the angels and the saints, wiping out all the loving handicraft of the old stonecutters. Once again molten lead ran in the streets of Rheims. Fire lapped the sculptured screen inside the western doors, and the lovely lavish chiseling has become a blurred, amorphous mass. Projectiles tore through the gaping windows and crashed against the opposite walls. Some of the burning timber from the overroof fell through the apertures of the vault's keystones and ignited the straw spread on the pavement for the wounded German soldiers who had been left behind when the invaders evacuated the city.

Let an eyewitness relate the burning of Rheims Cathedral: "It stood enveloped in flames, one towering flame itself. Before the outrage something surged unchained at the root of our being. Our cathedral! Our hearts broke as we watched its desecration. An aged woman of the city intoned solemnly: 'This will bode them no good!' ('Ca ne leur portera pas bonheur!') We stood in groups watching with fierce anger the conflagration. We walked, we spoke, but like automatons, for our souls were groaning with anguish. Our cathedral! *Première page de France! Geste des aïeux! Legs des siècles devenant aujourd'hui, en ce poignant martyre, l'hostie nationale!*" Suddenly word came that the German wounded inside the church must be saved. The archpriest of the cathedral, Canon Landrieux (to-day a bishop), called for aid from the onlookers. He was answered by angry murmurs: "What! must we then risk our lives to save these bombarders of hospitals, these incendiaries of cathedrals?" Then a young girl's voice rose, trembling with tears: "*On est de France, nous autres!*" And instantly men stepped forward to aid the heroic priest save their enemies from the flaming furnace.

Poor martyred Rheims! Its once illuminated western front is battered and corroded past restoral, and is falling flake by flake. With a touch of the finger the stone crumbles into dust. The towers are mutilated. One after another the rapt and fearless angels on the buttresses have been toppled down. As the incessant rain of fire and iron came from the northeast, the transept's northern entranceway is wrecked—its historic statues mere unsightly stumps. Never again will the hardy lesson of the Last Judgment be preached at the ruined portal.

No more will the triple-winged seraphim chant hosannas in the great western rose. No coming generations of travelers will carry away an undying memory of the sunset hour in the great church, when the western inclosure became a resplendent sheet of flame, and those who paced up and down the basilica gazed with awe at that majestic spectacle of Art and Faith. The XIII-century windows of the clearstory are pulverized; scarcely a fragment is left of the forty lancets of the nave where, in superimposed rows, the kings of France stood, with the archbishops who had crowned them, big-eyed barbaric images, so intense of hue that one remembers them as blood-red rubies. The loss of the windows of Rheims has been expressed poignantly by Pierre Loti, who spent a Sunday in October, 1915, in the cathedral. He found the silence of death within its ravaged walls that for centuries had echoed the music of the liturgy. Only a cold wind now and then made fitful psalmody. When it blew strongly he could hear a patter as of delicate light pearls. It was the falling to oblivion of what still remained of the ancient windows.

The hammer of Odin and of Thor has gone on beating down relentlessly the national church, and a Berlin poet has sung, exultantly: "The bells sound no more in the two-towered Dom. We have closed with lead, O Rheims, thy house of idolatry." Rheims was hated of old. In its cathedral of 1119 Calixtus II, of the blood of the Capetians, had excommunicated the would-be autocrat of Europe, the German emperor, who had proved himself an unnatural son, a treacherous neighbor, and one who laid sacrilegious hands on holy things. As the pope pronounced the sentence the four hundred prelates gathered in the cathedral dashed down their candles. Yes, Rheims was hated.

Every check to the invader's troops in the trenches was immediately revenged on the defenseless church. *Rheims Cathedral bombarded* became a tragically recurrent line in the war's official bulletin. On October 14, 1914, a hole, meters wide, was torn in the most beautiful of Gothic apses. On February 21 and 22, 1915, the bombardment surpassed in savagery the horrors of the fateful September 19th. On March 29, 1915, a German airship dropped inflammable bombs on the choir, and before many months of this rain of iron and fire the masonry roof began to give way. During the half year preceding the armistice a veritable avalanche of shells fell on the stricken city, where remained only a few hundred of its hundred and thirty thousand inhabitants. From June 15 to June 28, 1918, over sixteen thousand shells fell on Rheims, and, strange to tell, amid it all Dubois' statue of Jeanne d'Arc mounted on her charger on the cathedral parvis stood unscathed.[121] On July 5th eight shells crashed into the western entrances; and so on runs the sinister record.

"We wait for a chastisement equal to the crime," is the word of Enlart, the archæologist. And the world's heart echoes the verdict. When on that fatal September day of 1914, the staggering almost unbelievable report first spread over France, "Rheims Cathedral is in flames" — many a strong man wept on the streets of French cities, and throughout the tragic night of the conflagration the French soldiers, camped over the plains for miles, watched in anguish the destruction of

---

[121] Sung in the French trenches:

"... Attila II s'en veng et brûle
Le baptistère de nos rois.
Un siécle d'art à chaque bombe
Se craquèle, s'effrite et tombe
Avec un râle, et tout d'un coup!
... Mais dans la ville ruinée,
Par l'incendie illuminée,
Jeanne d'Arc est encor debout!"

—(THÉODOR BOTREL, Refrains de guerre (Paris, Payot, 1915)).

their patrimony, of their ancestress cathedral, *l'holocauste de la patrie*. In Jeanne's century it had taken a long and cruel war and the sacrifice of her who was the incarnation of France to remake the stricken soul of the nation, and again an overwhelming martyrdom was needed to set right the grievous *pitié* there was in the country of France.

The city of Rheims is to-day a shapeless mass, resembling a place wrecked by ancient barbarism. The archiepiscopal palace, whose two-storied chapel was built by the same hands that laid the choir stones of Notre Dame, is entirely demolished. The cathedral, though ravaged irreparably, still towers above the ruined city. Had Amiens been subjected to the same bombardment as Rheims, it would have collapsed long ago. It is the surplus strength of Rheims' foundations, somewhat criticized by architects, that has saved the church from utter destruction. Notre Dame of Rheims was built for eternity.

The mystic wonder of the severed head of St. Nicaise has been repeated. Immolated Rheims has stirred anew the latent crusading blood. "Honor" and "sacrifice" and all the brave words of the days of chivalry are again on the lips of Frenchmen, and many a scoffer has been beaten to his knees by the same spirit which actuated the generations who built the cathedrals and, building them, welded a nation's unity. Those who committed the sacrilege of Rheims forgot that when mankind is robbed of a heritage it sets the criminal in the pillory of history. To-day Rheims Cathedral lies wounded on the field of honor; Rheims Cathedral is forever the symbol of a people's resurrection. *À la peine!... À l'honneur!*

AMIENS CATHEDRAL[122]

There have been, in humanity's story, only two great schools of art—that of Greece, and that of the Gothic era. For only then was expressed the ideas and the religious spirit of the peoples that gave birth to them. The Greeks rendered the Pagan spirit, the Pagan emotion; they left us the Parthenon. The Gothic School rendered the Christian idea, the Christian spirit. It has left us Notre Dame of Amiens.

—ÉMILE LAMBIN.[123]

---

[122] Georges Durand, *Monographie de l'église Notre Dame, cathédrale d'Amiens* (Paris, Picard et fils, 1903), 2 vols., folio; *ibid., Description abrégée de la cathédrale d'Amiens* (Amiens, Yvert et Tellier, 1904); *ibid.,* "La peinture sur verre au XIIIᵉ siècle et les vitraux de la cathédrale d'Amiens," in *Mémoires de la Société des antiquaires de Picardie* 1891, 4ᵉ série, tome I, p. 389; Jourdain et Duval, "Le grand portail de la cathédrale d'Amiens," in *Bulletin Monumental*, vols. 11, 12, *passim; ibid., Cathédrale d'Amiens, les stalles et clôtures du chœur* (Amiens, 1867), 8vo; T. Perkins, *The Cathedral Church of Amiens* (London, Bell, 1902); Rodière et Guyencourt, *La Picardie historique et monumentale* (Paris, Picard, 1906), 4to; Camille Enlart, *Monuments religieux de l'architecture romane et de transition dans la région Picarde* (Amiens, Yvert et Tellier, 1895); Taylor et Nodier, *Voyages pittoresques ... dans l'ancienne France. Picardie,* (Paris, Didron, 1835-45), 3 vols.; Émile Mâle, *L'art religieux de la fin du moyen âge en France* (Paris, Colin, 1910); A. de Colonne, *Histoire de la ville d'Amiens* (Paris, 1900); Demogeon, La Picardie (Collection, Les régions de la France), (Paris, L. Cerf).

[123] Emile Lambin, *La flore des grandes cathédrales* (Paris, 1897).

The terrors and the thunder of the World War menaced Amiens through the long four years, but the grand doctrinal temple, almost superhuman in its majesty, was spared the fate of Rheims, Soissons, and the noble church of St. Martin at Ipres, begun in the same twelvemonth as itself. The statues at the portals of Amiens have seen pass the great personages of the mediæval centuries. The kings of this world felt honored to visit the church of Our Lady and St. Firman. Its reconciliation Mass put the seal on a treaty of goodwill between France and England, and united the English ruler with his rebellious people; St. Louis, the peace maker, prayed in its sanctuary. On its very enemies it imposed veneration. When Charles le Téméraire attacked the city in 1471 he ordered his troops to respect the cathedral.

While the upper vaulting of Chartres was being finished and the choir of Rheims was building, there was laid the first stone of Notre Dame of Amiens in 1220. Amiens is the Gothic cathedral par excellence, recognized from the first as a masterpiece—the Parthenon of Gothic—and immediately taken as a model. The cathedrals of Tours and of Troyes, already begun, were now continued like the big church of Picardy. The Sainte-Chapelle in Paris was modeled on the Lady chapel of Amiens. The cathedrals of Clermont, Narbonne, Rodez, and Limoges are "daughters of Amiens." Its influence extended to the church of St. Sauveur at Bruges, to the cathedral of Prague, and to the choir of Cologne, the latter being almost a replica.[124]

Amiens carried the Gothic principle of equilibrium farther than Rheims. The aisles were made higher, the bays wider, the points of ground support fewer, and the piers less heavy. No energy was wasted. Each part was made just strong enough. To go beyond this culminating point of constructive boldness was inevitably to decline.

No one has better summed up the amplitude of this inspired church than M. Georges Durand, its latest historian, whose monograph is a model: "A vast space inundated with air and light has here been covered by stone vaults, as light and solid as possible; those vaults have been raised to a height never before attained; no longer any walls; the solidity of the edifice is assured by a play of pushes and resistances; flying buttresses exactly meeting the necessary spot to counterbut the great vault; the system of equilibrium perfectly known, and applied with a rigor and audacity unbelievable; the least possible sharpness given to transverse arches; the collaterals raised to a great height—all contribute to give this interior its expression of immensity."

Amiens is a "triumphal chant." The "vast space inclosed" produces an impression that is confounding. When first you step inside the western doors of Amiens, you pause in awe. The emotion felt has the efficacy of a prayer.

The edifice is prodigious and appears so; only St. Sophia, Cologne Cathedral, and St. Peter's at Rome cover larger areas. Now in St. Peter's each detail was enlarged in proportion to the giant scale chosen; thus, a cherub would have a thigh

---

[124] L. Reau, *Cologne* (Collection, Villes d'art célèbres), (Paris, H. Laurens); L. Leger, *Prague* (Collection, Villes d'art célèbres), (Paris, H. Laurens); Henry Hymans, *Bruges et Ipres* (Paris, H. Laurens).

the size of an elephant's. The result is that the great church appears less than its real size. The method of the mediæval architect was precisely opposite. He saw no advantage in making his edifice appear smaller than it really was. He observed that no matter how big a tree might grow, its leaves were no larger than those on smaller trees. The mediæval architect took for his scale of measurement the height of man. His doorways were made for man to walk under. In the bases of his piers, in the triforium arches, in the normal size of his sculpted flora and fauna, he recalled to the eye the scale of a man, his chosen *échelle*: "And he measured the wall thereof ... the measure of a man, which is of an angel."[125] No matter how large a Gothic church might be, the statues decorating it did not increase in scale. To those who prefer a cathedral of the north there will always seem to be a touch of the artificial, of the *tour de force* in St. Peter's.

The name of the master mind who designed the cathedral of Picardy was Robert de Lusarches, recorded in a labyrinth formerly in the nave's pavement, as were his two successors, Thomas de Cormont and his son Renaud. The occasion for a new structure was the fire of 1218 which partly destroyed the Romanesque cathedral. As its old choir was preserved sufficiently to serve for a while longer, the new cathedral was begun by the nave, not the usual procedure. The nave rose in one supreme effort; from start to finish its plan never deviated. It has been taken as the typical masterpiece. "The façade of Paris, the tower of Chartres, the sculpture of Rheims, the nave of Amiens" is a popular summing up.

---

[125] Apocalypse xxi:17.

The Transept of Amiens Cathedral (1220-1280)

By 1236 the nave of Amiens was finished, whereupon the Romanesque choir was replaced by a Gothic one whose plan had been drawn by Robert de Lusarches at the same time with that of the nave. His feeling for proportion was unfaltering; the relation between every part of his church is perfect. The interior elevation in three vertical stories was to become classic—a pier arcade—which is one-third of the entire height, and of the remaining upper wall a clearstory which occupies two-thirds and a triforium one-third. The church is three times as wide as the side aisle is high, and height and span correlate with length. Subtlety of calculation is seen everywhere. The perspective view became a kind of classic type. As you gaze down the church toward the curving east wall which closes the vista, you see beneath the pier arcades of the *sanctum sanctorum* the windows of the apse chapels behind; they appear to fill the apertures symmetrically, whereas at Beauvais, where the side aisle is exceedingly high, the windows of the chapels rise to merely half the height of the pier arches. The cathedrals of Tours and Clermont followed the more satisfactory arrangement of Amiens.

In the last days of Gothic architecture the dislike of the horizontal line was to be carried to such an extent that even the capitals, which the custom of all nations had approved for three thousand years, were eliminated. At Amiens a sane balance was kept. Under its triforium runs a deeply carved band of foliage broken only at the triumphal arches of the transept-crossing. Only there does the ascending line rise unobstructed from pavement to vault. And yet no church ever soared more confidently. The very hall-mark of genius is Amiens' strong horizontal leaf garland—just the needed touch to give variety to regularity as grandiose as this. In the nave the frieze was cut before the posing of the stones, but in the choir the sculpture was done *in situ.*

The fenestration of this cathedral of St. Louis' reign shows the national art in its prime. The glazed triforium is a kind of pedestal for the clearstory, with which it is bound in a single composition by means of continuous mullions. The original glass was of the Sainte-Chapelle type, made by the Paris school which led in the second half of the XIII century, and were it still in existence the interior of Amiens would be a gorgeous sight. Only vestiges have survived; in some of the choir chapels are patchwork panels of ancient fragments. No one denies that the light enters this cathedral too profusely for the mystic seclusion beloved of the soul.

The prelate who laid the foundation stone of Amiens in 1220 was Evrard de Fouilloy, cousin of that archbishop of the great house of Joinville who was a builder at Rheims. Intimate with Innocent III, connoisseur in notable men, the bishop of Amiens was one of the many building prelates who attended the Lateran Council whose séances must often have appeared like an *Amis des Cathédrales* reunion. Bishop Evrard's splendid bronze tomb, cast at one flow, escaped the smelting pot of the Revolution, and with that of his successor, Geoffrey d'Eu, who chanted the first Mass in his cathedral in 1236, the year of his death, is now placed under the pier arcades of the nave. "Here lies Evrard," runs the inscription, "a man compassionate to the afflicted, the widows' protector, the orphans' guardian, who fed the people, who laid the foundations of this structure, to whose care the city was given." The hand of the bishop is raised in a grave gesture of power. The image of Geoffrey d'Eu is less personal. "Bright-shining man of Eu," runs his epitaph, "by whom the throne of Amiens rose into immensity." The saintly bishop used to encourage even the beggars to give their penny toward raising the new house of God.

By 1245 bells were placed in the western towers; then came a lull in the work, from 1247 to 1257, for the bishop had accompanied St. Louis to the holy wars. Louis IX was in Amiens on several occasions and his Sainte-Chapelle at Paris proved his admiration for the classic church. As the XIII century closed, a chapel was added to Amiens by her bishop, the learned Guillaume de Mâcon, a personal friend of St. Louis, and present at his death in Tunis, 1270. The son and successor of Louis IX sent Guillaume to Rome to solicit his father's canonization. During the XIV century other side chapels were added, and in the one erected by Bishop La Grange, from 1373 to 1375, appeared for the first time in France some of the characteristics of Flamboyant Gothic—the flame tracery and ramified vaulting. As early as 1270, however, Amiens had made a sporadic use of supplementary ribs, in the square over the transept-crossing, employing them there, no doubt, in order to break up the immense expanses of infilling.

Though the cathedral of Amiens has lost its stained glass, it has retained that other glory of decorative art—its sculpture. The three western entrance arches, in nine orders, are sovereign compositions. Probably as a scheme of dogmatic theology Amiens is even more complete than Chartres or Rheims. The main façade, with its strong buttress lines unbroken from ground to tower, would be the grandest of all the Gothic frontispieces had it been completed as first planned. But only in its lower stories is it of the XIII century, and the towers scarcely rise above the enormous parallelogram.

At the trumeau of the central door stands *le Beau Dieu* of Amiens, of stronger personality than that of Rheims, a Christ of the West more than the East. "He is the master, wise, steadfast, fraternal, with the patience and the human sympathy that comprehend man's eternal weaknesses."[126] He treads on monsters that symbolize Satan and Sin: "Thou shalt walk upon the asp and the basilisk; the lion and the dragon shalt thou trample under foot."[127] About him stand the best loved of all the saints, the apostles—plain, primitive men in whose upturned foreheads shines the serenity of certitude. We are His witnesses, they seem to be saying, and our testimony we sealed *usque ad sanguinem*: "That which we have seen and have heard we declare unto you...." "We were eyewitnesses of His greatness...." "This Voice we heard brought from heaven...." "These things we write to you that you may rejoice and your joy be full." The prophets and patriarchs at Amiens' portals lack the assurance of joy which shines in the faces of the humble men chosen for the hierarchy of the New Law; the earlier ones had not themselves seen and heard and touched.

Never was the meaning of the Messiah's coming set forth more sublimely than in this archetype cathedral. The soul of the Middle Ages had brooded over the Gospels till it had pierced to their spiritual sense. "The house of the Lord built upon the foundation of the apostles and prophets, Jesus Christ himself being the chief corner stone in whom all the building being framed together, growing up into an holy temple in the Lord."[128]

When the apostles were placed at the cathedral doors, the tradition was to

---

[126] Emile Mâle, *L'art religieux de XIIIᵉ siècle en France* (Paris, Colin, 1908).
[127] Psalm xc:13.
[128] Eph. ii:20-21.

have St. Peter stand to the right of his Master, and St. Paul to the left; the latter was substituted for Matthias, elected to Judas' place. St. Peter, tonsured, carried the key and a cross; his beard was short and curly. St. Paul bore a sword, since his Roman citizenship had saved him from death by crucifixion; he was represented with a bald forehead and a long beard. St. Andrew carried the peculiar-shaped cross on which he died; St. Bartholomew a knife, emblem of his martyrdom.

At the western doors of Amiens is an Annunciation group in which the Virgin is the prototype of the gentle *Ancilla Domini* at Rheims. The St. Elizabeth of the Visitation group is a noble aged woman; the St. Simeon of the Presentation has been called the *Nunc dimittis* in person. Local saints are in a position of honor at the right-hand door, the chief here being St. Firman, the first bishop of Amiens, and the pioneer who preached the Word in Picardy, where he was martyred in 289. On his tomb rose the first cathedral of the city. His statue at the trumeau is a masterpiece of its period.

In his *Bible of Amiens*,[129] Ruskin gives enlightening interpretations of the quatrefoils adorning the wall under the big images at the western entrance. Little genre studies of agricultural life typify the seasons, and the vices and virtues are rendered with movement and subtlety. There is a connection between certain of the small bas-reliefs and the large statues standing above them.

About 1288 they carved the images at the transept's southern portal. Fifty years had elapsed since the making of the western entrance, and already the early reverential awe had passed away. Our Lady is now shown as a radiant young matron whose smile is somewhat mannered, but to call the charming *vierge dorée* "the soubrette of Picardy," as did Ruskin, is an absurd exaggeration. The apostles are no longer of the ideal type. They are mediæval schoolmen, debating some point of dialectics.

Each century was to add to the sculpture of Amiens. André Beauneveu, an illustrious French-Flemish master, made buttress statues of Charles V and his sons, realistic portrait work. The king was one of the four Valois brothers who were, with the Avignon popes, the chief art patrons of the XIV century. As Amiens Cathedral suffered comparatively little during the two cataclysms which emptied the churches of France, it is still a museum of treasures. When, in 1562, the Huguenots, sword in hand, rushed into the church to shatter the altars, the town's tocsin sounded and the citizens assembled in such numbers that they saved their church. Again, during the Revolution, when brutal soldiery began to mutilate the choir screen's groups, the women of Amiens who lived about the cathedral lustily beat the vandals with chairs. Of course the Revolution set up here the usual altar with its living Goddess of Reason, Marat's bust was honored, and over the portal was inscribed the grandiloquent boast: "Fanaticism is destroyed: Truth triumphs."

The tombs, bas-reliefs, and paintings were left intact, as well as the famous carved stalls finished in 1522. In the choir-screen sculpture of XVI-century Gothic the Renaissance had only just begun to appear. St. Firman's mission was related

---

[129] John Ruskin, *The Bible of Amiens*, vol. 33, Complete Works (London, Cook & Wedderburn, 1908). Illustrated; chap. iv, "Interpretations."

quaintly—no prudery shown in the scene of the baptism of Amiens' first Christians. The life of St. John the Baptist was set forth because crusaders had brought his relics to this church from Constantinople. The tourist guide enjoys leading his clients behind Amiens' sanctuary to show them a plump little cupid weeping a marble tear over the tomb of some good canon who founded a local orphanage. M. Durand remarks that for one who appreciates the magnificent bronze tombs of the bishop-builders, or the realistic late-Gothic groups of the choir screen, there are ten who are moved by that banal little *ange pleurant*.

In the transept are some marble slabs inscribed with the names of the presidents of a religious-literary association called Puy-Notre-Dame. Such Puys (from podium, or platform) were poetic contests that sprang up in the XIV century, with the disappearance of the wandering minstrels, and they led in turn to a real literary movement.[130] At Amiens it was the custom each year for a new picture in honor of Notre Dame to be presented to her church, and at the festival a poem was read in her praise. Eventually statues were substituted for pictures, which explains the wealth of XVII-century sculpture in the side chapels and aisles of Amiens Cathedral. A number of the ancient paintings have been placed in the Museum of the city, whose walls have been embellished by Puvis de Chavannes' *Ave Picardia nutrix*.

---

[130] Abbeville, close by, also had its Puy, in whose competitions figured Froissart, the historian, as laureate. The magnificent portal decorations (1548) of the Flamboyant Gothic collegiate church of St. Wulfran were contributed in this way.

Émile Deliguières, *L'église Saint-Vulfran à Abbeville* (Abbeville, Paillart, 1898); *Congrès Archéologique*, 1893.

CHAPTER VI

SIX OF THE LESSER GREAT CATHEDRALS: BOURGES, BEAUVAIS, TROYES, TOURS, LYONS, LE MANS

Cathedral of Bourges—Only XIII-century cathedral without a transept—Inner aisle has its own triforium and clearstory—Chevet built by St. Guillaume, 1200 to 1209—Over main portal is best Last Judgment (c. 1275)—Bourges famous for its stained glass—Jean, duc de Berry, and Jacques Cœur, the late-Gothic art patrons of Bourges—Their gifts to the cathedral—Orléans Cathedral destroyed by Calvinists (note).

Cathedral of Beauvais—A mighty fragment: only a choir and transept—Begun in 1247, derived directly from Amiens—Transept façades masterpieces of late-Gothic—Is Flamboyant Gothic of English origin?—Le Prince family of glassmakers.

Cathedral of Troyes—Its choir built by Bishop Hervé, 1206 to 1226—Martin Chambiges designed the Flamboyant west façade—Magnificent XIII- and XIV-century windows of Troyes Cathedral—St. Urbain's church begun by Pope Urban IV in 1262—Carried the Gothic principle of equilibrium to its limit—Churches of Troyes treasure-houses of stained glass and sculpture—Cultivated court of Champagne's rulers—To the Gothic school of Champagne belongs the Cathedral of Châlons-sur-Marne—Châlons another center for stained glass.

Cathedral of Tours—Choir begun about 1210—Has the classic note of the Touraine landscape—Cathedral windows set up between 1260 and 1270—Venerable ecclesiastical souvenirs of Tours—Tours, the center for the Region-of-the-Loire school of sculpture—Michel Colombe, last of the great Gothic artists, worked here—Environs of the city rich in Flamboyant Gothic.

Cathedral of Lyons—Lyons boasts an apostolic succession for its bishops—Early Christian martyrs of Rome's chief city in Gaul—St. Martin d'Ainay's abbatial dedicated in 1107—Cathedral choir late XII century—With Vienne Cathedral (note) it alone in France used incrustations—Nave of Lyons Cathedral building through the XIII century—Stained glass of Lyons of exceptional quality—All

Christendom was represented at the Ecumenical Council held in Lyons Cathedral in 1274—Church of Brou built by Marguerite of Austria (note)—Moulins Cathedral and Souvigny's abbatial and tombs (notes).

Cathedral of Le Mans—XII-century nave built by notable prelates—Bishop Hildebert de Lavardin (1097 to 1125) a poet and scholar—Guillaume de Passavent made the Angevin vaults (c. 1150)—Geoffrey the Handsome, nicknamed Plantagenet, and his son, Henry II of England, born in Le Mans—Trinité church at Vendôme (note)—Le Mans' Gothic choir built from 1218 to 1254 by Bishop Geoffrey de Loudon—Le Mans ranks next to Chartres and Bourges for its wealth of stained glass—Rayonnant-Flamboyant transept of the XIV and XV centuries—The groups at Solesmes a final expression of Gothic sculpture (1495 to 1550)—Collegiate church at St. Quentin, in size a cathedral, XIII-century choir—Villard de Honnecourt, probably the architect of St. Quentin.

Every work of art truly beautiful and sublime throws the soul into a gracious or serious reverie that lifts it toward the Infinite. Art of itself is essentially moral and religious, since it expresses everywhere in its manifestation the eternal beauty, or else it is false to its own law, to its own genius.

—Victor Cousin, Du vrai, du beau, et du bien.

SCATTERED over France are a number of cathedrals that would stand in the first rank in any other land but one in which were such supreme churches as Chartres, Rheims, and Amiens. It is convenient to group here six of these lesser Great Cathedrals, since they will not fall properly within the coming four chapters, which deal with the regional schools of Normandy, Burgundy, the Midi, and Plantagenet Gothic.

According to the classification used by M. Lefèvre-Pontalis, there are six schools of Gothic architecture in France. Their differences lie in secondary characteristics such as ground-plan, ramifications of ribs, and the form of piers, window tracery, and ornamentations. Of the Ile-de-France and Champagne schools we have already gained some idea in tracing the first steps of the national art, and in following its highest development at Paris, Rheims, and Amiens. Of the six cathedrals here grouped that of Beauvais belongs to the Ile-de-France Picard school and that of Troyes to the Gothic of Champagne. But the four others—Bourges, Tours, Lyons, and Le Mans—show the influences of two or more schools and therefore fit more reasonably into this heterogeneous chapter. In speaking of Gothic schools it is well to recall that in the Flamboyant development there were no distinct regional groups. A similar Gothic style was used in the Midi as in Normandy, in Picardy as in Burgundy.

Though not of the greatest, these six churches are splendid monuments. With hesitation one places such a cathedral as Bourges in a secondary group. Had Beauvais and Le Mans been completed on the same scale as their grandiose choirs, they would stand with the foremost. At Troyes are windows, of the same epochs as the stones framing them, that for splendor are second only to those of Chartres and Bourges. The cathedral of Tours is the personification of the equipoise of Touraine's art, and its storied windows are notable. The metropolitan church of Lyons possesses a grave individuality of the most singular interest, and its windows, too, are masterpieces.

During an astonishing century—roughly speaking from 1170 to 1270—France built about eighty Gothic cathedrals, and more than three hundred fine churches. And the miracle is that each had its own distinct personality, which etches itself clearly on the traveler's mind. Such was the super-abounding joy of creation in the golden age of the national art that no two churches are alike.

THE CATHEDRAL OF BOURGES[131]

One goes before the Lord's altar, one bends the knee, one stays there in an attitude of prostrate humility, and *perhaps*, in it all, one has not rendered to God a single homage. Why? Because religion does not consist of inclinations of the body, or of modesty of the eyes, but of humbleness of spirit, and not for an instant has the spirit been one with those demonstrations of respect and adoration.

One visits the hospitals and prisons, one consoles the afflicted, one tends the sick and helps the poor, and *perhaps* the very one who displays in all this the most assiduity and zeal is he who possesses the least Christian mercy. Why? Because he is carried on by a certain natural activity, or an entirely human pity touches him, or is it any other motive, except God, that leads him.

[131] *Congrès Archéologique*, 1849 and 1898; Amédée Boinet, *La cathédrale de Bourges* (Collection, Petites Monographies), (Paris, H. Laurens, 1911); *ibid.*, "Les sculpteurs de la cathédrale de Bourges," in *Revue de l'art chrétien*, 1912; also published by Champion (Paris, 1912); Gaston Congny, *Bourges et Nevers*; Buhot de Kersers, "Les chapelles absidioles de la cathédrale de Bourges," in *Bulletin Monumental*, vol. 40, p. 417; *ibid.*, *Histoire et statistique monumentale du département du Cher* (Bourges, 1875-98), 8 vols., 4to; Girardot et Durant, *La cathédrale de Bourges* (Moulins, 1849); G. Hardy et A. Gandillon, *Bourges et les abbayes et châteaux de Berry* (Collection, Villes d'art célèbres), (Paris, H. Laurens, 1912); Cahier et Martin (P. P.), *Monographie de la cathédrale de Bourges; vitraux du XIIIe siècle*; Des Méloizes, *Les vitraux de Bourges postérieurs au XIIIe siècle* (Lille, 1897), folio; *ibid.*, *Les vitraux de Bourges*, 1901; *ibid.*, "Note sur un très ancien vitrail de la cathédrale de Bourges," in *Mémoires de la Soc. des Antiquaires du Centre*, 1873, vol. 4, p. 193; Champeaux et Gauchery, *Les travaux d'art exécutés pour Jean de France, duc de Berry* (Paris, Champion, 1894), folio; Buhot de Kersers, "Caractères de l'architecture religieuse en Berry à l'époque romane," in *Bul. archéol. du Comité des Travaux hist. et scientifiques*, 1890, p. 25; F. Deshoulières, "Les églises romanes du Berry," in *Bulletin Monumental*, 1909, p. 463; Raynal, *Histoire de Berry*; Vacher, *Le Berry* (Collection, Les régions de la France), (Paris, L. Cerf); Sauvageot, *Palais, châteaux, hôtels et maisons de France*; Sir Theodore Andreas Cook, *Twenty-five Great Houses of France* (London and New York, 1916).

—*On True and False Piety*, Bourdaloue (1632-1704; born in
Bourges).

The cathedral of St. Étienne stands on a slight hill in the center of Bourges, and is a landmark for forty miles over the Berry plains that are the tranquil heart of France. The best architectural view of it is obtained from the park once attached to the archbishop's palace and said to have been laid out by Le Nôtre, master of this type of cold distinction which is so eminently French. As the entire south flank of the church is exposed to view there, the absence of a transept is what first strikes the attention. Bourges is the only XIII-century cathedral without the extended arms of the cross. Had it a transept it might appear short, whereas now its four hundred feet of length make the most imposing effect.

Bourges, Paris, Troyes, and Clermont are the only cathedrals with double aisles about choir and nave. Bourges is exceptional in that the inner aisle is twice as high as the outer—so high that it possesses its own triforium and clearstory; so high that the pier arches around the middle church rise to more than half the height of the edifice. Indeed, many an English cathedral could stand under the pier arches of Bourges. Each pillar is encircled by eight shafts—an arrangement that accentuates its loftiness. It may be claimed that there is over-emphasis in a procession of such giant columns about the interior of a church, and that there is something spectacular in a colonnade of such stupendous arches. Certainly the main clearstory is dwarfed by comparison, and the contrast in height between inner and outer aisle is too violent. Bourges must pass as a superb experiment rather than the restrained achievement from which emanates a school. Subsequent architects preferred to take as model the more classic division of Amiens' interior wall elevation.

None the less is this most original basilica magnificently and romantically beautiful. Upon entering the church for the first time one feels the gripping sensation of beholding a thing audacious and gigantic. And yet the impression conveyed is not that of overweening pride. There is reverence here. Bishop Durandus tells us that the piers of a church are the bishops and doctors who sustain the temple of God by their doctrines, that the length of a church representeth fortitude which patiently endureth till it attain heaven; its breadth, charity; its height, courage that despiseth prosperity and adversity, hoping to see the gladness of the Lord in the land of the living. The windows are hospitality with cheerfulness, and tenderness with charity. They are Holy Scriptures which expel the wind and the rain—that is, all things hurtful—but transmit the light of the true Sun—that is, God—into the hearts of the faithful.[132] So wrote the wise old XIII-century Midi bishop for whom the whole world and everything in it were symbols.

Sound doctrine, fortitude, and warm protecting hospitality—such are qualities supremely understood of Bourges. There is awe in this church and there is magic. Of the boundless imagination of dreams are certain sunset aspects here, when from the wide western window of Jean de Berry gleams of light strike athwart these vast arches of wonderland, across these sixty big pillars of stone,

[132] *Rationale Divinorum officiorum*, tr. by Neale and Webb of the Camden Society (Leeds, Green, 1843).

and night-time hours—during the May evening services of Our Lady—when the great church as in fearsome meditation is shrouded in shadow.

The Apse of Bourges (1200-1225)

Some four or five cathedrals have stood, in turn, on the same site which was close by the Gallo-Roman city walls. For the early Christians were despised as pariahs, and allowed to build only on the outskirts of cities, until the edict of Constantine permitted them to exercise their religion with honor. All over France churches are to be found abutting on the ancient ramparts of towns. Of the early cathedrals of Bourges only the core of the present crypt remains. From the Romanesque edifice immediately preceding the present cathedral come its XII-century side portals.

There are strong analogies between the ground-plan of St. Étienne of Bourges and that of Notre Dame of Paris, especially if one recalls that the cathedral of Paris, as first designed, possessed no transept. Probably the plans of both were made at the same time, but the work in the capital of the royal demesne started immediately in 1163; hence it retained the galleries over the side aisles—a Romanesque tradition—whereas, at Bourges the actual building began only in the last decade of the XII century, when such tribunes were passing out of vogue. Bourges thereupon undertook to modify its first design, and it tried the startling experiment of making an inner aisle whose height comprised both aisle and tribune.

The crypt of Bourges,[133] one of the most spacious in France, was begun by Archbishop Henri de Sully (1184-99), brother of Bishop Eudes who helped build the west façade of Paris Cathedral. When Henri died, the decision was left to his brother in Paris, as to which of three Cistercian abbots should be the succeeding archbishop in Bourges. The nomination fell to St. Guillaume Berruyer (1199-1208) of the house of Nevers, whose counts had built the admirable Romanesque St. Étienne in that city. Guillaume had watched both Paris and Soissons' cathedrals rising; he had been a monk in Pontigny, whose church was the earliest Gothic venture in Burgundy, and he was abbot of Châalis, where the church also was Primary Gothic. This holy Cistercian was loath to leave his cloister, and always wore his white robe and fasted like a genuine son of St. Bernard. In his face shone his purity of soul, and it is said that his manner was merry.

Only a saint could have made the ambulatory of Bourges, a place apart from the world's fret, fashioned for meditative prayer, its walls hung with gospel parables of mosaic glass. It is thought that while the new Gothic choir was building, services were held in the Romanesque cathedral, which may have been partly open to the elements, since St. Guillaume caught a chill in it while preaching, from the effects of which he died in 1208. Ten years later, the first ceremony held in the completed choir was for his canonization; without the usual process of investigation the pope declared him a saint.

From 1236 to 1260, a nephew of St. William's, Blessed Philippe Berruyer, was archbishop of Bourges and carried forward the nave; and the saint's great-niece, the Countess Matilda of Nevers, contributed generously. Bourges commemorated her saintly bishops in the clearstory of her inner aisle. The window wherein St. Guillaume is pictured shows his niece as the donor.

Never was monument set on a more majestic base than the choir end of Bourges. There the crypt stands above the ground, owing to the slope of the land. The chevet of St. Étienne is incomparable. In every part of the edifice good mason work was done, save in the upper vaults, where the necessity of economy led to skimping. It is apparent that, as the eastern curve of the cathedral was rising, the architect modified his plan. In his apse walls he inserted small chapels, each standing on two columns and an engaged shaft and each roofed by a stone pyramid. Not only does the circlet of little shrines add to the beauty of the chevet, but each chapel serves the practical purpose of a buttress. That they were afterthoughts is proved by the ambulatory windows not being set symmetrically over the crypt windows. However, the chapels must have been added during the building of the procession path, because the latter's vaulting shows no sign of reconstruction.

---

[133] Rodin should have placed his "Thinker" here: "Le Penseur aurait été au diapason dans cette crypt; cette ombre immense l'aurait fortifié!"

—RODIN, LES CATHÉDRALES DE FRANCE.

The cathedral of Bourges is not well documented. Only by a study of the stones themselves can it be dated. Its eastern end was building during the first part of the XIII century; in 1266 the chapter contributed toward the works, their donations being used probably for the completion of the nave. At the end of the XIII century porches were added to the side doors retained from the Romanesque cathedral. Work continued on the west façade during the early part of the XIV century, but when, in 1324, St. Étienne was dedicated, it had been completed in its main parts for forty years.

This makes the west front of Bourges about a century younger than its apse. The five deeply recessed portals correspond to its five aisles, and the western towers are set clear of the aisles, as at Rouen; that to the southwest is now braced by a flying buttress and detached buttress pile. In 1506 the northwest tower collapsed. It was rebuilt by alms, given as thank-offering for the privilege of eating butter during Lent, hence its name Tour de Beurre. Such butter towers may be called the XVI century's method of charity bazaar to raise money for church repairs. During the heyday of Gothic, the fervent layman gave voluntarily, asking for no return, and in that spirit rose the *clocher vieux* at Chartres. Compare that sublime monument with the elegant, mundane late-Gothic "butter towers" of France, and you comprehend how inevitably the spirit of builders reveals itself in the work of their hands.

Of the five western doors of Bourges, only the central one is wholly of the XIII century (c. 1260-75). Its representation of the Last Judgment, adjudged to be the best ever set up at a cathedral door, the *Dies Iræ* warning in stone, is derived from Job, St. Paul, St. Matthew, and the Apocalypse. In the upper zone Christ is enthroned; in the lower is shown the arising of the dead from their tombs. Between these scenes is the splendid panel of the Judgment, with the stately archangel as its central figure, holding the scales of justice. To his left malign demons seize on the damned to plunge them into the jaws of the Leviathan described in Job. To his right the blessed ones smile with complacency as they move toward Paradise, here represented by a hieroglyphic—supposed to be Abraham's bosom, out of which peep some little souls smuggled safely away.[134] St. Peter stands at the gates of Paradise, holding the keys, a doctrinal symbol of his power to bind and to loose, until in time popular fancy pictured him as the actual gatekeeper of heaven.

[134] "There is a charming detail in this section. Beside the angel, on the left, where the wicked are the prey of demons, stands a little female figure, that of a child, who, with hands meekly folded and head gently raised, waits for the stern angel to decide upon her fate. In this fate, however, a dreadful big devil also takes a keen interest; he seems on the point of appropriating the tender creature; he has a face like a goat and an enormous hooked nose. But the angel gently lays a hand upon the shoulder of the little girl—the movement is full of dignity—as if to say, 'No; she belongs to the other side.' The frieze below represents the general Resurrection, with the good and the wicked emerging from their sepulchers. Nothing can be more quaint and charming than the difference shown in their way of responding to the final trump. The good get out of their tombs with a certain modest gayety, an alacrity tempered by respect; one of them kneels to pray as soon as he has disinterred himself. You may know the wicked, on the other hand, by their extreme shyness; they crawl out slowly and fearfully; they hang back."—HENRY JAMES, *A Little Tour in France* (Boston, Houghton Mifflin Company, 1900), p. 105.

Among the elect is represented a king holding the flower of sanctity, probably meant for St. Louis. Beside the king is a cord-girdled monk—hence the name "cordeliers" for Franciscans—showing how popular was the new Order.

The fall of the north tower caused the ruin of the portals near it, and when rebuilt in the XVI century an iconographic error was made which would have been impossible with the trained scholastics of an earlier day—the mother of the Saviour was placed on his left, instead of in the seat of honor on his right. In the fatal year 1562, when from end to end of France the churches were mutilated, the Calvinists attacked the portal images of Bourges and flung the carven stones into the breaches of the town walls. They went so far as to mine the giant piers in order that the great edifice might totter to its fall; but happily their control of the city was cut short, or the tragedy of Orléans might have been enacted.[135]

Bourges is a chosen spot for stained glass, second only to Chartres. Students have made the study of its windows a lifetime enthusiasm. Nowhere can the epochs of the vitrine art from the XII to the XVII century be more easily studied. The school of St. Denis, however, is not represented. Two small panels, now set in a window beside the south portal, are earlier in date than Suger's windows; their flesh tone is purplish; perhaps they are the oldest colored glass extant in France.

Of the XIII-century school of Chartres are the twenty and more lancets in the ambulatory, legend-medallion windows ranking with the best ever made. They repeat some of the themes used by the artists at Chartres, such as the parables of the Prodigal Son, presented by the tanners, and of the Good Samaritan, which latter lancet at Bourges is an exception in having its story begin at the top. Ancient windows are to be read usually from the bottom upward. The first window in the choir aisle, as you enter it from the north, shows the beggar Lazarus despised and suffering on earth, then carried by angels to Abraham's bosom, wherein (in the topmost medallion) he sits cozily ensconsed, but Dives, the bad rich man, is snatched by demons from his earthly scenes of plenty and thrust into hell. The lancet which, at Bourges, is devoted to the Apocalypse, is held to be a subtle commentary on the vision of Patmos. To the fifth large window of the ambulatory, called the New Alliance, the Jesuit fathers, Cahier and Martin, have devoted over a hundred pages—a veritable treatise on symbolism—in their monumental study of the earlier stained glass in this church. "Prophecies in action," our friend Joinville called the prefiguring of the New Law by the Old, so popular during the Middle Ages. New Alliance windows are to be found in various cathedrals—their theme

---

[135] The chief piers of Orléans Cathedral were mined by Théodore de Bèze and blown up on the night of March 23, 1567. The portal, part of the choir, and the apse chapel escaped. The XII-century nave had double aisles with tribunes; the frontispiece also was XII century. The choir, begun in 1287, was finished by 1297, and a new Gothic nave was in progress at the time of the civil wars of religion. Henry IV undertook to rebuild Orléans Cathedral, and with his bride, Marie de Medici, laid the first stone in 1601. But a bastard-Gothic edifice is not compensation for earlier work. H. Havard, éd., *La France artistique et monumentale*, vol. 6, p. 122, "Orléans," G. Lefenestre; *Congrès Archéologique*, 1854 and 1892; G. Rigault, *Orléans et le val de Loire* (Collection, Villes d'art célèbres), (Paris, H. Laurens); E. Lèfevre-Pontalis et Eugène Garry, on Orléans Cathedral, in *Bulletin Monumental*, 1904, vol. 68, p. 309.

being the substitution of Gentiles for Jews by the merit of the Cross.[136] The guild of butchers was the donor of this abstract doctrinal window of Bourges.

The only break in the XIII-century glass of the choir aisle is in the axis chapel, where the windows—of the XVI-century Renaissance—belonged originally to the Sainte-Chapelle of the ducal palace that once existed in Bourges; other windows from the same source have been reset in the cathedral's crypt. The small scenes at the base of each lancet—the signatures as they are called—show that here, as at Chartres, the larger number of these priceless treasures of art were donated by the little people of the Lord—carpenters, weavers, coopers, money changers. A window given by the stonecutters, in the choir aisle of Bourges, is devoted to St. Thomas, the apostle, patron of builders. Bourges and Chartres afford the best opportunity for a more intimate study of the legends and symbols then most popular. Here, as at Chartres, the *Golden Legend* should be one's inseparable companion.

In the high-windows of the middle choir the apostles are ranged on one side of Sancta Maria, and the prophets on the other—another of the many contrasts of the Old and New Testaments. The nave's clearstory is chiefly XIII-century grisaille. The XIV-century artists, in their desire for more light, gave up the profound colors of their mosaic-like windows for that coldly elegant phase of the vitrine art, when the use of white was carried to excess and each figure set in its own panel was pictured like a statue with architectural niche and dais.

About 1370 Duke Jean of Berry, born connoisseur like his brothers Charles V, Philippe of Burgundy, and the Duke of Anjou, presented to Bourges Cathedral its immense western window. Before the Medici, this Valois prince collected cameos and medals and bric-à-brac. Among the twenty castles he built were those of Poitiers, Riom, and Bourges, on which were employed the noted Flamboyant Gothic architects, the Dammartin brothers. When the Sainte-Chapelle of the palace in Bourges was destroyed (1759), the duke's tomb, which his nephew Charles VI had ordered of Jean de Cambrai (1477-83), was brought to the cathedral. The sarcophagus was once surrounded by alabaster statuettes, some of which are in the Museum. The arrangement of mourners came from his brother's world-famous tomb in Dijon. In his old age the spendthrift, unstable Jean de Berry married the very youthful Jeanne de Boulogne, and kneeling images of both duke and duchess have been placed on either side of the entrance to the axis chapel of the cathedral. Apparently art-loving John of France was in person the homeliest of men. The Revolution damaged these images, which were restored by means of drawings made of them by Holbein in the time when Bourges was a Mecca for the artists of Europe. Some of Duke Jean's friends presented early XV-century windows to the side chapels of Bourges Cathedral. His physician, Aligret, gave one.

The Hundred Years' War put a stop to the accumulation of art treasures in the metropolitan church. When Charles VII, "the little king of Bourges," as the English had dubbed him ironically, went with the victorious Maid of Orleans to be

---

[136] *Nouvelle Alliance* windows are to be found at Chartres (sixth window in the nave's north aisle), at Le Mans (the east window of the long Lady chapel), at Tours (in the axis chapel), in the transept of Sens Cathedral (in five lights below the north rose), and in the apse curve of Lyons Cathedral.

crowned king at Rheims, his gentle queen, Marie of Anjou, stayed in Bourges with her mother, Yolande of Aragon. Marie's brother, then a youth under Jeanne's command, was to become the good King René of history. To Bourges Jeanne herself came later. She lodged with an estimable widow of the town who, years afterward, during the inquest conducted for the Maid's rehabilitation, bore testimony to the young girl's simple goodness. She told how gallantly Jeanne mounted a horse and how adroitly she managed a lance so that "everyone was in admiration of her, for no knight could have done better."[137]

Then when "*Jehanne la bonne Lorraine*," as Villon called her, had given France a new soul, when the blight of the Great Schism of the West was over, and France accepted the same spiritual chief as the remainder of Europe, there came about the energetic, happy, restless manifestation of art which we call Flamboyant Gothic. Bourges then possessed a Mæcenas in the person of a merchant (son of a tradesman of the city) whose ships covered the sea. Jacques Cœur, from 1443 to 1452, built himself, in his native town, the finest burgher's house in France, to see which René of Anjou — great-nephew of Jean of Berry — came especially to Bourges. Its walls were carved with quaint devices and images,[138] and, like Van Eyck's, were the charming little angels painted on its chapel vaults. No civic monument in the land excels it; it ranks as the best with Rouen's Palais de Justice and the Hôtel Cluny at Paris.

The same merchant-prince built in Bourges Cathedral a private chapel for his family, and beside it a rich Flamboyant Gothic sacristy. The Annunciation window in the chapel (1450) is held to be the best glass of its century, uniting the better drawing of the later day with a plain, firm, general design. The face of the Angel Gabriel has been said to be a portrait of Jacques Cœur. St. James is represented in pilgrim garb because of the fame of his shrine at Santiago Compostela. It is thought that Jacques Cœur donated the row of richly damasked windows in the west façade beneath Jean of Berry's big sheet of glass, made fifty years earlier. Colors have become richer and the figures show a tendency to escape from the rigid attitude of statues, but not yet has absolute congruity between the hues been achieved.

Jacques Cœur was not to be buried in the chapel he had prepared. He served the same master who had let the Maid of Orleans perish at Rouen without striking a blow to save her. With money provided by the merchant-banker of Bourges, Charles VII had reconquered Normandy, but he let the estate of his faithful servant

[137] The happy chance of travel led the writer, in May of 1914, to the ceremony of the unveiling of a statue of Jeanne d'Arc in the cathedral of this city, that has not known invasion — the military arsenal of France. As the preaching bishop exhorted modern France to remake her soul else she would perish, over that spellbound congregation seemed to pass a premonition of portentous events looming ahead. Within three months the World War opened, *forte et aspre guerre*, as they said in Jeanne's day, war the chastiser, war the purifier: "*Il y a des guerres qui avilissent les nations, et les avilissent pour des siècles; d'autres les exaltent, les perfectionnent de toutes manières*," wrote Joseph de Maistre.

[138] Carved on Jacques Cœur's house in Bourges are mottoes such as, "*A vaillans cœurs rien impossible*," or "*Dire, faire, taire, de ma joie*," or "*En bouche close, n'entre mousche*." Vallet de Viriville, *Jacques Cœur*; Pierre Clément, *Jacques Cœur et Charles VII*.

be rapaciously confiscated without a trial, and left him to languish in prison for two years before being banished from the kingdom by the mockery of a law process. Jacques Cœur died in exile in 1461, but his good name was exonerated, and his son Jean, archbishop of Bourges, was buried in the cathedral's choir. The merchant-prince's chapel passed with his mansion into the hands of the Laubespine family, whose kneeling statues now adorn it.

With the XVI century there opened another golden period of the vitrine art in Bourges. A local master, Jean Lecuyer, won fame. He made the Tullier window (1532) in the tenth bay (south) of the cathedral. The donor, Canon Tullier, and his father, mother, and various ecclesiastic relatives, are being presented by their patron saints to a distinguished-looking Madonna. The architectural background shows what headway the foreign Renaissance had made in France, though the chief figures are still true to French traditions. The colors are faultlessly balanced and certain exquisite half-tones are noticeable. In the upper panels, in a fair blue sky, are entrancing little angels giving a celestial concert, fiddling, beating a drum, singing with all their hearts, for this is the shrine built by St. William, who knew how to be holy and merry as well.

The Tullier light has been called the loveliest of XVI-century windows. And yet no one can deny that enamel painting on glass was a deterioration of the art. The old masters had followed a sounder tradition when they subordinated their windows to their architecture, making them an integral part of it, and not merely isolated painted pictures. Jean Lecuyer also composed the window (1518) relating the lives of St. Stephen and St. Laurence in the cathedral's nave (south side), and several brilliant lights in St. Bonnat's church. Even the XVII century produced interesting work at Bourges; in the Martigny chapel of the cathedral (north side of nave) the portrait of the donor is as realistic as a miniature.

THE CATHEDRAL OF BEAUVAIS[139]

C'est alors que se constitue cette merveilleuse discipline, vrai fondement de la culture intellectuelle et de la science, qu'est la discipline scholastique.... Toute la connaissance est tournée vers la science de l'être, vers la métaphysique, plus haut encore vers la théologie; plus haut encore, vers théologie vécue, vers la contemplation.

[139] *Congrès Archéologique*, 1905, "Beauvais," Chanoine Barsaux; P. Dubois, *La cathédrale de Beauvais* (Collection, Petites Monographies), (Paris, H. Laurens, 1911); Abbé P. C. Barraud, "Beauvais et ses monuments," in *Bulletin Monumental*, vol. 27, *passim*. He gives studies on the Le Prince and other windows in the cathedral and St. Étienne, in *Mémoires de la Soc. Académique de l'Oise*, 1851-53, vol. 1, p. 225; vol. 2, p. 537; vol. 3, pp. 150, 277; Louise Pillion, on St. Étienne's glass, in *Revue de l'art chrétien*, 1910, p. 367; Eug. J. Woillez, *Archéologie des monuments religieux de l'ancien Beauvoisis pendant la métamorphose romane* (Paris, 1839-49), folio; Graves, *Notice archéologique sur le département de l'Oise* (Beauvais, 1856); Gustave Desgardins, *Histoire de la cathédrale de Beauvais* (1875); Abbé L. Pihan, *Beauvais, sa cathédrale, ses monuments* (1905); *ibid., Esquisse descriptive des monuments historiques dans l'Oise*; see Gonse and Palustre on the portals of the cathedral; Monseigneur Barbier de Montault, "Iconographie des Sibylles," in *Rev. de l'art chrétiens*, 1874.

—JACQUES MARITAIN.

The cathedral of Beauvais derived directly from Amiens, and no expression of the Gothic principle was ever carried farther. It consists of a mammoth choir and transept. As the height of the edifice is three times its width, the nave which now is lacking would need to have been of enormous length. Instead of that much-needed nave, there nestles under the truncated west end a modest little Carolingian edifice called the *Basse-Œuvre*, built by the fortieth bishop of Beauvais, Hervé (987-998). The small cubic stones and occasional courses of brick tell of the antiquity of this, the best-preserved monument in France, dating before the year 1000.[140] Most of the Romanesque churches of the Oise copied it. Scarcely, however, had the Ile-de-France Picard Romanesque school developed than the privileged region gave birth to the national art.

In 1227 Beauvais planned a new cathedral, spurred on thereto by the magnificent nave rising in neighboring Amiens. But the works were not started till 1247, for the bishop, more a feudal baron than a pastor, was for a time entirely engrossed in mercenary wars in Italy and in quarreling with Blanche of Castile, the queen-regent. Finally Bishop Milon began his cathedral in Beauvais on a scale beyond the resources of the diocese. Despite his own and the chapter's generous donations, and the exemption of workmen and all building material from taxes, the choir was not finished till 1272, two years after the choir of Cologne. Scarcely was it done when, in 1284, its upper vaulting fell; a few years earlier a partial collapse had occurred. To remedy the disaster new piers had to be inserted between the old ones, which explains the sharp-pointed arches of the pier arcade. Only in the ambulatory, which was untouched by the falling masonry, is the original vaulting to be found. The required addition of flying buttresses was no improvement to the symmetry of the exterior. Instead of being able to proceed to the erection of a nave, forty years were wasted in repairs.

Then came the calamities of the Hundred Years' War when building activities flagged all over France. Never again were profiles to be virile. The apogee hour of Gothic was forever past. With English, Burgundian, and French troops roving the country, Beauvais was kept on the alert. In 1429, the citizens, roused by Jeanne d'Arc's success at Orléans, expelled their bishop, who was in sympathy with the foe, and was none other than the unworthy Pierre Cauchon, soon to sit as miscreant judge at the Maid's trial in Rouen. Two years after Jeanne had been burned, Beauvais was besieged by English troops, and so gallant was the behavior of the women of the city, notably Jeanne Hachette, that forever after was accorded to

[140] Carolingian work aboveground is rare; besides this *Basse-Œuvre* at Beauvais, there is St. Philibert de Grandlieu (Loire-Inférieure), part of the small church under the flank of Jumièges' ruined abbatial, portions of St. Jouin-de-Marnes (Deux-Sèvres), and vestiges in the walls of La Couture at Le Mans. There are Carolingian crypts at St. Quentin, Amiens, Chartres, Orléans, Auxerre, Flavigny. More exceptional still are Merovingian remains, such as the crypt of Jouarre, the small tri-lobed church of St. Laurent at Grenoble, the crypt of St. Léger at St. Maixent (Deux-Sèvres), a crypt at Lyons, in St. Martin d'Ainay, and apsidal chapels in St. Jean's baptistry at Poitiers. A list of the Romanesque monuments of the Ile-de-France and bordering districts is to be found in Arthur Kingsley Porter's *Medieval Architecture*, 1909, vol. 2, pp. 13-49.

them the right to march in the place of honor in all processions, directly behind the clergy. When the Duke of Burgundy, England's ally, besieged the city in 1472 he burned the episcopal palace, to which the two sturdy towers near the *Basse-Œuvre* originally belonged. Once more the women of Beauvais fought side by side with the men, while the children and the aged gathered in the cathedrals to supplicate Heaven for protection.

No city in the land had better cause to rejoice over peace and the invader's expulsion than Beauvais. And nowhere did Flamboyant Gothic take on nobler expression than in the stately transept now added to the cathedral, a masterpiece worthy to be joined to the giant choir. On its north front worked Martin Chambiges, who gave to Troyes and Sens their admirable façades. Over-ornamentation was a pitfall for the late-Gothic masters, but not for Chambiges, who kept Beauvais' strong lines of construction unobliterated by lavish detail.

Flamboyant Gothic was essentially a decorative art. Therein only did it differ from preceding schools, for it developed no new principles of construction. Because of the flamelike undulations of its window tracery, the Norman archæologist, M. de Caumont, who had brought into use the name Romanesque, invented the equally useful term Flamboyant.[141] Capricious, overladen, disturbingly restless, this final phase of the national art may often be (it has been called more terrestrial than celestial), it was inclined to exhibit its technical dexterity; but none the less it was keenly alive and a vast improvement on the over-formalized geometric Rayonnant Gothic to which it succeeded. In both, the profiles were prismatic, fluid, and weak. Discipline which made for robustness was forever lost.

A century before the characteristics of Flamboyant art developed in France, they were in use in England, and there called Curvilinear or Decorated Gothic. Window mullions undulated, arches were crowned with reversed curves and sculptured finials, secondary, connecting ribs were added to the vaulting, bases were elongated, there were interpenetrating molds, hanging keystones, piers without capitals, and such new models for foliate sculpture as the deeply indented leaves of parsley and curly cabbage. When capitals were given up, the ribs died away weakly in the piers. The Gothic of England had changed to its cold Perpendicular phase by the time that the architects across the Channel adopted the features called Flamboyant in France.

---

[141] Among the Flamboyant monuments of France are St. Wulfran's frontispiece at Abbeville, begun in 1481, overcharged with ornament but with portals of great beauty; St. Riquier near by, also overcharged; the churches of Rue and Mézières; façades of cathedrals at Sens, Senlis, Auxerre, Troyes, Tours, and Limoges; Vendôme's frontispiece, and Albi's porch; towers at Bordeaux, Rodez, Saintes, Chartres, Auxerre, Bourges, Rouen, and many other cities in Normandy; the cathedrals of Toul and Metz; St. Maurice at Lille, a well-restrained Flamboyant monument; the magnificent church of St. Nicholas-du-Port near Nancy; the choir of Moulins; St. Antoine at Compiègne and a number of civic halls such as Compiègne's and St. Quentin's. The beautiful Flamboyant Gothic church at Péronne (1509-25) has been wiped out in the World War. Artois and Flanders were especially rich in late-Gothic edifices. Normandy was a Mecca of Flamboyant work—from Rouen, to that gem of the final phase, the choir of Mont Saint-Michel. Monseigneur Dehaisnes, *Histoire de l'art dans la Flandre, l'Artois et le Hainaut* (Lille, 1886), 3 vols.

M. Camille Enlart has developed the idea that the last phase of the national architecture was a product of the English occupation during the Hundred Years' War, that from elements of decoration introduced by England, the French composed a style which differed somewhat only from that in vogue across the Channel from 1300 to 1360. In France, flowing tracery and ogee arches were not used before 1375. France need feel no diminution of her claim of leadership in Gothic architecture because she adopted, for her XV-century traits, certain decorative details developed first by others, since the Gothic of England was originally of French derivation.

The theory of an English origin for French Flamboyancy is contested by M. Anthyme Saint-Paul, who thought that from the same elements of XIII-century Gothic one country developed its own Curvilinear style and the other its own, Flamboyant Gothic.[142] M. de Lasteyrie agreed with the thesis that there is a French origin for French late-Gothic manifestations. That Flamboyant art is in part indigenous and partly of foreign derivation is probably nearest the truth. Certainly sporadic cases of florid features appeared in French art during the XIII and XIV centuries, but it is clear that in various places long held by the English there appeared the first or the fullest expression of late-Gothic art.

Before the Flamboyant Gothic transept of Beauvais was finished, the foreign Renaissance had arrived in France. And it showed here in the richly sculptured doors. The sibyls, all ten of whom are represented, are, as pagans, kept outside the church. With skilled gradation the carving grows deeper and bolder toward the top of the doors, farthest away from the eye. Jean Le Pot carved the southern doors in faultless taste. He was a glassmaker as well, and in St. Étienne's church are his windows beside those of his father-in-law, Engrand Le Prince, who, with his sons Jean and Nicholas, made the north and south rose windows of the cathedral and its splendid Peter and Paul window. Their tree of Jesse, in St. Étienne's choir, is considered a masterpiece of color and design. To-day a Le Prince window in any French city is a matter of civic pride.

The old saying ran: "The choir of Beauvais, the nave of Amiens, the portals of Rheims, the towers of Chartres" make the most beautiful cathedral in the world. One hundred and fifty feet high curve the upper vaults of Beauvais choir. Beneath them could be set the belfries of Notre Dame of Paris. As at Bourges, the lofty aisle possesses its own triforium and clearstory, but here the clearstory of the central choir has not been dwarfed as a result of the stupendous pier arcades. Beauvais dared to make its upper windows eighty feet high. Think what its interior would be had it retained the original stained glass! Its towering choir windows would scintillate like those of Sainte-Chapelle, since it was the Paris school that supplied XIII-century Beauvais.

---

[142] André Michel, éd., *Histoire de l'Art*, vol. 3, 1ère partie, "Le style flamboyant," Camille Enlart (Paris, A. Colin), 1914, 10 vols.; Camille Enlart, "Origine anglaise du style flamboyant," in *Bulletin Monumental*, 1886, 1906, p. 38; A. Saint-Paul, "L'architecture religieuse en France pendant la Guerre de Cent Ans," in *Bulletin Monumental*, 1908, p. 5; *ibid., Les origines du gothique flamboyant en France* (Caen, 1907); Arthur Kingsley Porter, *Medieval Architecture*, vol. 2 (New York and London, 1907), 2 vols.

Such a sweep of fragile glass was possible because the play of thrusts and counterthrusts had been calculated to a certainty. Technically, Beauvais is the extreme expression of the Gothic theory. It perfected the pier by making it elliptical, widest where fell the greatest strain, north and south. It is said that its error lay in certain false bearings, that some of the intermediate buttresses were balanced half on air without direct ground supports. That may have been temerarious, since building material of perfect quality is required when chances are taken. Certainly Beauvais pushed to its rigid consequences the law of equilibrium, allowing no excess in the supporting members, but it was not a builder's folly.

M. de Lasteyrie has called its plan a *chef-d'œuvre* of lightness. Though the architect pushed his technique to the extreme limit of the law of thrust and counterthrust, he did not pass beyond the possible, and had he employed the hard, resistant stone of Burgundy the history of the cathedral church he built would not be a tale of disasters. What brought about the collapse of Beauvais' vaults was the use of inferior stone.

Sometimes one feels in the hardihood of this cathedral a trace of everweening pride, as if its certitude of excelling tended to virtuosity. The stupefying ascending lines, strong-willed and carried out with science, seem as much to vaunt the enterprise of their builder as pay homage to the Creator. Some of the lesser churches, that humbly and tentatively reached out toward perfection, make a deeper appeal than does stupendous Beauvais. Was man meant for the superlative on earth? And one remembers that Bishop Milon de Nanteuil was a proud man of the world, very unlike that true pastor of souls, Maurice de Sully, who with unpretentious diligence raised Notre Dame of Paris. Such criticisms would be silenced, perhaps, had Beauvais a nave from which could be viewed its overwhelming choir. Truncated as it now is, it is necessary to crane the neck in order to see its clearstory windows. So colossal a thing should be led up to gradually; it cries out insistently for its missing nave.

Fatality seemed always to pursue Beauvais. After terminating a noble Flamboyant transept, the ambitious citizens were lured into the scheme of a central tower, when a church of such height should have at its crossing merely a slender spire. Instead of proceeding to build a nave, they raised a lantern that lacked merely a few feet of the enormous height of St. Peter's dome in Rome. It was a day of tower building in France, and Beauvais, ever hopeful beyond its resources, thought to outvie all others. On feast days lights were hung in its spire's open stonework for the illumination of the entire countryside. For five years only the giant beacon stood. On Ascension Day of 1573, just after the congregation had left the church to walk in procession, the tower fell with an appalling noise, covering the whole town with dust. Only one bay of the nave has been built, its piers have disappearing moldings, amorphous profiles, and no capitals whatever. Beauvais stands a massive fragment, and there seems little chance that the truncated church will ever be completed.

THE CATHEDRAL OF TROYES[143]

With travail great, and little cargo fraught,
See how our world is laboring in pain;
So filled we are with love of evil gain
That no one thinks of doing what he ought,
But we all hustle in the Devil's train,
And only in his service toil and pray;
And God, who suffered for us agony,
We set behind, and treat him with disdain.
Hardy is he whom death doth not dismay.
The feeble mouse, against the winter's cold
Garners the nuts and grain within his cell,
While man goes groping, without sense to tell
Where to seek refuge against growing old....
The Devil doth in snares our life enfold.
Four hooks he has with torments baited well;
And first with Greed he casts a mighty spell,
And then, to fill his nets has Pride enrolled,
And Luxury steers the boat and fills the sail,
And Perfidy controls and sets the snare.
Thus the poor fish are brought to land.

—COUNT THIBAUT IV of Champagne.[144]

Beneath the present choir of Troyes Cathedral are Gallo-Roman walls, and a succession of edifices have stood on the same site. From the cathedral of the V century started the bishop, St. Loup, "the friend of God," when he went forth to check Attila the Hun, "God's scourge," and the barbarian was touched by spiritual fear and retired. That same good bishop of Troyes was the companion of St. Germain of Auxerre, on the notable journey north, when they blessed the gentle child Geneviève in a village near Paris, marking her as a vessel of election.

Probably the cathedral immediately preceding the present one was in large part early-Gothic. Fire wiped it out, in 1188, and preparations for a new basilica were started by the energetic Bishop Garnier de Trainel, who went on the Fourth

[143] *Congrès Archéologique*, 1902; V. C. de Courcel, *La cathédrale de Troyes*, (1910); L. Morel-Payen, *Troyes et Provins* (Collection, Villes d'art célèbres), (Paris, H. Laurens, 1910); F. Arnaud, *Description historique de l'église cathédrale de Troyes*; J. B. Coffinet, "Les peintres-verriers de Troyes," in *Annales Archéologiques*, vol. 18, pp. 125, 212; A. J. de H. Bushnell, *Storied Windows*, chapters 32 and 33, on Troyes (New York, Macmillan Company, 1914); Ch. Fichot, *Statistique monumentale du département de l'Aube*, vol. 1, *Arrondissement de Troyes* (Troyes, 1884), 4to; R. Koechlin and J.M. de Vasselot, *La sculpture à Troyes et dans la Champagne méridionale au XVIe siècle* (Paris, A. Colin, 1900); Raymond Koechlin, "La sculpture du XIVe et du XVe siècle dans la région de Troyes," in *Congrès Archéologique*, 1908; Paul Vitry, *Michel Colombe et la sculpture française de son temps* (Paris, 1901); Louis Gonse, *La sculpture française depuis le XIVe siècle* (Paris, Quantin, 1895), folio; D'Arbois de Jubainville, *Histoire des ducs et des comtes de Champagne*, 1859, 7 vols.; Bontier, *Histoire de Troyes et de la Champagne méridionale* (Troyes, 1880), 4 vols.; Amédée Aufauvre, *Troyes et ses environs*.

[144] Translation from XIII-century French by Henry Adams.

Crusade, and was among those, says Villehardouin, who scaled the walls of captured Constantinople along with his friend Nivelon, the bishop-builder of Soissons.

The first stone of the new cathedral at Troyes was laid in 1206 by Bishop Hervé (1206-23), an able man who had been advanced by the observant prelate of Paris, Eudes de Sully. For almost twenty years Bishop Hervé worked on the choir, considered one of the best chevets in France. During his episcopate Troyes was a brilliant center of European trade and culture. Blanche of Castile and young Louis IX passed some time in the city when Thibaut IV the Singer, related to the royal line, was attacked by the clique of rebellious barons who plotted against the boy king. There had been considerable romancing about the volatile, inconstant Thibaut's admiration for Queen Blanche, who was a married woman before he was born. His own mother, Blanche of Navarre, another of the able women rulers of that day, gave generously to the new cathedral of her capital city.

In 1228 a storm damaged the rising structure, necessitating years of tiresome repairs. Pope Urban IV, as a native son of Troyes, contributed. During the last forty years of the XIII century the transept was building. It showed traces of English feeling derived perhaps from Edmund Plantagenet, a son of the builder of Westminster Abbey, who had married the dowager Countess of Champagne. His ward Jeanne, Thibaut the Singer's granddaughter, inherited the countship of Champagne, the kingdom of Navarre, and by marriage became the queen of France.

Slowly during the XIV and XV centuries, one bay of the nave was added to another; the changes from the precise lines of Rayonnant tracery to the undulating mullions of the Flamboyant day are easy to follow. The long delays were caused by lack of funds and the repeated need for consolidating the parts already built. The soil on which the church stood was unsuitable, and from the first, security was jeopardized by using the soft, native stone in those parts of the edifice which were out of sight, in order to economize on the firm stone imported from Burgundy.

Several times during the difficulties of reconstruction, the cathedral chapter turned for advice to noted masters—to Raymond du Temple, Charles V's architect, and to André de Dammartin, patronized by the king's brothers of Berry and Burgundy. Work ceased altogether during the English occupancy.

Then in 1429 the city opened its gates to Charles VII on his way to be crowned at Rheims. Jeanne d'Arc, during her trial in Rouen, told of an incident of their entry into Troyes. Some of the townspeople were fearful lest the heroine of Orleans came of the devil, so they had a holy preacher march out to exorcise her. Scattering holy water and making repeated signs of the Cross, Brother Richard approached the Maid. "Draw near without uneasiness," Jeanne assured him, in her pleasant manner. "I won't fly away."

The city by its reception of the king evinced eagerness to wipe out the infamy of the Treaty of Troyes, signed here in 1420 by Queen Isabeau of Bavaria, wherein she repudiated her son Charles VII and gave France over to the foreign invader. The people's renewed hope and self-respect expressed itself in some of the most lovely Flamboyant foliage ever chiseled—the deeply undercut leafage on the gable of the north portal (1462-68).

Work on the cathedral was taken up with energy after Jeanne, carrying her standard, had hallowed the streets of Troyes. As the XV century closed, the nave's radiant late-Gothic windows were installed. They are of the *Biblia pauperum* type, and are surprisingly like big translucent woodcuts. They tell the story of Daniel, Tobias, Joseph and his brethren, Job—a window especially to be noticed—some parables, too, and edifying legends. The scenes are set quite as they appeared in the mystery plays, the costumes being not of Syria, but of the very stuffs and damasks bought in their own international fairs. The same masters of Troyes, Verrat, Godon, Lyénin, Macadré, who signed a rose window of Sens transept, put their signatures here.

Bible stories such as these suit the layman's part of a church, for they serve to hold the attention of the average man. In the choir of Troyes are thirteen large windows of an earlier day, profounder in color and more spiritual in suggestion. They are like a jeweled cloistral screen around the Holy of Holies. In the upper central windows are the Passion scenes, and on either side rise tier on tier of martyrs who witnessed to the Faith—bishops, abbots, and a few important personages, such as Pope Innocent III, Bishop Hervé, the builder, and the archbishop of Sens, the learned Pierre de Corbeil. On one side of the choir Henry I, emperor of Constantinople, of the house of Champagne, is pictured, and Philippe-Auguste, suzerain of Champagne. And opposite in the fourth window are donjons and fleurs-delys showing that the queen-regent, Blanche of Castile, was generous here as elsewhere.

The upper choir windows of Troyes allowed more light to pass than had their immediate predecessors, the lancets of Chartres. Their colors were clear and bright; only such stone mullions were used as were absolutely required for the support of the glass. The eight lateral windows of the upper choir belong to the XIII century, the five at the eastern curve to the XIV century. In the lower choir are various ancient windows, liberally restored, the Tree of Jesse, of Byzantine character, being the best. Two hundred years later another Tree of Jesse was made by Lyénin,[145] for the clearstory of the nave. It gave Christian folk a feeling of pride to record the Lord's high ancestry according to Isaias and the Acts. This cathedral of Troyes was one of the first to glaze its triforium, even before St. Denis' abbatial. The present triforium lights are, in most part, modern.

By 1504 the clearstory windows of the nave were all in place. Among their donors was represented a mayor of Troyes with all his family. The golden-hued west rose was put up in 1546. And even into the XVII century the vitrine art of this exceptional city maintained its high traditions of five hundred years. In 1625 Linard Gontier made the *Pressoir* window, the swan-song of good Renaissance glass. There is a translucent picture of Our Lady in the nave's south aisle, with stars leaded into holes that were cut out of an entire plate of glass; any apprentice who could perform that difficult feat of glazing was promoted to be a master craftsman.[146]

[145] Generation after generation, the Lyénin, Macadré, Verrat, and Gontier families produced noted artists. Assier, *Les arts dans l'ancienne capitale de la Champagne.*

[146] The same feat can be seen in St. Nizier at Troyes, rebuilt in 1528 and literally filled

For the building of the cathedral's west front, the chapter, in 1506, called on the noted late-Gothic master, Martin Chambiges, who had made his reputation with transept façades at Beauvais and Sens. Together with other artists, his son, Pierre (who won fame with Senlis' transept façade, and who, in 1539, began the château of St. Germain-en-Laye), carried on Troyes' frontispiece during fifty years, so that its imagery—badly damaged by the Revolution—shows the ermine of Anne of Brittany, the porcupine of Louis XII, and the salamander of Francis I. Troyes, with its record of four hundred years, was, of all the cathedrals of France, the longest in building.

In spite of its double aisles, its wide transept, its noble, deep choir, and its astounding wealth of storied windows, it is clear when standing before the Flamboyant Gothic front of this chief church of Champagne's capital, that it is a cathedral of secondary rank. The flaw here is one of proportion. With such width—and this is the widest cathedral in France—the church should be thirty feet higher. However, no traveler with harmony in his soul thinks of technical criticism once he steps across the threshold and walks beneath the joyous terrestrial windows of the nave and the seraphic lights of the sanctuary.

ST. URBAIN AND OTHER CHURCHES AT TROYES[147]

Madame, je vous le demande,
Pensez-vous ne soit péché
D'occire son vrai amant?
Oïl voir; bien le sachiez.
S'il vous plaît ne m'occiez;
Car, je vous le dis vraiment,
Quoique l'amour soit tourment,
Si vous m'aimez mieux vivant.

with XVI-century glass. Its best window is in the transept (1552), and shows the beasts of heresy trampled upon, for that day was nothing if not controversial. In a central window of the choir, the Descent of the Holy Ghost, the artist made the hands of a figure in one panel appear in the neighboring panel, regardless of the stone mullions. In 1901 an anarchist bomb exploded in St. Nizier, and in 1910 a terrible storm wrecked more of its windows. The church possesses a *Saint Sépulcre* and a *Christ de Pité* in which the Gothic spirit lingers. Its reredos, now in the Museum, was from the Juliot *atelier*. Her international fairs early accustomed Troyes to foreign influences. Flemish realism had fortified her sculptors and vitrine artists, and during the first third of the XVI century (when the trade of the city tripled itself) the new Italian ideas found favor. For a generation the just and loyal measure of Champagne's own Gothic tradition held the leadership, but finally the Italian Renaissance conquered. When abstract types were substituted for types precisely observed, imagery became cold, declamatory, and pretentious. In several of the churches of Troyes will be found the Education of the Virgin by her mother, St. Anne, a theme for which this city had a partiality.

[147] Abbé O. F. Jossier, *Monographie des vitraux de St. Urbain de Troyes* (Troyes, 1912); E. Lefèvre-Pontalis, "Jean Langlois, architecte de St. Urbain de Troyes," in *Bulletin Monumental*, 1904, vol. 64, p. 93; Albert Barbeau, *St. Urbain de Troyes* (Troyes, Dufour-Bonquot, 1891), 8vo; Viollet-le-Duc, *Dictionnaire de l'architecture*, vol. 4, pp. 182-192; Abbé Lahore, *L'église Saint-Urbain* (1891).

Je n'en serai point fâché.

—Thibaut IV of Champagne, in lighter mood.

St. Urbain's famous collegiate church, a forerunner of XIV-century Rayonnant Gothic, was founded by a son of Troyes, who sat in Peter's chair, Urban IV. He tells us that "in the desire that the memory of this our name might remain forever in the city of Troyes even after the dissolution of our body," he began, in 1262, a church on the site where his father's shop had stood, choosing for its tutelary the saint-pope, Urban, who had succored the early martyrs in Rome. His father was a prosperous shoemaker in the day when tradesmen gave princely gifts to their parish churches. Urban IV himself had been a choir boy in Troyes Cathedral.

He died before his church was finished, but his nephew, Cardinal Pantaleone Ancher, continued the edifice, which was completed in 1276. Urban's successor, Clement IV, also a Frenchman, patronized the new works at Troyes. While the choir and transept were done by one generation, many a century was to pass before the westernmost bay and façade were finished.

St. Urbain at Troyes (1264-1276)

In archæological circles St. Urbain is noted, Viollet-le-Duc being the first to discuss its ingenuity. As construction it is a small masterpiece, a model of elasticity, perhaps the lightest and most fragile of all Gothic edifices. To an economy in stone we owe this structural feat. Were the principle of equilibrium pushed a step farther, metal, not stone, would be required. Ground supports have been lessened, and flying buttresses attenuated to the last limit. Despite its science, St. Urbain is not doctrinaire, but immaterial and seductive. On first entering it Montalembert exclaimed, *"Quelle délicieuse église!"*

The architect, Jean Langlois, here created the most elegant form of Rayonnant window tracery. At his porch appears the first French arch of double curvature, the earliest interpenetration of archivolts. We know his name because in 1267 a papal bull summoned him to account for sums advanced on the edifice, and Jean was not forthcoming, because he had disappeared in the East, crusading. The chief church at Famagusta, in Cyprus, begun in 1300—the only completed French-Gothic cathedral of the XIV century—shows such analogies with St. Urbain at Troyes that apparently Langlois' architectural influence had spread in the Orient.

M. Lefèvre-Pontalis has called Troyes' lantern church inundated with light one of the most original monuments of the Middle Ages. Ten feet above the ground its walls change to opalescent glass. No grisaille is more exquisitely decorated with natural foliage outlines; set in the expanses of the opal-tinted white glass are colored medallions of extreme beauty. The lower row of lights around the choir are of this character. Above them, and almost a part of them, are the choir's upper windows—big prophets and patriarchs with the Crucifixion in the center—transition windows between legend-medallion glass, and the XIV century's single figures in a vitrine architectural frame. The arms of France, Champagne, and Navarre appear in the borders of the choir windows.

The transeptal chapel to the north of the choir shows in its quatrefoils some interesting heads of men, women, and children. From the windows of the south transeptal chapel some panels were stolen, but St. Urbain's curé, Abbé Jossier, a learned enthusiast, was able, by sending photographs all over France, to trace his lost panels in a private collection, and it is to be hoped they may be returned.

In his short pontificate, 1262-64, Urban IV, besides creating this enduring memorial, instituted the feast of Corpus Christi. He requested a liturgy for his new feast from St. Thomas Aquinas, who composed the *Pange lingua gloriosi*, the last stanzas of which are sung daily throughout the Christian world, the familiar *Tantum ergo*. To Aquinas is ascribed the *Verbum supernum prodiens* hymn whose ending is the lovely *O Salutaris Hostia*. Doubt and heresy have always been instrumental in clarifying doctrine and in enriching the liturgy and art. So in a later day was made, in reaction against the XVI-century desecration of the Eucharist, such windows as the Wine Press of Troyes and that of Conches.

In 1906, soon after St. Urbain's church had celebrated the completion of its western portal, it became the scene of a conscientious objection on the part of its parishioners, who protested against the taking of an inventory, they deeming it an unlawful interference with their private affairs. They sat in their church till the police broke in the doors; even then they continued to sing canticles, and were expelled only by having a hose turned on them. Six centuries earlier, St. Urbain's had been the scene, on the completion of its choir, of a suffragette-like demonstration by a community of nuns, who claimed part of the land on which the church stood. They smashed various things on the premises, and, it is whispered, even slapped a high dignitary's face. Apparently St. Urbain's is destined to pass into history under various aspects.

For four hundred years the ancient capital of Champagne was an active center of the stained-glass industry. Overpowering is the wealth of storied windows to be found in its churches, the majority being of the Flamboyant-Renaissance day. In the suburbs, and farther afield in the hamlets of Champagne, there is the same prodigal display of colored windows and interesting statues.[148] From father to son, from generation to generation, was passed on the art skill of this ancient city on the highway of international trade.

In Troyes there were so many churches that the old saying ran: "You arrived from Troyes? And what are they doing there?" "*On y sonne.*" Next to St. Urbain's, for its wealth of art treasures, comes the Madeleine church built about 1175, and reconstructed during the Flamboyant enthusiasm when this city readorned almost every shrine it possessed. Contemporary with its noted *jubé*, or rood screen (1508-17), is the statue of St. Martha, one of the gems of French sculpture, entirely of the national school, unaffected work as ample and robust as the best period of the XIII century. St. Martha is represented, in this church of Troyes dedicated to her sister, with the holy water by which she exorcised the legendary Tarasque of Tarascon. She was the patroness of housekeepers, and it is said that the servant maids of Troyes presented to their church this memorial of the plastic genius of Champagne.[149]

---

[148] Within walking distance of Troyes are Ste. Maure, with a Jesse tree by Linard Gontier; Les Noës, with good sculpture and a Jesse-tree window of 1521; St. André-lès-Troyes, with a lovely St. Catherine statue; St. Parre-les-Tertres, with a Vision of Augustus in *camaïeu* like a magnificent enamel on white glass, and another grisaille-like Vision of Augustus at St. Léger-lès-Troyes (1558); Chapelle St. Luc, with a triptych on wood, sculpture of the Three Maries, and good glass; Torvilliers, Pont-Ste.-Marie, and Montgueux, with other *objets d'art*. Eight miles away, at Verrières, is the best portal of the region and more late-Gothic glass. There are storied windows at St. Loup, St. Ponanges, Rosnay, Brienne, Rouilly (with a good Virgin image), Pouvres, Chavanges, Bar-sur-Seine, Bar-sur-Aube (with a statue of St. Barbara), Mussy-sur-Seine, Montier-en-Der, Arcis-sur-Aube, and Ceffonds, whose windows were the gift of Étienne Chévalier (1528). Some thirty miles away lies St. Florentin (six miles from Pontigny), where are twenty splendid Renaissance lights, among them a Creation window (1525), with God the Father wearing the tiara, one of 1528 telling St. Nicolas' life in quatrains describing each scene, and a 1529 window devoted to the Apocalypse. Between Troyes and St. Florentin lies Ervy, where is a Crucifixion window (1570), showing the Saviour nailed to a Tree of Knowledge Cross with apples and leaves on its top, and Adam and Eve standing below. There are also the noted windows of the Sibyls (1515), representing twelve instead of ten prophetesses, each accompanied by the event of the New Law which she is said to have foretold, and the window called the Triumph of Petrarch (1502).

[149] Of the same appealing type as St. Martha at Troyes are the Virgin and Madeleine of the Holy Sepulcher group at Villeneuve l'Archevêque (Yonne), where are also some beau-

Champagne's special aptitude for sculpture appeared in the XIII-century gargoyles of St. Urbain's church, each of which was almost a complete figure. Later her imagery grew mannered for a few generations, with the Madonna's face of a formal type, and an exaggerated throwing out of the hip. The advent of Flemish realism, through the Franco-Flamand school at Dijon, renewed the vigor of French idealism, and before the XV century closed a truly French Renaissance had set in, retaining the equipoise of the old school and quite free of Italian classicism.

Eventually the imported standards checked that renewed national movement. It was not the big men of Italy's revival who came to Champagne, but secondary artists whose work was often pretentious or coldly abstract. From 1540, under the leadership of the Italian, Domenico Rinnuccini, called Florentino, the foreign Renaissance prevailed at Troyes. In the church of the Madeleine, besides its *jubé* and St. Martha statue, is some of the best XVI-century glass. A window of 1506 tells the life of St. Eloi, the goldsmith-bishop of Noyon; a window dated 1517 is devoted to St. Louis; Jean Macadré I made a Jesse tree; and there is the celebrated Creation in which God the Father wears the papal tiara, significant of the reaction that followed Luther's attacks on Rome. There are, also, two good XV-century windows, the Lord's Passion and the Magdalene's story.

So vast is the accumulation of treasures in the sanctuaries of Troyes that one can indicate merely a few of them. In St. Jean's church—Flamboyant Gothic mainly, with a XII-century tower and a XIV-century nave—is a Visitation (1520) by Nicolas Haslin, a meeting of two pleasant dames of Troyes, wearing robes of Burgundian fullness, a group in which there appears a first evidence of transalpine influence. The reredos, from the Juliot studio, that led in the transition from French Gothic art to the neo-classic standards, has conventional images somewhat overgestured. In the flat eastern wall of St. Jean is a *maîtresse vitre* (1630) by the Gontier brothers, delicate in hue, yet radiant, with half tones such as mauve, salmon pink, soft grays, pomegranate, celadine green. Eagerly the Renaissance masters seized on the new invention of *verre double*, which allowed them a fuller palate. Their over-use of opaque enamel-painting on glass led to the deterioration of the vitrine art, for the picture-painter soon swamped the glazier and draftsman who had worked in subordination to the architect.

In the church of St. Pantaléon, where Lyénin II worked, the windows are in one or two tones, gray-brown with silver-stain yellow and flesh color, a style better suited to domestic interiors or to civic halls than to churches. The church boasts a statue of St. James and a Charité by Domenico Florentino, and a St. Crespin group by a son of Troyes, François Gentil, influenced by the Italian. To Gentil is attributed the Christ at the column and the Christ bearing the Cross in the church of St. Nicolas, where are also images of St. Anne and St. Joachim from the Juliot studio, a St. Bonaventure from the same source whence emanated the adorable statue of St. Martha, and more of the grisaille picture-glass. In St. Martin-ès-Vignes the

---

tiful portal images of the XIII century. M. Ch. Fichot has brought forward testimony that would indicate the image called St. Martha in the church of the Madeleine is really one of St. Mary Magdelene herself. However, the majority of those who have written on the sculpture of Champagne continue to call it a St. Martha.

window of St. Anne (1623) is attributed to Linard Gontier; in Ste. Sabine are some painted wood panels, and a carved keystone of great beauty; in the hall of the library of Troyes are thirty panels by Linard Gontier, made in commemoration of Henry IV's visit in 1598.

CHÂLONS CATHEDRAL[150]

It so happens that in most of our communes the church remains the only witness of the olden times and of departed generations. It thus becomes a symbol, legible for the humblest, of the duration of our race, of the persistence, through the dead, of a special group of French families on a special corner of French soil. The village church gives the lesson of lineage, of the solidarity of efforts, of the communion of men.

—EDMOND BLANQUERON, Inspecteur de l'Académie de la Haute-Marne, in the crusade to save the churches of Champagne, notably Vignory, one of the oldest in France (c. 1050).

The cathedral of Troyes and the church of St. Urbain belong to the Champagne school of Gothic, to which we have devoted no separate chapter because some of its monuments, such as St. Remi at Rheims and Notre Dame at Châlons, we grouped with the Primary Gothic churches, and the cathedral of Rheims with the Great Cathedrals, classifications used solely for greater clarity.

From its inception, the Gothic of Champagne kept pace with the Ile-de-France Picard school, and in certain characteristics even took the lead of its neighbor. Gerson, Racine, La Fontaine, Gaston Paris, are among the sons of this province whose Gothic art, formulated centuries before them, displays qualities which embody aspiration, sublimity, sanity always and just measure, a singular ease and grace, patience, and science.

From Champagne came the gracious arrangement of planting slender columns and stilted arches at the entrance to radiating chapels. Champagne was the first to use the pier composed of twin columns, first to employ a passageway round the church at the level of the aisle windows, and to place lancets side by side in each bay for the better lighting of the edifice. The region was conservative in clinging to certain Romanesque traits, such as apsidal chapels projecting from the eastern

---

[150] *Congrès Archéologique*, 1855, 1875, and 1911, p. 447, the cathedral of Châlons; p. 473, Notre-Dame-en-Vaux; p. 496, St. Alpin; p. 512, Notre-Dame-de-l'Épine; E. Lefèvre-Pontalis, "L'architecture dans la Champagne méridionale au XIIIe et au XVIe siècle," in *Congrès Archéologique*, 1902, p. 273; *ibid.*, "Les caractères distinctifs des écoles gothiques de la Champagne et de la Bourgogne," in *Congrès Archéologique*, 1907, p. 546; Louis Demaison, *Les églises de Châlons-sur-Marne* (Caen, 1913); E. de Barthélemy, *Diocèse ancien de Châlons-sur-Marne. Histoire et monuments* (Paris, 1861), 2 vols.; E. Hurault, *La cathédrale de Châlons-sur-Marne et sa clergé au XIIIe siècle*; A. J. de H. Bushnell, *Storied Windows*, chapter 34, on the windows of Châlons (New York, Macmillan Company, 1914); Abbé E. Musset, *Notre Dame-de-l'Épine près Châlons-sur-Marne. La légende, l'histoire, le monument et le pèlerinage* (Paris, Champion, 1902); Chanoine Marsaux, "La prédiction de la sibylle et la vision d'Auguste," in *Bulletin Monumental*, 1908, p. 235.

wall of the transept. It employed, as did Normandy and Burgundy, a circulation passage under the clearstory windows. Champagne's influence spread far afield to Sens, Auxerre, St. Quentin, St. Denis, Metz, Toul, Ipres, Tournai, Avila, León, and York.[151]

Lest these pages should become overloaded, we can merely touch on the beautiful Champagne cathedral of Châlons-sur-Marne, an old city which is another treasure house of colored glass. The most interesting windows are in the small church of St. Alpin, whose apse celebrates the Eucharist, the souls in Purgatory, the Corpus Christi procession, lately mocked by the Calvinists. Its Manna in the Desert window is a symbol of the Eucharist. In St. Alpin are the most successful examples of that distinguished phase of vitrine art called *camaïeu*—of cameo or chiaroscuro effect, using brown-gray hues, the yellow of silver-stain, a pale blue for the sky, and an occasional single touch of superb ruby red. One of the windows of Raphaelesque design represents St. Alpin, bishop of Châlons, meeting Attila the Hun; another, dated 1539, is a rendering of the Vision of Augustus, a theme most popular then.

Peter the Venerable called Châlons "great and illustrious." Guillaume de Champeaux, one of the most learned men of the age, whose schoolroom was really the beginning of the University of Paris, was bishop of Châlons in 1115 when a young Burgundian named Bernard came to be consecrated abbot of Clairvaux. In the monk of twenty-five, unknown yet to fame, the great teacher was swift to recognize a supreme spiritual genius. In 1147 St. Bernard preached at the dedication of the Romanesque cathedral of Châlons before Pope Eugene III, who had been one of his own Cistercian monks at Clairvaux. The present tower to the north of the choir belonged to the church that Bernard knew. The south tower, its mate, is of the XIII century. The placing of belfries on either side of the choir was a Rhenish trait.

In 1230 Châlons Cathedral was wrecked by lightning. Its reconstruction began with the choir, under Bishop Pierre de Nemours, whose brothers were building-prelates at Noyon, Paris, and Meaux. In 1250 work on the nave was going on, and at the end of the century was built the transept's excellent north façade. The XVII century erected the unsuitable neo-classic west frontispiece, yet at the same time, curiously enough, the two westernmost bays were constructed in perfect imitation of Apogee Gothic. It remains an open question whether the same Renaissance century made the apse chapels after a fire in 1668. Some say they are of the XIV century, that the choir, as first built, had no ambulatory, but that one was added soon after, with radial chapels.

There is a noble purity in Châlons Cathedral, due in large part to its soaring monolithic piers. No church is richer in tombstones, and its stained glass is plenteous. In the eastern clearstory are three lovely silver and blue XIII-century windows; the north rose of the transept is early XIV century and the first window in the nave's south aisle is another good example of that period. The same

[151] *Congrès Archéologique*, 1890, Toul. In the series of *Villes d'art célèbres*, published by H. Laurens (Paris), are studies on Tournai, Ipres, and Avila: Henri Guerlin, *Ségovie, Avila, Salamanque*; Henri Hymans, *Gand et Tournai* and *Bruges et Ypres*.

aisle shows a brilliant XV-century light, ruby red in effect, and a window of 1509, wherein the Blessed Virgin's life is explained by quaint inscriptions. Some XII-century glass from Châlons Cathedral is in the Trocadéro Museum at Paris.

Just as Champagne had proved herself a pioneer in the first days of the national art, so she distinguished herself in later times when Rayonnant Gothic turned to Flamboyant art. Among the few churches built during the transition between those two phases is the cathedral-like Notre-Dame-de-l'Épine, in the fields a few miles from Châlons-sur-Marne, a link connecting St. Urbain at Troyes with the goodly array of Flamboyant buildings that sprang up in the ancient capital of Champagne. The interior proportions of Notre-Dame-de-l'Épine resemble those of Rheims Cathedral, and its rood screen recalls the *jubé* of the Madeleine church at Troyes.

But *revenons à nostro matière*, as dear Joinville, seneschal of Champagne, would say. The reason for the wealth of architecture and its allied arts and crafts in the region of which Troyes is the center was because the ancient city, so unnoted in to-day's activities, lay on the mediæval highway of commerce, and under its enterprising rulers became the scene bi-yearly of a fair to which all Europe flocked. To this day we use Troy weight. The counts of Champagne safeguarded the visiting merchants and fostered commerce by wise laws. Their money passed in Rome and Venice as freely as in Provins and Troyes. Lavish and art-loving were the Champagne rulers; one of them founded Clairvaux in lower Champagne; another rebuilt the Cistercian church of Pontigny, just over the border in Burgundy. They were indefatigable crusaders, some of them winning thrones in the East. And their alliances constantly enriched their stock with new qualities, as when Count Henry the Magnificent wedded, in 1164, the daughter of Louis VII by Aliénor of Aquitaine. That Countess Marie—the *suer comtessa* to whom her half brother, Richard Cœur-de-Lion, addressed his famous prison song—made of her court of Champagne a school of good manners with all the ceremonial of the Midi's *cour d'amour*. What M. Gaston Paris calls poet-laureates' work, *poésie courtoise*, became the vogue, and the Countess Marie herself wrote in the troubadour manner. She encouraged the best of the XII-century poets, Crestien de Troyes (d. 1175), suggesting to him the romances of the Breton cycle, Lancelot, Tristan, and Percival.[152] Through Crestien the story of the Holy Grail spread over Europe. In him the trouvères new ideals of chivalry met the Midi's refined gallantry, and the Celtic themes which he versified brought what was needed of passion and profundity.

[152] L. Petit de Julleville, *Histoire de la langue et de la littérature française*, dirigée par (Paris, Colin et Cie, 1841-1901), 8 vols. In vols. 1 and 2 the Middle Ages are treated by Léon Gautier, Gaston Paris, and Joseph Bédier; Gaston Paris, *La littérature française au moyen âge* (Paris, Hachette, 1890); *ibid., Les origines de la poésie lyrique, en France au moyen âge* (Paris, 1892); Léon Gautier, *Origines et histoire des épopées françaises* (Paris, V. Palme, 1878-94), 4 vols.; Joseph Bédier, *Les légends épiques* (Paris, H. Champion, 1908-13), 4 vols.; P. Tarbé, *Les chansonniers de Champagne* (1851); Delaborde, *Notice historique sur le château de Joinville. Haute-Marne* (Joinville, 1891); Natalis de Wailly, éd., *Jean, sire de Joinville, texte original accompagné d'une traduction*. Translated into English, Bohns' Antiquarian Library, VI, London; Bouchet, éd., *Villehardouin* (Paris, 1891). English translation by Sir F. T. Marzial (London, Everyman's Library, 1908).

All Europe then drew its poetic inspirations from the *matière de France*, as France in her turn was enriching herself from the inexhaustible *matière de Bretagne*. The XII-century French trouvères were imitated by the German Minnesingers, by the early songsters of England, Spain, and Portugal, and in Italy the precursors of Dante preferred the use of the Romance tongues of France. In the fecund hour wherein our modern civilization was conceived, France gave to the Western World her architecture, her sculpture, and her poetry. At the cathedral doors of Verona, Roland and Oliver were sculpted.

The international city of Troyes saw the creation of the Templars Order at her Council of 1128, whither had come Hugues de Payns, a knight related to the reigning counts. Taking part in the First Crusade, he proved himself a true *prud'homme* in Palestine by forming a band of volunteer knights to escort unprotected pilgrims. At the Council of Troyes he won recognition for his monk-knights. St. Bernard championed them, drew up their rule, and gave them their white robe and red cross. With the birth of the national art rose this great military Order and with its decline it was stricken down. When the lust of gain replaced aspiration, men no longer went crusading or built cathedrals.

The ancient city of Troyes is not only associated with epic poetry — "history before there are historians" — but is linked with the earliest two historians who wrote in the vernacular, Villehardouin and Joinville. "*Mes lengages est buens car en France fui nez,*" boasted the Champagne poet, who tells us that God listened by preference to his speech, since he had made it lighter and better than any other, of more brevity, of nobler amplitude. Villehardouin's record of the Fourth Crusade, the *Conquête de Constantinople*, possesses the same powerful simplicity as the greatest of all chansons-de-geste, *Roland*. He was born near Troyes, in whose convents lived two of his daughters and his two sisters, and to whose churches he left property.

Our good friend Joinville grew up in the cultivated court of the Countess Marie's grandson, Thibaut IV *le Chansonnier*, born in Troyes. Thibaut's songs blended the courteous poetry of the troubadour tradition with the attic salt of his own most civilized Champagne. In his gallant company Joinville acquired his good manners and inimitable mode of expression.

The last countess of this land of gay singers and soldier-historians was Thibaut's granddaughter, Jeanne, who inspired Joinville to write his memoirs, helped to build Meaux Cathedral, and founded the College of Navarre where Gerson and Bossuet were to be trained. But, alas! the liberal young heiress of Champagne married the legist king of France, Phillipe le Bel, the executioner of the Templars. When he struck a blow at the international fairs of Champagne by persecuting Lombards and Jews, the great day for Troyes was over. When Jeanne d'Arc—born on the confines of Champagne—revived the nation's pride, the art traditions latent in the citizens of Troyes flowered once more with magnificence. Only the slow accumulation of centuries could have produced the unemphatic beauty of the gracious St. Martha in Troyes' Flamboyant Gothic church of the Madeleine.

THE CATHEDRAL OF TOURS.[153]

A religion is the heart of a race; it expresses the emotions of a people and elevates them by giving them an aim: but, unless a God be visibly honored, religion does not exist, and human laws are powerless.... Thought, the fountain of all good and evil, cannot be trained, mastered, and directed except by religion, and the only possible religion is Christianity, which created the modern world and will preserve it.... France is being saved and lost perpetually. If she wants to be saved, indeed, let her go back to the laws of God.

—HONORÉ DE BALZAC (1799-1850; born in Tours).

The cathedral of Tours does not startle. One is not carried away by it, at first. Its charm is that of the tranquil horizons of the Loire, *fleuve de lumière, de vie doucement heureuse, partout de plein effets de lenteur, d'ordre*, so Rodin saw it. The beauty of Touraine increases with familiarity because it is touched with that measure, that justness of soul inherited from the classic spirit, that has ever tempered, in the art manifestations of this nation, the sublime overimpassioned consistencies of the Celt and the lofty overexaggerated dreams of the Teuton.

The cathedral of Tours does not aspire to the impossible. It is a rather cold, high-bred church at one with its environment, the gracious garden of Touraine, a satisfying, discreet church and most intensely French. While one rejoices that a Robert de Lusarches aspired to the Infinite at Amiens, one approves the architect of Tours who worked within human possibilities. The choir of the cathedral possesses both delicacy and force. Toward its erection Louis IX granted a quarry and some forest lands near Chinon. The choir must have been nearing its completion when in 1255 the king visited Tours, whose archbishop, Geoffrey de Martel, had lately died a crusader in Palestine.

During the fifty years prior to 1270 the cathedral was building. In 1269 the relics of St. Maurice and his companions from Thebes, who were martyred in Gaul under Diocletian, were transferred to the sanctuary. Those early Christians were the tutelary saints of Tours Cathedral up to the XIV century. Then St. Gatien, the first to preach Christianity in this region, was chosen as patron. *La Gatienne* the people call their chief church. The cult of the early missionary had been a favorite

[153] Chanoine Boissonnot, *La cathédrale de Tours* (Tours, 1904); Paul Vitry, *Tours et les châteaux de Touraine* (Collection, Villes d'art célèbres), (Paris, H. Laurens, 1905); *ibid.*, *Michel Colombe et la sculpture française de son temps* (Paris, 1901); Marchand et Bourassé, *Verrières du chœur de l'église metropolitaine de Tours* (Paris, 1849), folio; A. J. de H. Bushnell, *Storied Windows*, chapter 22, on Tours (New York and London, 1914); Charles de Grandmaison, *Tours archéologique* (Paris, 1879); Abbé Bossebœuf, *Tours et ses monuments*; Monseigneur Chevalier, *Promenades pittoresques en Touraine* (Tours, 1869); Abbé J. J. Bourassé, *Recherches hist. et archéol. sur les églises romanes en Touraine* (1869); L. Courajod, *La sculpture française avant la Renaissance classique* (Paris, 1891); Louis Gonse, *La sculpture française depuis le XIVᵉ siècle* (Paris, 1895), folio; Giraudet, *Histoire de la ville de Tours* (Tours, 1873), 2 vols.; Chalmel, *Histoire de Touraine* (1841), 4 vols.; Henri Guerlin, *La Touraine* (Collection, Provinces françaises), (Paris, H. Laurens); L. Barron, *La Loire* (Fleuves de France), (Paris, H. Laurens); C. H. Petit-Dutaillis, *Charles VII, Louis XI et les premières années de Charles VIII* (Paris, Hachette, 1902).

devotion of St. Martin, third and greatest bishop of Tours, who died as the IV century drew to a close.

Like Lyons, Tours has eminent ecclesiastical memories. The shrine of St. Martin, the most popular saint of Gaul, made the city a frequented pilgrimage for Europe. Gregory of Tours, who ruled this see from 573 to 595, has described the richness of the Byzantine church that stood over the tomb of the great thaumaturge. Like most of the prelates who saved Latin civilization from the Barbarian's submersion, Bishop Gregory was of Gallo-Roman stock, of a senatorial family of Auvergne who boasted descent from an early Christian martyr of Gaul. In the present southwest tower of la Gatienne are traces of the VI-century cathedral built by this bishop-historian of Gaul, whose pages are a chief source for Merovingian times.[154]

The city of Tours always had two great monuments—the cathedral within the ramparts, the basilica of St. Martin outside the walls. St. Martin's abbey was the nation's intellectual leader when the Saxon scholar Alcuin became its abbot (796-804). He made of Tours a Christian Athens. They buried him in his abbatial, where four years earlier Charlemagne's wife, Luitgarde, had been laid. To-day only two towers stand of St. Martin's basilica—the Tour Charlemagne, begun by the Blessed Hervé, abbot in 997, hence one of the oldest memorials of the rebirth of architecture associated with the year 1000, and a former façade tower mainly of the XII century. One of the busiest streets of Tours runs up what once was the nave of the abbatial, but, not discouraged, the people of Touraine have erected a new Byzantinesque basilica of St. Martin on the site of the transept's southern arm. Those two tragic frenzies of forgetfulness, 1562, that scattered St. Martin's ashes—for which St. Eloi, bishop-goldsmith of Noyon, had made a priceless reliquary—and 1793, that laid in ruins his church in Tours and Marmoutier's Apogee Gothic abbatial that marked the rock-hewn cells where he had lived a hermit across the Loire, those two blind hours when men thought to erect barriers between themselves and their past, destroyed monuments which, did they exist still, would rank Tours, architecturally, among the first cities of Europe. St. Martin's church, built by Hervé, became a *monument-type*,[155] copied by Ste. Foi, Congnes, St. Martial,

---

[154] Behind the choir of Tours Cathedral, in the Place Grégoire de Tours, a veritable nook of the Middle Ages, are XII-century vestiges of the Episcopal Palace, a mansion of the XV century, and near by is the rue de la Psalette, in which Balzac set the scene of his *Curé de Tours*. Why has not Tours named her chief square and residential street for Balzac, her own son, instead of for Emile Zola? Balzac's sister has told of the profound impression made on him by the cathedral of Tours, especially by its marvels of stained glass, so that all through the novelist's life the mere name "St. Gatien" had the power to rouse him to the dreams and aspirations of his youth.

[155] R. de Lasteyrie, *L'église St. Martin de Tours* (Paris, 1891); Monsuyer, *Histoire de l'abbaye de St. Martin*; Henri Martin, *Saint-Martin* (Collection, *L'art et les saints*), (Paris, H. Laurens); Ed. Chévalier, *Histoire de l'abbaye de Marmoutier* (Tours, 1871), 2 vols. There are papers on the church of St. Julien de Tours in the *Mémoires de la Soc. archéol. de Touraine*, 1909, p. 13, and on St. Martin de Tours, 1907; also in the *Bulletin Monumental*, 1873, p. 830, on St. Symphorien de Tours. The abbatial of St. Julien, a contemporary of Tours Cathedral, is exceptionally pure Gothic. Its tower is Romanesque and in part dates before 1000.

Limoges, St. Sernin, Toulouse, and the cathedral at Santiago.

It is said that twenty centuries of human effort are represented by the stones of Tours Cathedral.[156] In the base of its façade towers are remains of the city's III-century walls, which had been constructed in their turn with the big stones stolen from the local Roman temples of 50 B.C. For sixteen centuries Mass has been said on this site. In the southwest tower are vestiges of Gregory of Tours' VI-century church, and in the northwest tower traces of the Romanesque cathedral on which worked the philosopher and theologian, Hildebert de Lavardin, the most popular poet of his age and one of the builders of Le Mans Cathedral before promoted to be Tours' sixty-fourth archbishop (1125-34). In refuting Berengar, a canon of Tours, who taught a confused doctrine concerning the Eucharist, Bishop Hildebert was the first to use the term "transubstantiation" in its theological sense. It is said that the custom of elevating the Host in the Mass resulted from the eucharistic controversies started by Berengar.

In 1167 a fire, caused by a quarrel over crusaders' treasure, between Louis VII and Henry II Plantagenet, destroyed the Romanesque cathedral of Tours. Bishop Joscion, who died in 1173, planned to construct a Plantagenet Gothic church, since Touraine was in large part under Angevin control, and to the church he began belongs the graceful *bombé* vault borne on eight slender branches beneath the northwest tower. In 1191 Richard Cœur-de-Lion came to his city of Tours to receive the crusaders' insignia before his venture to the East. His ransom drained the land of building funds. For that cause or another, the projected work at Tours languished. The actual choir was begun only about 1210, when the city had become a part of the royal domain, and its new master Philippe-Auguste wrote that he held the church of Tours to be one of the chief jewels of his crown, and that whosoever molested it touched his (the king's) person.

We do not know who was the original architect of *la Gatienne*. Étienne de Mortagne, who designed the Benedictine church at Marmoutier, is mentioned, in 1269, as master-of-works at the cathedral, but by that time its choir was completed. That choir, while making no pretense of being sublime, is a monument of noble robustness, displaying within and without the veriest genius of good taste. The vista closing the eastern end of the church is one of the most satisfactory in France, owing to its right proportion. In this, Tours derives directly from Amiens. Its pier arcade comprises one-third of the interior wall elevation; and the triforium and clearstory make up the other two-thirds—clearstory being double the height of triforium. At Tours the relation of span and height is admirable, and both are well correlated with length. Seen in perspective down the nave, the three stories of colored glass around the sanctuary are the supreme impression of this church

[156] Many a Council has been held in Tours. In 1055 came Gregory VII, the reformer. In 1095 Urban II preached the First Crusade, and dedicated a Romanesque abbatial at Marmoutier. In 1107 Pope Paschal II came, in 1119 Calixtus II, in 1134 Innocent II, and Alexander III in 1163. At the Council of 1163 the new archbishop of Canterbury, Thomas Becket, pleaded for St. Anselm's canonization, and the builder of Lisieux Cathedral, the politic Arnoul, delivered an address that urged the unity and liberty of the Church; yet later he upheld Henry II in his dispute with St. Thomas Becket. Tours can even boast a pope, for Martin IV (d. 1285) had long been a canon in St. Martin's abbey.

interior, and seldom does one pass from its west portal without turning back for a lingering look at that harmonious chevet of consecrated light. Through the pier arches can be seen symmetrically the windows of the apse chapels. The design of the glazed triforium is excelled by no other in France; though serving as a kind of pedestal for the upper lights, it retains its own entity.

When the choir of Tours was completed, the builders proceeded at once to erect the transept which, the stones themselves say, must have been finished as the XIII century closed. The nave's easternmost bays touching it belong to the first years of the next century, as do the two rose windows of the transept. The northern rose is irreproachable in design and of the same scintillating jewel tradition as XIII-century glass.

The Hundred Years' War, here as elsewhere, checked building activities. When they were resumed at Tours, happily the first plans were adhered to, so that choir and nave are homogeneous. As the church advanced toward the west, the window tracery changed from Rayonnant to Flamboyant, the profiles grew prismatic, and the sculpture of the capitals became naturalistic rather than an architectural interpretation of foliage. The nave was made narrower than the choir, probably with the intention of joining it to the XII-century façade. Of the four triumphal piers at the transept-crossing, the two westernmost ones stand closer together than those flanking the choir, whose spacious procession path causes the side aisles of the nave to appear meager.

What might seem an overreasonableness in the architecture of Tours metropolitan church is offset by the glory of its jeweled windows. Between 1260 and 1270 the choir's upper lights were placed, and considering their date, they are exceptional in still being of the legend-medallions type rather than large single figures. Blue is set in greenish white with good effect, contrasting happily with certain contemporary windows at Paris, where the juxtaposition of blue and red produced melancholy purple. The joyous sparkling tone of Tours' lights proves a skillful use of pot-metal yellow. More care was taken to tell the legends plainly than to put borders round each medallion.

The glass of Tours belongs to the Paris school, though made, doubtless, by local workers. Were a floor laid below the triforium of the choir, its fifteen upper windows, composing a veritable pavilion of glass, would be almost a replica of the Sainte-Chapelle, and one recalls that it was Archbishop Odo of Tours who on April 25, 1248, dedicated for St. Louis his new shrine at Paris. The donors of Tours' great windows were churchmen and laymen, the lowly and the mighty. Bishop Geoffrey de Loudon, builder of Le Mans' glorious choir, presented a light, as did Tours' own prelate and a group of parish priests. Small craftsmen were donors, drapers, and day laborers, and of course Queen Blanche's donjons of Castile are to be seen. Her window, devoted to St. James, the patron of Spain, is splendid in hue.

The fourth clearstory window on the north excels in color harmony. They call it the Adam window, after the first tiller of the soil. It was presented by plowmen, and relates their field labors as well as the story of Genesis. On one side of the central light of the clearstory is a dazzling Tree of Jesse, the gift of a furrier and his wife. Next to it is a window devoted to St. Martin, whose story is told again, in the late XIII-century glass of an apse chapel. More French churches have been dedicated to St. Martin than to any other patron save Notre Dame. The windows of the sanctuary north of the axis chapel, though mixed in design, excel all others in exquisite color, being composed of fragments from St. Martin's abbatial reset here. The New Alliance window in the Lady chapel has medallions of Christ bearing His Cross and the Crucifixion accompanied by such symbols and prefigurings as Elisha resuscitating the child, Jonah issuing from the whale's jaws, the brazen serpent, and Moses striking the rock.

All the world was a symbol to the men of those Ages of Faith. The interlinked petals of the transept's northern rose meet in a symbol of the Divinity—a knot without beginning or end—the *forma universal* visioned by Dante. There are Frenchmen who think that the splendid rose windows in their Gothic cathedrals suggested to the exile of Florence his conception of the empyrean. Heaven as Dante visioned it had neither roof of gold nor pillars of jasper, but was an expanded, supernal, white rose.

Once the nave of Tours Cathedral was filled with late-Gothic windows, but storms wrecked many of them. Some of its glass has been set in a line of lights beneath the transept's north rose, XV-century panels representing members of the Bourbon Vendôme family, that was to mount the French throne with Henry IV. Jean Fouquet might have drawn them. Under the XVI-century rose in the west façade is another row of windows containing good portraits of art patrons as munificent as the Bourbons—the Laval-Montmorency family. All over France we find them as donors of beautiful things.

The hour when Tours was an individual leader in art came during the late-Gothic development.[157] Then was finished the cathedral's nave, chapter

[157] Such is the architectural wealth within reach of Tours that one can draw but a few monuments to the traveler's attention. At Amboise is St. Hubert's marvelously sculptured little chapel (c. 1491) and the church of St. Florentin (c. 1445). At Loches is Anne of Brittany's oratory, a Virgin statue of Michel Colombe's school of Tours, and the tomb of Agnes Sorel, attributed to the master who made Souvigny's ducal tomb, Jacques Morel. The collegiate church of St. Ours is of exceptional interest to archæologists; its narthex (now the first bay), covered by a tower, was built by Fulk II of Anjou; the porch, also with a tower over it, was added in the XII century. To that date belong the two bays of the church covered by hollow pyramids, said by Mr. A. Kingsley Porter to be an attempt to make a stone roof without wooden centering. At Beaulieu-lès-Loches, founded by Fulk Nerra, the choir is late-Gothic (1440-1540). At St. Catherine de Fierbois, where Jeanne d'Arc found her sword, is a charming Flamboyant Gothic church. There are Plantagenet Gothic vaults at Chinon. Nine miles from Chinon, at Champigny-sur-Veude, is a rich mass of Renaissance glass attributed to Pinagrier, with Bourbon-Montpensier portraits.

Some twenty miles from Blois is the Romanesque church of Fleury Abbey at St. Benoît-sur-Loire, with a superb XI-century narthex of three bays, surmounted by a tower. In 1562 the Huguenots wrecked the church. Also, between Orléans and Nevers, beside Sancerre, is the abbey church of St. Satur, a forerunner of Flamboyant Gothic, as early as 1361. The Benedictine church of La Charité-sur-Loire derives chiefly from the Burgundian Romanesque school, influenced by Berry and Auvergne. Its central and west towers, its nave, and chevet belong to the second half of the XII century, the transept is earlier; there was a reconstruc-

house, library, cloister, and the psaltery with its pretty Renaissance stair. The cathedral canons, *Messires de la Gatienne*, sacrificed a forest for the nave's overroof. The elaborate Flamboyant façade was set up. Jean Papin was its architect, and Jean de Dammartin, fresh from Le Mans' transept, worked on it. It was begun under Archbishop Philippe de Coëtquis (1427-41), one of the learned men whom Charles VII summoned to interrogate Jeanne d'Arc. He pronounced her entirely sincere.

In Tours Cathedral, April, 1429, knelt St. Jeanne for a solemn benediction before she went forth to accomplish her feat at Orléans. An artist of Tours made for her the banner she loved better than her sword. When Tours heard that she was taken prisoner, public prayers were ordered and a procession marched with bare feet, in penitential intercession for her deliverance. Charles VII had been married in Tours to his cousin Marie of Anjou, who was, says the modern student, more his incentive to patriotism than Agnes Sorel. The son of Charles, Louis XI, also was married in the cathedral of Tours, and preferred to live in the environs of the ancient ecclesiastic city.

Under the saintly Archbishop Robert de Lenoncourt, installed here in 1488, were finished Tours' western portals. Their foliage is tormented, serrated, and deeply undercut, almost too prodigally and delicately sculptured for an exterior decoration. The entranceways are to-day shorn of their imagery, the statues having been shattered in 1562. In the Renaissance day the façade's twin towers were gracefully topped; *deux beaux bijoux*, Henry IV called the belfries of Tours.

Throughout the Loire region an astounding number of monuments rose during the last half of the XV century and the early part of the XVI. Tours was the foyer for a school of sculpture that spread to Le Mans, Angers, Nantes, Poitiers, and Bourges. From 1480 to 1512 the school of the Region-of-the-Loire, as M. Paul Vitry calls it, was at its prime. It culminated in the ducal tomb at Nantes and the entombments at Solesmes. Dijon, the leader of the first half of the XV century, benefited Tours by its realism, and the Italian artists, gathered here in the dawn of the foreign Renaissance in France, contributed certain qualities. But the art of Michel Colombo is predominatingly of the Middle Ages, and a product of Touraine, a measured, contained, and charming art, *de pur esprit français*. Colombe simplified the draperies of the Franco-Flamand school and eschewed the Dijon roughness. His grace is never petty, however, nor his idealism conventional. As the XVI century opened he made, in his Tours studio, the statues for the ducal tomb at Nantes. In 1509 his nephew, Guillaume Regnault, sculptured the recumbent images of the children of Anne of Brittany and Charles VIII for the sarcophagus, now in the cation of the nave after 1559.

Louis Serbat, "La Charité-sur-Loire," in *Congrès Archéologique*, 1913, p. 374; Abbe Bosseboeuf, *Amboise*. For Loches, see *Congrès Archéol.*, 1869, 1910; G. Rigault, *Orléans et le val de Loire* (Collection, Villes d'art célèbres); F. Bournon, *Blois, Chambord et les châteaux du Blésois* (Collection, Villes d'art célèbres); A. Marignan, "Une visite à l'abbaye de Fleury à St. Benoît-sur-Loire," in *Revue de l'art chrétien*, 1901-02, p. 291; L. Cloquet et J. Casier, "Excursion de la Gilde de St. Thomas et de St. Luc dans la Maine, la Touraine, et l'Anjou," in *Revue de l'art chrétien*, 1889-90, vols. 42, 43; *La Touraine artistique et monumental; Amboise* (Tours, Pericet, 1899); Sir Theodore Andreas Cook, *Twenty-five Great Houses of France* (New York and London, 1916).

thedral of Tours, the base of which was covered with arabesques by Jerome of Fiesole. Colombo's contemporary, Jehan Fouquet, a son of Tours, delighted in painting the regional types. He decorated the walls of Notre-Dame-la-Riche, but his work is lost, though some of the dazzling Renaissance windows of that late-Gothic church of Tours have survived. A certain Jean Clouet emigrated from Brussels to Tours in those days, and his son and grandson, born by the Loire, are two of the French *primitifs* whose work the traveler does not care to miss in any gallery that can boast their Holbein-like canvases. During the Revolution, plans were afoot to destroy the cathedral of Tours, but two artists of the city (so loyal through centuries to art interests) risked their lives to save their noble Gothic church.

THE CATHEDRAL OF LYONS.[158]

What Christian does not approach with veneration this city that was in France the cradle of the true religion, and where amid persecutions and tortures rose for the first time the Cross of Christ? Who does not tread with veneration the soil impregnated with the blood of so many martyrs and forever consecrated by the glories of a see that justly claims the title Primate of Gaul?

—Charles de Montalembert, visiting Lyons in 1831.

In its early Christian memories Lyons outrivals all other cities of France. It claims a clear apostolic tradition, and boasts that, next to Rome, it shed most Christian blood witnessing to the planting of the Cross. And modern Lyons is the center of the Society for the Propagation of the Faith, which sends forth to non-Christian lands more missionaries than any other group in western Christendom—apostles who obey the mandate given to Lyons' first martyr-bishops: Go, teach ye all nations, baptizing in the name of the Father, of the Son, and of the Holy Ghost.

Imperial Rome, that foreshadowed many things, chose Lyons, before the birth of Christ, as starting point for her network of highways and aqueducts over Gaul. Augustus made it the capital of Celtic Gaul. It was the bishop of Smyrna, St. Polycarp (d. A.D. 166), the disciple of St. John the Beloved (d. A.D. 100), who sent the first two bishops of Lyons to Christianize Gaul, Pothinus (d. A.D. 177), an Asiatic Greek, and Irenæus (d. A.D. 202), one of the most remarkable writers of the early Christian era, lettered in Greek literature and writing in Greek. With profound

[158] Lucien Bégule et C. Guigue, *Monographic de la cathédrale de Lyon* (Lyon, 1880); Lucien Bégule, *La cathédrale de Lyon* (Collection, Petites Monographies), (Paris, H. Laurens); *ibid., Les vitraux du moyen âge et de la Renaissance dans la région lyonnaise* (Lyon, A. Rey et Cie, 1911); *ibid., Les incrustations décoratives des cathédrales de Lyon et de Vienne* (Lyon, 1905); H. Havard, éd., *La France artistique et monumentale*, vol. 3, p. 80, C. Guigue; Émile Mâle, *L'art religieux du XIIIe siècle*, pp. 52-59, on the glass of Lyons Cathedral; *Congrès Archéologique*, 1907, p. 527, on St. Martin d'Ainay; Abbé Martin, *Histoire des églises et chapelles de Lyon* (1909); André Steyert, *Nouvelle histoire de Lyon* ... (Lyon, Bernoux et Gamin, 1895), 3 vols.; Meynis, *Grands souvenirs de l'église de Lyon* (Lyon, 1886); Charletz, *Histoire de Lyon* (Lyon, 1902); Hefele, *History of the Christian Councils*, 12 vols.; H. d'Hennezel, *Lyon* (Collection, Villes d'art célèbres), (Paris, H. Laurens); Léon Maitre, "Les premières basiliques de Lyon et leurs cryptes," in *Revue de l'art chrétien*, 1900, p. 445; Henri Foeillon, *Le Musée de Lyon* (Paris, H. Laurens); L. Barron, *Le Rhone* (Collection, Fleuves de France), (Paris, H. Laurens).

knowledge of Christian doctrine, he advocated, for the guidance of the Church, tradition, or the spoken word of the Apostles, as well as their written word. Often with just pride did Irenæus boast that his doctrine came direct from the contemporaries of the Saviour: "I could describe to you the very spot where the blessed Polycarp sat when he preached God's word.... His discourse to the people is engraved in my heart. He had talked with John and the others who saw the Lord."

For twenty years St. Irenæus served as priest in Lyons under Bishop Pothinus, and then when that holy prelate, at ninety years of age, was martyred during the persecutions of the Christians under Marcus Aurelius, Irenæus went to Rome to be consecrated primate of Gaul in his place. When the pagan judge asked Pothinus who was the Christians' God, the aged man made answer: "Merit him and you will know him." For twenty years, till his death in 202, St. Irenæus evangelized the country with such success that Lyons was almost a Christian city when the persecution of Septimus Severus broke out. Then followed evil days when the streets of Lyons ran red with blood, and her learned bishop perished with nineteen thousand Christian martyrs.

During the first persecution, in 177, the Christians of the city wrote a famous letter describing how forty-eight of their number were tortured day after day in the Roman Forum of Lyons, till even the pagans allowed that never a woman had suffered so much and so long as the fragile slave Blandina. The letter of "the servitors of Christ who inhabit Vienne and Lyons in Gaul, to the brothers of Asia and Phrygia who partake of our Faith and our hope in the Redemption," is not only an historical document, precious for Lyons, but, as Renan said, is "one of the most extraordinary pages that any literature possesses."[159]

The hill of Fourvière looms over the scene of the martyrdoms, the *forum vetus*, the forum of Trajan, which gave its name to the neighboring eminence to which many generations have come as to a pilgrimage shrine. On the flank of the hill a hospice marks where St. Pothinus breathed his last. The sumptuous new basilica that stands on the crest of the hill beside an ancient chapel, now its annex, persistently dominates the old, gray city. Lyons fulfilled its war vow of 1870 by the erection of this church wherein are strange echoes of Greek, Sicilian, Byzantine, and Gothic art that surely will make archæologists in the far future wonder at much in our civilization. On its walls the city's proud apostolic traditions are set forth in mosaics.

Equally venerated is the ancient church of St. Martin d'Ainay which marks the holy ground where many of the martyrs were slaughtered at the confluence of the Saône and the Rhone. There once had stood the temple of the sixty nations of Gaul consecrated to the glory of Augustus. Haunted by imperial visions, Napoleon at St. Helena suggested that his burial site be where the Rhone met the Saône. No city is more nobly girdled than Lyons. From the altar to Augustus came the four pillars at the transept crossing of St. Martin's; two lofty classic columns were cut in two to make them. The Burgundian queen, Brunehaut, of tragic memory, rebuilt Ainay's

<hr>

[159] Paul Allard, *Histoire des persécutions* (Paris, 1892), 5 vols.; *Histoire littéraire de la France*, vol. 1, pp. 290, 324, on St. Irenæus and the churches of Lyons and Vienne (Paris, 1733).

original oratory over the Christian martyrs' bones, and founded the monastery which is one of the oldest in France. In the course of time it became affiliated with the world-power, Cluny. The present church of St. Martin was blessed in 1106 by Paschal II, who on this same journey had dedicated various new basilicas in northern Italy. In the XII and XIII centuries St. Martin's outer aisles were added. The crypt under the chapel of Ste. Blandine is not later than the V century. A contemporary of St. Martin's is the little Romanesque building touching the cathedral's façade, the *Manécanterie* (to sing in the morning).[160] Originally it formed the outer wall of a gallery of the cloister.

The cathedral of St. John the Baptist faces the hill of Fourvière and its apse overlooks the Saône. The Baptist was the first teacher of St. John Evangelist to whom the city traces its Christianity. A preceding Romanesque cathedral, building in 1084 and completed by 1117, was destroyed during disorders between the two warring local authorities, the archbishop and the counts of Forez. Lyons for a time was under the titular jurisdiction of the Holy Roman Empire, but to all intents and purposes was a free city with well developed communal rights. While the Romanesque cathedral was building, St. Anselm of Canterbury passed sixteen months in Lyons as guest of Archbishop Hugues.

The present cathedral was undertaken by Archbishop Guichard (1165-80), and in its foundation walls were incorporated some of the polished stones from the forum of Trajan, hallowed by the martyrs' blood. So thick were the apse walls made that flying buttresses were never needed. The windows were set in deep embrasures. The absence of an ambulatory, and the flat roof, are reminders that this city neighbors the Midi. The cathedral's apse, as seen from across the Saône, is admirable. Over the arms of the transept are towers whose breadth indicates that the tower of St. Martin d'Ainay created a school in the district. In comparison with the transept towers, the western belfries of the cathedral appear meager.

The nave of Lyons rises twenty-five feet above the choir, and, furthermore, is covered by an inappropriate high-pitched roof. Within the church, the difference in height between the two main parts has been gracefully veiled by piercing, in the flat wall over the triumphal arch of the choir, a rose window and two lancets.

---

[160] The church of St. Nizier also possessed a *manécanterie* in which Alphonse Daudet, as *Le Petit Chose*, spent some happy years. Another romance based on reality whose scene is Lyons is René Bazin's *l'Isolée*. An ancient crypt under St. Nizier, shaped like a Greek cross, dedicated to St. Pothin since the IV century, has been ruined by restorations; the actual church is Rayonnant and Flamboyant Gothic, with a portal of the Renaissance by a son of Lyons, Philibert Delorme (d. 1570). Jean Perréal was also born here, as was Coysevox, who made the Virgin of St. Nizier (1676). Eminence in religious or idealistic mural painting has been attained by two sons of Lyons, Puvis de Chavannes (1824-98), who decorated the Museum with *Le Bois Sacré*, and Flandrin (1809-64), who frescoed the walls of St. Martin d'Ainay. Meissonier (d. 1891) was born here; so was Ampère, scientist and Christian believer (d. 1836). In the hospital of fifteen thousand free beds which opened its doors in the VI century and has never since closed them, worked a loved physician who was father of Frédéric Ozanam, the founder of the Society of St. Vincent de Paul. St. Vincent's heart is treasured in a chapel of the cathedral. Another of the leaders of the Catholic reform, St. Francis de Sales, died in Lyons in 1622.

In size this church may be modest, but its sincere, grave dignity is such that the impression conveyed is that of a very great cathedral. The nave derived from the north. The choir emanated from the south, and its creamy, sculptured marbles and Greco-Italian incrustations compose an interior of sober elegance, the peer of any sanctuary in the land. A unique feature in France is Lyons' incrustations—patterns cut in white marble and filled in with a reddish-brown cement—found only here and in the cathedral of Vienne.[161] St. Sophia in Constantinople first used the decoration, which was imported into Italy and thence passed up the Rhone.

The choir of Lyons' Cathedral, up to its vault-springing, is Romanesque, of the Burgundian and Provençal type. The classic pilaster strips are channeled; on each arm of the transept is an apsidal chapel. The prelate who began it, Guichard, had, while abbot of Pontigny, been the host of St. Thomas Becket, and in Pontigny's church he was buried in 1180. His successor, Jean de Bellesmaine (1180-93), born in Canterbury, was another of Becket's friends, and soon after he was transferred here from the see of Poitiers, then under English rule, he inspired the building of a collegiate church dedicated to the new English saint. Archbishop John undertook the second campaign of works on Lyons' choir, which was now vaulted in the Gothic way. On the capitals of the upper walls are the familiar crockets of the north.

In the transept is to be seen the same change from the round arches and fluted pilaster strips of the Romanesque day to the Primary Gothic characteristics. During the first third of the XIII century the transept was vaulted, its two towers raised, and the choir's four easternmost bays built. Lyons was then governed by one of its best rulers, Archbishop Renaud de Forez, who laid here the base for

[161] The see of Vienne was founded A.D. 160. The cathedral of St. Maurice, well set on the Rhone, contains vestiges of the church consecrated in 1106 by Paschal II, and which had been aided by that archbishop of Vienne, of the first line of Burgundy's Capetian dukes, who became Pope Calixtus II in 1119. The present edifice is due to Bishop Jean de Bernin (1218-66), and was consecrated by Innocent IV in 1251. Only in 1533 were its façade and the four bays behind it finished. There is no transept. The XV century made the northern entrance, and the XVI century that to the south. The red incrustations form friezes, in the choir, below both triforium and clearstory.

A V-century bishop of Vienne was Claudianus Mamertus, who upheld Latin culture against the Barbarians, like his friend and fellow poet, Bishop Apollinaris Sidonius at Clermont. To Vienne's bishop is attributed the noted hymn *Pange lingua gloriosi proclium certamini*, and the institution of the Rogation days of penance and procession before the Ascension, in that hour when earthquakes and volcanic eruptions had terrorized central France. In 1312 Vienne was the scene of a general Council of the Church at which the Templars were suppressed by a pope cowed into obedience by the king of France, who arrived at the Council with an escort of the size of an army. The majority of the bishops present held that to abolish the Order was not a legal act, since the charges against them were unproven. Therefore, Clement V was forced to fall back on the expedient plea of solicitude for the public good.

Congrès Archéologique, 1879; J. Ch. Roux, *Vienne* (Paris, Bloud et Cie, 1909); M. Reymond, *Grenoble, Vienne* (Collection, Villes d'art célèbres), (Paris, II. Laurens); Lucien Bégule, *L'ancienne cathédrale de Vienne-en-Dauphiné* (Paris, II. Laurens, 1914); Paul Berret, *Le Dauphiné* (Collection, Provinces françaises), (Paris, II. Laurens).

several centuries of prosperity. Circumstances forced him into the position of a leader of armies, but his natural inclination led him to the cloister's peace to end his days. In 1226, as president of a free city, he received Louis VIII, shortly before that king's sudden death.

This capable churchman presented to his cathedral the seven magnificent lancets in the curving sanctuary wall, that glow with the sparkling jewel-radiance achieved before 1220, but never equaled afterwards. The windows at Lyons are linked with those at Sens, and Sens' lancets we know to have been related to the earlier school of Chartres. What differentiates Lyons' medallions from those in the north was their use of certain Byzantine arrangements, such as the Virgin reclining on a couch in the Bethlehem grotto, or the representing St. John with a beard.

The first light in the Lyons' chevet celebrates the local martyrs. The axis window is a New Alliance, wherein the Old Law symbolizes the New. The meaning of its animal allegories was first explained by Père Cahier, who observed that they were taken from the ancient book called the *Bestiaires*. M. Mâle further discovered that Lyons' New Alliance window showed only those animals spoken of in Honoré d'Autun's popular *Mirror of the Church*. Honoré, who taught in Autun's cathedral school early in the XII century, was the initiator of animal symbolism in French cathedrals.

In the upper lights of Lyons' choir are some XIII-century archaic figures of big gaunt patriarchs with strange white eyes. The upper choir's triplet windows of different heights are most artistic. Under the north rose of the transept is a large lancet of surpassing effect, and in the transeptal chapel, close by, is a window that is like a sublimated topaz. The small pieces of glass used, their varied thicknesses and roughnesses are causes producing such sparkle. One cannot stress too strongly the exceptional character of Lyons' glass. Centuries later, in the Flamboyant day, this city produced again a bevy of notable masters.

The nave of Lyons Cathedral advanced, bay by bay, in slow progress all through the XIII century, and sculpture and tracery in triforium and clearstory show the gradual change to Rayonnant design. The nave of northern Gothic conformed itself with sound instinct to the Romanesque southern choir. This is a cathedral that kneels more than it soars. The ancient city exulted on Fourvière's hill, but it thought best to keep its cathedral as a solemn cenotaph for its white army of unburied martyrs.

There came to Lyons, while its nave was building, the great Englishman, Robert Grosseteste (d. 1253), who at Lincoln made an angel-choir, "one of the loveliest of man's works," to shrine the relics of his predecessor, St. Hugh of Avalon, born in this semi-southern region. And many another enthusiast for the art of the builder studied the nave of Lyons in the course of its construction. Here gathered in 1245 a general Council of the Church. Modern congresses are sometimes dull affairs, but they must have been thrilling in the days when cathedrals were building and each prelate championed his regional ideas and yet looked about eagerly to seize on new ones.

The two westernmost bays of Lyons Cathedral were finished by 1310, and then were sculptured the façade portals with hundreds of little panels as full of frolic and fancy as the marginal gaieties of illuminated missals. A few years earlier the transept doors at Rouen had made similar medallions. Vice in them was rendered hateful. Where Lot's story should have been was left a blank space. Not until Flemish realism entered French art, in the XV century, were certain gross scenes rendered. The medallions at Lyons are "Gaulois but without obscenity."

From 1308 to 1332 the wide, plain west façade of St. Jean's cathedral was done. Two of the Avignon popes were crowned here in those days, Clement V, the builder of Bordeaux's choir, and John XXII. The great dukes of the west, Philippe le Hardi and his son Jean sans Peur, being hereditary canons of the cathedral, often sat in its choir stalls. Of their time is the astronomical clock in the transept. For ten years, prior to 1429, Jean Gerson lived in the old Christian city, teaching little children their catechism, and the only payment he craved was that they should pray: Lord have mercy on your poor servant Gerson. He had been worsted by his century's treachery, bloodshed, foreign rule, and church schism; but after his death Lyons revered him as a saint, and carved his device, *Sursum Corda*, on a chapel in the church of St. Paul. Scholars have decided against Gerson as author of the *Imitation of Christ*, yet during two centuries he was so believed to be, and his memory will be dear to those who have found inspiration in that precious book.

Lyons played so important a part in the revival of late-Gothic art that it was called the French Florence. Its new school of glassmakers decorated the church of Brou, at Bourg-en-Bresse, not far away.[162] Two elaborate Flamboyant Gothic

---

[162] About thirty miles to the north of Lyons lies Bourg-en-Bresse, in whose suburbs is the church of Brou. The eighteen windows of the school of Lyons were installed when the church was finished in 1536. Marguerite of Austria built it in fulfillment of a vow of her mother-in-law, a Bourbon princess, Marguerite herself being daughter of Mary of Burgundy, a line, like the Bourbous, that gloried in sumptuous mausoleums. She intrusted the work to the Lyons master, Jean Perréal, who called on his aged friend, Michel Colombe, for the imagery of the tombs. Colombe designed Duke Philibert's *gisant* and the six winged genii, executed later, with liberties, by Conrad Meyt, and his brother (artists trained at Lyons), and some Italians. Disagreements rose, and Perréal was superseded by Loys van Boghem, who erected a bastard Gothic church of the same heavy Flemish type popular then at Toledo and Burgos. The three rich overcharged tombs are in the choir. Marguerite almost became the wife of Charles VIII, late-Gothic builder, and for a short time was married to the only son of Isabelle and Ferdinand, whose tomb is a boast of Avila. When the early death of the Duke of Savoy left her a widow she governed the Netherlands for her nephew, the Emperor Charles V. Her father's tomb at Innsbruck is one of the noted ones of the world, and the heraldic tombs of her mother and her grandfather (Charles le Téméraire of Burgundy) are in Bruges.

If the traveler hopes to find flat, suburban Brou as described by Matthew Arnold, "mid the Savoy mountain valleys, far from town or haunt of man," he will be disappointed. Moreover, no reflections fall from ancient glass, owing to the patina or coating added by time to its exterior surface. Poetic license is allowed, and "The Church of Brou" adds to this heavy votive monument the charm it needs:

"... So sleep, forever sleep, O marble Pair!
Or, if ye wake, let it be then, when fair
On the carved western front a flood of light

tombs were put up in the cathedral—that of Archbishop de Saluces (d. 1419) by Jacques Morel, and that of Cardinal Charles de Bourbon, a grandson of John the Fearless of Burgundy, and son of the Bourbon duke commemorated by the Souvigny tomb. From 1486 to 1501, he and his brother Pierre de Bourbon, son-in-law of Louis XI, added to Lyons Cathedral the splendid chapel of their name whose walls are carved with their winged stag and the device Espérance. Unfortunately the windows, made by the Lyons master Pierre de la Paix, exist no longer, save a few upper panels, in one of which is an angel of rare beauty holding the Bourbon arms. Frequently in France one meets the donations of Henry IV's art-loving forbears, at Chartres, Tours, Souvigny,[163] Champigny-sur-Veude. Henry was mar-

> Streams from the setting sun, and colors bright,
> Prophets, transfigured saints, and martyrs brave,
> In the vast western windows of the nave;
> And on the pavement round the Tomb there glints
> A checkerwork of glowing sapphire tints,
> And amethyst, and ruby—then unclose
> Your eyelids on the stone where ye repose,
> ... And looking down on the warm rosy tints
> Which checker, at your feet, the illumined flints,
> Say: 'What is this? We are in bliss—forgiven.
> Behold the pavement of the courts of Heaven.'"

V. Nodet, *L'église de Brou* (Collection, Petites Monographics), (Paris, H. Laurens); C.J. Dufay, *L'église de Brou et ses tombeaux* (Lyon, 1879); Paul Vitry, *Michel Colombe et la sculpteur française de son temps* (Paris, 1901), p. 365; Dupasquier et Didron, *Monographie de Notre Dame de Brou* (Paris, 1842), in 4º et atlas in fol.

[163] In the XV century the dukes of Bourbon filled their capital of Moulins with art treasures, and Souvigny's abbatial, close by, was their necropolis. The present choir of Moulins Cathedral, originally the chapel of their palace, was begun by Agnes of Burgundy, daughter of Jean sans Peur, and finished by her sons, Jean II de Bourbon and Pierre II sire de Beaujeu, who in 1475 wedded the daughter of Louis XI and governed France with his wife during the minority of Charles VIII. Jeanne of France and her husband are portrayed on the folding doors of the splendid triptych (1488-1503), by some unknown French *primitif* now in the sacristy of Moulins Cathedral, and again in one of the three windows—warm in color and with fine, clear portrait work—in the square east wall of the chevet, glass that belongs to the transition from Gothic to Renaissance as the XV century merged in the XVI. Fifteenth-century windows are comparatively rare, so the twelve possessed by Moulins' chief church are precious. Cardinal Charles de Bourbon, who beautified Lyons Cathedral, also appears in the Bourbon dukes' window with his two brothers. The nave of Moulins Cathedral, in black-and-white Volvic stone, is a modern rendering by Lassus and Millet of the Primary Gothic of the region.

Souvigny was a Cluniac priory, in which died the two great Cluny abbots, St. Majolus (d. 994), who brought to France the noted William of Volpiano, the organizer of the Romanesque renaissance of architecture, and St. Odilo (d. 1049). In 1095 Urban II stayed in Souvigny, and so did Paschal II in 1106. The XII-century church was largely reconstructed in the late-Gothic day when the prior Dom Geoffrey Chollet wished to house fittingly the splendid new Bourbon tombs. That of Louis II (comrade in arms of Dugueselin) has been attributed without proof to Jean de Cambrai, who made the Berry tomb at Bourges. M. Guigue has ably assigned to Jacques Morel the tomb of Charles I and Agnes of Burgundy. The Bourbon line, direct in descent from St. Louis, mounted the French throne with Henry

ried in Lyons Cathedral, in 1600, to Marie de Medici, daughter of another line of connoisseurs.

Like many a cathedral of France, Lyons was at its richest when it was sacked most piteously both in 1560 and 1562. Every church in the city was devastated by the cruel Baron des Adrets, who led the Huguenots one year, the Catholics the next, for in those bitter civil wars religion was often the thinnest cloak. The Huguenots destroyed the tomb of Cardinal de Saluces, with its eighteen alabaster statuettes, smashed the Bourbon chapel and tomb, broke up the Flamboyant rood screen, and dragged through the streets a silver statue of Christ that had surmounted it. On the west façade some fifty large statues were brought down, though happily the lovely little scenes chiseled under their brackets were spared. It is told how an archer shattered Our Lady's image, but when he attempted to dislodge that of God the Father, on the pignon, it fell and killed him. Lyons was again the scene of saturnalian havoc during the Revolution, when by the thousand her citizens were mowed down with grape shot because they chose to adhere to the old régime. A passageway was broken open in the walls of the cathedral to permit the entry of a chariot bearing the Goddess of Reason.

Of all the happenings in Lyons Cathedral, the most momentous was the Ecumenical Council of 1274. Christendom never witnessed a greater gathering. At the Council held at Lyons in 1245, Innocent IV had preached his famous sermon on the five wounds of the Church, but he was less concerned with healing them than with excommunicating Frederick II. St. Louis tried in vain to make peace between pope and emperor on his visit to Lyons in those days. When the saint-king died on his last crusade his ashes rested in honor in Lyons Cathedral on their long journey from Tunis to St. Denis. Till the death of Frederick II, the pope lived in Lyons, whose independent position, neither wholly of France nor of the Empire, caused it to be a chosen spot for exiles. Innocent contributed toward the building of a stone bridge over the Rhone to replace one that had collapsed under the troops of Philippe-Auguste and Cœur-de-Lion as they marched to the Third Crusade.

The Council of 1245 had been held in a cathedral of whose nave only four bays were completed. For the far greater gathering of 1274, Lyons Cathedral could seat over two thousand prelates and princes. The chief visitors were placed in the choir with Gregory X (formerly a canon of this church). Among them was Aragon's king, Jaime el Conquistador, mighty builder of churches and untiring crusader, Guy de la Tour, the bishop-builder of Clermont Cathedral, and the bishop
IV.

Congrès Archéologique, 1913, p. 1, Chanoine Joseph Clémat; p. 182, Doshoulières; J. Locquin, *Nevers et Moulins* (Collection, Villes d'art célèbres), (Paris, II. Laurens); H. Aucouturier, *Moulins* (1914); R. de Quirielle, *Guide archéologique dans Moulins* (1893); Abbé Requin, "Jacques Morel et son neveu Antoine le Moiturier," in *Revue des Soc. des Beaux-Arts des Départements* (Paris, 1890); L. Courajod, "Jacques Morel, sculpteur bourguignon," in *Gazelle archéol*, 1885, p. 236; A. J. de H. Bushnell, *Storied Windows* (New York, 1914); L. du Broe de Segange, *Hist. et description de la cathédrale de Moulins* (Paris, 1885), vol. 2, Inventaire des richesses d'art de la France; L. Desrosiers, *La cathédrale de Moulins, ancienne collégiale* (Moulins, 1871); H. Faure, *Histoire de Moulins* (Moulins, 1900), 2 vols.; G. Depeyre, *Les ducs de Bourbon* (Toulouse, Privat, 1897).

of Mende, Guillaume Durandus, author of the universally read liturgical treatise. St. Bonaventure, whose book of meditations was soon to inspire Giotto, preached at the opening Mass. His fellow teacher in Paris University, St. Thomas Aquinas, journeying north to attend the congress at Lyons, had died suddenly in the prime of life.

The Council of 1274 was not political, as had been that of 1245; its main purposes were the Holy War in the East and the reconciliation of the Greek and Latin churches. The Emperor of Constantinople had sent officials to reconcile him with Rome, and to this day memorials of that short reunion—Greek and Latin processional crosses—stand behind the chief altar of Lyons Cathedral. The emperor's ambassadors solemnly abjured the twenty-six propositions condemned by Rome, then took the oath of fidelity to the pope. With swelling heart the vast throng rose to chant the *Te Deum*. Gregory X intoned the *Credo* in Latin, and the Greek patriarch repeated thrice the *Filioque* phrase which, centuries earlier, had been the occasion of the break with Rome, *qui ex Patre Filioque procedit*. Before the century ended the union was a dead-letter, though the emperor till his death remained faithful to his pact. The Greek priesthood proved irreconcilable.

The day before the Council closed St. Bonaventure died, and around his grave, in the Franciscan church at Lyons, stood the most imposing group of mourners recorded in history, pope, kings, and five hundred princes and prelates of note. The sermon was preached by Bonaventure's pupil of the Paris schoolroom, the learned Pierre de Tarentaise, archbishop of Lyons, soon to mount Peter's chair as Innocent V. All Christendom was bidden to offer up a prayer for the soul of Brother Bonaventure. The city adopted him as a patron. In 1562 the ashes of the Seraphic Doctor were flung into the Rhone, but there still stands in Lyons a late-Gothic church that bears his name.

LE MANS CATHEDRAL[164]

[164] *Congrès Archéologique*, 1860, 1863, 1871, 1878, and 1910, p. 267, on the cathedral; p. 280, on Le Mans' two Benedictine churches; Abbé A. Ledru et G. Fleury, *La cathédrale St. Julien du Mans* (Mamers, Fleury et Dangin, 1900), folio; Gabriel Fleury, *La cathédrale du Mans* (Collection, Petites Monographies), (Paris, H. Laurens); E. Lefèvre-Pontalis, *Étude historique et archéol. sur la nef de la cathédrale du Mans* (1889); Abbé A. Ledru, *Histoire des églises du Mans* (Paris, Plon-Nourrit, 1905-07); R. Triger, *Le Mans à travers les âges* (Le Mans, 1898); E. Hucher, *Vitraux peints de la cathédrale du Mans* (Paris, Didron, 1865), folio and supplement claques; A. Echivard, *Les vitraux de la cathédrale du Mans* (Mamers, 1913): *Bulletin Monumental*, studies on Le Mans, in vol. 7, p. 359; vol. 14, p. 348 (Hueher); vol. 26, on the Geoffrey Plantagenet enamel; also vol. 31, p. 789; vol. 37, p. 704; vol. 39, p. 483 (Dion); vol. 44, p. 373; vol. 45, p. 63 (Esnault); and vol. 72, 1908, p. 155 (Pascal V. Lefèvre-Pontalis); De Wismes, *Le Maine et l'Anjou, historique, archéologique et pittoresque* (Paris, A. Bry), 2 vols., folio; Guénet, *Le Maine illustré* (Le Mans, 1902); Abbé R. Charles, *Guide illustré du Mans et dans la Sarthe* (Le Mans, 1886); Kate Norgate, *England Under the Angevin Kings* (London, 1887), 2 vols.; Mrs. J. R. Green, *Henry II* (London, 1888); see also Davis (London, 1905); Robert Latouche, *Histoire du comté du Maine pendant le Xe et XIe siècle* (Paris, H. Champion, 1910); H. Prentout, *Le Maine* (Collection, Les régions de la France), (Paris, L. Cerf); *Histoire littéraire de la France*, vol. 11, p. 250, "Hildebert de Lavardin"; p. 177, "Geoffrey, abbé de Vendôme" (Paris, 1759); on Hildebert, see A. Dieudonne (1898) and P. Déservellers.

> A cathedral is a book, a poem, and Christianity, true to its promise, has drawn voice and song from stone, *lapides clamabunt.*
>
> —FRÉDÉRIC OZANAM.

Like Bourges and Lyons, the cathedral of Le Mans shows the influence of different schools. An Angevin architect made the *bombé* vaults of its nave, and from the Ile-de-France and Normandy came the masters who designed its mammoth choir. The nave of Le Mans is a masterpiece of Romanesque despite its diagonals; the choir a masterpiece of Apogee Gothic. In the nave appear different stages of pre-Gothic art, and in the choir, the transept, and the nave's masonry roof are represented—Primary, Apogee, Rayonnant, and Flamboyant Gothic.

To read the stones of this composite church with intelligence, one must trace its story step by step. It is named after the first bishop of the city, St. Julian, who brought Christianity into the region. Several earlier cathedrals succeeded each other on the site. The one erected after the Northmen sacked Le Mans was falling into ruin when, about 1060, Bishop Vulgrim began a new cathedral, carried on by his successor, Arnould. Their Romanesque choir exists no longer, but vestiges of the church are to be traced in the walls of the present nave, and in the gable of the Psallette, a building to the north of the cathedral, which in Bishop Vulgrim's day formed part of his transept's north tower.

The nave of Le Mans as we have it to-day shows three distinct campaigns of work undertaken by the three bishops, Hoël, Hildebert de Lavardin, and Guillaume de Passavant. Bishop Hoël (1085-97), a Breton, able, handsome, patriotic, continued the Romanesque transept and the towers that terminate its arms. His works exist in the base of the southern tower and also in those two pier arcades of the nave that touch the transept. The groin vaulting of the side aisles is of Hoël's time, as well as the aisle walls, decorated with blind arcades, the capitals of whose shafts are carved crudely with chimerical animals. As the capitals opposite those of the engaged shafts show more skill, they must have been done later in the XI century.

Good Bishop Hoël, in famine time, sold the gold and silver plate of his cathedral to feed the poor, and on his deathbed distributed his possessions among them. After a visit to Rome, he accompanied Urban II back to France, on the momentous occasion of the launching of the First Crusade. When the Council of Clermont ended, the pope came to Le Mans, in February of 1096, to visit his friend the bishop, to the intense pride of all the city. Such episodes reflect clearly the unison of aspiration which was presently to express itself in mighty movements. The Greek princess who saw the first crusaders arrive in Constantinople has told in graphic phrases how Europe, unloosed from its foundations, hurled itself on Asia, and with a like impetuosity western Christendom was about to fling itself toward heaven in cathedrals.

The church on which Bishop Hoël had worked was destroyed in large part by fire, and his successor, the illustrious Hildebert de Lavardin (1097-1125), began a reconstruction about 1110. Hildebert was the most popular poet of his day and in the mediæval schools his letters were committed to memory. A lover of the Latin authors, he composed verses of such facture that some of them have been mistaken for ancient classics. He was philosopher, orator, and architect as well. The best years of his life were passed in Le Mans, though he was to die in Tours as archbishop of that city. While a teacher in Le Mans' cathedral school, he accompanied Bishop Hoël on his travels, and knew well Cluny and its great abbot Hugues, whose biographer he became. Hildebert possessed *esprit*, a sound judgment, and much independence. Life tested him harshly. The ordeal of prison he suffered several times, and the worse ordeal of calumny, which is disproved by the affectionate friendship felt for him by St. Anselm, St. Bernard, and Bishop Ives of Chartres. No man, he himself said in one of his sermons, should be a bishop whose life has not always been irreproachable. His contemporaries called him "a prelate attentive to the distribution of the bread of the word of God," a man zealous for discipline, charitable to the poor, and with a love for the House of Prayer that made him a builder both at Le Mans and Tours.

Le Mans' Choir (1217-1254). The Double Aisles

Like St. Anselm, he was bullied by William Rufus. Maine lay between Anjou and Normandy and was fought for by each of those expanding powers, a duel settled only by the marriage of the heiress of Maine to the heir of Anjou, the son of which union was Geoffrey the Handsome, the first Plantagenet so called, who married the heiress of Normandy and England. Geoffrey's son, Henry II of England, inherited Maine, Anjou, and Normandy before he fell heir to the kingdom across the Channel.

When William Rufus captured Le Mans in 1097, he exacted the demolition of the cathedral's towers on the charge that they dominated his residence. Annoyed that Hildebert had been elected bishop without his deciding voice, he pillaged his palace, confiscated his possessions, and kept him chained in prison for a year. The bishop was imprisoned as well by Maine's designing neighbor to the south, the Count of Anjou, and once while in the south of France he almost met death at the hands of Saracen pirates.

Despite vicissitudes, he found time for writing poetry and for building. He obtained a monk-architect named Jean from the noted Geoffrey, abbot of Vendôme,[165] author, writer, and the intimate of many popes. Later, when Abbot Geoffrey asked for the return of his architect, Hildebert retained him, and a tart letter of the abbot to the bishop exists; it appears that monk Jean was sent, in consequence, on a penitential pilgrimage to Palestine. Bishop Hildebert's part in Le Mans' actual cathedral is the semicircular pier arches discernible in all the bays of the nave save the two touching the transept, the alternate circular piers, and the west façade, wherein were retained older portions, and against which leans a big menhir of immemorial age: "*Il y a dans la cathédrale toute la simple beauté du menhir qui l'annonce*," is one of Rodin's vivifying phrases.

Bishop Hildebert consecrated his new cathedral in 1120, and it is related how, on that day, Fulk V of Anjou, the widower of the heiress of Maine, about to start for the Holy Land, set his little son of seven, Geoffrey, on the high altar of Le Mans Cathedral, and said with emotion: "O holy Julian, to thee I commend my child and my lands. Defend and protect them both." His prowess in Palestine was eventually to win for him the heiress of Jerusalem, so that when he had married his son Geoffrey to a woman of great fortune, he sensibly left him as sole ruler in Maine and Anjou, contenting himself with his Oriental kingdom.

Two fires in quick succession damaged the Romanesque cathedral of Le Mans.

---

[165] The abbey church of the Trinité has in its transept walls parts of the edifice dedicated in 1040. At the beginning of the XIII century that transept was vaulted in the eight-rib Plantagenet way, the keystones being well carved. The ambulatory and radiating chapels are early-Gothic; the choir is late XIII century; the easternmost bays of the nave are of the XIV, and its westernmost bays of the XV century. The façade is a gem of Flamboyant Gothic. There are also windows of the XIII and XV centuries, and some well-known carved choir stalls. The Merveille of Vendôme, its tower of 1140, prototype for the Primary Gothic ones at Chartres and Rouen, stands free of the church. From the earlier abbatial was saved a famous XII-century window of the St. Denis school, a Byzantinesque Madonna.

Congrès Archéologique, 1872; Abbé Plat, *Notes pour servir à l'histoire monumental de la Trinité* (Vendôme, 1907); La Martellière, *Guide dans le Vendômois* (Vendôme, 1883).

Ordericus Vitalis tells how "in the first week of September, 1134, the hand of God punished many sins by fire, for the ancient and wealthy cities of Le Mans and Chartres were burned." In the necessary changes that followed practically all the central nave was redone by Bishop Guillaume de Passavant (1145-86). The triforium, the clearstory, and the masonry roof are his, and he constructed the pointed arches under the semicircular ones of Bishop Hildebert's pier arcade. The four immense square vault sections (c. 1150) over Le Mans' nave are of the heavy rib Plantagenet type, like the so-called domical vaults of Angers Cathedral. Their crown, or keystone, being ten feet higher than their framing arches, a pronounced concave shape results. The addition of a heavy stone roof necessitated the englobing of each alternate monolithic column by a square pier cantoned with shafts.

Bishop Guillaume developed the door in the south flank of the nave, whose column images, though much mutilated, are allied with those at Chartres' western entrances. At the door joints, in bas-relief only, are Peter and Paul; an additional step was taken when the other images were made to stand almost free of their columns. Guglielmo, the Lombard, had used jamb-sculpture at Modena Cathedral as the XII century opened. This door of Le Mans, among the earliest of French imaged portals, belongs to the decade before 1150. The porch leading to it was built in time for the consecration of the cathedral in 1158.

Guillaume de Passavant was another of the outstanding men of his age. He, too, wrote Latin verses, and even as he lay dying composed a little satire on his attendants, whom his clear eyes observed to be more concerned over the coming recompense from his estate than for the loss of their bishop. Like St. Bernard, who had loved him as a youth, he was a tireless reader of the Bible. Daily at his table the poor were fed. He presented to his cathedral a cloth of gold studded with gems, for which he wrote verses, saying that in case of famine it was to be sold to feed the destitute. Another princely gift he gave to Le Mans Cathedral was the enameled tomb of Count Geoffrey the Handsome, of which only one large panel has survived, now the treasure of the Museum. Both kinds of enamel were used, the flat surface, or champlevé, and the cloisonné method. The technique is Limousin, not, as some have said, Rhenish; between Le Mans and Limoges were many links.

Geoffrey the Handsome was the thirteenth count of Anjou, though the capital of Maine was always his favorite residence, rather than Angers, the chief city of his father's patrimony. He won the nickname "Plantagenet" because of the sprig of broom he used to stick in his cap. True to his race's instinct for territorial aggrandizement, he married, when not yet twenty, a woman twice his age, Matilda, daughter of Henry I of England, the Conqueror's son. Geoffrey died in 1151 on his return from the Second Crusade, where he had fought for his half brother, Baudouin III, king of Jerusalem. His son, Henry II, was born in Le Mans (1133) and baptized in its cathedral. Henry had revered Guillaume de Passavant from childhood, yet once, in an Angevin passion, because the aged bishop had crossed his will, he sent messengers from England to order the sacking of the prelate's palace. Thomas Becket, then Henry's chancellor, gave secret advice to the envoys to tarry long on their journey to Maine. On the third day after their departure he wrung from the king, who fancied his order was already carried out, a counter-order, which he rushed through to Le Mans.

Henry Plantagenet loved Le Mans better than any city in his wide dominions, and his heart broke when his rebellious son, Richard Cœur-de-Lion, drove him out in 1189. Two months later he died in Chinon castle and was carried for burial to Fontevrault; the ancient prophecy had said that Anjou's ruler of his generation would lie shrouded among the shrouden women.

If Fulk Nerra's wild blood had passed to Henry, so had his shrewdness and progressive statesmanship. He, too, like his father, before twenty, wedded a woman much older than himself, the richest heiress in Christendom, Aliénor of Aquitaine. Possessing Anjou, Maine, and Touraine, Normandy and Aquitaine, this king of England ruled more territory in France than did the French king. And Philippe-Auguste, son of the French monarch, whom Aliénor had discarded, bent his resourceful genius and fox-like policies to change so abnormal a state of affairs. The Capet-Plantagenet duel was to last for centuries.

Both Henry and Philippe were munificent patrons of the new architecture. Henry sponsored that individual phase of it called Plantagenet Gothic; under Philippe, French Gothic reached its highest development. And the cathedral of Le Mans records them both, Plantagenet in its nave, northern French in its choir. When Maine, Anjou, and Touraine, because of John Lackland's crimes, passed willingly to the French king, the art of the Ile-de-France found favor in southwest France. Then it was that the XI-century Romanesque chevet of Le Mans Cathedral was replaced by the present stupendous Gothic choir.

In 1217 Bishop Hamlin obtained the consent of Philippe-Auguste to destroy the Gallo-Roman city walls in order to extend the apse of his church, and the next year the choir was started. The bishop, trowel in hand, spent hours on the new work. His two successors continued the enterprise. From 1234 to 1255 Bishop Geoffrey de London was its princely benefactor. In 1254 the choir was dedicated, "a day of benediction" for our land, said the people with tears of fervor. Men and women worked voluntarily to clear the edifice of builders' rubbish, even the little children of four carrying out the sand in their frocks. For the happy ceremony, each guild of the city, chanting psalms, brought a candle of two-hundred-pound weight, to be set up in a majestic circle round the high altar.

The choir, then blessed for God's service, is one of the vast designs of Gothic architecture. "Words are powerless to paint the majesty of this sanctuary," wrote M. Gonse. Here, as at Bourges, is the note of dream beauty that haunts the memory, the something mysterious and superlatively picturesque. Were the church completed on the same scale it would rank with the supreme cathedrals of France. From the exterior the contrast between the XII-century nave and its towering neighbor is painfully abrupt. The nave's outer walls are stark and unadorned, the round arched windows insignificant in size. But who would be willing to forfeit the venerable monument built by the poet-theologians, Hildebert de Lavardin and Guillaume de Passavant, wherein history has been lived, and whose interior aspect is of so grave, white, and primeval a simplicity?

Overawing in size is Le Mans' Gothic choir. The ground falls away to the cast of the church, and then opens out in the Place des Jacobins, whence can be obtained an unobstructed view of the stupendous edifice. Its numerous apse chapels are of exceptional length. The forked flying buttresses allowed the insertion of ambulatory windows. As at Bourges and Coutances, the inner aisle is sufficiently high to possess its own triforium and clearstory, but Le Mans improved on Bourges by omitting altogether the triforium of its middle choir in order not to dwarf its clearstory.

Archæologists have traced the handiwork of three different men in Le Mans' choir. First, an architect of the Ile-de-France made the general plan, and built the thirteen radiating chapels. Then a Norman worked on the eastern curve, and it is thought he was Thomas Toustain, cited here as master-of-works, since Toustain is a Norman name. Perhaps he was the same genius who had already planned the high inner aisle at Coutances Cathedral. Very Norman are Le Mans' circular capitals, the sanctuary's twin-column piers, the carved band under the clearstory, the sharp-pointed arches beneath arches, and the foliate sculpture covering the spandrels of the aisle's triforium. The third master-of-works must have been a native of the Ile-de-France, for the upper choir and the two bays nearest the transept belong to that school.

There is a progressive enlarging of the bays of the choir from its entrance to its end, done too regularly to have been accidental. Professor Goodyear has developed the thesis of these intentional refinements in Gothic monuments.[166] Mr. Arthur Kingsley Porter thinks that undoubtedly there are cases when it was done with subtle design, but more often the irregularities resulted from the sound artistic taste of the old masters who preferred a free-hand drawing to mechanical perfection. "There is no excellent beauty that hath not some strangeness in the proportion," said Bacon. Some think that at Le Mans the desire was to counteract the perspective narrowing. Others say that the builder thought thus to conform the wide choir to the ancient nave of lesser breadth.

Not till the day of Rayonnant Gothic was Le Mans' transept begun, and it proved exceptional in continuing building while the foreign wars ravaged France; the chapter taxed itself heavily to meet expenses. As the XIV century closed, the southern arm was finished; it is entirely blocked by the ancient tower, to which were then added two stories. Midway in the vertical wall of the northern arm (begun in 1403) appears Flamboyant tracery. As cracks soon showed, the chapter called in a new architect, Jean de Dammartin, whose grandfather and great-uncle had beautified Dijon, Bourges, and Poitiers. When in 1430 the English captured Le Mans, he passed to Tours, on whose west façade he worked.

---

[166] W. H. Goodyear, "Architectural Refinements in French Cathedrals," in *Architectural Record*, 1904-05, vols. 16, 17; *ibid.*, "Architectural Refinements, a reply to Mr. Bilson," in *Journal of the Royal Institute of British Architects*, 3d series, 1907, vol. 15, p. 17; Anthyme Saint-Paul, "Les irrégularités de plan dans les églises," in *Bulletin Monumental*, 1906, p. 135.

Professor Goodyear's theory of intentional asymmetry in mediæval buildings—such irregularities as curves of alignment, vertical curves, want of parallelism in walls and piers, deflection of axis—has not found favor with various French and English archæologists, but much of what he has noted may some day be accepted as self-evident.

Because the Gothic transept of Le Mans was confined to the same space as the Romanesque one it replaced, it may seem too narrow for such tremendous height. It is a monument as stately and cold as the glass it frames. Window over window rises the fragile audacious sweep of color that closes the transept's northern vista, each part being bound by stone traceries into the monumental whole. White and the yellow produced by silver-stain is the general theme, with brilliant touches of green, flashed ruby, violet, and blue. It has been said that what XV-century glass needs, to give it character, are the strong black cross-hatchings of the earlier schools. In the row of lights below the big rose, a damasked background to the figures was used with good effect. Among those represented are good King René, faithful amateur of art, and his mother, Yolande of Aragon, the regent dowager of Maine and Anjou. Her son-in-law Charles VII contributed toward the transept of Le Mans.

For its wealth of storied windows Le Mans comes second only to Chartres and Bourges. It has suffered from hail-storms which wrecked many of its XIII-century treasures. The majority of the choir lights were set up between 1250 and 1260. Those in the radial chapels are somewhat earlier; in the long Lady chapel is a notable Tree of Jesse. The upper windows, contemporaries of those at Tours, have large figures with signatures that tell us their donors were canons, Benedictines,[167] Cistercians, architects, drapers (the donors of the fourth window), furriers (who gave the fifth), innkeepers and publicans (who presented the sixth). The seventh window—in the center of the apse—was the gift of Bishop Geoffrey de Loudon. In the thirteenth window bakers pour grain into sacks and take bread from the oven.

In the clearstory of the inner aisle the legend-medallion type of window is retained. The first two bays were filled by Bishop Guillaume Roland (1255-58) here portrayed. The vintners presented the next light, for, on the "day of benediction" in 1254, when each of the town guilds brought a giant candle, the vintners chose to donate a light that would burn longer, so they set up this dazzling window of St. Julian.[168] Over the entrance to the Lady chapel Bishop Geoffrey is again portrayed, and in the eleventh bay Pope Innocent IV appears.

A hundred years separate Le Mans' splendid specimens of XIII-century art

[167] In Le Mans are two Benedictine churches of archæological interest. *De Cultura Dei* is now Notre-Dame-de-la-Couture. When the church was rebuilt after a fire in 1180, big Plantagenet Gothic vaults, each section with eight ribs, were flung over the wide nave, which originally had possessed side aisles. Vestiges of a Carolingian church, built a decade before 1000, are in the crypt and the lower walls of choir and transept, where alternance of stone and brick work appears. The chevet is the oldest example now extant of an ambulatory and radiating chapel. In the XII century the upper choir was rebuilt, and again it was retouched during the XIII and XV centuries. The façade and the well-sculptured portal are late XIII century. A charming XVI-century Virgin, by Germain Pilon, on a pier opposite the pulpit, is to be classed with the prolongation of the Region-of-the-Loire school of sculpture whose center was Tours. Across the Sarthe lies the other Benedictine church, the former St. Julien-du-Pré, a Romanesque edifice of the XI and XII centuries, revaulted in the Flamboyant Gothic day.

[168] "O noble peuple d'artisans! Si grands, que les artistes d'aujourd'hui n'existent pas auprès de vous!" —RODIN, *Les cathédrales de France.*

from certain small lancets in the cathedral's nave, made probably by Suger's own workers of St. Denis, who came here when they had finished the three lancets in Chartres' façade. M. Mâle has proved that all the XII-century windows in the west of France derive from St. Denis. Le Mans' lancets show the same robes, the same borders of medallions as in the Suger lights at Chartres. The up-gazing apostles in Poitiers' Crucifixion window resemble the apostles in Le Mans' Ascension. The large much-restored light in the west façade, relating the story of St. Julian, though modeled on the St. Denis school, must have been executed by local craftsmen; it is rougher workmanship than the XII-century lancets in the nave aisles.

Le Mans suffered woefully in 1562 when the Huguenots worked their will for three months on the cathedral's treasures. A choir screen with three hundred figures, a contemporary of that at Albi, was demolished, windows by the dozen were broken, and there was a holocaust of carved altars and tombs. After the Revolution, the XIII-century tomb of Berengaria of Navarre, the childless widow of Richard Cœur-de-Lion, was set up in the transept. For thirty years, as chatelaine of Le Mans, she watched its new Gothic sanctuary rising. They have mistakenly called hers the house of a XV-century lawyer in the Grande Rue.

The earliest Renaissance tomb in France is in Le Mans Cathedral, that of King René's brother, made by Laurana from beyond the Alps. The effigy reposes in Christian fashion, but near by, on the later tomb of Guillaume du Bellay, the deceased is represented reclining at ease amid his mundane books.

THE SAINTS AT SOLESMES.[169]

> No one can speak with the Lord while he prattles with the whole world.
>
> —HILDEBERT DE LAVARDIN, bishop of Le Mans (1097-1125).

Bishop Hoël, who worked on the nave of Le Mans Cathedral, used to retire for meditation to the priory of Solesmes, farther down the Sarthe, a house founded in 1010 by the lord of Sablé and given to the Benedictines of the *Cultura Dei* at Le Mans. Closed by the Revolution's hurricane, Solesmes was reopened in 1833 through the devoted efforts of Dom Prosper Guéranger, who made it a modern Cluny for erudition, for arts and crafts, and above all for church music. Solesmes restored to the church the Gregorian chant in its purity. Cowled architects of the XIX century rebuilt their monastery. On their own printing press the monks brought out books. Guests came here to find peace of mind and inspiration. At Solesmes Montalembert wrote the noble chapter on the Middle Ages that prefaces

[169] De la Tremblay, Dom Coutil, *L'église abbatiale de Solesmes* (Solesmes, Imprimerie St. Pierre, 1892), folio; Paul Vitry, *Michel Colombe et la sculpture française de son temps* (Paris, 1901); Dom Guépin, *Description des deux églises abbatiales de Solesmes*, and also his *Solesmes et Dom Guéranger* (Le Mans, 1876); Dom Guéranger, *l'Année Liturgique* (Paris, 1888), 12 vols., tr. Worcester, England, *The Liturgical Year*, and also his *Études historiques de l'abbaye de Solesmes*; Cagni et Mocquereau, *Plain chant and Solesmes* (tr. London, 1902).

Among those who have taken part in the discussion as to who made the sculptural groups at Solesmes are L. Palustre, Girardet, Charles and Louis de Grandmaison, Benj. Fillon, Célestin Port, Lambin de Lignin, E. Cartier, A. Salmon, and Abbé Bosseboeuf.

his *History of St. Elizabeth of Hungary.*[170]

The traveler from Le Mans to Angers should quit the train at Sablé and walk two miles to the now deserted monastery on the Sarthe. In the transept of its church are the groups of images called *Les Saints de Solesmes*, work that ranks with the most vigorous final samples of the national art, and that are in spirit profoundly a part still of the Middle Ages despite Renaissance arabesques and pilasters.

What master, or masters, made the Solesmes groups has led to animated controversy. They belong to the Region-of-the-Loire school, of which Tours was the center, and, like Michel Colombe's work, in them the harsh realism of the preceding school of Burgundy has been softened, and the draperies made supple and less overwhelming. If the *Maître de Solesmes* is not Colombe himself, he was some one trained in his art school at Tours, perhaps some monk in this priory.

The entombments at Solesmes are the best of the Middle Ages, with that of Ligier Richier at St. Mihiel.[171] Interest centers chiefly in the Entombment of Christ, the earliest and finest group, made about 1496 under Prior Cheminart, whose crest is cut on the stones. No Holy Sepulcher can compare with this in contained and sustained emotion. Its classic moderation is very different from the dramatic, almost violent, sculpture soon to be made popular by the Renaissance from Italy.

The two men who lower the dead Christ into the tomb, Nicodemus (bearded) and Joseph of Arimathea (shaven, for such was the ritual in the mystery plays), are powerful images, and the latter is indubitably a portrait study, but of whom is not known. The Christ type could not be nobler. The Virgin's grief is rendered without emphasis, and St. John, supporting her, is an admirable image. But the supreme saint of Solesmes is the Magdalene, seated beside the tomb, her head bowed, her lips pressed against her crossed hands. She is garbed in as homely fashion as her sister Martha in St. Madeleine's church at Troyes—sisters in blood and sisters by the heart are these two admirable conceptions of late-Gothic sculpture. Nothing could be gentler, more discreet, more poignant in emotion, than the Magdalene of Solesmes, "the exquisite flower of the art of the Loire region," says M. Paul Vitry, "one of the masterpieces of French imagery of all times."

"She is alive, she breathes gently," wrote Dom Guéranger, "her silence is at the same time both grief and a prayer." Dom de la Tremblaye asks what Italian master of the Renaissance has rendered faith more profoundly than this Magdalene, whose desolation is closer to a smile of ecstasy than to the contraction of grief. Even the neo-classic XVII century admired this image, and Richelieu wished to transport it to his château in Poitou.

[170] The church of St. Elizabeth, in Marburg, is one of the earliest Gothic monuments in Germany, 1235-83. The saint was linked with the new system of building. For the king of Hungary, Villard de Honnecourt built Kassovic church. Her aunt was the gentle Agnes of Méran, married to Philippe-Auguste. Her half sister, Yolande, wedded that other builder of churches, Jaime el Conquistador, from whom sprang Yolande of Aragon, King René's mother, also a builder. St. Elizabeth's niece, daughter of the king of Hungary, married Charles II d'Anjou, who began the best Gothic church in Provence, at St. Maximin.

[171] Amédée Boinet, *Verdun et St. Mihiel* (Collection, Petites Monographies), (Paris, H. Laurens).

Some fifty years later, while Jean Bougler ruled Solesmes, was made the Burial of the Virgin, whose setting is entirely of the Renaissance, though the imagery remains faithful to the French Gothic spirit. It is said that the monk at Our Lady's feet represents the prior, Jean Bougler (1515-56), who returned to the lord of Sablé the eternal answer of the spiritual to the temporal powers. Accosted one day on the bridge over the Sarthe by the baron, against whom he had just maintained the priory's rights, the irate layman cried out: "Monk, if I did not fear God, I should throw you into the Sarthe." "If you fear God, Monseigneur," replied the prior, "I have nothing to fear."

ST. QUENTIN'S COLLEGIATE CHURCH[172]

Out in the night there's an army marching ...
Endless ranks of the stars o'er-arching
Endless ranks of an army marching ...
Measured and orderly, rhythmical, whole,
Multitudinous, welded and one ...
Out in the night there's an army marching,
Nameless, noteless, empty of glory,
Ready to suffer, to die, and forgive,
Marching onward in simple trust....
Endless columns of unknown men,
Endless ranks of the stars o'er-arching....
Out in the night they are marching, marching ...
Hark to their orderly thunder-tread!

—ALFRED NOYES, *Rank and File*.[173]

In size, if not in name, the church that tops St. Quentin's hill is a cathedral, an achievement of the apogee hour of Gothic fitted to close this group of stately churches. Throughout the World War battles raged round St. Quentin. The saints buried in its crypts, the cloud of witnesses in its window and sculptured groups, listened year after year to the marching millions, marching in the hope that a better world might emerge from the chaos, *ready to suffer and die and forgive.*

St. Quentin has always stood in the path of invading armies. Much of its precious glass was destroyed in 1557, when Philip II of Spain attacked the town on St. Laurence day, and in memory of his victory built the Escorial. The siege of 1870 damaged the city dedicated to Caius Quintinus, the Roman senator's son who

---

[172] Amédée Boinet, *St. Quentin* (Paris, H. Laurens); Ch. Gomart, "Notice sur l'église de St. Quentin," in *Bulletin Monumental*, 1856, p. 226; and 1870, p. 201; Pierre Bénard, *Monographie de l'église de St. Quentin* (Paris, 1867), 8vo; also his studies in the publication of the *Société Académique ... de Soissons*, 1864, p. 260; and 1874, p. 300; Lecocq, *Histoire de la ville de St. Quentin* (St. Quentin, 1875); J. B. A. Lassus, éd., *L'album de Villard de Honacort* (Paris, 1858; and London, tr. by Willis, 1859); Jules Quicheral, *Mélanges d'archéologie et d'histoire* (1886), vol. 2, on Villard de Honnecourt's album; Camille Enlart, *Hôtels de ville et beffrois du nord de la France* (Paris, H. Laurens, 1919); *ibid.* on Villard de Honnecourt, in *Bibli. de l'École des chartes*, 1895.

[173] Alfred Noyes, *Collected Poems* (London, Methuen; New York, Fred. A. Stokes Co.).

evangelized this region where he met a martyr's death. In August of 1914 the invaders passed in swift advance on Paris. When the Marne battle drove them back, they dug themselves into trenches a mile from St. Quentin's suburbs and there, with tragic monotony, the giant battle fluctuated. On August 15, 1917, suddenly, like a candle in the night, St. Quentin's great church flamed up, lighting the country for miles around. The projectiles came from the south where the invaders, not the Allies, were intrenched. From beneath this hill, in April of 1918, started the final desperate thrust toward Paris. Four months later the Allies, taking the offensive, swept all before them, and in October the Germans quitted the city in too great haste to destroy the big church, as the bored holes in every one of its piers would indicate had been their intention. A ghost of its former self is the collegiate of St. Quentin to-day. The venerated crypt, part of which dated from 840, was blown up with gunpowder before the evacuation (1918). The notably good XIII- and XV-century windows are wrecked, and the Flamboyant Gothic Town Hall, close to the church, is a ruin.

About 1115 was begun the present collegiate as a Romanesque edifice; the north arm of the easternmost transept and the side wall between it and the larger transept are pre-Gothic. St. Quentin is an exception, in France, in possessing two transepts. When in 1257 St. Louis came to St. Quentin for the removal of the martyrs' relics to the new crypt, the Gothic choir was completed. Three of the small chambers in the XIII-century crypt are of Carolingian origin, and vestiges of Carolingian work remain in the west tower, placed directly before the church, and serving as a kind of vestibule to it. Till the present nave was extended to meet that ancient belfry, it stood isolated.

Fissures showed in the new constructions and much time was wasted in consolidations. Only as the XIV century opened was the big transept between choir and nave begun; it was made twenty feet wider than the transept between apse curve and choir. The tracery in the rose windows of both cross inclosures is most artistic. The nave continued building all through the XIV century. It repeated the shafts which, in the choir, had been later additions needed for consolidation. Only by 1470 was St. Quentin's nave completed by joining it to the ancient west tower. Three different campaigns of work built this church, and three breaks in its axial line are distinctly visible. Toward its repairs the good king Charles V contributed, and Louis XI bore the expense of remaking the small transept.

To Villard de Honnecourt is attributed the plan of St. Quentin, since there are details in his sketchbook—the thirty-three parchment leaves now a treasure of the National Library at Paris—to substantiate the claim. His annotations are in the Picard dialect. St. Quentin's ordinance followed that of Rheims Cathedral sketched by Villard. The planting of columns between axis chapel and ambulatory—a Champagne feature—is the kind of charming novelty which would have appealed to the eager traveler who, at Kassovie, made a church for the king of Hungary wherein he repeated the unique fan-spreading eastern end of St. Yved at Braine.

Thus he opened his precious book: "Villard de Honnecourt salutes you, and he begs all those who work at different classes of studies contained in these pages, to pray for his soul and remember him, for in this book can be found great help in teaching oneself fundamental principles of masonry and church carpentry."

CHAPTER VII

PLANTAGENET GOTHIC ARCHITECTURE[174]

Plantagenet Gothic fused the cupola of Aquitaine and the diagonals of north—Lasted a hundred years, from 1150 to 1250—For clearness divided into three periods: I. Heavy diagonals, II. Eight slight branches, III. Multiple ribs—English fan tracery a derivation of Angevin Gothic.

Cupola churches of Aquitaine: St. Front at Périgieux, begun after a fire, 1120, and finished by 1180—Cahors Cathedral has Romanesque portal of beauty (note)—Cathedral of Angoulême, begun 1109—Its façade a notable page of French decoration—Rich façades distinguish Poitou's Romanesque school—Fontevrault abbey church, built in the first half of the XII century—Plantagenet tombs at Fontevrault—Aliénor of Aquitaine buried there in 1204 beside her husband, Henry II, and her son, Richard Cœur-de-Lion—Aliénor's descendants notable builders of churches.

Cathedral of Angers—Its nave vaulted with First-Period diagonals, about 1150—Anjou rulers a remarkable race—Fulk Nerra, the great builder, died 1040—Choir of Angers Cathedral extended after 1274—In the nave is XII-century glass of St. Denis derivation—Cathedral's Apocalypse tapestries—Fortress of Angers, built by St. Louis, 1228 to 1238—Church of Toussaint had a ramified vault of the Third Period—St. Jean's hospital hall, endowed by Henry II, a gem of Plantagenet art—Choir of St. Serge, 1220 to 1225, a masterpiece of lightness.

Saumur—Another center for the study of Plantagenet Gothic—Historical fête called the Non-Pareille took place in its castle in 1241—St. Pierre's church shows different kinds of Angevin vaults—Church of St. Martin at Candes, a Plantagenet masterpiece—St. Florent-les-Saumur shows one of the first eight-branch vaults—Puy-Notre-Dame and Asnières beautiful examples of Plantagenet art (note)—Plantagenet vaults at Le Mans, Vendôme, Chinon, and

[174] J. Berthelé, "L'architecture plantagenet," in *Congrès Archéologique*, 1903, p. 234; E. Lefèvre-Pontalis, "L'architecture plantagenet," in *Congrès Archéologique*, 1910; Prosper Merimée, *Notes d'un voyage dans l'Ouest de la France* (1836); Choyer, "L'architecture des Plantagenets," in *Congrès Archéologique*, 1871, p. 257; Célestin Port, *Dictionnaire de Maine-et-Loire*, 3 vols.; Abbé Bossebœuf, *L'architecture plantagenet*(Angers, Lachène, 1897).

Tours.

Cathedral of Poitiers, begun by Henry Plantagenet and Aliénor of Aquitaine, 1160—In adopting the gracious Plantagenet vaulting it remained true to Poitou's Romanesque traditions—XII-century Crucifixion window the most glorious in the world—Spirit of Poitiers' bishops, St. Hilary and Fortunatus, inspired it—Church of Ste. Radégonde is Plantagenet vaulted—St. Hilaire's abbatial has curious octagonal cupolas—St. Jean's baptistry, the oldest building in France, dating from the IV century—Clement V at Poitiers in 1307 carried on the Templars' process—Hall of the count's palace rebuilt by Duke Jean de Berry—Jeanne d'Arc examined there in 1429, found to be sent of God.

Il n'y a pas seulement deux principes opposés dans l'homme. Il y en a trois. Car il y a trois vies et trois ordres de facultés. Il y a trois espèces de dispositions l'âme bien différentes: la première, celle de presque tous les hommes, consiste à vivre exclusivement dans le monde des phénomènes qu'on prend pour des réalités. La deuxième est celle des esprits les plus réfléchis qui cherchent longtemps la vérité en eux-mêmes ou dans la nature.... La troisième enfin est celle des âmes éclairées des lumières de la religion, les seules vrai et immuables. Ceux-là seuls ont trouvé un point d'appui fixe.

—MAINE DE BIRAN (1766-1825; born in Périgord).

HE Gothic of the southwest grew out of the meeting of the cupola church of Aquitaine with the intersecting ribbed vault of northern France. It rose and spread in a region then under Plantagenet rule, Anjou, Poitou, Maine, and Touraine. As the first known vault of the Angevin type was dated approximately 1150, and as the system died out about the middle of the XIII century, Plantagenet Gothic was but an incident of a hundred years in French architecture. However, it was a phase which produced monuments of such remarkable individuality and grace that the school deserves more notice than has hitherto been given it.

The dominant feature in Plantagenet Gothic is its cup-shaped vaulting. The French term *"bombé"* is more exact than such expressions as "domical" and "domed." The panels of an Angevin vault do not form parts of a spherical dome. The keystone of each section is raised higher than the four arches framing the section. Similar vaults were built during the first trials of diagonals by other Gothic schools, in districts where there were no cupola churches to serve as models. They were the result of inexperience in constructing ribbed-groined vaults, and their *bombé* shape disappeared as soon as architects learned to raise their transverse and wall arches, by stilting and pointing them, to the level of the keystone. While the so-called domical vault in other schools had been a transitional step, in Plantagenet Gothic it was intentionally persisted in and became the most distinguishing characteristic of the school.

In principle and in construction, the Plantagenet school is truly Gothic. The cells are carried on the backs of diagonal ribs. The Angevin builders recognized at once the advantage of concentrating the thrust of the stone roof at fixed points and counterbutting and grounding the load at those points only, so they followed close on the northern architects in adopting the new system. At the same time they felt that the cupola tradition in their region was not to be wholly set aside. M. Anthyme Saint-Paul well expressed it when he said that southwestern France *"s'est conduit en nation tributaire et non soumise."*

There can be little doubt that the presence in the Plantagenet territories of churches covered by a number of small cupolas encouraged a decided curve in the newly imported diagonals. It was not for nothing that near Angers and Saumur, the two cities where Angevin vaults were first constructed, lay the famous abbatial of Fontevrault, a masterpiece of the cupola school. Had not the arrival, midway in the XII century, of the northern French type of masonry roof checked the construction of such churches, it is probable that they would have extended farther north. From the meeting of the two schools developed the Plantagenet phase of Gothic.

Before proceeding to a description of the successive steps taken by Plantagenet architecture in its best-known examples at Angers, Saumur, and Poitiers, it is well to touch on the cupola churches of southwestern France, building for a century before the beginning of the regional Gothic school. M. de Lasteyrie has divided Romanesque architecture into some half dozen schools—those of Normandy, Burgundy, Auvergne, Poitou, the Midi, Champagne, and the scarcely enunciated Picardy Ile-de-France school. To these he added two isolated developments of short duration, one typified at Tournus, in Burgundy, where half barrels are placed transversely across a nave; and the other consisting of cupola-covered edifices which were building from Saintes to Fontevrault in the same hour as the Poitou-Romanesque churches surrounding them. For three generations the cupola haunted the imagination of southwestern France. The majority of them came into existence by hazard, as it were. They were not in the first plan of the church, but were built to replace other roofs, and in France they have been set on every kind of pedestal.[175] They were a variant of the barrel vault of the region preferred because less material was required.

How the cupola arrived in Aquitaine is still an open question. M. de Lasteyrie

[175] Saintes lies on the Charente, some fifty miles from Angoulême. In the venerable XII-century church of St. Eutrope cropped out one of the early sporadic uses of diagonals. Its crypt, which is one of the largest in France, is braced on heavy, semicircular arches. The exterior of the apse is decorated. Nothing is left of the original nave; the present one is transitional work. The choir and part of the transept are of the XV century. The superb tower, with corner-turret effects that rise from base to summit, was finished with a spire by 1480. It is said that John XXII, who promulgated the Angelus by his bull of 1318, had learned its usage from a custom of St. Eutrope. The church of St. Pierre, at Saintes, rebuilt in 1117, and again in 1450, has another Flamboyant Gothic tower of good design, which is now much wasted by decay. See *Congrès Archéologique*, 1894; 1912, pp. 195, 309; also *Bulletin Monumental*, 1907, vol. 71; J. Laferrière et G. Musset, *L'art en Saintonge et en Aunis*; Ch. Dangibeaud, *L'école de sculpture romane saintongeaise* (Paris, 1910).

has belittled the explanation of an Oriental source, since the mode of construction in France differed from that of cupolas in the East. His idea is that the use of the cupola never died out from the earlier days in Gaul, and that the domed churches of France may be considered to be fairly indigenous. M. Enlart has contended that no matter how or when the use of the cupola got into France, its origin was undeniably Byzantine, since Rome took the feature from Byzantium. He has dwelt on the fact that it was while such churches were building in France, the men of western Europe were going on pilgrimages, on crusades, and on trading ventures into countries where the cupola was a common feature.

ST. FRONT AT PÉRIGUEUX.[176]

Is it not better to dwell a little sadly far from the world, under the hand of God? The world gives but vain pleasures. You will be like others beguiled by it and hardened. You will hear many evil conversations, you will see many contemptible pushing people with distinguished names, you will feel malignant envy, many will be the faults with which you will reproach yourself.... Nothing is good apart from Peace. Peace is the mark of God's finger. All that is not Peace is but illusion, and disturbing self-love.... Be simple and insignificant, and Peace will be your reward. It is only you yourself who can trouble your own Peace. It is in forgetting self that Peace comes.

—FÉNELON (1651-1715; born near Périgueux).

The most discussed of the cupola churches is St. Front at Périgueux. For a while it was considered a mother church of the school, but such well-constructed domes are a culmination, not a beginning. One of the oldest cupolas extant is that of St. Astier, near Périgueux, finished in 1018; there are two large domes over Cahors Cathedral, in which church Pope Calixtus II blessed an altar in 1119.[177] The

[176] *Congrès Archéologique*, 1858, 1901, and 1910; Chanoine Roux, *Monographie de St. Front de Périgueux* (Périgueux, 1920); J. A. Brutails, "La question de St. Front," in *Bulletin Monumental*, 1895, p. 125; 1906, p. 87; 1907, p. 517; Anthyme Saint-Paul, on St. Front, in *Bulletin Monumental*, 1888, p. 163; 1891, p. 321; 1906, p. 5; Félix de Verneilh, *L'architecture byzantine en France*, 1851; R. Michel-Dansac, *De l'emploi des coupoles sur la nef dans le sud-ouest Aquitain*; Corroyer, *L'architecture romane*, 1888; *ibid.*, *L'architecture gothique*, 1899; Ch. H. Besnard, "Étude sur les coupoles et voûtes domicales du sud-ouest de la France," in *Congrès Archéologique*, 1912, vol. 2, p. 118; Abbé Pécout, *Périgueux*; R. Phené Spiers, "St. Front de Périgueux et les assises à coupoles," in *Bulletin Monumental*, 1897; 1907, p. 175.

[177] The cathedral of Cahors was damaged by earthquake in 1303, after which its apse was rebuilt as Gothic, but not too much out of harmony with the rest of the church. The ancient frescoes are full of interest. At the north end of the transept is a now unused portal, whose sculpture belongs to the same Midi school as Moissac, but later and calmer work. The Christ of its tympanum is classed with Vézelay, Chartres, and Beaulieu—the supreme Christ images of Romanesque art. M. Forel praises the angels' magnificent gesture of adoration. The XIV-century west front resembles those of the Brunswick churches whose façade and towers comprise one massive up to the roof. John XXII (1316-33), the second Avignon pope, was born in Cahors, where he founded the university, contributed toward the cathedral, and built a bridge over the Lot which is considered the handsomest of the Middle

two cupolas over Cahors' unaisled nave appear in the exterior view, but were not well enough constructed for their inner surfaces to be left uncovered by coats of plaster, whereas the interior masonry of St. Front is beautifully finished, proving that in point of time it was separated from St. Astier.

Long and heated have been the controversies over the date of the cathedral of Périgueux. As much space has been devoted to the discussion as to the little Morienval in the Ile-de-France. At first it was taken to be the church begun before 1000 and dedicated in 1047. To-day no one dreams of saying it predates the fire of 1120. A few of the bays of the ancient church, burned in 1120 with much loss of life, were retained as parish rooms and now stand to the south of the present cathedral's façade. It is very evident that they never were intended to be incorporated in the new church.

Once it was thought that the actual St. Front, which is in the shape of a Greek cross, with a dome over each of its arms, copied St. Mark's at Venice. St. Mark's was modeled on the church of the Apostles at Constantinople, destroyed by Mohammed II in 1464. However, its domes were added only when the basilica was rebuilt, in 1063. And furthermore, there are indications at St. Front to show that the original design was to lengthen its nave by another bay, which would have changed the plan from a Greek cross to the universally used Latin cross.

The present St. Front was begun after 1120 and probably was completed by 1180, in which year a record says that Bishop Pierre de Mimet (1169-80) moved the ancient tombs into the basilica. During some modern repairs parchments were discovered in a scaffold hole thirty feet from the ground and closed only by a loose stone. The MSS. were in the Romance dialect of the XII century, and were abusive of Henry II of England, who besieged Périgueux in Bishop de Mimet's time. Such a hiding place for compromising papers might well have been thought of during the last stage of a building while yet the scaffolding stood in place.

St. Front's interior possesses a fine, plain solidity of its own, but its garish white walls cry out for mosaics or fresco. The cupolas rise above the big arcades without any vertical foundation members. Each is divided into a hemispherical dome and a drum having the shape of spherical triangles. So massive are the square piers supporting the cupolas that narrow corridors have been threaded through them. Those dense piles of masonry saved St. Front when the Huguenots lighted bonfires at the base of the piers. St. Étienne, formerly the cathedral of Périgueux, was devastated then, so that only two of its cupolas remain; the westernmost one is rougher, earlier work.

The restorer, Abadie, took deplorable liberties with St. Front, but it is an exaggeration to call it a modern church studied from a Romanesque original. Abadie from 1865 to 1875 reconstructed the great broad arches hitherto slightly pointed, and the actual sanctuary is entirely his work. Oriental and un-French as is the ex-

---

Ages. In the diocese of Cahors is Rocamadour, the most picturesque pilgrim shrine of Our Lady in France, visited by St. Louis. E. Rey, *La cathédrale St. Étienne de Cahors* (Cahors, J. Girma, 1911); *Congrès Archéologique*, 1907, p. 413; Alexis Forel, *l'Voyage au pays des sculpteurs romans*, vol. 2, p. 52; "Le cloître de la cathédrale de Cahors," in *Bulletin Monumental*, 1883, p. 110; E. Rupin, *Roc-amadour* (Paris, Baranger, 1904).

terior of Périgueux Cathedral with its white domes, its neo-minarets, its immense tower each of whose stories is lesser in size than the one below it, and whose summit is a pavilion covered with the inverted tiles called pineapple scales, one has to accept the disconcerting fact that it was building in the same year with the cathedrals at Paris and Laon. Well has St. Front been called an archæological monster defying the laws of that science.

THE CATHEDRAL OF ANGOULÊME.[178]

If we wish to know all that is worthy of being imitated, we must make of legends a part of our studies and observations. The marvel of the lives of the saints is not their miracles, but their conduct.

—JOUBERT, *Pensées* (1754-1824; born in Périgord).

Angoulême Cathedral. A XII-century Cupola Church of Aquitaine with a Typical Façade of Poitou's Romanesque School

[178] *Congrès Archéologique*, 1847, 1903, and 1912; Biais, *La cathédrale d'Angoulême* (Paris, H. Laurens); H. de la Mauvinière, *Poitiers et Angoulême* (Collection, Villes d'art célèbres), (Paris, H. Laurens, 1908); J. George, *La cathédrale d'Angoulême* (Angoulême, Cha 1901-04); Michon, *Histoire de l'Angoumois*, 1846; *ibid., Statistique monumentale de la Charente*, 1844; Viollet-le-Duc, *Dictionnaire de l'architecture* (see article *coupole*); Sharpe, *A Visit to the Domed Churches of Charente* (London, 1876); J. A. Brutails and Spiers, "Les coupoles du Périgord et de l'Angoumois," in *Bulletin Monumental*, 1895, 1897, 1906, and 1907.

The cathedral of Angoulême shares with St. Front and Fontevrault the distinction of being the finest cupola church in France. It is unsurpassed in the setting on the edge of the city's steep hill above the Charente valley. In ancient Angoumois, now the department of the Charente, are over five hundred XII-century Romanesque churches.[179]

Angoulême Cathedral was begun in 1109 by Bishop Gérard (1101-36), who had taught at Périgueux in the cathedral school and no doubt learned there to admire cupolas. His first dome at Angoulême—the easternmost one—is slightly later than the older cupola of St. Étienne at Périgueux. Bishop Gérard had the moral courage to rebuke the sinful union of the troubadour-duke, Guillaume IX, and the fair Vicomtesse Malbergeon, whose portrait he wore on his shield when he marched into battle. Guillaume informed Gérard that only when hair grew on his bald, prelate pate would he give up the lady of his affections. Gérard was papal legate in Gaul for Pascal II, Calixtus II, and the second Honorius, and was the prelate chosen, because of his eloquence, to be spokesman for the bishops who opposed Paschal II's compromise with the German emperor on the question of investitures. And yet this able man, because Innocent II had not renewed his dignities, joined the anti-pope faction and took with him Guillaume X of Aquitaine. Only the passionate genius of St. Bernard was able to end the scandal.

The cathedral built at Angoulême by Bishop Gérard, like most of the churches of the southwest, lacks the charm of perspective, since it has neither curving processional path nor side aisle. A note of force is given to the interior by the strong projection of the buttress piers, more salient within the church than without. Farther to the south, when the Gothic day had dawned, buttresses were to be disguised as walls between the side chapels. The three cupolas that roof the nave—each covering a large square bay—are among the largest in France. The side walls are divided at mid-height: below is a huge blind arch, while above are two round-headed windows. Angoulême's hemispherical domes on pendentives were sufficiently well constructed to dispense with plaster coatings, an advance over Cahors Cathedral and St. Étienne at Périgueux.

At the transept-crossing is an immense dome forming within the church a lantern lighted by a series of round-headed windows that open in its pedestal. The arrangement derives directly from the Orient and is rare in France. A very fine tower, whose stories lessen as they rise, covers the northern arm of the transept,

---

[179] Four miles from Angoulême is the curious octagonal church of St. Michel d'Entraignes (1137), built up to its big dome, as it were. Close to it is Fléae, whose three cupolas have no separate bases, but are pierced directly by the big arcades, which is more the Byzantine way of making a cupola than the French. Six miles from Angoulême are the ruins of La Couronne abbatial, where once was a Plantagenet Gothic choir; and ten miles away, at Roullet, is a remarkable sculptured façade. Aulnay's fine church has a decorated front, well-cut capitals, and a ribbed cupola, without distinct pedestal. Pont l'Abbé possesses one of the best Romanesque façades in France. At Ruffec and at Civray are others. There is a church at Charroux with the curious plan of three aisles round a central octagon. Cupola churches are to be found at Plazzac, Bassac, Gensae, Cognac, Souillae, and Solignac, six miles from Limoges. Studies of these churches by E. Lefèvre-Pontalis, L. Serbat, and André Rhein are to be found in the *Congrès Archéologique*, 1912.

and till the cathedral was sacked, during the XVI-century wars, a similar tower spanned the transept's southern limb.

Angoulême's elaborate XII-century façade is one of the noted pages of monumental decoration in France, a frontal more of ornate beauty than of power, in which M. André Michel finds the influence of old ivories. Tier on tier rise its carven scenes, with a Christ in Majesty crowning the whole. The XIX-century restorer, M. Paul Abadie, who worked such havoc at Périgueux, took equal liberties here. He made the upper story with its turrets topped by conical spires, and over-restored the principal sculptural groups. These pre-Gothic churches of southwest France obsessed his imagination, for when he came to design a church of his own he put up on the Mount of Martyrs in Paris a neo-Byzantine, neo-Gothic basilica most strangely reminiscent of Aquitaine as it stands in exotic isolation under the cold, northern sky.

Angoulême's west façade had not long been completed when under its portal passed John Lackland to be married to the fourteen-year-old daughter of the Count of Angoulême, Isabella, already affianced to a Lusignan. Henry III of England, the builder of Westminster Abbey, was the fruit of that union. Twenty years later Isabella married the son of her discarded fiancé, and her jealousy filled France with war. Jezebel, the people called her. She rests in effigy at Fontevrault, beside the tomb of her great father-in-law, Henry II, the first Plantagenet.

FONTEVRAULT ABBEY CHURCH.[180]

A trait peculiar to this epoch is the close resemblance between the manners of men and women.... Men had the right to dissolve in tears, and women that of talking without prudery. The women appear distinctly superior. They were more serious, more subtle. Richard Cœur-de-Lion, the crowned poet-artist, a king whose noble manners and refined mind, in spite of his cruelty, exercised so strong an impression on his age, was formed by the brilliant Aliénor of Aquitaine. St. Louis was brought up exclusively by Blanche of Castile, and Joinville was the pupil of a widowed and regent mother.

—Gareau, *Social State of France During the Crusades.*

The art of the cupola church may be said to have culminated in the abbatial at Fontevrault on the confines of Anjou, Poitou, and Touraine, and practically

---

[180] *Congrès Archéologique,* 1862 and 1910; L. Magne, "L'ancienne abbaye de Fontevrault," in *L'architecte,* 1910, p. 60; A. de Caumont, "Fontevrault," in *Bulletin Monumental,* 1867, p. 73; Bernard Palustre, "Les coupoles de Fontevrault," in *Bulletin Monumental,* 1898, vol. 63, p. 500; Honorat Nicquet, *Histoire de l'ordre de Fontevraud,* 1642; G. Malifaud, *L'abbaye de Fontevrault, notices historiques et archéologiques* (Angers, 1866); Abbé Bosseboeuf, *Fontevrault, son histoire et ses monuments* (Tours, 1867); Édouard, *Fontevrault et ses monuments* (Paris, 1874), 2 vols.; Joseph Joubert, "Les mausolées des Plantagenets à Fontevrault," in *Mém. de la Soc. d'arts d'Angers,* 1903; and 1906, p. 61, Chanoine Urseau; Vietor Pavie, "Westminster et Fontevrault," in *Mém. de la Soc. d'arts d'Angers,* 1866, p. 229; *Histoire littéraire de la France* (Paris, 1756), vol. 10, p. 153, "Robert d'Arbrissel."

the northernmost point to which attained the cupola development of Aquitaine. Undoubtedly it would have spread farther afield had it not been checked—even while Fontevrault was building—by the advent of ogival ribs which initiated a new manner of masonry roofing. In Fontevrault's bourg is a village church covered gracefully in the Plantagenet Gothic manner.

The untenable theory was advanced by a French architect that the cupola church was the egg out of which hatched the radical organ of Gothic architecture, that the first ribs were employed to stiffen a dome.[181] No one to-day concedes this. Yet, though cupola monuments may not have affected French Gothic in general, they certainly exerted a local influence on the Gothic of the West. The hemispherical domes at Fontevrault were directly under the eye of the first architects of Plantagenet Gothic.

An abbess ruled over men at Fontevrault. Its founder, the Blessed Robert d'Arbrissel, had been impressed by the Saviour giving St. John into the spiritual guidance of the Virgin. So he organized a new Order comprised of four communities ruled by a woman: a main house for nuns and another for men; a hospital dedicated to St. Lazarus, and a house for repentant Magdalenes. Robert d'Arbrissel was a Breton, schooled in Paris, and noted for his eloquence, which so impressed Urban II, who heard him preach at the dedication of Angers' church of St. Nicolas, that he named him an apostolic missionary to spread the First Crusade.

Feeling need of spiritual renewal, Robert had retired for meditative peace to these forests when one day he was attacked by bandits. He yielded all he possessed on condition that they give him their souls to guide, and, having converted them, the name of their chief, Evrault, was given, it is said, to the congregation that gathered in cells about the holy man. Pious folk came and sinners, the rich and the poor, the halt and the hale, and the impetuous Robert called them one and all "the poor of Christ." "I never read of a hermit," said honest old Samuel Johnson, "but in imagination I kiss his feet; never of a monastery but I fall on my knees and kiss the pavement."

In 1106, Paschal II approved the Order and in Blessed Robert's lifetime some five thousand gathered at Fontevrault. Abbot Suger, who was a young student at that time near the new abbey, testified to the edification it gave. A sermon by the Blessed Robert converted the fair Bertrada de Montfort, who had quitted her ignoble husband, Fulk IV of Anjou, to marry Philip I, king of France, which illegal union kept churchmen busy during sixteen years; she callously brought her second master to visit her first. The fight which Rome waged to preserve monogamy in western Christendom deserves the highest praise. Bertrada died the second abbess of Fontevrault. The historic names of France compose the list of abbesses. The young widow of the only son of Henry I of England retired here, after the loss of the White Ship, and her father, Fulk V of Anjou, came to visit her as he quitted his career in Europe to take up his new role as king of Jerusalem. Margaret of Burgundy, the builder of Tonnerre's hospital hall, and second wife of Charles d'Anjou, St.

[181] Louis Corroyer, *L'architecture gothique* (Paris, 1899), p. 1. "La coupole, sous sa forme symbolique, est l'œuf d'où est sorti un système architectonique qui a causé une révolution des plus fécondes dans le domaine de l'art."

Louis' brother, was educated at Fontevrault by her aunt the abbess. About 1500 Abbess Renée de Bourbon built the Renaissance cloister. To-day the famous house serves as a state prison.

Fontevrault church played a part in the Gothic story. Its earliest cupola, over the transept-crossing, differs from those over the nave in that its base is not distinct from its dome. Angers copied it in its churches of St. Nicholas and St. Martin, and so did Saumur in St. Pierre. When in 1119 Calixtus II dedicated Fontevrault, the church consisted of the present choir and the transept. During the first quarter of the XII century the aisleless nave was spanned by four cupolas on clearly defined pedestals. Perhaps from Angoulême Cathedral came the fashion of domes on pendentives, after some Fontevrault monks had gone on legal business, in 1117, to the capital of Angoumois.

The *abbaye-double* was favored both by the Angevin rulers and their Poitevin neighbors, the dukes of Aquitaine. Henry II's father and mother, Geoffrey the Handsome of Anjou and the ex-empress Matilda of England, gave generously toward the building of the new church, and so did Aliénor of Aquitaine's forbears of the illustrious house of Poitiers; hence it was fitting they both, Henry and Aliénor, should lie in burial there. When Henry Plantagenet died in 1189 in his castle at Chinon, which the old chronicler tells us rises steeply from the Vienne "straight up to heaven"—the Chinon whither Jeanne d'Arc was to come to give France a new soul—the dead monarch was carried to Fontevrault church near by, instead of to the Grammont he favored, the mother-house of a new Order founded by Stephen de Tierney in 1176. The archbishop of Tours came to Fontevrault to conduct the funeral, and Henry's rebellious son, Richard Cœur-de-Lion, stood by while they lowered into the tomb the great administrator who gave us the germs of our jury system, the man of the same unbridled passions, the same strong leadership in arms and statecraft, as his ancestor, Fulk Nerra, who had won this strip of middle France by sheer ability. And well Richard might feel serious, for the nine generations of increasing prosperity, promised to Fulk I of Anjou, ended with him.

In 1199 the Lion-hearted himself was brought to Fontevrault for burial; he had begged to be laid in penitence at the feet of the father he had defied, like the true Angevin he was. As his elder brother had said: "It has ever been the way with Plantagenets for brother to hate brother, and for son to turn against father." The ceremony for Richard in Fontevrault abbey church was conducted by St. Hugh from Lincoln, where he was raising a splendid Early-English cathedral. He had come to France to protest to Richard against further spoliation of his see. At this 'shrouding of a second Angevin among the shrouden women,' Aliénor stood beside the nuns, and, the ceremony over, St. Hugh, so wise and holy amid such seething passions, proceeded to comfort the widowed Berengaria.

Richard, like his father, was a cosmopolite. "*Miey hom e miey baron, Angles, Norman, Peytavin et Gascon,*" he sang in his prison lay, and indeed one would be puzzled to know which of them were the countrymen of him whom Guizot called "the bravest, most inconsiderate, most passionate, most ruffianly, most heroic adventurer of the Middle Ages."

In 1204 his equally turbulent, able, and seductive mother, Aliénor, was buried at Fontevrault beside the husband against whom she had stirred up undutiful sons, and who in his last years had kept her shut away from further mischief. From 1122 to 1204 stretched her full life; queen of France for fifteen years, queen of England for fifty, a pernicious influence upon them both, but always a most sensible ruler for her own Aquitaine. She passed her final years in peaceful Fontevrault, but her stormy destiny was to be troubled to the end. In 1204 her grandson, Arthur of Brittany, besieged her in a Midi castle where she was visiting, and when John Lackland heard of his mother's plight he came by forced marches to her relief and captured Arthur, who soon after was foully murdered. Aliénor had seen the rise of Gothic at St. Denis, whose corner stone her French husband laid, and she lived to found churches of the gracious Plantagenet phase of the new art. But true daughter of the Midi that she was, an Aquitaine cupola church is her rightful funeral monument. In her, as in her own Midi of that age, culture and corruption were precocious.

The fourth of the famous Plantagenet tombs at Fontevrault which England has tried to get for Westminster Abbey, is that of Isabelle of Angoulême (d. 1247), the wife of John Lackland. And there once were two others, the tomb of Richard Cœur-de-Lion's favorite sister, Jeanne (d. 1199), who became the fourth wife of Raymond VI of Toulouse, and that of her son, Count Raymond VII (d. 1249), of the Albigensian wars—tombs swept away either by the Huguenots or during the Revolution. As the XIX century opened, the Plantagenet tombs lay forgotten in a cellar. When England became aware of their value they were shipped to Paris in 1846, to be taken across the Channel. Luckily, however, an Angevin, M. de Falloux, became minister on the declaration of the Second Republic, and the four precious mausoleums were returned to Fontevrault church.

Aliénor was ninth in descent from that Duke of Aquitaine who had founded great Cluny itself. Her grandfather, Guillaume IX, the troubadour duke, was a benefactor of the newly established Fontevrault. When her father resigned his dominion in penitence, his will was that Aliénor, his heiress, should wed the son of the king of France. So in Bordeaux Cathedral, in 1137, Aliénor married the future Louis VII. No temperaments could have been more opposite. In 1249 she took the Crusader's cross from St. Bernard, at Vézelay—where the monks were building their glorious basilica. At Constantinople her troublous beauty roused admiration, and scandal at Antioch, where the ruler was her own handsome young uncle, Raymond of Poitiers.[182] Her union with Louis became an irksome bond and she clamored for its dissolution on the ground of consanguinity. The flouted French king was only too happy to be rid of her, but Abbot Suger, foreseeing all too clearly the national calamity that would be precipitated should Aliénor's great domains pass to a rival of France, held together the mismatched pair. When he died, in 1152, headstrong Aliénor broke loose, and as she rode away from the court of France the great lords came out to woo her—one of them even tried to kidnap her. Because she craved a strong arm to revenge herself on her first husband, she chose

---

[182] *"Dans ces choses-là on eu dit plus qu'il n'y en a, mais aussi il y a souvent plus qu'on eu dit,"* says the discreet historian Mézerai.

as consort young Henry Plantagenet, Count of Anjou and Maine, and Duke of Normandy; she was thirty, Henry not yet twenty. Thus began the long Capet-Angevin duel, not to be fought out to a finish until 1452, when all that Henry II had possessed on the Continent and all of Aliénor's wide domain were in the hands of the king of France. It needed a St. Jeanne to atone for the very unsaintly Aliénor.

The Plantagenet Tombs at Fontevrault

From this unscrupulous, mischief-making, virile, and capable queen of the XII century sprang a vigorous brood of men and women, passionate in both good and evil, and most of them enlightened art patrons, builders of churches, and writers of verses. Cœur-de-Lion was a troubadour. John Lackland's son built Westminster Abbey. Aliénor's daughter, the queen of Castile, had an Angevin architect help in the building of Las Huelgas, by Burgos. Her daughter of Champagne set the trouvères singing of Lancelot, Tristan, and Iseult. Another Eleanor of her lineage had her funeral journey marked by sculptured crosses from Lincolnshire to Charing Cross. It was given Aliénor to make some atonement for the evil she brought on France in her youth; at eighty years of age she went into Spain to bring back her granddaughter, Blanche of Castile, as bride for the grandson of the discarded Louis VII, and Blanche gave France the saint-king who illuminated his realm with fair churches. Another of Aliénor's great-grandsons was a saint-king, Ferdinand, the conqueror of Seville, who founded many a church. Even as the cruelty and craft of John Lackland cropped out in Charles d'Anjou, whom the Sicilian Vespers punished, so the culture and inconsistency of Cœur-de-Lion appeared again in his nephew of Champagne, Thibaut IV, the maker of songs. From Aliénor descended Bishop Eudes de Sully, who built the western portals of Notre Dame at Paris, and

Henry de Sully, who had the plans drawn for Bourges Cathedral. Herself an outstanding figure in the early day of Gothic art, and ancestress of enlightened builders, much can be forgiven Aliénor. All of which brings us back to the starting point of our chapter, the formation of the Plantagenet Gothic school of architecture.

PLANTAGENET GOTHIC

The XII and XIII centuries were a period when men were at their strongest; never before or since have they shown equal energy in such varied directions or such intelligence in the direction of their energy; yet these marvels of history—these Plantagenets; these scholastic philosophers; these architects of Rheims and Amiens; these Innocents and Robin Hoods and Marco Polos; these crusaders who planted their enormous fortresses all over the Levant; these monks who made the wastes and barrens yield harvests—all, without apparent exception, bowed down before the woman. The woman might be the good or the evil spirit, but she was always the stronger force.

—Henry Adams.

There have been various divisions of this school, and it is always well to bear in mind that such cut-and-dried classifications are arbitrary and made use of merely for the greater ease of the student. By dividing Plantagenet work into three periods—preceded by a brief incubation hour, the twenty years before 1150—it is easier to follow the evolving steps of this brilliant phase of the builder's art.

During the short introductory stage before 1150 the cupola had the upper hand and imposed its construction on the intersecting ribs just imported from the north. The earliest *bombé* vaults with ribs are really cupolas still, since the stones of their infilling were laid in concentric rings round and round. Only a small number of these ribbed cupolas were built.

Then in the first phase of Plantagenet Gothic appeared the ascendency of ribbed vault over cupola. The dome was lowered and the stones of the infilling were laid like those of a true Gothic vault, not horizontally, round and round, but vertically, with the courses running parallel with the ridges of the triangular compartments traced by the diagonals. Each of the four triangular cells was concave in both directions, with a groin defining its axial line. Hence eight panels, not four, composed the *bombé* vault, groin ridges alternating with ribs.

Such groin lines called for strengthening ribs beneath them, since a curving surface has more need of a bone skeleton to stiffen it. Given the *bombé* shape, it was inevitable for the architect to arrive soon at the use of ridge ribs between the diagonals. The Plantagenet vault *par excellence* is made up of eight ribs that branch from a central keystone, those ribs being of the same slight graceful profile as the arches framing each vault section.

For a time the rib molds of the First Period were enormously heavy and wide, like the diagonals of the nave of Angers Cathedral—the oldest Angevin Gothic work extant (c. 1150). Their profile shows two large round molds with a flat space between. Before long the level space tended to swell into a roll molding, which in time predominated over the lateral ones; such are the diagonals of the Trinité church at Angers (c. 1170). Finally, the side rolls died out altogether, leaving one slender uniform torus, a characteristic of the Second Period of Plantagenet art.

When the lateral and transverse arches adopted the same delicate profile as that of the eight branching ribs, there was achieved the slender elegance and rare distinction typical of the best Plantagenet interiors. Keystones were richly carved, and pretty figures and heads were added where the vault ribs met the framing arches. During the last quarter of the XII century the Plantagenet school was building vaults of this type, and they remained in vogue till the cuplike shape died out altogether. In Plantagenet art the ramification and intercrossing of ribs had a structural reason, since they were the logical result of the concave outline of the vault and not, like the supplementary ribs of Flamboyant Gothic, mere ornamentations.

In the third and final period of Plantagenet Gothic, the ribs ramified more and more. They had first been increased about the windows of apses, because an eight-branch vault was better suited to a square than to a curve. During the years preceding 1250, the ramification of the ribs grew very complicated. All divisions between the vault sections were eliminated, and the masonry roof appeared to be continuous, one bay melting subtly into the next—in reality a cradle vault, *à pénétrations*, carried on intercrossing, branching Gothic ribs. The construction of such stone roofs was no easy matter and comparatively few of them were built.

It is interesting to note that a germ of the Angevin school when carried to England, then under the same Plantagenet rule, developed into what is a unique architectural glory, English fan tracery vaulting.

Most of the monuments of Angevin art fall under the three main divisions here given. Like a beautiful hybrid, the Plantagenet stone roof passed through a continuous series of transformations, while in northern France, once a satisfactory masonry vault had been achieved, it was adhered to faithfully as a classic type until the Flamboyant, or final, phase.

Frequently a Plantagenet church is extremely plain outside, in striking contrast with the aërial grace of its interior. The cause is a structural one, hence satisfactory. The thrust of a *bombé* vault is not altogether concentrated on branching ribs, piers, and buttresses, but in part is borne by the inclosure walls. Hence these latter were made thick and pierced merely by lancet windows; with such walls there was no need of flying buttresses. When the piers were somewhat relieved of the roof load by the thick walls, they could be made exceedingly slender. There is an effect of gracious winsomeness in certain Plantagenet churches, to be described only by such words as "fairylike" and "Saracenic." The transient perfect moment of the art of northern France was seized and rendered by the curving transept at Soissons, an ideal vision of the Beyond. In southwestern France the first, fine, careless rapture nothing can recapture is to be found in St. Serge at Angers, of lesser genius than Soissons, but, like it, possessed of an enthrallment that is enduring.

THE CATHEDRAL OF ANGERS.[183]

A mon avis, ceux qui n'ont pas au moins le tourment religieux
ignorent la moitié de la vie, et la plus belle, la moitié de la pitié. Un
esprit est bien incomplet s'il ne s'élève pas jusqu'à sa destinée, et
un cœur est bien faible s'il n'a que des motifs humains d'agir, de
se contraindre, et de se donner ou de pardonner.

—RENÉ BAZIN (born in Angers, 1850).

No city in southwestern France is a more satisfactory center for a comparative study of Plantagenet Gothic than Angers—the old Black Angers of history,
which owed its importance not to any pre-eminence of site, but to the powerful
line whose cradle land it was.

Each phase of the regional school of Gothic can be found in Angers. In the
tower of St. Aubin, a vestige of an ancient abbey named after a VI-century bishop
of the city, is a ribbed cupola, typical of the incubating period of the school.[184] It
is more a cupola than a Gothic vault. The stones are laid horizontally in concentric
rings, and the ribs are more decorative than structural, being in part embedded in
the infilling. The abbot who erected it ruled from 1127 to 1154.

The First Period of the Gothic of Anjou is represented at Angers by a masterpiece of elemental force—the nave of the cathedral. Three huge so-called domical
vaults, truly Gothic in construction, span the sixty-foot unaisled nave of St. Maurice. The stones are laid parallel with the groin line of each triangular panel between the intersecting ribs. Those diagonals are needlessly heavy, for the builders
were still experimenting. The crown of each vault section is ten feet higher than the
framing arches—wall arch and transverse arch. The exceptional span of Angers'
three massive vaults is due to a reconstruction of the nave undertaken in the XII
century, at which time the side aisles of the Romanesque cathedral were eliminated and the entire width of the edifice thrown into an unobstructed hall.

[183] *Congrès Archéologique*, 1910, the cathedral of Angers; p. 161, Chanoine Urseau; p.
182, St. Serge; p. 228, the château; p. 232, l'évêché; Louis de Farcy, *Monographie de la cathédrale
d'Angers* (1910), 3 vols. and album; *ibid., Les vitraux de la nef de la cathédrale d'Angers* (1912);
J. Denais, *Monographie de la cathédrale d'Angers* (Paris, 1899); John Bilson, "Angers Cathedral, the Vaults of the Nave," in *Journal of the Royal Institute of British Architects*, 1911-12, p.
727; also in the *Congrès Archéologique*, 1910, vol. 2, p. 203; V. Godard-Faultrier, *Répertoire
archéologique de l'Anjou* (1865); L. Halphen, *Le comté d'Anjou au XIᵉ siècle* (Paris, Picard, 1906);
Léon Palustre, *La Renaissance en France* (3 vols.), vol. 3, Anjou et Poitou (Paris, Quantin); H.
Jouin, *Les musées d'Angers* (Paris, Plon, 1885), 4to; Péan de la Tuilerie, *Le Maine et l'Anjou*;
Wismes, *Le Maine et l'Anjou, historiques, archéol. e pittoresque* (Paris), 2 vols., folio; E. Lelong,
"Histoire et mon. d'Angers," in *Angers et l'Anjou* (1903); Lecoy de la Marche, *Le roy René, sa
vie, son administration* (Paris, 1875), 2 vols.; Kate Norgate, *England Under the Angevin Kings*
(London, 1887), 2 vols.; De Solies, *Foulques Nerra*; Célestin Port, *Dictionnaire historique, géographique, et biographique de Maine-et-Loire* (Paris and Angers, 1874-78), 3 vols. also his *Notes
et notices angevins* (Angers, 1879); A. J. de H. Bushnell, *Storied Windows* (New York, Macmillan Company, 1914); Sir J. H. Ramsay, *The Angevin Empire*, (London, 1903).

[184] Ch. H. Besnard, "La coupole nervée de la Tour St. Aubin d'Angers," in *Congrès
Archéologique*, 1910, vol. 2, p. 196; L. de Farcy, "Tour St. Aubin," in *Bulletin Monumental*,
1906, p. 558.

Mr. John Bilson, the eminent English archæologist, belittles the influence of the cupola church in Angevin Gothic, the shape of whose vaults he attributes to a structural cause. He thinks that the extreme width of Angers' nave made it essential to raise the keystone above the crowns of transverse and wall arches in order to prevent its settling. The diagonals were made more obtuse than the equilateral framing arches lest they might tower too high. Given the form adopted for the arches, the *bombé* vault web resulted inevitably. Arch curves determine the forms of a vault. None the less is M. Berthelé's account of the Plantagenet school sound both ethnically and æsthetically. The Angevin architect chose to persist in the use of *bombé* vaults over narrow spans where there was no structural need to raise the keystone.

A succession of cathedrals had stood on the site of Angers' actual church. To that of the IV century, St. Martin, Gaul's apostle, presented relics of St. Maurice and his legion of Theban soldiers. A Merovingian cathedral mentioned by Gregory of Tours was succeeded by a Carolingian basilica, and after the year 1000 the chief church of Angers was rebuilt several times as Romanesque. A dedication occurred in 1030. In 1032 the cathedral was wiped out by a fire caused by that remarkable personage, Fulk Nerra, the Black Falcon, who raised Anjou from an insignificant under-fief to be one of the chief powers in France.[185] To atone for his feudal excesses, Fulk built many shrines and made many pilgrimages; in Palestine, with the same melodramatic instinct for the picturesque which his descendant, Cœur-de-Lion, was to display, he walked barefooted in the streets of Jerusalem, flagellated by his own servitors, as he lamented, "Lord be merciful to a perjured, unfaithful Christian wandering far from his native land."

All over Anjou, and in Touraine, Fulk III put up abbey churches and castles; "the great builder," he was called. One day, from his castle on the rock of Angers, his falcon eyes saw a dove fluttering over a certain spot beyond the river, and there he founded the abbey of St. Nicholas in 1020, and his wife at that period (he had a succession of wives, one of whom he is said to have killed) founded a nunnery

---

[185] Beginning with a Breton woodsman, five counts of Anjou ruled before Fulk III the Black (989-1040). He held Vendôme, Amboise, and Loches, where he founded Beaulieu Abbey, and he won Chinon, and Saumur, where he established St. Florent-les-Saumur. His grandfather, Fulk II the Good, a canon in St. Martin's at Tours, and a poet, had said, "*Rex illiteratus est asinus coronatus*," which Henry I of England was fond of repeating. The son of Fulk Nerra was Geoffrey Martel (d. 1060), who won Tours and Le Mans, but later lost the overlordship of the latter to William the Conqueror. He founded the Trinité at Vendôme. Geoffrey and Fulk, his two nephews, succeeded in turn, but Geoffrey was kept imprisoned in Chinon for almost thirty years by his unnatural brother Fulk Rechin, or the Quarreler, who had all the greed, subtlety, and turbulance of his line, without its genius for statesmanship. He is counted as the first historian of the Middle Ages. (See *Hist. littér. de la France* (Paris, 1750), vol. 9, p. 391.) Fulk Rechin's son by the beautiful Bertrada de Montfort (who deserted him for the king of France) was Fulk V, who wedded the heiress of Maine. When later Fulk V won a second heiress in the East, he left Anjou and Maine to his son Geoffrey the Handsome, and reigned as king of Jerusalem (d. 1143). Geoffrey (d. 1151), nicknamed Plantagenet, married to the heiress of Normandy and England, always preferred Le Mans to Angers. His son became Henry II of England and a leader in Europe because of his territorial possessions on the Continent and his ability as a statesman.

close by to which was once attached the church of the Trinité. In the XVI century St. Nicholas was called Ronceray, because a bramble-rose insisted on pushing its way up through the choir's pavement.[186] A superman was Fulk the Black, highly dowered intellectually, with enormous capacity for organization, but of shameless wickedness, calculating, subtle, unscrupulous as to the means by which he pursued his designs, and of demoniac temper—marked traits in his race from generation to generation.

Vestiges of the cathedral of Angers which rose after the fire of 1032, and in which Urban II preached the First Crusade, are in the actual nave, built by Bishop Ulger[187] (1125-49). He taught in the cathedral school, which school was the nucleus of the present University of Angers. His successor, Bishop Normand de Doué (1149-53), at his own expense, substituted for the timber roof of the new nave its massive Angevin vaults. When we recall that only fifteen years earlier Abbot Suger, who started Gothic architecture on its triumphal career, was building the heavy diagonals to be seen in the antechurch at St. Denis, we can understand what pioneers were the builders of southwest France in the use of the cardinal organ of the new system.

Angers Cathedral continued building during the final years of the XII century, under Bishop Raoul de Beaumont (1177-97), who erected the southern arm of the transept and added a short choir; the city walls at that period prevented the farther extension of the apse. Along the west façade, the same prelate built a spacious porch, twenty-five feet deep, which stood till 1806, when, in spite of episcopal protest, the civic authorities tore it down rather than trouble to repair it. Sorely does the western entrance need that softening portico. Angers' portal images are

---

[186] The abbatial of St. Nicolas-du-Ronceray is in a lamentable state; its nave serves as a hall for the Arts and Crafts school, the transept's north arm is a laundry, and its south arm a roofless ruin. The dome at its crossing is without distinct pedestal. The nuns of this house erected at the side of their own sanctuary, the Trinité church for parish use. The present admirable Trinité was built after a fire in 1062. Its chevet and transept are the oldest parts, and then rose the nave, covered with First-Period Angevin vaults (c. 1170). Chapel-like niches are lost in the thickness of the walls.

Angers' abbatial of St. Martin contains Gallo-Roman, Merovingian, and Carolingian vestiges, and parts of the XI, XII, and XV centuries. Fulk Nerra rebuilt it on returning from one of his pilgrimages. Over its transept-crossing is a dome modeled on the one at Fontevrault, without separate pedestal. The church possesses one of the earliest eight-branch Gothic vaults extant; King René added the Flamboyant parts. Chanoine Pinier at his own expense is restoring the choir and transept.

Congrès Archéologique, 1910, vol. 1, p. 211, "St. Martin," Chanoine Pinier; and vol. 2, p. 12, "St. Nicolas-du-Ronceray," E. Lefèvre-Pontalis.

[187] Bishop Ulger carried forward, too, the episcopal palace which stood on V-century walls over the Roman citadel and is connected with the cathedral's transept. Its ancient façade is the finest civic monument in Angers (1101-49). The ground floor was used as a stable; over it rose Bishop Ulger's synodal hall, and under the rafters was made a library in the XV century. Angers is exceptionally rich in late-Gothic and Renaissance mansions. G. d'Espinay, *Angers et l'Anjou* (Angers, 1903); *ibid., Notices archéol., Les monuments d'Angers, Saumur et ses environs* (Angers, 1875), 2 vols.

of the same archaic column-statue type as those at Chartres' western doors, and here, too, in the tympanum is a Byzantine Christ in an elliptical aureole, surrounded by the symbols of the evangelists. Bishop Raoul de Beaumont came of one of the illustrious races of crusaders, statesmen, and prelates, the *ancienne chevalerie* in which France was so prolific for centuries. A XIII-century Beaumont, marshal of France, stood by Joinville in voting against the knight's return to Europe until they had redeemed their servitors from captivity; a XIV-century Beaumont was instrumental in giving Dauphiny to France; a Beaumont in the XVIII century was the archbishop of Paris, who warned the nation that if it de-Christianized itself it would be denationalized. Bishop Raoul's nephew, Guillaume de Beaumont, became bishop of Angers, and in 1236 donated land from his garden for the erection of the northern arm of the transept. Eight-branch Plantagenet vault sections cover transept and choir.

The choir of Angers Cathedral was extended after 1274, when permission was obtained from St. Louis' brother, Charles d'Anjou, to demolish part of the city ramparts. Heavy buttresses mark the junction of the old part and the new. By the extension of the eastern limb the church became a bold Latin cross. Secluded nooks in dim religious corners are not to be found in these unaisled churches of southwestern France. In them is no curving procession path, no picturesque perspective effects. Though they possess their own quiet nobility, seldom does their grave reverence rise to sublimity. The exterior of Angers Cathedral was made equally simple, without radiating apse chapels or flying buttresses.

The cathedral's nave boasts some windows which were donated before 1180 by a generous canon. Borders of the St. Denis glass were repeated in them. The third window (north), which has an inimitable deep blue background and a wide border, relates St. Catherine's life; the fourth portrays, the Burial of the Virgin; and the fifth is devoted to St. Vincent. Probably local workers allied with the St. Denis school made these lights. In the nave's southern wall is a good Renaissance lancet, transferred here from a ruined château. When the choir was completed, its windows were filled with glass of the Paris school a century later than the nave's windows. The transept roses are Flamboyant Gothic.

Angers Cathedral tops a high hill, so that its towers are landmarks, visible for thirty miles around. Its west façade has been so reconstructed that it now presents the ungainly proportions of the church fronts in Hanover and Brunswick. After a fire, in 1516, when the towers were renewed, stone spires were added by the well-known Flamboyant Gothic master, Rouland Le Roux, who elaborated the frontispiece of Rouen Cathedral. Then, in 1533, a third tower was built between the original two. One of its walls rested on the west façade, but the other three have mere arches for foundations, so that the tower hangs in space, as it were, the kind of feat applauded by the tourist guide, but which the true lover of structural sincerity can dispense with. Jean de l'Espine, a local master of whom Angers is proud, designed the curious central tower, and two sculptors who had worked on groups at Solesmes made the façades eight warrior images which have been restored.

Scarcely was Angers Cathedral newly dressed when came the tragic year 1562, to wreck the gathered treasures of generations. The Huguenots broke into the transept from the bishop's garden—and ever since that door has been walled up in disgrace. For a fortnight they intrenched themselves in the church, looting its treasures, destroying tombs and images. More than a hundred splendid tombs lined the walls of the church. The neo-classic canons of the XVII and XVIII centuries lost so entirely the comprehension of the national art that they sent priceless bronze tombs to the smelting pot, even that of Bishop Raoul de Beaumont, the builder. A silver-gilt altar given by Bishop Normand de Doué who spanned the nave with its vaults of magnificent proportions, was sold, as was another altar, the gift of Bishop Guillaume de Beaumont, and with the proceeds was erected the pseudo-classic baldaquin over the high altar. They did away with the lower panels of the precious XII-century windows in order that a new metal balustrade might show to better effect. In a final attack of *bon goût*, those worthy canons proceeded to whitewash the entire inside of the cathedral, including the tombs and statues. The Revolution broke up the elaborate funereal monument of good King René, on which several generations had worked; Jacques Morel, who sculptured the Souvigny sarcophagus, was putting final touches to it when he died in Angers in 1453. For years after 1793 its chiseled stones were used by the city's masons to adorn chimney pieces in civilians' houses.

Anjou, after returning to the French crown in the XIV century, was again given as an appanage to a king's son, to Louis,[188] son of Jean le Bon, and brother of those art-loving Valois princes, Charles V and the Dukes of Berry and Burgundy. Louis I d'Anjou had made for his palace chapel at Angers, in 1378, some tapestries telling the Apocalypse wonders. His grandson, good King René, presented them to the cathedral, where first they were hung for a visit of Louis XI. In the days when the cathedral walls were being whitewashed those one hundred and fifty yards of textile art, made by Parisian weavers after Flemish models—and the oldest-dated tapestries extant—were put up for sale, but, not finding a purchaser, were used to cover greenhouses and to line stables. When in 1843 the bishop of Angers was able to rescue a hundred yards of the Apocalypse, he was mocked for his taste for rubbish. Three hundred francs was all he paid for over sixty sections of the embroidery, and when one section was recently loaned to the exhibition at Ghent it was insured for forty thousand dollars.

Louis II d'Anjou married Yolande of Aragon, a statesman-like woman of sound character and good taste, and together they built the pavilion that stands within the fortress inclosure, and the chapel adjoining it (finished in 1411), whose *bombé* vaults are carried on ribs of prismatic profile. Yolande's two sons, Charles and René, ruled Anjou. The claims of Louis XI to the duchy caused his uncle, King

---

[188] The first line of Anjou's counts came to an end when John Lackland did away with his nephew, Arthur of Brittany. The region of the Loire became then most willingly a part of Phillipe-Auguste's royal domain. Anjou was given as an appanage to St. Louis' brother Charles d'Anjou, whose first wife brought him Provence, and who by invitation and conquest became king of the Two Sicilies. His son, Charles II, built the church of St. Maximin in Provence. He left only one daughter, who married the Count of Valois, like herself of St. Louis' direct line. The son of that union mounted the French throne as Philip VI. It was his son, Jean le Bon, who again detached Anjou from the French crown for his son Louis, who began the short-lived third line of Angevin princes.

René, to spend his latter years in Provence, but never did he forget his birthplace, and to Angers Cathedral he sent the green marble Roman bath mounted on lions, now used as a holy-water font. René wrote poems and plays, composed church music, painted and illuminated, and throughout a long life of misfortunes proved himself a loyal knight and Christian philosopher. Shortly after his death Anjou returned to the French crown.

The ramparts within whose somber walls was the palace[189] of the counts and dukes of Anjou's three lines of rulers, was constructed by St. Louis, from 1228 to 1238, though begun by his grandfather, Philippe-Auguste. For the precincts of his huge fortress St. Louis was compelled to take lands from the congregation of Toussaint. With the compensation money the religious rebuilt their church and roofed it with a Plantagenet Gothic vault of the elaborate final phase of the regional school. The interlocking ribs had three lines of keystones, like the vault of Airvault (Deux-Sèvres).

Toussaint had been founded in the XI century by a pious canon, as a refuge for the poor and stricken, and the duty of its clergy was to visit the sick and bury the dead. That every forlorn soul might feel under the protection of his own chosen patron saint, the name All Saints was chosen. The Revolution suppressed the asylum of charity and in 1815 Prussian cavalry were stabled in the neglected church. The roofless nave now serves as an archæological museum. The vaults of the choir were made early in the XVIII century on the same model as the nave's XIII-century Plantagenet roof.

The fortress built by St. Louis on the Toussaint property was saved from demolition by the seneschal of Anjou, who, when Henry III's orders came to destroy the ramparts, had the tact to proceed in so leisurely a fashion that after seven years, when he was able to get the order revoked, little more was destroyed than the upper stories of the towers. A kneeling image of that truly patriotic seneschal, Donadieu de Puycharic, is now in the museum installed in the XII-century hospital of St. Jean.

That hospital of St. Jean was begun by another enlightened seneschal of Anjou, but before long (c. 1180) Henry Plantagenet undertook to finish and endow it, some say to expiate the assassination of St. Thomas Becket. The oldest parts of St. John's establishment are the granary and the north and east corridors of the cloister; the latter's south gallery was built (1538) by Angers' local architect, Jean de l'Espine. The hospital hall was undertaken between 1174 and 1188, and at first was roofed in wood.

Shortly after 1200 the Knights of St. John Hospitalier of Jerusalem were put in charge of Angers hospital, and governed it till 1232. During their occupancy the

[189] That a portion of Angers' palace walls dates from Gallo-Roman times is indicated by the courses of brick in the small stones. When such brick courses alternate with big material, the work was done after 1000. Of the red flint-stone castle built by Fulk Nerra only fragments remain. A fire in 1132 and later disasters wiped out the counts' residence, to which Henry Plantagenet had added. L. de Farcy, "La chapelle du château d'Angers," in *Revue de l'art chrétien*, 1902; Henri René, *Le château d'Angers* (Angers, 1908); H. Havard, éd., *La France artistique et monumental*, vol. 2, "Angers," H. Jouin.

hall was covered by its twenty-four small cuplike sections, each of which is carried on four slender ribs. The effect of the three aisles of little *bombé* vaults is alluring. The slender torus usually distinguished the eight-branch Plantagenet type, and its use here for simple diagonals is an exception. The chapel attached to the hospital was also built in two campaigns; over part of it was employed the eight-rib vault, while portions were roofed in the more complicated Plantagenet way.

The singular grace of St. Jean's hospital hall, with its slender columns and multiple little *coupoliformes* vaults, inspired the small choir of St. Serge, which many hold to be the most exquisite example of Plantagenet Gothic. The church[190] once formed part of an ancient Benedictine monastery named for the pope, who had instituted the triple chanting of the *Agnus Dei* in the Mass. Hitherto the Angevin masonry roof had been applied to churches without side aisles. The ground plan of the cupola church had been adhered to. The Plantagenet architects now began to copy another regional model, Poitou's Romanesque church, whose side aisles were almost as high as the principal span they buttressed; hence the light came entirely from the lateral corridors. One roof covered all.

Poitiers Cathedral was among the first to use Poitou's pre-Gothic plan in Plantagenet architecture. The choir of St. Serge developed the same idea in its own small, gracious way. No doubt the harmonious effect obtained in St. John's hospital by the three aisles of *bombé* vaults inspired the architect of St. Serge, who built his choir, from 1220 to 1225. Six fragile-looking columns, thirty feet in height, support with ease the twelve little Plantagenet vaults, which are of the eight-branch type, with elaborate keystones, and minute figures at the intersection of the ribs and the framing arches. At the choir's square eastern end the ribs ramify considerably around the windows. It is impossible to say wherein lies the witchery of this small monument—all elegance and lightness. Some call it Saracenic because of its exotic loveliness. Its science of construction is perfect. Certainly some individual genius designed it.

SAUMUR[191]

L'ancienne Grand' Rue de Saumur ... la rue montueuse qui

---

[190] The nave of St. Serge is a mediocre XV-century structure. In its transept walls are vestiges of earlier churches; the cordons of brick in the stonework date from Carolingian times. *Congrès Archéologique*, 1871 and 1910; V. Godard-Faultier, "Le cœur de St. Serge à Angers," in *Bulletin Monumental*, 1866, vol. 32; J. Denais, "Histoire et description de l'église St. Serge à Angers," in *L'inventaire des richesses d'art de la France*, vol. 4, p. 20, Province, monuments religieux (Paris, Plon).

[191] *Congrès Archéologique*, 1862 and 1910; Prosper Merimée, *Notes d'un voyage dans l'Ouest de la France* (Paris, 1836), pp. 345-358; G. d'Espinay, *Notices archéologiques. Les monuments d'Angers, Saumur et ses environs* (Angers, 1875), 2 vols.; Célestin Port, "Les stalles et les tapisseries de St. Pierre de Saumur," in *Revue des Sociétés savantes*, 1868, p. 278; *ibid.*, *Dictionnaire historique, géographique, et biographique de Maine-et-Loire* (Paris and Angers, 1874-78), 3 vols.; V. Godard-Faultrier, *Monuments antiques de l'Anjou, arrondissement de Saumur* (Angers, 1863); Jules Juiffrey, "Tapisserie du XVe siécle à l'église Notre Dame-de-Nantilly à Saumur," in *Revue de l'art ancien et moderne*, 1897, vol. 4, p. 75; Eugène Müntz, Jules Juiffrey, Alex. Pinchart, *Histoire générale de la tapisserie* (Paris, 1879-84), 3 vols.

mène au château, obscure en quelques endroits, remarquable par
la sonorité de son petit pavé caillouteux, toujours propre et sec ...
la paix de ses maisons impénétrables, noirs, et silencieuses—l'histoire de France est là, tout entière.

—BALZAC, *Eugénie Grandet* (whose scene is Saumur).

Close by Angers lies Saumur on the Loire, "well-loved, well-set city." It comprises, with its environs, another center for the study of Plantagenet Gothic. The
town is topped by its castle, now in main part of the XIV century. In its former
great hall, built by Henry Plantagenet, took place, in 1241, that celebrated fête
called the *Non-Pareille* which Joinville has described. His memory of it was so
fresh, after sixty years, that he could tell the color of Louis IX's robe and surcoat;
perhaps it was the first time that Joinville saw the saint-king who was to become
his closest friend. He was not yet twenty when he accompanied his suzerain of
Champagne, Thibaut IV, the maker of songs, to the feast held in Saumur château
for the knighting of Alphonse of Poitiers, the king's brother.

The Plantagenet Gothic Choir of St. Serge at Angers (1220-1225)

The bodyguard of St. Louis were a Bourbon, a Coucy, and a Beaujeu, behind whom stood ranged a host of barons and knights in silk and cloth of gold. The future king of Portugal and a prince from Thuringia, the son of St. Elizabeth of Hungary, waited on the table of the queen-mother, Blanche of Castile, who, when she heard the name of the princeling from beyond the Rhine, called him to her side and placed a kiss upon his brow, since there, she said, his saintly mother must often have blessed him. Jealous passions, too, burned behind the glitter and show. Isabelle of Angoulême, the widow of John Lackland, married now to a Lusignan who had to render homage to his new suzerain, cried out, imperiously, "Am I a waiting woman that I should stand while they sit at ease?" and she proceeded to stir up war.

Below the castle of Saumur lies the XII-century unaisled church of St. Pierre, whose masonry roof belongs to different phases of Angevin Gothic. Over the transept-crossing is a ribbed cupola without distinct pedestal, inspired evidently by the small unribbed cupola of Fontevrault's crossing. The stones are laid in horizontal concentric courses like a true dome. Though archaic in structure, St. Pierre's *croisée* is of skilled execution. It belongs to the last third of the XII century.

Over the choir and transept are the heavy diagonals of the First Period of the Plantagenet development, and the nave's vault sections are carried on the eight branches of the Second Period. Powerful transverse arches separate the wide, square bays, and against the inclosure walls are other strong arches beneath the windows. The walls of St. Pierre's choir are not parallel, but draw closer together at the eastern end, for undoubtedly there was much intentional asymmetry in mediæval monuments. The Flamboyant day gave to St. Pierre its well-carved choir stalls and some exquisitely toned Flemish tapestries executed by local weavers.

Other superb tapestries adorn Notre Dame-de-Nantilly, a church patronized by Louis XI, who added to it the south aisle and a Flamboyant oratory. The body of the edifice belongs to the first half of the XII century; its barrel vault is braced by slightly pointed transverse arches. At the transept-crossing is a ribbed cupola, without distinct pedestal, like that of St. Pierre. Against the fourth pier, to the south, is the epitaph which good King René himself composed and set up because of his affection for his old nurse, Dame Tiphaine, for whose soul he begs a pater-noster of all who pass by. Against the fifth pier is the Limousin enamel crozier of the archbishop of Tyr, keeper of the seal for St. Louis, who was buried here in his native city in 1266.

Behind the Gothic Town Hall is the now unused chapel of St. Jean, a small example of the Third Period of Angevin architecture, when ribs branched considerably; in the square chevet they ramify to the number of twenty.

A mile down the river lies what is left of St. Florent-les-Saumur[192] re-estab-

[192] From Saumur, eight miles down the Loire, can be visited the magnificent Romanesque church at Cunault, XI and XII centuries. It has noticeable capitals, mural paintings, and Plantagenet vaults with sculptured keystones and figurines. Two miles below it lies Gennes, whose church has Angevin vaults of the First Period. To be reached, *via* Doué-la-Fontaine, are both Puy-Notre-Dame and Asnières, the latter called "the most beautiful ruin in Anjou." Its square-ended XIII-century choir resembles St. Serge's. Slender pillars divide

lished by Fulk Nerra when he conquered Saumur in 1026. Its narthex, now the chapel of a nuns' community, shows one of the earliest uses of the Plantagenet vault of eight branches (1170-1200). At St. Florent was living the daughter of the exiled poet-duke of Orléans, with her young husband, the Duke of Alençon, when one day in 1429 word came that at Chinon, near by, where Charles VII was staying, had arrived an inspired maid, and young d'Alençon, soon to be Jeanne d'Arc's lieutenant—her *gentil duc*—galloped along the banks of the Loire to see the wonder. So delighted was he with Jeanne's management of spear and horse that he presented her with a palfrey, and she came to St. Florent-les-Saumur for a four days' visit to his duchess, promising[193] that anxious young wife that she would bring back her husband safe and sound.

Fontevrault's abbatial, where culminated the art of the cupola church, is the chief excursion to be made from Saumur. It can be reached by a ten-mile trolley ride. Only three miles from Fontevrault, and a pleasant cross-country walk from it, is the beautiful Plantagenet Gothic church of St. Martin, at Candes,[194]

---

that wide chevet into three aisles of equal height, composing one of the most graceful specimens of the school's Third Period. One arm of the transept has heavy diagonals of the first phase; and over the other are the eight-branch type. The Huguenots wrecked Asnières in 1569. The present nave is a restitution. A society of artists saved the choir and transept from demolition.

The abbatial of Puy-Notre-Dame is very beautiful. Heavy diagonals of the First Period cover the transept's south arm; eight-branch vaults cover the nave and the transept's north limb; over the choir, which resembles St. Jean's chevet at Saumur, is a much-ramified Plantagenet vault. The lofty side aisles and clustered piers make this interior one of the best of XIII-century Angevin works extant. At St. Germain-sur-Vienne (Indre-et-Loire), two miles from Candes, the choir has the complicated multiple-ribbed vault of the Third Period, with three lines of keystones.

Congrès Archéologique, 1910, p. 128, Cunault and Gennes; p. 65, Puy-Notre-Dame and Asnières; E. de Lorière, "Asnières-sur-Vègre," in *Revue hist. et archéol. du Maine*, 1904, p. 95.

[193] At the battle of Jargeau, Jeanne reminded the duke of her promise. D'Alençon himself has related the episode: *"Je lui fis observer que c'était aller bien vite en besogne que d'attaquer si promptement: 'Soyez sans crainte,' me dit-elle, 'l'heure est bonne quand il plaît à Dieu, il faut besoigner quand s'est sa volonté: agissez, Dieu agira! Ah, gentil duc,' me dit-elle quelques instants après, 'aurais-tu peur? Ne sait-tu pas que j'ai promis à ta femme de te ramener sain et sauf?'"* Alas, for the deterioration of character brought about in those troubled years of foreign invasion and misrule; Jeanne's *gentil duc* was later to plot with the English and to be impeached.

At Chinon are specimens of Plantagenet Gothic (*Bulletin Monumental*, 1869). In the Loire-et-Cher department are some fourteen churches of the school. The other Plantagenet monuments usually seen by the traveler before his arrival in Angou are the eight-branch vaults at Vendôme, in the transept of the Trinité; the vault under the northwest tower of Tours Cathedral; and in Le Mans, the cathedral nave and the church of the Couture. At Mouliherne (Seine-et-Loire) every type of the Plantagenet development is present.

Congrès Archéologique, 1910, vol. 1, p. 130, "St. Florent-les-Saumur," André Rhein; vol. 2, "Les voûtes de l'église de Mouliherne," André Rhein; p. 247, "Les influences angevines sur les églises gothiques du Blésois et du Vendômois," F. Leseur.

[194] *Congrès Archéologique*, 1910, p. 33, André Rhein, on Candes; Abbé Bourassé, "No-

crowned with battlements, on the highland above the confluence of the Vienne and the Loire. In the ancient abbey here St. Martin died as the IV century closed. A chapel to the north of the choir marks the site of his cell, and its window recalls the pious piracy of his loyal parishioners of Tours, who claimed his body for burial, but who, knowing that Candes would not give it up, came by night and stole it away; and quite rightly they had judged, for when, centuries later, the Northmen invasions forced Tours to send its great relic for safe-keeping to Auxerre, it took an army of six thousand men to get it back.

The present choir of St. Martin's at Candes was built in the latter half of the XII century (c. 1180). Fifty years later rose the nave, justly considered one of the most brilliant examples of Plantagenet Gothic architecture, its model, not the unaisled cupola-church, but the Romanesque church of Poitou, whose side aisles are so high that their lancets are the only lighting of the edifice. St. Martin's hall-like interior of three spacious aisles is inundated with light. The well-proportioned clustered piers rising from pavement to vault-springing are placed considerably out of alignment, and in a number of other arrangements the architect here followed his personal bent. In the western porch the ribs of several Plantagenet vault sections fall on a central pillar.

THE CATHEDRAL AT POITIERS[195]

Vexilla Regis prodeunt	Abroad the regal banners fly
Fulget Crucis mysterium	And bear the mystic Cross on high,
Qua vita mortem pertulit	That Cross whereon Life suffered Death
Et morte vitam protulit.	And gave us Life with Dying breath.
Impleta sunt quæ concinit	That which the prophet-king of old
David fideli carmine,	Hath in mysterious verse foretold
Dicendo nationibus	Is now accomplished whilst we see
Regnavit a ligno Deus.	God ruling nations from a Tree.

—Fortunatus, bishop of Poitiers (599-607).[196]

---

tice historique et archéologique sur l'église de Candes," in *Mémoires de la Soc. archéol. de Touraine*, 1845, p. 141; Suppligeon, *Notices sur la ville et la collégiale de Candes* (Tours, 1885).

[195] *Congrès Archéologique*, 1843, 1884, and 1903, "Poitiers," André Rhein; H. L. de la Mauvinière, *Poitiers et Angoulême* (Collection, Villes d'art célèbres), (Paris, H. Laurens, 1908); Abbé Auber, *Histoire de la cathédrale de Poitiers* (Poitiers, 1849), 2 vols.; *ibid., Histoire civile, relig. et littéraire du Poitou* (Poitiers, 1856), 8 vols.; J. Berthelé, *Recherches pour servir à l'histoire des arts en Poitou*; Alfred Richard, *Histoire des comtes du Poitou*, 788-1204 (Paris, Picard et fils, 1903), 2 vols.; Dreux-Duradier, *Histoire littéraire du Poitou*; Alexis Forel, *Voyage au pays des sculpteurs romans* (Paris and Geneva, 1913), 2 vols.; Raynouard, *Choix des poésies originales des troubadours* (Paris, Didot, 1816), vol. 5, "Richard Cœur-de-Lion"; R. P. Largent, *St. Hilaire de Poitiers* (Collection, Les Saints), (Paris, Lecoffre); J. Robuchon, *Paysages et monuments du Poitou* (Paris, 1890-1903), folio; (on Poitiers, Mgr. Barbier de Montault); Benj. Fillon, *Poitou et Vendée*; A. J. de H. Bushnell, *Storied Windows* (New York, Macmillan Company, 1914); Boissonnade, *Le Poitou* (Collection, Les régions de la France), (Paris, Cerf, 1920).

[196] The *Vexilla regis prodeunt* hymn is sung on Good Friday when the Blessed Sacrament is carried from the Repository to the main altar, and as a vesper hymn from the Saturday before Passion Sunday to Maundy Thursday. It has also been incorporated in

The noblest Gothic monument due to Henry Plantagenet and Aliénor of Aquitaine is the cathedral church at Poitiers, founded by them in 1162 about the same time that, in Paris, Louis VII witnessed the laying of the corner stone for a new chief church in his capital. Never were contemporary edifices more unlike in their form and their informing spirit. In Notre Dame of Paris breathes the struggle of human existence and that Christian resignation voiced by the XIII-century Franciscan in the *Dies Iræ*. St. Peter's Cathedral at Poitiers rings with Christian joy, with the triumphal strains of the hymn composed by its VI-century bishop for the arrival from Constantinople of the True Cross relic. From the hour that the ancient ecclesiastical city marched forth with banners flying to meet the Cross, Poitiers has held it to be a tree of royal honor, not of pathetic agony. Her greatest bishop, St. Hilary, was western Christendom's champion for the Son's divinity when the Arian heresy attacked it. Clovis defeated the Arian Visigoths at Poitiers in 508; Charles Martel checked the Mohammedans at Poitiers in 732.

A city's spiritual history speaks by its monuments. In the high place of honor in Poitiers' cathedral of St. Peter, hangs a gleaming canticle of translucent mosaic, a window which many hold to be the finest in the world. It celebrates God ruling nations from a tree. It is a passion and a triumph, an agony and an apotheosis. Eight centuries divide the inspiration of the Crucifixion window from St. Hilary's struggle with Arianism, six centuries from the canticle of Bishop Venantius Fortunatus, but Hilary's affirmation and the rejoicing of Fortunatus live in it, and through it have been passed on to us.

Poitiers Cathedral is a spacious hall-church illuminated by large lancets that seem to be chanting Alleluias, yet whose piety is plain and robust. It is a church loyal to indigenous art traditions, yet blending those sober Romanesque inheritances of Poitou with the delicate grace of Plantagenet Gothic. Its loveliness is severe, its slenderness is sturdy. St. Peter's both imposes and allures.

Poitiers was the cradle of Aliénor of Aquitaine's brilliant and debonaire line of troubadours, crusaders, and church builders. Charlemagne gave them the title of Duke of Aquitaine for their services against Islam. The first warrior duke died a hermit at St. Guilhem-le-Désert, which became a Midi pilgrim shrine where, in the Gothic dawn, appeared a very early use of diagonals, profiled like those of the Ile-de-France. A duke of Aquitaine founded Cluny, the greatest building energy of the ages. Another of the dynasty of the Guillaumes aided Bishop Fulbert to build Chartres, and, when fire wiped out Poitiers Cathedral, reconstructed it in Romanesque form. Guillaume VIII and Guillaume IX built at Bordeaux the churches of Ste. Croix, St. Seurin, and St. André. In Poitiers they raised anew Notre Dame-

---

the Roman Breviary for feasts of the Holy Cross. There have been a host of translations. In his *Medieval Hymns and Sequences*, London, 1813, Dr. J. M. Neale thus rendered the first quatrain:

> "The royal banners forward go.
> The cross shines forth with mystic glow,
> Where He in flesh, our flesh Who made,
> Our sentence bore, our ransom paid."

la-Grande and St. Hilaire, and founded Montierneuf,[197] blessed by Urban II in 1096. Aliénor's grandfather, Guillaume IX, the first-known troubadour, especially favored Fontevrault. Her father was that Guillaume X, with the appetites of eight men, an open boaster of his crimes, whom it took St. Bernard to beat to his knees in penitence, after which he passed out of history in the odor of sanctity as pilgrim to Compostela.

With the art of the builder Aliénor's own links were multiple. When Bishop Geoffrey de Lèves took charge of her as a young bride in Bordeaux, he was raising at Chartres the most beautiful tower in the world. She assisted at St. Denis' dedication and knew Abbot Suger well; at Vézelay she watched the Burgundians sculpting a portal of paradise. Through all her crowded life, with all her reckless sins upon her, Aliénor was loyal to her own region. She began Poitiers Cathedral in the same decade that she had her favorite son Richard the Lion-hearted installed as ruler of Aquitaine—another troubadour duke—seating him in the abbot's chair at St. Hilaire's, according to ancient custom. She blended with her own Poitou's Romanesque what was choicest in the Gothic art of her Angevin husband.

Poitiers Cathedral was the prototype of monuments such as Candes and Puy-Notre-Dame, in whose interiors Aliénor's own "high grace, the dower of queens," seems incarnate. An Angevin architect probably designed St. Peter's at Poitiers. The works started at the east end, which is square, and rises from the down-slope of the hill like a solid fortress, a hundred and fifty feet in height; Coligny's troops were one day to riddle with bullets that big quadrangular target. So thick was the eastern wall that the round chapels ending the choir disappeared in its depth.

The easternmost bays and the south arm of the transept were built about the same time, soon after 1160, and their masonry roof belongs to the first phase of the Gothic of the West. Over the crossing is a six-branch vault; for the rest of the church, the eight-branch type was used. The lower half of the inclosure walls is ornamented with a blind arcade above which runs a circulating gallery carried on corbels carved with fantasy. Again was used the artifice employed in Poitiers' Romanesque church of Notre Dame-la-Grande, whereby from the eastern end onward the edifice grew slightly wider and higher. The axial line deviates considerably, and it is known that this cathedral rose during different periods.

While the plan and the beginning of the work were of Aliénor and Henry's day, the greater part of the church was erected under their great-grandson, Alphonse of Poitiers, the brother of St. Louis. When he died in 1271, the two westernmost bays were incomplete. After a lull, the work was resumed at the close of the century. In the XIV century was erected the not very interesting west frontispiece

---

[197] Montierneuf was founded in 1078 by Guillaume VIII (d. 1086). Only eight of the nave's eleven bays remain. The chevet was rebuilt in the XIV century. The abbey was sacked in 1562. St. Porchaire's tower is all that remains of an XI-century church, a contemporary of Notre Dame-la-Grande and Montierneuf. It was to be destroyed in 1843, but luckily some visiting archæologists saved it. From St. Porchaire's belfry rang the summonses of Poitiers University. De Cherge, "Mémoire historique sur l'abbaye de Montierneuf de Poitiers," in *Mém. de la Soc. des antiquaires de l'Ouest*, 1844; *Deux étudiants de l'Université de Poitiers, Francis Bacon et René Descartes*, 1867, p. 65.

which stands below the street level and which is too wide for its height; it would have been better had the towers been set in a line with the aisles and not planted beyond them like the towers of Rouen and Bourges. The first of the Avignon popes, Clement V, builder of the Rayonnant Gothic choir of Bordeaux Cathedral, watched Poitiers' Rayonnant façade rising during the sixteen months that he spent in the city. While here he learned that fire had damaged St. John Lateran's at Rome and ordered it to be reconstructed. The last windows in St. Pierre's Cathedral have the Flamboyant tracery of Jean de Berry's time. That amateur of art—sixth in descent from Henry and Aliénor—left his mark all through middle France.

The interior of Poitiers Cathedral is an ample parallelogram of eight bays, divided into three aisles of equal height, by a dozen widely spaced piers, each of which is a cluster of lovely shafts rising from pavement to vault-springing. The eighteen *bombé* vault sections are grace itself. As the light floods in from the big lancets in the side walls, one scarcely notices that this church has ground supports.

The plan of Poitou's Romanesque churches—seen at its best at St. Savin[198]— shows adroit construction, since it employed the aisles to buttress the principal span, and used one roof to cover the entire structure.

Poitiers' memorable Crucifixion window is in the flat, eastern wall of the central aisle. The three windows in that square chevet belong to the transition be-

[198] St. Savin lies thirty miles from Poitiers. Its choir and transept belong to the early part of the XII century, and its nave was erected about thirty years after. Its donjonlike tower was crowned later by a spire, the highest in southwest France with St. Michel's at Bordeaux. Like Etruscan vase ornamentation are its unique frescoes giving Genesis, Exodus, and the Apocalypse. On the route from Poitiers to St. Savin lies Chauvigny, "the pearl of Poitou," with the ruins of several castles. Its church of St. Pierre has a decorated apse and some eight-branch Plantagenet vaults; its church of Notre Dame possesses some XV-century frescoes.

Another of the chief Poitou-Romanesque churches is at St. Maixent, thirty miles from Poitiers, *via* Niort. The nave is XII century, the choir, Angevin Gothic, and the tower, Flamboyant; its crypt capitals are noticeable.

The abbey church at St. Jouin-de-Marnes, near Montcontour, has a good façade, a fine Romanesque tower, a transept of the end of the XI century, and a XII-century choir and nave, only three of whose vault sections, however, are the primitive ones. In the XIII century the present elaborate masonry roof was substituted. It belongs to the Third Period of the Plantagenet school, with three lines of keystones. Airvault abbey church, not far away, built a similar much-ramified vault, the prototype for that of Toussaint, at Angers.

Parthenay can be included in the trip from Poitiers to St. Jouin-de-Marnes. In its venerable church took place the scene when St. Bernard rose in majesty at the altar and compelled the giant sinner Guillaume X of Aquitaine to repent.

Three miles from Poitiers lies St. Benoit's Romanesque church, with a XIII-century spire, and five miles away is Ligugé, where St. Martin, under St. Hilary's guidance, founded the first monastery in Gaul. Dom Prosper Guéranger restored Ligugé in 1864, and here J. K. Huysmans lived, as he has described in *l'Oblat*. The XV-century church was rebuilt by that prelate of the Renaissance, Geoffrey d'Estissac, whom Rabelais came to visit.

Congrès Archéologique, 1910, St. Savin; p. 119, Airvault; p. 108, St. Jouin-de-Marnes, and the latter also in the *Congrès* of 1903; Prosper Merimée, *Les peintures de St. Savin* (Paris, 1845), folio; Ch. Tranchant, *Guide pour la visite des monuments de Chauvigny en Poitou* (Paris, 1901).

tween the XII and XIII centuries. That to the north was the gift of Maurice de Blason, who became bishop of Poitiers in 1198, and who is supposed to have been also the donor of the Crucifixion, whose date has given rise to controversy. The straight saddle-bars still used in it were abandoned after 1200. In the lower panel of the central light, the founders of the cathedral, Henry and Aliénor, are pictured kneeling. Aliénor knew well Suger's school of glassmakers, and as M. Mâle has proved that all the XII-century windows in western France proceed from those of St. Denis, very likely the ex-queen of France was instrumental in spreading their fame. At Poitiers the apostles gaze upward in quite the same attitude as those in the Ascension window at Le Mans, an accepted work of Suger's craftsmen.

Blue as profound as sapphires and a crimson that glows like blood-red rubies make of Poitiers' Crucifix an unapproachable glory. The genius who conceived it had brooded over the ecstatic hymn composed for the glad celebration of November 19, 569. This is the Tree of Life, effulgent in fecundity, on its branches hanging such fruit as the Ransom of the World, the vine that gives sweet wine of the red blood of the Lord. No agonizing Christ on Poitiers' Cross *ornata regis purpura*. The Saviour's eyes are wide open to indicate that the Christ dies not. The arms are extended to great length as if embracing the entire world.[199] The halo is marked by the Greek cross, emblem of divinity. In many other chevets of France the Crucifixion holds the central place, in the Lady chapel at Tours, in the clearstory at Rouen, in the ambulatory at Bourges, in St. Remi's wide gallery at Rheims, in the square east wall of Moulins, and at Ervy. And in many ways was the Sacrifice presented; sometimes the Cross became an apple-decked Tree of Knowledge with Adam and Eve beside it; sometimes the Saviour's arms were high uplifted and angels received the precious blood in chalices. Never was the meaning of Calvary presented with more profundity than at Poitiers, whose ancient bishops had suffered exile to defend the Son and written verses to exalt him.

The other lancets of the cathedral are in most part XIII-century work of the closely woven pattern type that produces scintillation; contrary to the more general usage the medallions are to be read from the top downward. As color schemes they have been composed with extraordinary care. Few church interiors can equal this for jeweled riches: 'And the building of the wall thereof was of jasper stone.... And the foundations of the wall were adorned with all manner of precious stones—jasper, sapphire, chalcedony, emerald, sardonyx, sardius, chrysolite, beryl, topaz, chrysoprasus, jacinth, and amethyst.'

Poitiers' ancient church of Notre Dame-la-Grande has the appearance of a cathedral, and its elaborate front, the best of all Romanesque façades, is classed among peerless works such as Vézelay's portico, St. Gilles' portal, and the Auvergnat apses. The pre-Gothic school of Poitou, formulated as early as 1050, excelled in sculptured frontispieces, decorated apses, and ornate window frames.

---

[199] Probably because of the magistral window at Poitiers, the Byzantine tradition of the crucified Christ lingered long in the art of midland France. Over an altar of the chapel of Bourgonnière, in the parish of Bouzillé, in Angers diocese, is a remarkable XVI-century polychrome image of the Saviour, unwounded, robed, and awake, with arms wide outstretched against the Cross.

Sometimes the side aisles bracing the principal span were made too narrow, as here in Notre Dame, but where the school reached its structural apogee as in St. Savin-sur-Gartemps (which has lofty ample aisles and splendidly carved capitals), it can hold its own with that of any region. Poitou has been called the paradise for lovers of Romanesque architecture.

In Notre Dame-la-Grande are some XII-century frescoes, but its modern experiment in polychromy is distressing. Many a gathering has the ancient church seen. When in 1100 a church council at Poitiers censured the illegal marriage of the king of France and the fair Bertrada de Montfort, Guillaume IX, the troubadour duke of Aquitaine who was present—and in much the same predicament, living with the wife of a neighboring lord—made a scene and indignantly left the hall. Stones were thrown at the churchmen who dared censure an open scandal. Then brave Robert d'Abrissel, founder of Fontevrault, tore off his cloak and stood forth, in token of his willingness to suffer in so good a cause.[200]

Poitiers' abbey church of St. Hilaire has much interest for archæologists.[201] The Vandals destroyed a church here, the Saracens burned another, twice was it wrecked by Norse pirates during the IX century when St. Hilary's relics were carried to Le Puy Cathedral for safety. Then a daughter of the Duke of Normandy, Emma, the mother of Edward the Confessor, had her architect, Gautier Coorland, rebuild the abbatial, which was dedicated in 1049. Owing to continuous reconstructions, little of that period remains, save in the ambulatory and in the tower which once stood isolated. The XII century added the oblong cupolas whose only counterparts are to be found at Le Puy. To support its new cupola-vaulting, St. Hilaire built two rows of pillars with a narrow passageway between, and when, in later times, outer aisles were added, the interior was given the uncommon aspect of triple aisles. A Huguenot sacking worked irreparable damage, and after the Revolution the westernmost bays of the church had to be demolished.

In Merovingian times the two most-visited shrines in France were St. Hilary's at Poitiers, and St. Martin's at Tours. When Hilary, the thirteenth bishop here (d. 368), returned from his exile in Phrygia, whither he had been driven for combating the Arian heresy, he brought back from the East a fondness for the interpretation of Scripture by allegory which was to have a strong influence on the iconography of Gothic cathedrals. To pray by St. Martin's tomb at Tours there came north the Italian poet, Venantius Fortunatus, who continued his pilgrimage to the tomb of St. Hilary, the master who had trained Martin in the spiritual life. Never was he to quit Poitiers, where, in 607 he died, its revered bishop.

[200] In 1106 gathered another council at Poitiers, a holy-war rally, but the war was to be waged on Christian Constantinople. The superb Bohemund, the new prince of Antioch, came to organize the expedition; he had gone on the First Crusade for booty, fierce as a Norman, astute as an Italian, in person like a Greek god, tall beyond man's normal height, broad-shouldered, and lithe—so the Greek princess at Constantinople saw him. Philip I gave him his daughter, and on Tancred, his cousin, a true hero of the holy wars, not a buccaneer, the king of France bestowed his daughter by the fair Bertrada de Montfort.

[201] E. Lefèvre-Pontalis, *Étude archéologique de St. Hilaire de Poitiers* (Caen, 1904); also in the *Congrès Archéologique* of 1903; De Longuemar, "Essai historique sur l'église Saint Hilaire-le-grand de Poitiers," in *Mémoires des antiquaires de l'Ouest*, 1856.

In those days, Radegund, the Thuringian wife of Clotaire, son of Clovis, had retired to Poitiers to pass her life in study and prayer. Scripture and the works of the church fathers were read in Greek and Hebrew, in her cloister. About her gathered pious maidens, chiefly of the Gallo-Roman stock, harried by the rougher peoples from the north. Fortunatus became for Queen Radegund and her Abbess Agnes a sort of self-appointed intendant; he sent them gifts of fruit with verses. Puvis de Chavannes has painted it all on the walls of Poitiers' Town Hall.

St. Radegund's tomb became a pilgrim shrine. The savants see no reason to doubt the genuine antiquity of the queen's sarcophagus of black marble now in the crypt of her church, part of which crypt escaped the fire of 1083 and so dates before 1000. The new apse was dedicated in 1099. The three big bays of the aisle-less nave are covered by Plantagenet Gothic vaults with eight branches, and along the walls are the same blind arcades and carved carbels as in the cathedral. The sacristy shows an octagonal dome on ribs. The church has no transept, but over the north portal is a XIII-century rose window of deep blue hue, between which and the apse are some XIV-century windows that experimented not very successfully with colored figures in white glass. The porch is good Flamboyant Gothic.

Poitiers boasts the oldest extant Christian church in France, the baptistry of St. Jean, in whose walls are Gallo-Roman IV-century vestiges.[202] There is VII-century Merovingian work in its apsidal chapels, and the later Romanesque and Gothic times added their quotas. The ancient well in which baptism by submersion was practiced has been preserved. A son of Poitiers feels doubly a Christian if baptized in the church of St. Jean's.

The venerable little edifice to-day lies many feet below the level of the city streets, for Poitiers escaped few of the sackings of history. For safety from the Barbarian invasions some rich Gallo-Roman must have buried the statue of Minerva exhumed in 1902, in the garden of a girls' school, and now in the town's museum. It is a most lovely Greek marble of the VI century, B.C.[203]

Henry Plantagenet and Aliénor of Aquitaine built in Poitiers the guard's hall of the Counts' Palace, in the center of the town, on its highest eminence.[204] The wall-arcading is like contemporary work in the cathedral and the church of St. Radegund. In late-Gothic times the south wall was remade. In this hall the second husband of Isabella of Angoulême made amends to his suzerain, Alphonse of Poitiers, for the war to which her jealous haughtiness had forced him. In this hall in 1307-08 the accused Templars were interrogated by Clement V, the pontiff who initiated the residence at Avignon, and the consequent papal subserviency to the

---

[202] De la Croix, *Étude du baptistère de St. Jean de Poitiers* (Poitiers, 1903); E. Lefèvre-Pontalis, "Les fouilles du R. P. de la Croix au baptistère de St. Jean à Poitiers," in *Bulletin Monumental*, 1902, vol. 66, p. 529; Mgr. X. Barbier de Montault, *Œuvres complètes* (various studies on the monuments of Poitiers and its region), (Poitiers, Blais et Roy, 1899).

[203] Like other Greek works of the period the Minerva at Poitiers shows the influence of Egyptian art in its stiff, regal attitude. The proud, full chin is uplifted. The shapely back is molded by a leopard's skin. The right arm is missing, but the left arm is honey-hued and as delicate as flesh in appearance. She bears the olive branch of peace, this wise Minerva.

[204] Lucien Magne, *Le Palais de Justice de Poitiers*.

French crown, Philippe le Bel cowed the pope, and the group of anti-cleric legists who controlled the king arranged that only picked specimens of the doomed military Order should appear at Poitiers. The royal coffers were empty and those of the Templars were full.

Torture and intimidation had wrung from all too many of the monk-knights false avowals of guilt. In Spain, where the investigation was carried on without torture, the bishops found no heresy in the Order; instead, they bore testimony to its exemplary standing. One brave old crusader raised his voice in honest speech: "Let him have a care," wrote Joinville, "this king who now reigns. Let him amend his ways, lest God strike him down without mercy." The Grand Master of the Templars, Jacques Molay, was burned publicly in Paris, calling on king and pope to meet him before God's judgment seat within the year. A month later Clement V died, and before 1314 closed, the young king met sudden death. And the people recalled that when Clement was crowned at Lyons, the tiara had been knocked from his head by a collapsing wall and one of its precious jewels lost.

Less discouraging were other doings of Clement V in Poitiers. Here he dated the nomination of John of Montecorvino (d. 1328), pioneer of Christian missionaries, to the see of Peking. Armed crusading had run its course; the crusade by preaching, prayer, and penance was to begin. Already in 1245 Innocent IV had sent Dominicans to Persia and Franciscans farther east, St. Louis had sent William de Rubruquis to the Mongols, and those astonishing Venetian merchants; the Polos, had roused the papacy to the spiritual needs of Cathay, the far Cathay of the mediæval tradition, to which Columbus was seeking a shorter route when he accidentally discovered America. For thirty years John of Montecorvino missionized Tartary. He translated the New Testament and the Psalms. To encourage missionary activity, Clement V ordered that Greek, Hebrew, and Arabic be taught publicly at Rome, Bologna, Paris, Oxford, and Salamanca.

The Hundred Years' War, so fatal to French architectural progress, surged round Poitiers. After Crécy, in 1346, the hall of the Counts' Palace was damaged by the English. In the environs of Poitiers took place the bitter French defeat of 1356, when King Jean le Bon was made prisoner. "*Et fut là morte toute la fleur de chevalerie de France*," says Froissart. The siege by Duguesclin to recapture the hill city from the English damaged its monuments. When the Duke of Berry, son of King Jean the Good, became master of Poitiers he undertook to restore the Counts' Palace, and he had noted Flamboyant Gothic masters construct for him the splendid triple chimney piece of the guard hall, decorated about 1383 by André Beauneveu with statues of Charles VI, of his wife Isabeau of Bavaria, and of Jean of Berry and his first duchess. In the pignon above the great fireplaces was set some XIV-century glass. Guy de Dammartin re-established the donjon tower called Maubergeon, now cut off at the third story. The images of the counts of Poitiers, decorating it, belong to that phase of French sculpture which preceded the Franco-Flamand school at Dijon. Before transalpine influences were imported, a truly national renaissance had begun. The Tour Maubergeon and the pignon of the great hall are all that remain of the palaces built at Poitiers by Jean de Berry; but what they were can be seen in his illuminated Book of Hours now in Chantilly's museum.

The historic hall of Poitiers has its memories of Jeanne d'Arc. Hither, in 1429, Charles XII brought her to be examined by learned men. When one of them told her, with condescension, that if God wished to deliver France he had no need of men-of-arms, swift was Jeanne's reply, "Man does the battling and God gives the victory." Finally her judges reported to the king that she was of sound sense and a true Christian and appeared to be sent of God, and that, given the desperate need of the kingdom, they advised the king to put her at the head of an army for the relief of Orléans. Decision momentous for the fate of France!

Jeanne, during her trial at Rouen, often referred to the answers she had given to her honest judges at Poitiers: "If you do not believe me, send to Poitiers, where I was questioned before.... It is written in the book at Poitiers." Cauchon might wear a miter, well she knew it was not the Church which persecuted her, though the English left no stone unturned to have it so appear. Jeanne in Poitiers lodged with Maître Jean Rabateau, advocate, and it was the duty of his good dame to spy on her night and day. Many years after she testified to Jeanne's habit of long prayer in the night-time. To test the maid's virtue the king's own mother-in-law visited her. That able Yolande of Aragon had brought up Charles VII. Her own son, the young knight René d'Anjou, was soon to fight under Jeanne, and Yolande, herself, convinced of the Maid's mission, helped with funds for the expedition to Orléans. They say that Jeanne made answer to the court ladies with such sweetness and grace that she drew tears from their eyes.

The old hill city of Poitiers, so ecclesiastical, so full of national memories, has had the good sense to keep itself *très province,* and its street directory still makes a sort of calendar of saints. At Bourges, the mania to wipe out its past has reached such a pass that the rue St. Michel is now the rue Michel-Servet and the rue St. Fulgent the rue Fulton. Poitiers has no desire to blot out her high historic memories.

CHAPTER VIII

GOTHIC IN THE MIDI

Cathedral of Clermont-Ferrand, begun in 1248—Gothic of the north, translated with a Midi accent—True character of Auvergne shown in its Romanesque churches—Notre Dame-du-Port, the classic type of Auvergne's Romanesque school—Abbey church of La Chaise Dieu, begun by Clement VI, 1344—Contains incomparable tapestries (note)—First Crusade proclaimed at Clermont by Urban II, 1095—Riom's Sainte-Chapelle, of the XIV century—Madonna of the Bird a masterpiece of late-Gothic imagery—Romanesque Cathedral of Le Puy (XII century) one of the most venerable shrines in France.

Cathedral of Bordeaux, like the city itself, is of the north and the south—Nave is composite and difficult to read—Clement V (d. 1314) built the Rayonnant Gothic choir—In the Romanesque church of Ste. Croix appeared the first diagonals of the region—Charlemagne laid Roland's olifant on the altar of St. Seurin—St. Bertrand-de-Comminges Cathedral built by Clement V—Cathedral of Bayonne (note).

Cathedral of Toulouse consists of two inharmonious parts—Unaisled nave with Angevin vaults building while Simon de Montfort besieged city—Gothic choir begun in 1275—Chief monument of Toulouse is the abbey church of St. Sernin (begun 1075)—Languedoc then excelled in sculpture: Moissac's portal and cloister (note)—Toulouse a center for brick architecture—Its Jacobins' church begun in 1229—St. Dominic's mission in Languedoc—Albigensian Crusade.

Albi Cathedral, the incarnation of the Midi wars: meridional Gothic—Aggressive Bernard de Castanets began it in 1282—Flamboyant and Renaissance riches were added to St. Cecilia's cathedral—Frescoes of its vault have never been surpassed (1509 to 1512)—Its choir screen equally noted—Auch Cathedral has famous XVI-century windows (note)—Cathedral of Rodez possesses a notable Flamboyant tower (1510 to 1526) (note)—Carcassonne Cité has been too much restored—Its ci-devant cathedral of St. Nazaire the best of XIV-century Gothic—Like a reliquary of colored glass—Carcassonne town has typical Midi Gothic churches.

Narbonne Cathedral, consisting of a vast Gothic choir, begun in 1272—
Its mechanical skill cold, but still Gothic of the grand style—Lovely XIV-century glass—Sack of Béziers, 1209—Perpignan Cathedral and Elne's cloister (note)—Abbey church of Fontfroide allied
with Poblet in Catalonia (note).

Montpellier Cathedral, formerly an abbey church, built by Urban V,
XIV century—Jaime el Conquistador, mighty builder of churches, born in Montpellier, 1208—Mende Cathedral and St. Victor's
abbatial at Marseilles built by Urban V (note)—Maguelonne, former cathedral of diocese, now the most aloof spot in Europe—Aigues-Mortes, begun by St. Louis, completed by his son—Fortress
unspoiled by restorations—Both crusades of Louis IX sailed
thence—St. Gilles' abbey church, partly a ruin, interesting to
archæologists; building from 1116—Noted portal of St. Gilles inspired Trinity Church, Boston—Loyalty of Provence to its Saintes-Maries traditions—Les Saintes-Maries church a pilgrim shrine
(note)—St. Martha's church at Tarascon (note).

St. Trophime Cathedral at Arles—Portal influenced by Gallo-Roman
sculpture—Its cloister the fairest Christian monument in the
city—Ruins of Montmajour near Arles—Frédéric Mistral should
be one's companion in Provence—Expresses the regional soul—
St. Maximin church the best Gothic monument in Provence—Begun by Charles II d'Anjou in 1295—Cathedral of St. Sauveur at
Aix-en-Provence is composite—Its south aisle originally a separate Romanesque church, XII century—Good King René gave the
triptych by a French primitif—Avignon's great day was the XIV
century under seven meridional popes, 1309 to 1377—Palace of
the Popes built from 1335 to 1358—Grandest fortress-palace in the
world.

The giant struggle we have witnessed is but the beginning of
a long and complicated historical crisis in which men will have to
make their choice between the unlimited augmentation of power
(by force, riches, and success) and a forward-moving moral progress (by justice, charity, and loyalty). If we live always in exterior
things, if we are always in movement, we become, little by little,
incapable of recollection and fecund meditation.

—Guglielmo Ferrero, 1917.

IT has been said that the Midi adhered long, if not always, to Romanesque architecture, even when employing the Gothic vault. Gothic
art was not an indigenous development in the south, but was
brought in the wake of political events, when central France and
Languedoc became one with the royal domain. It proceeded, in
part, from the architecture of southwest France, and in part from the

classic Ile-de-France Picard region.

The realization of the local type of Midi Gothic was Albi's fortress cathedral, which comprises a wide unaisled hall covered by twelve bays of diagonal vaults whose span is sixty feet — the width of Amiens' nave being merely forty-five feet. The buttress are disguised as walls between the side chapels, the windows are long, narrow lancets, there is no triforium, and the roof is flat. Ogival art such as this has retained all the grand simplicity of Romanesque.

The chief care of the Midi architect was to avoid the flying buttress; he had inherited Rome's admiration for wide, unincumbered interiors, and its aversion to showing the structural skeleton. His warm sun precluded the use of wall inclosures that were composed entirely of stained glass, which fragile screens would have necessitated wide-spreading buttresses. He seemed to disdain sculpture. And yet, during the pre-Gothic day, Languedoc had excelled in that important branch of the builder's art, as Moissac's wealth of imagery and Elne's lovely cloister show.

Various causes led to the nudity of sculpture in the later churches of the south. The Gothic cathedrals of the Midi were erected after two generations of the Albigensian strife had impoverished the race. The new mendicant Orders of Francis and Dominic advocated austerity; the best Gothic of Provence is the Dominican church of St. Maximin. The building material available in some of the central and southern provinces did not lend itself to ornamentation; the lava of Auvergne, the granite of Limousin, and the brick of the Toulouse region are unyielding to sculpture.

The chief Gothic churches of the Midi were built in the second half of the XIII and the first part of the XIV centuries. First there rose in central France the sister cathedrals of Clermont and Limoges — northern Gothic infused with the regional spirit. Directly derived from them are the cathedrals of Toulouse and Narbonne. Albi Cathedral was not begun till 1282. The choir of Bordeaux, built by the first of the Avignon popes, is a classic of Rayonnant Gothic, and so is that jewel of Carcassonne Cité, the whilom cathedral of St. Nazaire. St. Sauveur, at Aix-en-Provence, the cathedral of Rodez, and Béziers' fortified church were the work of the successors of the apogee period of Gothic. At Montpellier, Mende, La Chaise Dieu, and Avignon, the XIV-century popes, all of whom were meridionals, built Gothic halls and chapels.

Memorable and interesting as are the Gothic monuments of the Midi, the traveler carries away the impression that the inmost soul of these central and southern provinces lingers most happily in the venerated shrines of Our Lady and St. Michael at Le Puy, in such churches as Notre Dame-du-Port, St. Sernin, St. Trophime, in the sculptured portal of St. Gilles, and in Maguelonne's isolated cathedral of St. Peter.

CLERMONT-FERRAND[205]

> Si c'est un aveuglement surnaturel de vivre sans chercher ce
> qu'on est, c'en est un terrible de vivre mal en croyant Dieu.... La
> conduite de Dieu, qui dispose toute choses avec douceur, est de
> mettre la religion dans l'esprit par les raisons, et dans le cœur par
> la grâce.

> —Pascal (1623-62; born in Clermont).

In mediæval reckoning that mountainous, central province of France which
was called Auvergne was counted in Languedoc. Therefore, to place the cathedral
of Clermont in this general group of Midi Gothic is permissible. It is a daughter of
Amiens, of the northern French type, and yet it belongs in a marked degree to its
own volcanic region of mountains and storms. In it is the endurance and sturdy individuality of Auvergne, the inmost heart of France, where the Romanesque work
may be said to be indigenous, so directly does it derive from the local traditions
of Rome grafted on those of Gaul, and scarcely touched by those of Byzantium.

The chief Gothic church of Clermont has in it much of Romanesque austerity.
The black lava of which it is built sets it apart among French cathedrals. "A pious
fear of God makes itself felt in this spot," wrote a son of Clermont, Gregory of
Tours, of the cathedral governed by Bishop Sidonius Apollinaris, Gallo-Roman
and "last zealot for Latin letters." And though not a stone of the present edifice is
of historian Gregory's day, one often murmurs in its precincts, *"Terribilis est locus
iste,"* and one often experiences in this abode of Jehovah the Lord, *un frisson d'âme
à la Pascal.* In Clermont, where even the serene Gothic art could not free itself of the
fire-torn mountains around, the somber soul of Pascal first experienced religion.
That he should overstress the fall of man and original sin, what wonder? But Jan-
senist in temperament though he was—overwhelmed by man's nothingness and
God's grandeur—the mystic Pascal was no rigid pessimist. Cathedral and man of
genius both preach the resurrection after the fall, both have the upward surge of
hope, even as the fearful summit of the Puy-de-Dôme, standing over Clermont,

---

[205] *Congrès Archéologique,* 1850 and 1895; Abbé Ph. Gobillot, *La cathédrale de Clermont*
(Clermont-Ferrand, F. L. Bellet, 1912); H. du Ranquet, *La cathédrale de Clermont-Ferrand* (Collection, Petites Monographies), (Paris, H. Laurens); *ibid.,* "Les architectes de la cathédrale
de Clermont-Ferrand," in *Bulletin Monumental,* 1912, vol. 76, p. 7; G. Desdevises du Dézert
et L. Bréhier, *Clermont-Ferrand, Royat et le Puy-de-Dôme* (Collection, Villes d'art célèbres),
(Paris, H. Laurens, 1910); Louis Bréhier, *L'Auvergne* (Collection, Les provinces françaises),
(Paris, H. Laurens, 1910); *ibid.,* in *Revue de l'art chrétien,* 1912, on the capitals of Notre Dame-
du-Port; G. Fraipont, *L'Auvergne* (Collection, Montagnes de France), (Paris, H. Laurens);
E. Vimont, *Les deux principales églises de Clermont;* R. de Lasteyrie, *L'architecture religieuse en
France à l'époque romane* (Paris, 1912); H. Stein, *Les architectes des cathédrales gothiques* (Paris,
1912); Prosper Mérimée, *Notes d'un voyage en Auvergne* (Paris, 1838); Alexis Forel, *Voyage au
pays des sculpteurs romans* (Paris and Geneva, 1913), 2 vols.; Saveron, *Les origines de la ville de
Clermont;* Ambrose Tardieu, *Histoire de la ville de Clermont;* G. Desdevises du Dézert, *Bibli-
ographie du centenaire des croisades à Clermont-Ferrand* (Clermont-Ferrand, 1895); D. Branche,
Auvergne au moyen âge (Clermont-Ferrand, 1842); Paul Allard, *St. Sidoine Apolinaire* (Collection, Les Saints), (Paris, Lecoffre); Taylor et Nodier, *Voyage pittoresque dans l'ancienne France.
Auvergne* (Paris, Didot, 1829-33), 3 vols.

outsoars the storm clouds hiding its base, to rear its head in sunlight.

For all its soberness, the cathedral of Clermont has the true Gothic sweep of the spirit *au-delà*. Happy the traveler who first approaches it at sunset, coming slowly across the mountain-walled plain, out of the Forez hills of rushing torrents where is set the Chaise Dieu. The cathedral crowns the foothill around which has settled the city, and as it stands silhouetted against a bluish haze of mountain—the extinct crater, the Puy-de-Dôme—it fulfills the ideal of a church crowning a city.[206] Seen from the town, the massed volcanic hills are sufficiently near for their woods and villages to add picturesque details to the ever-changing views, yet not so close that they hang oppressively over the city. Other views of the cathedral can be gained from the foothills around Royat, whose small, sturdy church was fortified to bar the valley into the huge mountain behind it.

Lava stone is dusty black, therefore on closer inspection Clermont Cathedral has somewhat the aspect of the smoke-stained churches in manufacturing centers. The gray-black Volvic stone is of better effect within the church, though at first that interior may strike a chill. Lava does not lend itself to sculptural decoration. However, the essential lines of Clermont are of such masterly proportions, of so grand a simplicity, that deeper and deeper grows the influence of this church on those who frequent it. The diagonals etched black against the white vault panels fall with peculiar ease and vigor on the tall dark piers. The slenderness of those clustered columns is not foolhardy, since lava has much resistant force. The single aisles of the choir and the double aisles of the nave rise to half the height of the church, and we have seen at Bourges and Le Mans that when pier arches are above the average height there is given to an edifice a note of exotic beauty. Like Amiens, the height of this church is three times greater than its width. Its vista is closed imposingly; the imaged windows of its high apsidal chapels appear symmetrically behind the arches that surround the sanctuary.

The story of the chief church of Auvergne interests the archæologist. The crypt belonged to the previous Carolingian church, and so did the two western towers until the XIX century. M. Viollet-le-Duc removed the ancient belfries, extended the nave by two bays, and built the present towers, whose sky-pointing spires are superb in the general view of Clermont, but whose details can be criticized, as, for instance, the blocking of corner niches by pinnacles when the purpose of a niche is to hold a statue. Modern Gothic is too often a cold, hard imitation. The stair approaches here lack the old-time amplitude of the triple portals.

The XIII-century cathedral of Clermont was practically the first Gothic monument raised in Auvergne, which province adhered stubbornly to its own excep-

---

[206] "Il est peu de constructions ogivales qui se présentent d'un façon plus dégagée et plus pittoresque. La sombre masse se détache de la ville aux rues tortueuses comme une haute statue de son piédestal. Les deux flèches hardies s'encadrent dans la cirque majestueux de montagnes volcaniques. Il semble que la cathédrale soit le Mont-Saint-Michel de cette baie aux lumières mouvantes. Tantôt silhouettée par de vigoureux éclairages, tantôt estompée par les vapeurs qui planent dans la vallée, et quelquefois, aux heures matinales émergeant de leur nappe grise, comme une haute mâture au-dessus de la mer tranquille, elle reste toujours fière, imposante, poétique."—Louis Gonse, *L'art gothique* (Paris, 1891).

tional Romanesque architecture. The first stone was laid in 1248, in the same year that Cologne Cathedral was begun. The founder, Bishop Hugues de la Tour, had attended the dedication of the Sainte-Chapelle at Paris, and then had returned to Clermont to begin his own cathedral. That same year he started out as a crusader, in the train of Louis IX, but as he died in Egypt the work on the church was not continued seriously till 1253, when St. Louis helped to raise to the see of Clermont his friend Guy de la Tour, nephew of Hugues. Belonging to a feudal family of great possessions, the new bishop, too, was able to be munificent toward his cathedral.

In 1254, when St. Louis was returning from his unsuccessful crusade, he paused in Clermont, to replenish his depleted treasury. Ten years later he presented windows to the cathedral, on the occasion of his son Philippe's marriage there to the daughter of Jaime el Conquistador of Aragon. The lights in the Lady chapel show the fleur-de-lis and the donjons of Castile, and are apparently the work of Paris craftsmen, who controlled the vitrine art of the later XIII century. That unskilled local workers set them in place would seem to be indicated by the armature bars which do not follow the contour of the medallions, as was then the custom. In the choir's clearstory are the single figures and grisaille that were in vogue during the next century.

Jean Deschamps made the plan of Clermont Cathedral. He may have studied in the north, since certain traits of Picardy appear here, but the spirit of the work is regional. His windows do not fill the entire upper space between the active members. Under Bishop Guy de la Tour he directed the building of the cathedral for almost forty years, till 1287. Perhaps he designed the cathedral of Limoges, in west-central France, since its plan and details closely resemble those of Clermont. Bishop Aymar de Cros, who carried on the works in Auvergne's capital, was another of the schoolmen who were builders of churches; such was his intellect that St. Thomas Aquinas willed to him his manuscripts in the hope that his *Summa* might be completed.

Under Bishop Aubert Aycelin de Montaigu a new master-of-works took charge—Pierre Deschamps (1287-1325), the son probably of Jean who had made the plans. He erected the four westernmost bays of the choir, the transept, and the easternmost bay of the nave in its lower parts. From 1340 to 1359 the master-of-works was Pierre de Cabazat, who added three more bays to the nave, and was employed in those same years in making, with Hugues Morel, the abbey church of La Chaise Dieu in the Forez mountains across the plain from Clermont.[207] An

[207] The Chaise Dieu monastery, founded by St. Robert in 1043, was later affiliated with Cluny. The present church was begun in 1344 by Clement VI, who built the choir and four bays of the nave. The abbatial was completed, after 1370, by his nephew, Gregory XI. Clement had Avignon artists prepare his funeral monument, which originally possessed over forty statuettes representing his relatives, for he came of the great lines of Beaufort and Turenne. The Casa Dei abbatial, though possessed of grandeur, is dull and heavy. The aisles are as high as the principal span. The octagonal piers with uncut capitals lack elegance and lightness, the windows are the narrowest lancets, and there are no flying buttresses. Molds die away in the piers above the capitals—an early appearance of Flamboyant Gothic. The cloister (1378-1417) is frankly late-Gothic. The denuded church once was filled with the tombs of local magnates, among them those of the Lafayette family, precious pages of

Avignon pope, Clement VI, was the patron who undertook that gaunt granite structure, as full of sorrow as the times that produced it. Clement had been abbot at La Chaise Dieu, so naturally he contributed toward the erection of the cathedral of Auvergne as did his successor at Avignon, Innocent VI (d. 1362), a former bishop of Clermont.

The city was fortunate to have one of the notable D'Amboise family for its prelate in the late-Gothic day, Jacques d'Amboise (1505-16), who as abbot of Cluny had built at Paris the stately residence called the Hôtel Cluny. Close to his Auvergne cathedral he set up the Fontaine d'Amboise, now on the Cours Sablon. The eloquent Massillon was a later bishop of Clermont (1717-42); he founded its town library and bequeathed his fortune to the sick poor of the Hôtel Dieu. Before the French Revolution had turned to violence and destruction, in Clermont Cathedral gathered the people, with hearts beating high with generous desire for reform, for the blessing of their National Guard banner, embroidered by a community of nuns. With all too tragic swiftness came the day when in the same church were lighted bonfires for the destruction of vestments and missals. Among the precious things then wrecked was a portrait statue of Louis IX, made while his friend Guy de la Tour was bishop. Only by chance did the cathedral itself, riddled with bullets, escape annihilation.

The see of Clermont has gone by various designations; so ancient is this city that it has been called successively by five different names. Here where is more Celtic blood than in any other region in France, save Brittany, the Celtic hero, Vercingetorex, inflicted on Cæsar his sole defeat. When Gaul became Christian, Clermont continued to be important. Her first bishop, St. Austremonius, was one of the seven whom Gregory of Tours says were sent into Gaul in 250 by Pope Fabian, with St. Denis of Paris, St. Martial of Limoges, St. Saturninus of Toulouse, St. Just of Narbonne, St. Trophimus of Arles, and St. Gatien of Tours. At the close of the V century Clermont's bishop, the celebrated Caius Apollinaris Sidonius, poet and scholar, son-in-law of an emperor, made his stand for Latin culture against Teutonic submersion. Dearly he loved his own enlightened Lyons, but of Clermont he said, "Such an horizon would make a stranger forget his native land." A generation later another outstanding Gallo-Roman bishop of Clermont was St. Gall, uncle of Gregory of Tours, who was so just to all that even Jews marched with lighted tapers at his funeral. Some twenty-six of Clermont's bishops have been canonized.

French history obliterated in 1562 and 1793. As if to shut out the funereal, humid aisles, the choir has been lined with tapestries (begun in 1492) unsurpassed in France. They reproduce the *Mirror of Perfection* and the *Bible of the Poor*, two books popular in the XIII and XIV centuries. Each episode of the Saviour's life is accompanied by scenes of the Old Testament, prefiguring it. On the outer wall of the choir screen is a sketch, a Dance of Death, with the grim skeleton stalking in and out, touching with his chill finger pope, baron, burgher, page, field laborer, and little child. No XIII-century church had allowed so gruesome a theme on its walls. This lugubrious allegory came into vogue after the Black Death of 1348, when a third of Europe's population perished. *Congrès Archéologique*, 1904, pp. 54, 402; E. Durand, *La Chaise Dieu* (1903); Maurice Fançon, *L'église abbatiale de la Chaise Dieu en Auvergne*; Émile Mâle, *L'art religieux de la fin du moyen âge* (Paris, Colin, 1910).

The third cathedral of the city, and that which immediately preceded the present one, was consecrated in 946 by Bishop Étienne II. Clermont had suffered grievously by Saracen invasion, followed by the Northmen inroads. After the second Norman sacking the ruined houses smoldered for a month, and in the streets corpses lay unburied, for the population in terror had fled to the countryside. The bishop called back his flock to remake their homes. In his new church was a precocious use of ambulatory and radiating chapels, a disposition which was to lead to the chief beauty in the Gothic cathedrals of the land, but which made its appearance in the Ile-de-France only in the XII century. Bishop Étienne's Carolingian cathedral became the prototype for the Auvergnat-Romanesque school.

In the good Étienne's church prayed the first crusaders when by papal bidding there gathered at Clermont a mighty council at whose tenth and last session was preached the First Crusade. Nature herself seemed to have prepared the people's minds for some vast enterprise, for all the chroniclers of western Christendom describe the sublime shower of astral stars, thick as snowflakes, which whirled in the sky. So in this same primeval Auvergne, some six centuries earlier, at the break-up of Rome's empire before the invading Barbarians, there had for three years been earthquakes and fiery volcanic eruptions.

Tradition says that the momentous gathering of 1095 took place in what is now the Place Delille and the adjacent Cours Sablon. Many of our building friends were present—Bishop Odo from Bayeux, Bishop Ives from Chartres, Bishop Hoël from Le Mans, the abbots Geoffrey of Vendôme, Jarenton of St. Bénigne, and St. Hugues of Cluny, and from Spain came the great Bernardo who ruled the see of Toledo. For the people of Clermont to-day, November 28, 1095, is as vivid a reality as any of the revolutions of yesterday. A statue of Urban II stands outside the cathedral. Even so he stood, said a witness, as one having authority, high above the vast throng, on one side of him the stunted Peter the Hermit of Picardy, and on the other the Norman-Italian Bohemund of Taranto, a veritable Greek god in build and feature. From end to end of France Urban journeyed to arouse the people. Now he used persuasion, now invective; sometimes he appealed to idealistic motives or propounded colonial policies very like modern ideas. Europe had good cause to be apprehensive. The Almoravids had advanced into Spain. The Seljukian Turks were a menace more serious than the Saracens. Urban understood the peril and raised his voice in warning. "Cease to be a terror to peaceful citizens," he exhorted the gathered barons. "Turn your arms to the defense of the soil trod by the King of Kings, of the tomb over which rose the sun of the Resurrection.... The great cities of Asia Minor have fallen a prey to the Mussulman, who has planted the crescent by the Hellespont, whence he menaces Europe.... Nation of the Franks, set beyond the mountains, nation cherished and chosen of God, as clearly your high deeds prove, nation distinct from others by your situation, by your faith, by your respect for Mother Church, to you I address my plea.... Who should right these wrongs but you who have received from on high agility of body, the training of arms and grandeur of soul?... Cease these mutual wars!... Jesus Christ died for you. You should be willing to die for him." And a great answering cry rose from the hundred thousand gathered there, "God wills it," to be the rallying call of the crusades.

Thus in the heart of France a French pope initiated the cosmic ventures which were to change European ways of life, ventures in which Frenchmen played a leading part so that to this day a European is called a Frank by a Mohammedan. One can easily see in the crusades only their failures and their crimes, one can sneer at them with Voltaire—who sneered at Jeanne d'Arc. Europe's aggression was needed then to save Christianity from Asiatic immobility. The benefits of the crusades outweigh their delinquencies.

Gesta Dei per Francos a monk called his chronicle of the First Crusade. And while those feats by God through the men of France in the East went on, other feats for God were ventured in France, the raising of Gothic cathedrals, sister movements that gave wings to the soul, purifying and molding the faith and the genius of those virile and faulty generations. Already the movement was stirring. On his way to Clermont, Urban II had seen Verona Cathedral building and S. Ambrogio's at Milan. He had blessed S. Abondio at Como. In France he blessed the new choir of St. Sernin at Toulouse and the material gathered for the cathedral at Carcassonne. Cluny's new choir he dedicated, and various other Romanesque churches. Before the Second Crusade set out Suger had built St. Denis.

Notre Dame du Port at Clermont-Ferrand. Typical XII-century Church of Auvergne's Romanesque School

In Clermont, though the cathedral of 1095 has been superseded by the present Gothic structure, there is intact a venerated sanctuary where Urban had a votive Mass chanted on the eve of the historic council. Every morning one can see the men and women of the city gather in the crypt of Notre Dame-du-Port to beg a blessing on their working day. They may not be able to put into words what it is each feels in that subterranean chamber impregnated by the petitions of those of their race who have gone before them, but each knows that here his prayer has plenitude and patriotic aspiration. A *custodia matutina* in Notre Dame-du-Port, *usque ad noctem* in the cathedral. One fears God in the cathedral, one loves God in Notre Dame.

Notre Dame-du-Port is a masterpiece of the Romanesque school of Auvergne.[208] When it was built lava stone was not in use for construction, but solely for decorative purposes. So curiously alike are all the pre-Gothic churches in this province that one architect might have planned them. The venerable crypt of Notre Dame-du-Port was built in the XI century. The Romanesque church above it was constructed during the XII century and has all the Auvergnese traits: a central tower in two stories set on a barlong which forms a kind of upper transept, a compact apse with snug absidioles whose exterior walls are decorated by colored volcanic stones in marquetry designs, a western narthex, and a principal span covered by a half-barrel vault undivided by transverse arches and buttressed by side aisles surmounted by tribunes, which meant that light entered the middle vessel indirectly. Auvergne, like Burgundy, attempted to light her upper church by a clearstory, but found the experiment hazardous and gave it up. Her churches have stood intact through centuries of harsh winters. The very mortar lines were made means of decoration; wide bands of red mortar were found to be effective with blocks of black lava.[209] In the volcanic soil of Auvergne were elements that rendered mortar as resistant as stone. The local Gallo-Romans had used the polychrome lava as decoration.

The interior apse of Notre Dame-du-Port is a gem of masoncraft. Around the tiny processional path stand engaged pillars that are decoration and buttresses, too. The regional skill in sculpture appears in the capitals of the main piers, where the story is related with animation, even if the figures are too squat and the heads too large. The armor indicates that the work was done early in the XII century. The doorjamb images at the southern entrance of the transept were sculptured in the years when St. Thomas Becket came to Clermont wearing the white robe of the Cistercians who had given him hospitality in France. Crowds gathered every day

[208] "Quiconque en a senti une fois la beauté forte et simple de ce vigoureux style roman-auvergnat, dont l'origine demeure mystérieuse, n'oublie plus ces églises, solides, trapues, ramassées, dont l'ordonnance extérieure, au lieu d'être un décor plaqué, reproduit en relief l'ordonnance intérieure. Vue du chevet surtout, avec l'hémicycle de leurs chapelles serrées, accolées contre la masse de l'édifice, elles donnent une saisissante impression d'aplomb et d'unité." —PAUL BOURGET, *Le demon du midi* (Paris, Plon-Nourrit et Cie, 1913).

The feast of Notre Dame-du-Port falls on May 15th, and the city is illuminated with myriads of little lamps.

[209] Polychrome decoration is to be found everywhere in Auvergne: Royat, Riom, Mozac, Saint-Saturnin, Orcival, Saint-Nectaire (where are some of the best carved capitals in the region), Issoire (observe *La cène* sculptured on one of its capitals), Le Puy, and Brioude. This latter is one of the most beautiful of XII-century churches, showing Burgundian traits as well as those of Auvergne and the Velay. The influence of the Romanesque school of Auvergne spread to Parthenay, Saintes, Nevers, Toulouse, Santiago, and Avila. *Congrès Archéologique*, 1904, p. 542, E. Lefèvre-Pontalis, on Brioude; *Congrès Archéologique*, 1895, pp. 96, 238, 292, on Saint-Nectaire; and p. 177, "École romane d'Auvergne," H. du Ranquet; *Bulletin Monumental*, 1909, vol. 73, p. 213, "Saint-Nectaire," Abbé G. Rochias.

to receive his blessing, for all Christendom held him to be a saint defending right and liberty. A cast of Clermont's archaic portal, whose charm is exceptional, with its seraphim of the mystic triple wings, has been placed in the Trocadéro Museum at Paris. When this side entrance was completed, Richard Cœur-de-Lion was making over his claims in Auvergne to his lifetime rival, Philippe-Auguste, which cession was to lead, in time, to the erection of the Ile-de-France Picardy cathedral of Clermont.

Some of the most admirably sculptured capitals in Auvergne are at Mozac, a suburb of Riom.[210] The nave of Mozac's abbey church was built from 1131 to 1147 by a brother of Peter the Venerable, who made Cluny's nave, and of the doughty abbot, Pons de Montboissier, who erected Vézelay's portico of paradise, all three of them belonging to a feudal family of Auvergne. The small abbatial holds a priceless treasure, the reliquary of St. Calmin, which an abbot presented in 1168. Its fourteen panels of Limoges enamel are ornamented in gold. A bold attempt was made to rob the church of this national heritage, so it is now protected by electric bells and every kind of burglar alarm.

"Clermont le riche, Riom le beau," so ran the old saying. Riom, the small but proud rival of the capital of Auvergne, was a town of magistrates who built themselves Gothic Renaissance houses as individual as the pre-Gothic work of the province. The church of St. Amable has a Romanesque nave and an early-Gothic choir. Jean, Duke of Berry, had Guy and André de Dammartin design the XIV-century Sainte-Chapelle for his palace at Riom. Its brilliantly cold stained glass was commanded for the wedding, in 1389, of sixty-year-old Duke John and the thirteen-year-old heiress, Jeanne de Boulogne. Froissart has described the curious union. Each window panel has a single statue under a canopy; the prophets and apostles carry appropriately inscribed scrolls. A XV-century window, representing the Bourbon dukes, Jean II and Pierre II, patrons of Moulins, contains a St. Marguerite so similar to one in the "Book of Hours" which Jehan Fouquet painted for Étienne Chevalier that the window is thought to be designed by the great *primitif* of Tours.

It may be to artists of Jean de Berry's entourage that we owe the most entrancing Madonna of Flamboyant art, the *vierge à l'oiseau,* an image in the regional stone which stands at the trumeau of the XV-century church of Notre Dame-du Mathuret. One student after another has discussed the date of this exquisite figure, so purely French in essence, whose simplicity is as ample and unaffected as the

---

[210] Those who visit Riom (which lies close to Clermont) should go to Aigueperse, eight miles away, to see Mantegna's St. Sebastian and a Nativity by a brother of Ghirlandajo. As the lord of the region, a Bourbon-Montpensier—who died in 1496, had married the sister of the Gonzaga ruler of Mantua, these treasures probably came through that source. *Congrès Archéologique,* 1895; and 1913, p. 124, Mozac, Abbé Luzuy; p. 144, Riom, P. Gauchery; Paul Mantz, "Une tournée en Auvergne," in *Gazette des Beaux-Arts,* 1886; Abbé R. Crégut, *La vierge du Mathuret* (Clermont-Ferrand, 1902); *ibid., Les vitraux de la Sainte-Chapelle de Riom* (1906); E. Clouard, *Les gens d'autrefois aux XVe et XVIe siècles.* (The controversy on the Madonna of the Bird is here summed up); Gondalon, *Riom et ses environs* (Riom, Jouvet, 1904); A. de Champeaux et P. Gauchery, *Les travaux d'art exécutés pour Jean, duc de Berry* (Paris, II. Champion, 1891); Camille Eulart, *Le musée de sculpture comparée du palais du Trocadéro* (on the *vierge à l'oiseau*), (Paris, H. Laurens, 1913).

best XIII-century art. Work as exceptional as this is of no date or school, but is due to some unrecorded individual genius. In that same late-Gothic day the spirit of St. Louis and Joinville lived again in *The Very Joyous, Pleasing and Diverting History of the Gentle Lord of Bayard, written by the Loyal Servitor.*

The serrated foliage of the Madonna's crown proves the sculpture to be late-Gothic. M. Gonse places it midway in the XIV century, M. Vitry early in the XVI, and M. Enlart thinks that it could not have been produced before the XV century. MM. Mâle, Palustre, Merimée, and others have discussed it. In the ideal innocence and dignity of the Virgin is Michel Colombe's charm. The legend was that in Egypt the infant Jesus modeled images of birds, then breathed on them, imparting life. This is the mystic moment which the unknown master of Riom chose to render; there is a brooding reverence in the young mother's face as she gazes at her Son, who ponders in a divine wonderment at a bird about to fly from his hand.

THE ROMANESQUE CATHEDRAL OF LE PUY[211]

Into whatever country you carry war, remember that children, women and churchmen and the poor are not your enemies.

—(Dying words of BERTRAND DUGUESCLIN,
killed near Le Puy, 1380).

Le Puy is hoary with history. Perched high on basaltic rocks near the source of the Loire, picturesque beyond description, it stood on the great pilgrimage route from Italy to Compostela, the *Via Francigena* by which French art and poetry passed into Spain and penetrated to Italy, along whose pilgrim roads are found portal images of the Round Table heroes and the sculptured tympanums of France.[212] The cathedral is built near the top of the town's hill, and above it on the hillcrest has been set a mammoth statue of Our Lady cast from cannon taken at Sebastopol. In the immediate suburbs rises another mass of volcanic rock, a needle some two hundred and fifty feet in height. The oldest part of the chapel crowning that extraordinary little basalt mountain dates before the year 1000. The sanctuary is trefoil, like the early-Christian churches at Rome, and like St. Laurent at Grenoble.[213] At the end of the XI century St. Michel d'Aiguille was enlarged irregularly. From time immemorial a shrine dedicated to the Archangel has crowned the pinnacle:

[211] *Congrès Archéologique*, 1904, pp. 1, 403; Noël Thiollier et Félix Thiollier, *L'architecture romane du diocèse du Puy* (Le Puy, 1900); Félix Thiollier, *Le Forez pittoresque et monumental*; Mallay et Noël Thiollier, *Monographie de la cathédrale du Puy* (Le Puy, 1904); Prosper Merimée, *Notes d'un voyage en Auvergne* (Paris, 1838), p. 242; Alexis Forel, *Voyage au pays des sculpteurs romans* (Paris and Geneva, 1913), 2 vols.; Paul Mantz, "Une tournée en Auvergne," in *Gazette des Beaux-Arts*, 1887, vols. 35, 36; Louis Villat, *Le Velay* (Collection, Les régions de la France), (Paris, L. Cerf); Mandet, *Histoire de Velay* (Le Puy, 1860), 6 vols.; De la Mure, *Histoire des ducs de Bourbon et des comtes de Forez*; Michel, *Auvergne et le Velay* (Moulins), 3 vols. and atlas; *Histoire littéraire de la France*, vol. 8, p. 467, "Adhémar de Monteil"; p. 514, "Urbain II" (Paris, 1747).

[212] Marcel Reymound et Ch. Girard, "La chapelle de St. Laurent à Grenoble," in *Bulletin Archéologique*, 1914-16, vol. 56, p. 176.

[213] Emile Mâle, "L'art du moyen âge et les pèlerinages" in *Revue de Paris*, Oct. 1919, Feb. 1920.

"In the presence of angels I shall sing my psalms."

The approach to the cathedral of Le Puy, while less difficult than the precipitous needle of St. Michel, is equally romantic and solemn. You mount the hill by the Street of Tables, so called from the days of pilgrimages, when the merchants' booths lined it. As you climb, the way changes to a broad flight of steps, more than a hundred, and up and up you mount, with the polychromatic façade of the cathedral rising before you on high. Then suddenly, almost before you are aware of what has happened, you pass right under that western front of the church, ascending always, climbing under the cathedral's western bays. Formerly you could have mounted right into the very sanctuary itself, coming to it through the pavement. To-day the stairway branches, and you enter the church at the side. Never was there such an approach to the House of Prayer as this, never a more sublime and grandiose conception than the shadowed stair over which hangs the façade. Halfway up, where stand red porphyry columns and doors of chiseled bronze, is carved, "If you do not fear crime, fear to cross this threshold, for the Queen of Heaven wishes a devotion without stain."

M. Thiollier has shown that the Romanesque school of the Velay region was an intermediary between Burgundy, Auvergne, and the Midi, with the meridional influences the strongest. Le Puy's choir, transept, and two bays of the nave were erected in the XI century, and of that date is the cloister walk that touches the church. The transept has a tribune at each end. Beyond the chevet stood a tower of which the actual one is a replica. As all the level space available was covered by these structures, it became necessary, when they wished to lengthen the nave in the XII century, to build out from the hill a vast masonry foundation as a platform. It is under those westernmost bays that mounts the stairway of Wonderland. Each bay of the nave is covered by an oblong cupola set on an octagonal base, of a type found again only at Poitiers, in the church of St. Hilaire. At Le Puy the side aisles buttress the cupolas.

No one should miss seeing a XV-century fresco discovered under whitewash, in 1860, in the library off the cloister. The Liberal Arts are symbolized by women of the type of Anne of Brittany with bombous foreheads, and at the feet of each sits a disciple. Thus Aristotle, with the sensitive face of a scholar, is seated at the feet of Logic, and Cicero learns of Rhetoric.

Le Puy in Old Auvergne

The cathedral of Le Puy has been venerated and visited by practically every ruler of France from Charlemagne to Francis I. This ancient city was almost chosen as the meeting place for launching the First Crusade. Urban II paused here in 1095, and the bishop of Le Puy, Adhémar de Monteil (1087-1100), accompanied him to Clermont, and when the pope's great rallying speech was ended it was Bishop Adhémar, his face shining with enthusiasm, who first stepped forward to take the cross. Urban appointed him the spiritual chief of the expedition, and his skill in military strategics proved of use since he had been a knight before becoming a churchman. This good man died in the grievous days at Antioch, worn out with his efforts to check disorders in the crusaders' camp. To Adhémar de Monteil has been attributed the *Salve Regina* called in the olden times the anthem of Puy. To Le Puy's famous shrine St. Louis presented a thorn from the Crown he had obtained from Constantinople, and on his way back from his first crusade he deposited in the church the curious image of a black Virgin given him in Egypt.

THE CATHEDRAL OF LIMOGES[214]

Bien me sourit le doux printemps,
Qui fait venir fleurs et feuillages;
Et bien me plait lorsque j'entends
Des oiseaux le gentil ramage.
Mais j'aime mieux quand sur le pré
Je vois l'étendard arboré,
Flottant comme un signal de guerre.
Quand j'entends par mont et par vaux
Courir chevalier et chevaux
Et sous leur pas frémir la terre,
Et gens crier: "A l'aide! A l'aide!"
De voir les petits et les grands
Dans les fossés roulers mourants.
A ce plaisir tout plaisir cède.[215]

—Bertran de Born (1140-1215).

Although in plan, in the mode of construction, in the covering of chapels and various details, the resemblances between the cathedrals of Clermont and Limoges are such that it is thought the same Jean Deschamps designed both, the cathedral of St. Étienne at Limoges possesses its own individual character because of the fine-grained, compact granite of which it is built and the unusual talent of its

[214] René Fage, *La cathédrale de Limoges* (Collection, Petites Monographies), (Paris, H. Laurens, 1913); Abbé Arbellot, *Monographie de la cathédrale de Limoges* (Limoges, 1853); A. Petit, "Les six statues du jubé de la cathédrale de Limoges," in *Bulletin Monumental*, 1912, vol. 62, p. 144. MM. Émile Mâle, André Michel, and Louis Gonse have written on the *jubé*; René Fage, "Le clocher limousin à l'époque romane," in *Bulletin Monumental*, 1907, vol. 71, p. 262; Anthyme Saint-Paul, "Archéologie limousin," in *L'Almanac limousin*, 1885; Charles de Lasteyrie, *L'abbaye de St. Martial de Limoges* (Paris, Picard, 1901); A. Leroux, *L'abbaye de St. Martial de Limoges* (Toulouse, 1901); *ibid.*, *Géographie et histoire du Limousin* (Limoges, 1892); Ernest Rupin, *L'œuvre de Limoges* (Paris, 1890); A. Meyer, *L'art de l'émail de Limoges* (Paris, 1896); P. Lavedan, *Léonard Limosin et les émailleurs français* (Collection, Les Grands Artistes), (Paris, H. Laurens). (The meeting for the *Congrès Archéologique*, 1921, is to be held at Limoges.)

[215] Rendered in modern French by J. Demogeot.

masons. M. Viollet-le-Duc considered the apse of Limoges one of the most scientific of Gothic constructions. The very beautiful leaf foliage is as crisply cut as when it came from the master's hand. Full of character are the profiles of the molds used in the triforium for decorative effect.

Because of the enduring quality of their building material, the Romanesque edifices of Limousin lasted so well that there was little temptation to tear them down in order to substitute Gothic churches. Till the Revolution, Limoges kept its great pre-Gothic abbatial of St. Martial, and its cathedral was, like that of Clermont in Auvergne, an isolated example of Gothic. Like Clermont's chief church, the western bays of Limoges were not built till the XIX century. The general aspect of St. Étienne is Rayonnant. Its Flamboyant Gothic additions were held in rigorous restraint. When Bishop Aimeric de la Serre (1246-73), a man of wealth, determined to remake his church, he willed his fortune to the enterprise. As Bishop Aimeric had just died, the first stone was laid on June 1, 1273, by Hélie de Malemort, doyen of the chapter. For over fifty years they built steadily till under Bishop Hélie de Talleyrand the choir was completed in 1327. A second period of work, from 1344 to the end of the century, resulted in the south arm of the transept whose rose is Rayonnant, whereas that to the north is Flamboyant. In its tendency to eliminate the horizontal line Limoges is eminently a church of the XIV century. The shafts before the piers rise unbroken from pavement to vault-springing; the pier arches at the apse curve are very pointed. Yet there is no geometric dryness in this interior. Plain wall surfaces above the main arcade and around the triforium and clearstory add to its robust aspect.

In 1370 the Black Prince sacked Limoges and left little but the cathedral standing. Froissart recounts that "there was no pity taken of the poor people who had wrought no manner of treason ... more than three thousand persons of all ages and both sexes were slain that day ... and the city clean brent and brought to destruction." It took time and treasure to repair the devastation. Only from 1458 to 1490 were the two easternmost bays of the nave erected.

The fourth period of energy at Limoges, from 1515 to 1530, created a gem of Flamboyant Gothic, the transept's north façade, which is called the Portail de St. Jean, as it stood near a church dedicated to the Baptist. Bishop Philippe de Montmorency began it, and his successor, César de Villiers de l'Isle-Adam, completed it, as their carved armorials bear witness. Because it stood on the emplacement of the old Romanesque transept, it was somewhat too narrow. To obviate that impression the corner buttresses were offset at an angle. The wooden doors of this, the main entrance to Limoges Cathedral, are of the Renaissance. They represent the stoning of St. Stephen, and the first Christian missionary of Limousin, St. Martial, to whom an early local martyr, St. Valérie, is presenting her decapitated head. The ring of St. Valérie gave symbolic investiture to the dukes of Aquitaine.

Limoges was active in the Renaissance days. Her bishop, Jean de Langeac, erected an elaborate *jubé* between choir and transept, a rood loft which is one mass of hanging keystones, channeling, bas-reliefs, and arabesque panels, with six big statues of the Virtues made in 1536 by an artist of Tours named Jean Arnaud. It is plain to see that the Renaissance was in full swing. The Labors of Hercules were set forth, and Bacchus was placed beside Ambrose and Augustine. Perhaps the huge *jubé* and the episcopal tomb both came from the studios of Tours, where had settled the earliest artists of the transalpine Renaissance. The master hand that made the bishop's tomb, says M. Mâle, followed Dürer, but his eight Apocalypse panels were an improvement over the designs of the German. Unfortunately the bronze recumbent figure of the munificent prelate whose pride it was to adorn his church was melted up for pennies in 1793. There are two other notable tombs in the choir's procession path—that of a bishop-builder, Raynaud de la Porte—the only funeral monument in France that represents stone curtains drawn aside by angels—and the tomb of his nephew, Bernard Brun (d. 1350). Three of the Avignon popes were natives of art-loving Limousin.

The Revolution robbed Limoges of the noble abbey church of St. Martial, which had been dedicated by the pope of the First Crusade in 1095. St. Martial had formed the center of the Château section of Limoges, ruled by its own counts with a totally different administration from that of the Cité division, where the cathedral stood, and whose civic master was the bishop. Many a feud had Cité with Château. The abbatial of the "apostle of Aquitaine" would tell us the story had not blind passion laid it in ruins.

For three hundred years no effort was made at Limoges to complete its cathedral's nave until, through the enterprise of Monseigneur Duquesnay, the first stone of the sorely needed western church was laid in 1876 and the structure finished in 1888. It was joined, by means of a narthex or forechurch, to the ancient tower which had been built isolated before the Romanesque cathedral of St. Étienne. In its three lower stories, now hidden by cumbersome masonry propping, save on the east side, the tower belonged to the cathedral which Urban II blessed in 1095 when he dedicated St. Martial's abbatial. Its four upper stories, mainly of the XII century, were begun by Bishop Sebrand-Chabot while the overlord of the province, Richard Cœur-de-Lion, was on his crusading venture. In this very region, at the castle of Chalus near Limoges, the Lion-hearted met his death in 1199.

The dialect of Limousin was considered the purest form of Provençal by the troubadours. Here in the west center of France, Cœur-de-Lion's troubadour friend, the malignant breeder of dissensions, Bertran de Born, had his castle of Hautefort south of Limoges. He excited Henry Plantagenet against his sons, and spurred on the sons to rebellion. Unlike the gentle Valérie who carries in her hands her own head with right Christian pride since she lost it to witness to the planting of the Cross, Bertran de Born, sower of discord, is represented swinging his severed head by the hair like a lantern. So Dante saw him in the ninth chasm of hell herded with the malicious ones who had abused the attribute of reason: "I made the father and the son rebels to each other," he wailed. "Because I parted persons thus united, I carry my brain, ah, me! parted from its source. Thus the law of retribution is observed in me."[216] And equally merciless has been the law of retribution for Limoges, than which no other city has suffered more from pillage, pest, and fire. Froissart tells us that during centuries the frontier lands of Limousin and Gascony exercised brigandage as a *métier*.

---

[216] *Inferno*, xxviii:112-142.

Like the three lower stories of the tower, the crypt belonged to the XI-century Romanesque cathedral of Limoges. On its groin vault was painted a Byzantinesque Christ surrounded by the symbols of the Evangelists. The cathedral has recently lost by theft some precious enamels. From father to son in Limoges passed the skill in this beautiful art craft. St. Eloi was apprenticed to a goldsmith in Limoges in the VII century. At Le Mans is the XII-century plaque of Geoffrey Plantagenet, at Mozac an unrivaled Limousin reliquary, and Jean, duc de Berry, prince of amateurs, once possessed the best XIII-century work of Limoges enamel, the gold King's Cup, now in the British Museum. In St. Pierre's at Chartres are the splendid Apostle plaques of the XVI century by Léonard Limosin. The earlier method had been to sink the enamel like a jewel in cells or *cloisons*, hence the name *cloisonné*, but the Renaissance artists used no inclosing ribbon of metal.

The only ancient windows remaining in the cathedral's clearstory are the two at the apse end, which a canon, Pierre de la Rodier, presented. When he became bishop of Carcassonne he built the south chapel that opens from St. Nazaire's nave (1323-30). In the cathedral chapels are some XV-and XVI-century lights, and fragments of earlier glass. On the same river, Vienne, which at Limoges is crossed by two noble XIII-century bridges, lies Eymoutiers, some thirty miles to the west, between Clermont and Limoges. Its remarkable collection of windows is entirely of the XV century; each panel contains a single figure in an architectural setting.

French writers claim that between Eymoutiers and Limoges took place the apparition of the Infant Jesus to St. Anthony of Padua which became a favorite theme with painters, but the Italians insist that Padua was the privileged spot. Limoges city has its St. Anthony tradition. In its square, they say, while the saint was preaching in 1225, his audience was untouched by a rainstorm that inundated the other townspeople. As we have seen that the building of great churches was preceded in most cases by a spiritual regeneration, it is not extreme to think that the fervor roused in the Midi by the great son of St. Francis had much to do with the laying of the corner stone of Limoges Cathedral in 1273.

THE CATHEDRAL OF BORDEAUX[217]

Celuy qui, d'une doulceur et facilité naturelle, mépriseroit les offenses reçues, feroit chose très belle et digne de louange: mais celuy qui, picqué et oultré jusques au vif d'une offense, s'armeroit des armes de la raison contre ce furieux appétit de vengeance, et aprèz un grand conflit s'en rendroit enfin maistre, feroit sans

[217] *Congrès Archéologique*, 1861; Charles Saunier, *Bordeaux* (Collection, Villes d'art célèbres), (Paris, H. Laurens); J. A. Brutails, *Les vieilles églises de la Gironde* (Bordeaux, Feret et fils, 1912); *ibid.*, "La cathédrale de Bordeaux," in *Le moyen âge*, 1899-1901, vols. 12-14; H. Havard, éd., *La France artistique et monumentale* "Bordeaux," L. de Foucaud, vol. 5, p. 105; Cirot de la Ville, *Origines chrétiennes de Bordeaux, ou hist. et descript. de l'église de St. Seurin* (Bordeaux, 1867); P. J. O'Reilly, *Histoire de Bordeaux* (Paris and Bordeaux, 1857), 6 vols.; C. Jullian, *Histoire de Bordeaux* (Bordeaux, 1895); L. Barron, *La Gascogne* (Collection, Régions de la France), (Paris, L. Cerf); *ibid.*, *La Garonne* (Collection, Fleuves de France), (Paris, H. Laurens); P. Courteault, *Histoire de Gascogne* (Collection, Les vieilles provinces de France), (Paris, Boivin et Cie).

doubte beaucoup plus. Celuy là feroit bien; et celuy cy, vertueusement: l'une action se pourroit dire bonté: l'aultre, vertu; car il semble que le nom de la vertu présuppose de la difficulté et du contraste. Nous nommons Dieu bon, fort, et libéral, et juste, mais nous ne le nommons pas *vertueux.*

—Montaigne (Mayor of Bordeaux from 1581 to 1585).

While Bordeaux has the warm fertility of the Midi, there is much of the north in the big commercial city. And its cathedral of St. André is typical of the dual temperament. The nave is the aisleless, wide hall preferred by meridionals, the choir has the procession path with its circlet of chapels loved by the north. Excepting Le Mans, Amiens, and Rheims, it is the longest cathedral in France.

Bordeaux was an important city in the wide possessions of the dukes of Aquitaine. In 1137 Aliénor, the daughter of the last William, was wedded in its cathedral to the prince who immediately ascended the French throne as Louis VII. When she left him after fifteen years and wedded Henry Plantagenet the rich city on the Garonne passed under English rule. In all the vicissitudes of the three hundred years that followed, from 1154 to 1453, Bordeaux' self-interest kept her faithful to her masters beyond the sea, the chief customers in her wine trade. Bordeaux remained French, however, in race and in the expression of race, architecture. Aliénor's second husband, Henry II of England, was, like herself, more French than English; of his thirty-four years' reign he passed only twelve in England, and his son, Cœur-de-Lion, was another Anglo-Frenchman.

The hardy, domelike vaults carried on diagonals that span the nave of Angers' Cathedral (c. 1150) have been considered the earliest extant examples of the Gothic of the West. And yet it is possible, thinks M. Brutails, the erudite archivist of the Gironde, that the vaults of the same type which were built over the nave of the present cathedral of Bordeaux antedated the notable ones of Angers. In Bordeaux occurred one of the premature isolated examples of Gothic ribs under the south tower of Ste. Croix. During a revival of builder's energy, from 1052 to 1127 (under the eighth and ninth dukes of Aquitaine), Ste. Croix and St. Seurin were reconstructed and St. André begun. It seems more reasonable to suppose, however, that Anjou, where first the cupola church of Aquitaine met the diagonal ribs of northern France, should have been the cradle of that phase of the new architecture which we call Plantagenet.

The nave of St. André is a difficult page to read, Romanesque, Gothic, and Renaissance as it now is. The Romano-Byzantine church here which Urban II blessed in 1096 exists only in vestiges in the lower walls on either side of the wide hall. Originally the church had side aisles, but they were obliterated when the XII century spanned the entire width with Angevin diagonals. The side walls were then made into two stories, a lower wall arcade surmounted by a window story, such as we have seen in the cathedrals at Angers and Angoulême. In 1437 an earthquake caused the collapse of the masonry roof of the four westernmost bays, which were recovered by a Flamboyant Gothic vaulting rich with supplementary ribs.

The west front of St. André never was developed, as the church abutted there on the ancient ramparts. The main entrance was the Porte Royale in the north flank of the nave, whose statues, made in the golden hour of St. Louis' reign, were used as models by Viollet-le-Duc when he refilled the empty niches of Notre Dame at Paris. There can be no clearer exposition of what qualities were lost in Rayonnant Gothic than to pass from this apogee portal to the smoother, more conventional images at the northern entrance to the transept; in the rugged apostles, full of character, is the touch which all time recognizes as genius; in the aristocratic churchmen of the XIV-century door is mere talent. To the nave of Bordeaux a XVI-century archbishop, Charles de Grammont, who initiated here the Italian Renaissance, added an elaborate buttress. That miniature façade is called the *contrefort de Grammont*.[218]

Under Archbishop de Mallemort (1227-60) St. André superseded St. Seurin as the cathedral of Bordeaux. As late as 1259 it lacked a suitable chevet. Gascony was in chaos in those years when Henry III, builder of Westminster Abbey, sent the Earl of Leicester, Simon de Montfort (son of the leader of the Albigensian Crusade), to straighten out the disorders. That strong administrator, who was on the constitutional liberal side in English politics, was frustrated by Midi corruption. Only as the XIII century closed was built the present splendid choir of Bordeaux Cathedral, a classic work of Rayonnant Gothic before that phase turned to geometric rule. How technique cramped and killed inspiration can be seen in the later Rayonnant church of St. Michel. At St. André, it is true, the capitals are slight and the profiles not overvirile. Decadence is foreshadowed, but not yet is the art academic and wiredrawn. The Midi appears in the clearstory and triforium, which do not fill the entire space between the shafts. The partiality of the meridional for unencumbered interiors had something to do with making the procession path thirty feet wide. Most grateful is the traveler for a curving aisle around the sanctuary after having sojourned among the cupola and hall-like churches of Anjou and Aquitaine. Bordeaux' choir possesses some good stained glass of its own period, and some of its buttress statues are among the best imagery of the XIV century. Mary Magdalene, carrying her vase of ointment, appears as a chatelaine of the Middle Ages with the bandeau under her chin then fashionable; Aliénor of Aquitaine could not have been very unlike her.

The most active patron of St. André's Gothic choir was the archbishop of the city, Bertrand de Got, who in 1305 became Clement V, the first Avignon pope. When he died, in 1314, the new choir was practically completed. His image stands at the trumeau of the transept's north door (the head and hand are reproductions), and around him are six prelates who may be intended to represent the French bishops whom Clement raised to the cardinalate. In technique these images may surpass the weather-beaten apostles at the Porte Royale (c. 1260), but they are their inferior in spirit. Five of the statues are studies from the same model. Casts of the transept portal of Bordeaux are in the Kensington Museum and in the Trocadéro. The Avignon popes were the chief art patrons of the XV century, with the four

---

[218] In the nave of the cathedral is the neo-classic tomb of Cardinal de Cheverus, who died, archbishop of Bordeaux, in 1836. Driven out of France at the time of the Revolution, he founded the see of Boston, Massachusetts, in the United States of America.

Valois princes—Charles V of France and his brothers at Dijon, Bourges, and Angers. No pontiff was more munificent than Clement V. While he was bishop at St. Bertrand-de-Comminges (Haute Garonne)[219] he renewed that small cathedral, which consists of two unequal parts, a Romanesque façade, donjon tower, and forechurch of the day when St. Bertrand had been bishop (1073-1123), and an unaisled Gothic choir, begun by Bertrand de Got, continued by him while pope and finished by Bishop Hugues de Chatillon, who died in 1352.

The Rayonnant chevet of Bordeaux Cathedral and its transept, two of whose towers are spire-crowned, compose an effective architectural group, with a detached campanile in the gardens. In order to give employment to the poor, Archbishop Pierre Berland, who had been a shepherd's son, erected the graceful, isolated tower for bells to hang in, "that God might be praised in the sky." And the same generations built St. Michel's tower (1472-92), the highest beacon in southwest France, mutilated mercilessly by M. Paul Abadie's restoration. The lifeless church before which it stands is proof of how much needed was the vim, even if often exaggerated and bizarre, of the late-Gothic movement. M. Enlart considers Bordeaux and Bayonne[220] to be two of the principal doors by which the English Curvilinear style entered France. There its name is Flamboyant Gothic. And yet in this same Midi, M. Anthyme Saint-Paul, who denies the English origin of French late-Gothic architecture, claims to have found proof of his theory that already in Apogee Gothic and in the Rayonnant hour were developing the characteristics of the final phase. One cannot help but feel that the English builders' partiality for exuberant decoration had something to do with the making of such towers as St. Michel and the Pey Berland. The landscape round Bordeaux is as rich in sky-pointing spires as Calvados in Normandy.

When, in 1451, the English surrendered Bordeaux, the great Dunois, Jeanne d'Arc's companion in arms, was received as conqueror in its cathedral (where in 1376 the Black Prince had accepted the citizens' oath of fealty to his father), and to the ringing of bells and cries of "*Noël*," Archbishop Pierre Berland and the chief men of the town swore to be loyal subjects of France.

Among the ancient churches of historic interest in Bordeaux is Ste. Croix, rebuilt by Charlemagne when Saracens destroyed it, and again remade (1099) as Romanesque according to the school of Poitou. Under its tower, Gothic ribs were used early in the XII century. The church was partly wrecked in 1179 and revault-

[219] The beautiful cloister of St. Bertrand-de-Comminges belongs to the XII century. In 1536 the Renaissance art prelate, Jean de Mauléon, presented the carved choir stalls. *Congrès Archéologique*, 1874, p. 249, J. de Laurière; and 1906, p. 79, Louis Serbat; Morel, *Essai hist. sur St. Bertrand-de-Comminges*; d'Agos, *Description de l'église cathédrale de Comminges*.

[220] The cathedral of Bayonne was begun about 1135 under Aliénor of Aquitaine's father. The choir is of that century; the nave was finished about 1335, and some of its sculptures, showing the national crest with the arms of both England and France, recall the short sovereignty in France of Henry V and Henry VI. The cloister of Bayonne ranks with those of Elne and Arles. A transept is indicated merely by the spacing of bays. The XII-century tower was rebuilt from 1501 to 1544. The interior of the cathedral is more firm than it is graceful, owing to the piers being six feet square and to an excessive sobriety in ornamentation. *Congrès Archéologique*, 1888.

ed at the end of the XIII century. In the sculpture of the rich façade is a certain Assyrian note. M. Brutails complains that Abadie, the restorer, made of the frontispiece a neo-Angoumois work and that the north tower is entirely of his building.

Memories of the great Emperor Charles haunt the former cathedral of Bordeaux, St. Seurin. Fundamentally it belongs to the cupola type of edifice, and though incessantly rebuilt up to the XV century, it presents the aspect of a Romanesque church. The south portal (c. 1260), sculptured with elaborate foliate ornament, has images of unequal merit. In St. Seurin, says tradition, Charlemagne paused, in 778, with the bodies of the heroes of Roncevaux to be buried at Blaye, his nephew Roland and that paladin's comrade, Sire Olivier, and Archbishop Turpin of Rheims, who fought pagans—*par granz batailles et par mult bels sermuns*. On the altar of St. Seurin the emperor laid the horn that Roland blew in his last extremity, the olifant which the Midi folk say still echoes in the Pyrenean gorges:

> Vient à Burdele la citet de valur,
> Desur l'alter seint Sevrin li barun
> Met l'olifant, plein d'or et de manguns,
> Li pélerin le veient ki là vunt.[221]

> (Came to Bordeaux the city of great price,
> And on the shrine of Baron St. Seurin,
> The olifant Charles laid, filled full with gold,
> And to this day pilgrims can see it there.)

The XX-century pilgrims to the old city on the Garonne must remember that the *Chanson de Roland* was written a long, long time ago, and that to-day the olifant of the paladin lives only in the pages of French history, where its place is as secure as the standard of Jeanne d'Arc. *À la peine, à l'honneur.* Without St. Seurin's church we might have forgotten a proud page of Bordeaux' past.

TOULOUSE[222]

> Ici, dans Toulouse, je sens palpiter
> La prodigieuse histoire du libre Languedoc!

[221] Léon Gautier, éd., *Chanson de Roland* (Tours, Mâme, 1895), section 297, l. 3684.

[222] *Congrès Archéologique*, 1874 and 1906; H. Graillot, *Toulouse et Carcassonne* (Collection, Villes d'art célèbres), (Paris, H. Laurens); Jules de Lahondès, *Toulouse chrétienne; l'église de St. Étienne, cathédrale de Toulouse; ibid.*, "Les chapiteaux de St. Sernin de Toulouse," in *Mém. de la Soc. archéol. du Midi de la France*, 1897; Anthyme Saint-Paul, "St. Sernin," in *Album des monuments du Midi de la France*, 1897; in *Bulletin Monumental*, 1899; and in *Revue de l'art chrétien*, 1905, vol. 48, p. 145; Abbé Lestrade, *Histoire de l'art à Toulouse* (Toulouse, 1907); H. L. Gillet, *Histoire artistique des ordres mendiants* (Paris, 1912); A. Marignan, *Histoire de la sculpture en Languedoc des XIe et XIIIe siècles* (Paris, Bouillon, 1902); Alexis Forel, *Voyage au pays des sculpteurs romans* (Paris and Geneva, 1913), 2 vols.; Roschach, *Le musée de Toulouse*, "Inventoire des richesses d'art de la France: ministère de l'instruction publique" (vol. 8), (Paris, 1908), 4to; Martin, *L'art roman en France* (Paris, 1910); H. Revoil, *L'architecture romane du Midi de la France* (Paris, 1873-90), 3 vols.; R. de Lasteyrie, *L'architecture religieuse en France à l'époque romane* (Paris, 1912); Vie et Vaissette, supplemented by Du Mège, Molinier, and Roschach, *Nouvelle histoire de Languedoc* (Toulouse, Privat, 1872-92), 15 vols.

Et je vois Saint-Sernin, la grande église romane, ...
Et le rempart où la pierre écrasa l'oiseau de
Proie que je ne veux pas nommer....

À Toulouse vivante, à Toulouse qui chante,
J'élève mon salut et je dis: Ville sainte!
Au soleil à jamais épanouis-toi puissante!...
L'âme du Midi réfugiée en toi,
Chevaleresque et digne, tu as traversé les âges!

—Frédéric Mistral, at the *Jeux Floraux* of Toulouse, 1879.[223]

If the influence of both the north and the south is felt at Bordeaux, the unadulterated Midi reigns at Toulouse. It is eminently the capital city of this fertile Languedoc, where art and luxury developed precociously in the earlier periods of the Middle Ages. Here the troubadour still sings in the regional tongue which might to-day be the speech of France (instead of a dialect) had a genius such as Dante written in the *langue d'oc*, the most gracious form of the Romance language. It is spoken in Aragon and Catalonia—lands where the architectural development followed the same trend as that of French Languedoc.

Modern Toulouse is not a handsome city like the Bordeaux of to-day. Its most imposing church is not its cathedral of St. Étienne, which is as ungainly outside as it is irregular within. The nave and choir make no pretense of following the same axis line, since they never were intended to form one edifice; were the north wall of the nave extended down through the choir, it would abut on the high altar.

The nave is of enormous span like that of Bordeaux Cathedral. It once had side aisles, but the entire width of the edifice was thrown into one hall when the church was remodeled in 1211. Simon de Montfort (whom Mistral, as a patriotic son of the Midi, refuses even to name in his verses) was besieging the city while the Angevin vaults of its cathedral were building, and Count Raymond VI of Toulouse ordered that the works should continue, war or no war.

The choir of Toulouse Cathedral belongs to the same current of northern Gothic that produced Clermont, Limoges, and Narbonne. Begun in 1275, it was inspired directly by Narbonne Cathedral, whose foundation stone was laid in 1273. The plan is of the north, but the feeling is meridional. After the death of the wealthy Bishop Bernard de Lille, the founder, the chapter had not sufficient funds to continue building on the same ambitious scale. Only in the XV century was the triforium level reached, and it was not until the XVII century that the masonry roof was added. Even then it was so skimped that the exterior aspect of the choir is deplorable. At St. Étienne there seemed to be a fatality against symmetry. When all hope was given up of replacing the Romanesque nave by one of the same character as the choir, it was decided to make its entrance more important; but instead of setting the new Flamboyant portal in the center of the west façade, it was placed to one side. The window dedicated to two sons of the Midi, St. Roch and St. Sebastian, is attributed to Arnaud de Moles who made the celebrated Creation, prophets, and sibyls of Auch Cathedral. Some of the grisaille in St. Étienne came

[223] Frédéric Mistral, *Poèmes* (Paris, Charpentier-Fasquelle, 1912).

from the Jacobins.

There are few church interiors in Europe more stately and unique than that of the brick abbatial in Toulouse, called the Jacobins', a name given the Dominicans because their Paris convent was in the rue St. Jacques. The house of wisdom is founded on seven pillars, Scripture tells us.[224] So the Friars Preachers planted directly down the center of their lofty hall church seven columnar piers that soar to an enormous height. The easternmost one is set in the middle of the apse and on it fall some fourteen ribs. The vault arches of white stone against the red brick infilling are of striking effect. No mediæval pillars—save those of the late-Gothic church of St. Nicolas-du-Port near Nancy—are higher than the seven giants of Toulouse. In the desecration of the edifice after the Revolution, its pavement was covered with soil, for the stabling of horses, but within the last ten years excavations have exposed the true bases of the piers.

The Jacobins' church was founded in 1229 by a rich citizen and his wife, who had vowed to devote a large portion of their fortune to God's service, should their only daughter recover from a desperate illness. The edifice, constructed with an audacious massiveness, as if for eternity, has been allowed to fall into general decay, and now appears more desolate than would a ruin of stone. Like alien images, gargoyles protrude forlornly from the red brick walls, so inconsistent is brick with the true Gothic spirit. The Midi was too wedded to classic traditions to excel in the national art, which it never took completely to its heart. There is little of the ogival style about these narrow loophole windows, these diagonals unbraced by flying buttresses. Gothic in the south has an accidental aspect.

---

[224] "Wisdom hath built herself a house, she hath hewn her out seven pillars."—Prov. ix:1.

The Jacobins', or Dominicans', Church at Toulouse (XIII Century)

To the greatest of Dominican churches the Avignon pope, Urban V, who covered the Midi with his monuments, gave the body of St. Thomas Aquinas, greatest of Dominican doctors. It was saved when the Jacobins were sacked in 1562, and is now in St. Sernin, whose collection of authentic relics is the richest in France—and some say in Europe.

Toulouse also had a Franciscan brick church, whose wall bordered on the city ramparts, so that passages of defense were thrown from buttress to buttress. That church of the Cordeliers (rich with memories of St. Anthony of Padua) was burned in 1870, and its lovely XV-century cloister now forms part of the Museum that is housed in the former convent of the Augustinians. The graceful octagonal brick tower of the Cordeliers,[225] saved from the wreckage, was modeled on that of the Jacobins', just as the Jacobins' tower, in lessening stories, was designed probably by the architect who made the top stories of St. Sernin's beacon. Artists have preferred the Jacobins' belfry to its prototype.

The paucity of stone in the province caused the creation of a school of brick architecture of which Toulouse was the center. One may prefer a stone architecture, but one cannot deny the lovely tones of brown and crimson madder acquired in time by these brick monuments of the Midi that seem created especially for resistance and long duration.

Not the cathedral of Toulouse, but its monastic brick church of St. Sernin, is the supreme religious monument of the city and the grandest Romanesque edifice in France. Its date has been discussed by MM. de Lasteyrie, Corroyer, Saint-Paul, and Jules de Lahondès. In the last quarter of the XI century the monks began the choir of the present church, which combined the characteristics of the Romanesque schools of Burgundy and Auvergne. Those influences had passed south by way of Conques, where the abbatial of Ste. Foi had been rebuilt a generation before St. Sernin. In 1083 Cluny monks replaced at St. Sernin the canons regular, and where Cluny reformed, building activities usually followed.

While the Toulouse monastery church was rising, its selfsame plan appeared in the northeast corner of Spain in the cathedral of Santiago Compostela, begun in 1082, too direct a copy to have been done by any but St. Sernin's own architect or his favorite pupil. In Spain the works went faster, so that Santiago Cathedral was completed long before the abbatial at Toulouse, and, being constructed in stone, its interior has not been marred by centuries of whitewashing.

"The entry of Urban II into Toulouse" is pictured by Benjamin Constant in the Museum. In 1096, on his journey through France, preaching the First Crusade, he blessed the unfinished choir and transept of St. Sernin. The aisles around the transept form the most imposing part of the church. As the XI century closed, the transept was continued and the nave begun under the direction of a monk-builder, St. Raymond Gaynard, a man of wealth before entering the cloister. He conceived the masterly plan of five aisles. The side aisles were covered by a quarter-barrel vaulting that serves the purpose of a continuous flying buttress. Perhaps it was

[225] From the Chapelle de Rieux at the Cordeliers came some curious statues which are now in the Museum of Toulouse. Their date is certain, 1324 to 1348, yet their realism is of the XV century. Again Languedoc proved precocious in sculpture. In the Museum is a XIV-century statue of Bishop Guillaume Durandus, author of *Rationale*.

when the original architect of St. Sernin had proceeded to Santiago Compostela that St. Raymond became master-of-works at Toulouse. In 1119, a year after his death, another pontiff, Calixtus II, blessed St. Sernin.

From 1120 to 1140 was made the south portal, which constitutes, with Moissac's[226] portal and cloister, the chief works extant of the Languedoc school of sculpture. That school needs a competent biographer who will do for it what M. Paul Vitry has done for the Region-of-the-Loire school, and MM. de Vasselot and Koechlin for the imagery of southern Champagne.[227] The high-water mark of the regions' sculpture was attained in the Annunciation group at Moissac, whose ethereal elongated figures in clinging draperies rouse the imagination. The monks of Moissac, being Cluniac and not Cistercian, found imagery profitable to their souls. What were Bernard's thoughts as he gazed at their haunting rendering of the Incarnation?

Puritan Bernard thundered against the bizarre grotesques carved in cloisters. Up to 1140 they were popular, since the untrained stonecutters found it easier to make a caricature than an image true to nature. The invasions of the Barbarians had wiped out the sculptor's art, and the men of the XI century had to rediscover it. While St. Bernard sojourned in Toulouse he lived in St. Sernin's monastery, a Cluniac house, and it is probable that he paused with the monks at Moissac on the memorable journey he made into Languedoc to combat the fast-spreading dualist heresy of the Catharists. He was accompanied by Bishop Geoffrey de Lèves of Chartres, the builder of the most beautiful tower in the world. Surely those en-

[226] When Moissac was affiliated with Cluny and reformed, its church was rebuilt by Abbot Durand, whose image adorns a pier of the cloister's east gallery. The walls of the nave belong to the edifice consecrated in 1063. That church of three aisles was remade with cupolas and blessed in 1180, and of the same date are the fortified narthex and its tower. Owing to those defenses the celebrated portal is in the south wall of the porch, not in the church axis. The Gothic ribs beneath the tower are rectangular and three feet wide. In the XIV century the cupolas were replaced by diagonals. The cloisters were begun about 1100 under Abbot Ansquitil, who made the pier images, also the marble parts of the portal, its trumeau, and the Visitation. Abbot Roger (1115-31) finished the cloisters, inscribing the carved Scripture scenes of the capitals. During the first quarter of the XII century Moissac's imagery passed from the squat, coarsely executed figures of the cloister piers to the appealing, etherealized types—*"fluides créations du Languedoc"*—the Annunciation group. Mr. A. Kingsley Porter thinks that door-jamb-figure sculpture was first used by Guglielmo at Modena Cathedral (c. 1100), and from Italy passed into southern France. The current of art flowed in the opposite direction, too, for the coupled colonnettes, typical of the Romanesque cloisters of Provence, Languedoc, and Spain, soon found their way across the Alps, where early examples are to be seen at Verona and Aosta, and at the cathedral door of Verona are Languedoc's elongated figures with crossed feet. The *Portico de la gloria* at Santiago sets forth the vision of John the Beloved at Patmos quite as Moissac's tympanum presents it. *Congrès Archéologique*, 1901, vol. 2, pp. 43, 303; E. Rupin, *Abbaye et les cloîtres de Moissac* (Paris, Picard, 1897); André Michel, "Sculpture romane de Moissac," in *Bull. de la Soc. Archéol. du Midi de la France*, 1899 to 1901; Roger Peyre, *Padoue et Vérone* (Collection, Villes d'art célèbres), (Paris, H. Laurens).

[227] The master of French iconography, M. Émile Mâle, is on the eve of publishing a work on XII-century imagery, of which he says, "The art of Languedoc undulates like a flame in the wind, that of Provence seems cast in bronze."

lightened men mused with spiritual benefit before the *Ecce ancilla Domini* at Mois-sac? But one very much doubts if Bernard could have approved of four hundred carven capitals in the abbatial at Toulouse.

Slowly the making of St. Sernin's nave advanced. At first it was built story by story, but later the more usual procedure of bay by bay was adopted. In 1217, from the roof of St. Sernin, the stone was thrown that killed Simon de Montfort, who was besieging Toulouse. To the end of time a character such as his will rouse both enthusiasm and detestation. His personal morals were exemplary, his own troops adored him. The leading men of Christendom regarded him as an instrument of Heaven and right progress. The Midi execrated him, and does to this day, even as Ireland execrates Cromwell, whom good Puritans consider a hero, for the religious psychology of those two born leaders was curiously alike. With God's name on their lips their troops felt righteous in butchering.

With the death of Simon de Montfort the Albigensian wars changed in char-acter. Simon's son, Amaury de Montfort, was incapable of retaining the principal-ity won by his father's sword, so he sensibly passed over his claims to the king of France. The struggle henceforth was purely political. Blanche of Castile's wise head solved the Midi tangle when she married her son Alphonse of Poitiers to the heiress of the Count of Toulouse, with the understanding that, should the young people die childless, Languedoc fell to the French Crown. Alphonse gave the Midi, says Molinier, the first intelligent administration it had received since the better times of the Roman Empire. When he and his wife died, returning from St. Louis' fatal crusade of 1270, the great southern land became a part of France.

The Albigensian wars—for with reluctance one calls those years of bitter strife a crusade—delayed the completion of St. Sernin, whose main façade is gaunt and bare, and whose westernmost windows lack stone casements. When the Midi came under French rule the monks attained sufficient prosperity to erect the octagonal tower in five stories—each of lesser dimensions than the one below it. The upper stories used the miter arch so suited to brick. M. Enlart has called attention to the affinity of the *clochers Toulousans* and the Lombard steeples. At present the under-pinning of the tower obstructs the transept-crossing, but propping is better than demolition, which is what M. Viollet-le-Duc proposed in his blind enthusiasm for unity of style. The townspeople indignantly protested and the supreme beacon of this patroness city of art was saved.

A proud boast of Toulouse is that the first Dominican monastery was estab-lished there, and by Dominic himself, the saint whom Dante called "the messen-ger and familiar of Christ."[228] The Friars Preachers, like the Franciscans (who,

[228] *Paradiso*, xii:70-73.

> "Dominico fu detto; ed io ne parlo
> sì come dell'agricola, che Cristo
> elesse all'orto suo per aiutarlo.
> Ben parve messo e famigliar di Cristo."

("Dominic was he named; and I speak of him as of the husbandman whom Christ chose for his orchard to bring aid to it. Well did he show himself a messenger and a familiar of Christ.")

because of a new appreciation of their founder's character, are found sympathetic by many who still call a Dominican a "bloody sort of monk"), were agents for the quickening of the religious fervor of the XIII century. Both Orders were protests against abuses such as luxury, love of gold, and selfish privilege, which feudalism had helped to foster in the clergy.

Dominic de Guzman was a Castilian gentleman, a trained scholar, a man whose luminous face won instant affection and respect. In the first years of the XIII century he came north with the bishop of Osma on a diplomatic mission relating to a royal marriage. As those two good men journeyed through Languedoc amid the fearful havoc wrought by heresy, the vocation of the younger priest took shape. Returning from Italy in 1206, he and the bishop of Osma laid aside pomp and comforts to evangelize according to primitive Christianity. Only too clear was it to them that heresy was fed by the unworthy priesthood of the Midi that had lost the people's esteem. Two generations earlier St. Bernard had lamented over the same evil. Innocent III rebuked the worldling prelate of Bordeaux, and asked the bishop of Narbonne if he had a purse in place of a heart. After ten years' heroic missionizing both before and during the Albigensian Crusade, Dominic won papal sanction for his new Order in 1216. He was then a man of forty-seven. When he died, at Bologna in 1221, he left flourishing houses all over Christendom.

The function of his Friars was to teach again Christian doctrine in its purity; hence it was only natural, when the Inquisition[229] was founded, after the death of Dominic, that it should be intrusted to such trained theologians. They were to be a kind of jury to ascertain whether a case was heretical; if it was so decided, then the civic authorities stepped in and took action, since heresy was a state offense.

The best minds of that day held the theory that the decline of religion was a menace to law and order. The violent repression of heresy to prevent the dissolution of society seemed then as necessary as the repression of anarchy seems to-day. It had not always been so. "Slay error, but always love the man who errs," was St. Augustine's maxim. St. Ambrose and St. Hilary reprobated physical violence toward heretics. Gregory VII had protested against the "impious cruelty" which had burned a man of Cambrai for heresy. "Heretics are to be taken by force of arguments, not by force of arms," said the vehement St. Bernard himself on one occasion. Gradually a different outlook had taken possession of men's minds, a change of view that was to cost the Church dear. Crusades against the infidel were on every side, in the Orient, in the Balkans, in Spain. When heresy took on so alien and perverse an aspect as the Catharist errors, which were at root the negation of Christian standards and a veritable antisocial menace, it needed but an incident to <u>start a crusade ag</u>ainst heretics in France.

[229] Douais, *L'Inquisition, ses origines, sa procédure* (Paris, 1906); A. Molinier, *L'Inquisition dans le Midi de la France au XIIIe et au XIVe siècles* (Paris, 1880); Vacandard, *L'Inquisition; étude historique et critique sur le pouvoir coercitif de l'église* (Paris, 1907), (tr. London and New York, Longmans, Green & Co., 1908); Jean Guiraud, *Histoire patiale, histoire vraie* (Paris, 1911); *ibid., Questions d'histoire et d'archéologie chrétienne* (Paris, 1906); *ibid., St. Dominique* (Collection, Les Saints), (Paris, Lecoffre, 1909), (tr. London, Washburne, 1913); C. M. Antony, *In St. Dominic's Country* (London, Longmans, Green & Co., 1912); Mortier, *Histoire des maîtres généraux de l'Ordre des Frères Prêcheurs* (Paris, 1903), 5 vols.

It should not be forgotten that had the Albigensians won the victory, the south of France would have been placed outside the pale of western civilization as effectively as was southern Spain under Moslem rule. Had the Midi wars been conducted by civil authority many a partisan of to-day would not hold them up as exceptional horrors, but, since all the thinking of the Middle Ages was expressed in religious form, unfortunately the term "crusade" was used for the embittered struggle in the south.

THE ALBIGENSIAN CRUSADE[230]

La vérité n'est point a nous, nous n'en sommes que les témoins,
les défenseurs, et les dépositaires.

—MASSILLON.

So interwoven is the architectural story of Languedoc with the Albigensian Crusade that to find the underlying significance of the southern monuments it is needful to comprehend the trend of thought of the Midi people. We have the unbroken testimony of five hundred years as to what were the tenets of Catharism, the final form taken by the Manichean heresy. They held that two principles, one good and one evil, ruled the universe. In the third century Manes in Persia had woven a curious tissue of beliefs, largely Zoroastrian with a tinge of Buddhism, and had coated it all with a thin veneer of Christianity of the gnostic type. The dualist idea and a complete rejection of the Old Testament were leading Manichean doctrines. Manes was put to death in Persia, but his teachings lingered on in the Orient, and after seven centuries crept into Europe by way of the Slav countries of the Balkans. Without a doubt, the intercourse of Europe with the Orient, through the crusades, fostered the gnostic superstitions. The dualist heresy cropped out in the north of France, but after the XII century was confined more or less to Languedoc, where the Visigoths' Arian beliefs had prepared the soil. From the XI to the XIII century these neo-Manicheans were called Catharists. The local name Albigensian came into usage because in the region round Albi, though not especially in that city itself, the new ideas flourished. Toulouse was the heretic's stronghold.

It has always seemed illogical that many Protestants who revere the Bible should be sympathetic toward the Midi heretics who reprobated the Jehovah of the Old Testament as a vindictive assassin, the creator of this the visible world, which is Hell. Life is a nightmare, they taught, and suicide a virtue. Moses was sorcerer and thief (and the Ten Commandments?). John the Baptist was a strong incarnation of the Devil sent to combat the coming Christ. Baptism by water was reprehensible. On this muddle of the Old Law was grafted some neo-Christian spiritism. Christ was the God of good who created the invisible world of spirits. He was a phantom being who never really lived on earth or suffered or died. The Albigensian denied His human nature. Man's body, living or dead, was Satan's (Je-

---

[230] Jean Guiraud, *Cartulaire de Notre Dame-de-Prouille* (Paris, Picard, 1907), 2 vols. Vol. 1 is the ablest exposition of the Albigensian tenets; A. Molinier, "L'Albigeisme languedocien au XIIe et XIIIe siècles," in *Histoire de Languedoc*, vol. 1 (Toulouse, Privat, 1872-92), 15 vols.; C. Douais, *Les Albigeois; action de l'église au XIIIe siècle* (Paris, 1889); A. Luchaire, *Innocent III; la croisade des Albigeois* (Paris, Hachette, 1905).

hovah's) creation and to be annihilated; respectful burial of the dead was frowned on; marriage was sinful, since to engender was to capture souls and imprison them in the material world or Hell. Libertinage was preferable to marriage, since it did not pose as virtuous. We find in an official recantation of his Albigensian beliefs by a Midi lord that he promises to accept the Church's tenet that marriage is not sinful, as was taught by his sect.

The Albigensian heresy was an anti-social peril. It is sophistry to say, as has Molinier, that we do not know what they taught, or to call their movement a step in freeing the human mind, as do certain modern rationalists. They had two moralities, one for the people, or Hearers, and a stricter code for the elect, or the Perfect. If a Perfect relapsed, he had, after death, to pass through another existence, or Hell, in another body.

This current of anti-Christian thought, flowing in from the East, brought with it the over-rigid asceticism of the Orient, but in the Midi few lived up to ascetic practices. There were minor divergencies in the tenets according to the different regions, but always, East or West, the heretics were one in their detestation of the Jehovah of the Old Testament, and of the Church and her sacraments, especially that of Holy Eucharist. The Church was held to be a prolongation of the abhorred synagogue, and, like it, an incarnation of Satan.

No one can deny the crying need of reform in the Midi church. But the Albigensians damned one half of the Creator's work—the visible world—and the perfection which they preached was race suicide. When, more recently, Mormonism struck at the root of the social fabric, the United States government took immediate action. Had the Mormons resisted, had they, for instance, murdered an ambassador from Washington and war resulted, would we not think that the use of force by the Federal government was legitimate?

From 1100 to 1208 Rome had sent one peaceful ambassador after another into Languedoc. St. Bernard, who was loved all over Europe, was stoned in the Midi streets. The Albigenses were aggressive wherever they outnumbered the orthodox, and as most of the Midi lords held the new tenets, it was the believer who was persecuted in Languedoc. Churches were attacked and bishops flung into prison. Because the Count of Béziers accepted a local council which had censured the heretics, he was murdered by the people of Béziers in the very church and on the very day where they themselves, forty years later, were massacred by the northerners. "On all sides is the image of death," wrote the visiting bishop of Tournai, in 1182, "villages are in ashes, churches in ruin, and the inhabitants living like beasts." Long before the crusaders arrived in Languedoc life there was a bloody feud, and like ravening wolves the heretic lords warred one on another; their repeated divorces were a flaunted scandal.

The Albigensian Crusade is no isolated page in the annals of the Midi. Read of the anarchy in the south, previous to 1208, and then pass from the XIII century to the gigantic duel between France and England in the Hundred Years' War. You will feel no sense of dislocation. The crusade methods were hideous, but not exceptional. In the later debacle, Froissart relates as a matter of course the pleasant little jaunt of the Black Prince, *fleur de toute chevalerie*, into Languedoc, in 1355,[231] when he burned some seven thousand houses in the faubourgs of Toulouse, when Carcassonne was twice sacked and burned, Narbonne wrecked, treasure seized, and all ages and sexes butchered "till a line of fire and blood stretched from Toulouse to the sea." And the Black Prince was succeeded by avowed freebooters who gnawed France to the bone, the Grandes Compagnies who, as said the harassed pontiff at Avignon, *mettaient tout la Crestienté à combustion*. It was in the dire times of the XIV century that the Midi churches fortified themselves.

War slackens architectural work in any period. A radical decay of builders' energy in the Midi was not the result of the Albigensian Crusade, since Languedoc erected its chief Gothic churches between those wars and the Hundred Years' War, a period, moreover, that was controlled by the newly functioning Inquisition. To generations torn by anarchy, the methods of that tribunal, hateful though they appear to us, were an advance in jurisprudence. Every leader of the day accepted them as a progress. The civil courts were not to be able, for centuries to come, to offer even such guaranty for justice. No balanced mind can read the lives of such chief inquisitors as, for instance, St. Raymond of Penafort,[232] and fail to comprehend that past history is not to be read in the light of modern prejudices.

Rome had carried on a hundred years' diplomatic negotiation with the Midi heretics. Finally, in 1208, the pope's legate was murdered by a henchman of the Count of Toulouse and hostilities were precipitated. Innocent III proclaimed a crusade. Later he regretted its excesses just as he had cause to deplore the divergence of the Fourth Crusade to filibustering purposes, but he was too entirely a man of his own epoch to regret the Albigensian Crusade itself. By 1209 the northern barons had invaded Languedoc and many a building-bishop was in their ranks.

The spirit of crusading was at first strong enough to prevent their attacking the rich trading city of Montpellier which lay in their path but which was singularly free of heresy. Yet their very next step was a sacrilege. The orthodox population of Béziers, when called on to deliver up their heretic citizens, answered they would sooner see themselves sunk in the deep sea. It would seem that from the first hour many Catholics of the Midi looked on the crusade as a war of conquest on the part of the barons of the north. Between north and south was deep-rooted antipathy. The more cultivated but more corrupted Midi scorned the rougher peoples beyond their confines, who in their turn despised the southerners. Inevitable was it that a clash between those opposite civilizations should acquire the character of

[231] "Les vainqueurs mettent à sac toutes les maisons au nombre de 7000.... Si trouvèrent en la ville grant avoir; si en prisent donquel qu'ils veurent et le remanant ils ardirent. Là eut grant persécution d'hommes, de femmes et d'enfans, dont ce fut pitié." —FROISSART, book I, chap. lxxvi.

[232] Paul Fournier, *St. Raymond de Pennafort* (Collection, Les Saints), (Paris, Lecoffre). St. Raymond's life, from 1175 to 1275, covers one of the most vital centuries in history. He helped St. Peter Nolasco found the Order of Mercy to redeem Christian captives from Islam; he founded chairs for the study of Oriental languages; he reformed morals by his preaching. A voluntary teacher of philosophy at twenty, then a trained lawyer, it was not till he was touching the half-century limit that he entered the Dominican Order, of which he became the head. For fifty more years he gave himself up to works for humanity's advancement.

racial hate.

Simon de Montfort, chosen leader of the crusaders after the sack of Béziers, soon overran the heretical region, whereupon many barons of the north, deeming that the ethical purpose of the Midi excursion was accomplished, returned to their homes. Henceforth the racial and political aspects of the struggle were accentuated. Cruelty and perfidy marked both sides. The Midi lords boasted that no crusader escaped them with eyes, fists, or feet, and they cut into little pieces the nephew of Albéric de Humbert, archbishop-builder of Rheims Cathedral. In retaliation Simon de Montfort cut off heretics' ears and noses.

By 1212 word was sent to Innocent III that hate and cupidity, as much as zeal for the Faith, actuated the invaders, whereupon the pope roundly ordered them to pass into Spain to fight Islam. It was too late to stem the tide. In 1215, at the Fourth Lateran Council, in which every power in Christendom, lay and ecclesiastic, had a voice, Simon de Montfort's retention of his Midi conquests was sanctioned. Simon's death, in 1218, led young Raymond VII of Toulouse to rise in arms and the wars that followed were frankly political. In 1229 peace was signed under the portal of Paris Cathedral and the only daughter of Raymond VII affianced to the brother of the king of France.

ALBI CATHEDRAL[233]

> Laissons-nous aller de bonne foi aux choses qui nous prennent par les entrailles et ne cherchons point de raisonnements pour nous empêcher d'avoir du plaisir.
>
> —MOLIÈRE.

The city which gave its name to the terrible episode of the XIII century lies forty miles east of Toulouse. The local saying is, "Who has not seen the cathedral of Albi and the tower of Rodez has seen nothing." Albi Cathedral yields to none in its gaunt majesty. It stands apart in one's visions of travel, as unique a memorial of past history as the Mount of the Archangel off the coast of Normandy, as Vézelay looking out over the soft valleys of Burgundy, as Le Puy on its basaltic pinnacles. Never was a monument more absolutely itself.

---

[233] *Congrès Archéologique*, 1863; Jean Laran, *La cathédrale d'Albi* (Collection, Petites Monographies), (Paris, H. Laurens, 1911); H. Crozes, *Monographie de la cathédrale de Ste. Cécile d'Albi*, 1873; E. d'Auriac, *Histoire de l'ancienne cathédrale et des évêques d'Albi* (Paris, 1858); Abbé A. Aurial, "La voûte de Ste-Cécile d'Albi," in *Revue de l'art chrétien*, 1913, p. 91; Prosper Merimée, *Notes d'un voyage dans le Midi de la France* (1835); B. L. de Rivières, "Les églises d'Albi," in *Bulletin Monumental*, 1873, vol. 39, p. 194; Taylor et Nodier, *Voyages pittoresques dans l'ancienne France. Languedoc* (Paris, Didot, 1833-37), 2 vols.

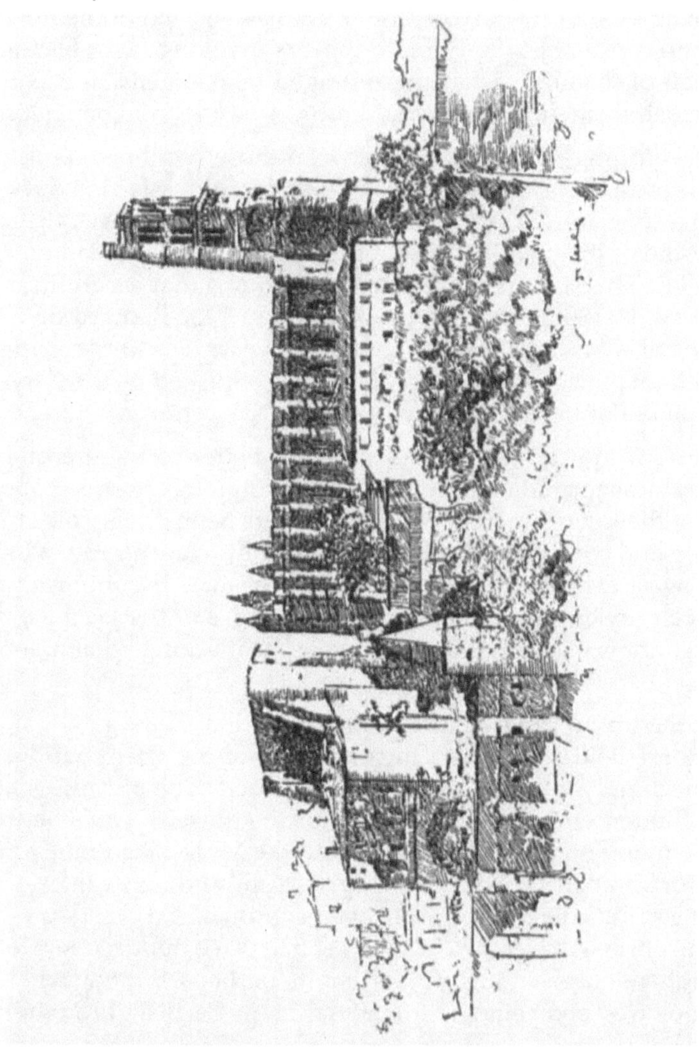

Albi Cathedral (1282-1399). A Midi Fortress Church

Unfrequented Albi was once in the stir of life, and over its stone bridge, built nine centuries ago, have passed the notable folk of the Middle Ages[234] as they wended their way to Santiago Compostela, whither all the world was going in those days. Time-scarred houses border the reddish Tarn; dark, decayed streets climb the hill. At a curve of the river, bastions and ramparts rise in terraces to a fortified episcopal palace and—crowning all—the enormous bulk of the cathedral. Its long, stark wall strikes the sky in a formidable straight line. The west façade is a massive donjon, four hundred feet above the Tarn. No welcoming west portals here, no extended transept arms of sacrificial mercy, no soaring buttress, no

[234] In the Romanesque brick church of St. Salvi, with its imposing tower and XII-century cloister, St. Bernard preached in 1145.

leaping pinnacles. Not the lore of Christ, "Do as you would be done by," seems to have inspired Albi, but the Hebraic spirit of breaking one's enemies' bones, as if the Jehovah of the Old Testament, outraged by Albigensian blasphemies, here asserted himself in a temple that would forever be a looming menace for heretics.

Albi's forbidding structure rose between those two harsh epochs—the Albigensian Crusade and the Hundred Years' War. Its aggressive mass was planned by a most aggressive churchman, Bernard, Cardinal de Castanets, the city's learned bishop detested of the people as their uncompromising feudal master, as well as a spiritual chief so harsh in his inquisitorial functions that a pontifical commission was appointed, in 1306, to repair his excesses. In 1282 Bernard de Castanets laid the first stone of Albi Cathedral and for twenty years he and the chapter contributed a twentieth of their revenues. The church was finished by the sixty-fifth bishop, Guillaume de la Voulte, in the last years of the XIV century.

To approach the cathedral at its apse end is not so picturesque as from the river side, but it is formidable enough. The prodigious apse rises abruptly, imperiously, from the town square. One fairly shivers beneath its Tolosan brick walls, overtowering and overpowering, broken merely by a few narrow windows—surely the narrowest ever made in a Gothic church—and by uniform bastion-tower buttresses. Gargoyles, of as alien an aspect as those of the Jacobins' at Toulouse, crane their gaunt necks from the upper walls, as if asking what manner of Gothic this is.

Albi Cathedral is the meridional interpretation of the national art. The traditions of Rome held tenaciously in southern France, where builders disliked to show the machinery by which their edifices stood. The buttresses at Albi are in larger part hidden within the church under the guise of walls between the side chapels. The flying buttress is uncommon in the Midi. Like Rome again, with her preference for an unencumbered floor space, Albi's immense interior is unbroken by aisles. The vault's diagonals spring over a width of sixty feet—a span unrivaled by any in the north. Albi Cathedral is a vast hall three hundred feet long, one hundred feet high, not high enough for its length, perhaps, but few will regret having the marvelous frescoed ceiling, "the missal of St. Cecilia," brought nearer to the eye.

The tutelary of this fortress-church is the gentle patroness of music. Half the fascination of Albi comes from its convincing inconsistencies. It would seem that not Cécile—doubly feminine and gracious under her French name—but Michael Archangel with a brandished sword, should guard this rugged pile. As if the good people of Albi felt the incongruity, they added, long after Bishop de Castanets' day, a southern portal preceded by a porch, the baldaquin, with all its elaborate Flamboyant tracery executed in a creamy-white marble in which surely Cécile, saint though she was, must have felt a personal satisfaction. An architect of genius set that marble porch of Albi against its red time-dulled walls, 'alabaster on corall'; one takes liberties with Chaucer's rime:

> And southward in a portal on the wall
> Of alabaster white on red corall

An oratorie riche for to see,
In honor of the Roman Cicily.

To ascend to the marble baldaquin one passes under a fortified sculptured gateway, erected by the Dominican bishop of Albi, Dominique de Florence (1392-1410). The marble portal and porch were executed under Bishop Louis I d'Amboise (1472-1502) and his successor, Louis II d'Amboise (1502-11) his nephew, belonging to an enlightened family all of whose members excelled in affairs, war, letters, and art, leaving their memorials at Chaumont on the Loire, their feudal seat, at Cluny, Paris, Clermont, Gaillon, and Rouen.

Louis I d'Amboise also adorned the interior of his cathedral by the sumptuous screen of white stone that surrounds the choir, leaving a passageway between it and the side chapels. The rood-loft, or *jubé* (so called because from its balcony the clerk chanted *Jube Domine dicere* before the gospel), is sculptured with the ermine of Anne of Brittany and the lilies of France, being made about 1499, when Anne wedded Louis XII. Bishop Louis at Albi was brother of the king's prime minister, Cardinal Georges d'Amboise.

Originally the choir screen of Albi was painted in colors. While the accessories indicate that the Italian Renaissance was obtaining headway in France, the images derive from the short, overdraped Franco-Flamand figures of Dijon. Perhaps the stonecutters who made Albi's choir wall came direct from Cluny, where a late-Gothic chapel, on which had worked Abbot Jacques d'Amboise, was adorned with prophets and apostles, each with his suitable text. On the inner wall of Albi's choir screen are sculptured homely but charming little angels, and the twelve apostles holding scrolls inscribed with phrases of the *Crédo*. Old Testament personages, who only heralded the Messiah, were not admitted to the *sanctum sanctorum*; the vestibule was their proper place. Prosper Mérimée called Albi's screen "a splendid folly before which one is ashamed to be wise." Inside and out it is exuberant with sculpture, though its extravagant caprices do not stifle a very real religious feeling in the images. Such a profusion of delicate ornament led the modern critic to suspect that the choir wall was modeled in cement, not chiseled in stone, but when a Sorbonne geologist analyzed the substance it was found to be a fine-grained white stone that grows harder with time.

Everywhere in St. Cecilia's cathedral is fragile loveliness set side by side, as an afterthought, with stern forcefulness. Bishop Louis II d'Amboise brought from Italy a group of artists to paint the panels of Albi's cyclopean vaulting, and the work accomplished by those men of northern Italy, from 1509 to 1512, remains the most splendid color decoration of the Middle Ages in France. Michael Angelo was painting the Sistine Chapel ceiling in those same years. Languedoc produced another superb array of color, the windows of Auch Cathedral,[235] and we must not

---

[235] The cathedral of Auch, which can be visited from Toulouse, was rebuilt (1371) by a nephew of Innocent VI, and again, after a fire in 1483. It is quite devoid of capitals. The façade is neo-classic. The choir stalls (1520-29) are masterpieces; Italianate fawns and Bacchantes are placed beside sacred personages. The magnificent windows, of the transition between Flamboyant Gothic and Renaissance, were the work of Arnaud de Moles (1507-13); their portrait studies are like Holbein's pictures. Abbé Canéto, Notice *sur l'église metro. de*

forget that the greatest of all Renaissance glassworkers, the friar who filled Arezzo with glory, was a Midi Frenchman.

Amid Albi's arabesques the artists from Bologna and Modena inscribed their names, and some young lovers wrote "Antonia, mia bella," and "Lucrezia Cantora, bolognesa." The frescoes give the genealogy of Christ. They recall Perugino, Francia, and Pintoriccio. Never was blue background more marvelous—a strong rare hue neither indigo nor Prussian nor peacock, but a blending of them all in a cerulean depth of color—an art as entirely lost to posterity as the blue background of Suger's windows. Chemical analysis has busied itself with Albi's frescoes, too; but though the blue color of the vault panels was found to be obtained from the precipitation of salts of copper by carbonate of potassium, how to produce a similar hue to-day remains unsolved. Over the blue background wind lovely arabesques, and the saints portrayed are stately Italians of the Renaissance. The diagonals and transverse arches are colored in old-gold. On the western wall of the church a XV-century fresco was painted directly on the bricks, a Last Judgment copied from popular woodcuts of the day, with the punishments of the seven deadly sins pitilessly set forth. The painting was ruthlessly cut into when a chapel was introduced under the western tower. The side chapels of Ste. Cécile are illuminated in gold and color like a Book of Hours. Never was there a church of such contrasts: within—a shrine of warm, polished, over-splendid beauty, and without—the most rugged feudal challenge of the Middle Ages.

CARCASSONNE[236]

> It is the first sharp vision of an unknown town, the first immediate vision of a range of hills, that remains forever, and is fruitful of joy within the mind ... that is perhaps the chief of the fruits of travel.

> —HILAIRE BELLOC.

The Cité of Carcassonne was long one of the most formidable fortresses of Europe, covering the route from ocean to sea and guarding a pass into Spain. These Pyrenean provinces of France gave Joffre and Foch to the World War. The lower walls of the Cité were of Rome's building; above came the Visigothic defenses; *Ste. Marie d'Auch* and *Congrès Archéologique*, 1901.

The cathedral of Rodez, some fifty miles west from Albi, built its grand Flamboyant tower, *la couronne*, from 1510 to 1526, under the Blessed François d'Estaing. The Romanesque cathedral at Rodez was supplanted by the present one in 1277. The works flagged, however, and the nave was built as late-Gothic by Bishop Guillaume de la Tour d'Oliergues and a nephew who succeeded him. The west façade was left bare, since there the church overlooked the ramparts; to it were added later a rose window and a Flamboyant gallery. G. de Cogny, in *Bulletin Monumental*, 1874, vol. 39; Bion de Marlavagne, *Cathédrale de Rodez* (Paris, 1875).

[236] *Congrès Archéologique*, 1868; and 1906, J. de Lahondès; Viollet-le-Duc, *La cité de Carcassonne* (Paris, 1858); H. Graillot, *Toulouse et Carcassonne* (Collection, Villes d'art célèbres), (Paris, H. Laurens); L. Fédié, *Histoire de Carcassonne* (Carcassonne, 1887); C. Douais, *Soumission de la vicomté de Carcassonne par Simon de Montfort*; Cros-Meyrevieille, *Histoire des comtes de Carcassonne* (1845), 2 vols.; Gaston Jourdanne, *La cité de Carcassonne* (1905).

then St. Louis extended the fortifications and his son completed them.

Within its double belt of walls and half a hundred towers is the precious little church of St. Nazaire, once of cathedral rank. Its western front was never opened by a portal because it stood near what were long the outer ramparts. The Romanesque nave is small and dark, without triforium or clearstory, and with high aisles that buttress the tunnel vault of the principal span, whose transverse ribs are slightly pointed. Piers and columns alternate. The materials to build this early church were blessed by Urban II in 1096 in the same month that he dedicated the new choir of St. Sernin at Toulouse. St. Nazaire was an entirely Romanesque church when Simon de Montfort ruled the Cité for ten years. In this church St. Dominic married Amaury de Montfort to a princess of Dauphiny. St. Dominic had held a public controversy of eight days with the heretics of Carcassonne in 1205, before the coming of the northern barons, and in St. Nazaire he preached the Lent of 1213. Simon de Montfort was buried temporarily in St. Nazaire, and there exists in a nave chapel a sculptured stone which some have thought to be part of his sepulcher, but which is more probably from the tomb of a brother of Count Raymond of Toulouse, who, having sympathized with the northern barons, was slain in consequence. The curious stone shows the engines of war described in the *Chanson de la Croisade*, and the costumes of that period.

Under Bishop Radulph (1255-66), who built the Gothic chapel beside the south arm of the transept, permission was obtained to replace the ancient transept and choir by a new one. Bishop Radulph won forgiveness for those citizens of Carcassonne who were expelled from the fortress in 1262, because they had conspired against the crown with one of the Trencavel dynasty, their old rulers, and the builders of the Cité's château. Louis IX, who governed Carcassonne through a seneschal, allowed the exiles to start the present town of Carcassonne beyond the river, in the plain below the citadel.

The erection of the Gothic half of St. Nazaire took place under Bishop Pierre de Roquefort (d. 1321) during the first twenty years of the XIV century. To him we owe the radiant glass lantern which is St. Nazaire's transept and choir, a structure that is really a big transept with seven chapels, equally high, along its eastern wall, the central of which chapels, and the longest, serving as choir. The windows in the chapels rise to the roof, and are filled with clear and brilliant glass ranked with the best of the XIV century; those in the first two chapels excel the others. Two windows show the arms of Pierre de Roquefort. St. Nazaire was one of the last to use the legend-medallion type of window; henceforth, in each panel, a single figure was placed in an architectural setting.

The seven eastern chapels of the transept open one on the other above a low dividing wall, and standing out from those walls, so that a narrow passage is made between them and the transept, are detached piers that rise powerfully from pavement to vault-springing. Above their capitals the molds die away in the column — a very early use of a Flamboyant characteristic. The two pillars flanking the entrance to the choir are decorated, midway up, with statues under canopies sculptured by northern artists before 1320.

Archæologists declare that the Gothic part of the Cité's ancient cathedral are the perfection of XIV-century construction, elastic in every part, each part fulfilling its own separate function. The ogival principle could not be carried farther. It is thought that some architect of the north made the plan, which local masons executed. The only Midi trait is the flat, tiled roof.

Modern restoration has overhauled the citadel of Carcassonne too radically. Imperiously set though it is, does it grip the imagination as entirely as Aigues-Mortes, lying flat on marsh lands, its time-stained walls untouched? Often in France one echoes Pius IX's response to Baron de Crozé, who proposed the restoration of the Coliseum: "Dear Son, I have read your memoir and I thank you for it; but do you not know that there are two sorts of vandalism, one which consists in destroying, the other in restoring? Never has the Coliseum been so beautiful as in its moving contrast of past splendor and magnificent present decay. To restore it is to annihilate the work of centuries, to recompose an ordinary pastiche with no *éclat*."

Not that Carcassonne, as redressed by M. Viollet-le-Duc, is deficient in *éclat*; it has too much of it. It is a vision of a feudal fortress too carefully prepared, too deliberately made ready for the tourist.

In the lower town are the typically meridional churches of St. Michel, the actual cathedral of Carcassonne, and St. Vincent whose aisleless hall is the widest in the Midi—a span of sixty-eight feet. Even when using diagonals, the south kept true to its favorite Romanesque traditions. Neither church has a triforium, the apse windows are long and narrow, over the entrance of each chapel is an eight-lobed rose, and the buttresses are disguised as walls between the side chapels. The tracery is Rayonnant. St. Vincent was built after the Black Prince burned Carcassonne in 1355. At its sculptured portal was placed a statue of the newly canonized saint-king, Louis IX, under whom this modern Carcassonne was founded.

NARBONNE CATHEDRAL[237]

Que chaque homme console un homme,
Fasse un bien, donne une pitié,
Ne t'occupe pas de la somme:
Ce pain sera multiplié.

—JEAN AICARD (born in the Midi, 1848).

At Narbonne one is at the very heart of the Midi. It is an ancient mother city of Europe, a capital of Celtic Gaul. Surpassed by nothing in the Roman world,

[237] Louis Serbat, in *Congrès Archéologique*, 1868 and 1906; L. Narbonne, *La cathédrale de Narbonne*, 1901; Victor Mortet, "Notes historiques et archéologiques sur la cathédrale de Narbonne," in *Annales du Midi*, vol. 10, p. 401; vol. 11, pp. 273 and 439—also printed separately (Toulouse, Privat, and Paris, Picard, 1899); F. Pradel, *Mono, graphie de l'église St. Juste de Narbonne* (Narbonne, Caillard, 1884); Ch. Lentheric, *Les villes mortes du Golfe de Lyon: Narbonne, Maguelonne, Aigues-Mortes, Arles, Les Saintes-Mariés* (Paris, Plon, 1883); "École gothique religieuse du Midi de la France," in *Positions des thèses soutenues par les élèves de l'École des chartes en 1909; Histoire littéraire de la France*, vol. 32, p. 474, on Gilles Aycelin, archbishop of Narbonne and Rouen, Léopold Delisle.

Narbonne kept its pre-eminence under both pagan and Christian Rome. It became the seat of the Visigothic royal line, and of their Moorish conquerors. Charlemagne made it a fortified outpost, and during the Middle Ages it was the richest of trading centers, a third of whose population was Jewish. In 1311, the same covetous king who abolished the Templars banished the Jews, to whom Charlemagne had given the freedom of this town for their support of his cause against Islam. To-day one walks its dust-white streets with a strange sensation of loneliness. Narbonne is a dead city.

When in the latter part of the XIII century the great Gothic cathedral of St. Just was begun, there seemed no reason why so flourishing a trading center could not succeed in the enterprise. Unlike Beauvais, where the chief church was from its inception out of all proportion to the population, Narbonne could easily have erected a nave to complete its mighty choir. In 1272 was laid the first stone of St. Just Cathedral.[238] Then there occurred here what happens to all rivers that communicate with the sea by means of lagoons: gradually the salt lakes silt up till they become marshes through which the river winds tortuously till suddenly it breaks a new path to the sea. In 1320 occurred this catastrophe for Narbonne. The Roman dike gave way and the river Aude left its ancient bed, quitting Narbonne to flow toward Courson, where it still is. The stagnant waters bred disease, and the metropolis, greeted by Sidonius Apollinaris for its salubrity, *Salve Narbo, potens salubritate*, became a pestilential site. Narbonne sank into silent decay. Over the shrunken city stands the ghostly fragment of the great cathedral, surpassed in height only by Beauvais and Amiens.

St. Just was begun in 1272, and three years later the cathedral of Toulouse was started on a plan and with profiles so closely resembling Narbonne's chief church that one master may have designed both. Both derive immediately from those northern Gothic churches translated with a meridional accent, the cathedrals of Clermont, whose choir was finished in 1265, and of Limoges, begun in 1273.

The Midi shows in Narbonne Cathedral in the simplified triforium which is framed by wall spaces, as are the clearstory windows, in the extremely high pier arcades, and in the stout buttresses that are disguised as dividing walls between the side chapels. The capitals are mere uncarved bands, and over them certain molds die away in the pier. M. Anthyme Saint-Paul's theory was that even in the XIII century began the evolution which was to end in Flamboyant Gothic. He pointed out, in Narbonne's chapels, windows with Rayonnant tracery side by side with

---

[238] For the other churches at Narbonne, see the *Congrès Archéologique*, 1906. M. Lefèvre-Pontalis devotes a study to St. Paul Serge (p. 345), whose choir was built from 1229 to 1244. In the transept are vestiges of the primitive church. Two bays of the nave are of the XIV century, and the others are XII-century work redone in the XIII. To bind together the bulging walls, flat arches were thrown over the central vessel at the level of the pier arches. The church presents such peculiarities in the Midi as circulation passages at different levels round the edifice. There are false tribune arches, and over the pier arcade a passageway is maneuvered. Sergius Paulus was the first to preach Christianity in the city. In Narbonne's valuable Museum are classic vestiges of the city's great day under the Roman Empire. Many of the classic marble columns are to-day in the mosque at Cordova. Ch. E. Schmidt, *Cordoue, Grenade* (Collection, Villes d'art célèbres), (Paris, H. Laurens).

flamelike undulations. M. Enlart thinks we cannot be sure that they were done at the same time. An unusual and graceful aspect was achieved in the choir's northern aisle by the setting of piers beyond the dividing walls of the chapels, making a kind of double aisle like that in the transept of St. Nazaire at Carcassonne.

An architect named Henri is cited as master-of-works at Gerona Cathedral whose chevet, begun after 1312, resembles that of St. Just. Henri was a name uncommon in the Midi. It is thought that he was the original architect of Narbonne. His successor at Gerona, Jacques de Favari or Favers, a name of the central plateau of France, is known to have directed the works of Narbonne's chief church. Catalonia, Aragon, and Languedoc were allied in architecture as in tongue. Poblet in Catalonia is directly the daughter of the abbey at Fontfroide, six miles from Narbonne.[239] The Gothic influence of Narbonne spread to the isles in the Mediterranean, to southern Italy and Cyprus.

Archbishop Maurin began Narbonne Cathedral after the tragic crusade of St. Louis in 1270. He had vowed that if ever again he saw the fair land of France he would offer thanksgiving by rebuilding his church. The corner stone and relics were sent by Pope Clement IV, originally a lawyer at St. Gilles, and then archbishop of Narbonne, whose crumbling cathedral of Charlemagne's time he had purposed to replace by a Gothic one, when his translation to the papacy intervened.

The apse chapels were built first. The main parts of the choir are the work of Archbishop Gilles Aycelin de Montaigu, (1292-1311), a noble of Auvergne, brother of the bishop who was building Clermont Cathedral and who had himself been a canon at Clermont. He also began the cloister, and to his own residence added a donjon tower. It is thought that the episcopal palace at Narbonne served as prototype for the palace of the popes at Avignon. In modern times, between its ancient towers a town hall has been constructed. In 1311 Gilles Aycelin was transferred to the see of Rouen, and Rouen's archbishop, Bernard de Farges (d. 1341), a nephew of the pope who built the choir of Bordeaux Cathedral, took his place at Narbonne, where he completed the giant choir. Services were held in it in 1320.

The truncated western end of the cathedral is a depressing sight. Work stopped after the completion of the east wall of the transept, whose window apertures had

---

[239] The Cistercian abbey of Fontfroide lies in a wild gorge some six miles from Narbonne. The church, begun in the middle of the XII century, was roofed with a pointed cradle vault. The cloister, like that at Tarragona, was covered with *bombé* vaults on eight ribs. Little marble columns support the Gothic masonry roof of the chapter house, which, like Poblet's, opens by arcades on the cloister. Twelve monks from Fontfroide founded Poblet in 1150. The countess who ruled Narbonne for sixty years confirmed the abbey charter in 1157: " I, Ermengarde, give to God and the Blessed Mary, to Abbot Vital and the present and future servants of God, the lands of Fontfroide," runs her deed of gift. Doubly is a nation robbed when monastic lands are held by private individuals who assume no responsibility toward the public, as did a majority of the ancient houses, before royalty named its favorites as their abbots. Even as vast tracts were granted to nobles that they might perform gratis the military defense of a land, so monasteries were expected to give payment for their domains, by voluntary services to civilization. J. de Lahondès, in *Congrès Archéologique*, 1906, p. 61; Calvert, *Études historiques sur Fontfroide* (1875); G. Desdevises du Dézert, *Barcelone et les grands sanctuaires d'art catalan* (Collection, Villes d'art célèbres), (Paris, H. Laurens).

later to be filled in; by the XV century all hope of completing the church was abandoned, and two west towers were raised. In the XVIII century the plan to build a nave was revived and part of the city ramparts were thrown down to allow for its extension. One bay of the proposed structure was begun in bastard Gothic, and then the enterprise collapsed. The present entrance is through a door contrived in one of the apse chapels. The exterior of that apse was fortified. From one turreted buttress pile to the other was maneuvered a crenelated gallery, and originally the passage communicated with the bishop's palace.

Although sadly needing a nave, Narbonne's choir is a proud and noble vessel. Critics have called it a work of mechanical skill more than of imagination. Its science is beyond cavil, each thrust being exactly counterbutted. Profiles, however are angular and there is a painful lack of sculpture. If, technically, Narbonne's chief church is somewhat hard and dry, it has retained sufficient of the emotional quality of Gothic, what has been called its *sursum corda*, to belong to the grand tradition of the national art. Moreover, one can kneel reverentially on the very steps of the altar instead of being kept at a stately distance. In the clearstory are the loveliest XIV-century windows in France, like rare-toned etchings or delicate spider-web, time-stained lace. As there is color in them, it is inexact to call such windows grisaille, but the subdued note of grisaille glass predominates.

Between Narbonne and Spain lies Perpignan's XIV-century[240] cathedral, and Elne's cloister, called a work of supreme elegance by the critical Prosper Merimée, and to the east at Béziers is a fortified cathedral with massive towers, begun in 1215 and building through the XIV century; it has good stained glass of this latter period.

One's interest in Béziers centers in the terrible massacre of 1209, the opening act of the Albigensian Crusade. Not that the mere sacking of a city would have roused such horror. In the course of its history eight massacres had occurred in Béziers. It was a day when such acts were the accepted methods of warfare and the northern leaders had discussed whether it were not good tactics to start their campaign by terrorization. It was the slaughtering of the citizens in the churches to which they had fled for sanctuary that violated the general standards.

Witnesses of the sacking of Béziers say that while the chiefs of the besieging army were considering how to spare those in the city who were not Albigensian,

[240] Perpignan's aisleless cathedral of St. Jean was begun in 1324 and finished, as the century ended, under the kings of Majorca, who then ruled the Roussillon. The transept ends are apsidal below and pentagonal above. Beside it stands an older St. Jean, dedicated in 1025. The see originally was at Elne, where the cathedral was rebuilt in the XI century; lotus leaves are carved on the capitals of its lovely marble cloister (c. 1175). *Congrès Archéologique*, 1868; and 1906, p. 109, Perpignan; p. 135, Elne; E. de Barthélemy, " Le cloître de la ville d'Elne," in *Bulletin Monumental*, 1857, vol. 23; Bernard Palustre," Perpignan et ses monuments," in *Revue d'hist. et d'archéol du Roussillon*, 1905; Auguste Brutails, " Notes sur l'art religieux du Roussillon," in *Bulletin archéol. du comité des traveaux hist. et scientifique*, 1892, No. 4; 1893, No. 3; P. Vidal, *Histoire de la ville de Perpignan* (Paris, 1897); P. Vidal et J. Calmette, *Le Roussillon* (Collection, Les régions de la France), (Paris, L. Cerf, 1909); J. de Gazanyola, *Histoire de Roussillon* (Perpignan, Alzinc, 1857); Isabel Savory, *Romantic Roussillon* (London, Unwin, 1919).

an assault was started through the skirmish of lawless hangers-on of the crusading army and a few townspeople. In the confusion that followed, the northern knights rushed to arms and the city was captured. A XX-century wrecking of the Louvain-Dinant-Termonde type followed, and some twenty thousand perished.

Modern scholars doubt that the famous *Tuez-les-tous* remark, attributed to Abbot Arnaud of Cîteaux, who died archbishop of Narbonne, was ever uttered. He is accused of saying, "Kill them all, God will know his own," when asked how the orthodox were to be told from the heretics. No contemporary chronicle mentions it and Albigensian historians would certainly have flung such words at the crusaders; equally would an ardent admirer of Simon de Montfort, who wrote his *Gestes*, have lauded the sentiment, if one is to judge by other happenings he thought praiseworthy. Neither enemy nor friend mentions the *Tuez-les-tous* phrase. It first occurs in the history of a German monk at Bonn, long after the Midi crusade, and the pages of that chronicler are so filled with discredited assertions that little he says should be taken seriously.

MONTPELLIER AND MAGUELONNE[241]

The tocsin sounded its lamentable notes of alarm over all the land of France. Fire? No. *War.* The voice of the bells long condemned to silence by the authorities suddenly rang out everywhere. From the high belfries spread the warning, and no one worried now to refuse to God, to the Inexplicable, the right of speech. From God's house alone came to France, waiting in tense agony, the announcement of the most terrible catastrophe that ever fell like an avalanche on humanity. Sunrise to sunset from east to west, from north to south rang out the coming of War, the world's misery.

—JEAN AICARD, on how the World War opened in the Midi.[242]

In Montpellier is a stately terrace called the Peyrou, built in the artificial, distinguished style of Louis XIV, from which one looks out on a most lovely landscape of Midi fertility.[243] Here Mistral in 1878 read his vibrant ode to the Latin

[241] Eugène Müntz, *Les constructions du pope Urbain V à Montpellier, 1364-70* (Paris, 1900); Jean Guiraud, *Les fondations du pape Urbain V à Montpellier* (Montpellier, 1899), 3 vols.; G. E. Lefenestre, *Le musée de Montpellier* (vol. 1, p. 189, "Inventaire des richesses d'art de la France: ministère de l'instruction publique"), (Paris, 1878); Émile Bonnet, *Antiquités et monuments du département de l'Hérault* (Montpellier, 1908); Abbé M. Chaillon, *Le bienheureux Urbain V, 1310-70* (Collection, Les Saints), (Paris, Lecoffre, 1911); A Germain, *Maguelonne, étude historique et archéologique*; A Fabrége, *Histoire de Maguelonne* (Montpellier, 1900), 2 vols.

[242] Jean Aicard, *Arlette des Mayons* (Paris, Flammarion, 1916).

[243] To the northwest of Montpellier, near Aniane, is St. Guilhem-le-Désert, with blind niches in its exterior apse wall that derive from such Lombard churches as S. Ambrogio at Milan. Lombard towers, arched corbel tables, and mural arcaded bands passed from northern Italy into Languedoc. The early intersecting ribs here were exceptional for the Midi in being profiled. The nave and aisles are of the first half of the XI century, the chevet and transept of the early XII, as is the cloister, which once had a second story. The narthex was built from 1165 to 1199. The first duke of Aquitaine, Aliénor's ancestor, died here, a monk. *Con-*

race, *la race lumineuse, la race apostolique*, and a generation later the people gathered here to listen to the belfries far and near ring out over that peaceful Claude Lorraine scene the hour of unity in battle array, for all Frenchmen—Latin and Celt and Frank. No longer a Midi and a North. The time was past for race hate or conquest to pose as a crusade. The time had come to end the silencing of Christian steeples under the guise of freedom. As one man, Midi and North sprang up in answer to the tocsin of August, 1914.

What to-day is the cathedral of Montpellier was built from 1364 to 1367 as a monastery church, so that it hardly falls within our scope. But if architecturally the city of Montpellier is of lesser importance, it has been for long centuries the intellectual stronghold of the Midi, and we know that cathedrals are built with more than stones. Montpellier's school of medicine was famous in the XII century. The city was free of Albigensian taint; no trading town was more flourishing during the XIII century. At the hour that the northern barons invaded the Midi, the heiress of Montpellier, whom the king of Aragon married for her dowry and immediately deserted, gave birth to one who was to build more churches than any monarch in Christendom. Twelve candles were set up in the chief church of Montpellier, each with the name of an apostle, and when the candle called James burned the longest the child was named Jaime. An inscription on the Tour du Pin, a vestige of the city ramparts that originally had twenty-five such towers, records the birth of Jaime el Conquistador, the scourge of Islam, the conqueror of Valencia and the Balearic Islands, and the builder of six thousand churches. His father was one of the victors of Las Navas de Tolosa, in 1212, where a vital blow was struck at Moorish domination in Spain; yet he was killed in the very next year in Languedoc, fighting on the heretic side.

Peter of Aragon looked on the Albigensian Crusade as a northern war of conquest, and if outsiders were to win new lands why had he not the same right. Jaime's mother fled to Rome, the sole court of arbitration then in Europe, and when she died there, she left her son the ward of Innocent III.[244] The pope compelled Simon de Montfort, who held the child as hostage, to return him to his Spanish subjects. Jaime's tutor was that Languedoc knight, St. Peter Nolasco (d. 1258), who founded the Order of Mercy to redeem captives from Moslem prisons, but no saint-tutor or saint-neighbor could tame this fierce young eagle, the scion of the French Midi and the Spanish Pyrenees. From the time he buckled on his sword as a boy, to his death in 1276, the weapon never left his side. He cut off the ear of the bishop of Gerona who had rebuked his free living, for Jaime's domestic relations

---

grès Archéologique, 1906, p. 384; "L'église abbatiale de St. Guilhem-le-Désert," Émile Bonnet; Joseph Bédier, *Les légendes épiques*, vol. 1, "St. Guillaume de Gellone" (Paris, H. Champion, 1908-13), 4 vols.

[244] Innocent III was the best type of the theory, enunciated by Boniface VIII as the XIII century closed, that civil rulers derive their power from religious authority. Leo XIII, in the encyclical *Immortale Dei*, November, 1885, set aside that claim. Each should keep to its own sphere, he said, one is not subordinate to the other; civil authorities are to attend to human affairs, and spiritual authorities to divine things. With every monarch in Europe appealing to him for his arbitration, it is little wonder that Innocent III should have held the views he did.

were on a par with those of the Languedoc lords and of his Mahommedan neighbors.

The church which now is Montpellier's cathedral consists of a modern choir of the meridional type, without ambulatory or flying buttresses, and a nave built as an abbatial by Guillaume de Grimoard, the best of the Avignon popes, Urban V. The nave is a wide, unaisled hall, with small clearstory windows. Even when the Midi used diagonals, says M. Enlart, it remained faithful to Romanesque traditions. At the west façade is an ungainly canopy held up by two round turrets of solid stone, the sort of thing which is a builder's notion, not the design of an architect. Urban was disappointed when he found that his architect from Avignon had erected a big chapel rather than a church. When he came to Montpellier in 1367 the new edifice was almost finished. He was honored as never man was before by any city. The townspeople marched out to meet him, every guild and corporation in the ranks, the lawyers carrying the image of the newly canonized St. Yves of Brittany. When the pope's visit ended, half the population walked for miles with him into the country, and the town authorities escorted him all the way back to Avignon.

Urban V had been educated in Montpellier and he loved its university, in which for years he had taught law in the school where Petrarch studied. He renewed the departments of law and art, put new life into the famed medical school (which to-day is housed in the former bishop's palace, fortified with propped machicolations), and founded a college for the free maintenance of a certain number of students. To this day Montpellier reveres him.

All over Christendom this energetic Midi baron endowed institutions of learning, supported hundreds of students, and built monuments. He founded the universities of Prague, Cracow, and Vienna, re-established that of Orvieto, made a school of music at Toulouse, began the cathedral of Mende,[245] near his birthplace, and in Marseilles rebuilt St. Victor's, where he had been abbot,[246] and where re-

[245] Mende lies in the mountains of western Languedoc. Its cathedral was begun (1365) under the auspices of Urban V, whose statue stands in the square close by. Practically it is a XV-century church, without capitals, flying buttresses, or transept. During twelve years the architect was Pierre Juglar, an associate, at Riom, of those Flamboyant Gothic masters, the Dammartin brothers. The cathedral was finished with its two towers in 1512. From 1286 to 1296 the bishop of Mende was Guillaume Durandus, author of *Rationale*, the famous book on church symbolism. He was governor under the popes of the marches of Ancona and the Romagna, and led the papal forces in battle. The Italian city of Castel Duranti was named after him. When he died at Rome in 1296, Giovanni Cosmati made his tomb, a masterpiece in the only Gothic church of Rome, Santa-Maria-sopra-Minerva. Urban V was generous also to St. Flour (which lies south of Mende), whose abbatial was rebuilt in the XIV century; John XXII had raised it to cathedral rank in 1317. *Congrès Archéologique*, 1857, Mende.

[246] Nothing now at St. Victor's, Marseilles, is earlier than the XI century. A pre-Gothic use of diagonal ribs (with Lombard rectangular profiles) cropped out here, yet when the upper church was remodeled in the XIII century, Romanesque vaulting was used. Urban V rebuilt the transept, made the square apse, and raised the battlemented towers. When he visited Marseilles in 1373 every man in the city ceased his work to welcome him. As it was his desire to be buried in his former abbey, his remains were brought hither in 1372, and his successor, Gregory XI, raised a sumptuous Gothic monument forty feet in height. Abbé A.

mains his towering tomb. At Avignon he continued the making of its walls of defense, for it was a day when the lawless *Grandes Compagnies* roved over France.

Urban was too wise a man not to perceive that his continued residence at Avignon was a detriment to the papacy, and he made a valiant effort to return to Rome. There, too, he was no sooner established than he initiated works of art.[247] Broken by the disorders round him with which he had not strength to cope, he returned to his beloved southern France, where he died almost immediately, in 1370. His successor, Gregory XI, inspired by St. Catherine of Siena, who journeyed to Avignon in 1376, was to be the pontiff who ended what Italy, sick to death, called "the Babylonian captivity."

Montpellier was not a bishopric till 1536, when the see was removed from Maguelonne here, and no sooner was the new see established when the city was sacked twice—in 1561 and again in 1565. Every tomb in the present cathedral was violated. Were its walls lined with those old-time memorials they would appear less bare. Neither side was distinguished by amenity in those long years of civil strife.

Maguelonne, the original bishopric, lies six miles from Montpellier on the Mediterranean. In ancient days it was a little island of volcanic formation, then in time an island in a swamp, connected artificially with the mainland. Climb to the flat stone roof of the ancient cathedral of St. Pierre, almost the only monument left standing here where civilization has followed civilization, and look across the lagoons that lie between France and the solitary dead city. Europe and the present seem no longer to exist in this the most aloof, self-effaced, most philosophic spot in the world.

Maguelonne had known all the peoples in their pride. During fifteen hundred years it played its part—Celt, Phœnician, Greek, and Roman ruled here in turn. Visigothic Wamba besieged it. Islam held it under the name of Port Saracen till Charles Martel drove the sea robbers from their stronghold by destroying the city; only the new church of St. Peter was saved. For the following three centuries Maguelonne lay deserted. Then in 1037 Bishop Arnaud undertook to restore the city, and the cathedral he rebuilt was blessed in 1054. Prosperity soon returned under a republican form of government, with the bishop as president. Maguelonne became an asylum for exiles and a retreat for scholars. Urban II blessed the island in 1095. When Pope Gelasius II, driven from Rome, landed at St. Gilles in 1118, he soon sailed thence for Maguelonne, and hither came Alexander III in 1162.

The cathedral of St. Pierre stood up a very rock of defense against the corsairs of Spain and Africa. On its flat stone roof engines of war were placed. The present XI-century church replaces that of Charles Martel's day; over an arm of its transept occurred one of the pre-Gothic early uses of diagonals. The transverse arches of the nave are slightly pointed. On the lintel of its portal of creamy-white marble—

d'Agnel, "L'abbaye de St. Victor de Marseilles," in *Bulletin historique et philosophique*, 1906, p. 364; Eugène Müntz, "St. Victor, Marseilles," in *Gazette Archéol.*, 1884.

[247] In his short time in Rome Urban V gave commissions for art works to Giottino and the sons of Taddeo Gaddi, and he had made the precious shrine for the relics of St. Peter and St. Paul in the Lateran. (See Eugène Müntz in the *Cronique des Arts* for 1880.)

Classic, Saracenic, Romanesque, and Gothic, with doorjamb bas-reliefs of Peter and Paul, key and sword—were inscribed by Bernard de Trevies in 1178 some Latin verses still legible:

> Ye who seek life's port to gain enter now this sacred fane.
> If ye pass these gates within, ye may break the chains of sin,
> So to pray thou must not fail, all thy cruel sins bewail;
> Know that all thy sins and fears may be washed away in
> tears.[248]

The cathedral of St. Peter was spared in the second annihilation of Maguelonne, which took place after the religious wars, when Richelieu's policy was to level every possible fort that rebellion might use. Stone by stone the other monuments of the city were carried away. When the canal from Cette to Aigues-Mortes was built, in 1708, Maguelonne became a useful quarry. St. Peter's church now stands alone, embalmed as in amber, preaching the sobering lesson, *Sic transit gloria mundi.*

AIGUES-MORTES[249]

> Aigues-Mortes! Consonnance d'une désolation incomparable! Dans le train si lent à traverser la Camargue je m'imagine ces mornes remparts qui depuis sept siècles subsistent intacts. J'évoque ces mystérieux Sarrasins, ces légers Barbaresques qui pillaient ces côtes et fuaient, insaisis, même par l'histoire. Aigues-Mortes, le vieux guerrier qu'ils assaillaient sans trêve, est toujours à son poste, étendu sur la plaine, comme un chevalier, les armes à la main, est figé en pierre sur son tombeau.
>
> —MAURICE BARRÈS.[250]

"I propose that we institute a pilgrimage," sighed Rodin, "to all monuments *de plein air* yet spared by restoration." Aigues-Mortes' big quadrangle set on the dead lagoons is precisely as it came from its builder's hand in the reign of Philippe III, son of St. Louis. No destructive restoration has ever chipped away the time stain of centuries. So shrunken is the little town of to-day, within those imposing ramparts with their fifteen towers and nine gateways, that it is as weird an experience to encircle the walls within as to make the solitary tour without.

No sooner did St. Louis take the crusaders' vow, in 1244, when he began to look about for a concentration camp on the southern coast. He was suzerain only in the south of France. Narbonne had its own counts and so had Provence; St.

---

[248] Translated by F. J. C. Kearns, O. P.

[249] *Congrès Archéologique,* 1909, p. 183; J. Ch. Roux, *Aigues-Mortes* (Paris, Bloud et Cie, 1910); F. Em. di Pietro, *Histoire d'Aigues-Mortes* (Paris, 1849); Marius Topin, *Aigues-Mortes* (Nîmes, 1865); Abbé H. Aigon, *Aigues-Mortes, ville de St. Louis* (1908); H. Havard, éd., *La France artistique et monumentale,* vol. 3, p. 145; Ch. Lenthéric, *Le littoral d'Aigues-Mortes au XIIIᵉ et au XIVᵉ siècles* (Nîmes, 1870); Vie. (Dom) et Vaissette (Dom), *Histoire de Languedoc,* vol. 7, p. 107, 3d éd.; Viollet-le-Duc, *Dictionnaire de l'architecture,* vol. 1, pp. 378, 390; vol. 9, p. 182.

[250] Maurice Barrès, *Le jardin de Bérénice* (Paris, Charpentier, 1894).

Gilles and Adge were in the Toulouse countship, and the Montpellier coast was under Aragon. Practically only swampy Aigues-Mortes was available. St. Louis purchased it from the monks of Psalmodi, and reconstructed an old tower on the site which had served as a fort during piratical attacks. The grand Tour de Constance, now standing outside the quadrangle fortification, is the only part of Aigues-Mortes of Louis IX's day. He deepened the tortuous canal of eight miles that led to the sea, since Aigues-Mortes never was directly on the Mediterranean. The Genoese architect, Boccanegra, who constructed the ramparts for Philippe III, followed the type of fortified town in the Orient; Aigues-Mortes especially resembled Antioch.

On both his crusades St. Louis started from his fort on the dead waters. When in 1248 the crusaders saw the low-lying spot so like the pestilential coasts of the East, many a heart felt oppressed. Again in 1270 the king's army arrived at Aigues-Mortes. Finding his transport ships delayed, Louis IX thought it best to move his warriors to the more healthful site of St. Gilles. There he held brilliant court, to keep up the idle army's spirit, and at the tourneys excelled his Provençal queen's nephew, the future king of England, Edward I. The crusaders left their mark on the walls of St. Gilles.

ST. GILLES[251]

Noms des Morts pour la Patrie,
Qu'on vous trie
Selons vos provinces; puis,
Pour propager votre culte,
Qu'on vous sculpte
Sur la borne et sur le puits!...

Mais d'abord, que votre zèle
Vous cisèle
Sur les maisons mêmes d'où
Pour aller vers le martyre,
Ils partirent
Dans le soleil du mois d'août.

... On lira sur la corniche
Pauvre ou riche:
"Mort pour nous ... un tel ... un tel...."
Trois fois, tous bas, comme on prie,
On s'écrie:
"Morts pour nous ... pour nous ... pour nous!"

[251] *Congrès Archéologique*, 1897, p. 98; and 1909, p. 168, L. H. Labande; J. Ch. Roux, *St. Gilles, sa légende, son abbaye, ses coutumes* (Paris, Lemerre, 1910), 4to; J. Hubidos, *Histoire et décoration de l'église abbatiale de St. Gilles* (Nîmes, 1906); De Lasteyrie, *Étude sur la sculpture française au moyen âge* (Paris, 1902); A. Marignan, *L'école de sculpture de Provence du XIIe au XIIIe siècle*; *Histoire littéraire de la France*, vol. 19, p. 268, Clement IV (Paris, 1838); Forel, *Voyage au pays des sculpteurs romans* (Paris and Geneva, 1913), 2 vols; W. Vöge, *Die Anfänge des monumentalen Styls.*

—Edmond Rostand (1868-1918; born in Marseilles).[252]

To this day on the stones of St. Gilles' abbatial are the graffiti of ships and warriors—a king among them—scratched by the swords of St. Louis' crusaders before they crossed to their death in Africa, 1270. The sadly dilapidated bourg which is St. Gilles to-day played a prominent part in the important centuries of the Middle Ages. Many were the popes and kings who visited it to venerate the tomb of the VIII-century hermit, Ægidius, from Athens, whose cult was widely spread over western Christendom, as many a church image and window showing the holy man and his fawn remain to tell.

The counts of Toulouse were the chief patrons of the abbey. On the First Crusade, Raymond IV of Toulouse bore the title Count of St. Gilles. Raymond VI held here, in 1208, an interview with the papal legate, Guy de Castelnau, the after-consequences of which precipitated the Albigensian wars. Angry words were uttered by the count when the legate rebuked him for shielding the heretics, and the next day the legate was murdered by one of the count's retainers as he was about to cross the Rhone. Thereupon Innocent III declared the Albigensian Crusade. In the following year Raymond VI performed penance before the church door of St. Gilles—the last public canonical penance of the Middle Ages. The disasters of the house of Toulouse diminished the abbey's building funds.

The discussions over the date of St. Gilles have been of importance because of its relation to the school of Provençal sculpture of which the most notable monument is its triple portal. Before St. Gilles' western end is a mass of composite imagery, of different dates and material, yet composing an architectural unit. Six bays of the nave are covered by a masonry roof of the XVIII century; only the piers and side walls of the edifice are ancient. Beyond the nave lie the ruins of the choir, in which has been installed an open-air archæological museum.

Did the choir of St. Gilles still stand, it would be the best Gothic monument in the south of France, exceptional in possessing an ambulatory and radiating chapels. At its entrance still exists a spiral staircase, the *vis de St. Gilles*, the first of its kind constructed, which many a mason of the Middle Ages journeyed hither to see. The steps compose an annular vault, winding like a corkscrew.

According to M. Labande, the choir of St. Gilles was built from 1140 to 1175, and at first there was no intention of vaulting it with diagonals. As the walls rose, however, a Gothic vault was prepared for. The nave, whose capitals have well-cut acanthus leaves, was erected from 1175 to 1209. It could not have been finished when in 1265 Clement IV rebuked his fellow citizens of St. Gilles for their delay in completing their church. Clement had been a local lawyer—a Romanesque house is still pointed out as his—by name, Guy Fouquet, or Fulcodi. The death of his wife caused him to embrace religion. When raised to St. Peter's chair, such was his dread of nepotism that he wrote to his daughters they were not to expect matches any more important than if he were a simple knight; we learn that the well-admonished young ladies failed to obtain any husbands at all. This pope, whom St. Louis

---

[252] Edmond Rostand, "Le nom sur la maison," in *Le vol de la Marseillaise* (Paris, Charpentier-Fasquelle, 1919).

called *"notre aimé et féal Guy,"* instigated the crusade of 1270, which was associated in the hour of its departure with his own town.

Despite his exhortation, St. Gilles' choir was joined to its nave only in the XIV century, as is proved by the rows of Rayonnant Gothic foliage on the capital of the nave's easternmost bay. The XVI-century religious wars devastated the abbey, which now was held by Calvinists, now by Catholics; and finally the Huguenots, after using the church as a citadel, ordered that it be razed. The tower was mined and its fall wrecked all around it, but the arrival of the king's troops saved the edifice from entire destruction; as the masonry roof had collapsed, a bastard-Gothic restoration of the nave was undertaken from 1650 to 1670. Then came the Revolution; the choir was sold and its stones carted away. So dead seemed all appreciation of the national art that the constitutional curé of St. Gilles clamored for the demolition of the famous triple portal, as its images "were insupportable reminders of past servitude, recalling the odious feudal régime, displeasing to lovers of liberty and equality." Till the middle of the XIX century the church was abandoned.

During excavations in 1765 a chamber, or bay, of rough workmanship was unearthed in the crypt, and in it was found a tomb inscribed as that of St. Gilles. This is all that remains of the church in which Urban II blessed an altar in 1096. On a buttress of the crypt an inscription states that its foundation was laid Easter Monday of 1116. The abbey had been damaged by an irate count of Toulouse, and Calixtus II asked Peter the Venerable to send from Cluny a new abbot to reorganize things.

The crypt's north and west walls rose first, but the work was dropped and taken up several times. All the vaulting, whether groin or diagonals, was an afterthought, for all the piers have been rearranged for the masonry roof they now support. Only a few of the westernmost bays of the crypt used diagonals, and as their profiles are the same as those in the choir, building from 1140 onward, they are probably contemporary. Inscriptions on the outer west wall of the crypt prove that in 1142 people were buried there, which would indicate that the present stair to the west portal was not yet arranged. Perhaps for a time they were not sure of making an upper church above the spacious basement. By 1209 that upper nave was built, because Innocent III buried his murdered ambassador beside the tomb of St. Gilles, and when Raymond VI had performed public penance before the portal, we are told that he was brushed against by the crowd, and escaped through the lower church, passing his victim's new tomb.

The imaged portal of St. Gilles, which inspired the porch of Trinity Church, Boston, is a composite mass of imagery begun in the XII century and continued till St. Louis' day. Pilfered fragments were made use of, as was only natural in a region where Rome had left many monuments. Some of the pillars are the fluted marbles of antiquity; others are of granite. Fourteen columns and fourteen large images of apostles and angels give unity to the composition, as does the continuous wide frieze.

St. Gilles' images, strong and short like the figures on the Gallo-Roman sarcophagi near the mouth of the Rhone, are perfectly proportioned to the place they occupy, cold, impersonal figures, more architectural than sculptural, the fruit of an old art, not the beginning of a new tradition, as was the theory of Herr Vöge, who would trace to Provence the origin of French Gothic sculpture. M. de Lasteyrie contended that the Porte Royale at Chartres—first of the Gothic portals, last of the Romanesque—with its long, slender figures in whose visages expression has been attempted, descends from the imaged portals of Burgundy, not from St. Gilles or St. Trophime, but from a nascent rather than a dying art tradition. The Lombard school gave to St. Gilles its lion caryatides, a very popular feature at church doors; Lanfranco, who remade Modena's cathedral in 1099, had been the first to plant pillars on the backs of lions, perhaps copying some lost work of antiquity.

"A world in itself," said Prosper Merimée of St. Gilles' sculptured portal. Under the biblical scenes of the frieze animals crouch and crawl. Some of the frieze groups, such as the Flagellation, are full of spirit, and must be of later date than certain other stiff archaic figures. The Kiss of Judas with its grimacing soldiers is probably a XVII-century restoration. The only time that the Expulsion from the Temple was treated in the older work was here. The sisters Martha and Mary and their brother Lazarus, with Mary Jacobi and Mary Salome, are all imaged at St. Gilles' door. The tradition of their arrival in Provence was gaining in favor every day while this portico was making.

The savants inform us, though not patriotic Provençal savants, that no mention of the saints of Bethany is to be found in Provence before the middle of the XI century. Monseigneur Duchesne of the Institute of France, who takes saints out of their niches as boldly as any Bollandist, tells us that it was the monks of Vézelay in Burgundy who first imagined the arrival in southern France of Mary Magdalene, in order to explain how it was they possessed her relics, the lodestar of their pilgrim shrine. Then, gradually, the legend grew till it was a remarkably full boatload that landed, in A.D. 40, at Les Saintes-Maries,[253] where the Little Rhone, on which stands St. Gilles, enters the Mediterranean: the risen Lazarus, whose relics were claimed by Autun in 1144; Martha, whose relics appeared at Tarascon in 1187 and caused a new church there to rise;[254] Marcella, the waiting woman

[253] Les Saintes-Maries is a desolate village of the Camargue, on the sea by the "Rhone of St. Gilles," six miles to the west of the big Rhone. The crenelated fortress-church replaced, in the XII century, one destroyed by Saracens. Its eastern end rises in three stories; below, in the crypt, is the shrine of Sara, the dark handmaiden; above is the high altar; and crowning all is the shrine (placed in St. Michael's care) in which Mary Jacobi and Mary Salome are honored. Their chapel opens on the church over the entrance to the Mass chapel. The sculpture resembles that of St. Trophime, at Arles; perhaps the much-eroded marble lions came from some monument of antiquity. Twice a year there are popular pilgrimages to Les Saintes-Maries, that of May being frequented by the gypsies. Monseigneur Duchesne, "La légende Sainte-Marie-Madeleine," in *Annales du Midi*, 1903, vol. 5; Georges de Manteyer, "Les légendes saintes de Provence," in *Mélanges d'archéol. et d'hist.: École de Rome*, 1897, vol. 17; Faillon, *L'apostolat des Saintes-Maries en Provence*. (This latter gives the Midi loyalists' point of view.) (1848, 2 vols.)

[254] *Congrès Archéologique*, 1897, pp. 95, 291, Tarascon; pp. 92, 333, Beaucaire; and 1909, p. 262, Tarascon. The church of St. Martha at Tarascon was dedicated in 1197, but reconstructed in the XIV century. The south portal, with its curious little gallery, is of the XIII cen-

of Martha and Mary; Maximinus, one of Our Lord's disciples; Simon the leper; St. Sidonius; Joseph of Aramathea; and the Blessed Virgin's sisters, Mary Jacobi, mother of James the Less, and Mary Salome, mother of James and John, and their dark handmaiden Sara, who became the patroness of gypsies.

Monseigneur Duchesne says that a grotto dedicated to the Virgin in the mountains east of Marseilles came to be regarded, by gradual unconscious fabrication, as the Sainte Baume where Mary Magdalene passed years of penitence, for the Midi wove the story of St. Mary the Egyptian with the saint of Bethany. All these holy people who had known the Lord fled from Syria after the martyrdom of St. Stephen and found asylum in southern France. The savants can prove what they will; while in Provence, in the "kingdom of sentiment," one believes every word of it. Read Mistral's *Mireille* and dare to be a skeptic! Under the leaden skies of Paris you may take the Institute's learning seriously. But gazing at *la grand bleu*, the frequented highway between Syria and Gaul when Roman Emperors ruled both, you say to yourself that it all *could* have happened. For hundreds of years the people of Provence have been made better and happier because they have believed that the historic family of Bethany who entertained the Lord were entertained by them.

---

tury. The honored relics are in the crypt in a heavy tomb of 1650. The simpler sarcophagus that once held them now stands by the side wall. All over France the defeat of paganism by Christian bishop or saint was symbolized by a dragon, and in the course of time the people often took the symbol for reality. The legend of St. Martha's Tarasque, or dragon, may be of this origin. Louis II d'Anjou began the castle of Tarascon, which was decorated by good King René. At Beaucaire, across the Rhone, is a tower built by St. Louis. The international fair of Beaucaire was famous. "Aucassin was of Beaucaire, of a goodly castle there":

> "'Tis of Aucassin and Nicolette....
> The song has charm, the tale has grace,
> And courtesy and good address.
> No man is in such distress,
> Such suffering or weariness,
> Sick with ever such sickness,
> But he shall, if he hear this,
> Recover all his happiness,
> So sweet it is!"

Turn to that cante-fable of the XIII century, and live again the Midi's days of chivalry. Turn to that XIX-century masterpiece of satirical generous humor, *Tartarin de Tarascon*, more likely to survive than many a more pretentious tale, so gay it is.

F. W. Bourillon, éd. and tr. of *Aucassin et Nicolette* (Oxford, 1896).

ST. TROPHIME AT ARLES[255]

Seigneur, des lois et voies
antiques, nous avions
quitté; l'austérité, vertus,
coutumes domestiques,
nous avions tout détruit,
démoli....

Seigneur, nous sommes tes
enfants prodigues; mais
nous sommes tes vieux
chrétiens: que ta justice
nous châtie, mais au trépas,
ne nous laisse point....

Seigneur, au nom des pauvres
gens, au nom des forts, au
nom des morts—qui auront
péri pour la patrie, pour leur
devoir, et pour leur foi!...

Seigneur, pour tant d'aversités,
de massacres, d'incendies;
pour tant de deuil sur notre
France, pour tant d'affronts
sur notre front,

Seigneur, désarme ta justice!
Jette un regard par ici-bas;
et enfin écoute les cris
de meurtris et des blessés!...

Seigneur, nous voulons devenir
des hommes; en liberté—
tu peux nous mettre!
Gallo-Romans et fils de noble
race, nous marchons droit
dans notre pays.

—(Literal French translation of Mistral's "Psaume de la pénitence," 1870.)

The western portal of the cathedral at Arles, less carefully executed than that at St. Gilles, was begun at the end of the XII century and finished in a couple of generations. Both were inspired by the same local classic influences of Rome and the subsequent Gallo-Roman development. The large statues, eminently architectural, at the famous door of St. Trophime, are as sturdy and squat as the images on early Christian tombs. Two of those ancient tombs, of the V and VI centuries, have been turned to ecclesiastic usage in this very church, as baptismal font and altar, and across the square from the cathedral many others can be studied in the Museum of Arles. The strong Byzantine influences apparent in St. Trophime's sculpture recall that Arles was the favorite residence of Constantine. From northern Italy came the animal-caryatides idea.

St. Trophime's Romanesque entrance leads into a somber church under whose

---

[255] *Congrès Archéologique*, 1876; and 1909, p. 213, L. H. Labande; L. H. Labande, "Étude historique et archéologique sur St. Trophime d'Arles," in *Bulletin Archéologique*, 1904, p. 459; J. de Louvière, "St. Trophime d'Arles," in *Bulletin Monumental*, 1876, vol. 42, p. 741; Abbé Bernard, *La basilique primatiale de St. Trophime d'Arles*, 2 vols., 8vo; Roger Peyre, *Nîmes, Arles, Orange* (Collection, Villes d'art célèbres), (Paris, H. Laurens, 1904); Georges de Manteyer, *La Province du I^e au XIIe siècle* (1908); F. Beissier, *Le pays d'Arles* (1889); Abbé Pougnet, *Étude analytique sur l'architecture de la Provence au moyen âge* (1867); H. Revoil, *L'architecture romane du Midi de la France* (Paris, Morel et Cie, 1873), 3 vols.; Martin, *L'art roman en France* (Paris, 1910); Rebatu, *Antiquités d'Arles* (1876); J. B. de Rossi, "Le cimétière des Arlescamps et sa basilique de St. Pierre," in *Bulletin Monumental*, 1875, vol. 41, p. 170; E. Leblant, *Les sarcophages chrétien de la Gaule* (1886); Alexis Forel, *Voyage au pays des sculpteurs romans*, vol. 1, chap. 1, "Arles-la-grecque" (Paris and Geneva, 1913), 2 vols.

barrel vault reigns a mellow gloom.[256] Begun before the middle of the XI century, it was reconstructed in the XII century; the painfully narrow high side aisles are covered by quarter circles that buttress the central vessel, whose undergirding arches are slightly pointed because the pre-Gothic masons had learned that the thrust of a broken arch was less. The XV century built the insignificant choir (without the vestige of a capital), exceptional only in having the sole ambulatory and radiating chapels in Provence. A prelate of the Grignan family built a chapel projecting from the transept, for, not far away, in Dauphiny, is the château of Grignan, where Madame de Sévigné died while staying with her daughter; one knows that she and XIII-century Blanche of Castile had been friendly.

The Mediæval Cloister of Arles

---

[256] "Saint-Trophime, humide et écrasé, dit une louange irrésistible â la solitude et s'offre comme un refuge contre la vie.... Arles, où rien n'est vulgaire." —Maurice Barrès, *Le jardin de Bérénice* (Paris, Charpentier, 1894).

St. Trophime's cloister, among the most beautiful in France, building from the XII to the end of the XIV century, is the fairest Christian monument of Arles.[257] This Midi art expands in the sunlight and grows melancholy under a masonry roof. Arles was a free town when it was begun, with its own podesta and consuls like a flourishing commercial city in Italy. About 1150, the north gallery was commenced, and the one to the east soon followed. The angle pier is composite (c. 1180), with St. Trophimus standing between St. John and St. Peter, the latter being sculptured in marble. The storied capitals of the cloister are exceedingly interesting. In the second half of the XIV century the west walk was begun, and almost immediately was followed by the south gallery, which is similar to it save for slight details. The cloister was completed under Bishop Jean de Rochechouart (1390-98).

Arles, like Lyons, claims a direct apostolic origin. A tradition says that St. Trophimus, her first bishop, was the disciple of the gentile of Ephesus, whom St. Paul mentioned in his epistle to Timothy. For centuries before the popularity of the Saints of Bethany legends in the Midi, St. Trophimus was revered. Pope Zosimus, in the V century, called Arles "the source from which flowed all over Gaul the rivulets of the Faith." Gregory of Tours voiced another tradition concerning St. Trophimus when he named him as one of the seven evangelists sent by Pope Fabian into Gaul in 250. At any rate, whether he lived in the first century or the third, St. Trophimus was the first bishop of Arles, and it is right that its primate church should be dedicated to him.

Arles, from which flowed over Gaul the rivulets of the Faith, is a city of ruins, and yet most gracious in aspect; *Arles la blanc*, Joinville called it as he sailed by on his way to the Sixth Crusade; *Arles la Grecque*. The women walk as nobly as the matrons of antiquity here where "the copper coins of Rome's republic and the gold of the emperors gleam in the sun amid the springtime wheat." "I tell you, and you can well believe me," sings Mistral, "that the damsel of whom I speak is a queen, for, know you, she is twenty years old and she is Arlésienne.... She descended with lowered eyes the steps of St. Trophime, and the stone saints by the portal blessed her as she passed, for she was ineffably good." There are books so typical of their race, or this period, that they belong to all time, and by them posterity can learn more of the basic forces that build monuments than from many a learned treatise. Such a book is Voragine's *Golden Legend*, such a book is the *Rationale* of Durandus.

---

[257] There is another cloister at Montmajour, four miles from Arles. Its transverse ribs are caught along the wall on corbels carved with grotesques. Nothing at Montmajour predates A.D. 1000. In the monastery church appeared (in the transept) some early diagonals; the crypt (middle of the XII century) is of a peculiar plan: a circular chapel in the middle of its apse with chapels radiating from the passage round it. From each arm of the transept projects an apse chapel. Under a hillock is a small shrine remade in the XIII century. In 1369 a tower of defense was added to the abbey. The curious chapel of the Holy Cross, in a meadow near by, is not of the time of its foundation, 1019, but a reconstruction of the XII century, probably intended for the chapel of a graveyard. Montmajour once rose from the sea marshes that for centuries came up to the gates of Arles. J. M. Trichaud, *Les ruines de l'abbaye de Montmajour-lès-Arles* (Arles, 1854); *Congrès Archéologique*, 1876, p. 362; and 1909, p. 154; Chantelon (Dom), *Histoire de Montmajour* (1890); L. Royer, *L'abbaye de Montmajour-lès-Arles* (Abbeville, Paillart, 1910).

The *Barzas-Breiz* teaches us to comprehend Carnac and the Calvaries of Brittany. Even so the soul of Provence has been interpreted by her own Mistral, who loved "the perfume of the ancient days when on the banks of the Rhone flourished a refined civilization that for a time bore the name, the Kingdom of Arles, but that really, through all the successive revolutions, was naught else but the direct survival, on French soil, of Rome's civilization."[258]

ST. MAXIMIN[259]

The cement, without which there can be no stability of the walls, is made of lime, sand, and water. The lime is fervent charity which joineth to itself the sand—that is, undertakings for the temporal welfare of our brethren. Now the lime and the sand are bound together in the wall by an admixture of water. Water is the emblem of the Spirit. And as without cement the stones cannot cohere, so neither can man be built up in the heavenly Jerusalem without that charity which the Holy Ghost worketh in them. The stones are built by the hands of the Great Workman into an abiding place in the Church: whereof some are borne and bear nothing, as the weaker members; some are both borne and bear, as those of moderate strength; and some bear and are borne of none save Christ the Corner Stone. All are bound together by one spirit of Charity as though fastened with cement, and these living stones are put together in the bonds of peace.

—BISHOP GUILLAUME DURANDUS OF MENDE (1220-96), RATIONALE.[260]

The bourg and church of St. Maximin lie about thirty miles east of Aix-en-Provence. Some rich Gallo-Roman noble of the V or VI century had his estate here, thinks Monseigneur Duchesne, on which he built a funereal chapel and crypt according to custom. That crypt with its early Christian sarcophagi is now under the church of St. Maximin, though why that saint is honored in the locality is not known. The first record of the site occurred when the estate was passed over to the monks of St. Victor's at Marseilles, who built a priory here (1038), and chose Max-

[258] "Sur cette terre élégante, au dessin si précis et si pur, sous cette lumière pénétrante, sur ces champs rouges où l'ovilier verse son ombre fine et grise, sur ces bords que la mer antique bat de sa flot court et rythmé, subsistent des œuvres et des souvenirs qui ne dépareraient pas la Grèce elle-même, mère de toute beauté. Le Pont du Gard, la Maison Carrée, les Arènes de Nîmes et d'Arles, Saint Trophime, Montmajour, Les Saintes-Maries, Les Baux, le Château des Papes à Avignon, les remparts de Saint Louis à Aigues-Mortes, le Peyrou à Montpellier, le canal du Midi, sont les monuments de cette activité séculaire qui recueillit l'héritage de Rome, et l'entretint tout le long de cette vallée du Rhône qui, à ses deux extrémités, comme deux phares, porte deux villes, deux républiques qui n'ont rien de supérieur par l'antiquité, l'activité, et l'éclat: Lyon et Marseilles."'—GABRIEL HANOTAUX.

[259] L. Rostan, *Monographie du couvent de St. Maximin*, 1874; Abbé Albanès, *Le courent royal de St. Maximin*; Monseigneur Duchesne, "La légende de Ste. Marie Madeleine," in *Annales du Midi*, 1893, vol. 5; L. G. Pélissier, *La Provence* (Régions de la France), (Paris, L. Cerf).

[260] *Rationale divinorum officiorum*, translated by Neale and Webb (Camden Society) as *The Symbolism of Churches and Church Ornament* (Leedes, Green, 1843).

iminus as its tutelary. It was only when some fertile brain, in Vézelay, said that St. Maximinus was one of the Lord's seventy-two disciples, and had accompanied Mary Magdalene to Provence, that Aix-en-Provence began to claim him as her first bishop. For two centuries Provence allowed Vézelay to boast of the possession of the Blessed Magdalene's remains. During Saracen inroads she had lost the relics of Lazarus and his sister, so the Burgundian church told her. Finally—we are quoting Monseigneur Duchesne, not a Midi savant—a patriotic Provençal whose mind was as fertile in inventions as the chronicler at Vézelay, arranged a rediscovery in 1279, in the crypt of St. Maximin, of the Magdalene's relics, whereupon the pilgrimages to Vézelay ceased.

Before witnesses and the ruler of Provence, Charles II d'Anjou (nephew of St. Louis), was opened one of the sculptured tombs in the Gallo-Roman noble's funeral crypt now under the nave of St. Maximin. In the sarcophagus was found a manuscript, in a wooden coffer, relating that in the year of the Incarnation, 716, on December 6th, under King Odoin, the body of Mary Magdalene had been moved from its alabaster tomb, in this same crypt, to the plainer tomb of St. Sidonius, in order to save it from those felons, the Saracens. The uncritical mind of the age accepted the obvious forgery as genuine. It was worded in XIII-century, not VIII-century Latin, the use of the term Incarnation for dating was an anachronism, and no such king as Odoin ever existed. Why should it have been expected that Saracens would spare one tomb more than the other, asks the courageous Monseigneur Duchesne. But why feel too critical of the pious fraud, since the genuine enthusiasm it aroused led to the building of the most imposing Gothic church in Provence and the one most pure in style, an edifice that inspired the imposing modern church of St. Vincent de Paul at Marseilles.

In 1295 Charles II d'Anjou[261] (1285-1309) began St. Maximin, which he passed into the care of the Dominicans. Abbé Albanès has discovered that the architect's name was Jean Bandier. During two centuries the Angevin rulers of Provence continued the church, and good King René finished it before he died in 1480. As the first plans were adhered to, the edifice possesses unity save for a few Flamboyant windows in the aisles. Those side aisles of St. Maximin are almost as high as the central vessel; they braced the main span and did away with the need of flying buttresses. Traits of Midi Gothic are the exceedingly narrow windows, the lack of a triforium, and uncut bands for capitals, though the omission of sculpture may be due to the fact that the abbatial belonged to a mendicant Order, vowed to poverty. St. Maximin's piers soar majestically from pavement to vault springing, nor has nobility of proportion been sacrificed in its severe granite interior.

---

[261] His son, St. Louis d'Anjou, died archbishop of Toulouse, having resigned his heirsships after captive years in Spain proved to him the futility of grandeur. Giotto painted him on the walls of Santa Croce, Florence. His chasuble, a masterpiece of embroidery, was preserved by the solid wardrobes of St. Maximin's XIV-century sacristy.

AIX-EN-PROVENCE[262]

Le désordre des malheureux est toujours le crime de la dûreté
des riches.

—VAUVENARGUES (1715—47; born in Aix-en-Provence).

The cathedral of St. Sauveur is a composite edifice needing skilled archæologists to decipher it. Its semicircular apse, without ambulatory or chapels, was
begun by Bishop Rostan de Noves. Its nave, of the XIV century (with typical capitals whose foliage is disposed in two bands), shows vestiges of a far more ancient
church. The nave's north aisle is neo-classic. The south aisle, called *Corpus Domini*,
is Romanesque, and was held to be the ancient cathedral, since it conforms to the
classic type of the regional Romanesque school, such as the Dom at Avignon.

M. Labande has demonstrated that this pre-Gothic portion of Aix Cathedral
was originally a church for the laity, built between 1150 and 1180 and dedicated to
St. Maximinus, and that it was planted along the side of a church for the canons,
dedicated to Notre Dame in 1108. Vestiges of this latter church are the ancient
parts in the actual nave of St. Sauveur.

The *Corpus Domini* has its own sculptured doorway, and three bays covered
by a barrel vault carried on pointed arches. Over the fourth bay is a shallow cupola
ridged with eight pilasters in a manner inherited from ancient Rome. Classic, too,
are the columns now arranged to form a baptistry.

Aix was the capital in Provence of the art-loving Anjou princes of the Capetian
line. Under them in 1476 was begun St. Sauveur's beautifully restrained Flamboyant Gothic façade and tower. In the nave is a stone reredos of 1470 called the
Tarasque, from the dragon of St. Martha represented in it, and under King René's
inspiration was made the splendid triptych of the Burning Bush by the French
primitif, Nicolas Froment, born in Avignon, but impregnated with the Flemish
spirit of Van Eyck. King René kneels in one panel, and his second wife, Jeanne de
Laval, in the other; the outer side of the folding panels is painted in grisaille. The
Burning Bush was taken as a symbol of the Virgin's integrity. The carved doors at
the west entrance of St. Sauveur, rich with prophets and sibyls, are ranked with the
noted doors of Beauvais and Rouen.

While the church of St. Maximinus, or the present south aisle of St. Sauveur,
was building, a student at the University of Aix, across the way from its cathedral,
was St. Jean de Matha (1156-1213), one of those good men of history who accomplished a great work but are overlooked by posterity. In Aix he passed his leisure
waiting on the poverty-stricken sick. Then he went up to the Paris schools to perfect himself in theology, and good Bishop Maurice de Sully, then building Notre
Dame, became interested in him, and with the prior of St. Victor's, after attending

[262] L. H. Labande, "St. Sauveur d'Aix-en-Provence," in *Bulletin archéological du comité
des travaux historiques et scientifiques* (Paris, 1912), p. 289; Abbé E. F. Maurin, *Notice historique
et description de l'église métropolitaine St. Sauveur d'Aix* (Aix-en-Provence, 1837); Prosper de St.
Paul, "La cathédrale d'Aix-en-Provence," in *Bulletin Monumental*, 1875, vol. 41, p. 442; J. Ch.
Roux, *Aix-en-Provence* (Paris, Bloud et Cie, 1907); L. Dimier, *Les primitifs français* (Collection,
Les Grands Artistes), (Paris, H. Laurens).

the young Midi noble's first Mass, prophesied that this was a soul chosen of God. Because Jean de Matha had been born in the south, a witness of Islam's piracies, he vowed himself at his first Mass to the redemption of Christian captives. His fellow student at Paris, Innocent III, approved the new Trinitarian Order called popularly Maturins because their Paris house was dedicated to St. Maturin. So rapidly did it spread that before long it had fifty houses in far-off Ireland, and as many in England. In its annals are the names of all the western nations. Jean de Matha, until his death, passed backward and forward to Africa. When the first boatload of redeemed captives landed at Marseilles a cry of thanksgiving rose in Christendom. Sometimes a brother of the Order would remain in a captive's place, when his funds for ransoming prisoners gave out. In Granada, Maturins were martyred. In the year 1260 five thousand Christians were redeemed from Islam prisons by these devoted men. And for five centuries the good work went on, so that we hear of Trinitarians freeing Christians from Mohammedans in the reign of Louis XIV. Cervantes was released from African captivity by the sons of St. Jean de Matha, else we would have no *Don Quixote*. All through the dark episodes of the Albigensian wars these lives of unobtrusive Christian charity endured. Their deeds have not been trumpeted to the winds. I dare say the historian who rings the changes on the *Tuez-les-tous* phrase never heard of St. Jean and his Maturins.

AVIGNON[263]

In abandoning Rome, their cradle, in departing from the venerated tomb of the Prince of the Apostle, in ceasing to reign on the site consecrated by the blood of martyrs, the popes failed to value the prop those august memories were for them. In their voluntary exile on the banks of the Rhone the popes were controlled by the king of France. Villeneuve's high towers, a French stronghold, threw too protective a shadow over the papal palace of Avignon.

—L. Salembier.

Architecturally Avignon does not fit into our category, but who can close a chapter on the Midi and not mention, among gems, this diamond? There is no more imposing, no more magnificent a palace in the world than that of the XIV-century

---

[263] *Congrès Archéologique*, 1882; 1897, p. 113; and 1909, L. H. Labande; André Hallays, *Avignon el le Comtat-Venaissin* (Collection, Villes d'art célèbres), (Paris, H. Laurens); F. Digonnet, *Le palais des papes d'Avignon* (after R. P. Ehrle, S. J.), 1907; L. Duhamel, *Les origines du palais des papes d'Avignon* (Tours, 1882); L. H. Labande, "L'église de N.-D.-des-Doms à Avignon," in *Bulletin Archéologique*, 1906; A. Penjon, *Avignon la ville, et le palais des papes* (1905); Léon Palustre, "Les peintures du palais des papes à Avignon," in *Bulletin Monumental*, 1874, vol. 40, p. 665; Eugène Müntz, "Les tombeaux des papes en France," in *Gazette des Beaux-Arts*, 1887, vol. 36, pp. 275, 367; *ibid.*, "Les sources de l'histoire des arts dans la ville d'Avignon pendant le XIVe siècle," in *Bulletin Archéologique*, 1887, p. 249; Verlaque, *Jean XXII, sa vie, ses œuvres* (Paris, 1883); Robert André-Michel, "Les fresques de la garde-robe au palais des papes à Avignon," in *Gazette des Beaux-Arts*, 1914-16, vol. 56, p. 293. (This study of the frescoes, discovered in 1909, was the author's last work. He fell in battle at Crouy-sur-Ourcq in 1914); Louis Guérard, R. P., *Les papes d'Avignon* (Paris, Lecoffre, 1910); Jean Guiraud, *L'église et les origines de la Renaissance* (chap. 2, on thé Avignon popes). (Paris, Lecoffre, 1902).

popes at Avignon.

Romanesque architecture is represented by the Dom and the bridge built by *frères-pontifes* over the Rhone (1177-85) under the inspiration of the shepherd boy St. Bénézet. Many a time has the river carried away its bays. The chapel on the bridge shows the work of three epochs, part being of Little Benedict's time, part of 1234, and an apse of 1513.

Notre Dame-des-Dom, as it was first built, belonged to the usual type of a Midi Romanesque church (1140-60), but to it have been added chapels and neo-classic decorations.[264] The west porch of the cathedral can claim to be one of the first conscious revivals of classic art in France, inspired by a Roman triumphal arch in neighboring Carpentras. Originally the inner walls of the porch were frescoed by Simone Martini of Siena, a friend of Petrarch. That humanist spent many years in Avignon, and it was at the door of the church of St. Clara that he first saw Laura, in 1327. If the Avignon popes employed Italian painters, their architects and sculptors were mainly local.

Avignon's great day was under the seven Roman pontiffs who lived here in succession during sixty-eight years, a period disastrous to the interests and prestige of the Church, but fecund for the art life of southern France. All seven of the popes were meridionals.

Clement V (1305-13), whom the patriotic Italian poet places in hell for his subservience to the French king, was the first to take up his residence in Avignon, but his building enterprises were elsewhere, at Bordeaux and St. Bertrand-de-Comminges, and he chose to be buried near Bordeaux, at Uzeste, his native place, where his tomb was mutilated in 1577. Clement is pictured on the walls of the Spanish chapel in Santa Maria Novella at Florence. Neither his statue at the chief portal of Bordeaux Cathedral nor his effigy on his tomb is a portrait.

After an interval he was succeeded by John XXII (1316-33), born in Cahors, where a tower of his palace still stands, as well as the most beautiful bridge of the Middle Ages, which he helped to build. John had been educated at Cahors, Montpellier, and Paris; he had taught law at Toulouse, and from 1310 was bishop of Avignon, so that he made it his permanent residence when elected to the papacy at seventy-two. John was an organizer of genius; he founded Perugia University and reformed those of Paris, Cambridge, and Oxford. The great treasure he left was the fund drawn on by his successors for the erection of their palace. His tomb in the cathedral of Avignon is like an immense reliquary, excessive lace stonework and pinnacles, though if some of the sixty statues that once embellished it remained,

---

[264] While the popes ruled in Avignon, churches rose from end to end of the city. In St. Didier (XIV century) is the bas-relief N. D.-du-spasme made for King René in 1476 by Francisco Laurana, one of the earliest Renaissance sculptors to work in France. He made the tomb for King René's brother in Le Mans Cathedral. The Gothic-Renaissance façade (1512) of St. Pierre is of singular grace; the date of its carved doors is 1551. There is a XV-century pulpit, and a retablo (1461) by Antoine Le Moiturier, born in Avignon, who finished the celebrated tomb of Jean Sans Peur now in Dijon's Museum. *Congrès Archéologique*, 1909, p. 17; A. Chaillot, *Les œuvres d'art dans les églises et chapelles d'Avignon*; G. Bayle, *Notes historiques sur l'église de St. Pierre d'Avignon* (Avignon, 1899).

there would naturally be more character in the ornamentation. The tomb has recently been claimed as a late-Gothic west-of-England work, similar to monuments at Exeter and Tewksbury.

His successor, Benedict XII (1333-42), was the pope who really began the Avignon palace which was to be completed in twenty-five years. While abbot of Cistercian Fontfroide, he had watched Narbonne's episcopal palace rising, and there are decided likenesses between it and the papal residence on the Rhone. Both were fortresses eminently of the Midi, not of Italy. Of Benedict it is related that when his father, a baker in the comté of Foix, came to visit him, dressed richly by courtiers who thought to save the pope's *amour propre*, the pope declined to recognize him till he garbed himself humbly. His was a complex character. He spent vast sums lavishly on his palace, bringing artists from Italy to decorate its walls and ceilings. His tomb, that had resembled his predecessor's, exists only in a few arcades housed in the Musée Calvert. The tomb called his in the cathedral is a composite affair. There is a statue of Benedict XII in the crypt of the Vatican.

The next pontiff, Clement VI (1342-52), a Limousin lord of great lineage, more knight than churchman, made the most beautiful parts of the papal palace, the conclave gallery, the Audience Chamber, the Pontifical Chapel over it, and the tower called St. Jeane whose chapels, *sotto* and *sopra*, were decorated by Martini. Petrarch had praised Clement for his liberality toward the Jews, who, driven out of other countries, found a home here, *"povres Juifs ars et escacés par tout le monde excepté en la terre d'Église dessous les clefs des papes."* For his burial Clement VI rebuilt, in the Forez mountains, the church of his former abbey, La Chaise Dieu, in the center of whose choir he placed his own sumptuous monument, whose forty-four statuettes represented his great relatives. In the religious wars of the XVI century the mausoleum was sacked and only the pontiff's marble effigy now remains.

Clement VI purchased the city of Avignon from Queen Joanna of Naples of the Anjou house. The Comtat-Venaissin, but not Avignon, formed part of the possessions that fell to the French Crown on the death of Alphonse of Poitiers and his wife in 1271. Philippe III gave it to the popes, to whom it had been promised by the last count of Toulouse.

The papal palace was finished by Innocent VI (1352-62), another Limousin. He made the tower applied to the south wall of audience hall and church, and he added to the city's fortifications. Across the Rhone he began the Chartreuse, later called Val de Bénédiction, a vast structure carried on by his family as a hereditary obligation.[265] To-day it is a mass of desolate ruins, and the pope's mutilated tomb is now housed in the hospice at Villeneuve-lès-Avignon.

Urban V (1362-70), *"moult saint homme et de belle vie,"* says Froissart, was a patron for art and letters throughout the Midi. At Avignon he continued the fortifications. His work is to be found in Montpellier Cathedral, also at Mende, St. Flour, and Marseilles, where his mausoleum towers in St. Victor's abbatial. His attempt

[265] *Congrès Archéologique*, 1897, p. 280; and 1909, p. 144, Villeneuve-lès-Avignon; Jules Formigé, *Rapport sur la Chartreuse de Villeneuve-lès-Avignon* (Gard), (Paris, 1909); Robert André-Michel, "Le tombeau du Pope Innocent VI à Villeneuve-lès-Avignon," in *Revue de l'art chrétien*, 1911, p. 204.

to re-establish the papacy in Rome failed, but his successor, Gregory XI—Count Roger de Beaufort, a nephew of Clement VI—went back definitely in 1377 to the Holy City, where a bas-relief on his tomb, in Santa Francesca Romana, records his triumphal entrance. The consequences of the long exile were deplorable. Immediately came the Great Schism of the West, during which some of the doubtful pontiffs resided at Avignon.

After their return to Rome the popes governed their small Midi principality by viceroys till at the time of the Revolution it passed to France. The palace was turned into a prison and barracks; when a local antiquarian society begged that they might be allowed to preserve the precious frescoes of Simone Martini in the chapels of Clement VI, the military governor replied that such notions were contrary to military custom. Happily the Palace of the Popes is now a national monument, and its judiciously accomplished renovation is one of those restorals against which no one can cavil.

CHAPTER IX

THE GOTHIC ART OF BURGUNDY[266]

Burgundy excelled in monastic architecture—The cradle of three great cloistral centers—Luxeuil, Cluny, Cîteaux—Luxeuil, founded by St. Columbanus (610), reorganized the VII century—Cluny, Christendom's supremest monastic congregation, founded 910—St. Hugues of Cluny (1049 to 1109) trained the leaders who remade Europe's civilization—Peter the Venerable, abbot from 1120 to 1156, continued building Cluny's vast church—Abélard died in a Cluny house, 1142—Revolution destroyed the glorious abbatial church—Paray-le-Monial, the favorite priory of Abbot Odilo (d. 1049) of Cluny, initiator of the Truce of God—Its Romanesque church has fluted pilasters (XII century)—Autun Cathedral's Romanesque portal the ancestor of the sculptured doors of Gothic cathedrals—Abbey church at Saulieu (note)—Beaune's collegiate of Notre Dame has lovely tapestries—Hôtel Dieu at Beaune (1444 to 1457), founded by Nicolas Rolin, contains Roger van der Weyden's best work—Hospital hall at Tonnerre (founded 1293) the prototype for Beaune's hospice—Fontenay, the oldest Romanesque Cistercian church extant—Dedicated by Eugene III in 1147—Avallon's church of St. Lazare blessed by Paschal II in 1107—Has a well-known Romanesque entranceway.

Some Primary Gothic churches in Burgundy—Montréal's collegiate can be visited from Avallon—Built by a returned crusader late in the XII century—Pontigny's abbatial the oldest Gothic in Burgundy—Its nave (1160 to 1180), with bombé vaults, was begun as

---

[266] *Congrès Archéologique*, 1907 and 1913; A. Kleinclausz, *La Bourgogne* (Collection, Régions de la France), (Paris, L. Cerf, 1905); *ibid.*, *Histoire de Bourgogne* (Paris, 1909); Dom. Urbain Plancher, *Histoire générale de Bourgogne* (1739-81), 4 vols.; Claude Courtépée, *Description du duché de Bourgogne* (1775-85); De Barente, *Histoire des ducs de Bourgogne de la maison de Valois* (Paris, 1825), 12 vols.; Ernest Petit, *Histoire des ducs de Bourgogne de la race capétienne* (Dijon, 1905), 9 vols.; A. de Caumont, "Rapport sur une excursion archéol. en Bourgogne," in *Bulletin Monumental*, 1852, vol. 18, p. 225; J. Calmette et H. Drouot, *La Bourgogne* (Collection, Provinces Françaises), (Paris, H. Laurens); A. Perrault-Dabot, *L'art en Bourgogne* (1897); J. L. Bazin, "La Bourgogne sous les ducs de la maison de Valois, 1361-1478," in *Mémoires de la Soc. Éduenne*, 1901, vol. 29, p. 33; Taylor et Nodier, *Voyages pittoresques et romantiques dans l'ancienne France, La Bourgogne* (Paris, Didot, 1863), 2 vols., folio; W. S. Purchon, "An architectural Tour in Central France and Burgundy," in *Journal of the Royal Institute of British Architects*, 1913-14, 3d series, vol. 21, p. 557.

Romanesque—Its choir used structural features as decorations—Three archbishops of Canterbury, St. Thomas Becket, Stephen Langton, and St. Edmund Rich, found refuge at Pontigny—Vézelay's abbatial of the Madeleine the stateliest church in Burgundy—Its Romanesque nave and Gothic choir belong both to the XII century—Its imaged portico (c. 1132) a supreme work of French sculpture—Second Crusade preached by St. Bernard at Vézelay, 1146—Philippe-Auguste and Richard Cœur-de-Lion rallied here for the Third Crusade, 1191.

Burgundy's best Gothic monuments—Collegiate of Notre Dame at Semur a gem of the Burgundian school, begun about 1225—Its sculpture exceptional—Auxerre Cathedral begun in 1215, the model of Gothic churches in the province—Auxerre's sculpture and its opaline glass rank with the first—Bishop Jacques Amyot (d. 1593) restored the cathedral after the Calvinists sacked it—Cathedral of Nevers has an apse at both west and east ends (note)—Dijon, the capital of Burgundy, led in art, under its four great dukes, 1364 to 1477—Flemish-Burgundian school began modern imagery—Dijon's cathedral of St. Bénigne, formerly an abbatial, is mediocre late-XIII century—Crypt of St. Bénigne begun 1001—Oldest monument of the Romanesque renaissance—William of Volpiano, abbot of St. Bénigne, initiated the revival of architecture after the year 1000—Rebuilt Tournus abbey church (note)—Church of Notre Dame, Dijon, is a gem of Burgundian Gothic (1220-1240)—Its subtleties of construction have never been excelled.

St. Bernard, abbot of Clairvaux (d. 1153), born near Dijon, the greatest son of Burgundy—His reform laid the spiritual foundations of Gothic cathedrals—His puritanic taste in architecture made Cistercian churches bare and simple—Cistercian Order, founded 1099, instrumental in spreading Gothic over Europe—St. Stephen Harding, its practical founder, welcomed St. Bernard at Citeaux in 1113—Five hundred Cistercian monasteries founded in Europe before the middle of XIII century—Spirit of St. Bernard, greatest of Cistercians, lives in the Imitation of Christ.

Be strong in humility and humble in authority:
Be austere in tenderness and tender in austerity:
Be amiable in sorrow and grave in prosperity.

—St. Columbanus' Antitheses.

URGUNDY, "a country placed on Europe's highways," was a land of monasteries. They dotted the fertile province. There were "prodigious Cluny," and Vézelay "the superb," scenes of historic gatherings; at Auxerre was St. Germain's monastery; at Dijon, the abbey of St. Bénigne, pioneer in the Romanesque renaissance of the region.

There were Cîteaux, the mother house of missions over the entire Christian world, Pontigny, that harbored three archbishops of Canterbury, Fontenay with its industrial forge, Tournus, Saulieu, Paray-le-Monial, and Flavigny, that reminded Chateaubriand of Jerusalem set on its hill. Up and down the land the laus perennis never ceased.

On the confines of the old kingdom of Burgundy, as the VI century closed, St. Columbanus founded at Luxeuil, between the sources of the Moselle and the Saône, an abbey which was to mold the religious life of the VII century, most fertile of epochs in the number and fervor of its religious institutions. Luxeuil became the popular school of Gaul, the mother house of hundreds of monasteries. Her monks filled the sees of France. The Celtic Rule was harsh, a compound of the Orient, of Lerens, and of Bangor in Ireland; even on feast days fish was a luxury. It was only the personal genius of the impetuous Irish missionary that caused it to be accepted for a few generations; then as the VII century closed, the Benedictine Rule which conformed better to human limitations superseded the Columban. "Where Columbanus sowed, Benedict reaped."[267]

Three hundred years later there rose in Burgundy the most splendid monastic institution that Christendom has ever known, Benedictine Cluny, that stood shoulder to shoulder with the reforming popes in their fight for the purification of the Church.[268] Cluny initiated the Truce of God, the peace movement of the XI century that permitted the art renaissance which was to culminate in the Gothic cathedrals. Peace meant an unmolested commerce, peace meant city charters and

---

[267] From Luxeuil derived Jumièges, St. Wandrille, Fécamp, St. Malo, St. Valéry, St. Bertin, Corbie, St. Riquier, Péronne, Lure, Rebais, Jouarre, Faremoutier, Remiremont, Dissentir, St. Gall, and Bobbio. St. Columbanus was born in Leinster in 543, the year that St. Benedict died at Monte Cassino. It is said that there was something supernatural in his appearance. Because of his comeliness he embraced the monastic life to flee temptation, entering the abbey of Bangor, a center of letters in what is now Ulster. All his life Columbanus was a lover of the classics; from his library at Bobbio was recovered Cicero's *De Republica*. At thirty came the call to missionize in Gaul. Ireland, on the outer verge of Europe, had escaped the Barbarian's wrecking so that her culture was intact. With twelve monks, among them his nephew, St. Gall (future founder of the noted Swiss abbey), Columbanus crossed to France. The king of Burgundy, a grandson of Clovis, gave him the region of Luxeuil, which the late invasions had turned into a desert. In twenty years Columbanus made it the center of spiritual life in Gaul. He was exiled in 610 because of his strictures on the evil living of Burgundy's rulers. After many wanderings he founded Bobbio, between Genoa and Milan, which abbey became another seat of learning. There he died in 615. Martin, *St. Columban* (Collection, Les Saints), (Paris, Lecoffre, 1909); Healy, *Ireland's Ancient Schools and Scholars* (Dublin, 1890); Ch. de Montalembert, *Monks of the West* (translated, London, 1896); Dalgairns, *Apostles of Europe* (London, 1876), vol. 1; Besse, *Les moines de l'ancienne France* (Paris, 1906).

[268] "On peut dire que vers le Xe siècle, le genre humain en Europe, était devenu fou. Du mélange de la corruption romaine avec le férocité des barbares qui avaient inondé l'empire, il était enfin resulté un état de choses que, heureusement peut-être, on ne reverra plus. La férocité et la débauche, l'anarchie et la pauvreté étaient dans tous les états. Jamais l'ignorance ne fut plus universelle. Le chaire pontificale était opprimée, deshonorée, et sanglante." —JOSEPH DE MAISTRE.

stable laws. A reformed clergy meant the renewal of the people's love of the altar, and their generous contributions toward the erection of churches. With Cluny as leader there was then formulated the architecture which was a stepping stone to a greater system.

Two hundred years after Cluny's foundation, Burgundy again gave birth to a monastic movement which was to carry to the ends of Europe the Gothic system of building. Cîteaux, in the extent of its conquests and its centralized administration, has been compared with the Roman Empire. Cistercian monks carried Burgundian Gothic to Spain, to Italy, to Greece, to England, Germany, and Scandinavia. Owing to the conditions of society and of the episcopacy, the cloister then was chief patron of art. Simony infected the bishoprics and it is not under unworthy prelates that churches are reared. Gregory VII, Cluny, that supplied him with his army of reformers, and St. Bernard, with his white-cowled brethren, warred unceasingly on simony, concubinage, and investiture (the tormenting question of layman control of churchmen). And since it was monasteries that fought that battle of regeneration, monastic churches and not cathedrals were the first tangible proof of the ethical rebirth of Europe. *À la peine ... à l'honneur.* When the reform achieved by Cluny and Cîteaux had filled the sees with worthy bishops, then were built the great cathedrals.

We have seen how the problem of roofing churches in stone caused the evolution from Romanesque to Gothic art. Burgundy's struggle to achieve a permanent stone roof was bolder than that of other regional schools in France, and perhaps it was overhardy, since her abbatials, in Gothic times, had to be buttressed to keep them standing. Though the Burgundian discarded too early the Romanesque principle of equilibrium by dead load, his temerity was a step forward in the march toward new principles of construction. These monks on Europe's highway made churches of ample width and height, and, rather than sacrifice their proper lighting, opened windows in the upper walls of the central vessel. However, they must have felt that their clearstory windows were an experiment, for they essayed, occasionally, an embryo flying buttress, keeping it hidden under the lean-to roof of the aisles.

The militant Romanesque school of Burgundy was too well developed for it to bow instantly before the new art. Not here did the generating member of Gothic architecture first come into common usage, but in that region of northern France whose pre-Gothic school was of less importance. The Burgundian clung stubbornly to his early ways of building, and even after other provinces had accepted the ogival style he erected thoroughly Romanesque churches; St. Philibert at Dijon is the contemporary of the cathedrals at Chartres and Paris. Flying buttresses at no time found favor in Burgundy. Groin vaults were persisted in simultaneously with diagonals, and the sexpartite vault used long after the north had dropped it. Firm plain profiles for archivolts and window molds were preferred.

Once the Burgundian frankly accepted the new system, his bold genius led him to push its principles to their limit. Within the confines of the duchy were the quarries of hard Tonnerre stone that permitted audacious experiments in building. He dared traverse his exterior buttresses by circulation passages, he dared catch his heavily weighted diagonals on corbels (carved with original heads), and to poise a mass of material on the slenderest of colonnettes. Often he surmounted his triforium by a passage that passed directly through the active wall shafts, as in cathedrals of Auxerre, Nevers, and Semur. By the middle of the XIII century Dijon achieved a marvel of Gothic technique in its church of Notre Dame. Despite much notable Gothic work one is inclined, none the less, to maintain that Burgundy found her fullest expression in her earlier monastic churches. Alas, that the greatest of them, Cluny, should to-day be but the phantom of its once colossal self!

CLUNY[269]

Time will be ending soon, heaven will be rending soon, fast
we and pray we: Comes the most merciful; comes the most terrible; watch we while may we.

—BERNARD DE MORLAIX, "JERUSALEM THE GOLDEN"[270] (C. 1140).

The "mother abbey of Europe" lies in a fertile valley some fifteen miles off the express route that passes through Mâcon. The property was given to the monks by a duke of Aquitaine, who thus anathematized future despoilers: "I conjure you O holy Apostles Peter and Paul, to cut off from life eternal all robbers, invaders, or sellers of that which I herewith donate with full satisfaction and entire free will."

When Cluny was founded in 910, the victory of Christianity over the Barbarians still hung in the balance. It was Cluny that weighed down the scale for justice and progress, Cluny that gave to Rome the needed reforming popes. Hers should be a name as honored in humanity's history as Athens: "We leave college," wrote Montalembert, "able to cite the list of Jupiter's mistresses, but ignorant, even to their names, of the founders of the religious Orders that civilized Europe." And the testimony of the Protestant Leibnitz is: "Without monks we should have no er-

---

[269] *Congrès Archéologique*, 1899, p. 48; 1913, p. 65, Jean Virey; *Millénaire de Cluny* (Mâcon, 1910), 2 vols.; Jean Virey, *L'architecture romane dans l'ancien diocèse de Mâcon* (Paris, 1892), 2 vols.; *ibid.*, *L'abbaye de Cluny* (Collection, Petites Monographies), (Paris, H. Laurens); Chanoine L. Chaumont, *Histoire de Cluny* (Paris, 1911); Migne, *Dictionnaire des abbayes* (Paris, 1856); Ch. de Montalembert, *Monks of the West* (trans. London, 1896); H. Pignot, *Histoire de l'ordre de Cluny depuis la fondation de l'abbaye jusqu'à la mort de Pierre le Vénérable* (Autun et Paris, 1868), 3 vols.; F. L. Bruel, *Cluny, 910-1910. Album historique et archéologique* (Mâcon, 1910), 4to; Ponzet, in *Revue de l'art chrétien*, 1912, on the capitals of Cluny's abbatial; David, *Grands abbayes de l'occident* (Paris, 1909); Lecestre, *Abbayes en France* (Paris, 1902); G. T. Rivoira, *Lombardic Architecture*, vol. 2, p. 104, Cluny; p. 112, Tournus. Tr. by G. McN. Rushforth (London and New York, 1910); Demimuid, *Pierre le Vénérable et la vie monastique au XIIe siècle* (Paris, 1895); A. Penjon, *Cluny, la ville et l'abbaye* (Cluny, 1884); *ibid.*, "Abélard et Pierre le Vénérable d'après Dom Gervaise," in *Annales de l'Acad. de Mâcon*, 1910, p. 393; *Histoire littéraire de la France*, vol. 7, p. 318, "Le bienheureux Guillaume, abbé de St. Bénigne"; p. 399, "Raoul Glaber"; p. 414, "St. Odilon" (Paris, 1746); vol. 9, p. 465, "St. Hugues"; p. 526, "Abbé Jarenton" (Paris, 1750); vol. 14, p. 211, "Pierre le Vénérable"; p. 129, "St. Bernard" (Paris, 1764).

[270] Dr. John Mason Neale, éd., *Rhythm of Bernard of Morlaix* (London, 1858). Dr. Neale has here rendered his translation like the XII-century original, dactylic hexameters divided into three parts.

udition, for it is certain that we owe to monasteries the preservation of letters and books." Four of the best among the popes came out of Cluny's cloister: Gregory VII, Urban II, Paschal II, and Urban V.

The XI-century Sanctuary of Cluny as It Was until the Revolution

The modern French school of mediæval archæology, delving into the past, has drawn Cluny from its long oblivion. In 1910 was celebrated with national honors the millennium of the Burgundian "abbey of abbeys," and to the festival the French Academy sent M. René Bazin as its representative to voice the gratitude of French letters to the "great Order of Cluny which in the France of the Middle Ages exercised in its plenitude the mission of civilizer, apostle of the Gospel, apostle of peace, guardian of the whole field of knowledge, founder then, of all works of charity, initiator of both literary and agricultural progress, creator of an art which she spread over Europe."

During the Middle Ages the silent Burgundian valley was a busy hive of arts and crafts[271] with goldsmiths' work, illuminating, carving in ivory and in stone, foundering of bells, and the making of stained glass. All that went toward the adornment of God's house was fostered in Cluniac schools, but above all was the master art of the builder honored. In bands of twelve the monks carried not only the Gospel, but the arts to every part of Europe, and even farther afield, for there were houses of the Order on Mount Tabor, in Nazareth, and in Bethany. No uniform Cluniac building lore was followed; it was the usual custom for the monks to conform to the local traditions in each different country.[272]

It was natural that the big abbey church at Cluny proper should have been Burgundian Romanesque. Hazelon, a monk of Cluny, was the master-of-works, a learned man who had once occupied a high position in the world; he is said to have himself worked here with trowel and mortar. The tunnel vaulting was braced by transverse ribs that were slightly pointed; clearstory windows were opened in the upper walls. The channeled pilasters were a heritage from the classic traditions of the region; near by, in Rome's former capital of Autun, were many monuments of antiquity.

Cluny's abbey church of St. Peter was the largest in the world, and covered an area about equal to that of the present St. Peter's at Rome. It was over five hundred and fifty feet long; the cathedral at Paris is not four hundred feet in length. There were double aisles and double transepts. St. Hugues of Cluny, the sixth abbot, "a man of God greatest among the great," "the pupil of the papacy's eye," ruled the Burgundian mother house during the sixty years that Cluny guided Christendom (1049 to 1109). No flattery, no subtlety could turn him from pure justice. Under him were trained Hildebrand, the future Gregory VII, who led the forces of church reform. "The giving up of justice is the shipwreck of the soul," said Gregory VII. Abbot Hugues trained also Urban II, who preached the First Crusade. Among the houses he founded were St. Martin-des-Champs at Paris, and St. Pancras at Lewes; in England there were thirty-five Cluniac establishments in the time of Henry VIII.

Twice St. Hugues went into Spain, where his niece was the Queen of Castile, engaged in substituting the liturgy of the Church universal for the Mozarabic rite. To the town of Cluny he granted a commune, and he built two of its parish churches, Notre Dame and St. Marcel.[273] When he felt death approaching, he had

[271] "Ah! ce Cluny!... ce fut vraiment l'idéal du labeur divin, l'idéal rêvé! Ce fut, lui, qui réalisa le couvent d'art, la maison du luxe pour Dieu." —J. K. HUYSMANS, *L'Oblat* (Paris, Plon-Nourrit et Cie).

[272] Some of the French houses affiliated with Cluny were Vézelay, the Trinité at Vendôme, the Trinité at Fécamp, St. Martin-des-Champs and St. Germain-des-Prés at Paris, St. Denis, the Caen abbatials, St. Ouen at Rouen, Jumièges, St. Wandrille, St. Remi at Rheims, Notre Dame at Châlons-sur-Marne, St. Bénigne at Dijon, Tournus, St. Maixent, St. Savin, Ste. Foy at Conques, Moissac, St. Sernin at Toulouse, and St. Eutrope at Saintes.

[273] The church of Notre Dame built in Cluny by St. Hugues was burned in 1233, and immediately reconstructed as Burgundian Gothic; the lower walls and some of the capitals are of St. Hugues' time. Consoles, sculptured with heads, such as those under the lantern, are frequent in the province, but a central tower is exceptional. In the XVIII century the narthex was destroyed. St. Marcel's church was rebuilt after a fire in 1159 by the abbot of

himself carried before the altar of St. Marcel, there to breathe his last on a bed of ashes, and a few days earlier than the Easter Tuesday of 1109 on which he passed away, his dear friend and frequent visitor at Cluny, St. Anselm of Canterbury, died, being privileged, he said, to go to meet his Saviour in time for the blessed Easter feast. Those two great men of the cloister by their ethical and intellectual leadership laid the basis for the Gothic cathedrals.

The choir of St. Peter's, at Cluny, was blessed by Urban II, in 1095, when he came into France to preach the First Crusade. He passed a week in his old home, after which he and his beloved master, St. Hugues, proceeded to the historic gathering at Clermont. The nave of St. Peter's was carried forward by succeeding abbots of Cluny, and many a pope was to watch the edifice rising. Paschal II passed the winter of 1106-07 in Cluny, and his successor, Gelasius II, died there in 1119; he had recently consecrated the new Romanesque cathedral of Pisa.[274] On the site of the wing of the cloister where he lodged now stands a XIV-century building called by his name. On his death the cardinals at Cluny held conclave, electing as pope a member of the ducal house of Burgundy, the bishop of Vienne, who took the name Calixtus II; in Cluny church he canonized the great Abbot Hugues.

St. Hugues' successor, Pons de Melgueil, after an estimable career, was led by pride to a downfall. On his resignation, Pierre de Montboissier, an Auvergne noble, known in history as Peter the Venerable, became the ninth abbot (1122-56). At that time he was but thirty years of age. Pons returned, seized Cluny abbey, and in the ensuing disorders the vaulting of the new nave collapsed. Abbot Peter restored the stone roof, and Innocent II dedicated the completed church in 1131.

The capitals then carved are to be seen in the town's Museum. Some of them personified the eight tones of liturgical music, for Cluny excelled in song, and every twenty-four hours her vast basilica echoed to the chanting of the entire book of Psalms; never, says the old chronicle, was there pause in the *saintes clameurs*, the *laus perennis* started by Irish Columbanus in the valleys of Burgundy. Some of the capitals from the abbatial are contemporaries of the statuary at Vézelay, where Peter the Venerable had been prior, and where his brother, Pons de Montboissier, was abbot. Vézelay was a pilgrimage church, so that its imagery was made of more popular character than that of Cluny, where worshiped an intellectual élite.

Cluny began the carving of the Bible for the Poor. The Burgundians were the first to develop the imaged portal which the Gothic cathedrals were to elaborate into their sumptuous triple entrances. While Cluny was building, a monk in the

---

Cluny, who was a great-nephew of William the Conqueror. The octagonal tower, capped by a XIII-century spire, is of exceptionally lovely proportions. *Congrès Archéologique*, 1913, p. 68. St. Hugues also founded the Charité-sur-Loire, whose church was dedicated by his pupil. Paschal II, in 1107, at which ceremony assisted Suger, then a monk at St. Denis. Only the transept and absidioles are of that time, for the choir, nave, and tower are Burgundian Romanesque of the second half of the XII century; the Lady chapel rose two centuries later. Once the abbatial was four hundred feet long, but a fire, in 1559, damaged it and only four bays of the nave remain. *Congrès Archéologique*, 1913, p. 374, Louis Serbat; André Philippe, "Charité-sur-Loire," in *Bulletin Monumental*, 1905, vol. 69, p. 469.

[274] De Foville, *Pise et Lucques* (Villes d'art célèbres) (Paris, H. Laurens).

monastery composed a poem of some thousand lines, opening with a vision of the heavenly Jerusalem. Bernard of Morlaix must have found inspiration in his own Burgundian basilica, which we know to have contained over three hundred windows of translucent mosaic. He dedicated his poem to his beloved abbot, Pierre de Montboissier.

Peter the Venerable was no Puritan in art, as was his friend St. Bernard, with whom he had many a skirmish, owing to their temperamental differences and the rivalship of their respective Orders. The abbot of Cluny never wavered in his reverence for the "fellow citizen of angels," as he called the abbot of Clairvaux, and Bernard saw in Peter, man of the world though he was, "a vessel of election full of truth and grace."

Like Abbot Suger, Pierre de Montboissier was the type of the liberal culture of the Benedictine, and he was to live again in the XVII-century scholars of the St. Maur reform, even as Bernard's uncompromising spirit reappeared then in De Rancy and his Trappists, a reform of Cîteaux. Like Suger, Peter the Venerable was a quoter of the classics, and a literary man. "To write was for an abbot of Cluny a hereditary tradition," said a XII-century historian. He had Arabic taught at Cluny for mission purposes. Journeying in Spain, he was the first to have the Koran translated for Europe; he held it to be Islam's best refutation. Very modern appears this old-time abbot in the zest with which he set out to travel, to inspect the houses of his Order. When he died in 1156, he was ruling over two thousand establishments, in every part of Christendom.

In person Peter was distinguished, and in character most generous, humane, and free from narrowness. He was wisely moderate always, and simple and direct. The letters of his which still exist make him a living personality. Though as keen a theologian as his friend Bernard, Abbot Peter kept the defeated Abélard with him at Cluny until his irritated spirit was soothed, and when the great schoolman died in 1142, Abbot Peter wrote to Héloïse, in her nunnery of the Paraclete, in Troyes diocese, to arrange that Abélard's body be brought there for burial, and he himself went to preach the funeral sermon.[275] In his letter to Héloïse he said that never had he seen truer humility and retirement than Maître Pierre's; "after which," as M. René Bazin remarks, "none of us need despair."

Cluny's abbatial of St. Peter was enlarged in the XIII century by a forechurch of several bays, with double aisles. An antechurch or narthex was a frequent addition to the Burgundian basilica; sometimes it was open as at Autun and Beaune, sometimes wholly inclosed as at Vézelay. Although Cluny's narthex was built as late as 1220, groin vaulting was used for the aisles.

In 1245 Innocent IV paused for a month at Cluny, having in his train a dozen cardinals and their suites, and Louis IX came for a fortnight's conference with the pope, accompanied by the queen mother, his brothers, and courtiers. The emperor

[275] Héloïse as a girl, in the convent of Argenteuil, studied Greek, Latin, Hebrew, philosophy, and theology; the women of that age were as eager for learning as the men. In 1817 her body and that of Abélard were removed to the cemetery of Père la Chaise at Paris. Le Roux de Lincy, *Les femmes célèbres de l'ancienne France* (Paris, Leroi, 1848), 2 vols. For Abélard, see de Rémusat (Paris, 1855) and E. Vacandard (Paris, 1881).

of Constantinople and the heirs both of Castile and Aragon were guests at that same time, and yet so immense was the establishment, that all were accommodated without the monks quitting their usual quarters. In 1248 St. Louis paused again in Cluny before his first crusade.

With material success came spiritual decline. The tale runs the same in most of man's organizations. As a reformer Cluny was succeeded first by the Cistercians, whose fervor lasted for a century, when were needed the two mendicant Orders of Francis and Dominic. The system that allowed the king to appoint abbots, initiated by the Concordat of 1516, proved fatal, and there is truth in the saying that the court prelates paved the way for the religious wars. Three times in those bitter years of strife was Cluny sacked, its famous library ravaged, and its art treasures burned.

The Revolution completed the ruin. The first mob that marched out from Mâcon to wreck the abbey was dispersed with firearms by the townspeople. The municipality of Cluny wrote to the National Assembly to tell of the constant benefits it had derived from the monks—so the rationalist Taine relates in his *Ancien Régime*—but the impious wrecking of the great monastery went on. Day after day cartloads of rare books were brought to feed the bonfires in the square. All through 1793 bands of looters came out from Mâcon to break windows and destroy images. The indignant townspeople looked on impotently at the vandalism that spelled their own material decline. At Napoleon's advent they sent petition after petition to try to save the big church, but the Mâcon merchant who had purchased it proceeded to open a road right up its nave and sold the stones as building materials. First the narthex was blown up with gunpowder; then a transept arm. When the huge central tower fell with stupefying noise the people shivered with a nameless fear. The history of France was being obliterated before their eyes.

To save what remained the town offered in exchange its communal lands and market halls. In vain; the grandest monastic church in the world was demolished piecemeal after the nineteenth century opened. Some seven or eight towers had crowned St. Peter's. In 1811 the one over the choir was destroyed. Gunpowder blew up the stately pillars of Pentelic marble and Italian cipolin set around his sanctuary by St. Hugues seven hundred years before. They destroyed the frescoes of the apse, which were so fresh that one who then sketched them said that they seemed to have come straight from the artist's brush.

To-day little of the abbey church is standing. There are vestiges of the choir, a small tower, and the south arm of the main transept with a big tower over it. There also remains the Flamboyant Gothic chapel built by Abbot Jean de Bourbon (1456-81), out of the smaller transept. In the town street are evidences of where the western doors of the abbatial once stood. The entrance arches to the abbey grounds are intact, and some few of the towers of the inclosure walls. The museum is now housed in the monastery's guest quarters built by Jean de Bourbon. His successor, Abbot Jacques d'Amboise (1481-1514), erected the pavilion which now serves as Town Hall. Both of those art-loving prelates constructed at Paris the Hôtel Cluny as town residence for the abbot of the Burgundian mother house.

THE ROMANESQUE ABBATIAL OF PARAY-LE-MONIAL[276]

> The world is very evil,
> The times are waxing late,
> Be sober and keep vigil,
> The Judge is at the gate!
> The Judge that comes in mercy,
> The Judge that comes with might,
> To terminate the evil
> To diadem the right.

—BERNARD DE MORLAIX, "Jerusalem the Golden."[277]

Not far from Cluny lies Paray-le-Monial, "a town very dear to heaven," said Leo XIII's brief of 1896. The monastery was founded by the second abbot of Cluny, St. Majolus, who was instrumental in bringing to France William of Volpiano, the leading spirit in the renaissance of architecture after the year 1000. The present abbatial resembles on a very small scale that of Cluny. Its barrel vaulting is braced by pointed arches and there are the channeled pilasters of Rome's tradition in the region. The exterior of the apse and the carven doorway are gems of pre-Gothic art. Towers and porch date from the end of the XI century, and the remainder about 1130. At present the monastery church (which is abominably marred with whitewash) is dedicated to the Sacré Cœur, a devotion that was initiated by the Blessed Margaret Mary Alacoque, who died in the Visitation convent of this town in 1690. Paray-le-Monial has become one of the pilgrimages of modern France.

St. Odilo, who governed Cluny for the half century preceding the sixty-year rule of Abbot Hugues, loved especially the priory of Paray-le-Monial. He inspired and organized the Truce of God, the *Treuga Dei*, by which war was prohibited on certain days and in certain holy seasons. The monk, Raoul Glaber, to whom Odilo was patron, has described in a chronicle covering the period from 900 to 1047 (an invaluable document for the sources of the Capetian line) how the war-wrecked populace flocked to the church councils that were their only hope, their hands uplifted, with the beseeching cry, "Peace! Peace! Peace!" In the rebirth of hope and energy that succeeded to the terrors of the year 1000, Glaber has told us how the earth reclothed herself in a white mantle of churches. He had been spurred on to write his history by the chief builder of the age, William of Volpiano. The great monastic churchmen of Burgundy were leaders in the movement that was to culminate, within four generations, in Gothic cathedrals. To Abbot Odilo is attributed, also, the founding of the feast of All Souls, which he set on the day following All Saints, as if to place the suffering ones in the care of the elect. From the observance of this feast in Cluny houses it spread to the entire Church.

---

[276] *Congrès Archéologique*, 1899; and 1913, p. 63, E. Lefèvre-Pontalis; Abbé Cucherat, *Monographie de la basilique du Sacré Cœur à Paray-le-Monial*, 1884; N. de Nicolai, *Générale description du Bourbonnais*.

[277] John Mason Neale, *Collected Hymns, Sequences, and Carols* (London, Hodden & Stoughton, 1914), p. 199, a translation of the XII-century poem of Bernard de Morlaix.

THE ROMANESQUE CATHEDRAL OF AUTUN[278]

Et c'est ainsi que Dieu travaille quand il veut nous châtier sans nous perdre, quand il ne veut pas que la guerre finisse, par le feu, le sang, la désolation générale, la ruine entière et le changement d'un État. *Il sépare les gens de bien*: il faut que les uns se mettent avec choix au parti qu'ils estiment le plus juste, et que les autres se trouvent dans le parti qu'ils approuvent quelquefois le moins. —LE PRÉSIDENT JEANNIN (1540-1622; born in Autun).

Autun's chief church, one of the few cathedrals in France which is Romanesque, was begun in 1120 and consecrated in 1132 by Innocent II. In that same year he blessed Cluny's nave and Vézelay's narthex. A friend of St. Bernard, Bishop Étienne de Baugé (1112-36), was its chief benefactor, as he was, also, of the Burgundian abbey of Saulieu.[279]

The Last Judgment over Autun's west door, signed by one Gislebertus, dates from that period. Its strange, elongated figures are not the culmination of an old art, but a first effort in a development that was to produce the imaged portals of Gothic cathedrals. Autun's curious tympanum was saved from the iconoclasts of the Revolution because the *gens de goût* of the XVIII century had covered it over with the neo-classic plaster ornamentation they preferred. The graceful trumeau images of Lazarus, Martha, and Mary are restorations. Before the western door an open narthex for the use of lepers was added about 1178.

In the first part of the XII century, the cathedral school was directed, during thirty years, by Honoré d'Autun, whose popular book, *The Mirror of the Church*, introduced the use of animal symbolism into the iconography of cathedrals. M. Mâle discovered that the New Alliance window in Lyons Cathedral copied his book verbatim. In the learned Honoré's day Autun Cathedral had not yet laid claim to the relics of the risen Lazarus. Originally the church was consecrated to St. Nazaire, which name was changed to Lazare after the Burgundian abbey of Vézelay had spread the story that Mary Magdalene had died in Provence. No one knew how Autun obtained the relics said to be those of Lazarus of Bethany. They

[278] *Congrès Archéologique*, 1899, p. 62; and 1907, p. 32, Joseph Déchelette; also p. 537; H. de Fonteray and A. de Charmasse, *Autun et ses monuments* (1889); Abbé Devoncoux, *Description de l'église cathédrale d'Autun* (1845); Claude Courtépée, *Description de la duché de Bourgogne*, vol. 6; H. Havard, éd., *La France artistique et monumentale*, vol. 5, p. 49, L. Paté, on Autun; Paul Vitry, in *Revue Archéol.*, 1899, p. 188; Montegut, *Souvenirs de Bourgogne*.

[279] The abbey of St. Andoche, Saulieu, was named for a companion of St. Benignus, a Greek missionary sent to evangelize Gaul, perhaps by St. Polycarp of Smyrna. The church was rebuilt early in the XII century, and of that period is the nave whose capitals present sculpture of different epochs: the barbaric earlier grotesques censured by St. Bernard, then a few acanthus leaves and medallions, and, finally, naturalistic work. Calixtus II dedicated Saulieu's abbey church in 1119. In 1339 the English sacked the choir and transept, which were rebuilt in 1704. That true son of Burgundy, Vauban, the celebrated engineer of Louis XIV, was born in a château near Saulieu in 1633: "The most honest man of his century, the simplest, truest, and bravest," according to St. Simon. He covered France with defenses whose worth was proved in 1914. One can comprehend qualities in a region's architecture by a knowledge of regional characters. *Congrès Archéologique*, 1907, p. 103, Pierre de Truchis, on Saulieu. The architect Soufflot, of M. Lefèvre-Pontalis' family, was a Burgundian.

were first exposed for veneration in the cathedral in 1147. Monseigneur Duchesne has thought that the legend grew by unconscious fabrications. It certainly did the Burgundian towns little harm to honor those whom the Lord had cherished. Through long centuries Burgundy delighted to call her sons Lazare.

The cathedral of Autun has a barrel vault undergirded by pointed arches. Channeled pilasters,[280] great and small, abound; they are on all four sides of the piers. In Autun stand gateways of Rome's empire to serve as classic models. The acanthus leaves of the cathedral's triforium can compare with those of the Porte d'Arroux. Autun was a Roman capital in Gaul, founded by Augustus. It covered then twice its present area. Agrippa, son-in-law of Augustus, built the great military road that ran from Lyons to Autun, Autun to Auxerre, Auxerre to Troyes, Troyes to Châlons-sur-Marne, Châlons to Rheims, Rheims to Soissons, Soissons to Senlis, Senlis to Beauvais, Beauvais to Amiens, and thence to Boulogne-sur-Mer.

The graceful central tower of the cathedral was added in the Flamboyant Gothic day by Cardinal Rolin (d. 1483), son of the builder of Beaune Hospital, Nicolas Rolin (a native of Autun), the self-seeking but able chancellor of Duke Philippe le Bon. Another son of Autun was Pierre Jeannin, president of the parliament of Burgundy and minister of Henry IV. His father, a tanner, was a man of civic importance in the town. President Jeannin's kneeling statue and that of his wife, Anne Gueniot, are now in the cathedral choir, being all that remained, after the Revolution, of his tomb made by Nicolas Guillan of Paris. No man ever had a truer passion for the public weal than this Burgundian magistrate who saved Burgundy from the stain of blood on St. Bartholomew's day in 1572. Word came from the king to kill, but the Catholic Jeannin on the governor's council at Dijon urged delay, saying that when a king's orders were given in anger, the wisest course was procrastination. He was to live long enough to aid Henry IV in drawing up the Edict of Nantes in 1598.

Jeannin's attitude in 1572 was all the more meritorious because Burgundy had suffered acutely from the Calvinists, who invited their co-religionists from Germany to fight their fellow citizens. In 1569 a band of the invaders left behind them a trail of four hundred burned villages. Cluny was attacked, and Cîteaux was sacked from top to bottom; to-day some XIV-century debris is all that marks the mother house of the Cistercian Order. The destruction of Cîteaux was irreparable for art, since during centuries its abbatial was the St. Denis of the first Capetian dukes who ruled Burgundy. The leading families of the province felt it an honor to be buried at Cîteaux. In its church was once the splendid tomb (now in the Louvre) of the seneschal of Burgundy, Philippe Pot (d. 1494). The effigy of the baron in armor is carried on the shoulders of eight black, cowled figures—a further development of the *pleurant* type of tomb.

In a chapel of Autun Cathedral is a beautiful modern statue of Pope Gregory the Great, presented to Cardinal Perraud (1882-1906) of the French Academy, as bishop of this ancient city whose prelate in the VI century had entertained Au-

[280] The cathedral of Langres in ancient Burgundy resembles Autun in its channeled pilaster strips and its acanthus-leaf sculpture. Its choir was rebuilt in 1100, using simultaneously groin vaulting and diagonals. The façade is neo-classic.

gustine and his monks on their way to missionize England. Cardinal Vaughan of Westminster was the donor of this grateful souvenir.

THE HOSPITAL AND ROMANESQUE COLLEGIATE AT BEAUNE[281]

L'art du Moyen Âge—aussi ennemi de l'art académique figé dans ses moules conventionnels que du désordre matérialiste— est une esthétique très simple, très certaine, très puissante et très libre. Cette esthétique n'invoque pas un idéal abstrait; elle impose le culte de la réalité, de la plus humble comme de la plus écla- tante; elle pourrait s'appeler un réalisme trancendant, respectant la forme telle que Dieu l'a faite, et en même temps la transfigurant par la grand frisson de l'au-delà.

—ROBERT VALLERY-RADOT.[282]

The Hospital of the Holy Ghost, built by Chancellor Nicolas Rolin from 1444 to 1457, is a gem of the province, reminding us of the close union of Burgundy and the Netherlands under the four great dukes of the West. The third of those rulers, Philippe le Bon, patronized Jean Van Eyck, as did the enterprising man who was the duke's chancellor during forty years. For a church at Autun, Rolin ordered of Van Eyck, in 1425, the magnificent Madonna now in the Louvre in which he kneels as donor—a shrewd, hard-featured, capable man.

For his new hospital at Beaune he commissioned Roger Van der Weyden to paint, in many panels, the Last Judgment now in the little museum of the estab- lishment, but originally installed in the large raftered hall. After the Van Eyck's Adoration of the Lamb it was the most important work of Flemish art undertaken. Philippe le Bon is portrayed in it twice, and so is the donor. The outside of the pan- els is painted in monochrome—what the French call *camaïeu* from its cameo effect, and the Italians call chiaroscuro. When this superb painting hung at the end of the hospital hall that ended in a chapel like the XIII-century hospice at Tonnerre, the patients could see it from their beds. The Hôtel Dieu at Tonnerre had been found- ed by Marguerite of Burgundy, in 1293. After the death of her husband, Charles d'Anjou, whose cruelty roused the Sicilian Vespers, she retired to the city of which she was hereditary countess, and with two other dethroned ladies, the Empress of Constantinople and the Countess of Tripoli, gave herself up to good works. *La bonne Reyne*, the people called this princess who passed her days serving the sick poor in a hospital where the spirit of the Beatitudes ruled. None was dismissed from its door without new cloak and shoes. To-day the great rafter-covered hall at Tonnerre lies empty; the raising of its pavement has somewhat impaired its

[281] *Congrès Archéologique*, 1899, p. 68; A. Kleinclausz, *Dijon et Beaune* (Collection, Villes d'art célèbres), (Paris, H. Laurens); Alphonse Germain, *Les Néerlandais en Bourgogne* (Bruxelles, 1909); Arsène Périer, *Un chancelier au XVe siècle, Nicolas Rolin* (Paris, Plon, 1904); H. Chabeuf, in *Revue de l'art chrétien*, 1900, p. 193, on the tapestries of Beaune; Abbé Bavard, *Histoire de l'Hôtel Dieu de Beaune* (Beaune, 1881); André Michel, éd., *Histoire de l'art*, vol. 3, première partie, "La tapisserie aux quatorzième et quinzième siècles," Jules Guiffrey.

[282] Robert Vallery-Radot, *Le réveil de l'esprit* (Paris, Perrin et Cie, 1917).

proportion.

Beaune's hospital hall, that indubitably copied Tonnerre's, serves still the charitable purpose for which it was founded. Its quiet courtyard is a vision of Flanders. In the kitchen the ancient iron crane of the fireplace is ornamented with I.H.S.; the Middle Ages made even work artistic. On feast days, such as Corpus Christi, the quaint half-timber hospice is hung with beautiful XV-century tapestry. It is deemed an honor for the leading families of the region to count one of its members among the nuns whose service is for a few years, after which they may return to their own people.

The collegiate church of Notre Dame at Beaune is a typical Burgundian Romanesque edifice of the XII century, to which the following century added a graceful open narthex of two bays. It possesses seventeen embroidered panels relating Our Lady's life, presented in 1500 by the Chanoine Hugues le Coq, and held to be among the most lovely tapestries in France, evoking memories of Memling and the Flemish primitives.

AVALLON, MONTRÉAL, FLAVIGNY, AND FONTENAY[283]

L'esprit humain, poussé par une force invincible, ne cessera jamais de se demander: qu'y a-til au delà? Il ne sert à rien de répondre: au delà sont des espaces, des temps, ou des grandeurs sans limites. Nul ne comprend ces paroles. Celui qui proclame l'existence de l'infini accumule dans cette affirmation plus de surnaturel qu'il n'y en a dans tous les miracles de toutes les religions. La notion de l'infini dans le monde j'en vois partout l'inévitable expression. Par elle, le surnaturel est au fond de tous les cœurs. L'idée de Dieu est une forme de l'idée de l'infini. Tant que le mystère de l'infini pesera sur la pensée humaine, des temples seront élevés au culte de l'infini. Et sur la dalle de ces temples, vous verrez des hommes agenouillés, prosternés, abimés dans la pensée de l'infini. Où sont les vraies sources de la dignité humaine, de la liberté, et de la démocratie moderne, sinon dans la notion de l'infini devant laquelle tous les hommes sont égaux?

—LOUIS PASTEUR (1822-95; born in Burgundy).[284]

---

[283] *Congrès Archéologique*, 1907, p. 4, Avallon, Charles Porée, and p. 129, G. Fleury; p. 97, Montréal, Charles Porée; p. 49, Flavigny, P. de Truchis; E. Petit, *Avallon et l'Avallonnais* (Auxerre, Gallot, 1867); R. Vallery-Radot, *Un Coin de Bourgogne; Avallon;* Abbé Villetard, "Les statues du portail de l'église St. Lazare d'Avallon," in *Bull. de la Société d'études d'Avallon*, 1899, 1900, and 1901; E. Petit, "Collégiale de Montréal," in *L'Annuaire de l'Yonne*, 1861, p. 121; G. T. Rivoira, *Lombardic Architecture* (tr. London and New York, 1910), vol. 2, on the crypt of Flavigny; L. Bondot et J. Galimard, *Restes de l'ancienne basilique de Flavigny* (1906); Claude Courtépée, *Description du duché de Bourgogne*, vol. 3, on Flavigny; Lucien Bégule, *L'abbaye de Fontenay et l'architecture cistercienne* (Lyon, 1912). There is also a study by Bégule of Fontenay in the Petites Monographies series published by H. Laurens; J. B. Corbolin, *Monographie de l'abbaye de Fontenay* (Cîteaux, 1882).

[284] *Discours de réception de M. Louis Pasteur à l'Académie Française*, 1882. Pasteur was born at Dôle (Jura), once a part of ancient Burgundy. A grandson, Robert Vallery-Radot, is

The hill town of Avallon, above the gorge of the Cousin, with a square that would do honor to any capital, makes a convenient center from which to explore various Burgundian churches. Its own church of St. Lazare still possesses the apse and absidioles of the edifice blessed by Paschal II in 1107. The remainder of the church was built in mid-XII century, and the portal (in five orders richly carved, with channeled and twisted columns) belongs to the end of the century. A copy of Avallon's door is in the Trocadéro Museum at Paris where it can be compared at close range with the two other notable Romanesque portals of the province—those of Autun and Vézelay. The interior of St. Lazare is excessively plain, having a high expanse of unbroken wall over the pier arches, with the clearstory opened merely by little circular windows.

Twenty miles from Avallon is the church of Montréal, like a feudal fort guarding one of the main passageways from Champagne. The lord of Montréal was among the few hundred barons who returned from the dire experience of famine, treason, and death which was the Second Crusade, on which had set forth a hopeful hundred thousand knights and pilgrims. In the latter part of the XII century he built Montreal's collegiate church, one of the earliest Gothic ventures in the province, showing a simultaneous use of Romanesque and Gothic vaulting. Its two westernmost bays were added early in the XIII century. The beautiful alabaster reredos of the XV century, and the carved choir stalls, are well worth studying. Beyond Montréal, to the north of Avallon, lies Tonnerre's hospital hall and to the south can be visited the abbatial at Saulieu and the XIII-century castle of Chastellux, a son of which ancient house fought in America with Rochambeau and was the good friend of George Washington.[285]

To the east, at Flavigny, set picturesquely on a hill near the last stronghold held by the Gauls against the Romans, stood one of the most interesting of abbey churches, of which portions of the XIII-century sanctuary remain, a few arches of the nave, and a Carolingian crypt built by the abbot who ruled here from 755 to 768, hence that subterranean chamber can claim to be the oldest dated monument extant in France. Over the choir of Flavigny was a cupola, and the Lady chapel was an XI-century octagon like that which William of Volpiano constructed for his abbey at Dijon. This precious Benedictine abbatial was destroyed in the XIX century. At Flavigny are two ancient parish churches. What is now the Pension Lacordaire was the Dominican convent opened in 1849 by that brilliant son of Burgundy, with funds donated by his admirers of Dijon.

To the northeast of Avallon, at Fontenay, near Montbard, is the oldest extant Romanesque church of the Cistercian Order, built from 1139 to 1147, on land given by the lord of Montbard, the maternal uncle of St. Bernard; on his mother's side one of the younger generation that comprehends the spiritual essence of the Middle Ages. He has written of the potency of his prayer in the church dedicated to holy Lazarus in his native Avallon. Another grandson, Jean Vallery-Radot, is a rising member of the school of mediæval archæology.

[285] Jean de Chastellux, *Travels in America, 1780-1782.* He was the first to have himself inoculated with smallpox in order to give confidence to the people. The heir of Chastellux was a hereditary first canon in Auxerre Cathedral, privileged to sit in its choir with a falcon on his wrist.

St. Bernard was of the blood of Burgundy's first line of Capetian dukes. The great abbot of Clairvaux himself conducted hither the twelve monks who were to found the new house and reclaim the marshy region; and for his brethren of Fontenay he wrote his treatise on Pride and Humility.

The first small sanctuary at Fontenay was soon replaced by the actual one, built on the same lines as the church at Clairvaux, which no longer stands. Both followed the Cistercian plan; no tower; no triforium nor clearstory; uncut capitals; the east end rectangular; square chapels opening on the eastern wall of the transept. Funds for the new constructions at Fontenay were provided by a wealthy English prelate who had retired here, Evrard de Montgomery, of the Arundel family, who, while bishop of Norwich, completed the long Norman nave of that cathedral. In 1147 the church was consecrated by Pope Eugene III, St. Bernard being present. As it was frequent in Cistercian monasteries to make a specialty of some branch of manual work, Fontenay conducted a forge, and the massive XII-century building which housed it still stands. The forge, the abbey church, and the refectory to-day comprise part of a paper factory whose proprietor has taken a patriotic pride in restoring these precious monuments of ancient Burgundy.

THE PRIMARY GOTHIC ABBATIAL AT PONTIGNY[286]

> Whatever draws us from the power of our senses, whatever makes the past, the distant, or the future predominate over the present, advances us in the dignity of thinking beings. Far from me and from my friends be the frigid philosophy as may conduct us indifferent and unmoved over any ground which has been dignified by wisdom, bravery, or virtue.... That man is little to be envied whose patriotism does not gain force on the plain of Marathon, or whose piety would not grow warmer among the ruins of Iona.
>
> —Dr. Samuel Johnson.

The oldest Gothic church in Burgundy is the Cistercian abbatial at Pontigny. "Cradle of bishops and asylum of great men," Pontigny is *parfumée de souvenirs*, to use a charming stilted French phrase. It was the first daughter of Cîteaux, founded in 1114. When a pious canon of Auxerre proposed to endow a house of the new Order, the abbot of Cîteaux, St. Stephen Harding, came to overlook the site on the confines of Champagne, and then sent twelve monks to found the house, under the leadership of Hugues de Mâcon, kinsman and childhood friend of St. Bernard.

The Cistercians had not the Benedictines' weakness for a noble site, but if they planted their monasteries in a marsh—as at Fontenay and Pontigny—their agricultural industry soon made the desert bloom. The earlier Cistercian churches obeyed St. Bernard's ascetic admonitions for architecture, a Puritanism that became monotonous in the Italian churches of the Order. In France the Cistercians ceased to

---

[286] *Congrès Archéologique*, 1907, p. 199; Abbé Henry, *Histoire de l'abbaye de Pontigny* (Avallon, 1839); Chaillon des Barres, *L'abbaye de Pontigny* (Paris, 1844); *Histoire littéraire de la France*, vol. 11, p. 213, "St. Étienne, troisième abbé de Cîteaux" (Paris, 1759).

adhere to church simplicity, raising sanctuaries such as Ourscamp, Longpont, and St. Julien-le-Pauvre at Paris.

No towers adorned Pontigny, and stained glass was eschewed, but the leaded design of the grisaille windows is so lovely that, as M. André Michel has said, "one could not be poor with more nobility." The architect of Pontigny made skillful use of certain essential constructive features to obtain his decorative effects. Thus, though monastic sobriety was followed by omitting the triforium, the bare wall between pier arches and clearstory was relieved (at the sanctuary curve) by carrying down the moldings from the upper windows; and in the procession path a fifth rib was introduced into each vault section, which rib fell on a corbel set above the entrance to each of the radiating chapels—a constructive subtlety by which was produced a graceful wall arcade.

The present abbatial was begun a generation after the foundation of Pontigny, with funds contributed by Thibaut the Great, Count of Champagne. The transept, which is Romanesque, rose from 1150 to 1160. While the walls of the nave were mounting, the master-of-works began to prepare for a Gothic vault over the principal span. The lower windows were round-headed; the upper ones used the pointed arch. As the keystone of the diagonals was raised far above the arches framing each section, a pronounced *bombé* shape resulted. From 1160 to 1180 this transitional nave of Pontigny was building, and the most famous of the English exiles, who sought the hospitality of Pontigny, must have watched the works. The choir, as first erected, had a rectangular eastern wall after the usual manner of Cîteaux's churches. Then, from 1170 to 1200, the present choir was erected with Gothic ambulatory and radiating chapels.[287] Alix of Champagne, daughter of the abbey's generous patron, and mother of the French king, Philippe-Auguste, was buried in the new choir, in 1208. From 1207 to 1213 Pontigny harbored a second archbishop of Canterbury, Stephen Langton, of Magna Charta fame. During the studious years he passed here he divided the Bible into chapters for the first time, and even the Greeks accepted his rulings. In later life Archbishop Langton often looked back to this byway of Burgundy; "his garden, his solace, his abode of peace," he called it.

His predecessor at Pontigny was St. Thomas Becket, one of the outstanding figures of the XII century, whose story is told in many a French window and sculptured group. If ever an Englishman was all of a piece it was that son of a Rouen merchant settled in London. During his life as a courtier Becket was so lavish in grandeur that when he passed through France as Henry II's ambassador, the countryside turned out to see him, since few were the king's retinues that could equal his. When Henry raised him to the highest post in the English Church he instantly dropped luxury. He stood firm as a rock in defense of ecclesiastical rights against the king's attempt at Church supremacy. Tennyson's "Becket" says, "I served King Henry well as Chancellor; I am his no more, and I must serve the Church."

---

[287] "The long prospect of nave and choir ends with a sort of graceful smallness in a chevet of seven closely packed, narrow bays. It is like a nun's church, or like a nun's coif."—WALTER PATER, on Pontigny, in *Miscellaneous Studies* (London, The Macmillan Company, 1895).

To the end of time such a character will be discussed; some for, some against, him; admired he certainly was by that sincerest and cleverest of men, John of Salisbury, who lived in his intimacy.[288] Both in England and France the populace felt that Becket was the champion of their civic rights by his defense of church independence—then the only supreme court against lay tyranny. Undeviatingly and enthusiastically they supported him all through his seven years' exile. One of the articles of the Clarendon Constitutions which Henry Plantagenet tried to impose on English ecclesiastics was that no peasant could become a priest without his lord's permission. The poet voiced the indignant outcry: "Hath not God called us all, bond or free, to his service?"

When Henry II, with his usual Angevin bad faith, duped his new archbishop into a promise to maintain the customs of the kingdom, and thereupon proceeded to revive obsolete customs, Becket, repenting the concessions he had made, fled, in 1164, to Sens, to lay the case before Alexander III. The pope decided that certain of the Clarendon propositions were impossible for any churchman to accede to. The abbot of Pontigny offered hospitality to the persecuted primate and Becket stayed with him till 1168, conforming to the severe Cistercian Rule. He quitted the Burgundian monastery when Henry, in a burst of vindictive anger, threatened to shut up every house of the white monks in England as well as in his continental possessions if they harbored the rebellious churchman. Soon after Becket's arrival at Pontigny, the irate king sent thither the primate's relatives and friends, turned out to beggary, in order that their plight might oppress the archbishop's spirit.

The third exile from Canterbury, and the saint who has given his name to Pontigny's abbatial, was a gentler spirit. St. Edmund Rich knew France as well as his native region of Oxford, having studied in Paris University and taught there for years. It is told how his mother, Mabel, sent him to the foreign schools with a hair shirt and a cord whip in his gripsack in order that he might learn to chastise and thus curb himself. She was a merchant's wife, and alone reared her family, to enable her husband to follow the call he felt for the cloister; two of her daughters died the saintly abbesses of Catesby. At the knee of that XIII-century mother the little Edmund, as a child, recited every Sunday the entire book of Psalms. While lecturing at Oxford he initiated the study of Aristotle. In Paris, St. Edmund watched the cathedral of Notre Dame perfecting itself, and at Salisbury, while treasurer, he assisted at the laying of the corner stone of the Gothic cathedral in 1220.

Worsted in the struggle to right crying abuses in English church affairs where the king kept bishoprics vacant for his financial profit, and the queen filled the sees with her own unpopular foreign relatives, the archbishop, accompanied by his chancellor, St. Richard, was on his way to Rome to remonstrate. He thought it wrong to condone further by his presence evils he was powerless to correct. He paused in Burgundy, and there death came to him in 1243. To-day his tomb stands over the high altar of the abbey church named St. Edmé, in his memory. Puritan

---

[288] J. C. Robertson, ed., *Material for the History of Thomas Becket.* Rolls series, 7 vols.; vols. 1 to 4 contain the lives written by John of Salisbury, Herbert of Bosham, etc. Other studies of St. Thomas of Canterbury are Morris (London, 1885); Kate Norgate (*Dictionary of National Biography*); L. Huillier (Paris, 1891), 2 vols.

Bernard most certainly would not approve the gymnastic-limbed angels that decorate the present Renaissance tomb of St. Edmund, but one fears that he would give his sanction to the whitewash that disfigures the interior of the interesting Primary Gothic church.

To the canonization ceremonies at Pontigny in honor of St. Edmund of Abingdon came St. Louis (who had known him well in Paris) and Blanche of Castile, and notables such as the archbishop-builder of Bourges Cathedral, and St. Richard, now become bishop at Chichester, in which cathedral his tomb was destroyed, in 1538, by order of Henry VIII. Few spots in France are more entirely apart from the come-and-go of modern life than is forgotten Pontigny, *parfumée de souvenirs.*

THE ABBATIAL OF VÉZELAY[289]

Il y a des lieux qui tirent l'âme de sa léthargie, des lieux enveloppés, baignés de mystère, élus de toute éternité pour être le siège de l'émotion religieuse ... l'héroïque Vézelay, le mont Saint-Michel, qui surgit comme un miracle des sables mouvants ... lieux qui nous commandaient de faire taire nos pensées et d'écouter plus profond que notre cœur. Silence! les dieux sont ici! Il y a des lieux où souffle l'Esprit.

—MAURICE BARRÉS, *La colline inspirée.*[290]

The supreme excursion from Avallon is that to Vézelay, ten miles away. One can drive to it or walk to it, since no railway touches the valley which once was the beaten thoroughfare for Christendom marching to crusades. A good way to approach it in the proper spirit of pilgrimage is to walk from the station at Sermizelle with the church of St. Magdalene as the lodestar to guide one's steps. Vézelay has the aspect of a hill city of Umbria. The abbey church, Gothic in its choir, Romanesque in its nave, transition in its forechurch, and practically all of it of the XII century, crowns the hill like a cathedral.

"Le grand nom de Vézelay sonne aux oreilles avec une sauvage poésie. La majesté du site est digne de la splendeur du monument."[291] Always afterward will you remember this abode of reverie with that uplift of the heart which high art and high thoughts arouse. Like loved sites in Umbria, this, too, is "one of the earth's oases

[289] *Congrès Archéologique*, 1907, p. 27; Charles Porée, *L'abbaye de Vézelay* (Collection, Petites Monographies), (Paris, H. Laurens); H. Havard, éd., *La France artisque et monumentale*, vol. 4, Vézelay; De George, "L'église abbatiale de Vézelay," in *L'Architecture*, 1905; L. E. Lefèvre, "Le portail de l'abbaye de Vézelay," in *Revue de l'art chrétien*, 1906, p. 253; also, 1904, vol. 54, p. 448, G. Sanoner; Crosnier, "Iconographie de l'abbaye de Vézelay," in *Congrès Archéologique*, 1847, p. 219; V. Flandin, "Vézelay," in *Annuaire statistique du département de l'Yonne*, 1841-45; A. Chérest, *Études historiques sur Vézelay* (Auxerre, 1868); Gally, *Vézelay monastique* (Tonnerre, 1888); Camille Enlart, *Le musée de sculpture comparée du Trocadéro* (Paris, H. Laurens, 1913); A. Thierry, *Lettres sur l'histoire de France*, chaps. 22-24; Joseph Bédier, *Les légendes épiques*, vol. 1, "La légende de Girard de Roussillon" (Paris, H. Champion, 1908), 4 vols.

[290] Maurice Barrès, *La colline inspirée* (Paris, Émile-Paul, frères, 1913).

[291] Louis Gonse, *L'Art Gothique* (Paris, Quantin, 1891).

of spiritual rest and refreshment."

The abbey was founded in the IX century by Girard de Roussillon[292] of *chanson de geste* fame, but its position as a leading pilgrim shrine was not established till Abbot Geoffrey was installed in 1037. Only then did the relics of the Magdalene appear here, given, it was claimed, by Charles Martel as reward for Burgundian aid during Saracen inroads in the Midi. Monseigneur Duchesne thinks that from Vézelay started the legends so loved in Provence, that the privileged family of Bethany, with others who had known the Lord, fled from persecution in Syria to the mouth of the Rhone about A.D. 40. Up to the XI century the Christian world had accepted Ephesus as the burial place of the Magdalene, and the tomb of Lazarus was claimed by Cyprus. In 899 the Emperor Leo VI had removed both bodies to Constantinople, where he built a church for them. Not a trace of the tradition concerning the Bethany sisters and brother is to be found in France before Vézelay monastery claimed the possession of the relics of the Magdalene and dedicated its church to her.

---

[292] St. Père-sous-Vézelay, below the hill, occupies the site where Girard de Roussillon's foundation was first established. The present church is a typical Burgundian Gothic edifice, partly of the XII and partly of the XIII century. Carved corbels catch the fall of certain diagonals, and in place of a triforium is an interior passageway that passes through the shafts. In the opening years of the XIV century was added the narthex, a noble porch of two bays whose capitals have foliage in little bunches set in two rows. The façade is decorated by big statues like that of the Madeleine church, a mile away, and at the corners of the tower, a landmark for the valley, are sculptured angels blowing trumpets. The choir of St. Père-sous-Vézelay was wrecked during the English wars, and was in large part rebuilt as late-Gothic. *Congrès Archéologique*, 1907, p. 16; Abbé Pissier, "Notice historique sur Saint-Père-sous-Vézelay," in *Bull. de la Soc. des Sciences de l'Yonne*, 1902, vol. 56, pp. 33, 275.

Vézelay's XII-century Abbey Church of the Madeleine

The founder of Vézelay freed its abbot of the control of local bishop or baron by establishing him as feudal proprietor of the town. The result was that the history of the abbey was a stormy one. The neighboring proprietors, resenting the abbot's independence, excited against him the townspeople who had grown rich from the fairs held during the pilgrimages. The burghers chafed at their serfdom to the monastery, and in 1106, during riots, they murdered Abbot Artaud. He probably was the builder of the Romanesque choir to which was originally attached the actual nave, since there is record of a dedication ceremony at Vézelay in 1104. As the archives were burned by the Calvinists in 1560, no precise dates exist for the church, but M. Lefèvre-Pontalis thinks that the crypt under the choir is of Abbot Artaud's time.

A fire in which hundreds perished occurred in 1120. The present nave could not have been in use before then. When it was completed the builders proceeded to erect a forechurch of three bays, and between it and the nave was opened the famous portico which has been called worthy of Paradise. Innocent II, in 1132, blessed the new parts of the abbatial. He had lately consecrated the cathedral of Piacenza, and at Pavia in that same year was blessed San Pietro-in-Ciel-d'Ore. North and south of the Alps the same energies were astir, but no sculpture of that period in Italy equals that of Vézelay. The date of the imaged portal of Ferrara Cathedral is 1135, and that of St. Zeno at Verona, 1183.

The nave at Vézelay had no triforium, nor was there a tribune over the aisles. However, in the narthex they built upper galleries, under whose lean-to roof was concealed a quarter-circle wall that did the work of a continuous flying buttress. The principal span was still further counterbutted by the side aisles themselves. Over the easternmost bay of the narthex appeared a vault section with Gothic ribs, but the diagonals were more decorative than functional; the vault web of rubble in a bed of mortar was molded on a temporary frame like a groin vault. Pointed arches were employed in the main arcade of the forechurch.

Vézelay's capitals rivet attention, so dramatic are the Bible stories related — the suicide of Judas, David and Goliath, Absalom, Moses, some symbolized vices and virtues, too, and a few *genre* studies. The capital of the fifth pier on the north side of the nave shows field laborers who carry cones which some say were used for scattering grain, and others think were for the vintage, or for honey-gathering; the same agricultural scene was represented at Cluny. Vézelay even ornamented with sculpture some of the bases of its piers.

The triple doors between narthex and nave are a supreme work. At the middle trumeau stands John the Baptist, he who was sent before to prepare the way, the announcer as well as the witness. On the disk which he holds was once carved the Lamb of God who taketh away the sins of the world. Observe that the trumeau was made narrow at its base, in order to let pass the pilgrim throngs. At each side of the door stand a few apostles, and among them M. Viollet-le-Duc cited St. Peter as one of the earliest attempts to escape the stereotyped Byzantine models by portraying individual expression in imagery.

In the tympanum is the Pentecost, or perhaps it may be called more exactly the Messiah's mandate to the apostles: Go, teach all nations. Christ is surrounded by a gloria, and the Greek cross of his nimbus symbolizes divinity. From his outstretched hands spread rays which touch the head of each apostle. The explanations of the lintel stone have been various. It would seem to represent the strange peoples of the world to be won by Gospel preaching. Around the tympanum are eight medallions, thought to interpret John the Evangelist and the seven churches of Asia he exhorted.

In 1136 an Auvergne noble, Pons de Montboissier, became abbot of Vézelay (d. 1161), when the forechurch was practically finished, but without doubt while its statuary was in progress, for certain uncut sides of the capitals prove that the stones were set up in the rough and carved *in situ*. Under Abbot Pons, Vézelay emancipated itself from Cluniac rule. He was the brother of Peter the Venerable of Cluny, who had become prior of Vézelay at twenty years of age. In vain the amenable Peter counseled Pons to show a more conciliatory spirit toward the restless townsmen, but Pons was as stubbornly convinced of the righteousness of his monastery's privileges as is many a modern landlord who holds vast areas among the unlanded millions. He held a stiff head against popular demands, the trouble grew aggravated, and the embittered burghers passed beyond their first fair demands and compromised their cause. Abbot Pons was driven out, but returned a victor after Louis VII had investigated the case and imposed a heavy fine on the citizens. Some have thought that the penalty money was expended on the elaborate sculptures of the abbey church. The people might oppose their feudal master, but they were aware that their material prosperity came from the pilgrimage church of the monastery, and each Burgundian was proud to show the visiting strangers the region's exceptional ability in stonecutting.

In Vézelay occurred two notable gatherings of mediæval history. Here, on March 31, 1146, St. Bernard preached the Second Crusade, on the hillside without the northern gate. Abbot Pons built on the site the chapel of the Holy Cross, wherein was preserved the tribune on which the saint had stood. The leaders of France flocked into this valley of Burgundy, Louis VII and his brilliant queen, Aliénor of Aquitaine.[293]

St. Bernard had been commissioned by the pope to set the new venture in motion, and he threw his whole passionate heart into the enterprise. Standing above the vast gathering, he read the papal letter that told of Odessa's fall, two years earlier, and the horrifying massacre of eastern Christians. It was sound statesmanship that discerned the menace of the Eastern Question; the advance of the Seljukian Turk was indeed a knotty problem for the XII century, when XX-century Europe, after oceans of blood, has not settled the trouble. We may be sure that Bernard of Clairvaux used no flatteries in addressing the throng at Vézelay, if his public word was as uncompromising as his private letters: "Up! soldier of Christ! Go, expiate your sins! The breath of corruption is on every side. The license of manners is unchecked. Brigandage goes unpunished. *Debout, soldats du Christ!*" We know that his words of flame swept the crowd, and that, as at Clermont, fifty years earlier, again rose the cry: "God wills it! The Cross! The Cross!" The seductive queen, whose equivocal conduct on this very crusade was to start centuries of calamity for France, threw herself at Bernard's feet, to receive from his hand the Cross. The lowly people jostled with the lords to take the vow, "*les menues gens et les gens de grand air,*" for crusades were democratic things that did more than aught else to break up feudal autocracy.

The eager men and women of 1146 knelt in the actual nave and narthex of

---

[293] In his *Via Crucis*, F. Marion Crawford has described the great gathering at Vézelay.

Vézelay's abbatial. The choir which we have to-day was not yet built. In 1165 a fire damaged the choir of the Madeleine. A year later the exiled archbishop of Canterbury, Thomas Becket, excommunicated his enemies in England from Vézelay's pulpit. The new choir was built mainly under Abbot Girard d'Arcy (1171-96), and is Burgundy's Primary Gothic, though a generation behind the work of that phase in the Ile-de-France. Unpracticed hands made its vaulting, whose web is not built elastically as in the true Gothic fashion; the stones were welded in a compact mass by a bath of mortar. Viollet-le-Duc suggested that Abbot Hugues, deposed by the pope in 1206 for indebtedness, may have expended more than he should on the church.

The choir was well advanced when, in July of 1191, the second great gathering at Vézelay occurred. Here Philippe-Auguste and Richard Cœur-de-Lion met, swore eternal friendship, and then marched south together for the Third Crusade. Before ever they reached Palestine their pact of good will was broken, as was only to be expected with the virus of the Capet-Angevin duel in their veins. Richard's mother, Aliénor, had flouted Philippe's father, her first husband, on the former great enterprise for the East which had been initiated at Vézelay. The Madeleine church reconstructed its west frontispiece in the XIII century in order to light better its narthex; the pignon is overheavy and rather odd.

Three times St. Louis came to pray in the famous Burgundian pilgrim church, his last visit being a few months before his death while crusading in Africa. Then, in Provence in 1279, was discovered what was claimed to be the real body of the Magdalene. Before the XIII century was ended the prestige of Vézelay's pilgrimages was a thing of the past. The monastery's ruin was consummated during the religious wars.[294] Such was the decrepitude into which the splendid church fell, that only a complete restoration by Viollet-le-Duc, from 1840 to 1858, saved the edifice from collapse.

Because Vézelay's nave belongs to Burgundy's school of Romanesque it is spacious and amply lighted; no gloom, no cramping here. Such a nave could lead up to a Gothic choir, without sharp contrast. The choir, taken by itself, may be a cold work, but the sublimity of its setting places it beyond criticism. There is no more romantically ideal a vista in architecture than the white choir of Vézelay, as it appears from the narthex through the imaged portico. Seen thus down the prospect of the sober nave four hundred feet away, it rises like the crusaders' dream of the Heavenly Jerusalem.

The dominant note of Vézelay's interior is serenity. Pace up and down its deserted aisles as a warm June day fades. The rose glow of sunset transmutes the coarse, porous stones to glory and the church seems voicing, *securo e gaudioso*, the grand old plain-chant psalmody which through long centuries echoed here. With you, like a tangible presence, is Faith's certitude, the certitude of John the Baptist who witnessed, the vision of John the Evangelist who loved, the impassioned tranquillity of Mary of Magdala. Here reigns the benignant gladness, *benigna letizia*,

[294] The Huguenot leader, Théodore de Béze, was born in the bourg of Vézelay. His brother, a canon in the church of St. Lazare at Avallon, espoused the opposite side with equal zest.

that Dante attributes to St. Bernard in Paradise. The luminous stillness of Vézelay testifies that he that cometh to God must believe that He is. Here Faith is an overwhelming acquiescence of the conscience as entire as was the belief of the men and women of the XII century who, when they heard the preacher's word, responded with the cry: "The Cross! The Cross!" In the solitary abbatial of to-day, half forgotten on a bypath of the world, breathes the living quietude, the active repose, the voluntary discipline of its old Benedictine builders. "Faith is the substance of things to be hoped for, the evidence of things that appear not. Without faith, it is impossible to please God."

Like the Tag, in India, there is here a supersensual art beauty that renews the jaded spirit. Both have been embalmed for eternity in a vivifying peace. "Without holiness no man shall see God," thought the faulty, vehement, crusading generations who prayed in Vezelay's church, and holiness, then, meant primarily the humble repentance of sins. Whoever it was built the tomb of the Indian princess at Agra, whoever it was built the church in Burgundy called after Mary of Magdala, he worked in something more than stones and mortar. At Agra you end by thinking that the secret of the enthralling magic lies in the marvel of atmosphere, the deep soft shadows which break the dazzling sun expanses. At Vézelay, in the groping effort to put its spell into words, you end by saying that the beauty lies in the space which the inclosing walls have so holily shut in. But what analysis or what detailed description can convey how the spirit is impressed by this shrine, named for the Sinner who poured out the precious ointment with a Faith and Love so complete that it washed her clean!

In such a church come flashes of insight, momentary liftings of the veil, periods of mental fecundity that make clear why the true mystic passes without loss from his isolated reverie of Divine Love to an intensely practical activity, and when you begin to understand that you are on the way to a comprehensive sympathy with that pillar of French Christianity, that apostle sent of God as surely as was Paul to the Gentiles—Bernard the Burgundian, who prayed and preached in this abbey church.

THE GOTHIC COLLEGIATE AT SEMUR-EN-AUXOIS[295]

> Les Français, fils ainés de l'antiquité, Romain par le génie, sont Grec par le caractère. Inquiets et volages dans le bonheur; constant et invincibles dans l'aversité; formés pour les arts; civilisés jusqu'à l'excès durant le calme de l'État; grossiers et sauvages dans les troubles politiques; flottants comme des vaisseaux sans lest au gré des passions; enthusiastes du bien et du mal; aimants pusillanimes de la vie pendant la paix; prodigues de leur

[295] *Congrès Archéologique*, 1907, p. 64, Pierre de Truchis; Abbé Bouzerand, *Mémoirs sur l'église Notre Dame de Semur*, 1864; *ibid., Histoire générale de Semur-en-Auxois*; Ledeuil, *Notice sur Semur-en-Auxois* (Semur-en-Auxois, 1886); Taylor et Nodier, *Voyage pittoresque et romantique dans l'ancienne France. Bourgogne* (Paris, Didot, 1863), folio; Max Quantin, *Répertoire archéol. du département de l'Yonne* (Paris, 1908); Eugène Lefèvre-Pontalis, "Les caractères distinctifs des écoles gothique de la Champagne et de la Bourgogne," in *Congrès Archéologique*, 1907, p. 546.

jours dans les batailles; charmants dans leur pays; insupportable chez l'étranger; tels furent les Athéniens d'autrefois, tels sont les Français d'aujourd'hui.

—CHATEAUBRIAND.

If the traveler has chosen little Avallon as the center from which to explore Burgundian churches, Semur-en-Auxois, lying a few miles to its east, will soon be visited. Picturesque and well kept, it is perched on a crest round which loops the river, a site such as a feudal baron chose, when possible, for his lair. The donjon towers at Semur belonged to a fortress built by Duke Philippe le Hardi.

The collegiate church of Notre Dame, included with the best Gothic work in Burgundy, derived indirectly from the choir of Auxerre Cathedral, through the church of Our Lady at Dijon. About 1225 the builders began to replace the XI-century Notre Dame at Semur by the present edifice, which reproduced the columnal piers with salient crockets that distinguish the most beautiful of Dijon's churches. By 1250 they had terminated the choir, transept, and the bay of the nave touching the transept. The nave and transept are too narrow for their height, because they followed the same ground plan as the antecedent Romanesque church. Burgundy seemed to enjoy a problem in construction. Here, the arches of the vault being excessively pointed, the flying buttresses were made with a radius greater than is to be found elsewhere.

Early in the XIV century, three new bays were added to the nave, as is shown by their main arches, which are more pointed than those of the earlier bays. Then about 1370, probably after a fire, the nave's stone roof was rebuilt and its triforium suppressed. The religious wars of the XVI century played havoc here in Notre Dame. During the Revolution, for two entire weeks, cartload after cartload of art treasures was carried away from the collegiate. Happily, the transept's northern portal escaped destruction, for it is a small masterpiece of Burgundian sculpture. Its tympanum relates the adventures in India of St. Thomas the Apostle, whose builder's rule was said to be of gold, in emblem of his spiritual masoncraft. St. Jerome would not sanction the Indian legends of the architect apostle, but the story of King Goldoforus and St. Thomas lingered in popular favor.

In one of the chapels of Semur's collegiate church is a XIV-century window dedicated to no saint, telling no Scriptural story, but merely setting forth, in large, clear panels, the working day of various artisans—dyer, vintager, butcher, tailor. The theologians who directed the iconography of mediæval churches permitted the old guildsmen to translate into sign language their sensible idea that honest work was prayer.

The keystone over the sanctuary of Notre Dame, where eight ribs meet, is the most beautiful ever carved—a Coronation of the Virgin. Throughout the church the sculpture is exceptional. In the choir and transept, carved heads lean out from the triforium's spandrels, heads of monarch, bishop, monk, nun, and chatelaine, with here and there a grinning mask or grotesque. The restorer has followed a wrong path when he makes the exaggerated images in XIII-century sculpture exceed the ideal or realistic ones. Semur's triforium is among the most beautiful in

Gothic art. On some of the capitals of the collegiate are vintage scenes, as was natural in this land of famous wines. There are noted modern vineyards, such as Chambertin and Vougeot, which were cultivated by the monks of Cluny and Cîteaux for many a long century.

THE CATHEDRAL OF AUXERRE[296]

J'erre à pas muets dans ce profond asile,
Solitude de pierre, immuable, immobile,
Image du séjour par Dieu même habité,
Où tout est profondeur, mystère, éternité ...
La voix du clocher en son doux s'évapore;
Et, le front appuyé, contre un pilier sonore,
Je le sens, tout ému du retentissement,
Vibrer comme une clef d'un céleste instrument ...
Les rayons du soir que l'Occident rappelle,
Éteignent au vitraux leur dernière étincelle,
Au fond du sanctuaire un feu flottant qui luit,
Scintille comme un œil ouvert sur cette nuit;
Alors, portant mes yeux des pavés à la voûte
Je sens que dans ce vide une oreille m'écoute,
Qu'un invisible ami dans la nef répandu,
M'attire à lui, me parle un langage entendu,
Se communique à moi dans un silence intime
Et dans son vaste sein m'enveloppe et m'abîme.

—LAMARTINE (1790-1869; born in Burgundy).

At Auxerre, on the Yonne, two Gothic edifices stand imposingly above the city, the cathedral of St. Stephen and the abbatial church named after that bishop of Auxerre, St. Germain, who foretold the sanctity of *la pucellette* Geneviève in the village of Nanterre by Paris, and whose own sanctity was so assured that more churches have been called for him than for any other saint of France save the supreme St. Martin himself. Paris put her church of St. Germain l'Auxerrois under

[296] *Congrès Archéologique*, 1850, p. 22; and 1907, p. 167, Charles Porée; p. 599, Camille Enlart, on the sculptured doors of Auxerre Cathedral: Camille Enlart, *La cathédrale d'Auxerre* (Collection, Petites Monographies), (Paris, H. Laurens): A. Chérest, *La cathédrale d'Auxerre. Conferences d'Auxerre* (Auxerre, 1868); Émile Lambin, "La cathédrale d'Auxerre," in *Revue de l'art chrétien*, 1897, vol. 47, p. 383; Charles Porée, "Le chœur de la cathédrale d'Auxerre," in *Bulletin Monumental*, 1906, vol. 70, p. 251; Louise Pillion, "Sculpture de la cathédrale d'Auxerre," in *Revue de l'art chrétien*, 1905, p. 278; Viollet-le-Duc, *Dictionnaire de l'architecture*, vol. 4, p. 131, on construction; vol. 9, p. 447, on vitrail; Victor Petit, "Description des villes et campagnes du département de l'Yonne" (Auxerre, 1876). In the *Annuaire de l'Yonne*, earlier studies on Auxerre are, 1841, p. 38, F. de Lasteyrie; 1843, p. 128, V. Petit; 1846, p. 207, and 1847, p. 141, Challe; 1872, p. 161, and 1873. p. 3, Daudin; André Philippe, "L'architecture religieuse au XIe et au XIIe siècle dans l'ancien diocèse d'Auxerre," in *Bulletin Monumental*, 1904, vol. 68, *passim*. Other notices on Auxerre in the *Bulletin Monumental* are, 1847, vol. 13, p. 153, and 1849, vol. 15, p. 145, Victor Petit; 1872, vol. 38, pp. 494, 744, Victor Petit; Abbé Lebeuf, *Histoire d'Auxerre*; E. Moulton, *La guerre au XVIe siècle* (Paris, H. Laurens).

his protection. He had been the ruler of this region of middle France under the Emperor Honorius, and was a soldier and devoted to sports; yet the old bishop of Auxerre, St. Amâtre, chose him as his successor, divining in him a man destined to do great things for God.

The splendid abbey church at Auxerre stands on the site of the oratory which rose over the grave of St. Germain. Queen Clotilde on her way to wed Clovis, pausing here in 490, renewed the shrine by a church, which became the nucleus for an abbey favored by all three dynasties of France—Merovingian, Carolingian, and Capetian.[297] The monastery was a noted school whither came St. Patrick, and many generations later St. Thomas Becket studied here after he had finished his law courses at Bologna.

In memory of Auxerre's reputation as a teacher, the cathedral has twice represented the Liberal Arts, in glass and in sculpture. The choir of St. Étienne Cathedral was begun about 1215 by a well-known schoolman, Bishop Guillaume de Seignelay, who undertook it at his own expense, stimulated thereto by some of the parish churches which had lately been rebuilt in the new way. The crypt (c. 1130), retained under the choir of the new cathedral, had been begun by the bishop, St. Hugues de Châlons, a friend of St. Bernard, and probably finished by his successor, Hugues de Mâcon (1137-51), the first abbot of Pontigny, and St. Bernard's kinsman and childhood intimate. Of the cathedral of their day only the present crypt remains.

When Bishop Guillaume de Seignelay was transferred to the see of Paris, in 1220, he worked on the west façade of Notre Dame of the capital, and his successor at Auxerre, Henri de Villeneuve, completed the choir of St. Étienne in 1234. Two lancets in the sanctuary are his gifts. The cathedral of Auxerre was building at both ends, while between lay the ancient Romanesque nave. The easternmost bay of the nave is XIII century, but the next five bays were erected only during the XIV century, at which time most of the statues of the western portals were done. With the choir's superb stained glass they form the supreme accessory of this cathedral. M. Enlart holds Auxerre's imagery to be, for delicacy and charm, among the best produced by the XIV century, and that the statuettes of the Liberal Arts, in the

---

[297] St. Germain's abbatial is less pure Gothic than the cathedral's choir. Beneath its sanctuary are two superimposed crypts, the lower one of the IX century, and that above it belonging to the XIII-century reconstruction of the abbey church. Conflagrations wiped out several early churches of the monastery. In the XII century rose the Romanesque tower—one of the best in France; until 1820 it was attached to the nave. A total reconstruction of the abbatial was necessary in 1277, but after the upper crypt and the choir were undertaken there came a pause. The abbot here (1309-39), who erected the crenelated inclosure walls of the monastery, resumed the church as Rayonnant Gothic. Urban V, the greatest of the Avignon patrons of art and letters, had been abbot of St. Germain (1352), and his arms were cut on a keystone of the new nave, to which he contributed, as did his successor, Gregory XI. Soon after the church was completed it was pillaged during the religious wars. Napoleon turned the establishment into a hospital, which it still is. *Congrès Archéologique*, 1907, p. 182, C. Porée; p. 627, Jules Tillet; Abbé V. B. Henry, *Histoire de l'abbaye de St. Germain d'Auxerre* (Auxerre, Gallot, 1853); Victor Petit, "Les cryptes de St. Germain d'Auxerre," in *Bulletin Monumental*, 1872, vol. 38, p. 494; Viollet-le-Duc, *Dictionnaire de l'Architecture*, vol. 3, p. 377.

spandrels over the canopies of the David-Balthazar groups, are equal to Greek terra-cotta figurines. The Judgment of Solomon by the northwest door is excellent. Within and without the stonecutting of the transept's southern façade should be observed. At that entrance appeared an early example of an accolated arch, cited by M. Enlart as an indication of the English derivation of Flamboyant Gothic in France, since during the XIV century they were masters of Auxerre for a time.

As the Hundred Years' War relaxed building enterprise, the nave was not covered by a masonry roof till the XV century, about the time when Jeanne d'Arc paused to pray in Auxerre Cathedral on her memorable journey of eleven days from Lorraine to Touraine, across a France ravaged by civil and foreign wars.[298] The gracious Flamboyant west front of Auxerre's chief church is an expression of the hope and national pride renewed in France by the Maid's feat at Orléans. The well-designed north tower proves that the final phase of Gothic art in France did not pass away in decrepitude; had only the south tower been raised above the roof, this frontispiece could claim foremost rank.

For bold and light construction Auxerre's choir is notable, and it made a school in Burgundian Gothic. It has only one radiating chapel—that in the axis—because it followed the ground plan of the Romanesque crypt, its foundation. The charming Champagne disposition of planting columns between chapel and ambulatory was made use of; perhaps the pillars and stilted arches of Auxerre are rather too frail in their proportions. The same feature was used in the abbey church of St. Germain, and when the church of St. Eusèbe[299] rebuilt its chevet, in the XV century, pillars were again placed to divide the curving aisle and the radiating chapels.

Auxerre Cathedral showed another trait of the Champagne school of Gothic—an interior passageway beneath the aisle windows. The plain wall below it is relieved by a kind of arched corbel course not very satisfactory; the arches and the capitals upon which they rest are present, but there is no shaft to support the capitals, from above each of which reaches out a well-sculptured head. One of these busts represents the Erythræan priestess referred to in the *Dies iræ*:

> That day of wrath, that dreadful day,
> When Heaven and Earth shall pass away,

[298] At her trial in Rouen Jeanne spoke of Auxerre Cathedral: "*En route, je traversai Auxerre, où j'entendis la messe dans la principale église.... Alors, j'avais fréquemment mes voix.*" Marius Sepet, *Au temps de la Pucelle, récits et tableaux* (Paris, P. Téqui, 1905).

[299] The abbey church at St. Eusèbe is of archæological interest. The octagonal tower over its altar, forming internally a lantern, is of the XII century, as are the piers and their arches. A pause came between the making of the nave's lower and upper parts, for the church did not follow the usual custom of advancing bay by bay, but was constructed story by story. The west front is full Gothic, and the ambulatory of the XIII century. The original choir was in large part replaced by the present well-built Flamboyant Gothic one, finished by 1530. What used to be the episcopal palace of Auxerre is to-day the Prefecture. It shows, in its wall on the river side, the Romanesque gallery built by Bishop Hugues de Châlons (1116-36). Its hall, with pignons alike at both ends, was erected by Bishop Guillaume de Mello (1247-70). *Congrès Archéologique*, 1907, p. 188; Corberon, *Auxerre, ses monuments*; Lescuyer, "Notice sur l'église de St. Eusèbe," in *l'Annuaire de l'Yonne*, 1839, p. 318; 1845, p. 103, "St. Eusèbe," Max Quantin.

As David and the Sibyl say.

The XIII century distinguished only that one sibyl whom St. Augustine's *City of God* had popularized as the prophetess of the Last Judgment, but later in the Middle Ages all ten of them were represented, and certain Renaissance windows represented as many as twelve pagan prophetesses.

The placing of sculptured heads in the spandrels of arches was not infrequent in Burgundy, though occasionally merely one salient crocket was used. The cathedral of Nevers,[300] south of Auxerre, went a step farther and chiseled a small figurine in the spandrels of its triforium, like the angels of Lincoln's choir. Moreover, the colonettes of Nevers' triforium are borne on the backs of small crouching caryatides—a Lombard echo. In France, Nevers' cathedral of St. Cyr was exceptional in having an apse at both east and west ends, like a Rhenish church. One is forced to relegate the beautiful little capital of the Nivermois to a footnote, which is what France herself seems to be doing to the well-set town on the Loire which in England or beyond the Rhine would be made into a small residence city. Its palace, parks, cathedral, and numerous churches, its faïence industry and fortifications give it the air of a little capital.

Auxerre is another Mecca of stained glass in France. Its choir possesses almost forty windows (1220-30) of the school of Chartres, half of them being in the ambulatory and Lady chapel. Unfortunately, the lower panels were wrecked in 1567, and the east window of the axis chapel was destroyed in the Franco-Prussian war; the grisaille design throughout is mastery. The opaline loveliness of the choir's clearstory grisaille has drawn from M. Viollet-le-Duc one of his most eloquent pages.[301] Each bay is filled with twin lancets surmounted by a rose; each lancet

[300] The west apse of Nevers' Cathedral, dedicated to St. Juliette, mother of the child martyr, St. Cyr, formed, with its crypt and transept, part of the XII-century Romanesque edifice. Late in the XIII century was built a Gothic nave, which was reconstructed after a fire in 1308, and again its outer walls were reconstructed in the Flamboyant Gothic day. The present choir dates from the XIV century. The fine tower at the transept's southern façade was built 1506 to 1528. Nevers' former ducal palace, of the XV century, stands on a park overlooking the Loire. The Romanesque abbey church of St. Étienne, founded, tradition says, by St. Columbanus, combines the schools of Auvergne and Burgundy, and is important to archæologists because the date of its building, 1063 to 1097, is certain. The expense of constructing it caused the Count of Nevers to forego the First Crusade. Bishop Ives of Chartres consecrated the church in 1097. *Congrès Archéologique*, 1913, p. 300, Louis Serbat; Gaston Congny, *Bourges et Nevers*; J. Locquin, *Nevers et Moulins* (Collection, Villes d'art célèbres), (Paris, H. Laurens); Monseigneur Crosnier, *Monographie de la cathédrale de Nevers* (1854); Abbé Sery, *Les deux apsides de la cathédrale de Nevers* (1899); Morellet, Barat, et Bussière, *Le Nivermois* (1840), 2 vols.; Paul Meunier, *Nevers historique et pittoresque* (1901).

[301] "Because the pearly white surfaces of the grisaille would make the adjacent colored surfaces appear heavy and opaque, they introduced, into these latter, limpid blues and yellows, very light reds, whites with a greenish or rosy tint. In the high windows of the cathedral of Auxerre they first tried this method, and here the grisaille is chased with a large and firm design that offsets the transparency of the colorless surfaces. Notice how the pedestal and the canopy, both very light, bind together the bands of grisaille on either side, while the latter is heavily painted with a trellis and rich ornaments. In Auxerre, the grisaille is found only in the lateral windows which are seen obliquely. The apse windows,

has a large figure set in uncolored glass—one of the first attempts made to give more light to an interior. Those crusading generations visioned their Heavenly Jerusalem in sculpture at Vézelay, in color at Auxerre:

> With jaspers glow thy bulwarks,
> Thy streets with emeralds blaze,
> The sardius and the topaz
> Unite in thee their rays:
> Thine ageless walls are bonded
> With amethyst unpriced;
> The saints build up its fabric,
> And the corner stone is Christ.
>
> They stand, those halls of Zion,
> Conjubilant with song,
> And bright with many an angel,
> And all the martyr throng:
> The Prince is ever in them;
> Their daylight is serene,
> The pastures of the blessed
> Are decked in glorious sheen.
>
> There is the throne of David,
> And there, from care released,
> The song of them that triumph,
> The shout of them that feast;
> And they who, with their leader,
> Have conquered in the fight,
> For ever and for ever
> Are clad in robes of white.[302]

In the roses of the two bays neighboring the central lancets are the Liberal Arts and virtues contrasted with vices. The choir aisle has a Creation window, and lancets of the popular St. James, St. Nicolas, and St. Eustace. The transept's south rose is Rayonnant. Its north one is Flamboyant, and with the eight golden lights below it was given by Bishop François de Dinteville, the younger (1530-52), who

---

meant to be seen, in face and from a distance, are filled with color. The lateral windows are sufficiently opaque to prevent the solar rays which pass through them from lighting the colored windows on the reverse side. At certain hours the luminous rays throw a pearly light on the colored windows, imparting to them a transparency of tone and a delicacy impossible to describe. The opalescent light from the lateral windows makes a sort of veil of extreme transparency under the lofty vaults, and is pierced by the brilliant tones of the apse windows, producing the sparkle of jewels. Solid outlines then seem to waver like objects seen through a sheet of limpid water. Distance changes values and gains a depth in which the eye loses itself. Hourly during the day these effects are modified, and always with new harmonies of which one never wearies trying to understand."

—Viollet-le-Duc, Dictionnaire de l'architecture, vol. 9, p. 447.

[302] John Mason Neale, translator of "The Rhythm of Bernard of Morlaix" (e. 1140), in *Collected Hymns, Sequences, and Carols* (London, Hodder & Stoughton, 1914), p. 19.

donated also the *Gloria in Excelsis* west rose. But no sooner were all these precious things installed when came the bitter civil wars of the XVI century. No place in France suffered more than Auxerre. An eyewitness of the 1567 sacking wrote: "All the woes of Jerusalem when it fell to the infidel are heaped on our city." Many a citizen died of grief at the town's desolation, and so devastated was every single church that for months no services were held.

A restoration was accomplished by Bishop Jacques Amyot (1571-93), the noted Hellenist, who first brought flexibility and amenity into French prose.[303] His translation of Plutarch—a French classic—molded the ideals of French youth for generations. Unfortunately, because imported foreign taste had won the victory over the national art, this enlightened Renaissance prelate removed some of the ancient windows to light his high altar. His marble bust adorns a pier of the choir of Auxerre Cathedral.

DIJON[304]

Eternal, je me tais; en ta sainte présence
Je n'ose respirer, et mon âme en silence
Admire la hauteur de ton nom glorieux.
Que dirai-je? Abîmés de cette mer profonde,
Pendant qu'à l'infini ta clarté nous inonde,
Pouvons-nous seulement ouvrir nos faibles yeux?

*****

Cessez: qu'espérez-vous de vos incertitudes,
Vains pensers, vains efforts, inutiles études?

---

[303] "Je donne la palme à Jacques Amyot sur tout nos écrivains français."—MON-TAIGNE.

"Quand il s'agit d'une jolie et gracieuse naïveté de langage, on dit aussitôt pour le définir: C'est de la langue d'Amyot."—SAINTE-BEUVE.

[304] *Congrès Archéologique*, 1907, on Dijon, Charles Porée; p. 546, "Les caractères distinctifs des écoles gothiques de la Champagne et de la Bourgogne," E. Lefèvre-Pontalis; A. Kleinclausz, *Dijon et Beaune* (Collection, Villes d'art célèbres), (Paris, H. Laurens); *ibid.*, "L'art funéraire de la Bourgogne," in *Gazette des Beaux-Arts*, 1901-02; *ibid.*, *Claus Sluter et la sculpture bourguignonne au XVe siècle* (Paris, 1906); Abbé L. Chomton, *Histoire de l'église St. Bénigne de Dijon* (Dijon, 1900), folio; G.T. Rivoira, *Lombardic Architecture*, vol. 2, chap. 1, on St. Bénigne (tr. London and New York, 1910); Chanoine Thomas, *Épigraphie de Notre Dame de Dijon* (1904); H. Chabeuf, "Tête sculptée à Notre Dame de Dijon," in *Revue de l'art chrétien*, 1900, vol. 43, p. 472; *ibid.*, *Dijon, monuments et souvenirs* (Dijon, Damudot, 1894); H. Havard, éd., *La France artistique et monumental*, vol. 6, p. 26, Cunisset-Carnot; Alphonse Germain, *Les Néerlandais en Bourgogne*, 1909; Raymond Koechlin, *La sculpture belge et les influences françaises au XIIIe siècle* (Paris, 1903); Louis Courajod, *Leçons professées à l'École du Louvre*, 1887-96. Vol. 2, *Origines de la Renaissance* (Paris, Picard et fils, 1901), 3 vols. On the sculpture at Dijon, see MM. Paul Vitry, Louis Gonse, Léon Palustre, André Michel; A. Humbert, *Sculpture en Bourgogne* (Paris, H. Laurens); Ernest Petit, *Hist. des ducs de Bourgogne de la race capétienne* (Dijon, 1905), 9 vols.; B. de Barante, *Hist. des ducs de Bourgogne de la maison de Valois* (Paris, 1825), 12 vols.; Petit-Dutaillis, *Charles VII, Louis XI, et les premières années de Charles VIII* (Paris, Hachette, 1902); Abbé Chevalier, *Le vénérable Guillaume, abbé de St. Bénigne* (Dijon, 1875).

C'est assez qu'il ait dit: "Je suis Celui qui suis."
Il est tout, il n'est rien de tout ce que je pense;
Avec ces mots profonds j'adore son essence
Et sans y raisonner, en croyant, je poursuis!

—BOSSUET, *Tibi silentium laus* (1627-1704; born in Dijon).

Notre Dame at Dijon (1220-1245). Burgundian Gothic

And finally we come to the capital of Burgundy, to a city of prime importance in the art history of France, although it can claim no one supreme monument.

Dijon's leadership was from 1364 to 1477, under the four art-loving Valois princes, Philippe le Hardi (1364-1404), Jean sans Peur (1404-19), Philippe le Bon (1419-67), and Charles le Téméraire (1467-77). "Never," says Brantôme, "were there four greater princes one after the other than the great dukes of Burgundy." Each in turn on his formal entry into Dijon came to the abbey church of St. Bénigne to take oath to defend the special privileges of his capital. Tradition says that St. Benignus was sent to Christianize Gaul by St. Polycarp, who had known John the Evangelist. The hypothesis is possible, since it is historically certain that Polycarp provided Lyons with its first two bishops. Many a son of Dijon has borne the revered name of Bénigne, none with greater honor for his native city than Bossuet, descended from ancient parliamentary stock. The neo-classic taste of the great preacher's day might prevent his knowing Gothic architecture rightly, but without the centuries that built mediæval cathedrals he had not been what he was.[305]

Dijon became the capital of Burgundy under the first line of Capetian dukes who governed the province from 1032 to 1361 and who gave the city its franchise and privileges. A duke of Burgundy led the right wing at Bouvines, another fought under St. Louis at Mansourah. From Burgundy's reigning line came Pope Calixtus II (1119-24), whose brother went crusading in Spain, where he founded the house from which descended Queen Isabella; Burgundian Capetians also reigned in Portugal. Cluny and Cîteaux were favored by the first line of Burgundy's dukes, to which belonged, by ties of blood, the two greatest abbots of their respective Orders, St. Hugues and St. Bernard. In 1361 the last duke died childless and the duchy returned to the French crown.

Three years later the Valois Capetian king, Jean le Bon, gave Burgundy to his youngest and favorite son, Philippe le Hardi, who won his surname of valiant when fifteen years of age through his defense of his father at the battle of Poitiers.

---

[305] "La gloire de Bossuet est devenue l'une des religions de la France; on la reconnaît, on la proclame, on s'honore soi-même en y apportant chaque jour un nouveau tribut. Bossuet, c'est le génie hébreu, étendu, fécondé par le Christianisme, et ouvert à toutes les acquisitions de l'intelligence, mais retenant quelque chose de l'interdiction souveraine. Il est la voix éloquente par excellence, la plus simple, la plus forte, la plus brusque, la plus familière, la plus soudainement tonnante." —SAINTE-BEUVE.

No city has been more prolific in notable sons than Dijon, where, as Voltaire said, *"le mérite de l'esprit semble être un des caractères des citoyens."* Among them are Rameau, the musician (1683-1764), who founded French opera and discovered important laws in harmony; he and his descendants were exempted from tithes by their native city; Dubois, the sculptor (1626-94), whose Assumption and the high altar of Notre Dame, Dijon, are his best works; the critic and philologist, La Monnaye (b. 1641); the playwright, Crébillon (d. 1762); Piron, the witty epigrammatist (d. 1773); the learned Président de Brosse (1709-77), whose *Lettres d'Italie* are full of Burgundian vivacity and salt, and whose friend, Buffon, the naturalist (1707-88), though born at Montbard, was educated in Dijon, where his father was counselor in the parliament. The grandmother of Madame de Sévigné, St. Jeanne Françoise de Chantal, founder of the Visitation Order, was born at 17 rue Jeannin, 1572. Her father was a president of Dijon's parliament. The sculptor Rude was a son of Dijon (d. 1855), and in this same city that had produced St. Bernard and Bossuet, the most eloquent preacher of the XIX century, Lacordaire, spent his childhood and youth, as his mother came of an old legal family here. Léon Deshairs, *Dijon, architecture des XVIIᵉ et XVIIIᵉ siècles* (Paris, 1910).

When Philippe, by the generous aid of his brother, King Charles V, wedded the richest heiress in Europe, the very plain Marguerite of Flanders, there resulted the political union of Burgundy with the Netherlands that was of important influence on French art. It led to the formation at Dijon of a French-Flemish school of sculpture. The robust middle region of France impressed its own character on the masters from the Lowlands who flocked to the semi-royal court of the dukes, and equally it assimilated the artists who came from Lyons and neighboring regions. The Flemish-Burgundian style controlled the first half of the XV century. Its fusion of national and local art traditions with Flemish realism renewed the vigor of French sculpture, and a truly French Renaissance had already set in before the advent of the Italian spirit. In Dijon took place the evolution that changed the sculpture of the Middle Ages to that of modern times.

The artists who had gathered around Charles V in Paris, were scattered by that king's premature death and the subsequent disorders in the royal domain, and they flocked to the Burgundian court of his brother. Among them were André and Guy de Dammartin, who erected outside the gates of Dijon the Chartreuse of Champmol (1388-96) as a burial place for the Valois line of dukes. The work of the Dammartin family—with whom Flamboyant Gothic became a heritage passing from father to son—can be found at Bourges, Poitiers, Tours, Le Mans, and Nantes.

What parts of the Chartreuse monastery now remain constitute an asylum. The sculptured portal of the church shows kneeling images of Philippe le Hardi and his duchess Marguerite, and in the cloister is the noted Well of the Prophets, conceived, and in part executed, by Claus Sluter in 1395, and finished by his nephew, Claus de Werve, in 1403. The *Puits de Moïse* was so called because the statue of Moses, alone of the six prophets, shows religious analogy with the biblical character it stands for. The others are realistic studies of tradesman, rich citizen, or Jew, in eccentric costumes that probably were copied from those in the mystery plays of the day. With these prophet images of Claus Sluter, modern sculpture took birth.

The two most regal tombs of the Middle Ages, those of Philippe le Hardi and his son Jean sans Peur, were originally in the Chartreuse church, but were broken up by the Revolution. They were reset, for a time, in St. Bénigne's church, and now are installed in the XV-century guard hall of the ducal palace, a part of Dijon's Art Museum, raising that collection to first-class rank. Near them are placed the elaborately carved and painted altarpieces brought from Termonde by the dukes. The pomp and pageantry of the knighthood described by Froissart and Commines breathes in the two grandiose tombs of Dijon, and the progeny of sumptuous funereal monuments they inspired. Cowled figures called *pleureurs* are set in niches around each sarcophagus. They seem like symbols of the lesser people's sufferings in the dire Hundred Years' War, when France became a field of carnage. Foreign invasion, the Great Schism of the West, pest, massacres, misrule, lawlessness— such was the accumulation of miseries that only the heaven-sent Jehanne la Pucelle, from the far borders of the land, could right the immeasurable *pitié* there was in the kingdom of France.

Though Burgundy suffered less than the royal domain, the lesser people had to pay heavily for the prodigal largess of their dukes. At times the lavish giving of Philippe le Hardi bordered upon folly; while on visits of state he was forced to put his jewels in pawn to obtain sufficient funds for his home journey. When he died, in 1404, it took six weeks for his funeral *cortège* to journey from Brussels to Dijon, and those of his household who accompanied the body were provided with Capuchin capes of black cloth. That is the procession represented by the statuettes around his sarcophagus, though, unfortunately, the original order of their march has been lost. Among the eighty *pleurants* of the two ducal tombs are only eight restorations.

Jean de Marville, a Lorraine master, designed Duke Philippe's monument, whose imagery is in greater part from the hand of Claus Sluter and Claus de Werve, Netherlanders (1384-1411). De Werve made most of Duke Jean's monument, a replica of his father's tomb; it was finished by an Aragonese sculptor, Juan de Heurta, and Antoine le Moiturier from Avignon. The latter was nephew of Jacques Morel of Lyons, trained in the Dijon studios, who made for the daughter of John the Fearless, the Duchess of Bourbon, a tomb in Souvigny's abbatial near Moulins, which M. Enlart has called the most masterly work in sculpture of the XV century.

Dijon built no XIII-century cathedral. What to-day is its cathedral was originally the abbey church of St. Bénigne, not of architectural pre-eminence, but rich in historic memories. Abbot Hugues d'Arcy began it in 1280, in the hour of hope and energy that followed on the Council of Lyons, where Greek and Latin churches fraternally united. In 1286 the choir was dedicated and the relics of St. Benignus transferred from the crypt to the new sanctuary.

St. Bénigne of Dijon is a secondary church compared with its neighbors, the cathedrals of Bourges and Lyons. The profiles are emasculated, the clearstory windows lack sufficient height, the wall surface above the triforium is monotonous, the denuded triforium of the nave lacks capitals, and despite the warm brown color of the stone, the general aspect of the interior is glacial. The Gothic effect has been marred further by the numerous busts and statues brought here from other churches after the Revolution.

Far surpassing in interest the somewhat pinchbeck Gothic upper church of St. Bénigne is its crypt, the oldest Romanesque monument in Burgundy. It lies beyond the actual apse. For eight hundred years it was the foundation of a rotunda church of the same type as the round church at Cambridge, England, the prototypes for both being certain Roman mausoleums. Originally the Dijon crypt opened westward on a crypt now lost—the basement for a Latin cross church—and where that juncture occurred are vestiges of buildings that antedate the actual crypt. The round church beyond the apse of St. Bénigne's Gothic abbatial was destroyed during the Revolution, and its crypt filled in and forgotten. In 1858, while digging foundations for a new sacristy beyond the choir, the circular chamber was unearthed, in which was found a tombstone, apparently the ancient one of St. Benignus. Once again the venerable subterranean shrine became a pilgrimage for Burgundy.

St. Bénigne's crypt has double circular aisles. Its sculpture is rude, even amor-

phous, and testifies to the extinction of the art during the Barbarians' immigra-
tions. These rough designs on the capitals of St. Bénigne are, as it were, the first
stutterings of the national pæans in praise of God and country that are the imaged
portals of Gothic cathedrals.

Abbot William of Volpiano, who made St. Bénigne's Romanesque rotunda
and its adjacent basilica, came from Cluny to reform the spiritual life of the Dijon
monastery and rebuild its church. Born on an island in the lake of Orta, he had
crossed the Alps with Abbot Majolus of Cluny. For over thirty years he exercised
his double function of administrative reformer and architect in Burgundy[306] and
in Normandy, introducing certain Lombard features such as alternating piers,
arched corbel courses, and superimposed arcades for decorative effect, this latter
being a Ravennate motive adopted by Lombardy. He began his two connecting
churches at Dijon in 1001, and completed them in 1018, when there was a solemn
dedication at which St. William preached most movingly. St. Bénigne is, therefore,
the first-recorded monument built after the terrors of the year 1000, described by
Raoul Glaber, who lived in this monastery.

William of Volpiano founded schools, taught the plain chant to children, re-
vised Gregorian music, and established centers for craftsmen. In manner he was
authoritative, but one on intimate terms with him wrote: "No one can tell to what
degree in him rose mercy and compassion. In famine time, he sold the gold plate
of the church to feed the people." To this day a gateway of Dijon bears his name,
the Porte Guillaume.

A century later Abbot Jarenton of St. Bénigne invited monks from Cluny to
reanimate the spiritual life of his monastery. Paschal II blessed the Dijon abbatial,
repaired after the fall of a tower in 1096. When in 1107 Aleth de Montbard, mother
of St. Bernard, died in her castle two miles from Dijon, Abbot Jarenton hastened
out to Fontaine-lès-Dijon to claim the body of the saintly woman for his hallowed
crypt of St. Bénigne, and an enthusiastic procession carried the Blessed Aleth to
the city. St. Bernard was an unknown lad at the time.

------

[306] Tournus abbey (Saône-et-Loire), when founded, was affiliated with the Columban tradition. From 946 to 980 the church was rebuilt, and again from 1008 to 1028, under
the auspices of William of Volpiano, abbot of St. Bénigne. On its outer walls are Lombard
mural arcaded bands. The massive forechurch, or narthex of three bays, has two stories of
different dates, the lower one about 950, and the upper about 980. The vault of the latter—a
cradle carried on brackets—is the earliest example extant in France of a wide-span masonry
roof at such a height. Tournus exemplified the militant spirit of Burgundy's Romanesque
school by experimenting with every kind of vault, cradle, half cradle, transverse cradle, and
groin. The pier arcades of the main church are of William of Volpiano's time. The transept
and choir are early XII century, and in that same period the reconstructed nave was covered
by an experiment in stone roofing which never made a school; it had been used in Persia
in the VI century. A series of half barrels borne on lintels were placed side by side across
the wide nave, from north to south, instead of one long tunnel vault from east to west. The
system allowed for the better lighting of the upper church, and as each barrel vault was
buttressed by the one next it, only at the east and west ends of the edifice was abutment
required. *Congrès Archéologique*, 1899, pp. 223, 236; and 1909; Clement Heaton, in *Journal of
the Royal Institute of British Architects*, 3d series, 1909.

In 1131, Pope Eugene III blessed the Dijon abbatial subsequent to still other restorations. Finally, in 1271, the easternmost church of William of Volpiano was wiped out by fire (though his rotunda church was to stand till 1792), and the present St. Bénigne was begun immediately on the site of the destroyed Latin cross basilica.

If the ex-abbatial which is now Dijon's cathedral is secondary in size and character, the parish church of Notre Dame is a veritable gem of Gothic architecture, faultless in construction and of singular purity and unity. Its influence on the Gothic art of the province was widespread. After a fire in 1137, which consumed half the city, a Romanesque Notre Dame had risen. It was cited, in 1178, as the first of the town, its bells sounding the opening and the shutting of the city gates and alarms for fire.

The present church of Notre Dame was begun about 1220; a record referred to it as in use in 1245. The architect had to contend with difficulties. His funds were so small that a minimum of building material was necessary. Three sides of his edifice were bounded by public thoroughfares; hence it was impossible to spread out the piles required by flying buttresses; at the same time the limited plot of ground made it imperative not to encumber the small interior by clumsy piers. How to construct a secure edifice without big piers, thick walls, or flying buttresses was the problem.

The builder showed his genius when he used the inclosure wall to counterbut the vault thrust and yet dared open these walls by generous Gothic windows. For ten feet above the ground the walls are heavy; then they become a mere shell, skillfully doubled by the use of colonnettes of durable stone, each slender shaft being so weighted that it stands with the security of iron.

The interior of Notre Dame appears charmingly spacious and airy. The XVII century added circular windows to the triforium of the apse, in character with the church, however. The exterior of the apse is plain and neat and, with the central lantern tower, composes an architectural group of simple elegance. The eastern buttresses fulfill a triple function as piers, as walls, and as counterbutting members. Technical subtlety is to be found throughout Notre Dame. The vaults of the side aisles were constructed to brace the principal span. The piers are uniform monoliths, but a sexpartite vault was built, though for a generation that system had been discarded in the north. The coping stones over the capitals of each alternate pier were enlarged to catch there the heavier weight.

There are so many points of resemblance between Notre Dame of Dijon and the choir of Auxerre Cathedral, begun in 1215, that M. Charles Porée has thought that the same architect designed both. Their profiles are alike, their capitals have similar salient crockets, and their colonnettes were cut from the quarry according to the rock's horizontal strata, and not by the usual method of vertical cutting.

In boldness of technique the small Dijon church is a masterpiece to which many an eloquent page has been devoted.[307] Beneath an apparent simplicity is

[307] Viollet-le-Duc, *Dictionnaire de l'Architecture*, vol. 4, pp. 131-147; Huysmans, *L'Oblat*, chap. 5, on Notre Dame of Dijon. In his story, which is the continuation of *En Route* and

unsurpassed scientific construction. The great engineer Vauban praised it, as did Soufflot, the XVIII-century architect of the Panthéon at Paris. The balanced equilibrium of the national art can be carried no farther, and only the use of hard Tonnerre stone permitted this successful audacity. Were a modern student to present such a plan to any commission, said M. Lassus, he would be dismissed as mad.

While the nave was building a narthex was added before the western entrance, consisting of a fifty-foot-deep porch. Notre Dame's west façade rides astride two rows of pillars set close together before the narthex, again a case of strength being attained by the able use of double walls. The façade's superimposed arcades, used merely as decoration, as at Pisa, prevented the employment of strong buttress ridges, and give to the western front of the church a most un-Gothic aspect. It cannot be said that the lamp of truth is upheld, since the frontispiece makes no pretense to express the three-aisled interior, but rises above the roof like an abstract screen. The gargoyles that alternate with some ancient superbly cut panels of foliage across the west front, date only from 1881, and, as usual with restorations, the grotesque element has been overemphasized. A manuscript of the XIII century relates that the original gargoyles were removed when a bridegroom (a money-lender) about to enter the church was killed by the fall of a protruding image that represented a man gripping a money bag.

The imagery of Notre Dame's portal has been entirely obliterated. When the Revolution voted to destroy "all signs of fanaticism," an apothecary of Dijon mounted a ladder each morning and leveled with his hammer all the stonecutters' work. The present image at the trumeau is a fragment saved from the late-Gothic Chartreuse of the Valois dukes. To Notre Dame Philippe le Hardi gave the Jacquemart[308] clock, one of his spoils from the sacking of Courtrai in 1382, whereat he had been assisted by the Dijon citizens *par loyauté et parfait amour.*

La Cathédrale, Huysmans described the closing of the Burgundian monastery of Val des Saints near Dijon. His theory is that by such acts the balance of good and evil in the world is destroyed, since no longer is propitiatory self-sacrifice and prayer offered to heaven for the sins being committed on earth: *"Il faut s'attendre à ce que le Bon Dieu tombe sur nous ... pour remettre les choses en place, et vous savez comment il procède, dans ces cas là, il vous accable d'infirmités et d'épreuves."*

[308] A clockmaker named Jacquemart made such works, hence their name. Originally only one figure struck the hours on the big bell. Then a wife, Jacqueleine, was given to the bell-knocker, and after a local wit had rallied the couple on their childless state, first one child, Jacquelinet, was added, and then another, Jacquelinette, and the industrious children now ring the quarter hours on the little bells.

SAINT BERNARD, AND CISTERCIAN INFLUENCE IN GOTHIC ARCHITECTURE[309]

What is genius? It is a mind in which imagination, intelligence, and feeling exist in an elevated proportion and in an exact equation. It is a mind which has a penetrating view of ideas, which incarnates them powerfully in marble, in brass, in language, and in that dust which we call writing, which also communicates to ideas an impulse from the heart to precipitate them, living, into the hearts of others. Genius is, with conscience, the most beautiful endowment of humanity.... Genius is the greatest power created by God for grasping truth. It is a sudden and vast intuition of the connections which bind beings together.... It is the faculty of rendering ideas visible to those who would not have discovered them by themselves, of incarnating them in speaking images, of casting them into the soul, enlightening it, subjecting it, thrilling it.

—Lacordaire (1802-61; born in Burgundy).

Although modern Dijon may momentarily blot out much in its past history by renaming the square before Notre Dame *Place Ernest Renan, auteur de "La vie de Jésus"* (which work depicts the Saviour as an unconscious charlatan), and christening the square before the cathedral *Place Blanqui, grand Révolutionnaire* (Blanqui being the Communist who founded the journal *Ni Dieu ni Maître*), although it may mark one street sign *Rue Babeuf, écrivain politique, démocrate très ardente* (the socialist, Babeuf, was executed under the Directory), and another with an equal pedantry that is most un-French, *Rue Diderot, auteur principale de l'Encyclopédie* (the encyclopedia which railed at the Christian religion), none the less will the greatest honor of the ancient capital of Burgundy be the monk in whom western monasticism culminated, Bernard of Clairvaux, who led Dante to the Supreme Vision in Paradise, "who spoke to kings as a prophet, to the people as their leader, and transported Christendom by his eloquence," the greatest of Cistercians, the greatest of Burgundians, and the last great Doctor of the Church.

As the XI century drew to a close, certain pious Benedictines, who regretted the laxity of rule in their own convent, retired to the marshy woods near Beaune, to Cîteaux, some twelve miles south of Dijon. There was started a new Order which languished during fifteen years, fever decimating the postulants, till the third ab-

[309] Works of St. Bernard, edited by Mabillon (Paris, 1669-90), tr. by Eales and Hodges (London, 1889), 4 vols.; E. Vacandard, *Vie de Saint Bernard* (Paris, Lecoffre, 1895), 2 vols.; other studies of the saint, by Eales (London, 1890) and R. P. Ratisbonne; De Dion, *Étude sur les églises de l'ordre de Cîteaux*; Arbois de Jubainville, *Étude sur l'état intérieur des abbayes cisterciennes et principalement de Clairvaux au XII siècle* (Paris, 1858); Lucien Bégule, *L'abbaye de Fontenay et l'architecture cistercienne* (Lyon, 1912); Camille Enlart, *L'architecture gothique en Italie* (Paris, 1893); *ibid., En Espagne et en Portugal* (Paris, 1894); *ibid.,* "Villard de Honnecourt et lex Cisterciens," in *Biblio. de l'École des chartes,* 1895; *Bulletin Monumental,* 1904, André Philippe, on Cistercian churches; John Bilson, *The Architecture of the Cistercians; Their Earliest Churches in England* (London, 1909); also in the *Journal of the Royal Institute of British Architects,* 1909; Marcel Aubert, on Cistercian churches in Germany.

bot, St. Stephen Harding, stormed heaven with petitions to spare his dwindling flock. And efficacious prayers they appeared to be, for one spring day in 1113 there came to the abbey gates (Cîteaux' name signifies *Sistite hic*, Halt here!) a group of thirty young nobles, whose conversion was to set all Burgundy talking.

Their leader was Bernard of Fontaine-lès-Dijon,[310] then in his twenty-fourth year. When he experienced the call to a monastic life, he drew after him brothers, cousins, uncle, and friends. His mother, the Blessed Aleth, had impressed ineffaceably on his soul her own ardent love of God. As Peter the Venerable said in that same generation: "With us the virgin, the wife, the mother, expand the soul of the country by the breath of their piety."

When the small band of enthusiasts were quitting the château of Bernard's father, the elder brother and heir, Guy, told Nivard, the youngest of the six sons of Aleth, that now he alone remained to inherit the estate. "Ah," cried the lad, "you would leave me the earthly reward while you gain the eternal? The exchange is not fair." And in time he, too, sought his brothers in the cloister as did his father, who died in a Cistercian robe.

All the nations of Europe were meeting then in the internationalism of monastic institutions. St. Stephen Harding, who was practically the founder of the Cistercian Order, who drew up its charter and began its centralized system of chapters-general, was an Englishman, educated in Sherborne abbey in Dorset, and later at Paris University. Feeling the desire to visit Rome in pilgrimage, he went there afoot, reciting each day, as he walked, the entire Psaltery. It is said that benignant joy shone in his face. To-day a Bible he translated is treasured in Dijon; he used to consult the learned rabbis of his acquaintance whenever in doubt concerning the Hebraic text. It was an hour of internationalism. A frequenter of St. Bernard's own Clairvaux was St. Malachy O'Morgair, archbishop of Armagh, who died in Bernard's arms in 1147. The Burgundian saint loved Malachy for his gentleness, his holiness, his delicacy of soul, and his noble majestic presence, and for him trained young Irish monks to serve in the reform needed then in the Celtic church, thus paying back to Ireland the debt incurred by the mission of Columbanus.

With such souls as Bernard and his kinsmen, the new Order governed by Abbot Stephen Harding took on fresh vigor. Pontigny was founded a year later, and in 1115 Bernard and twelve companions were sent to establish Clairvaux[311] in a former robber haunt given by the Count of Champagne, a valley of wormwood which they turned into a valley of light. By the middle of the XIII century there were five hundred Cistercian houses in Europe. In England, from 1125 to 1200, rose a hundred monasteries of the white monks, Fountains, Furness, Tintern, Kirkstall, "God's castles," wrote a contemporary, "where the servants of the true anoint-

[310] The castle of Fontaine-lès-Dijon was held by Bernard's lineage till the XV century. To-day the site is covered by an unfinished commemorative church. The village church is of the XVI century.

[311] As at Cîteaux, scarcely an ancient vestige remains at Clairvaux. The XII-century monastic storehouse now serves as a house of detention. All trace of St. Bernard's tomb has been lost. The Revolution finished what the Huguenot wars and the absentee commendatory abbots began.

ed King do keep watch, and the young soldiers are exercised in warfare against spiritual evil." Many a Cistercian house was in Scotland and Ireland—Melrose, Mellifont, Boyle; in Germany and the north—Maulbronn, Arnsberg, Warnhem, and Sorö; in Spain—Poblet and Santa-Creus; in Portugal—Alcobaça. St. Bernard himself founded Chiaravalle near Milan, and on the spot of the Roman Campagna where St. Paul was beheaded flourished the Cistercian house of Tre Fontane, whose first abbot, trained under Bernard at Clairvaux, mounted Peter's Chair as Eugene III.

Wherever the Cistercians went they promulgated the new Gothic building lore of France. Their churches with square east end, square chapels opening on transept arms, and neither tower, triforium nor clearstory, were built exactly alike whether it was in the far north as at Alvastra in Sweden, or in the far south as at Girgenti in Sicily. Burgundy's abbatial at Fontenay is the type at its purest.

M. Camille Enlart was first to draw attention to the active rôle played by Cistercian monks in the dissemination of Gothic architecture in Europe.[312] All Cistercian churches were dedicated to the Mother of God, and the use of the gracious

----

[312] M. Enlart calls Fossanuova, on the Appian Way between Rome and Naples, the first Gothic church in Italy, begun in 1187 by Burgundian Cistercians. Mr. Porter thinks that the infiltration had begun thirty years earlier through various channels. In 1208 Innocent III dedicated Fossanuova; in 1274 St. Thomas Aquinas died there, en route to the Council at Lyons. The same plain Burgundian plan was followed at Casamari (1217), and a daughter house of the latter was S. Galgano (1218), from which went monks who are cited as the masters-of-works of Siena Cathedral, the best Gothic edifice of the peninsula. Monks from French Clairvaux built the three Chiaravalle churches of Italy, and monks from Pontigny raised S. Martino near Viterbo. Later, Italy felt the influence of different French schools; thus the Naples churches are Gothic of Provence because southern French architects accompanied Charles d'Anjou, count of Provence, when he became king of the Two Sicilies. At Assisi the church of S. Francesco shows the Gothic traits of Burgundy, Provence, and Champagne. The Cistercians introduced the torus profile of diagonals, but they long clung to round-headed windows. The Provence masters introduced pointed arched windows. In Spain, Cîteaux found a rival in the monks of Cluny for the dissemination of the new art. In the XII century a large number of Spanish bishoprics were filled by Cluny monks. Sometimes they built according to their own native architecture, as in Lugo Cathedral, San Vincente at Avila, and churches in Seville, which are Burgundian Romanesque. Sigüenza Cathedral is Burgundian both in its Romanesque and Gothic parts. Zamora Cathedral, consecrated 1174, and the old cathedral of Salamanca, show traits of Aquitaine; both sees were occupied by Bishop Jerome, who came from Périgieux. The Cistercians of Spain did not confine themselves, as in Italy, to typically Burgundian Gothic churches. Poblet and Santa-Creus (1157) derive from the early Gothic of Midi France, as well as from Burgundy. Las Huelgas, the Cistercian house for nuns near Burgos, finished about 1180, shows slight Burgundian and much Plantagenet Gothic influence. The foundress was the daughter of Henry II and Aliénor of Aquitaine. In Spain, as in Italy, the later Gothic monuments conformed to the standards of northern French Gothic. Portugal was more exclusively a Cistercian field of art. In 1148, Alcobaça monastery was founded by the son of a Burgundian prince, progenitor of Portugal's royal line. While it shows Angevin Gothic traits, its plan is the sober Cistercian Burgundian type. In the military Orders of Spain and Portugal the Cistercian Rule was used. The king of Sweden, in 1143, obtained Cistercian missionaries from Clairvaux; in Denmark the abbey church of Sorö is Burgundian Gothic. Camille Enlart, *Les origines de*

term *Notre Dame* spread from their abbatials to the cathedrals. Dante opens the final canto of the *Paradiso* by a eulogy of the Queen of Heaven, put into the mouth of St. Bernard, who never flagged in her praise, culling from Scripture every mystic and lovely name for her. *Io sono il suo fedel Bernardo*, the Burgundian proudly boasts in Paradise. Though Bernard's devotion to his *Dame souveraine* was poles apart from Puritanism, his rules for ecclesiastic plainness were as rigid as those of the Puritans. His severe ideas concerning art restrained the earlier Cistercian churches, though his apostolate quickened the spiritual forces that soon were to rear the cathedrals.

It has been said that to relate St. Bernard's life is to resume the history of the XII century during half its course. He ended the schism of an anti-pope; he went up and down Europe preaching unity and peace and reconciling enemies; he journeyed into Languedoc to combat, by word, the Catharist heresy; fearlessly he rebuked scandal in high places. He drew up the Rule for the Military Order of Templars. His *Book of Considerations*, written for Eugene III, became a manual of behavior for the papacy. His treatise on Grace and Free Will defined so perfectly the Church doctrine of Justification that almost textually it was repeated by the Council of Trent. No man ever received more overwhelming ovations than Bernard; at Toulouse they crowded to kiss his hand till his frail arms were swollen past all movement; at Albi a jeering crowd was subjugated by one sermon; in northern Italy, such was the reverence for the maker of peace between the rival cities, that Genoa chose him as a patron, and Milan placed herself under his protection. As he crossed the Alps, word passed among the mountaineers, and his way became a triumphal procession. He was worn to a shadow in the service of Christendom when Eugene III commissioned him to preach the Second Crusade, and when the expedition proved a lamentable failure, Heaven sent this strong man, who had passed unscathed through the intoxication of human glory, the severer test of human disgrace.

The figure of the greatest proselytizer since St. Paul is no vague one in history. Bernard was tall and slender, with chiseled features like polished ivory; his hair was red-blond; in his blue eyes was a flame of celestial purity. Many have testified to the serenity of his visage, the modesty of his attitude, and the almost superhuman influence he exerted on those who saw him. They say that the very sight of him preached. Apart from the numerous descriptions of him by his contemporaries, there are over four hundred of his own letters extant, letters straightforward, abrupt, ironic here and there, fearless, and warm-hearted. He swayed emperors and kings, yet retained always his personal humility. Reluctantly he tore himself from the peace of Clairvaux to direct the affairs of Europe, and eagerly he returned to the life of prayer and brotherly love. A preacher, he said, must be a man of prayer if he would convert men. He must be a reservoir kept full and overflowing, not merely a canal that can run dry.

---

l'architecture gothique en Espagne et en Portugal (Paris, 1894); *ibid., L'architecture gothique en Italie* (Paris, 1893); *ibid., Notes archéologiques sur les abbayes cisterciennes de Scandinavie* (Paris, 1894); *ibid.,* "Villard de Honnecourt et les Cisterciens," in *Biblio. de l'École des chartes,* 1895; *ibid., L'art gothique ... en Chypre* (Paris, 1899), 2 vols.

Some to whom the spiritual life is a dead letter have called the abbot of Clairvaux unsympathetic and superhuman. Others, while admiring him, regret his brusqueness and hardy invectives. It was not a day when controversialists handled their adversaries with gloves; witness Abélard's onslaughts on those who disagreed with him on the most abstract theological points. No doubt, in some cases, Bernard's zeal exceeded propriety; perhaps his father had touched exactly on the defect of his qualities when he advised him to keep measure in all things. But who that appreciates this great man would tone down his splendid vehemence? His love for morality and pure doctrine was a glorious passion. He struck at the sin, not the sinner. Such censures are the anger of love.

And remark how the men whom Bernard rebuked accepted the humiliation of his public censures. When he asked the archbishop of Sens—the feudal lord, Henri le Sanglier, who began that cathedral—if he thought justice had disappeared from the rest of the world as it had from his own heart, the proud churchman set about curbing his autocratic tendencies, and died an honored pastor. No disputants ever more soundly berated each other than Abélard and Bernard, yet their reconciliation, brought about by kindly, large-minded Peter of Cluny, was frank and complete. And we have seen how Abbot Suger changed his worldly ways of life, how he reformed his monastery, and how the revenues hitherto wasted on a retinue of sixty horsemen were devoted to building the first Gothic monument in France.

St. Bernard was, without question, the most eloquent preacher of the Middle Ages, but the conversions he wrought were due as much to the purity, charity, and humility of his own life as to his unparalleled powers of persuasion. The ideal of that harsh age, despite its shortcomings, was saintliness, and when men found it incarnate in this Burgundian, they accepted him as their leader. Bernard held that it was false principles that led to social corruption, and to punish the evil act while the mental crime which led to it went unchastened, was illogical. So whenever the purity of Christian doctrine was threatened, this champion of the Cross emerged from his seclusion full armed for its defense. His vigilance was not bigotry. When a fanatical German monk preached a persecution of the Jews, the abbot of Clairvaux came to their defense: "The Just," an old rabbi called him, "without whom not one among our people had saved his life. Honor to him who came to our succor in our hour of mortal anguish."

In all Bernard's writings is not one word of disloyalty to what he thought was right, not a trace of the hypocrite. If he thundered against ambition, cupidity, and that hypocrisy which moves about in dim corners, *perambulante in tenebris*, he knew that scandals there have been and will ever be, since even among the chosen twelve Judas betrayed, Peter denied, and Thomas doubted. He might flagellate ecclesiastic disorders as openly as Luther himself, but the pope called him the pillar of the Church and its guide. Towering above his fellow men morally, he took up his Master's cord whips to drive the traffickers from the temple, but he left an altar in the sanctuary and a high priest at the altar, and his own life was blameless.

The choicest spirits of the age sought Bernard's friendship. He was loved by St. Norbert, whose new Order of Prémontré spread over Europe with the same rapidity as that of Cîteaux. He had links with the mystics in St. Victor's abbey at Paris; Hugues de St. Victor submitted cases of conscience to him; Richard de St. Victor asked of him criticism on his book on the Trinity; and the Latin hymns of Adam de St. Victor breathe the selfsame spirit as that of the Burgundian mystic. Geoffrey de Lèves, who built the tower at Chartres, traveled with him in Italy and Languedoc. Pierre de Celle, who built the choir of St. Remi, at Rheims, wrote of Bernard: "His life, his fame, his works, his writings, his miracles, his faith, his hope, his charity, his chastity, his abstinence, his words, his visage, his gestures, the attitude of his body, all, in a word, rendered homage to his sanctity. He was the well-beloved disciple of the Lord, in whose honor he built, not only one basilica, but all the basilicas of the Order of Cîteaux. If, then, thou wouldst touch the pupil of Our Lady's eye, write against Bernard." And the bishop of Paris, who worked on the façade of Notre Dame, the schoolman, Guillaume d'Auvergne, testified that Bernard "lived in the highest perfection," that his "wisdom proceeded not from human instruction, but from divine inspiration." The first great master of scholasticism, Guillaume de Champeaux, the progenitor of Paris University, was bound to Bernard in loving friendship till his death, and asked to be buried in the abbey church at Clairvaux.

Detachment from the things of the world never weakened this saint's human affections. What cry from a stricken heart is more moving than Bernard's lament for his brother Gerard? That elder brother was following a knight's career when Bernard won him for God's service in the cloister. There for twenty-five years they lived side by side. They had just returned together from Italy when Gerard suddenly died. Dry-eyed, Bernard attended the burial, and dry-eyed he went about his daily tasks. He mounted the pulpit to continue an exposition of the Canticle of Canticles which he was conducting, and all at once his grief broke forth irresistibly in one of the sublime elegies of literature, recorded by a monk of Clairvaux who heard it: "What is there in common between this Canticle of joy and me who am in bitter anguish!... I have done violence to my heart.... Grief shut in but wounds with deeper sting. It has vanquished me. What I suffer must have its way. I must pour out my trouble before you, my sons, who knew the faithful comrade I have lost and the justice of my sorrow. You knew his vigilance, his sweetness; you knew my need of him. When I was weak in body, he strengthened me; when I hesitated he spurred me on; when I grew negligent he cautioned me. My Gerard! why have you left me to stumble alone on the road we two trod together, my brother by blood but still more by religion! Ah! I would know if you still think of one whom you loved, if, in God's presence, you can lean toward our distress? You have shed your mortal weaknesses, but surely not your human tendernesses, for charity endures, says the apostle. No! my Gerard does not forget me in eternity! It was our joy to be together, inextricably were our spirits interlinked, the same thoughts, the same emotions, the same will; one only heart, one only soul between us; with one blow, the sword has pierced my heart and his.... That I might have tranquillity he took on his own shoulders the material cares of the convent. It was his heart bore my troubles. His eyes led my steps. Now, when a need rises I turn to where I think to find him, and he is not there!... I am deprived of the best part of myself and I must not weep. My heart is torn from my bosom, and I must not suffer.... But my courage is not of stone.... I suffer, I weep, and my grief is ever before me...."

And so on it runs, this lamentation with its Hebraic note of sorrow's passion. Impregnated through and through was Bernard with the Bible, and his speech fell naturally into its cadences. To mark the biblical references in his works would be, says the student, to fill half the pages with annotations.

There is a book of interior consolation, precious to humanity, which has preserved for us intact the spiritual teachings of this Cistercian abbot who led the XII century. Scholars say that the *Imitation of Christ* bears the direct impress of St. Bernard's spirit, that it reproduced and analyzed his writings. Whoever its author, his prayer *Da mihi nesciri* has been answered.

Those who have been comforted by the book which, next to the Bible, has been chief solace for the stricken heart, have leaned unaware on the purpose, the faith, and the purity of the greatest saint of the Middle Ages, the man who made Burgundy as illustrious by its Cistercian reformers and missionary builders as it had been by its Benedictines when Cluny was a world power.

CHAPTER X

GOTHIC ART IN NORMANDY[313]

Monastic architecture best expression of Norman character—Normandy, like Burgundy, was a land of monasteries—Bernay's abbey church an ancestress of Norman Romanesque (note)—Bec Abbey, the Cluny of Normandy—Lanfranc made the school of Bec world-noted—At Bec, St. Anselm began the philosophical movement of the Middle Ages—William of Volpiano pioneer in the rebirth of architecture in the duchy—Jumièges, the first Norman church of architectural pretension, begun 1040—Only vestiges remain of St. Wandrille abbey—Caen, the Mecca of Norman Romanesque and the queen city for towers—Three good towers at St. Pierre-sur-Dives—St. Georges de Boscherville the best type of Norman Romanesque—Fécamp's Primary Gothic abbatial rose after the fire of 1169—Gothic abbatial at Eu built after the death of St. Laurence O'Toole, 1180—Mont-Saint-Michel the greatest of Norman abbeys—Its Merveille (Gothic halls), building from 1203 to 1228—Choir of Mont-Saint-Michel, the best work of Flamboyant Gothic, begun 1450.

Rouen Cathedral, not local in character—Its tower of St. Romain begun in 1145—Its transept façades and Lady chapel XIV-century Rayonnant work—Abbatial of St. Ouen a gem of Rayonnant Gothic—No city richer than Rouen in Flamboyant Gothic monuments—Trial of Jeanne d'Arc at Rouen in 1431 and her Rehabilitation in 1456.

[313] *Congrès Archéologique*, 1908; V. Ruprich-Robert, *L'architecture normande aux XIe et XIIe siècles* (Paris, 1897), 2 vols.; A. de Caumont et Ch. de Beaurepaire, *Mémoires historiques sur la Normandie: antiquités, monuments, histoire* (1827-36); *La Normandie monumentale et pittoresque. Seine-Inférieure, Calvados, Eure, Orne, Manche* (Le Havre, Lemale et Cie), 8 vols, folio; Léon le Cordier, "L'architecture de la Normandie au XIIIe siècle," in *Bulletin Monumental*, 1863, vol. 29, p. 513; Chanoine Porée, *L'art normand* (Paris, 1914); Taylor et Nodier, *Voyages pittoresques ... dans l'ancienne France. Normandie* (Paris, Didron, 1825), 2 vols., folio; Henri Prentout, *La Normandie* (Collection, Les provinces françaises), (Paris, H. Laurens, 1910); Lechandé d'Anisy, *Les anciennes abbayes de Normandie* (1834), 2 vols, and atlas; Ordericus Vitalis, *The Ecclesiastical History of England and Normandy* (London, Bohn Library, 1856), 4 vols.; Albert Sorel, *Pages normandes* (Paris, Plon, 1907).

On Normandy's history, see Stubbs, Freeman, Palgrave, H. W. C. Davis, G. B. Adams, Sir J. H. Ramsay, Miss Kate Norgate, Mrs. J. R, Green, etc. A. Thierry in his *Conquête de l'Angleterre* gives details of the oppression of the Anglo-Saxons by their Norman conquerors.

Lisieux Cathedral the earliest Gothic cathedral in Normandy—Begun after 1160 as Ile-de-France Gothic—Its Lady chapel built by Bishop Pierre Cauchon, Jeanne d'Arc's venal judge.

Évreux Cathedral not homogeneous, but has much charm—Its choir (1298-1310) a gem of Rayonnant Gothic—XIV century's best array of glass in its choir.

Séez Cathedral modest in size—Norman in style—Its choir a forerunner of Rayonnant Gothic—Has XIV-century windows.

Bayeux Cathedral the Gothic of the duchy at its best—Romanesque part of its nave remarkable—Bishop Odo, brother of the Conqueror, built the crypt, and of his time is the Bayeux Tapestry—Choir of Bayeux a masterpiece of Normandy's elaborate Gothic.

Coutances Cathedral loveliest in Normandy, begun after the fire of 1218—Its three towers notable—Aisles of choir are of different height.

Gothic art of Brittany—Brittany more a land of shrines than cathedrals—Her religious soul best expressed by her Calvarys—XIII-century cathedral at Dol has fine eastern window—Cathedral at Nantes possesses the last great work of Gothic sculpture—Cathedral of Quimper very Breton in spirit—St. Pol-de-Léon Cathedral entirely complete—The Kreisker is Brittany's grandest tower—St. Yves of Brittany helped build Tréguier Cathedral.

Summing up—Gothic art gave way before the pagan Renaissance and the contempt for legends roused by the Reformation. In the World War France again displayed the spirit that had built cathedrals. Unquenchable idealism of the French race.

The cathedral was perfected slowly and passionately. The Romans brought to it their force, their logic, their serenity. The Barbarians brought to it their naïve grace, their love of life, their dreamful imaginations. From this unpremeditated collaboration sprang a work modelled by times and places. It is the French genius and its image. It did not progress by fits and starts; it was not the servant of pride. It mounted in the course of centuries to complete expression. And that expression, one throughout the country, varies with each province, with each fraction of a province, just enough to make interesting the chain that joins all the pearls of this monumental necklace of France.

—RODIN, LES CATHÉDRALES DE FRANCE.[314]

---

[314] Rodin, *Les cathédrales de France*, (Paris, A. Colin, 1914).

IRTUALLY the land conquered by the vikings received its civilization from monasteries. Like Burgundy, Normandy was a very Egypt, a Thebaid, for the number of its religious houses. Each baron sought to have one on his domain. In the capital of the duchy was St. Ouen, whose abbot owned half the city; on the same Seine lay Jumièges, a center of letters and arts, and farther down the river was St. Wandrille, "nursery for saints" — three noted houses that inherited directly the apostolate of Celtic Columbanus. From St. Wandrille went monks to establish Fécamp, favorite of the Norman dukes, with an early-Gothic church equal to a cathedral. Other monks from Fontenelle reorganized the most romantic pile of monastic buildings in the world, Mont-Saint-Michel, guarded by the patron of the kingdom of France, Sanctus Michael in periculo maris.

When that man of genius, William of Volpiano, abbot of St. Bénigne, at Dijon, came to Normandy to reform its houses, he himself rebuilt the abbatial church at Bernay which architecturally is an ancestress for such Romanesque work as Cerisy-la-Forêt, Lessay, the Caen abbatials, and St. Georges de Boscherville. At Mortain, at St. Sauveur-le-Vicomte, at St. Évroult, were monastery churches, and the picturesque ruins of Hambye cause one to mourn that Primary Gothic abbatial wrecked by the Revolution. St. Pierre-sur-Dives and the collegiate at Eu are later monastic works of the province. For its influence as a world power — what we may call the Cluny of Normandy — was Bec abbey that became, under Lanfranc the Lombard, and St. Anselm the Piedmontese, the intellectual leader of the West. Its mammoth church has gone the way of Cluny's — scarcely stone left on stone.

BEC ABBEY[315]

O beata solitudo!
O sola beatitudo!

— (Inscription on a Benedictine monastery in France.)

In Bec, theology for the first time spoke the language of philosophy. Herlouin, an unlettered knight, who learned to write only at forty, founded, in 1034, an abbey on his lands on the banks of a beck in the valley of Brionne. With the monks who gathered round him, he was engaged in building with his own hands his convent when, one day in 1042, Lanfranc of Pavia arrived in their midst, the learned one needed by those simple, good men. Lanfranc had been teaching at Avranches, and was journeying to Rouen when brigands seized him in a forest near Bec, stripped and tied him to a tree to perish. Before aid came to him, as he faced death during long hours — learning that despite his scholarship he was incapable of reciting one single psalm to support his soul — a new comprehension of life dawned on him,

[315] Chanoine Porée, *Histoire de l'abbaye du Bec* (Évreux, impri. de Hérissey, 1901); *La Normandie monumentale et pittoresque Eure*, vol. 2, p. 221, "Bec," Chanoine Porée (Le Havre, Lemale et Cie, 1895); Ragey, *Histoire de Saint Anselm* (Paris, 1889); Martin Rule, *Life and Times of St. Anselm* (London, 1883). Other studies of St. Anselm by Rémusat (Paris, 1853); R. W. Church (London, 1870); J. M. Rigg (London, 1896), and in *Lives of the Archbishops of Canterbury* (London, 1860-75); *Histoire littéraire de la France*, vol. 8, p. 260, "Lanfranc" (Paris, 1749); vol. 9, p. 398, "St. Anselm"; p. 369, "Gondulfe, évêque de Rochester" (Paris, 1750).

and he vowed himself to the triumph of religion.

The school which he opened in Bec abbey soon drew students from all parts of Europe. From northern Italy came young Anselm, destined twice to succeed his master, in Bec as prior, in Canterbury as archbishop. Lanfranc, practiced in the affairs of the world, a born statesman, was better fitted to be primate of England than was Anselm with his childlike, tender nature, and his subtle, speculative brain. Bec gave still a third archbishop to the see of Canterbury, Theobald, the patron of St. Thomas Becket; Martin, whilom abbot of Bec, built Peterborough Cathedral.

For thirty-three years St. Anselm wrote and taught in Bec abbey, student first, then monk, then prior, and in 1078 abbot. There at night, while all the house slept, he wrote the books which have won for him the title of founder of the Christian philosophy of the Middle Ages. A forerunner of scholasticism, he was among the first to set forth the conformity of Christian doctrine with human reason. Dante places him in Paradise among the great contemplatives. The union of the mystic and the rational in theology, in the Norman abbey ruled by Anselm, started impulses which were to pass down through the centuries. An immediate result was the quickening of the mental life of the XII century. Among St. Anselm's pupils at Bec was Anselm de Laon, whose classes, with those of Guillaume de Champeaux, are regarded as the nucleus of the University of Paris.

What is of interest to us here is that, from the hour of the opening of men's minds to scholastic learning, rose the architecture of France, that the giant energy which built cathedrals had its source in a faith that *believed in order that it might understand*, which is St. Anselm's own proposition, *Credo ut intelligam*, as well as it is the apogee flight reached by Plato, what the Greek philosopher called *the wings of the soul*. And Plato's peer, XIII-century Aquinas, voiced the Greek's vision, and repeated Anselm's thought, in a hymn whose subtle stanzas are sung daily over Christendom: "*Præstat fides supplementum sensuum defectui*" ("Faith for all defects supplying where the feeble senses fail"). Anselm, with his "face of an angel," naïvely enthusiastic over his metaphysical proof of God, writing alone in Bec, in the silence of the night, was digging unaware the foundations for Chartres, Rheims, Amiens, and those other visions of the Beyond to which man gave tangible shape in the scholastic-trained centuries because, *believing*, he *understood*.

Sorely against his will St. Anselm left the peace of Bec to take up the duties of England's primacy in an hour when the eternal lay-ecclesiastical controversy was embittered. The wanton and despotic William Rufus was the opponent who overwhelmed him. His sole friends were the little people for whom, at that time, any churchman who maintained independence against layman tyranny was a champion of civic liberties. The scholar of Bec was the only prelate of the many crossing from Normandy to England who displayed loving kindness for the downtrodden Saxons. Homesick in England, St. Anselm used pathetically to sign his letters to his intimates, "Brother Anselm by the heart, Archbishop of Canterbury by coercion."

At Le Bec-Hellouin to-day little remains of the abbatial whose choir once soared on twenty immense piers. Again and again the church was reconstructed. In 1077 Archbishop Lanfranc crossed the Channel for a dedication. Early in the

XIII century the master-of-works at Rouen, Enguerrand, proceeded to Bec to superintend a new Gothic edifice. A fire in 1263 caused another renewal of the choir. In the Rayonnant day the nave was rebuilt on the same lines as St. Ouen's abbatial. The religious wars of the XVI century damaged the church, whose demolition was continued as late as 1814. What now remains are a portion of the transept, a chapter house of the XII century, and the isolated tower of St. Nicholas (1467-80), another memorial of Normandy's rejoicing to be free of foreign rule. Eight large statues adorn its upper walls.

Bec had been pillaged by Henry V's troops before Jeanne d'Arc's advent, and the abbot then appointed by the invaders was one of the sixty university professors and ecclesiastics who condemned the Maid to death in Rouen, 1431. Ten abbots of Normandy thus tarnished their great names, but it is well to bear in mind that in each case the delinquent monastery had recently been sacked because of its patriotic stand against the foreigners, and that it was governed by a tool of the victors. Fifty Norman abbeys honored themselves by their absence from the torture of a young girl who had all England against her, half of France, as well as the perverted learning of Paris University.

NORMANDY'S ROMANESQUE SCHOOL[316]

The Christian world made no mistake when, in calm confidence, it sought, under the wing of the Benedictine abbeys, that strong education of the Western races which made possible all the marvels of faith, courage, fervor, and humility with which Europe was illuminated from the XI to the XV century, from Gregory VII to Jeanne d'Arc.

—CHARLES DE MONTALEMBERT, THE MONKS OF THE WEST.

Normandy's hardy personality showed at its best in her Romanesque monastic churches. Their design is decisive and vast, their construction solid—the Norman excelled in masoncraft—and as art they have never been surpassed for grave impressiveness. In the Norman minsters is a primeval energy admirably restrained, a massive grace, a something of reasoned simplicity lost in the Gothic cathedrals of the region. One who fell under the spell of Normandy's Romanesque architecture has told how its repose "appeals to men and women who have lived long and are tired, who want rest, who have done with aspiration and ambitions,

[316] V. Ruprich-Robert, *L'architecture normande aux XIe et XIIIe siècles* (Paris, 1885-87); G. T. Rivoira, *Lombardic Architecture*, vol. 2, on Normandy (London and New York, 1910), translated from *Le origini dell'architettura lombarda* (Milano, 1908); Canoine Porée, *L'art normand* (Paris, 1914); Camille Enlart, *Manuel d'archéologie française* (Paris, Picard et fils, 1904), 2 vols.; R. de Lasteyrie, *L'architecture religieuse en France à l'époque romane* (Paris, 1912); John Bilson, "The Beginnings of Gothic Architecture," in the *Journal of the Royal Institute of British Architects*, Third series, 1898-99, vol. 6, pp. 289, 322, 345; 1901-02, vol. 9, p. 350; René Fage, "La décoration géométrique dans l'école romane de Normandie," in *Congrès Archéol.*, 1908, vol. 2, p. 614; Louis Engerand, "La sculpture romane en Normandie," in *Bulletin Monumental*, 1904, vol. 68, p. 405; Arthur Kingsley Porter, *Medieval Architecture*, vol. 1, pp. 285 to 332, gives the chief Norman Romanesque monuments (New York and London, 1907); *ibid.*, *Lombard Architecture* (New Haven, Yale University Press, 1917), 3 vols. and atlas.

whose life has been a broken arch.... The quiet strength of these lines, the solid support of the moderate lights, the absence of display, of effort, of self-consciousness, satisfy them as no other art does. They come back to it to rest after a long cycle of pilgrimage—the cradle of rest from which their ancestors started."[317]

No church earlier than the year 1000 has survived in Normandy. The Norseman, while still an unbaptized buccaneer, laid low every Merovingian and Carolingian edifice. All was in ruin. "From Blois to Senlis," says the old record, "not an acre is plowed, for none dare work in the fields." Then, Rollo, chief of the marauders, baptized in Rouen, settled down in the duchy granted him in fief by the harassed king of France. In an incredibly short time the erstwhile pagans became the most indefatigable of church builders. For Normandy, the date 911 is as important a landmark as is 910 for Burgundy, the year of Cluny's foundation.[318]

The Norman Romanesque school made general use of the roll molding at window and portal, of griffes at the base of piers, blind arcading, intercrossing wall arches (that became monotonous in the Anglo-Norman school), and very frequently it contrived an interior passage at the clearstory level, whose effect was heightened by the use of arches of different designs in its outer and inner walls.

Certain archæologists contend that the predominant influences in the development of Norman Romanesque were Lombard, and that in this it differed from other French schools which in main part derived from local Carolingian work. As the Norman's creative genius was not on a par with his constructive abilities, it seems reasonable to look for foreign influence when finding its school precociously formed by the middle of the XI century. The Lombards used, before the Normans, the alternate system of ground supports, cubic capitals, transverse arches, compound piers, crypts, and raised choirs, and their most striking feature of exterior decoration was the arched corbel table that made a continuous cornice. Mr. Arthur Kingsley Porter says that diagonals were used in Lombardy early in the XI century as an expedient to economize wood, groin vaults being molded on a temporary wooden substructure, but as the Lombard never counterbutted his intersecting ribs, such vaults proved unsatisfactory and were given up after 1120. If the Norman had an early knowledge of diagonals through the Lombard, like the Lombard he failed to derive from them their constructive consequences. That fact of creative genius no one can deny to the Ile-de-France. Even if the controversy as to who first used Gothic ribs should be decided in favor of the Anglo-Norman school, and behind their use of it, traced to Lombardy's Romanesque builders, none of them saw in it what Abbot Suger did—the radical member of a new system of building.

William of Volpiano, a Lombard, and an architect as well as a reformer, spent

<hr>

[317] Henry Adams, *Mont Saint-Michel and Chartres* (Boston, Houghton Mifflin Company, 1913).

[318] Normandy's *Millénaire* of 1911 was celebrated fitly. Among the books it called forth are: Gabriel Monod, *Le rôle de la Normandie dans l'histoire de France* (Paris, 1911); H. Prentout, *Essai sur les origines et la fondation du duché de Normandy* (Paris, 1911); A. Albert, *Petit histoire de Normandie* (Paris, 1912). In 1915 appeared Charles Homer Haskins, *The Normans in European History* (Boston, Houghton Mifflin).

many active years in Normandy, where he died in 1031. At Fécamp he is said to have trained a group of masons. A decade after his death, Lanfranc, born in northern Italy, became a leader in the duchy, and under him was built the present nave of the Abbaye-aux-Hommes at Caen. It seems very natural to suppose that such men, alert as they were to architectural progress, should have exerted influence on the Norman school. However, M. Lefèvre-Pontalis thinks it wiser not to exaggerate the immediate influence from beyond the Alps. He holds that the Romanesque school of Normandy proceeded in main part from the same element as the other pre-Gothic schools of France, elements derived somewhat from Barbarian sources, but chiefly from Rome's occupation of Gaul. In the case of Normandy the Barbarian influences would be largely Scandinavian, and there has been considerable speculation over the Norseman's wooden structure and the Norman's partiality for the pleated capital.

Mr. John Bilson is unsympathetic to Mr. Kingsley Porter's ideas of Lombard influence in Normandy, and he considers the early dates ascribed to Lombard diagonals most improbable. Why, he asks, if the solution was reached in Lombardy about 1025, did it take three quarters of a century for the Normans, directly in contact with the builders of Italy, to arrive after long experimenting at the same intersecting ribs? He claims that the Ile-de-France was indebted to Normandy for diagonals, which were not in use in the royal domain before 1130, but that, once that school came into possession of intersecting pointed arches and flying buttresses, it developed from them a new system of construction, clothing it with a new expression, which we call Gothic. The controversy is by no means closed.

Normandy's Romanesque school spread far afield.[319] It passed into Picardy and penetrated as far south as Chartres. It crossed the Channel with the adventurers who descended on England, and with other free lances who carved out distant kingdoms for themselves, its characteristics appeared in southern Italy and Sicily.

The ornamentation of the Norman school came in part from Oriental or Byzantine sources already in use in the Carolingian era, and in part from Scandinavian. Unlike Burgundy, this province, despite its good stone, never won distinction in sculpture either in the Romanesque or the Gothic day. Never was Norman decoration equal to Norman construction, otherwise this school would be without a peer. Its ornamentation lacks variety and imagination. Geometric designs were endlessly repeated. Both in England and in Normandy the traveler grows weary of the zigzag or chevron motive, taken from Merovingian interlacings, or Carolingian triangular outlines, and very weary, too, of its variants, the dog-tooth or star ornament, and the fret or meander which reproduced a classical motive. The Carolingian billet molding was also overused. Such monotony of decoration was probably the defect of a good quality—caution and thoroughness. The Norman seldom attempted what he could not put through, hence his churches were usual-

---

[319] E. Lefèvre-Pontalis, "Les influences normandes au XIe et au XIIe siècle dans le nord de la France," in *Bulletin Monumental*, 1906. vol. 70; Camille Enlart, *L'influence extérieure de l'art normand au moyen âge*; F. Chalandon, *Histoire de la domination normande en Italie et en Sicile* (Paris, 1907); Ch. Diehl, *Palerme et Syracuse* (Collection, Villes d'art célèbres), (Paris, H. Laurens, 1907); Émile Bertaud, *L'art dans l'Italie méridionale*.

ly completed, even to having their towers crowned by stone spires. The builders of the Ile-de-France were less cautious, but more sublime.

THE ROMANESQUE ABBEY CHURCH OF JUMIÈGES[320]

> Aucun pays n'avait fourni au moyen âge plus de mission-
> naires chrétiens qu'Irlande, ni d'hommes empressés de répandre
> chez les nations étrangères les études de leur patrie.
>
> —A. Thierry.

The first Romanesque church of Normandy with architectural pretensions, the first to present the regional school fully formed, was the abbatial of Jumièges, begun about 1040. That virile, rugged "château de Dieu" stands on a semi-island of the Seine where the river makes a gracious twenty-mile meander, or rather, there stand the "incredible masses of masonry" which are the ruins of Jumièges, a wall of the big central lantern, a roofless nave, and two gaunt façade towers, the only Norman towers entirely of the XI century. In all France is no more austere, stark, and grandiose a ruin.

How from such a predecessor as Bernay's abbatial the Norman could immediately evolve an architectural feat as tremendous as Jumièges seems explicable only by some strong exterior impetus. Here is the Lombard alternance of ground supports over whose origin in Normandy much printer's ink has been spilled. As the Lombard groin vault embraced two bays, a strong pier was needed only for the transverse arch separating the large square vault sections; or if a timber roof was used, a reinforced pier was required only for the bigger tiebeams. Now, at Jumièges, the lower structure proves (say certain archæologists) that never was a masonry roof planned for, so it is probable that the open timber roof required heavy tiebeams only at every other bay, hence an alternance of substantial and slight piers to correspond to the alternance of big beams and little beams. Jumièges also used the Lombard engaged shaft. Its uniform *hautes colonnes*, without capitals, rise from soil to roof, serving as interior buttresses, and some say as supports for the tiebeams, since they rose too high to be intended for a masonry roof. They bind together the three stories, and æsthetically their rhythm breaks the monotony of the plain walls. Mr. John Bilson thinks that the wall shafts of Jumièges can have had no other motive than to support a vault over the principal span, and cannot have been the supports of mere tiebeams. They may have been planned, suggests Prof. Baldwin Brown, to carry an undergirding arch such as occurs beneath some wooden roofs.

---

[320] Roger Martin du Gard, *L'abbaye de Jumièges, étude archéol. des ruines* (Montdidier, 1909); *ibid.*, "Jumièges," in *Bulletin Monumental*, 1909, vol. 73, p. 34; John Bilson, on "Jumièges," in *Revue de l'art chrétien*, 1901, p. 454; F. Lot, *Études critiques sur l'abbaye de Saint-Wandrille* (Paris 1913); *La Normandie monumentale et pittoresque. Seine-Inférieure*, p. 219, "Jumièges," Alfred Darcel; p. 353, "St. Wandrille," Abbé Sauvage (Le Havre, Lemale et Cie); Abbé Julien Loth, *Histoire de l'abbaye royale de St. Pierre de Jumièges* (Rouen, 1882-85), 3 vols.; David, *Les grandes abbayes de l'Occident* (Lille, 1907); Lefèvre-Pontalis, *Les influences normandes au XIe et au XIIe siècle dans le nord de la France* (1906), also in *Bulletin Monumental*, 1906, vol. 70.

Normandy's invention of the sexpartite vault came about, thinks M. Anthyme Saint-Paul, through her predilection for multiple lines. With such Gothic vaults—each section of which embraced two bays—she proceeded to reroof various of her Romanesque abbatials, whose already existent alternated piers were thus made logical. Almost it would seem as if the presence of ground supports, substantial and slight, had called into being the new type of masonry roof. St. Denis used a sexpartite vault in 1140, and M. Lefèvre-Pontalis suggested, at one time, that Normandy derived the idea from the Ile-de-France. In the royal domain, however, no steps are to be found leading up to it, whereas in Normandy can be seen sexpartite vaults of primitive design, such as those covering the Abbaye-aux-Dames, which consist merely of two diagonals with a transverse rib crossing their apex. In the Abbaye-aux-Hommes, where the timber roof of the nave was replaced by a Gothic vault as early, perhaps, as 1135, the vault web is warped to the intermediate transverse rib. It has been suggested that the sexpartite vault originated from the employment of the diaphragm arch.

Jumièges abbey church was dedicated "with great spiritual joy," so an old chronicle relates, by saintly Archbishop Maurille of Rouen, in the presence of William the Conqueror and Matilda. Maurille had been trained at Fécamp under the great William of Volpiano. A Gothic choir, added to the abbatial later, was blown up after the Revolution by a contractor who acquired the monastery in order to sell its stones as building material. Under the flank of the now roofless nave nestles a ruined little church of the XIV century, St. Peter its tutelary. Two of its bays incorporate parts from a Carolingian church built by Rollo's son, William Longsword (928-943). They are of archæological interest in being the oldest examples extant of twin arches beneath a common arch for the tribune-opening on the middle vessel. The arrangement became popular in the Romanesque churches of Normandy and England, and can be seen at Mont-Saint-Michel, Rochester, Ely, Gloucester, Peterborough, and Winchester.

Jumièges was an ancient foundation of Clovis II and Queen Bathilde. They granted forests on the Seine to St. Philibert (d. 684), who had been an intimate at the Merovingian court, of St. Ouen and St. Wandrille. To obtain the Celtic rule of Columbanus at its source, Philibert visited Luxeuil and Bobbio, and he dedicated a chapel of his abbatial at Jumièges to the Irish missionary. His own cult was to crop out at Tournus and Dijon when the Norse piratical inroads drove the inmates of wrecked monastic houses into Burgundy.

Jumièges was a scene of pillage and massacre during the last acts of the Capet-Plantagenet duel, when Henry V, the victor of Agincourt, overran Normandy. The abbot, then appointed, sat in judgment on St. Jeanne in 1431, and fell down dead three months later. After Charles VII had entered Rouen as conqueror, in 1449, he retired to Jumièges. During the feasts of rejoicing *la dame de beaulté*, Agnes Sorel, died in a manor close by, and her memorial stone in Jumièges abbatial recorded her "pitiful loving kindness to all men and especially the poor and children." Days of decline came for Jumièges under her commendatory abbots. A XVII-century revival of learning was led by the reformers of the Congregation of St. Maur, but the famous establishment went under completely during the Revolution. The sequence is the same for most French abbeys.

Farther down the Seine, at what once was Fontenelle, stand the less imposing ruins of St. Wandrille's abbatial, consisting of a transept of the XIII century and a Flamboyant Gothic cloister, whose *lave-mains* is a gem of Renaissance delicacy. The house was founded in 649 by St. Wandrille, of Merovingian blood. Like his friend, Philibert of Jumièges, he sought the rule of St. Columbanus at its fountainhead, though the more equable rule of St. Benedict was to prevail in French religious establishments before the VII century closed. St. Wandrille trained many of the saints who planted monasteries over northern France, and in later centuries the Duke of Normandy chose monks from St. Wandrille's abbey to institute a Benedictine house of prayer on the rock of St. Michael-in-peril-of-the-sea.

THE ROMANESQUE ABBATIALS AT CAEN[321]

Clochers légers, clochers aigus,
Clochers de France,
Par quel attrait d'élan pieux
Emportez-vous si vite et si haut dans les cieux
Nos regards et notre espérance?...
Longs et pareils à ces lances pointus
Que les géants piquaient au sol,
Vous montiez d'un seul jet pour défier le vol
Des hirondelles éperdues.

—GEORGES LAFENESTRE, "Clochers de France."[322]

Caen played a prominent part in the builder's story of Normandy. It has been called the Romanesque Mecca. Its church of St. Nicolas (c. 1180-93), one of the most interesting Romanesque edifices of the duchy, is dismantled, but the Abbaye-aux-Hommes or St. Étienne, and the Abbaye-aux-Dames, or Ste. Trinité, are in good repair. All the world knows how William the Conqueror and his good and gentle Matilda of Flanders each founded an abbey in Caen, "that God might be served by both sexes and thus pardon their transgression." Their marriage disobeyed Church regulations concerning consanguinity and a canonical atonement

---

[321] *Congrès Archéologique*, 1883 and 1908; H. Prentout, *Caen et Bayeux* (Collection, Villes d'art célèbres), (Paris, H. Laurens, 1909); V. Ruprich-Robert, *L'église Ste. Trinité et l'église St. Étienne de Caen* (Caen, 1864); E. de Beaurepaire, *Caen illustré, son histoire, ses monuments* (Caen, 1896), folio; Bouet, *Analyse architecturale de l'abbaye de St. Étienne de Caen* (1868); *La Normandie monumentale et pittoresque. Calvados*, pp. 1, 49; Arcisse de Caumont, *Statistique monumentale du Calvados* (Caen, F. Le Blanc-Hardal, 1898), 6 vols.; Camille Enlart, *Manuel d'archéologie française* (Paris, Picard, 1902), 2 vols.; John Bilson, "The Beginnings of Gothic Architecture," in *Journal of the Royal Institute of British Architects*, Third series, 1898-99, vol. 6, pp. 289, 322, 345, and p. 259, his answer to M. de Lasteyrie. Reprinted in part in *Revue de l'art chrétien*, 1901, vol. 44, pp. 369, 462.

In the excellent public library of Caen are to be found the *Congrès Archéologique*, the *Bulletin Monumental*, and other archæological publications. Also the *Catalogue des ouvrages normande de la Bibliothèque municipale de Caen* (Caen, 1910-12).

[322] Georges Lafenestre, *Gloires et deuils de France* (Paris, Hachette, 1918).

was required. Matilda's tomb rests in the middle of the choir she built. Her epitaph was inscribed in letters of gold: "Consoler of the needy, lover of piety, a woman who, having lavished her treasures in good works, was poor to herself, but rich to the unfortunate. Thus she sought the fellowship of eternal life on the second of November, 1083."

The Crypt of the Abbaye-aux-Dames at Caen (1059-1066)

The Abbaye-aux-Dames, begun about 1059, was dedicated in 1066 by the same Archbishop Maurille who blessed the new church at Jumièges. A few weeks after the ceremony, William descended on England, which his knights and villeins conquered to the chant of the *Chanson de Roland*, written by some unknown poet who, like themselves, looked to the Archangel of the Peril for inspiration. Yet a few decades more and Roland's war song was sung by the first crusaders before Jerusalem. Architecture, crusades, language, literature—many were the vital movements then coming to birth.

On the day of the blessing of Matilda's convent of the Holy Trinity, her little daughter, Cécile, was laid on the altar and dedicated to God's service. For almost fifty years her aunt, Matilda, daughter of Richard II and the fair Judith of Brittany, ruled the Abbaye-aux-Dames, and then Cécile succeeded as second abbess; *Dame de la ville de Caen*, her brother Henry I of England called her. Cécile was one of the learned ladies of her day, having studied philosophy and belles-lettres under the patriarch of Jerusalem. One recalls that it was a contemporary abbess—at St. Odile in Alsace—who made the first attempt to compile an encyclopedia. Several English princesses were nuns of the Trinité, among them the daughters of Henry III and Edward I. In a later century Charlotte Corday was a pupil of the convent.

It has been thought that Gundulf, a monk of Bec, called to Caen by Lanfranc, was architect of the Abbaye-aux-Dames, where his mother had retired as a nun. This learned and pious man had entered Bec in the same year as St. Anselm, and when he had become the bishop of Rochester he remained faithful to Anselm, then the primate of England, facing bitter troubles with the king. The saint came to attend the good bishop on his deathbed. Gundulf rebuilt Rochester Cathedral, whose crypt and western bays are of his time (1076-1108); Rochester Tower, too, he raised, and the chapel of St. John in London Tower. It was said of him that he was the most skilled of all men in masoncraft.

The apse of the Trinité is considered one of the best things in Caen. It stands over a crypt whose sixteen piers are in four rows. When the choir was renovated, after 1100, some of its sculptures were modeled on certain Byzantine ivories that had been brought as gifts to Abbess Cécile by her crusading brother. The abbatial's triforium is a blind arcade behind whose wall was essayed some very primitive flying buttresses. The present sexpartite vault was an early trial of that Norman form of the Gothic masonry roof, and is really a quadripartite vault divided by a transverse rib, the web being unwarped to that intermediate member. Though the XII century replaced the original timber roof of the Trinité by this sexpartite one, exactly when it was done is not known. But those interested in claiming priority for Normandy in the use of diagonal ribs place it before the sexpartite vaulting of St. Denis. The XIII century added a handsome Gothic chapel to the transept of Matilda's convent church.

As the expiatory abbatial erected by the Conqueror was on a far larger scale than the Abbaye-aux-Dames, it took longer to build; perhaps the same Gundulf of Bec and Rochester was its architect. Over the aisles are deep tribunes, some of whose bays have retained their primitive vaults of the same type as those at Tournus in Burgundy—half barrels placed side by side on lintels at right angles to the axis of the church. The original roof of the principal span was replaced by the actual sexpartite vault (whose web is warped to the six branches) about 1130, said M. Régnier; other archæologists have placed it a generation later. By the addition of a sexpartite vaulting the much-discussed Lombard alternate piers were no longer inconsequent. The height to which the wall shafts of the nave are carried indicates that the cowled architect had not purposed originally to cover his main span with a stone roof. When the Gothic vaulting was added the clearstory was changed in the interior of the church, but the exterior was left as first built.

William and Matilda made Caen their chief residence in Normandy, and Lanfranc was brought from Bec in 1063 to be prior of the duke's new monastery. He opened a school in Caen to which his pupil, Pope Alexander II, sent his relatives as scholars. In the peaceful cloister of St. Étienne the able Italian composed a treatise—to counteract Berengar's heresy on the Eucharist—which is considered a small masterpiece of Christian controversy. Lanfranc was dialectician, administrator, builder, subtle lawyer, and statesman. His genius reached its highest development in the organization of a Norman hierarchy for England. He rebuilt his own church at Canterbury, and two former monks of St. Étienne, Caen, rebuilt the cathedral of Winchester and St. Alban's abbey. Other memorials of Lanfranc's primacy in England are the crypt and eastern end of Gloucester Cathedral, the work of a monk of Mont-Saint-Michel, the crypt at Worcester, choir chapels and ambulatory at Norwich, and the western transept of Ely Cathedral, erected by a monk from St. Ouen, Rouen. It is said that during the century and a half from the Conqueror to John Lackland the Norman prelates in England erected over four hundred churches as expiatory offerings for the grievous wrong perpetrated in the Norman conquest.

In Caen, Lanfranc built the nave of the Abbaye-aux-Hommes, a monument of magnificent proportions, compact, tranquil, and sincere. When archbishop of Canterbury he returned to Caen in 1077 for the dedication of his abbey church. Another ten years and in St. Étienne's choir took place the sinister burial of William the Conqueror. In the town was raging a fierce conflagration which was to wipe out half the place. As they lowered into the tomb the proud and wrathful overman whose strength had been so pitiless, whose will so inflexible, a poor townsman stepped forth to forbid the burial, claiming he had been robbed of that special parcel of land. In the disorders that ensued the corpulent body of the dead king was injured, and though incense was burned to purify the infected air, the people deserted the church in horror. *Sic pulvis es.*

In 1210 the Romanesque choir of the Abbaye-aux-Hommes was replaced by the present Gothic one. Normandy apparently used annulets about the clustered shafts at a much later date than the Ile-de-France, and it continued to employ its pre-Gothic zigzag decoration. The chapels round the choir were made to open one on the other above low dividing walls; Bayeux and Coutances repeated this, as they did the turrets at the birth of the apse. The exterior aspect of the edifice was enhanced by a row of small rose windows each of which lighted a bay of the choir's tribune. A generation later the same arrangement was employed in the collegiate church at Mantes.

The new Gothic choir of St. Étienne at Caen was joined with skill to Lanfranc's grave Romanesque nave. Maître Guillaume is cited as architect of the new works, and he probably crowned the two western towers that so grandly dominate the city. Few architectural views in France surpass the stark majesty of the fortresslike church built by the Conqueror, as it appears from across the town, from the rue des Chanoines, when one stands near the convent church of Queen Matilda. St. Étienne's towers were the prototypes for the other notable ones at Caen.

During the XVI-century religious wars the Abbaye-aux-Hommes was twice pillaged and the Calvinists scattered the Conqueror's ashes. They stripped the roofing of its lead, which soon caused the collapse of the central lantern and the choir vaults. During two generations the great church lay unused save as a stone quarry. Then the prior, Jean de Baillehache, in 1609, undertook a restoration, carried through so judiciously that were it not for the monastery's official record, and a slight poverty in the sculpture, it would be impossible to detect the new parts from the old.

For the making of towers Caen is a queen city. In descending the rue des Chanoines one passes the church of St. Pierre, whose much-admired Renaissance apse (1518-45) was the work of a regional master, Hector Sohier. But it is the tower of St. Pierre which is its glory and the boast of Normandy. It served as model for belfries throughout the duchy and in Brittany. Built from 1308 to 1317, it stands as proof that the tradition of Apogee Gothic continued till the opening of the Hundred Years' War. Apart from the natural rise and fall of things human various causes contributed to the decline of Gothic art after the XIII century. A soulless mechanical dexterity that crystallized the principles of Gothic architecture succeeded to the creative genius that had made glorious the reigns of Philippe-Auguste and Louis IX. Symbolism and true mysticism gave place to doubt, and—when internal dissensions and foreign invasion rent the land—to superstition. With the blurring of spiritual vision passed the vigor of construction.

The XIV century in France opened under a king who debased the coinage, overtaxed the clergy, persecuted the Jews, and who, by the outrage of Anagni, struck a fatal blow at the prestige of the papacy. Soon followed the Black Death, when a third of Europe's population perished. Radical deterioration of the national art set in after France "went to pieces at the Battle of Crécy" (1346). The royal domain was a field of brigandage: "From the Loire to the Seine, and from the Seine to the Somme, the peasants being killed, all the fields lay uncultivated, and this during many years," wrote Bishop Bérenger of Le Mans. In Paris Cathedral a foreigner was crowned king of France.

What horrors reigned in Normandy, many an old record relates. More than a thousand patriot leaders perished when English gold was given for each decapitated corpse. "Houses are without occupants, fields without workers," wrote a XV-century bishop of Lisieux. Bedford's troops pillaged and massacred. Near Falaise twelve thousand civilians were butchered in one day. "The land of Normandy was grievously oppressed and *le pauvre peuple détruit*," wrote Monstrelet. "Men and women fled for their lives, by land and by sea, as if in peril of fire. Nobles gave up their fiefs, clerks their benefices, burghers their patrimony, rather than take oath to the invader."[323] *Normannia nutrix* lay almost uninhabited.

[323] An old chronicle related how the young widow of the lord of La Roche-Guyon *"mieux aimer s'en aller denuée de tous bien, avec ses trois enfants, que de rendre hommage au roi d'outre mer et de se mettre ès mains des anciens ennemies du royaume."* Anthyme Saint-Paul, *L'architecture française et la Guerre de Cent Ans* (Paris, 1910); Siméon Luce, *La France pendant*

Such is the French version. Naturally the English outlook was different. "The false Frenchman," sings Drayton in his Agincourt ballad. Freeman falls into a vein of self-congratulation. "Go from France proper into Normandy," he writes, "and you at once feel that everything is palpably better; men, women, horses, cows, all are on a grander, better scale. The good seed planted by the old Saxon and Danish colonists, and watered in aftertimes by Henry V and John, Duke of Bedford, is still there. It is not altogether choked by the tares of Paris."

Gothic art deteriorated, but so persistently lingered the simplicity, the spiritual poignancy of the XIII century that in the late-Gothic day it was still possible to produce the mystic loveliness of Riom's Madonna of the Bird, and the humble prayerfulness of Solesmes' Magdalene.

In the unspoiled years of the XIV century was built the tower of St. Pierre, at Caen. Its shaft rises in a virile, unbroken ascent from soil to spire tip. On the busiest street corner of the city it stands like a perpetual call to recollection and joy. The Norman will boast with legitimate pride that it is the most beautiful tower in France, excelling those of Chartres and Senlis, whose shafts, he will tell you, are either too high or too short, whereas his loved tower of St. Pierre has spire and shaft in perfect accord. When Caen added this stately monument to its wealth of churches it was as rich a metropolis as Rouen, and it had contributed more than London toward the ransom of Richard Cœur-de-Lion from Teuton captivity. Just before the defeat of Crécy, this, the intellectual capital of Normandy, was besieged by English troops, and all its wealth pillaged, and its streets strewn with dead. Amid havoc wrought, the towers of the Abbaye-aux-Dames were destroyed.

---

la Guerre de Cent Ans (Paris, Hachette, 1893); H. Dénifle, *La désolation des églises, monastères, et hôpitaux en France pendant la Guerre de Cent Ans* (Paris, Picard, 1899); H. Martin, *La guerre au XV*^e *siècle* (Paris, H. Laurens); G. Lefèvre-Pontalis, "Épisodes de l'invasion anglaise. La guerre de partisans dans la Haute-Normandie" (1424-29), in *Bibliothèque de l'École des chartes*, 1893 to 1895, vols. 54, 55, 56.

**Belfry of St. Pierre at Caen (1308-1317). Prototype for the Gothic Towers of
Normandy and Brittany**

All over the department of Calvados are towers.[324] A Romanesque one
crowns the church of Vaucelles, a suburb of Caen. At Ifs, and near Bayeux, at St.
Loup (c. 1180), are others. The monk's church of Norrey, a dependency of St. Ouen,
at Rouen, noted for the lavishness of its foliate ornamentation, has a tower of the
XIII century, and near it, also ten miles from Caen, is Secqueville's Gothic beacon.

[324] A. de Caumont, "Les tours d'églises dans le Calvados," in *Bulletin Monumental*,
1847, vol. 23, p. 362; E. Lefèvre-Pontalis, "Les clochers du Calvados," in *Congrès Archéologique*,
1908, vol. 2, p. 652; G. Bouet, "Clochers du diocèse de Bayeux," in *Bulletin Monumental*, 1872,
vol. 38, p. 517; Abbé Édeline, *Norrey et son histoire; La Normandie monumentale et pittoresque.
Calvados*, p. 231, "Norrey," G. Lavalley; p. 349, "Secqueville"; *Congrès Archéologique*, 1908, p.
193, "Bernières"; p. 338, "Norrey"; p. 349, "Secqueville."

There are belfries at Bernières-sur-mer (c. 1150), at Langrune, Thaon, Tour, and Basly.

Three of the most beautiful towers in Calvados crown the abbatial of St. Pierre-sur-Dives, an edifice, too much a patchwork of five centuries to be altogether pleasing, but linked with a memorable hour of the Gothic story, 1145. Popular enthusiasm then aided Abbot Haimon to reconstruct his church, as he wrote, in a much-quoted letter to the English monks at Tutbury. The same wave of fervor was raising the Primary Gothic towers of Chartres and Rouen. The western towers of St. Pierre-sur-Dives are of Haimon's day only in their lower stories; that to the south has a XIII-century top, and that to the north was finished in the XIV century.[325]

Throughout the final phase of Gothic, Normandy continued to excel in towers. Witness Rouen's Flamboyant beacons. In quiet country places and lesser towns rise belfries as stately as those of cathedrals: at Carville is the "Giant of the Valley" (1512-14), at Harfleur is a most beautiful tower, and still another at Verneuil (1506-30), built by a son of the town, Arthur Fillon, curé of St. Maclou, Rouen, and vicar-general of that lover of noble structures, Cardinal Georges d'Amboise; when he became bishop of Senlis, he helped to finish the Flamboyant Gothic transept of that cathedral.

THE ROMANESQUE ABBATIAL OF ST. GEORGES DE BOSCHERVILLE[326]

> I have borne for forty-two years with happiness the sweet yoke of the Lord.
>
> —ORDERICUS VITALIS (XII Century).

From Rouen a pleasant six-mile walk through the forest of Roumare leads to the abbatial of St. Georges de Boscherville, an example of the best Anglo-Norman

[325] In the abbatial of St. Pierre-sur-Dives there is XII-century work in the ambulatory walls, in the piers and side walls of the nave, and in the lower parts of the façade towers. To the XIII century belong most of the choir's piers and the apsidal chapels, also the beautiful chapter house. The transept then was put into harmony with the nave, and its tower built, which latter now is braced by clumsy obstructions within the church. In the XIV century rose the west façade, and the north tower was rebuilt. The XV century rehandled the high vaulting and clearstory, where appear die-away moldings and flamelike tracery. The abbey was founded by Richard II (d. 1020) and his beautiful duchess, Judith of Brittany. Its Romanesque abbatial was dedicated in 1067 by Archbishop Maurille in the presence of the Conqueror and Matilda. In 1107 the abbatial was burned by Henry I of England, who accused the abbot of siding with his elder brother, with whom he was at war, but in atonement the king contributed toward the reconstruction of the church; *Congrès Archéologique*, 1861, 1862, and 1908, p. 278; J. Pépin, *Saint-Pierre-sur-Dives* (Caen, 1879); Abbé Denis, *Église de Saint-Pierre-sur-Dives en 1145* (Caen, 1869); *Bibliothèque de l'École des chartes*, vol. 21, p. 120, gives Abbot Haimon's letter, which also was published in Rouen, 1851, by L. de Glanville.

[326] *Congrès Archéologique*, 1908; A. Besnard, *Monographie de l'église et de l'abbaye Saint Georges de Boscherville* (Paris, Lechevailier, 1899); J. A. Deville, *Essai historique et descriptive sur l'église et l'abbaye de St. Georges de Boscherville* (Rouen, 1827); *La Normandie monumentale et pittoresque. Seine-Inférieure*, p. 235, Abbé A. Tougard.

Romanesque. Some have thought it belongs to the first decade of the XII century, but M. Besnard places it a generation earlier. Mr. John Bilson claims that, like its contemporary, the cathedral at Durham, the piers show that from the start the design was to construct ribbed groin vaults over the wide span, and he thinks that the same is true for the now disused Romanesque abbatial of St. Nicolas, at Caen (1083-93), building twenty years before Durham's choir. He has cited the diagonals of Lessay's choir and those of the transept of Montvilliers as the primitive Gothic of Normandy, vaults which M. de Lasteyrie considered to be contemporary with Suger's St. Denis. The German archæologists, Dehio and von Bezold, give priority to Normandy.

The actual intersecting ribs at St. Georges de Boscherville are a XIII-century reconstruction. So solid were the church walls made that no flying buttresses have been needed. The tribune at the end of each arm of the transept is supported by an isolated pillar, apsidal chapels project from the eastern wall of the transept, and the central lantern is one of the best in Normandy. The entire church, save its west façade flanked by slender turrets, was the work of some six or seven years only. About 1157, under Abbot Victor, was erected the chapter house that nestles beneath the transept's northern arm. The French students who did not know, or who have not accepted, Mr. John Bilson's theory of Anglo-Norman priority in the use of the essential organ of Gothic architecture, have claimed that the diagonals of St. Georges' chapter house are among the earliest extant of the province, of the same decade as the vaulting of the lower hall of St. Romain's tower at Rouen. Mr. John Bilson's championship of Anglo-Norman pioneer work, and Mr. Arthur Kingsley Porter's theory of Lombard priority, have both found supporters among leading French archæologists; the English scholar is patriotically disgruntled at the American's advocacy of the Italian claims.

It would seem that during the XI century the Normans, like the Lombards, used what Mr. Bilson calls ribbed groined vaults, occasionally, for one reason or another. The Norman developed tentatively the ribbed vault, always associating it with the semicircular arch, and without comprehending the wonderful results that were to be derived from concentrating the weight of a masonry roof at fixed points. The possibility of those results was perceived first in the Ile-de-France, and from there, when Gothic architecture had taken on its special characteristics, it entered Normandy by way of the Seine at Rouen and Boscherville, then at Fécamp and Lisieux. The first Gothic cathedrals of Normandy show purely French influence and only gradually were regional ogival traits developed. In the controversy as to who first used diagonals, one can take whichever side one prefers; the question remains open. Light will be thrown on it, doubtless, by a forthcoming paper by Mr. Bilson in the *Archeological Journal*, tracing the evolution of the diagonal rib in Normandy.

The abbey at Boscherville was founded by the lord of Tankerville, high chamberlain of the Conqueror and Henry I. In its abbatial, when his grandson, hereditary constable of Normandy, was knighted, he laid his sword on the altar, and to redeem it presented property to the monastery. If we would comprehend the society that built these churches, we must understand that such donations were voluntary and a matter of civic pride. "If I cannot myself attend to the works of God," runs an ancient deed of gift, "at least I can assure a home for those with whom God loves to dwell. It is only natural to enrich our Holy Mother the Church, and thus to take a hand in caring for Christ's poor."

THE GOTHIC ABBATIAL AT FÉCAMP[327]

It is a usage bequeathed to us from our ancestors, never to let anyone depart from our abbey without a gift.

—(FROM AN OLD LATIN CHRONICLE OF FÉCAMP.)

If one would enjoy, without critical comparison, the Gothic of Normandy, her churches should be visited before the taste has become sensitized by loiterings in the Ile-de-France. In that classic region of the national art is found a simplicity, a purity, a restraint, a something of imaginative genius that makes of its work the touchstone by which all other manifestations of Gothic are judged. Of the Norman churches, the Trinité, at Fécamp, is most closely related to the Primary Gothic work of the royal domain. Its architect must certainly have come from the Ile-de-France. Monks trained in the Celtic rule by St. Wandrille founded Fécamp, which was wrecked by Norse pirates in 876. William Longsword, the first duke's son, built his palace here, and his son, Richard I the Fearless (d. 996), began a new monastery. In his will Richard ordered: "Bury not my body within the church, but deposit it on the outside, immediately under the eaves, that the dripping of the rain from the holy roof may wash my bones as I lie and may cleanse them of the spots of impurity contracted during a negligent and neglected life." He desired that on every Friday a sarcophagus be filled with wheat and grain for the poor. His son, Richard II the Good (d. 1020), finished Fécamp abbatial, and was laid to rest beside his father. The dukes of Rollo's line especially favored Fécamp, which held a front rank among Normandy's institutions, and was the richest of her monasteries down to the Revolution. Henry Plantagenet presented Fécamp town to the monastery.

After Duke Richard the Good had brought that man of administrative genius, William of Volpiano, into his duchy to reorganize its spiritual life, architectural activities took on new vigor. William himself directed the construction of Bernay's[328] church; the abbatial of Mont-Saint-Michel rose when he reformed that

[327] *Congrès Archéologique*, 1908; Doctor Coutan, *La Trinité de Fécamp* (Caen, 1907). He also describes the Trinité in *La Normandie monumentale et pittoresque. Seine-Inférieure*, p. 465; the churches at Dieppe, p. 279; the church of Harfleur, p. 393; Le Havre, p. 381; Carville, p. 177, and Notre Dame at Caudebec-en-Caux, of which Abbé Sauvage has published a separate monograph (1876); A. Leport, *Description de l'église de la Trinité de Fécamp* (Fécamp, 1879); Leroux de Lincy, *Essai historique sur l'abbaye de Fécamp; Histoire littéraire de la France*, vol. 7, p. 318, "Le bienheureux Guillaume, abbé de St. Bénigne de Dijon" (Paris, 1746); vol. 10, p. 265, "Herbert Lozinga, évêque de Norwich" (Paris, 1756).

[328] The abbatial of Bernay (Eure), to-day a corn exchange on the market place, shows in its transept the earliest instance of an arcaded wall passage, the feature that, when placed at the clearstory level, became one of the most frequent characteristics of Anglo-Norman architecture, both Romanesque and Gothic. Bernay was founded between 1013 and 1019 by Richard II and Judith of Brittany, the same who invited to their duchy the Lombard, Wil-

house; and the church of Jumièges followed immediately after his reformation there. The Blessed William, in his thirst for souls, used to loiter at the crossroads to gather in the stricken of body or spirit. He passed away in Fécamp in 1031, and his ashes are still preserved in a chapel of the present Gothic abbatial. In 1034, in the Romanesque Trinité, Robert the Magnificent gathered the chief men of Normandy to have them swear allegiance to his sturdy little bastard son of seven, who was to be known in history as William the Conqueror, after which Duke Robert started on his pilgrimage to the East, from which he was never to return. The abbey church of Fécamp long consisted of the nave begun by Richard I, and a choir built by Abbot Guillaume de Ros (1082-1108), under whose rule the Trinité won the admiration of Europe. He is said to have introduced into Normandy the ambulatory and its radiating chapels. Two of the radial chapels which he constructed at Fécamp have survived. While they were building, there lived in the Trinité convent, as prior, Herbert de Lozinga, who, obtaining the bishopric of Norwich, erected on the Norfolk downs a stately Norman cathedral (1096-1119). Abbot Guillaume de Ros carried out the instructions of Richard I to give a loaf of bread to every beggar asking it, and when Fécamp was dissolved at the Revolution its abbot was distributing daily some twelve thousand free loaves of bread.

In 1169 fire wrecked the Romanesque Trinité, whereupon the present Gothic edifice was begun immediately, and in it two of the groin-vaulted chapels from the choir of Guillaume de Ros were incorporated. Abbot Henri de Soullay (1139-87) built the Primary Gothic choir, transept, and half of the nave. After the fifth bay of the nave a new architect took up the work, as is shown by differences in the pier profiles, but the cessation of activities must have been of short duration, as the church is homogeneous. The nave was finished under Abbot Raoul d'Argence (1190-1220), who organized Normandy's first literary academy—a confraternity of jongleurs. Its character was more Norman than the choir, though regional traits had early appeared in the turrets at the birth of the apse and the square central lantern.

To increase the impression of length in the nave its side walls were marked by double the number of arcades that divide the middle church from the aisles. This was accomplished by introducing a fifth rib into each vault section of those side corridors, which rib fell on a shaft engaged in the side walls. Like the minsters of England, Fécamp is more remarkable in its length than in its height.

liam of Volpiano. William is known to have worked on the Bernay abbatial, which shows resemblances to Burgundian churches at Auxerre and Nevers, and he may have brought to Normandy the Lombard trait of absidal chapels projecting from the eastern wall of the transept. Bernay, however, did not use the Lombard alternance of ground supports. Mr. Bilson thinks that the tall attached stripes were intended for a vaulted, not for a timber roof. The nave's side walls and piers are of Abbot William's time; two bays of the choir belong to later years of the XI century. William the Conqueror is said to have finished the church. It was grievously sacked during the religious wars. The church of Ste. Croix in Bernay, begun, 1373, enlarged 1497, contains tombs from Bec, of former abbots there. *Congrès Archéologique*, 1908, vol. 2, p. 588, Chanoine Porée; *Bulletin Monumental*, 1911, vol. 75, p. 396, Chanoine Porée, and p. 403, John Bilson; G.T. Rivoira, *Lombardic Architecture*, translated by G. Mc. N. Rushford (London and New York, 1910); Chanoine Porée, *Bernay* (Caen, H. Delesques, 1912).

Abbot Thomas de Saint-Benoît (1297-1307) decided to suppress the deep gallery over the choir's ambulatory, making the chapels that open on the curving aisle of exceptional height. He changed the southern aisle, giving it a coldly elegant Rayonnant aspect, but happily not that to the north, or we would have lost the two interesting Romanesque chapels of Abbot Guillaume de Ros. Some of Fécamp's later abbots were Clement VI, builder of the palace of the popes at Avignon and of the Chaise Dieu in the mountains of Auvergne, and an abbot of the patriotic Estouteville family, who was driven out by the English when Fécamp was besieged in 1415. The tool who succeeded him sat in judgment on Jeanne d'Arc.

The abbot of Fécamp during the transitional Flamboyant Renaissance day was Cardinal Antoine Boyer (1492-1519), a Mæcenas who adorned his beautiful church with Italian marbles. He had sculptured, in the same studio at Genoa that provided Louis XII with the Orléans tombs for St. Denis, an Entombment more spectacular in character than the famous one at Solesmes. Girolamo Viscardo made for him a tabernacle (for the choir's procession path), after the style of Mino da Fiesole. The lovely marble screens that close the side chapels are due to this generous prelate. For him Jacques Le Roux, the noted architect of Rouen, lengthened the Lady chapel. The only later change of importance in the Trinité was the erection of its neo-classic façade.

THE GOTHIC ABBATIAL AT EU[329]

La Nature a bien des manières de sourire. La Normandie est
le plus beau sourire de la nature temperée.

—O. Reclus.

The tutelary of Eu is St. Laurence O'Toole, archbishop of Dublin, son of a prince in Leinster, an active continuer of the reforms begun by St. Malachy of Armagh, who died in St. Bernard's arms at Clairvaux. St. Laurence had crossed the Channel to plead with Henry Plantagenet for certain of his flock in disgrace (1180). Arriving at Eu's convent, then belonging to the congregation of St. Victor, he felt a premonition of his approaching death, and exclaimed, as he crossed the threshold, "Here is my abode of rest forever." He was worn out in the struggle to uphold the weak against the strong in those difficult years of the Anglo-Norman seizure of the eastern coast of Ireland. As his end drew near a monk suggested that he make his testament. "I thank God that I have nothing to bequeath," he said.

So impressive was the death of Archbishop Laurence in Eu monastery that the little people of the Lord soon began to pray beside his tomb. When the monks reconstructed their church they placed the saintly man's relics in the new crypt. From 1186 to 1226 the choir, transept, and one bay of the nave were built without interruption, in a Gothic more of the Ile-de-France than regional, though the placing of towers between transept and choir and the central lantern followed the Norman tradition.

[329] *Congrès Archéologique*, 1895; Abbé A. Legris, *L'église d'Eu* (1913); Desiré Le Beuf, *La ville d'Eu* (1884); Doctor Coutan, in *La Normandie monumentale et pittoresque. Seine-Inférieure*, vol. 1, p. 333; Viollet-le-Duc, *Dictionnaire de l'architecture*, vol. 1, p. 198; vol. 2, p. 364; vol. 5, p. 359; Gonse, *L'art gothique*, p. 210 (Paris, Quantin, 1891).

Archbishop Laurence O'Toole was canonized in 1225, and to the joyous ceremony when his relics were set above the high altar came the archbishop of Rouen—then building his cathedral, and Bishop Geoffrey, the "shining man of Eu by whom the throne of Amiens rose into immensity." For eight days the throng pressed to pray near the relics of the canonized Irish prelate, and with the gifts that poured in the monks were able to finish their nave by 1230. It is a gem of Norman Gothic, sober, elegant, of perfect unity. The first plan called for tribunes over the aisles, as in the choir. Before they were constructed, however, the idea was given up, but it was decided to keep the arches by which the tribunes would have opened on the middle church. The same effect of false tribunes had been used earlier in the nave of Rouen Cathedral.

In 1426 lightning caused the collapse of the central tower, and in the reconstruction of the transept and choir, undertaken after the invaders were driven from Normandy, Flamboyant work was set side by side with Primary Gothic. From 1511 to 1534 rose the transept's florid south façade. After the Revolution the church of St. Laurent was restored by the Orléans family, who own the château and park at Eu.

MONT-SAINT-MICHEL[330]

Chaque peuple a son ange, disait Daniel le prophète. Le nôtre ne peut pas, même indignes nous délaisser.... Plus encore que Saint Jacques était le patron des espagnols, Saint Michel voulut être le Baron de France. Il mit les trois lys dans ses armes et fit passer sur le royaume l'éclair de son glaive. Avoir suscité Jeanne d'Arc et par elle libéré la France.... Voilà bien le plus beau miracle dû à l'archange. Il constitue pour le pays une promesse de perennité.

—JOSEPH LOTTE (born in Normandy, 1875;
killed in the World War, 1914).

Surpassing all the abbeys of Normandy is the outpost of the archangel that lies offshore, at the junction of Normandy and Brittany, a conicle mass of "rock on rock, keep on keep, century on century," sand-locked one hour, and the next rising from the Atlantic. *Tremor immensi oceani* is the motto of the Mount. Before the days of crusaders it was one of Europe's chief points of departure for the Eastern pil-

[330] Paul Gout, *Le Mont-Saint-Michel* (Paris, Colin, 1910), 2 vols.; Ch. H. Besnard, *Mont-Saint-Michel* (Collection, Petites Monographies), (Paris, H. Laurens, 1911); Ch. de Beaurepaire, *Curieuses recherches sur le Mont-Saint-Michel* (Rouen, 1873); Ed. Corroyer, *Description de l'abbaye du Mont-Saint-Michel et de ses abords* (Paris, 1877); Dubouchet, *L'abbaye de Mont-Saint-Michel* (Paris, 1895); Sir Theodore Andreas Cook, *Twenty-five Great Houses of France* (London and New York, 1916), chap. 1; Henry Adams, *Chartres and Mont-Saint-Michel* (Boston, Houghton Mifflin Company, 1913); Léopold Delisle, éd., *Cronique de Robert de Torigni* (Paris, Soc. de l'histoire de Normandie, 1872-75), 2 vols. On Robert de Torigny see *Histoire littéraire de la France*, vol. 14, p. 362 (Paris, 1817); Siméon Luce, éd., *Cronique de Mont-Saint-Michel: la défence nationale* (1879-86); O. de Poli, *Les défenseurs du Mont-Saint-Michel, 1417-50*, (Paris, 1895); Huynes, *Histoire générale de Mont-Saint-Michel* (Rouen, 1872); Brin, *St. Michel et le Mont-Saint-Michel dans l'histoire et la littérature* (Paris, 1880).

grimage. Like Jerusalem, it has been one of the sites of the earth that has impressed itself with historic signification on the imagination of mankind.

Many have felt the kindred spirit of the *Chanson de Roland* and the granite, military monastery. They are both of the same high lineage. To the paladin Roland, dying at Roncevaux, as he held up his right glove to God, his suzerain, there came, to fetch his soul to Paradise, the very special St. Michael of the Mount that stood in peril of the sea, in *periculo maris*.[331] Scholars think that the most virile, the most

[331] From the *Chanson de Roland*, édition Léon Gautier (Tours, Mâme et fils, 1895).

> "Li quens Rollanz se jut desuz un pin;
> Envers Espaigne en ad turnet sun vis.
> De plusurs choses à remembrer li prist;
> De toutes teres que li bers ad cunquis,
> De dulce France, des humes de sun lign,
> De Carlemagne, sun seignur, ki l'nurrit,
> Ne poet muer n'en plurt e ne suspirt.
> Mais lui meïsme ne voelt metre en ubli;
> Cleimet sa culpe, si priet Deu mercit:
> 'Viere paterne, ki unkes ne mentis,
> Seit Lazarin de mort resurrexis
> E Daniel des leuns quaresis,
> Guaris de mei l'aume de tuz perilz
> Pur les pecchiez que en ma vie fis!'
> Sun destre gant à Deu en puroffrit,
> E de sa main seinz Gabriel l'ad pris.
> Desur sun braz teneit le chef enclin:
> Juintes ses mains est alez à sa fin.
> Deus li tramist sun angle chérubin,
> Seinz Raphael, seinz Michiel de l'Péril,
> Ensemble od els seinz Gabriels i vint,
> L'aume de l'Cunte portent en pareïs."

("Roland the brave lay prone beneath a pine,
Toward Spain his face was turned as conqueror,
Of many things came back the memory sharp,
The host of places he had won in war,
Thoughts of sweet France and of his parentage,
Of Charlemagne, his lord, who nurtured him;
And tears and sighs rose as the memories surged.
Nor did he wish his own self to forget.
Demanding grace of God, he told his sins:
'Our Father true, who never yet has lied,
Who from the grave raised Blessed Lazarus,
Who Daniel saved from lions, save my soul.
Pardon the sins that I have stained it with!'
Toward God he held his right-hand gauntlet up,
Archangel Gabriel took it from his hand.
Then on his arm his head sank slowly down,
Hands clasped in prayer his spirit passed beyond.
God to him sent his angel cherubim,
Archguardian Michael, him called of the Peril,

heroic of the *chansons de geste*, wherein already was *la douce France* loved beyond the regional cradle, was composed by a Norman who lived in the marches within the cult of the Angel of the Peril.[332]

The Hall of the Knights at Mont-Saint-Michel (1203-1228). Second Story of the Merveille

Alas, in our day Mont-Saint-Michel-au-péril-de-la-Mer is in very deadly peril of the land, for it looks as if the covetousness of financiers was to defraud France of this rock of glory *"qui s'émeut et s'achève en prière."* Dikes and dams, to reclaim coast lands, will before long cause the historic crag to rise from green woods as it did some geological periods ago.

Citadel, palace, cloister, church, and town, the Mount is a thing of romance that not all the vulgarity of daily tourist crowds can tarnish. Charlemagne himself chose its tutelary archangel for the national patron saint, and the cowled guardians here were in truth through long centuries what the great emperor called monks: "Knights of the Church, of the willing vassalage and chivalry of Christ."

The Northmen destroyed the ancient shrine. Then Richard the Fearless, grandson of the pirate Rollo, placed on the rock the sons of St. Benedict, trained at St. Wandrille. Richard II, in 1017, came to the Mount to ask a blessing on his union

St. Raphael and St. Gabriel with him came
And bore the Count's soul straight to Paradise.")
[332] Léon Gautier, *Les épopées françaises* (Paris, V. Palme, 1878-94), 4 vols.; Joseph Bédier, *Les légends épiques, recherches sur la formation des chansons de geste*, vol. 3, "La légende de Roland" (Paris, H. Champion, 1908-13), 4 vols.

with Judith of Brittany, whose beauty was such that the old chronicle exclaimed *corpore et moribus usque ad miraculum elegantem*. The duke's marriage gift enabled the monks to supplant their Carolingian church by a bigger one. The discarded X-century chapel was discovered in 1909 by M. Paul Gout, the Mount's latest historian. Until 1780 it had been used as Notre Dame-sous-Terre, but during the building of the foundations for the ugly west façade of the upper church it was walled up.

With Richard the Good's donation, Abbot Hildebert II erected his new church on the very summit of the rock, but as there was not sufficient level space, he built out from the hillcrest a platform of masonry to support the nave. From William of Volpiano's school at Fécamp came skilled journeymen. The church at Mont-Saint-Michel was begun in 1020, and still building in 1057. Abbot Roger I, formerly chaplain to William the Conqueror, erected the nave. William prayed at the Mount before undertaking the conquest of England, and the abbot fitted out for him an entire fleet.

In 1103 the northern wall of the Romanesque nave collapsed one night as the monks were chanting matins in the choir. It was restored immediately in the same style, and Abbot Roger II took the opportunity to reconstruct the monks' quarters. Above the crypt called Aquilon (c. 1112) he built a cloister, which later was vaulted with diagonals, and over that *promenoir* was made a dormitory on the same level as the church. During the years that followed the Mount was governed by a man of genius, Robert de Torigni (1153-80), whose chronicle is the most important history of France for that epoch. In the *promenoir* he entertained, at a banquet in 1158, his sovereign, Henry II, and Aliénor of Aquitaine. They chose him as godfather for their daughter, who, later, as queen of Castile, built the convent church of Las Huelgas by Burgos. Abbot Robert was a pupil of Bec, whose higher standards of intellectual life he brought to the Mount, where he formed a library, built monks' quarters, and added western belfries to his abbatial, though the façade of his day no longer exists.

As the XIII century opened, Normandy became once more a part of the royal domain, after being three centuries under dukes of its own. When Rollo's strong breed ended in the debased John Lackland, the northern province gladly accepted Philippe-Auguste as ruler. How whole-heartedly, how unreservedly French it became it was to prove by its heroic resistance to the English invaders during the Hundred Years' War.[333]

In the frays of 1203, fire had spread from the town that hugged the rock's edge, to the monastic buildings on the summit. Philippe-Auguste, always wisely conciliatory toward new subjects, contributed toward the restorations. With the gift from the king under whom most of the Gothic cathedrals of France were begun, Abbot Jourdan (1191-1212) built the supreme architectural work of the citadel,

---

[333] "Il y a des provinces qui ont le doit de se dire françaises par excellence.... La Normandie et la Picardie sont de celles-là.... Elles ont apportés, dans le cours des siècles, à la vieille Ile-de-France, leur aînée, le concours loyal de leur bras, de leur courage, de leur génie." —GABRIEL HANOTAUX, "La Normandie dans l'unité française," in *Société normande de géographie*, 1900, vol 22.

what is called the Merveille, and a marvel indeed are its three stories that rise, one above the other, hall over hall, two hundred feet in height above the sea, ridged heavily outside by stout buttresses and graced within by pillars, arches, and a sky-gazing cloister.

From the brain of some unknown cowled genius sprang this *mâle* and splendid conception, built in the very prime of Gothic. Who else but one enamored of meditation would have set his cloister atop of his monastery under the open sky, or have opened on that courtyard of peace a monks' refectory, where, in a flooded stillness of light, the brethren could sit pondering as they listened to one of their number reading from the stone lectern the book which is the spirit of Bernard of Clairvaux incarnate: "Give all for all; seek nothing; call for nothing back. Thou shalt be free in heart and the darkness shall not overwhelm thee." And around them there spread the wide horizon of the sea one hour, of the white ashes of sand the next.

Pacing the lovely skyward cloister one has time to brood on life and death, on God and one's own soul; it refutes a hundred calumnies against monastic life just by being what it is. Serious men enamored of voluntary seclusion carved it unstintingly and set its columns quaintly in triangular order. Love and science contrived the diffused, soothing luminousness of the brothers' dining hall. The present gable windows there are innovations. Originally when one entered one could discern no window, and yet light was everywhere. The side walls, that from the door appear to be blind arcades, are in reality a succession of narrow panel windows—thirty to a side—deeply recessed in stone embrasures that are triangular in shape, because they serve the purpose of buttresses. To have carried the exterior buttress ridges to such a height as is this refectory, set audaciously up in the sky on the Merveille's third story, would have been an awkward procedure; so the nameless monk-architect, because he was a XIII-century man, let his genius lead him, and, "master of the living stone" that he was, contrived a supreme beauty of decoration out of a structural necessity.

The Merveille was erected under a succession of abbots, in one consecutive radiant effort, from 1203 to 1228—a Titan's work. Each of its three stories is divided into two halls; on the ground floor are the almonry, where the pilgrims fed, and a groin-vaulted cellery or storehouse; the top story, as we have seen, consists of open cloister and monks' refectory; and between the upper and lower stories are two of the most vigorous halls ever built; that over the almonry called the Salle des Hôtes because in it were entertained the guests of the monastery, and that to the west, over the cellery, acquiring the name Salle des Chevaliers, from the Order of the Knights of St. Michael, whose members met here. The latter is divided by rows of stout pillars, and served as the common room of the community, where the tireless scholar-scribes illuminated missals and copied manuscripts.

The charter for the military Order of the Archangel, founded in 1469 by Louis XI, welded the name of St. Michael, whom every good Frenchman knew kept a specially friendly eye on France, with that of Jeanne the Maid, who had quitted Domrémy-on-the-Meuse because the voice of her dear archangel rang insistent in her ear: *Fille Dè, va! Je serai à ton ayde. Va!* It was St. Michael who first roused her to the sense of the great misery there was in the kingdom of France, and in her hour of victory after Orléans she spoke of going to the rescue of the besieged Mount in Normandy. At her trial in Rouen she dwelt on the comfort he had given her.[334] He appeared to her, she said, in the guise of *"un très vrai prud'homme"* — the term loved of St. Louis, who once told Joinville that to be *prud'homme* meant to be knight in heart, as well as outward bearing. "I believe the words of St. Michael who appeared to me," said Jeanne, at her trial, "as firmly as I believe that Our Lord Jesus Christ suffered death and passion for us. And what leads me so to believe is the good counsel, comfort, and good doctrine St. Michael gave me."

On the completion of the Merveille, the monks continued building. They had finished the officiality hall by the entrance gate of the monastery before the visit of St. Louis to the Mount in 1254, when he came to return thanks for his safety during his late crusade. The XIV century added more defenses till the rock became the most forceful example of mediæval military architecture. Strong walls were needed during its siege by the English who invaded Normandy under Henry V. The Mount's abbot, Robert Jollivet, whose name figures among the well-paid judges at Rouen in 1431, allied himself with the victorious foreigners who had quickly overrun the province. His monks repudiated him, led by their prior, Jean Gonault. Defended by the gallant knight Louis d'Estouteville, they endured the longest siege recorded in history, 1415 to 1450, when, as Jeanne had proclaimed, the invaders were *"boutés tous hors de France."*[335]

In 1429, during the memorable siege, the Romanesque choir of Mont-Saint-Michel's abbey church collapsed. It was impossible then to rebuild it; they had even to sell their altar vessels to carry on the defense. When Normandy was again a part of France the erection of a new choir was undertaken by the abbot of the Mount, who was none other than the distinguished Cardinal Guillaume d'Estouteville, the chief agent in the vindication of Jeanne d'Arc's memory. His layman brother had directed the defense of the Mount during many years. In 1450 were laid down the crypt's nineteen mammoth piers, among the most powerful ever planted. The upper church reached its triforium story by 1469, the year when Louis XI came to the rock to establish his new Order of knighthood, and about 1513 the choir was

---

[334] The court at Rouen asked Jeanne at the fourth interrogation, February 27, 1431: "Whose was the first voice you heard when you were about thirteen?" Jeanne replied: "It was St. Michael's. I saw him before my eyes; he was not alone, but was encircled by angels of heaven. I saw him with my bodily eyes as clearly as I see you. When they left me, I wept; right gladly would I have gone with them, that is — my soul." At the seventh interrogation, March 15, 1431, when asked how she knew it was St. Michael, Jeanne replied: *"Par le parler et le langage des anges...."* He told me I was a good child and that God would aid me, and to come to the aid of the king of France. He related to me the *grand pitié qui était au royaume de France."* — E. O'REILLY, *Les deux procès de condamnation et la sentence de réhabilitation, de Jeanne d'Arc* (Paris, Plon, 1808), 2 vols.

[335] *Le procès Jeanne d'Arc,* eighth interrogation, March 17, 1431. When asked by her judges if God hated the English, Jeanne replied: "Of the love or the hate which God has for the English, or of what He will do with their souls, I know nothing. But this I know: that they one and all will be driven out of France, except those who here die, and that God will send victory to the French against the English."

completed. Many hold it to be superior to all other late-Gothic works in France. There are no capitals, the moldings die away in the shafts, the triforium is glazed. It belongs to the fleeting splendor of Flamboyant art, but without capriciousness. There is no overexuberance, no virtuosity in this vigorous, glad memorial of the nation's reconquered freedom:

> Sainte Jeanne went harvesting in France,
> And oh! what found she there?
> The brave seed of her scattering
> In fruitage everywhere.
> And where her strong and tender heart
> Was broken in the flame,
> She found the very heart of France
> Had flowered to her name.[336]

Building activities at the embattled abbey ceased after the erection of its beautiful florid choir. The evil consequences of commendatory abbots—those named by royal whim—bore bitter fruit from end to end of France in the relaxed spiritual life of the monasteries. The XVII-century reformers of the Congregation of St. Maur found the Mount's abbot to be a princeling of Lorraine, five years of age. Those scholarly Benedictines carried on excellent research work in local history, but to their neo-classic generation Gothic art was a sealed book.

Deplorable changes went on during three hundred years: an apsidal chapel of the church was made into a staircase, irregular windows were opened in the halls of the Merveille, the cloister was planted as a garden, to the deterioration of the lower structures, and when, in 1776, fire weakened the abbatial, its three westernmost bays were demolished and the present ugly façade put up. After the Revolution pillaged the monastery it became a state prison called Mont Libre, and so continued until 1863. The church was floored midway to serve as a convicts' hat factory. The modern restoration of Mont-Saint-Michel has been, like that which saved the palace of the popes at Avignon, a truly national benefit.

THE CATHEDRAL OF ROUEN[337]

[336] Marion Couthouy Smith, "Sainte Jeanne of France," in *The Nation* (London, 1915.)

[337] *Congrès Archéologique*, 1859 and 1868; Abbé Loisel et Jean Lafond. *La cathédrale de Rouen* (Collection, Petites Monographies), (Paris, H. Laurens, 1913): Loisel et Alline, *La cathédrale de Rouen avant l'incendie de 1200* (Rouen, Lecerf fils, 1904); Louise Pillion, *Les portails lateraux de la cathédrale de Rouen* (Paris, Picard et fils, 1907); A. Deville, *Tombeaux de la cathédrale de Rouen* (Paris, Levy, 1881), folio; Camille Enlart, *Rouen* (Collection, Villes d'art célèbres), (Paris, H. Laurens, 1904); Émile Lambin, "La cathédrale de Rouen," in *Revue de l'art chrétien*, 1900; Abbé Julien Loth, *La cathédrale de Rouen* (1879).

Other descriptions of Rouen's monuments can be found in the general works of Henri Havard, André Michel, Louis Gonse, Émile Mâle, Paul Vitry.

Cheruel, *Histoire de Rouen sous la domination anglaise au XVᵉ siècle* (Rouen, 1840); A. Fallue, *Histoire de l'église métropolitaine et du diocèse de Rouen* (Rouen, 1850), 4 vols.; Ch. de Beaurepaire, *Notes historiques et archéol. concernaut le département de la Seine-Inférieure* (Rouen, Cagniard, 1883); *ibid., Dernières mélanges historiques et archéol. Seine-Inférieure* (Rouen, 1909);

One can say that nothing great ever was accomplished in the Church without women bearing a part. A host of them stood among the martyrs in the amphitheater; they disputed with the anchorites the possession of the desert. Constantine set up the Labarum on the Capitol, and St. Helena raised the True Cross on the walls of Jerusalem. Clovis, at Tolbiac, invoked the God of Clotilda. Monica's tears won the conversion of Augustine. Jerome dedicated the Vulgate to the piety of two Roman ladies, Paula and Eustochium. The first lawmakers of monkish life, Basil and Benedict, were seconded by their sisters, Macrina and Scholastica. The Countess Matilda held up the tottering throne of Gregory VII. The wise judgment of Queen Blanche dominated the reign of St. Louis. France was saved by Jeanne d'Arc. Isabella of Castile led in the discovery of the New World. And in times closer to our own we see St. Teresa mixing with bishops, doctors, and the founders of Orders by which the reform in Catholic ranks was operated. We see St. Francis de Sales cultivating like a rare flower the soul of Madame de Chantal, and St. Vincent de Paul passing over to Louise Marillac the most admirable of his designs, the establishment of the Sisters of Charity.

—Frédéric Ozanam.

So much for the abbey churches of Normandy. Many another might be described, but with six Gothic cathedrals to consider, one must refrain. Of the six—Rouen, Lisieux, Évreux, Séez, Bayeux, and Coutances—that of Rouen shows the earliest Gothic work and its character is more French than Norman, as if the river, flowing down from Paris, carried with its waters the characteristics of the art life astir on the banks of the Seine, Oise, Aisne, and Marne.

The least local of Normandy's cathedrals, Our Lady's church at Rouen, has a magnetism distinctly its own—from its florid romantic west front, the most lavish screen ever set up, to the imposing sentry columns that guard its sanctuary. The northwest tower is Normandy's best Primary Gothic, the southwest tower the supremest belfry that sprang up to commemorate the freeing of France from foreign yoke. The façades of the transept and the Lady chapel (whose tombs mark dates in the art history of France) rank with perfect Rayonnant work. Its storied windows are among the richest ever dight by mediæval guildsmen.

Not but that a dozen flaws might be picked in the metropolitan church at Rouen. Were it to be strictly ranked among French cathedrals, it could not be placed among the foremost. But it has gone on embellishing itself century after century with a self-respect so sincere that few care to dispute its claim to stand in the front rank.

On a first visit to Rouen many an amateur prefers the regularity of St. Ouen's abbatial, which in size equals Westminster Abbey.[338] St. Ouen, the classic of Ray-

---

Cook, *The Story of Rouen* (London, 1899); Perkins, *The Churches of Rouen* (London, 1900).

[338] St. Ouen derived its name from the bishop who succeeded St. Romanus and gov-

onnant design, geometric in tracery, accentuating the ascending line, coldly perfect in construction, possessed still the true *sursum corda* of Gothic, though the art was fast crystallizing into formulas. The capitals were lessened, and the glazed triforium united to the clearstory in a single composition. Made of fine-textured gray stone St. Ouen is a stately vessel, but, add the critics, "its uniform excellence is average." Gothic lore has not degenerated, but has simply gone too far in the development of its principles, says the mechanical artistry of the last built of the great monastic churches of France, planned before the tragedies of the Hundred Years' War had petrified the national genius.[339]

The cathedral of Normandy's capital is not uniform, but its excellence surpasses the average. It is not homogeneous, its proportions are not absolutely harmonious, but it has profundity, personal character, and flashes of genius. The better it is known the deeper grows affection for it, which is not the case with St. Ouen. In the latter one feels that the cult is the main concern; in the cathedral there is piety of heart.

The early history of Sainte-Marie at Rouen follows the usual course. Norse marauders wrecked the ancient cathedral. Rollo, the first duke, endowed another which was radically reconstructed under an XI-century archbishop, a son of Duke Richard II. In 1063, that Romanesque church was dedicated by Archbishop Maurille (whose tomb is in the present ambulatory) in the presence of William

erned Rouen for forty years in the VII century, aiding the founders of Jumièges, Fécamp, and St. Wandrille. He had been blessed as a child in his father's castle near Braine by a passing guest, the Irish missionary, St. Columbanus, and he loved to trace thence his vocation. So rich grew the abbey of St. Ouen that it ruled half the city as temporal lord. In the XV century the English expelled Abbot Jean Richard, a builder of the present nave, to substitute a prelate docile to themselves who sat as judge at Jeanne's trial. But the pope restored Jean Richard in 1434, and he lived to entertain Charles VII in his monastery when that king came as victor to Rouen in 1449. Vacandard, *Vie de St. Ouen* (Paris, 1902).

[339] To a Romanesque abbatial of St. Ouen, burned in 1136, belonged the two-storied chapel called the Chambre-aux-Clercs, now set against the northern limb of the transept. In 1318 Abbot Jean Roussel, called Marc d'Argent, began the present abbatial, making its choir and transept in twenty years, as well as one bay of the nave. After a pause, two more bays were finished by 1390. Another cessation of work came during the Hundred Years' War. Alexander Berneval set up the transept's south rose (1439), made the pretty southern portal (1441) called after the marmosets decorating it; his son put up the north rose. Both architects repose in the same tomb in the church. Many hold the central lantern (c. 1490) to be a prime success of Flamboyant art. Flame tracery appeared in the XV-century windows, but the Rayonnant first plan was adhered to for the chief lines, so that the church, whose building extended over two centuries, is homogeneous. The abbatial was finished under Abbot Bohier (1491-1515). The Huguenots stripped it of its tombs, and lighted bonfires in the church. In the XIX century was added the mediocre west façade.

La Normandie monumentale et pittoresque. Seine-Inférieure, p. 105, "St. Ouen"; p. 129, "St. Maclou"; H. Havard, éd., *La France artistique et monumentale*, vol. 2, p. 79, "St. Ouen," L. de Foucaud; p. 85, "St. Maclou"; Dom. Pommeraye, *Histoire de l'abbaye royale de St. Ouen* (Rouen, 1662), folio; Jules Quicherat, "Documents inédits sur la construction de St. Ouen de Rouen," in *Biblio. de l'École des chartes*, 1852, vol. 3, p. 454; H. de la Bunodière, *Notice sur l'église St. Ouen de Rouen* (Paris, 1895); Camille Enlart, "L'architecture gothique au XIV siècle," in *Histoire de l'Art* (éd., André Michel), vol. 2, partie 2 (Paris, Colin, 1914).

the Conqueror and his good Matilda. Vestiges of the Romanesque edifice are in the first bay of the choir aisle. In it were interred the prodigious Rollo, the Norwegian sea-robber, who sacked half Normandy, sailed up the Seine to terrorize Paris, and up the Loire to overrun Auvergne and Burgundy, and yet, no sooner was he granted the duchy of northern France than the buccaneer gave way to a ruler whose laws were so respected that golden bracelets were left exposed and remained unstolen for years in the forest of Roumare. Rollo was baptized a Christian in Rouen, in 912, and there he wedded a Carolingian princess. When his son, William Longsword, died in 945, he was wearing a gold key that opened a casket containing a monk's robe for his burial; the new rulers were swift to comprehend that monasteries were the chief civilizers in that formative age.

Near Rouen, in 1087, died the Conqueror, sixth in descent from Rollo. "Pirate jostled statesman" in him, too. Mortally wounded at Mantes, he was brought to the priory of St. Gervase—beneath which suburban church still exists intact a V-century crypt—and as he heard the bells of Rouen Cathedral ringing, there rose to haunt him the curses, not loud but deep, of the oppressed Anglo-Saxons, and most piteously he petitioned the Queen of Heaven to draw Her Son's attention to all the religious houses he had built for the people's good on both sides of the Channel. No sooner was he dead than his retainers stripped and robbed him, and through private charity he was carried to his horror-inspiring burial at Caen.

To Rouen, because of its generosity to him in his captivity, Richard Cœur-de-Lion bequeathed his heart. In 1203 the last duke of Normandy, John Lackland, fled from Rouen after the murder of his nephew, Arthur of Brittany, of which the popular voice accused him. Philippe-Auguste entered the city in triumph in 1204, and the building of the new Gothic cathedral started apace.

Notre Dame at Rouen is associated closely with the return of Normandy under French rule. On Easter night, 1200, fire ravaged the city and its chief church. Whether the cathedral then wrecked was that blessed in 1063 by Bishop Robert de Maurille is uncertain. Some think that it was a Romanesque choir and transept which were burned, and a recently built Primary Gothic nave. It may have been an entirely new Gothic church which was destroyed. At any rate, the northwest tower, named after the VII-century bishop, Romanus, and the side doors of the main façade escaped the fire. The preservation of the tower was due, probably, to its position beyond the side aisle. The doors, built about 1180, are ornamented with Oriental incrustations such as are to be seen in the cathedral at Genoa, with which seaport Rouen had trade links.

The Tour Saint-Romain, whose prototypes were the towers at Étampes, Vendôme, and Chartres, was long counted as the oldest Primary Gothic work extant in Normandy, with the chapter house at St. Georges de Boscherville and the chapel of St. Julien, Petit-Quevilly.[340] But as many archæologists now say that the

---

[340] Henry II, the first Plantagenet, made for his own residence the chapel of St. Julien in a faubourg of Rouen, Petit-Quevilly. Simultaneously Romanesque and Gothic, the small edifice is one of the most elegant specimens of Normandy's XII-century architecture. Only the choir bay has retained the polychrome decoration which once covered the interior. St. Julien's sexpartite vault has been replaced by a wooden roof.

Gothic vault of St. Étienne's nave at Caen may be 1130 just as well as 1160, and that there are still earlier diagonals in the duchy, it remains an open question where the oldest extant ogival work of Normandy is. Mr. John Bilson claims that the diagonals of Lessay's choir pre-date any in the Ile-de-France. However the controversy over the priority of diagonals may be decided, the tower of St. Romain is the first Norman monument that shows the incontestable influence of Gothic of the Ile-de-France type.

The spirit of religious ardor that expressed itself in the northwest tower of Rouen Cathedral was described by Bishop Hugues d'Amiens in a letter, in 1145, to a brother prelate. He tells how volunteers were quitting Normandy to aid in the making of the new tower at Chartres: "In like manner, a large number of the faithful of this, our diocese, and of neighboring regions, put themselves to work on the cathedral church, their mother, forming associations to which no one is admitted unless he has confessed his sins, fulfilled his penances, laid down at the foot of the altar every enmity and revenge, and become reconciled with his enemies in a true peace. Under the lead of one in the band, who is chosen as chief, the people drag heavy wagons in humility and silence." The writer of this famous letter had been a monk of Cluny, and while ruling the see of Rouen he taught school there; he had inherited the traditions of Bec's scholarship through Anselm of Laon. The lower hall of the cathedral tower then begun is considered faultless. Before the close of the century the upper hall was completed, but the belfry story was not added till the late-Gothic day.

After the fire of 1200 work on the new cathedral was pushed on with energy. A master called Jean d'Andely is cited as the architect, a native, probably, of Les Andelys farther up the Seine, where there are two churches so closely resembling the cathedral of Rouen that they are doubtless from the same hand.[341] Another architect, named Enguerrand, is mentioned as quitting work on the cathedral of the capital in 1214, to undertake the abbatial at Bec. A keystone of Notre Dame, of the date 1233, is inscribed by one Durand, mason. He is thought to have been the son-in-law of the original architect, Jean d'Andely.

Doctor Contan, *Monographie de St. Julien, Petit-Quevilly*, and his account, p. 239, in *La Normandie monumentale et pittoresque. Seine-Inférieure*; Duchemin, *Le Petit-Querilly et le prieuré de Saint Julien.*

[341] The church of St. Sauveur in Petit-Andely, begun in 1215, finished in 1245, contains excellent XIII-century glass. Of the same date are the façade, nave, and square-ended choir of Notre Dame at Grand-Andely. Its central tower is of the XV century; the transept is a gem of Flamboyant Gothic. The most brilliant of its windows date from 1540 to 1616. Above the smaller Andely stands Château Gaillard, the "Saucy Castle," which Richard the Lion-hearted built in a year. Its capture in 1204 by Philippe-Auguste ended the English resistance in Normandy at that period. Five miles away are the remains of the magnificent château of Gaillon, where every master of the Renaissance in France was employed. Begun in 1454 by Cardinal d'Estouteville, it was carried forward by Cardinal George I d'Amboise and Cardinal de Bourbon. Its bas-relief of St. George and the dragon is one of the three authenticated works of Michel Colombe. A façade of Gaillon is now in the courtyard of the Beaux-Arts at Paris. Abbé Porée, *Guide historique et descriptive aux Andelys*; *Congrès Archéologique*, 1853; *La Normandie monumentale et pittoresque. Eure 1*, pp. 147, 163 (Le Havre, 1895); E. A. Didron, "Les vitraux du Grand-Andely," in *Annales Archéol.*, vol. 22.

The first plan of Rouen Cathedral called for tribunes over the aisles, but the idea was given up in order to have the side aisles twice as high as originally designed. The arches by which the tribunes would have opened on the central vessel were retained, however, as was done later with the false tribunes of the abbey church at Eu. In the side aisles, resting on the capitals of the nave's piers, are ringed colonnettes that rise to the ledge above—a ledge constructed to catch the tribune's diagonals (which never were built). By this graceful expedient they cloaked architectural members prepared but not used. The passageway carried from pier to pier above the main arcade of the nave is exceptional. An apsidal chapel projects from each arm of the transept, as in the Romanesque edifices of the region.

The archbishop under whom Notre Dame of Rouen was begun was Walter of Coutance, *Gautier-le-magnifique* (1184-1207), who willed his fortune to the cathedral, since it was he, devoted public servant of the Plantagenets, and long the chief justice of England, who had urged the chapter to sell its treasure to help ransom Cœur-de-Lion from captivity after the Third Crusade. He himself went as hostage into Germany in order that Richard might be released before his full ransom was raised. Learned, liberal, and affable, Bishop Walter was a man of whom all spoke well.

The choir of Rouen Cathedral showed more the regional characteristics; the arches were more acute and the moldings multiple. The circular piers about the sanctuary have Norman round capitals. We know that in 1235 a bishop was buried in the choir, which must have been entirely finished when, in 1255, St. Louis spent Easter in Rouen as the guest of his friend and counselor, Archbishop Eudes Rigaud (1247-74), a Franciscan, who was to accompany the king on his fatal crusade. The choir's upper windows were reconstructed during the XV century.

About 1280, architect Jean Davy began the south façade of the transept, the Portail de la Calende, so called because there was carved there a mythical animal of that name, considered in ancient times as a symbol of the Saviour, since the superstition was that the sight of a Calende cured illness. The transept façades of Rouen are among the best works of the Rayonnant phase. Their sculpture, says M. Enlart, has not yet the fluid indecision of XIV-century draperies. A pronounced feature of that period are the openwork gables, which, though they may be superbly decorative, are none the less a step away from constructive sincerity, since drip stones made of lacework masonry fail to fulfill their practical function.

The northern door of the transept was named from the canon's library beside it. It, too, like the earlier Calende portal, was paneled with medallions over which many a pharisee has shaken his head. The Middle Ages were neither pharisaic nor prudish. Rouen's little sculptured groups are merely fantastic and popular. They embody no satire against the clergy, as some would intimate; nor are they obscene. To place a centaur or an acrobat in proximity to a scriptural group seemed then no more profane than to illuminate the margins of missals with meaningless frolics. Leeway was allowed the artistic imagination, which here ran largely to grotesques. The medallions of the Calende door were in better sequence and of more vigorous character than those of the Portail des Libraires. Beside this latter entrance is the courtroom of the archepiscopal palace adorned with statues representing Solomon's judgment, in souvenir of the old usage of rendering justice before church doors.

From 1302 to 1320 rose the Rayonnant Gothic Lady chapel of impeccable mechanical skill but not inspired. Long centuries later, during the Revolution, its tomb of the cardinals d'Amboise,[342] in which Gothic sculpture culminated, escaped destruction because the axis chapel served as a granary. Clement V, the builder of Bordeaux' Rayonnant choir, arranged that his nephew, who was archbishop of Rouen and had got into difficulties with the Norman nobles, should exchange his see with Gilles Aycelin, the prelate who was erecting Narbonne Cathedral, brother of the bishop-builder of Clermont's nave. A little later another archbishop of Rouen became the Avignon pontiff who built the audience hall and the chief chapel of the palace on the Rhone. Other XIV-century additions to Rouen Cathedral are the side chapels; every guild and corporation craved thus to honor its own particular patron.

Those contemporary works, Rouen's Lady chapel, the choirs of Bordeaux and Narbonne, Avignon's halls, belong to the phase of the national genius which we call Rayonnant because of its geometric window tracery, a phase aptly designated as metallic by M. Gonse. Artists were fast losing their exquisite feeling for the silhouette; the vertical line was over-accentuated; triforium and clearstory had become one composition. Pitiless logic was drying up the spring of inspiration. When the cathedral of Rouen remade three bays of the nave's triforium, the model taken was the geometric design of that masterpiece of Rayonnant Gothic, the abbatial of St. Ouen. Before the XIV century closed the façade of the cathedral was redressed with arcatures and statues like the west frontispieces of Wells, Salisbury, and Litchfield.

The XV century carried through the chief supplementary works of Sainte-Marie of Rouen in a style frankly florid. Normandy, Artois, and Picardy reveled in the last development of the national art, regions all of them having close links with England. For if much of Flamboyant Gothic was indigenous, as M. Anthyme Saint-Paul contends, if it enveloped and absorbed Rayonnant Gothic, it seems fairly well proved that its two most pronounced traits, the flamelike window tracery and arches of double curvature, came from England. M. Enlart says that ramified vaults were built at Ely, Lincoln, and Litchfield, during the XIII century. By 1304 accolade arches were used; at Merton College, Oxford, is a flame-tracery window

---

[342] Opposite the tomb of the d'Amboise cardinals (1513-25), predominantly Gothic in character, is the purely Renaissance monument of Louis de Brézé (1536-44), seneschal of Normandy, son of the daughter of Charles VII and Agnes Sorel. The kneeling figure on the tomb is the notorious Diane de Poitiers, his widow. The critics say that if the De Brézé mausoleum is not the work of Jean Goujon, Diane's favorite sculptor, then there must have been living here an unknown XVI-century master of the first order. Jean Goujon was in Rouen, making the wooden doors of St. Maclou, at that time.

Paul Vitry, *Jean Goujon* (Collection, Les Grandes Artistes), (Paris, H. Laurens, 1908); Louis Gonse, *La sculpture française depuis le XIVe siècle* (Paris, 1895); Léon Palustre, *La Renaissance en France*, vol. 1 (Paris, Quantin, 1888), 3 vols.

of 1310, features not to be found in France before 1375.[343] In the Rayonnant phase lines break; in the Flamboyant they undulate. Rayonnant capitals were diminished; capitals disappeared altogether in the later period, and molds melted into the piers.

Normandy expressed her renewed national dignity with enthusiasm in the flowery, happy architecture we call Flamboyant:

> Le Temps a laissié son manteau
> De vent, de froidure et de pluye,
> Et s'est vestu de broderye
> De soleil raiant, cler, et beau.

So sang Charles, Duke of Orléans, come back from twenty years in English prisons to witness the expulsion of the invader from Normandy:

> Il n'y a beste ne oiseau
> Que en son jargon ne chante ou crye;
> Le Temps a laissié son manteau
> De vent, de froidure et de pluye.[344]

How they built in Rouen! With what vim and emancipated energy! St. Ouen carried forward its nave and raised a central tower. From 1437 to 1480 was built the gallant little church of St. Maclou with a central tower that is one of the best in Normandy, and whose curving front of five arcades is profusely elegant. Similarly large, ornate portals became the vogue in late-Gothic Norman construction. St. Maclou is to the Gothic art of the XIII century what the reel is to the minuet, said an English architect.[345]

In the cathedral of Rouen one noted master succeeded another. Guillaume Pontifs put the belfry on St. Romain's tower (1463-77); built the canon's library, to which he made a staircase from the cathedral's transept; and made the decorated portico leading from the rue St. Romain to the court before the Portail des Libraires. No approach to a church possesses more entirely the atmosphere of the Middle Ages than that. Pontifs began a masterpiece of Flamboyant architecture,

[343] Camille Enlart, on the origin of Flamboyant Gothic, in the *Archæological Journal*, 1886, and in *Histoire de l'Art* (éd. A. Michel), vol. 3, 1ère partie (Paris, Colin, 1914); *Bulletin Monumental*, 1906, vol. 70, pp. 38, 483, 511, the controversy between M. Saint-Paul and M. Enlart, on the origin of Flamboyant Gothic; Anthyme Saint-Paul, *L'architecture française et la Guerre de Cent Ans* (1910); *ibid.*, *Les origines du gothique flamboyant en France* (Caen, 1907).

[344] Charles d'Orléans, *Poésies*, éd. Ch. d'Héricault (Paris), 2 vols.

[345] St. Maclou, says Mr. F. M. Simpson, expresses the *joie de vivre*, even as the stiff angular lines of a contemporary style—the English Perpendicular—show the gloom that prevailed in England after the War of the Roses. Cardinal Guillaume d'Estouteville contributed toward St. Maclou, which was dedicated only in 1521, by Cardinal Georges II d'Amboise. Jean Goujon probably made the richly chiseled doors. St. Maclou has XV-century windows; its rose windows are of the XVI century. There is Le Prince glass in the late-Gothic church of St. Vincent, and other XVI-century windows in St. Patrice. Abbé Ouin-Lacroix. *Histoire de l'église et de la paroisse de St. Maclou de Rouen* (1846); Edmond Renaud, *L'église St. Vincent de Rouen* (1885); Arthur Kingsley Porter, *Medieval Architecture*, vol. 2, pp. 389 to 416, "Flamboyant Gothic Monuments."

the Tour de Beurre (1485-1509), that, as it rises, grows more and more sumptuous, though it never loses its architectural lines. Unfortunately the stone used was of poor quality, which necessitated a coarse sculpture. The transition from square to octagon was gracefully achieved by the one constructive arrangement which originated during the final stage of the national art: to unify the design, flying buttresses were sprung from the corner turrets and the face-shafts to the octagon.[346]

From 1497 to 1507 the master-of-works at Rouen Cathedral was Jacques Le Roux, who continued the Tour de Beurre, finished by his nephew, Rouland Le Roux (1507-20), an artist of the first order. He redressed the upper part of the main frontispiece in order to put it into character with the Tour de Beurre and St. Romain's belfry. After completing the middle portal of the façade he reconstructed the central tower, whose platform he raised a story higher. When Rouen's lantern tower was burned in 1822 the present iron skeleton was contrived, a structure too mechanical to be architecture, but of good effect in the distant views of the city.

The oft repeated renewals of the famous frontispiece of Rouen Cathedral account for its failure to express the interior church structurally, but though merely a screen, it is deservedly popular, "one of the dreams of the Middle Ages," M. Émile Lambin has called it. By moonlight its effect is romantic, almost spectacular. Most popular, too, is another work of Rouland Le Roux, the Palais de Justice which he built with Roger Ango, from 1493 to 1507, for the parliament of Normandy. A pomp and a pageantry carried almost to folly distinguished the generations that raised monuments such as these. In 1520, when Francis I met Henry VIII, not far from Rouen, at the Field of the Cloth of Gold, many a lord, says the chronicler, carried on his back his mills and his forests and his meadows. One of the most curious houses in France, Rouen's Hôtel du Bourgtherould, now a bank near the Old Market, is decorated exteriorly by reliefs of the Field of the Cloth of Gold.[347] M. Léon Palustre discovered that the sculpture on its tower, originally polychrome, was a copy of a Flemish tapestry in the possession of that prince of pageantry, Philippe le Hardi of Burgundy.

The archbishop of Rouen from 1493 to 1510 was none other than the Mæcenas of his age, Cardinal George I d'Amboise, chief minister of Louis XII. All over France we have traced the work of that art-loving family—at Paris, Cluny, Cler-

---

[346] Notre Dame at Caudebec-en-Caud, called by Henry IV "the most beautiful chapel of my kingdom of France," has its "tiara" united to its shaft by flying buttresses. Other Flamboyant Gothic monuments in Normandy are Louviers' lacelike portal (1493); churches at Dieppe; the transept of Évreux Cathedral; St. Jacques at Lisieux; St. Pierre at Coutances; Les Andelys, Elbeuf, Gisors, and the joyous festival of stone of Notre Dame at Alençon, where the shady north side of the nave is adorned with Old Testament scenes, and the sunlit southern wall opened by spacious Flamboyant traceries that frame the New Testament; its Jesse tree is unusual. Notre Dame at St. Lô (which has a Becket window) shows Perpendicular traits. Its west portals are strangely dissimilar, as are its monumental towers. Near Fécamp, the Estouteville family founded Valmont abbatial (1116) now unroofed save its Lady chapel, in which are splendid tombs, a reredos of the Annunciation that is a gem of XVI-century realism, and a window that inspired Eugène Delacroix's palette.

[347] Sir Theodore Andreas Cook, *Twenty-five Great Houses of France*, chap. 12 (New York and London, 1916).

mont, Chaumont, Albi. A nephew of the same name held the see here until 1545, and saw to the erection of his uncle's tomb, designed by Rouland Le Roux, with sculpture by artists of the Michel Colombe tradition as well as those of the Italian Renaissance.

Rouen was so active a center for glassmaking that, in 1317, Exeter obtained windows here, as did Gloucester and Merton College, Oxford. Next to Troyes, Rouen contained the richest collection of colored glass in France. Until the Revolution her eighty lesser churches were filled with it. The best windows left are six lancets in the ambulatory of the cathedral. They belong to the XIII-century school of Chartres and are exceptional in being the only signed windows; "Clement of Chartres" was their maker. The first, given by a company of boatmen, relates the legend of St. Julian Hospitator, who ferried strangers day and night over the river, a story recounted by Gustave Flaubert, a son of Rouen.[348] The other five lancets are of the *Biblia pauperum* type, teaching dogma to the people. The cold, limpid hues of the XIV century appear in the Lady chapel, and in the chapel of St. Jeanne d'Arc is an interesting Pentecost window of that century; contemporary are the apse lights in the upper choir, where the unsuccessful experiment was tried of continuing the subject from one panel to another—here the arms of the Crucified Lord extend into the lateral lights. The cathedral's west rose is of the XV century; in the transept is a XVI-century window devoted to the ancient bishop Romanus. The abbatial of St. Ouen has, with the choir of Évreux, the best array extant of XIV-century canopy glass figures. So loath were the vitrine artists to give up an architectural design in glass that when the XV century composed scenes instead of single figures for each panel, even those small groups were set in grisaille frames.

The iconoclastic 1562 worked havoc in Rouen. For twenty-four hours a Huguenot mob wrecked tombs, altars, and windows in the cathedral, to such an extent that it lay unused during half a year. One mourns the loss of the cenotaph of good Charles V, made in 1369 by the same Jean de Marville who designed the famous Dijon tomb of the king's brother. Ten years later, in 1572, the Rouen Catholics retaliated by massacring some eight hundred Calvinists in the city on St.

[348] Flaubert, born in Rouen, 1821, died near the city, at Croisset, in his ancient house that formerly belonged to the monks of St. Ouen. The increased river activities during the World War have encroached on his property. His pupil, Guy de Maupassant, born near Dieppe, was associated with his mother's city, Rouen, where stands his statue (1853-93). The house of the great Corneille (1636-1709) is near Rouen's Old Market. Other sons of Rouen were La Salle, the explorer (d. 1687), and the painter Géricault (1791-1824). Nicholas Poussin (1594-1665) was born at Les Andelys; Jean-François Millet, near Cherbourg (1814-74); Auber, the composer (1782-1871), at Caen, as was the poet Malherbes (1555-1628). Mézerai, whose history is considered the best account of the XVI-century religious struggle in France, and his brother, Jean Eudes, founder of the Eudists, were born near Caen. The great seamen, Tourville (1642-1701) and Du Quesne (1610-88), were Normans; so were Laplace, the mathematician (1749-1827), Alexis de Tocqueville (1805-59), Bernardin de Saint-Pierre (1736-1814), Octave Feuillet (1821-90), Léon Gautier (1832-97), Barbey d'Aurevilly (1808-89), and savants such as Simeon Luce (d. 1892), Gabriel Monod (d. 1912), Albert Sorel, Paul Allard, Leopold Delisle (d. 1910). The latter was led to decipher ancient manuscripts by C. de Gerville, who, with that other Norman, Arcisse de Caumont, was a pioneer in mediæval archeology.

Bartholomew's Day.

In the World War Rouen became almost an English city again. This time, however, England, the ancient combatant of France, came not as a detested invader, but as her ally in dire years of distress. It is pleasant to learn that devotion to the Maid of Orleans was not infrequent among the English troops of 1914-18.

JEANNE D'ARC'S TRIAL IN ROUEN[349]

> De ma part, je répute son histoire un vrai miracle le Dieu. La pudicité que je vois l'avoir accompagnée jusques à sa mort, même au milieu des troupes; la juste querelle qu'elle prit; la prouesse qu'elle y apporta; les heureux succès de ses affaires; la sage simplicité que je recueille de ses réponses au interrogatoires qui lui furent faits par les juges du tout voués à sa ruine; ses prédictions qui, depuis, sortirent effet; la mort cruelle qu'elle choisit dont elle se pouvoit garantir s'il y eût de la feintise en son fait; tout cela dis-je, me fait croire (joint les voyes du ciel quelle oyoit) que toute sa vie et histoire fut un vrai martyre de Dieu.
>
> —Testimony of ÉTIENNE PASQUIER (1529-1615).

So swiftly followed the fruitage of the sacrifice offered up in the Vieux-Marché on May 21, 1431, that in every part of the ancient city of Rouen sprang up exuberant, vigorous, Flamboyant monuments. The most momentous and the saddest happening in the history of Normandy's capital was the burning at the stake of Jeanne la Pucelle whose relief of Orléans, only two short years before, had saved the nation in its last gasp.

From the church of St. Saviour on the market place they brought her the cross for which she begged on that tragic morning, that the pillory on which her Lord

---

[349] Jules Quicherat, the archæologist, was the first to place before the public the records of Jeanne d'Arc's two trials. He printed (1841-49) five volumes in Latin for the *Société de l'histoire de France*. Accounts of Jeanne have been written by Wallon (Paris, 1877); Marius Sepet (Tours, 1885); Ayroles, S. J. (Paris, 1902), who dwells much on the nefarious part played by Paris University in her condemnation: Siméon Luce; G. Hanotaux (Paris, 1911); Petit de Julleville (Les Saints Collection, Paris, Lecoffre, 1907); Andrew Lang (London, 1908): Mrs. Oliphant (Leaders of the Nation Series, New York); D. Lynch, S. J. (New York, 1919); Sarrazin, *Jeanne d'Arc et la Normandie au XVe siècle* (Rouen, 1896); F. Poulaine, *Jeanne d'Arc à Rouen* (Paris, 1899); Ch. Lemire, *Jeanne d'Arc en Picardie et en Normandie* (Paris, 1903); Le P. Denifle et Chatelain, *Le procès Jeanne d'Arc et l'université de Paris* (Paris); U. Chevalier, *L'abjuration de Jeanne d'Arc*; C. de Maleissye, "La prétendue abjuration de St. Ouen," in *Revue des Deux Mondes*, February, 1911, p. 610. The study of Anatole France on Jeanne d'Arc is written from the rationalist standpoint that considers hers a case of hysteria fitted for medical science. No book on Jeanne equals the contemporary records. The report of her two trials in Rouen, and the testimony gathered from end to end of France to vindicate her memory in 1456, have been marshaled and clarified in a skilled legal manner by a magistrate of Rouen: E. O'Reilly, *Les deux procès de condamnation ... et la sentence de réhabilitation de Jeanne d'Arc* (Paris, Pion, 1868), 2 vols. This masterly work should be translated into English. It is an example of the right way to write history. For Charles VII see Thomas Basin and Vallet de Viriville.

had hung might be held up before her eyes, to strengthen her in her last hour. Long afterward, in 1450, Massieu, the priest-sheriff of her trial, a weak man but less unsympathetic than many in that grim gathering of rascals, testified: "The English feared her more than the whole army of the king of France.... It was they who held the trial and paid its costs. She was taken to the Viel-Marché, having beside her Brother Martin and me, and accompanied by more than eight hundred men at arms, with spears and swords. On the way she made pious lamentation so touchingly that my companion and I could not keep back our tears. She recommended her soul to God and the saints with such devotion that those who heard her wept. All distressed, she exclaimed, 'Rouen, Rouen, must I die here!'"

When the Old Market was reached Jeanne heard herself sermonized as a limb of Satan, a blasphemer guilty of diabolical malice, of pernicious crimes, and infected with the leprosy of heresy. Her sentence read, she fell on her knees and addressed to God prayers so ardent that even the foreign masters of Rouen were moved. Her dear St. Michael she petitioned, too. "As soon as the flames reached her," relates an eyewitness, "she cried out more than six times, *'Jhésus!'* and then a final time, in a loud voice, with her last breath, *'Jhésus!'* And her cry was heard from end to end of the market place, and almost everyone was weeping.... A shiver passed over the assembly.... The people pointed at her judges and said that Jeanne was the victim of a great injustice.... They murmured that such an evil deed should have taken place in their city.... That evening the executioner went to the Dominican convent and confessed in fear, 'I have burned a saint!'... The secretary of the English king turned away from the lamentable spectacle, muttering: 'We are lost. We have burned a saint!'" Surrounded by her brutal jailers, at dawn that May morning, Jeanne had said, with confidence, "With God's aid, I shall be this night in His Kingdom of Paradise." As her final cry to her Redeemer rang out, a canon of Rouen Cathedral prayed aloud, "Would to God my soul were where I believe is the soul of this Maid."

The young priest-secretary, the clerk of the court, Manchon, who took down her trial (and let his irresistible admiration for her run over in marginal notes, "*Superba responsio!*"), testified later: "Never did I weep so much over any grief that has come to me, and for a month I could not be appeased. I bought a little missal with the money that came to me from the trial, that I might have cause to remember her in my prayers." The verdict of all impartial men in Rouen, that somber May morning of 1431, was that the whole business from beginning to end had been violence and injustice.[350]

---

[350] Boisguillaume, second clerk of the Rouen court in 1431, Manchon's assistant, testified before the three inquests for Jeanne's rehabilitation. He drew attention to the fact that all who had been culpable of the Maid's death had come to a swift or shameful end. Estivet was found dead in a gutter at the gates of Rouen; Loyseleur, the false confessor, was struck down suddenly; Cauchon expired ignominiously. "I call you to judgment before God for what you have done," rang out Jeanne's words to these unworthy churchmen on her last day. Nicolas Midi, of the Paris Parliament, who drew up the odious twelve accusations, and who sermonized Jeanne in the Old Market, was stricken with leprosy. A year after the execution died the young Duchess of Bedford, who had inflicted a gross outrage on Jeanne, and her death detached from the English cause her brother, the Duke of Burgundy. Her

A packed jury had judged her. The president of the tribunal, the renegade selected to prove a saint a sorceress, was Bishop Pierre Cauchon, driven from his see of Beauvais by loyal Frenchmen, as the enemy of his own country. Because the see of Rouen was unoccupied, the English preferred to hold Jeanne's trial there rather than at Paris, where the bishop was not their creature. How abject a tool Cauchon was is to-day shown by old receipts which prove that he was the recipient, on each day of the trial, of a hundred *sols tournois*. For the same ignoble reason many a learned professor "charged his soul."

There was not the faintest shadow of fair play in the process. After Maître Jean Lohier had said to Cauchon that the proceedings were not valid because Jeanne was allowed no counsel, nor were the hearings in public court, and those present had not freedom to express their true opinion, that honest Norman lawyer saw that his only safety lay in quitting the city. "It is an affair of hate," he said to young Secretary Manchon one day as they stood together in Rouen Cathedral. "Deliberately they try to trap her. If only she would not say in regard to her apparitions, 'I know for certain,' but, 'It seems to me,' I do not see how she could be condemned."

Some canons of the cathedral who criticized the trial were thrown into prison, and the English locked up a citizen who remarked that since Jeanne had been judged innocent by the doctors at Poitiers, in a court presided over by the archbishop of Rheims, a second trial was illegal. Three of the younger judges who at first dared to give their true opinion were berated by Cauchon, who bade them quit their ecclesiastical quibbling and let the jurists decide the matter. The testimony of the aged bishop of Avranches, then a resident of Rouen, was set aside because he advised that in matters doubtful touching the faith the case should be referred to a council or to the pope. Because Massieu, the humble court usher, said to a townsman, "I can see nothing but goodness and honor in her," he was threatened with a prison cell where never again would he see sun or moon. The secretaries, Manchon and Boisguillaume, were beaten by the English. A man on the street who spoke well of Jeanne was chased by Lord Warwick with a drawn sword and almost killed. Passions ran high. Lord Stafford drew his dagger on Jeanne in her cell one day because she said that the English would be driven out of France. Even after her execution, when a Dominican in the city spoke kindly of her, he was flung into prison for a year.

Her judges sought to tire Jeanne out by long hours of interrogation; the lawyers themselves came away exhausted from the sessions. Virulent against her was Beaupère, rector of Paris University, who, when routed by the young girl's replies, called her sly. When Cauchon wished to have it appear that she refused to submit to the Church, he made the scribes omit her statement that gladly she appealed to a general council or to the pope. "Ah," cried Jeanne, "you write all that is against me, but you do not write anything for me." The lawyers' subtle questions rained on her thick and fast till she would call them to order with admirable courtesy, *"Beaux seigneurs, faites l'un après l'autre."* Whenever she wished to make no reply

husband, John of Lancaster, regent-duke, brother of Henry V, died in full youth, three years later, and was buried in Rouen Cathedral. His nephew, Henry VI, was dispossessed of his English crown, imprisoned, and murdered.

to a question came her concise, "*Passez outre.*" Secretary Manchon testified before an inquest, twenty years later, "Never could Jeanne have defended herself as she did in so difficult a cause, against so many and such learned doctors, if she had not been inspired."

Sublime to tears are some of the answers made by this young country girl not yet twenty, who could barely read and write, who knew only *Pater* and *Ave*. When sheeringly asked were she in a state of grace, she replied: "A serious question to answer. If I am, may God keep me so; if I am not, may God put me in his grace. I would rather die than not have God's love." Awe fell on the assemblage and for that day the session broke up.[351]

Yet Jeanne was very human at her trial, too. It was just the well-brought-up country maid, the Jeannette they all loved in Domrémy, who boasted before those callous men: "For sewing and for spinning, I fear no woman in Rouen." Those housewives of Rouen, the "little people of the Lord," to whom Jeanne's thoughts turned in homely fashion, dared only murmur beneath their breath that her process was "a crying injustice," and shame it was that so evil a *cause célèbre* should take place in their good town. Rouen was terrorized into silence by her foreign master.

Jeanne's five months' imprisonment and final execution at Rouen was a political crime covered with the cloak of religious zeal by a very genius of hypocrisy. John Plantagenet, Duke of Bedford, together with the boy king's great-uncle, the cardinal of Winchester, were the movers behind the scenes. Jeanne never quitted her prison in the castle built by Philippe-Auguste—only a tower of which is extant to-day. From that stronghold the English governed Normandy. Since the opening of the World War an erroneous inscription, placed by partisan politicians in the wall of the episcopal palace of Rouen, has been changed, for it sought to convey the idea that from the prelate's court of justice Jeanne was led forth to her death. Never did she set foot in that officiality building; she was held from the first day to the last in an English prison. From a dark cell in the tower fortress she was conducted through corridors of the same castle to the hall where sat her judges. Massieu, the usher, used to let her slip into the castle chapel for an *Ave* as she passed its open door, but even that solace was stopped by Estivet. That venomous agent of Cauchon accused Jeanne of ironic replies ill suited to a woman.[352]

---

[351] "'Si j'y suis, Dieu m'y tienne; si je n'y suis, Dieu m'y veuille mettre: j'aimerais mieux mourir que de ne pas avoir l'amour de Dieu!' A cette réponse, les juges restèrent stupéfaits et rompirent sur-le-champ."—Testimony of the second clerk of the court, Bois-guillaume, in 1450, before the inquest for the rehabilitation.

[352] The Norman, Siméon Luce, has written of Jeanne: "La Pucelle n'est pas seulement le type le plus achevé du patriotisme, elle est encore l'incarnation de notre pays dans ce qu'il a de meilleur. Il y a dans la physionomie de l'héroïne du XVe siècle, des traits qui la rattachent à la France de tous les temps, l'entrain belliqueux, la grâce légère, la gaieté prisesantière, l'esprit mordant, l'ironie méprisante en face de la force, la pitié pour les petits, les faibles, les malheureux, la tendresse pour les vaincus. De tels dons appartiennent à notre tradition nationale, et la libératrice d'Orléans les a possédés à un si haut degré que cette face de son génie a frappé tous ses admirateurs."

Cauchon tried to coerce the young priest-secretaries of the trial, Manchon and Boisguillaume, to falsify their notes, but they proved incorruptible. And twenty years later they, with Massieu, became the chief vindicators of the Maid when the inquests for her rehabilitation were started. Jeanne had felt their unspoken sympathy. Once with pleasant humor she told them not to ask her the same question twice or she would pull their ears. We know from contemporaries that Jeanne's way of intercourse was natural and friendly, *enjouée*, that her attitude was modesty itself, that her voice had a feminine note of sweetness, that she was strong and comely and well shaped, that her hair was dark.

Born in 1412, by the Meuse, in Domrémy, on the old Roman road from Langres to Verdun, in French territory, on the borders of Champagne and Lorraine, she was not yet eighteen when she crossed the ravaged land in the winter of 1429 to rouse Charles VII, then in Chinon Castle. In March of that year she raised the siege of Orléans; in July she witnessed the coronation of her *"gentil dauphin"* at Rheims; in September occurred the assault on Paris, from which siege Charles VII, counseled by traitors, retired, and all winter Jeanne was kept in semiactivity, though chafing to free the land from the foreign yoke. Especially she longed to go to the aid of the besieged Mont-Saint-Michel, and to liberate from his English prison the poet-duke of Orléans, even, she said, if it meant going to London Tower itself. In May, 1430, she was captured by her enemies, the Burgundians. Jeanne's active mission covered only a year. "Several times in my presence," testified the Duke d'Alençon,[353] her companion in arms, "Jeanne told the king she would last but a year, and to look well that he made right use of her." But Charles VII failed her.

After her capture Jeanne spent some months in prisons in northern France, and finally she was sold to the English for a king's ransom. Never in their minds was there any mistake as to who had turned the tide against them. "They had for her a mortal hate," said, in later years, Pierre Minier, one of the judges cowed by the Duke of Bedford; "they thirsted to bring about her death, no matter by what

[353] The Duke d'Alençon testified, in 1455, concerning Jeanne: "I have heard captains who took part in the siege of Orléans declare that what passed there touched on the miraculous, that it was no human work. Apart from things of war Jeanne was a simple young girl; but for things of war, wielding the lance, massing the army, preparing the battle, arranging the artillery, she was remarkably skilled. All marveled that she should show the ability and foresight of a captain who had warred for thirty years. Especially in her control of artillery was she admirable."

Equally convincing is the testimony, in 1455, of the bastard of Orléans, the great Dunois: "I believe that Jeanne was sent of God and that her conduct in war was more a divine than a human act.... I heard the seneschal of Beaucaire, whom the king had appointed to watch over Jeanne in the wars, say that he believed there never was a woman more chaste. I heard Jeanne say to the king one day: 'When I am distressed that credence is not given that it is Heaven has sent me to your aid, I withdraw to a quiet place and I pray and complain to God, and, my prayer finished, I hear a voice saying, *"Fille Dè, va, va, va! Je serai à ton ayde, va!"* 'And in repeating what the voice said, Jeanne was—an extraordinary thing—in a marvelous ravishment, in a sort of ecstasy, her eyes lifted to heaven." E. O'Reilly, *Les deux procès de condamnation et la sentence de réhabilitation de Jeanne d'Arc* (Paris, Plon, 1868), vol. 1, pp. 153, 156, 200, 214, 2 vols.

means."

From December, 1430, to May, 1431, Jeanne's martyrdom at Rouen endured. "An iron cage was made for her, and at night she was chained up," declared Secretary Boisguillaume, at the inquest of 1450. "She was incarcerated in Rouen Castle; her guardians were English soldiery of the lowest type; day and night they kept watch ... they made her the object of their mockeries; often she reproached them for it. Her feet were held in irons which were attached to a post." There were scenes in that dark cell, vouched for by witnesses, which are too painful to transcribe.[354] Only when she fell ill was the severity with which she was treated relaxed, lest by a natural death she escape public burning. One day Estivet so vilified her that she had a relapse of fever. Every detail is set down in the process for her rehabilitation, for which the Dominican Bréhal traveled from end to end of France, gathering testimony from those who had known Jeanne. But the chief instrument of her vindication is the word-for-word record of her trial at Rouen in 1431. Not in all history is there a more personal and appealing document. One can hear Jeanne's very accent in her valiant replies to her tormentors. *"Répondes hardiment,"* her voices admonished her.

Why did Charles VII, who, before Jeanne appeared, was about to pass into foreign exile, strike no blow to rescue her who had given him back his kingdom? A difficult question to answer. Charles was no hero, though his quality of perseverance was ultimately to make him the instrument that ended the centuries-old Capet-Plantagenet duel. Charles was surrounded by counselors who were jealous of Jeanne's leadership, who represented her captivity as the result of her headstrong character.

In 1449 Charles, *le bien servi,* but not the duly grateful, entered Rouen "in triumph and magnificence as never king in city." Bells rang out and children cried, *"Noël!"* in welcome. In the cathedral the festal throng gathered. Beside the king stood Jacques Cœur, the merchant-prince, who had provided the funds for the reconquest of Normandy, and whose splendor of apparel on this triumphal entry was so to excite the barons' envy that within four years their machinations had him impeached, despoiled, and banished. He who was building at Bourges the finest bourgeois mansion in France, must have observed with interest the host of Flamboyant monuments then arising in Rouen. With Charles VII came, too, his commander in chief, the great Dunois, who had fought with Jeanne, the half brother of the Duke of Orléans, who that day was singing:

> "Resjoys-toy, franc royaume de France!
> À présent Dieu pour toy se combat."

When Normandy was again French, not many years were to pass before Rouen exonerated herself of the crime of Jeanne's execution. The chief mover of the rehabilitation was the archbishop of the city, the Norman, Guillaume d'Estouteville, son of the hero who in 1415 held Harfleur against the entire army of Henry V,

---

[354] Testimony of Isambeau de la Pierre, in 1450, before the inquest for the rehabilitation: "Je la vis éplorée, son visage plein de larmes, défigurée et outragée en telle sorte que j'en eus pitié et compassion."

brother of the knight who led the defense of Mont-Saint-Michel, and nephew of Archbishop d'Harcourt, who gave up his see of Rouen to live in exile, rather than swear fealty to a non-French master. Cardinal d'Estouteville saw the propriety of clearing not only Normandy but France and the Church of what had been the political crime of foreigners. Through his efforts Pope Calixtus III, in 1456, revoked the legal decision of 1431, as "iniquitous, malicious, calumnious, and fraudulent." The unworthy Cauchon was excommunicated. A formal reading of the sentence of rehabilitation took place in the big hall of Rouen's episcopal palace: "Considering the quality of the judges and of those who directed the trial, considering that her abjuration was extorted by fraud and violence, in presence of the executioner and under threat of fire, without the accused understanding its full content and terms, considering finally that the crimes charged against her are not proven whatsoever by the process"—thus runs the decree declaring Jeanne's two sentences of condemnation in 1431 to be the work of iniquity. It was ordered that the rehabilitation be read publicly, not alone in Rouen, but in all the chief towns of France.

Rouen celebrated with gladness the justice rendered to the Maid who had saved France in her darkest hour. A solemn procession, in which marched Jeanne's brothers, who had been ennobled by the king, proceeded to the graveyard beside St. Ouen's abbatial, where, twenty-five years earlier, Jeanne had sat alone on a platform above the crowd, just a week before her execution. They had there read to her the twelve accusations—dubbing her witch and wanton—which a doctor of Paris University had drawn up, and then a preacher thundered in vituperation. Jeanne listened gently till she heard Charles VII abused, whereupon she, who had the mystic cult of royalty, lifted up her head bravely: "By my faith, sire," she cried, "my king is a noble Christian. Say what you will of me, but leave my king alone." "Hush her up!" angrily cried Cauchon.

In that cemetery of St. Ouen occurred what now is called proper self-defense on Jeanne's part. She could write her name, but with a smile she signed with a circle, emblem of mockery, and a cross, meaning negation. She hoped to be transferred to the prisons of the Church, where she clamored to be placed. Jeanne signed a paper consisting of seven lines, and afterward they produced an abjuration of fifty lines. Her judge might be a bishop, but never once did she confuse the Church she revered and the unworthy clerics who sat in judgment on her. During the ceremonies of the rehabilitation at Rouen, a great procession marched to the Old Market where had stood Jeanne's funeral pyre, and with solemnity the twelve accusations against her were torn into shreds and burned. Rouen felt happier after rendering that justice, and her renewed self-respect found natural expression in her Flamboyant Gothic monuments.

However, many a long year was to go by before France fully comprehended the martyr of Rouen. Voltaire libeled Jeanne as vilely as the XV-century savants of Paris University. The rationalists of a later day have patronized her as self-hallucinated. But the tide has mounted. "The day that all the bells of the world ring in honor of Jeanne d'Arc, they will sound abroad the glory of France," said Leo XIII, in 1896. The Maid of Domrémy-on-the-Meuse was declared Venerable in 1904, Blessed in 1909, and canonized a saint in 1920. *St. Jeanne d'Arc, ora pro nobis!*

THE CATHEDRAL OF LISIEUX[355]

One must live as one thinks, or else, sooner or later, one finishes by thinking as one lives.

—PAUL BOURGET.

Lisieux Cathedral is, with that of Rouen, the least Norman in the province. It claims to be the first built of the Gothic cathedrals of Normandy and the most vigorous. The preceding Romanesque cathedral was grievously damaged by fire in 1136. Arnoul, a prelate who had gone through the disillusioning experience of the Second Crusade, began the present church. Similarities between it and Laon Cathedral, and various other indications, prove that it was building from 1160 to 1190.

Bishop Arnoul, of a line of shrewd Norman diplomatists, profited materially by his ability to keep on good terms with both husbands of Aliénor of Aquitaine, Henry of England, and Louis of France. In Lisieux Cathedral he married Aliénor to Henry II, which act was to take three hundred years of war and Jeanne's sacrifice to undo. Arnoul was the English king's chief adviser before Becket's ascendancy. It is said that he counseled Henry, after his first quarrel with Becket, to detach one by one the English bishops from their primate, which policy of *divide et impera* came only too easily to an Angevin-Anglo-Norman. Four times did Bishop Arnoul journey to Sens to negotiate for Henry with the pope, during the Becket controversy. Some of the leading men of his day admired the prelate of Lisieux; but soundly honest men such as Abbot Robert de Torigny of the Mount, and the bishop of Chartres, John of Salisbury, distrusted him entirely—the latter remarked on his political sense in bestowing benefits when he wished to convince a man of his point of view.

Under Bishop Arnoul the nave of Lisieux rose in one campaign, a monument severe and pure, fog-colored like the wintry sky over it, say the townsmen. A note of force is imparted by the sturdy cylindrical piers. There is a narthex bay at the western end—a Germanic influence. No trace of vaulting shows in the deep gallery over the aisles, though the triforium arches that open on the central vessel are better suited for a tribune than a blind arcade. Behind that arcade now stands a poorly constructed wall opened here and there by doors, reminding us that once it was the custom for crusaders to store their valuables in the upper galleries of cathedrals.

---

[355] *Congrès Archéologique*, 1858, 1870, and 1908, p. 300, Louis Serbat; Abbé V. Hardy, *La cathédrale St. Pierre de Lisieux* (Paris, Impri. Fazier-Saye, 1917); *La Normandie monumentale et pittoresque. Calvados*, pp. 91, 103, "Lisieux," Abbé Marie (Le Havre, Lemale et Cie, 1875); Ch. Vasseur, *Études historiques et archéologiques sur la cathédrale de Lisieux* (Caen, 1891); Émile Lambin, "La cathédrale de Lisieux," in *Revue de l'art chrétien*, 1898, vol. 45, p. 448; A. de Caumont, *Statistique monumentale du Calvados* (Caen, 1867), vol. 5, p. 200; V. Ruprich-Robert, *L'architecture normande au XIe et XIIe siècles* (Paris, 1897), 2 vols.; H. de Formeville, *Histoire de l'ancien évêche-comté de Lisieux* (Lisieux, 1873), 2 vols.; *Histoire littéraire de la France*, vol. 14, p. 304, "Arnoul, évêque de Lisieux" (Paris, 1817); A. Sarrazin, *Pierre Cauchon, juge de Jeanne d'Arc* (Paris, 1901). Other studies of the judges of Jeanne d'Arc, by Fabre (Paris, 1915), and Ch. Engelhard (Le Havre, 1905).

Some have suggested that Guillaume de Sens was the architect of Lisieux, whose resemblances with his known works at Sens and Canterbury are discernible. Lisieux adhered to the Romanesque tradition of salient transept arms; that to the north lacks a portal; that to the south is an excellent example of plainest Primary Gothic. The transept has an eastern aisle, an arrangement found at Durham, Lincoln, Salisbury, and Peterborough. The first two bays of the choir were built, like the nave, in the XII century; the birth of the apse is marked by a staircase, as at Caen, Boscherville, Fécamp, and Eu.

The ample central tower of Lisieux, not in the first plan, was erected as the choir was gradually extended. In the later-constructed straight bays of the choir, and at the apse, finished under Bishop Jourdain du Hommet, no annulets broke the ascending line of the clustered shafts, quatrefoils were cut in the spandrels, and more and more the structure took on regional characteristics. Arches were set under arches, some of them being acutely pointed, because the Norman preferred to use the same opening of the compass for all his arches, wide or narrow. It gave his eye pleasure to multiply molds, and his sense of exactitude craved a support for every roll molding. Lisieux' choir, however, avoided what was to become an excessive complication of parts in the Anglo-Norman school. The cathedral is essentially vigorous and severe.

In 1226 a fire necessitated repairs, and Bishop Guillaume de Pont-de-l'Arche took the opportunity to make three ambulatory chapels. He built the façade towers whose lower walls retained Romanesque parts of the XI century. When the southwest tower fell in 1553 it was replaced by one of pre-Gothic design. The northwest belfry had as prototype the famous one of St. Pierre at Caen. The axis chapel—longer than the XIII-century one it replaced—is a gem of Flamboyant art. On its walls are some small funereal bas-reliefs erected by the cathedral canons.

The builder of Lisieux' Lady chapel was Pierre Cauchon, president of the tribunal that sentenced Jeanne d'Arc to death. He did not erect his chapel, as some intimate, in expiation of his conduct at Rouen in 1431, for he remained to the end the creature of his country's invaders. His detestation of Jeanne, moreover, was a personal affair, since it had been her triumph at Orléans, creating a national hope, that put heart into the citizens of Beauvais to expel their pro-English bishop. The English sent him to buy Jeanne from her captors. After the happenings in St. Ouen's cemetery, by law Jeanne should have been passed into the control of the Church, but Cauchon ordered her back to her English prison, and when she again donned male attire, and again asserted that she had heard her voices, her unscrupulous enemies were enabled to accuse her of being a relapsed heretic and wanton, to start a new trial, and condemn her to death. Cauchon himself hastened to the fortress to witness Jeanne's "relapse," and with Lord Warwick he is said to have chuckled over it—"This time she's well caught!" The morning that Jeanne was led to her execution she faced Cauchon fearlessly: "Bishop, I die by your hand. Had I been placed in the prisons of the Church, this would never have happened. You have left me in the clutches of my enemies. I call you before God, the great judge, to answer for the wrong you have done me." Even as she so spoke a spirited statue now represents Jeanne in Cauchon's Norman cathedral, while her judge is a condemned felon before the bar of history.

Like Arnoul, builder of Lisieux' nave, Cauchon knew how to act a better part. As rector of Paris University he had been esteemed for his learning. But, coming to the parting of the ways, he chose the broad and easy path, and the rest followed. His influence encouraged the University of Paris in its pernicious betrayal of France after Henry V's invasion. Cauchon won the see of Beauvais by defending Jean Sans Peur of Burgundy, in 1407, when the latter had murdered his cousin, the Duke of Orléans,[356] in the streets of Paris. And in the same hour that he thus truckled for advancement, Jean Gerson, the chancellor of Paris University, denounced the ducal crime—destined to be for France of incalculable consequence—and had his house sacked by Burgundians.

Ten years later, at the Council of Constances, in Switzerland Cauchon upheld the murderer, and Gerson rebuked the crime, whereupon he felt it to be wiser to quit Constances in disguise and to pass his latter life in retirement. Cauchon became the butcher of Jeanne d'Arc, his name forever an infamy; Gerson, dying in poverty and defeat at Lyons, was thought worthy, during two centuries, to be called the author of the *Imitation of Christ*, and before he passed away in July, 1429, it was given to him to learn that the Maid had triumphed at Orléans, and to testify that her mission was of God: *Gratia Dei estensa est in hac puella; a Domino factum est istud.*

Cauchon, ex-bishop of Beauvais, having placed his learning and energies at the service of his country's invaders, ambitiously hoped to obtain Rouen as his thirty pieces of silver, but the Duke of Bedford compromised matters by bestowing on him the lesser see of Lisieux, in 1432. As the national cause prospered the traitor was more and more detested by the populace. When the Burgundian partisans of the English were expelled from Paris, the properties of the bishop of Lisieux in the capital were seized and he himself was mobbed. In 1442 he fell dead suddenly one day while his barber was shaving him. A few years later, when Jeanne was rehabilitated and her judge excommunicated, the populace broke open Cauchon's tomb in the cathedral and flung his bones into the mire. His successor at Lisieux, Bishop Pasquier de Vaux, also one of Jeanne's faithless judges, died alone, deserted, on the day that the French army entered his city as victors, in 1449. The after history of Lisieux Cathedral followed the same course as others in France; 1562 and 1793 wrecked its monuments and smashed its stained glass. In the Flamboyant Gothic church of St. Jacques—where not a capital breaks the ascending line—are some XVI-century windows, making it the first church with such remaining.

---

[356] The murdered Duke of Orléans, a son of the art-loving Valois king, Charles V, built the châteaux of La Ferté-Milon, on the Oureq, and Pierrefonds, in the forest of Compiègne, in the courtyard of which latter stands his equestrian statue. His sons were the poet-duke, Charles d'Orléans, and Dunois, his acknowledged bastard, the chief instrument in ridding France of her invaders. Two grandsons of the builder of Pierrefonds ascended the French throne, Louis XII and Francis I, and those who undertake an architectural journey over France will soon become familiar with the porcupine of the one and the salamander of the other. Sir Theodore Andreas Cook, *Twenty-five Great Houses of France* (New York and London, 1916); Viollet-le-Duc, *Dictionnaire de l'architecture*, on Pierrefonds.

Lisieux can boast of no bishop canonized by the Church, but her citizens are doing all in their power to let Christendom know of the gentle Norman girl, Thérèse Martin, the "Little Flower," who died in the odor of sanctity (1897) in the Carmelite convent of the town, before she had reached her twenty-fifth year. Her extraordinary cult, especially among soldiers during the World War, proves that the thirst for sainthood is as strong as ever in the peoples who went crusading and flung themselves toward heaven in cathedrals. Art springs from emotions such as that felt by Frenchmen for the "Little Flower." To ignore such manifestations, as do the rationalists who still are insisting, as dogmatically as before 1914, that France, at root, is the land of Voltaire, is a willful shutting of the eyes to the basic forces that make history.

Those good people of Lisieux who are mystic-minded, who *believe in order that they may understand*, as Anselm taught at Bec near by, as Plato taught in Greece, feel subconsciously that their "Little Flower," who said that only after her death would begin her real mission, is atoning for Pierre Cauchon.[357]

THE CATHEDRAL OF ÉVREUX[358]

Il en coûte cher pour devenir la France. Nous nous plaignons, et non sans droit, de nos épreuves et de nos mécomptes. Nos pères n'ont pas vécu plus doucement que nous, ni recueilli plus tôt et à meilleur marché les fruits de leurs travaux. Il y a dans le spectacle de leurs destinées de quoi s'attrister et se fortifier à la fois. L'histoire abat les prétentions impatientes et soutient les longues espérances.

—Guizot.

The cathedral of Évreux is not homogeneous like that of Lisieux, but, gathering of different styles though it is, Romanesque, Gothic, early and late, neo-classic, it possesses its own distinct personality. A church of whose choir it has been said

[357] A professor in a Norman college, Joseph Lotte, who fell on the field of honor at Arras, in December, 1914, thus apostrophized the "Little Flower" of Lisieux: "Enrôlez-nous, petite sœur céleste! Enrôlez-nous sous vos bannières. Nous avons battu bien des pays, couru bien des aventures, dissipé bien des dons: il nous reste la fidélité. Nous serons derrière vous les vieux routiers qui escortaient Jeanne d'Arc. Notre France ne veut pas mourir. Apprenez-nous à aimer. Il faut qu'un tel amour monte de nous à Dieu qu'il tourne à nouveau sa face vers notre terre de France et, retrouvant son peuple, décide de le sauver. Mais ne l'a-t-il pas déjà décidé, puisqu'il vous a envoyée?" P. Pacary, *Un compagnon de Péguy, Joseph Lotte; pages choisies* (Paris, J. Gabalda, 1916).

[358] *Congrès Archéologique*, 1864, 1889, and 1908; Abbé Jules Fossey, *Monographie de la cathédrale d'Évreux* (Évreux, 1898); Abbé Forée, *Les clôtures des chapelles de la cathédrale d'Évreux* (Évreux, Hérissey, 1890); A. J. de H. Bushnell, *Storied Windows* (New York, Macmillan, 1914); N. H. J. Westlake, *A History of Design in Painted Glass* (London, Parker & Co., 1881); *La Normandie monumentale et pittoresque. Eure*, vol. 1, p. 1, Évreux; p. 31, Conches; p. 61, Verneuil; p. 89, Tillières; p. 93, Nonancourt; p. 119, Vernon; p. 147, Les Andelys; p. 191, Gisors; vol. 2, p. 1, Louviers; p. 23, Gaillon; p. 97, Pont-Audemer; p. 63, Pont-de-l'Arche; p. 183, Bernay; p. 221, Bec-Hellouin; p. 245, Beaumont-le-Roger. In most of these churches the colored windows are remarkable.

by one so competent to compare the cathedrals of his native land as M. Louis Gonse, that it is "one of the fairest bits of Gothic architecture in France," surely can hold its own among more brilliant companions.

Two Romanesque edifices stood in succession on the site, not to speak of the Merovingian and Carolingian cathedrals here. Évreux is the *Evora* of Gallo-Roman times when it was ranked with Rouen and Tours. St. Patrick came hither in 432 for his consecration as bishop before his apostolate to Ireland. The first of the Romanesque cathedrals was dedicated in 1072 by Archbishop Lanfranc of Canterbury, but in 1119, when Henry I of England was besieging the city, it was destroyed for strategic purposes, by consent of its bishop, who was in the king's camp. Henry and all his barons gave generous compensation, we are told by Ordericus Vitalis, the English monk who spent most of his life in the Norman monastery of St. Évroult, "delighting in obedience and poverty," writing a history which is the chief XII-century record of the duchy.

The second Romanesque cathedral was begun in 1126. To it belonged the pier arcade of the present nave and the entire westernmost bay, as well as portions of the façade towers. At one time it was thought that the arches adjacent to the transept were part of the earlier church blessed by Lanfranc, inasmuch as they differ from the profiles of the other pier arches. Further study has demonstrated, however, that the entire arcade belongs to the XII century, since it was not the usage, before 1120, to flank a pier's four faces by columns, as was done here throughout.

The second Romanesque cathedral of Évreux was also destined to be of short duration. In 1194, Philippe-Auguste laid the city in ashes as chastisement for John Lackland's black deed. John had allowed a French garrison into Évreux during his intrigues with the French king, while Richard the Lion-hearted was on his crusade. When word came that his brother was returning to his possessions, John, hoping to placate him for his own treachery, invited the French garrison of three hundred to a feast and, it is said, foully murdered them all. The bishop of Évreux had accompanied Richard Cœur-de-Lion to the East and in Cyprus had crowned his bride, Berengaria of Navarre. In the course of time the counts of Évreux became kings of Navarre, through the marriage of Berengaria's sister to the Count of Champagne.[359] The niece of Richard and John, Blanche of Castile, brought in her dowry Évreux to the French Crown, when she married (1200) the son of that wily augmenter, Philippe-Auguste.

The renewal of the cathedral as Gothic proceeded slowly. By 1230 the nave

[359] The son of that union was the trouvère poet, Thibaut IV of Champagne and I of Navarre, of which latter domain he was chosen king in 1234, on the death of his mother's brother, Sancho, the chief victor of Las Navas de Toloso. His niece, Jeanne, inheriting both Champagne and Navarre, united them with the royal domain by her marriage to Philippe le Bel. Three of her sons ruled successively as kings of France, and then the Valois branch— sprung from a brother of Philippe le Bel—came to the throne. Whereupon the Navarrese elected, as their ruler, the Count of Évreux, who had married a daughter of Jeanne's. His son was Charles the Wicked (1319-87), Count of Évreux, king of Navarre, who in turn was succeeded by his son, Charles the Noble (1387-1425). One and all of them were linked with the architectural story of France: at Troyes, Provins, Meaux, Mantes, and Évreux Cathedral.

had merely reached the triforium level. A horizontal sculptured band, such as surmounts it, was not used after that date. The clearstory of the nave is contemporary with the Sainte-Chapelle in Paris, and when Louis IX came to his mother's dower city, in 1259, for the consecration of its bishop, who was his personal friend, he and the group of building-prelates with him, from Rheims, Rouen, Coutances, and Séez, must have discussed the new works at Évreux with interest. The choir of the cathedral was not undertaken till the close of the century. From 1298 to 1310 it was built in a Rayonnant style fully as advanced as the later abbatial of St. Ouen, at Rouen, with glazed triforium, capitals that are slight bands of foliage, and precocious prismatic profiles. The only distinctly Norman trait is the balustrade of the triforium. As the choir was made fifteen feet wider than the nave, its westernmost bay was canted to join the transept, but the effect is not displeasing.

The Hundred Years' War caused a cessation of works at Évreux. Dire years were they for the city ruled by Charles le Mauvais, a "demon of France," "perfidy in person." He plotted ceaselessly against the national party, not because he leaned to the English side, but that he was obsessed by his own superior claims to the French crown, being by both father and mother directly of St. Louis' line. His high abilities—and he was learned, eloquent, and handsome—were wasted in mischief making. In 1365 he gave up his city of Évreux to the flames. Charles the Wicked is pictured in the cathedral's clearstory windows, in the fourth on the north side of the choir, and across the sanctuary from him, in another light, is his wife, a Valois, sister of the French king, Charles V, and his art-loving brothers at Dijon, Angers, and Bourges. She possessed Mantes by her dower right, and added to its collegiate church the Rayonnant chapel of Navarre, in which are portrait statuettes representing her daughters. Her four brothers, says M. Anthyme Saint-Paul, were the paramount influences in the formation of French Flamboyant Gothic, from 1365 to 1415.

The best array of XIV-century glass[360] in France is that of the choir of Évreux. The windows are not forceful, like XIII-century medallion-mosaics, any more than the Rayonnant stonework framing them resembles hardy Apogee Gothic. The hues, while limpid and pleasing, show none of the lovely half-tones which the Flamboyant-Renaissance day was to achieve. Large plates of glass were employed in order that fewer leads might darken the window. White was overused, as well as the recently discovered yellow, called silver-stain, obtained by fusing the surface of white glass with a solution of silver. Pot-metal glass—that colored in the mass—had hitherto been used exclusively. Effective backgrounds were obtained by damasked patterns. In each panel was a single figure in an architectural setting of grisaille and silver-stain, which frames grew so elaborate, by the middle of the century, that perspective was represented.

---

[360] In Normandy, glass of the XIV century is to be found in the cathedrals of Séez and Coutances, at Carentan, Pont-de-l'Arche, Nesle-St.-Saire, and in Rouen's big abbatial. Elsewhere in France there are XIV-century windows at Mantes, Beauvais, Amiens, Dol, Limoges, Toulouse, Bordeaux, Narbonne, Béziers, Carcassonne (in St. Nazaire), Chartres (in St. Pierre), and Poitiers (in Ste. Radégonde). In St. Urbain's at Troyes is some of the earliest glass of this century.

The earliest example of a canopy type of window is in Évreux' upper choir—the third light on the north side. It was the gift of the *grand queux*, or cook, of France, Guillaume d'Harcourt, who died in 1327. The two windows presented by the bishop of Évreux, Bernard Cariti (1376-83), show progress in architectural backgrounds, and the donor is drawn from life. In the canted bay of the choir (north) is a XV-century window of the Saintes Maries, whose alleged relics were given to the bishop here by good King René of Anjou. The window commemorates Normandy's newly acquired freedom, hence its portraits of Charles VII, his son, the future Louis XI, and the seneschal of Normandy, Pierre de Brézé. It is also a memorial of the Great Schism of the West, ended by the Council of Constance, at which the bishop of Évreux was present. Foliate designs cover the grisaille lights of the triforium. The quarries (white, parallel pieces of glass framed together in a lead pattern) are enlivened by strips of colored glass and heraldic ornament.

Louis XI built the Lady chapel of Évreux, in whose windows he depicted his coronation. In the lily-petals formed by the Flamboyant tracery of the mullions are pictured the barons who attended the king's investing. Instead of the single figures in each panel, hitherto popular, small groups were now set under the vitrine canopies, and subjects heretofore unknown in western iconography appeared, such as the Transfiguration, the Woman of Samaria, the Marriage at Cana. They were pictured just as the mystery plays of the day presented them on the stage. In the Tree of Jesse, at the end of the chapel, the new process of abrasion was employed, by which the color of flashed glass was ground away in places, and on the white surfaces thus exposed were enameled new colors, so that one piece of glass could exhibit a variety of hues. These windows of Évreux' Lady chapel belong to the transition hour between the earlier tradition that treated a window as an adjunct of the architecture, and the later tradition that composed a window as an independent painted picture.[361]

When, in 1441, Évreux opened its gates joyously to the national troops, new works were begun in the cathedral. The actual Flamboyant transept was substituted for a decrepit Romanesque structure, whose ground plan it followed, hence it is too narrow for its height; seen from the interior of the church, the octagonal lantern appears cramped. The lacework stone spire of the crossing was one of the first

[361] Normandy's XV-century glass, besides that of Évreux' Lady chapel, can be studied at Rouen, in the cathedral, and the churches of St. Ouen and St. Maclou, at Caudebec, Bernay, Vereuil, Beaumont-le-Roger, St. Lô, Carentan, Falaise, Pont-Audemer, Bayeux, and Coutances. Elsewhere in France glass of this period can be seen in Amiens Cathedral, in the Vendôme chapel of Chartres, in the choir of Moulins, in the north transept of Le Mans, and the windows presented to Bourges Cathedral by the Duke of Berry and Jacques Cœur. There is also XV-century glass at Clermont-Ferrand, Eymoutiers, Riom, in some of the churches of Paris, such as St. Sévérin, and in Brittany, at Dinan, Plélan, Les Iffs, and in Quimper Cathedral. Windows of the XVI century abound in Normandy. The most imposing array is near Évreux, at Conches, whose church of Ste. Foi is on no account to be missed. Aldégrevier, a pupil of Albert Dürer, designed the seven tall apse windows, about 1520. There are eighteen other lights (1540-53), very Raphaelesque in type; the *Pressoir* window and the apotheosis of the Virgin are typical of that heated hour of controversy. Andre Michel, éd., *Histoire de l'art*, vol. 4, 2{ème} partie, "Le vitrail français au XV{e} et au XVI{e} siècle," Émile Mâle; A. Bouillet, *L'église Ste. Foi de Couches (Eure) et ses vitraux* (Caen, H. Delesque, 1889).

in the region. For sixty years during the XVI century two prelates of the prominent Tillières family held the see; to Ambrose le Veneur is due the superlatively ornate Flamboyant north front of the transept, an unanswerable proof that if Gothic art was soon to end it was not of inanition it expired. To put the northern flank of his church in accord with the façade's festival of lace stone he re-dressed the chapels along nave and choir. His nephew, Bishop Gabriel le Veneur, undertook to remake the west frontispiece in a style so neo-classic that M. Léon Palustre, the historian of the Renaissance, exclaimed, *"Pour cette fois le moyen âge est bien fini!"* And yet only thirty years separated the façades of uncle and nephew. The southwest tower has been left uncrowned; that to the northwest is an imposing heavy mass in which is the sonorous bell of Évreux, called Gros-Pierre.

THE CATHEDRAL OF SÉEZ[362]

> Il y a plus d'une sorte de chevalerie, et les grands coups de lance ne sont pas de rigueur. À défaut d'épée, nous avons la plume; à défaut de plume, la parole; à défaut de parole, l'honneur de notre vie.
>
> —Léon Gautier, *La Chevalerie.*

"Prudent, modest, and gracious," reads the epitaph of Bishop Jean de Bernières, who, having in large part built the choir of Séez Cathedral, impressing on it his personal qualities, departed this life on Holy Thursday of 1292. Séez has been called a little sister of Chartres. It is well set, but of unpretentious dimensions. Its twin spire-crowned western towers will be improved when the masses of masonry now propping them are removed. The interior is white and clean, almost to prudery, which may be due to the renewal of choir and transept in modern times.

Never from its inception have restorations ceased in this church. Not that Séez overstepped the possibilities of Gothic equilibrium, but it made incautious use of the calcined foundations of the Romanesque cathedral to which it succeeded. That earlier church had been erected by Bishop Yves de Bellême after two cathedrals had been wiped out by the Norse invasions. Brigands had nested beside his church, and in seeking to dislodge them he had set fire to his own sanctuary, for which act he was rebuked by Leo IX at the Council of Rheims in 1049. He took as his penance the replacing of the cathedral at his own expense, and since he was connected with the rich Norman princes of Italy funds soon poured in. The edifice he erected was destroyed in the unceasing petty wars waged against each other by the husbands of Aliéner of Aquitaine.

[362] V. Ruprich-Robert, *La cathédrale de Séez* (Paris, Morel, 1885); Abbé L. V. Dumaine, *La cathédrale de Séez, son histoire et ses beautés* (Séez, 1894); H. Tournouër, "La cathédrale de Séez," in *Bulletin de la Soc. hist. et archéol. de l'Orne,* 1897; Marais et Beaudouin, *Essai hist. sur le cathédrale et le chapitre de Séez* (Alençon, 1878); Robert Triger, "La cathédrale de Séez," in *Revue hist. et archéol. du Maine,* 1900, vol. 47, p. 287; *De la Sicotière et Poulet-Malassis, Le département de l'Orne, archéol. et pittoresque* (Laigle, Beuzelin, 1845), folio; *La Normandie monumentale et pittoresque. Orne,* p. 101, on Séez, Abbé Barret; p. 1, St. Germain at Argentan, with a central lantern and elaborate late-Gothic porch; p. 41, Notre Dame at Alençon; p. 77, St. Évroult-de-Montfort, a late-XI century abbatial; p. 245, the monastery of La Trappe, in Séez diocese, established in 1122, and reformed in 1662 by the noted Abbé de Rancy.

The nave of the actual cathedral, the part first undertaken, rose from 1220 to 1240 under Bishop Gervais, a member of the Order of Prémontré. After the pause of a generation, its upper vaulting was constructed. All the traits loved by the Norman are here; friezes below triforium and clearstory, balustrades, sharp twin lancets under equilateral arches, multiple ridges and multiple supports, circular capitals and bases, interior passageways contrived skillfully. Subdivision and multiplication of parts reign supreme; merely for the pleasure it gave his eye the Norman increased the molds of his archivolts. There are diagonals here of so generous a profile that little vault-web shows. The Norman was partial to shadow decoration. He covered his walls with holes cut into foiled shapes which lent themselves to ever-changing contrasts of light and shade. In each spandrel of the main arcade is cut an elaborate rosette before which stands the shaft that mounts to the vault-springing. No Ile-de-France architect had thus obstructed his pierced ornament.

The choir of Séez was begun soon after the nave, but about 1270 was entirely reconstructed as a Rayonnant vessel, designed audaciously to weigh as little as possible on defective foundations. The sanctuary was raised above the ambulatory, with no screen between. The capitals were slight. Here again appeared a trait of Norman redundancy—rain-guards or weather-drips over the main arches and the wall arcading; an Ile-de-France master had relegated such crocketed gables where they belong—to the exterior walls of a church.

Like Évreux, Séez Cathedral possesses a uniform array of XIV-century glass. Above and below the canopied figures in the clearstory lights are panels of grisaille. The triforium was among the first to become one composition with the upper windows, by means of stone mullions; its quarry designs are bordered with strips of colored glass. The transept, built from 1290 to 1330, has in its side walls excellent images of the prophets. Its roses are linked by mullions with the row of windows below; the north rose traces a star with rays. In 1373 a fire damaged the edifice, and its reconstruction continued through the foreign wars. The Bishop of Séez, Robert de Rouvre, proved loyal to the national cause and quitted his city for the wandering court of Charles VII, rather than take oath to Henry V. This patriotic Norman prelate knew Jeanne d'Arc, not at her trial at Rouen, but in her triumphal hour of the coronation at Rheims.

The cathedral of Séez was twice pillaged during the religious wars. The Huguenots tore the lead from the roofs, and piled the art treasures in the aisles for bonfires. One doubly regrets the loss of the nave's windows which would have completed the coherent scheme of color decoration that distinguishes the church. Séez was neglected for centuries, its decrepitude becoming such that the priests at its altars were inconvenienced by wind and rain, and not so inconsequent, after all, then seemed the interior weather-guards. The much criticized restoration of M. Ruprich-Robert was a necessity, even though it may have been too radical.

Of the six Norman cathedrals, that of Séez is the least known, yet it lies but a few miles beyond Falaise, visited by most travelers in Normandy. In the streets of the Conqueror's birthplace they still sing, *"Vive le fils d'Ariette, Normans, vive le fils d'Arlette!"* A statue of William faces the Trinité in which parish he was baptized

(1027). The XIII century built the Trinité's transept, the XVI century its choir (beneath which passes a street), and the Renaissance appears in a porch of faultless taste.[363] The donjon of the castle belongs to the XII century, though the guides will point out a window whence Duke Robert the Magnificent first beheld the maid Arlette.

THE CATHEDRAL OF BAYEUX[364]

> Mais c'est toujours la France, ou petite ou plus grande
> Le pays des beaux blés et des encadrements,
> Le pays de la grappe et des ruisslements,
> Le pays de genêts, de bruyère, de lande.

—CHARLES PÉGUY.

In the cathedrals of Rouen, Lisieux, and Évreux, the Norman traits are subordinate to those of the Ile-de-France; at Séez all is Norman, and altogether Norman, too, are Bayeux and Coutances, the gems of the duchy's Gothic school. The cathedral of Bayeux stands on the site of one burned in 1046. After that fire Bishop Hugues began a Romanesque cathedral which was continued by his successor, Odo de Conteville, a half brother of the Conqueror. The fair Arlette, the tanner's daughter of Falaise, after the death of Duke Robert the Magnificent, was joined in lawful wedlock with a Norman baron. Her son, Odo, without the slightest vocation, was made a bishop at seventeen—precisely the feudal debasing of the priesthood which Gregory VII was combating. At the battle of Hastings, when he had blessed the troops, he sprang to his charger and led the cavalry. A XII-century canon of Bayeux, Robert Wace, in his rimed history of the Norman dukes, the *Roman de Rou*, tells how, at Hastings, the Norman minstrel, Taillefer, "famed for song, mounted on a charger strong, rode on before, awhile he sang of Roland and of Charlemagne, Oliver and the vassals all, who fell in fight at Roncevals."

---

[363] St. Gervais, at Falaise, has a good Romanesque tower consecrated in the presence of Henry I of England. The nave's southern pier arcade is Romanesque, but the arches on the north side were reconstructed as Gothic at the same time that the vaults were redone during the XIII century. See *Congrès Archéologique*, 1848, 1864, and 1908, p. 367; Louis Régnier, "Falaise et la vallée d'Auge," in *Annuaire normand*, 1892; Langevin, *Recherches historiques sur Falaise*; Meriel, *Hist. de Falaise* (1889); Black, *Normandy and Picardy, Their Castles, Churches, and Footprints of William the Conqueror*.

[364] *Congrès Archéologique*, 1853 and 1908, vol. 1, p. 145; Henri Prentout, *Caen et Bayeux* (Collection. Villes d'art célèbres), (Paris, H. Laurens); Abbé Lelieve, *Bayeux, la cathédrale, les églises* (Bayeux, Deslandes, 1907); Jean Vallery-Radot, *La cathédrale de Bayeux*, Thèse: École des chartes (1911); De Dion et Lesvignes, *La cathédrale de Bayeux* (Paris, A. Morel et Cie, 1861); Rev. R. S. Mylne, *The Cathedral of Bayeux* (London, 1904); Chigonesnel, *Histoire de Bayeux* (1867); Paul de Farcy, *Abbayes du diocèse de Bayeux* (Laval, 1886-88), 3 vols, (on Cerisy-la-Forêt, etc.); Arcisse de Caumont, *Statistique monumentale du Calvados* (Caen, F. Le Blanc-Hardel, 1898); G. Bouet, "Clochers du diocèse de Bayeux," in *Bulletin Monumental*, vol. 17, p. 196; vol. 23, p. 362; vol. 25, 1859, p. 165; vol. 49, p. 465; Engerand, "La sculpture romane en Normandie," in *Bulletin Monumental*, 1904; *Histoire littéraire de la France*, vol. 13, p. 518, "Robert Wace, chanoine de Bayeux, historien-poète"; V. Bourrienne, in *Revue catholique de Normandie*, on the bishops Odo de Conteville and Philippe d'Harcourt, vii to

As governor of Kent, Bishop Odo deepened, by his injustices, the hate of the dispossessed Anglo-Saxons for their new masters. On an excursion against Durham he so harried the countryside that it lay waste for a hundred years. When to his misgovernment was added the folly of grandeur—for this unbalanced feudal bully intrigued to wear the papal tiara, to succeed to the great-hearted champion against iniquity, Gregory VII—his brother, William, thought it best to shut him up. From 1047 to 1096 Odo held the see of Bayeux. The Romanesque cathedral which he completed was blessed in the presence of William the Conqueror and Matilda, in 1077, on which occasion the bishop presented to his church a candelabrum such as can be seen at Hildersheim. Bayeux' crown of light hung from the high vaults until wrecked by the Calvinists in 1562.

Of the cathedral built by this anomalous prelate very little remains. The crypt is of his time, parts of the outer walls, and the body of the west towers in their lower halls; their upper stories were re-dressed later. The crypt was forgotten till 1412, when, in digging for a certain bishop's tomb they unearthed it. Odo's cathedral was in part destroyed in 1106 when Bayeux was besieged and burned by Henry I of England. Another fire in 1160 made rebuilding imperative, and even before the latter disaster Bishop Philippe d'Harcourt (1142-62) had begun a new Romanesque church. To it belonged the core of the actual transept-crossing's piers and the lower part of the nave, which is considered the richest Romanesque[365] work extant. The flat wall above the pier arcade is covered with geometric designs, interlacings, and chevrons. The curious carved disks, in the spandrels of the arches, represent Oriental animals and the grotesques that are to be found in Celtic illuminations. Some have thought that the exotic sculptures of Bayeux derived directly from an ivory coffer, of the IV-century Hegira, brought home by crusaders for the treasury of their cathedral. Oriental Byzantium was their common origin.

---

x, xviii to xxiii.

[365] The term Romanesque was put into usage by the archaeologist, Arcisse de Caumont (1802-73), to whom Bayeux has erected a statue. He also originated the useful term "Flamboyant." His Norman Society of Antiquarians was a pioneer in the study of mediæval monuments. Another son of Bayeux, honored by a statue, is the poet, Alain Chartier (1386-

The Choir of Bayeaux Cathedral (1210-1260). Typical of Normandy's Elaborate Gothic.

The choir of Bayeux is a masterpiece of Norman Gothic erected by Robert des Ablêges (1206-31), who died a crusader, and by the two successive bishops. In the nave those prelates surmounted the Romanesque lower walls with Gothic win-

1449), who lived to see his master, Charles VII, the conqueror of Normandy.

dows and vaulting; a balustrade marks the division between the dissimilar parts. They reinforced the façade towers, and made five western doorways—although the church behind possessed only three aisles.

The student who would comprehend at a glance the difference between the æsthetic equipoise of the Ile-de-France and the sumptuous Gothic of Normandy can do nothing better than to place side by side the pictures of Bayeux' choir and the curving transept end of Soissons. Those whose taste has been formed by English minsters may prefer Bayeux, those whose loiterings have made them familiar with the cradle-land of the national art of France will find their ideal in the classic restraint of Soissons. Scarcely a square foot of Bayeux' choir is unadorned. Each spandrel is pierced by trefoils and quatrefoils, and at the apse the triforium spandrels are entirely covered with foliage. There are acutely pointed arches, and arches under arches. Mold has been added to mold, and each roll molding has its own colonnette. There are carved friezes at different levels, and the horizontal line is still further accentuated by balustrades. At the sanctuary curve double pillars stand one behind the other. Even the vault web is decorated with the portraits of bishops. As the choir surmounts Odo de Conteville's crypt it is raised above the procession path. Some of its side chapels open, one on the other, above a dividing wall, as in the Gothic choir of the Abbaye-aux-Hommes at Caen, an arrangement repeated with beautiful effect at Coutances. At the birth of the apse are turrets; there are corner towerettes with staircases on each of the western belfries.

The Norman façade, as a rule, is very plain, lacking rose window and galleries, and with undeveloped portals. Two marked stories usually divide it—that of the entranceway and the big window story over it. Often the towers are disengaged awkwardly from the massive, nor is the transition from shaft to pyramid accomplished with subtlety. Yet the Norman church has great compensations to offer. Few edifices in the classic region of the Oise, Seine, and Marne present a more complete exterior than this chief church of Bayeux that stands so proudly over the flat little city, unencumbered by houses, raised on a dignified platform where the ground slopes to the east.

The cathedral's transept is Rayonnant Gothic of the XIV century, in which day were added the various side chapels whose tracery is geometric. When Jeanne d'Arc had given France a new soul, Bayeux raised its lordly central tower "to praise God in the sky." It was undertaken by a wealthy prelate, Louis d'Harcourt (d. 1479), of the same family as the bishop who had built the Romanesque wall of the nave. He planted his Flamboyant octagon on the square XIII-century lantern, but the actual top story of the transept-crossing tower is modern. Bayeux almost lost her notable beacon in the XIX century, when fissures appeared, and a zealous restorer thought to demolish it whereas all that was needed was consolidation. The ancient Romanesque piers at the four corners of the *croisée* were found incased in XIII-century masonry.

Opposite the cathedral in the town library is an invaluable historical document, the Bayeux Tapestry,[366] the oldest extant large amount of the art of design

[366] A. Levé, *La tapisserie de Bayeux* (Paris, H. Laurens, 1919); Hilaire Belloc, *The Bayeux Tapestry* (London and New York, 1914); J. R. Fowke, *The Bayeux Tapestry* (London, G. Bell,

in the mediæval centuries. Many a vicissitude it has had: lost from view till Montfaucon, the learned Benedictine of St. Maur's reform, unearthed it in 1720, and again, during the Revolution's disorders, used as covering for ammunition carts till an enlightened citizen redeemed it. Originally it comprised one seamless piece, just sufficient to encircle the nave of Bayeux Cathedral, for which, indubitably, it was made. Every summer solstice, on the dedication day of Odo's church, it adorned the cathedral, "the toilet of St. John," it was named, a very simple toilet, for, though called a tapestry, it is really a drab linen band twenty inches wide, two hundred and thirty feet long, with the design alone worked in worsted of eight colors.

The scheme is the perjury of Harold and its punishment, hence its suitableness as an embroidery for a church. It begins with Harold and ends with his death at Hastings. His oath of allegiance to William, given at Bayeux, is pictured. Odo is shown saving the Normans from retreat at the battle of Hastings. Some have thought he would not have dared to glorify himself till after the death of his brother, William. The tapestry was made, probably, from 1067 to 1077, immediately following the successful conquest of England, and is a contemporary, therefore, of the *Chanson de Roland*, composed by a Norman anterior to the First Crusade. The embroidery was done before 1085, since the Conqueror's seals of that date show armor similar to that pictured in the canvas; the sequence of the scenes indicates they are subsequent to Wace's poem (c. 1160).

Critics have thought, from the inscriptions, that Anglo-Saxons made the tapestry. It is known that the textile art flourished in Kent, the province ruled by Odo; in Normandy, too, the industry was popular. M. Levé, in the most recent monograph of this precious legacy from the past, contends that a Norman who was favorable to William the Conqueror made it, and that the popular attribution to Queen Matilda is not unlikely. She may have had the work done as a gift for Bayeux Cathedral while Odo was still in royal favor. The war-like bishop died as a crusader journeying East, and lies buried in Palermo Cathedral. The people despised Odo, and would openly mock as he passed, "Fie on the bishop who married adulterous King Philip to adulterous Bertrada de Montfort."

A century after Harold's oath to Duke William, in Bayeux, and in the same hunting-seat, at Bures, near the city, occurred a scene of passion whose consequences were momentous. Bishop Henri de Beaumont was at work on the cathedral's transept and upper nave when Henry II came to Bayeux to spend the Christmas season of 1170. For seven years western Christendom had watched his feud with the exiled primate of Canterbury. The lesser people of France and England considered that the prelate defended their liberties by his defense of church liberty. For how, they asked, can a churchman rebuke lay injustices if he owes his position to the very culprits he should censure?

A pretense of reconciliation between Henry and his whilom intimate had recently been brought about. Becket felt its hollowness, since none knew better than he that the Angevin monarch's besetting sin was duplicity and a merciless vindictiveness when his will was successfully crossed. As he parted with the king he had

1898); Lefebvre des Mouettes, in *Bulletin Monumental*, 1912, p. 213; 1903, p. 84.

looked steadily at him, saying, with meaning: "I think I shall never see you again," and Henry Plantagenet had cried, vehemently, "Do you take me for a traitor?" Soon after word was brought to the king that Becket, newly arrived in England, was again stirring up difficulties. Henry flew into one of his madman passions hereditary in his blood from Fulk Nerra, from the Conqueror, too; frenzied words broke from him, their purport being the upbraiding of his followers that he lacked a friend to rid him of this upstart priest. Immediately four of his courtiers started for England, and as December of 1170 closed, Canterbury Cathedral was the scene of a bloody assassination.

Becket dead was more formidable than Becket alive. Frightened by the indignation roused by the murder, Henry conceded what the primate had contended for. The Canterbury martyr became a frequent theme with the mediæval artist. At Coutances, Chartres, Angers, and Sens are medallion windows that relate his story. Twice he is honored in Bayeux Cathedral, in the sculpture of the southern portal and in a window of the transept. The popular voice of Europe canonized St. Thomas, and his grave at Canterbury became the loadstone of an international pilgrimage. The XIV-century poet has related how Merrie England rode down to Kent in the first spring days, when that Aprille with his shoures sweet hath pierced to the root the drought of Marche, and with the new-liveried year the *wanderlust* awakes:

> Then longen folk to goon on pilgrimages ...
> And specially, from every shires ende
> Of Englelond, to Caunterbury they wende,
> The holy blisful martir for to seke
>
> That hem hath holpen, whan that they were seke.[367]

THE CATHEDRAL OF COUTANCES[368]

Art is the stammering of man driven from his terrestrial Paradise but not yet arrived at the heavenly Paradise. Ever has he recalled, ever will he recall, the lost beauty. He is fallen: beauty's sanctuary is shut to him, but the exile traces a sketch of his original home in the strange land where he finds himself. Does not art fill in the intellectual life the same place that hope does in the moral? Art is man's trial to embody his ideals, it is a presentiment and a souvenir.

---

[367] Chaucer, *Canterbury Tales*, "Prologue."

[368] *Congrès Archéologique*, 1883; and 1908, p. 247, "La cathédrale de Coutances," E. Lefèvre-Pontalis, also published separately by H. Delesques, Caen, 1910; Abbé E. H. Pigéon, *Histoire de la cathédrale de Coutances* (Coutances, Salette fils, 1876); Alfred Ramée, "Cathédrale de Coutances," in *Revue des Soc. Savantes*, 1880, p. 94; A. de Dion, in *Bulletin Monumental*, 1884, vol. 50, p. 620; 1865, p. 509, G. Bouet; 1872, p. 19, Regnault; Gabriel Fleury, in *Revue ... archéol. du Maine*, 1909, on the architect, Thomas Toustain; Regnault, *Revue monumentale et historique de l'arrondissement de Coutances* (St. Lô, 1860); C. de Gerville, "Recherches sur les abbayes de la Manche," in *Mém. de la Soc. des Antiquaires de Normandie*, vol. 2, p. 77; *ibid.*, *Études géographiques et historiques sur le département de la Manche* (Cherbourg, 1854).

—Ernest Hello, Philosophie et Athéisme.

If the exterior aspect of Bayeux is admirable, that of Coutances Cathedral is superb. The high hill of the town is its pedestal. Few architectural views in France are finer than the silhouette of Coutances against the sky. And when its crowning cathedral is seen rising from a mist, it appears to ride the clouds like a mighty ship—a vision of Norman energy as memorable as the Mount of the Archangel off this very coast, in the bay of St. Michael.

As the archives of Coutances Cathedral were destroyed by the Huguenots, documentary proof of its date is lacking. Midway in the XIX century even serious students contended that this Apogee Gothic edifice was the church dedicated in 1056 by a hero of Hastings' battle, Bishop Geoffrey de Mowbray. Like Odo of Bayeux, the sword, not the crozier, should have been his emblem. He was the holder of two hundred lordships. He it was who, in Westminster Abbey, in 1066, mounting a tribune, asked the cowed Anglo-Saxons if they would consent that Duke William of Normandy assume the title, king of England, and the next day an enormous tax was imposed on the conquered race as "joyous tribute" to their new rulers. Geoffrey gave up residence in his Norman see to be castillan of Bristol, but, taking part in Odo's intrigues, he was driven from the country with the cry, "Gallows for the bishop!"

This ambitious baron-prelate obtained donations for his Romanesque cathedral when he journeyed in southern Italy and the East, where ruled his Norman kinsmen. When the archæologists Bouet, A. de Dion, and Abbé Pigéon found parts of Geoffrey's church englobed in the present nave and façade of Coutances, the heated controversy over the date of the cathedral ceased. The core of each façade tower is Bishop Geoffrey's, as are some of the piers in transept and nave, and the nave's upper wall (re-dressed as Gothic about 1230). The tribune of the fighting bishop lies unused behind the present triforium, whose wall arcades plainly show a succession of transformations.

The Romanesque cathedral was injured by fire in 1218. Bishop Bivien de Champagne planned a new church which his successor, Hugues de Morville (1208-38), started. That prelate, and his two successors, built the choir with its double aisles of different height, and the central tower carried on triumphal piers of multiple molds. "What inspired idiot dared fling those stones toward the sky!" exclaimed the great engineer, Vauban, before the lantern of Coutances. The transfused gentle light that falls from its windows tranquilizes the entire church. Even the laie-haunted Viollet-le-Duc likened it to St. Christopher bearing the Christ Child before an image of the Virgin, in her honor. Joinville would have called it prayer in action.

The *Deus absconditus* impression conveyed by the mystical choir of Coutances is another of its ravishing qualities. As at Bourges and Le Mans, the inner aisle is so high that it possesses its own triforium and clearstory; however, it avoided the stunted aspect of Bourges' main clearstory by omitting the triforium altogether in the central vessel. The choir of Coutances has retained more of the warmth of atmosphere that induces piety of soul than any other Norman cathedral, save that of Rouen. Not mere brilliant talent, but genius and faith, built it. It is almost triple-aisled, inasmuch as columns were planted in the outer aisle slightly before the walls that divide the radiating chapels. Throughout the church are these lesser arrangements that charm—such, the opening of the nave's chapels, one on the other above the dividing walls. The ends of the transept have tribunes like many Romanesque churches of the duchy. There are the usual Norman characteristics of a double-walled clearstory with different tracery in each wall, friezes of sculptured foliage, balustrades, acutely pointed arches, pierced ornament, and a generous multiplication of molds, each with its own support.

Two architects designed the church; one made the nave and the other—thought by M. Lefèvre-Pontalis to be the same Thomas Toustain who planned the apse of Le Mans Cathedral—constructed the choir, lantern, transept, and perhaps the spires of the western towers. Under Bishop Jean d'Essay (1251-74) the cathedral was finished. Louis IX was the guest of that prelate when he came to render thanks at the national shrine of St. Michael for his safe return from Palestine.

The west façade of Coutances is very Norman: plain portals, no rose window, and a staircase on a corner of each belfry. The lines of the towers rise uncrossed by horizontal bar from ground to tapering point. "Ponder them well," old Villard de Honnecourt would have said before the faithful sentinel towers of Coutances, that seem planted "like the spear of a man-at-arms." This severe church front was not meant for romance like the façade of foreign-trading Rouen, or for royal pageants like that of wine-growing Rheims. The basic forces that lead to architectural character were different here. Northern men in an outpost of France facing the dangers of the sea, built the façade of Coutances, men who had won this province by the sword, who with the sword were seekers for new conquests to the north, to the south. Taken with the central tower, the belfries of Coutances compose an unequaled group. The apse exterior is equally admirable; the flying buttresses, as at Notre Dame, at Paris, clear both aisles of the choir by a single hardy leap.

The adventurers of Normandy who made the brilliant, if ephemeral, kingdoms of Apulia, Sicily, and Antioch, were the sons and grandsons of a Norman knight called Tancred de Hauteville,[369] whose manor lay not far from Coutances.

[369] Near Hauteville-sur-mer are the ruins of Hambye Abbey, whose destruction was an irreparable loss for art, since its church was Primary Gothic. On the road from Coutances to Cherbourg is the abbatial of Lessay (a contemporary of St. Étienne at Caen), said by M. Arcisse de Caumont to be one of the purest models of Norman Romanesque, an austere monument of the XI-century type. Differences in the pier's profiles show where, in the nave, the XII century resumed work. In this latter period Gothic ribs were prepared for from the planting of the piers, but the actual diagonals of the nave were built in the XIII century. Mr. John Bilson claims that the Gothic ribs of the two sections preceding the apse are of the XI century, which again brings up the controversy of priority in the use of diagonals.

The Cistercian church of La Blanche at Mortain was another abbatial of the Manche, dedicated in 1206. At Cerisy-la-Forêt the abbey church was begun (c. 1130) by the Fécamp school of William of Volpiano, continued by Duke Robert the Magnificent, and finished by his son William the Conqueror. The nave was built from west to east in the last quarter of the XI century, the apse slightly after 1100, the actual vaulting a century later. The religious wars and the Revolution sacked the abbatial; in 1811 its demolition was still going on.

The people have chosen to call certain statues on their cathedral's northern outer wall by the names of Roger and Robert de Hauteville, and their descendants of the next generation—Bohemund, who used the Holy Wars to push his own fortunes, and his cousin, Tancred, the idealist of the First Crusade. Probably the "Tancred" statues—which now are restorations—were intended by the XIII-century sculptors for Hebrew kings. In the southern kingdoms founded by the stalwart offshoots of a simple knight of Normandy, the local architectural traits predominated, but such Norman influences appear as the central lantern and intercrossing arches (at Monreale), acutely pointed arches, and lobed rosettes cut in the spandrels (in the hospital at Palermo), west towers with corner staircases in turrets, an aisle preceding the chapels that open on the east wall of the transept (the cathedral of Cefalu, c. 1145). There are Norman traits in the cathedrals of Bari and Barletta, the latter having false tribunes like those of Eu and Rouen.[370]

At Coutances the XIV century added side chapels to the cathedral. During a siege in 1356, English stone bullets damaged the church; Charles V had it restored and fortified. Bishop Silvester de Cervelle (1371-86) built the Lady chapel, some lateral chapels, and added to the façade its only ornamentation—the colonnade connecting the towers. When Jeanne d'Arc's good name was to be vindicated, a bishop of Coutances was named by Rome as one of the three judges in the process of rehabilitation. "Would to God," exclaimed the pope, "that I had bishops of Coutances. The Church would be well governed." Olivier de Longueil, *vir gravis, vir bonus, vir mutis* (like his own cathedral), was endowed with the ideal qualities for a judge—independence and firmness. His boyhood friends were the Estouteville brothers, one the defender of the Mount, and the other the most active agent in the clearing of the Maid's name.

The cathedral of Coutances suffered much in the religious wars. So devastated was it in 1562, when from end to end of Normandy, as at a given signal, priests were slaughtered at the altar, tombs violated, church windows broken, and images shattered, that it lay long unused. The collapse of some vault sections made a thorough restoration necessary.

To the south of Coutances, at Avranches,[371] once stood another cathedral of Normandy, begun in 1109, dedicated in 1120, and later changed to Gothic. It was exceptional in having no transept. An inscription in the street marks the spot where, before its northern portal, Henry II of England did public penance in 1172,

Congrès Archéologique, 1908, p. 242, "Lessay," Lefèvre-Pontalis; p. 553, "Cerisy-la-Forêt," André Rhein; *Congrès Archéologique*, 1860, on Cherbourg; *La Normandie monumentale et pittoresque. Manche*, p. 173, "Lessay"; p. 1, "St. Lô"; p. 51, "Carentan"; p. 73, "Cerisy-la-Forêt"; p. 153, "Hambye"; R. Le Conte, *Études hist. et archéol. sur les abbayes bénédictines en général, et sur celle de Hambye en particulier* (Bernay, 1890).

[370] Camille Enlart, *L'influence extérieure de l'art normand au moyen âge*; ibid., *Origines françaises de l'architecture gothique en Italie* (Paris, Thorin, 1894); Ch. Diehl, *Palerme et Syracuse* (Collection, Villes d'art célèbres), (Paris, H. Laurens, 1907); Miss C. Waern, *Medieval Sicily* (London, 1910); Émile Bertaud, *L'art dans l'Italie méridionale*; F. Chalandon, *Histoire de la domination normande en Italie et en Sicile* (Paris, 1907); E. Curtis, *Roger of Sicily* (New York, 1912).

[371] Doctor Coutan, *La cathédrale d'Avranches* (Rouen, Cagniard, 1902); *La Normandie monumentale et pittoresque. Manche*, vol. 2, p. 65, "Avranches."

and received absolution from the papal legate for his guilt in the murder of St. Thomas Becket. Alas! like the cathedrals of Cambrai and Arras, the Revolution brought about the ruin of Avranches. *"L'égalité s'était faite dans les ruines,"* says one of its biographers. After the sacking of 1794 the historic church collapsed. Ruskin has nobly lamented its loss: "Did the cathedral of Avranches belong to the mob who destroyed it any more than it did to us who walk in sorrow to and fro over its foundations?"

THE GOTHIC ART OF BRITTANY[372]

Chez les Bretons un double courant: l'esprit de liberté, l'esprit de tradition; et pour les concilier, les pousser tous deux vers un même but et vers un but supérieur, la flamme, la passion de l'idéal, si ardente chez nos bardes et nos saints, si vivante, si puissante toujours dans l'âme bretonne, et qui l'a jetée tout entière dans la religion de l'idéal par excellence: la foi du Christ. Liberté, tradition, idéal: voilà le triple facteur de la vie intime et de la vie publique, de la vie nationale des Bretons.

—Léon Séché.

Brittany was a late comer in the national art and much is it to be regretted, for had her building energies been aroused during the Romanesque epoch, her storm-worn granite rock would have then best expressed her regional character. Among the few Romanesque works of Brittany are the crypt of Nantes Cathedral; the nave of St. Aubin's church within the corselet of stone at Guérande; a stalwart central tower over monastic Redon—cradle of Breton history-making, St. Gildas de Rhuys, which M. Lefèvre-Pontalis places in the first quarter of the XI century; the church of the Holy Cross, at Quimperlé, radically remade after the fall of its tower in 1862 (the Gothic-rib masonry roof beneath that tower dating before 1150); a Templar's church at Loctudy; the Bréléverez church beside Lannion. Equally rare are Brittany's Gothic monuments of the first part of the XIII century, Dol Cathedral being one of the few. As the era of Apogee Gothic drew to a close the cathedrals

[372] Anatole Le Braz, *La Bretagne* (Collection, Les provinces françaises), (Paris, H. Laurens); *ibid., Histoire de Bretagne* (Collection, Les vieilles provinces de France), (Paris, Bouvin); *ibid., Au pays des pardons* (translated, London, Methuen, 1906); Abbé J. M. Abgrall, *Architecture bretonne; études des monuments du diocèse de Quimper* (Quimper, 1904); *ibid., Paysages et monuments des Côtes-du-Nord*; Gautier du Mottay, *Répertoire archéol. des Côtes-du-Nord*; H. du Cleuziou, *Bretagne artistique et pittoresque* (Paris, 1886); *Bulletin de la Soc. archéol. du Finistère,* 1901, vol. 28, p. 264, "Le vieux Morlaix"; and 1902, vol. 30, p. 24, "Le vieux Quimperlé"; A. de Lorme, "L'art breton du XIIIe au XVIIe siècle," in *Bulletin de la Soc. archéol. du Finistère,* 1901, vol. 28, p. 264; Taylor et Nodier, *Voyages pittoresque ... dans l'ancienne France, La Bretagne* (Paris, Didron, 1845-46), 2 vols.; André, *La verrerie et les vitraux peint dans l'ancienne province de Bretagne* (1878); Léon Palustre, *La Renaissance en France,* vol. 2, "La Bretagne" (Paris, Quantin, 1885), 3 vols., folio; De la Borderie, *Histoire de Bretagne,* vol. 3, from 995 to 1364, and vol. 4, from 1364 to 1522 (Rennes, 1896-1900); *ibid., Mosaïque bretonne* (Rennes, Plihon et Hervé); De la Villemarqué, éd., *Barzas-Breiz; chants populaires de la Bretagne,* ninth edition (1892), 2 vols.; F. M. Luzel, *Gwerziou Briez-Izel* (epics) and *Soniou* (lyrics), (Lorient, 1868-74), 3 vols.; Siméon Luce, *Histoire de Bertrand Duguesclin et de son épogue* (1883); Leroux de Lincy, *Vie de la reine Anne de Bretagne* (1860); A. Robida, *La veille France, Bretagne* (Paris, 1891).

at Quimper, St. Pol-de-Léon, and Tréguier were rising. So was that rude mass of granite, the cathedral at St. Brieuc, and the churches of Rosporden and Guingamp.

In the XIV century was built the Kreisker tower, parent of a generous progeny. Sea-going people are lovers of high towers, and Brittany is dotted with them. Over the flat, bleak land of Léon the *clochers à jour* are a glory. With passion the Breton admired his landmarks. As he sailed home from long months in the northern fisheries, they were the first signals of welcome. To express his affection, he sometimes inscribed the Canticle of Canticles on his tower: "Who is this that cometh up from the desert flowing with delights?" No village felt itself too humble to attempt an imitation of the Kreisker at St. Pol-de-Léon.

By far the greater number of Breton churches belong to the Flamboyant Gothic day, and at that time the most energetic builder was Finistère, the far-western stronghold called Armorica before the Celts from Britain fled in the V and VI centuries from invading Saxons to the inviolate refuge of these other dwellers by the sea. St. Jean-du-Doigt was built from 1440 to 1513, and when almost completed, Anne, duchess of Brittany and twice queen of France, visited it to pray for a cure. Her daughter, Claude, also queen of France, was equally generous to the shrine. St. Jean's Pardon of the Fire, in the latter days of June, is one of the five big Pardons of Brittany.

Anne of Brittany's device, the ermine, is carved on many a façade of France. Both her husbands were notable art patrons. For her Charles VIII rebuilt the château at Amboise, and for her Louis XII began the château at Blois, and at Loches made an oratory that bears her name. The *Book of Hours* of Anne of Brittany has never been surpassed. It was for her a liberal education to live in contact with her second husband's minister of state, Cardinal Georges I d'Amboise, who is said to have employed practically every Flamboyant and Renaissance architect and sculptor of the time on his château at Gaillon, and whose tomb in Rouen Cathedral retains much of the truly French spirit of Michel Colombe's school. Brittany benefited artistically by the royal marriages of her last duchess: Anne gave the Breton Colombe the opportunity to make his *chef-d'œuvre*—the splendid ducal tomb in Nantes Cathedral.

The ermine of Anne of Brittany adorns the lintel of Folgoët, to which she added a tower, after her visit in 1505. That stately late-Gothic collegiate church, standing in a little Breton village above Landerneau, possesses an apostle porch—a feature popular in Brittany—a richly sculptured *jubé* of three arcades, and altars of green Kersanton granite. On one of its altars the corporation of masons carved compass, rule, and hammer. And in like manner, as emblems of patriotic service, might be inscribed the names of the twelve villagers who, at personal sacrifice, when their church was to be demolished in 1808, bought it as a gift for their commune. On many a shrine can modern Finistère inscribe the names of those of her sons who fought for their country in the World War. Just as it was given Breton sailors of the XV century to raise the siege of Mont-Saint-Michel, so at Dixmude, in the autumn of 1914, they checked the drive toward Calais of other invaders of French soil. Brittany, with her profound cult of the dead, will consecrate one of her noblest Calvaries to the memory of Dixmude's heroes:

Que ces noms soient sur l'église!
Qu'on les lise
Sur le granit des piliers ...
Que, sur la roche sévère
D'un Calvaire,
Solitairement inscrit,
A travers la pastorale
Vespérale

Le nom du mort pousse un cri![373]

Other Flamboyant Gothic monuments of the ancient duchy are the choir of the cathedral of St. Pol-de-Léon; the cloister, porch, and central tower of Tréguier Cathedral; the chapel of Notre Dame-des-Portes at Châteauneuf-du-Faou; Notre Dame in the little city of Vitré, that claims to be, with Avignon, the most entirely mediæval walled town in France; St. Jean and Notre Dame at Lamballe, which latter XIII-century church, with foundations hewn out of the solid rock, was rebuilt and fitted with XVI-century windows; St. Mélaine, at Morlaix, rebuilt, 1482, and possessing a towering baptismal font of carved wood; and Notre Dame at Kernascleden, between Le Faouët and Guéméné, the work of two brothers named Bail.

The making of stained glass flourished in the later Middle Ages at Quimper, Tréguier, and Vannes. Good windows are to be found at Dol, Quimper, Guérande, Ploërmel (where the church has a rich Flamboyant façade pignon), at Kergoat, Moncontour, Les Iff (where the donors were the Laval-Montmorency family), at Plélan, Plogonnec, and at Penmarc'h, whose Pardon of the Rosary occurs on the first Sunday of October. Because the popular gatherings called pardons are among the basic forces that have helped to mold the architecture of the ancient duchy, they are important for the student of the builder's art.

The late-Gothic churches that cover Brittany are rich in ecclesiastical furniture, carved baptismal temples, and panels sculptured with the quaint usages of burial and marriage, or with agricultural scenes, such as those at St. Goueznon (1615), at Bannalec (1605), at La Roche-Maurice near Brest, and at Notre Dame-la-Grâce, near Guingamp, the latter two churches possessing some "storied windows richly dight." At Kerdévot is a wooden reredos, at Roscoff a very beautiful alabaster one of the XV century; at Lambadec a *jubé* dated 1480; at St. Fiacre-du-Faouët (whose pardon comes on the first Sunday of July) a rood-loft of richly carved wood, unfortunately painted in crude colors; at Quimperlé, in the church of Ste. Croix, that is fashioned in memory of the sepulcher shrine at Jerusalem, is a *jubé* almost wholly of the Renaissance.

Because of her pardons, Brittany's religious ceremonies took place largely in the open air, even as each of her tribes, each *plou*, in prehistoric times had gathered around her solemn menhirs and dolmens. Hence the Breton made much of churchyards, placing in them his Calvaries, profound expressions of a people's emotions carved primitively in the regional coarse granite. The Lord's Passion had vivified the Celtic soul ever since Christianity took possession of it. As granite is

[373] Edmond Rostand, "Le nom sur la maison," in *Le vol de la Marseillaise* (Paris, Charpentier et Fasquelle, 1919).

unyielding to sculpture, many a Breton turned to wood to express his verve, carving his church beams like the prow ends of ships.

Morlaix[374] is a good center from which to visit many of the notable revered places. Close by, in the village of Plougonven, is the oldest Calvary extant (1554). A few miles away is that of St. Thégonnec (1610), a shrine invoked for the cure of beasts, where beneath a statue of Our Lady is inscribed: "We beg you, *Madame Vièrge*, to accept our first bull." Near the church is one of the isolated chapels called ossuaries in which were gathered the bones of the past generations when they had had their turn in the churchyard's consecrated ground. The chapel bears an inscription from Maccabees: "It is therefore a holy and wholesome thought to pray for the dead, that they may be loosed from their sins." Bedrock in the Breton is his instinct to join his progenitors and his descendants in a permanence of spiritual emotion.[375] No other people of the earth risk life more freely than these frequenters of the deep-sea fisheries; nowhere is the cult of the dead more tenacious, because it is considered that they who have fallen asleep with Godliness have great grace laid up for them.

Near St. Thégonnec, at Guimiliau, is another Calvary (1581), and another ossuary and triumphal arch. The capacious church porch is lined with statues of the apostles. At Carhaix, Pleyben (1650), Cronan, and Penmarc'h, are Calvaries, and that at Lampaul is united in the same composition with the graveyard's triumphal arch. Brittany's most imposing *Calvaire*, and the most wonderful wayside shrine ever made, comprising over two hundred images in all, is at Plougastel-Daoulas, a memorial of the epidemic of 1598. The greenish Kersanton granite of which it is made is quarried close by in the harbor of Brest, and acquires with time the endurance and appearance of bronze. Breton peasants are represented playing on Breton pipes in the Entry-into-Jerusalem scene. Late comers these rough-hewn sculptures may be in the national art, but in so far as character goes they might easily belong to the XII or XIII century.

The theorist may say that the racial exclusiveness of Brittany is one of the reasons why it has not excelled in architecture and the kindred arts. That may be so. The chief concern of the Celt has ever been to save his soul. The architectural purist is prone to carp at Breton Gothic, and some even dare say that the Kreisker itself errs, in that its shaft is not sufficiently welded with its spire. Without a doubt the absence of symmetry in many churches of the ancient province is at first disturbing, but soon one comprehends that one travels in Brittany not for its architecture,

---

[374] A son of Morlaix, Émile Souvestre (1806-54), has written lovingly of Brittany: "Il y a quelque chose de bien supérieure à la louange; la conscience que l'on a été compris et que l'on est aimé pour son œuvre. *Aimé pour son œuvre!* Je sais mieux que personne ce qui manque à ce que j'écris. Il faut quelque chose d'ondoyant. J'appartiens à cette terre Celtique où les monuments sont des pierres non taillées."

[375] "Campagnes bretonnes, qu'on dirait toujours recueillies dans le passé ... grandes pierres qui couvrent les lichens gris ... plaines où le granit affleure le sol antique.... Ce sont des impressions de tranquillité, d'apaisement, que m'apporte ce pays; c'est aussi une aspiration vers un repos plus complet sous la mousse."

—Pierre Loti, Mon frère Yves.

but for the unconquerable soul of a people who, while devoted to tradition, have ever stood up uncowed, unswerving in their antagonism to despotism. The sensitive traveler—that is, the man with kindly, plain loyalties—will let himself grow attached to the mediocre, irregular churches of this individual land.

Some of those irregularities are startling enough. The pilgrimage church of Guingamp has a curious two-storied triforium, and flying buttresses inside the choir over the aisles. Its nave is an amalgam, one wall Gothic and its vis-à-vis a fluted-pilastered Renaissance affair. The sculptor gave his initiative full scope in the apostle's porch—a revered spot on the days of Guingamp's famous pardon, that precedes the first Sunday of July. At Dinan, in the church of St. Sauveur—in whose transept is treasured the heart of Duguesclin, born not far away—a Romanesque wall faces a Flamboyant Gothic one. In the corsair stronghold of St. Malo,[376] breeder of strong men, the cathedral's walls make no pretense to be parallel.

The Breton has been too engrossed in keeping warm in his churches the spirit of devotion to bother about such details as symmetry. Eagerly he added chapel to chapel, aisle to aisle, regardless how difficult it might be for a stranger to orient himself on entering. The wise traveler will accept Brittany as she is, for if he does not, Brittany, like Spain, will exasperate him by her tranquil indifference to his criticisms. On a mediæval tower of the castle at St. Malo was inscribed:

> Grumble who will.
> So shall it be
> As pleases me.[377]

THE CATHEDRAL AT DOL-EN-BRETAGNE[378]

> Bretagne, ô mon pays, garde ta foi naïve,
> Car Dieu se plaît surtout dans la simplicité;
> C'est comme le miroir d'une source d'eau vive,
> Où vient se réfléchir, l'astre de vérité.

> —JOSEPH ROUSSE, *Poésies bretonnes*.

Brittany may be a land of shrines more than of churches; nevertheless, some five of its former nine bishoprics are of interest in the Gothic story—Dol, Nantes,

[376] The men of St. Malo have been pioneers under one aspect or another, sea rovers, like Duguay-Trouin, Surcouf, or Jacques Cartier, who, in 1535, knelt in the cathedral, where an inscription marks the pavement, to receive episcopal blessing before he sailed to discover Canada. Other sons of St. Malo have been the astronomer, Maupertius (1698-1756); Lamennais (1782-1854); and Chateaubriand (1768-1848), who chose for his burial the barren island of Grand Bé, offshore.

[377] "Quiqu'en grogne, Ainsi sera: C'est mon plaisir."

[378] André Rhein, "La cathédrale de Dol," in *Bulletin Monumental*, 1910, vol. 74, p. 367; A. Ramé, "La cathédrale de Dol; tombeau de l'évêque Thomas James," in *Mélanges d'archéologie bretonne*, 1858, vol. 2, p. 10; T. Gautier, *La cathédrale de Dol*; Ch. Robert, *Guide de tourist archéologique à Dol* (Dol-de-Bretagne, 1892); Léon Palustre, *La Renaissance en France*, vol. 2, "La Bretagne," p. 87, on Dol (Paris, Quantin, 1885); Paul Vitry, *Michel Colombe et la sculpture française de son temps* (Paris, 1901); A. de Montaiglon, "La sculpture française à la Renaissance: la famille des Juste en France," in *Gazette des Beaux-Arts*, 1875, vol. 12, p. 394.

Quimper, St. Pol-de-Léon, and Tréguier.

The hardy outpost of Dol, in the north, has stood many a siege, fought many a battle, and its church walls are crenelated where they face the city ramparts. The tutelary of the *ci-devant* cathedral is St. Samson, whose name keeps alive the memory of the arrival of the harassed Celts of Britain who poured "like a torrent" into Armorica during the dark centuries of the Middle Ages when the migrations of the Barbarians had wiped out Rome's civilization in England. In Dol's great eastern window, St. Samson and some monk companions are shown crossing the Channel.

The cathedral of Dol—which Stendhal admired beyond others in France—is a melancholy severe granite edifice, though probably the best Gothic of the province. Characteristics both of Normandy and the Ile-de-France appear in it. Two of the wholly detached colonnettes of each pier are now clamped with metal bands, and the wide arches of the triforium would be better suited to open on a gallery than as they are at present—set close to a blank wall; a few doors in the wall give on the lean-to roof over the aisles. The structure of the church demonstrates that, as the works rose, extra supports were added for stability.

The cathedral was begun by its nave soon after a conflagration of the town, in 1203, caused by the troops of John Lackland. Vestiges only of the wrecked church were retained. The façade's southern tower is late work, despite its Romanesque character, and its fellow belfry to the north is in larger part of the XVI century. Out of the nave's southern flank opens a graceful XIII-century porch. The choir, which ends in a flat eastern wall, was finished by 1265, when was installed its splendid big window of eight medallion panels that set forth the Last Judgment. In the XIV century was opened the arch leading to the Lady chapel of that same date, wherein were used various supplementary ribs, around windows and in corners, to obviate the difficulty of vaulting a square-ended edifice. To the XIV century, too, belong the side chapels of the choir, and the big porch of St. Magloire before the transept's southern door.

Against the blank wall that closes the north arm of the transept stands the much-discussed Renaissance tomb of Bishop Thomas James. It is an initial work of the Juste brothers of Tours, the ablest among the Italians who brought the new art standards across the Alps. The bishop's recumbent image has disappeared. From 1482 to 1504 he held the see of Dol, though only in residence after 1486, as he lived in Rome, the papal guardian of the castle of St. Angelo. In his testament he requested a simple burial, but his nephews—whose profiles adorn the tomb—chose to erect this elaborate monument, whose cream-colored fine-grained stone, delicately arabesqued, contrasts happily with the dark granite walls. One of the nephews had known the Juste, or Betti brothers, in Florence, and through him those artists came to France. In his prime Jean Juste made the tomb of Louis XII and Anne of Brittany for the Royal Abbey at St. Denis.

THE CATHEDRAL AT NANTES[379]

Très crestien, franc royaume de France,
Dieu a les braz ouvers pour t'acoler,
Prest d'oublier ta vie pécheresse:
Requier pardon, bien te vendra aidier
Nostre Dame, la très puissante princesse,
Qui est ton cry et que tiens pour maistresse.
Les saints aussy te viendront secourir,
Desquelz les corps font en toy demourance.
Ne vueilles plus en ton péchié dormir
Très crestien, franc royaume de France!

—CHARLES D'ORLÉANS (1391-1465).

The cathedral of St. Peter, at Nantes, the third on the site, is a late-Gothic structure, not overvirile, somewhat artificial, but ingenious and elegant, even as is the contemporary verse of Charles d'Orléans, who was taken prisoner at Agincourt and passed half a lifetime in exile. M. Gaston Paris has drawn attention to the similarity between XV-century architecture and XV-century poetry. Is not that bijou of artistry, the chapel of St. Hubert, which Anne of Brittany's first husband set on the cliff edge at Amboise, of the same quality as a rondel of the poet-duke's? Is not Villon's ironic, tragically-true note reflected in the Dance of Death painted on church walls during those years of pest and internecine strife? Brittany has retained one of the only two surviving *danses macabres*, in the hamlet of Kermaria,[380] the house of Mary, that lies between the villages of Plehedel and Plouha. In Auvergne, at La Chaise Dieu, is the other.

In 1431 Jean V, of the third ducal line of Brittany, the de Montforts, decided to remake the cathedral of the outpost city wherein stood his castle. Nantes never was *Bretagne bretonnante*, being differentiated from Finistère amid its rocky seacoast, by its position on the Loire of commerce and art. That wonderful river, in an eight-hundred-mile course from Languedoc to Brittany, passes some of the fairest monuments of France: Le Puy, Nevers, La Charité, St. Satur, St. Benoît, Orléans, Blois, Chaumont, Amboise, Tours, Langeais—where Anne of Brittany wedded Charles VIII—Saumur, St. Florent, Gennes, Cunault, and the castle and cathedral of Nantes.

Under ducal patronage the nave of Nantes Cathedral rose apace; the capitals of its north side have deeply undercut curly-tipped foliage, but on the nave's

[379] *Congrès Archéologique*, 1856 and 1886; Guilhermy, "Monuments des bords de la Loire; Nantes," in *Annales archéol.*, 1845, vol. 2, p. 87; J. Montfort, "La crypte de la cathédrale de Nantes," in *Bulletin Monumental*, 1884, vol. 50, pp. 368, 449; Paul Vitry, *Michel Colombe et la sculpture française de son temps* (Paris, 1901); Lambin de Lignum, *Recherches historiques sur l'origine et des ouvrages de Michel Colombe*; Benj. Fillon, *Poitou et Vendée* (1846); Travers, *Histoire ... du comté de Nantes*, 3 vols.

[380] Félix Soleil, *La danse-macabre de Kermaria-an-Isquit* (St. Brieuc, 1882); Émile Mâle, *L'art religieux de la fin du moyen âge en France*, chap. 2, "La danse macabre" (Paris, Colin, 1910); Lucien Bégule, *La chapelle de Kermaria Nisquit et la danse des morts* (Paris, 1911); Abbé J. M. Abgrall, *Le mobilier artistique des églises bretonnes* (Quimper, Cotonnec, 1898).

south side the piers lack capitals altogether. The interior of the church is of glacial aspect; light floods it pitilessly. Its eastern end is modern. In 1886 was unearthed a Romanesque crypt which Abélard must have known, for he was born in a manor close by Nantes, and returned to live here in 1136.

Guillaume Dammartin, of the notable family of Flamboyant Gothic architects, is mentioned as working on Nantes Cathedral, and M. Arthur de la Borderic, Brittany's historian, has discovered that an artist of Tours, Mathelin Rodier, was master-of-works when the western portals were sculptured (1470-80), and while the stately inner-court façade of the duke's château was rising. In that castle Anne of Brittany was born in 1477, became a reigning duchess at twelve years of age, and in its chapel was married, in 1499, to Louis XII. On her deathbed she willed her heart to her native city. She completed the castle of Nantes by what is called the Horseshoe Tower overlooking the river.

Anne must have known the master, Mathelin Rodier, who made the portals of the cathedral, decorating them with the same undercut leaf foliation, the same lavish splayed ornaments as adorn the contemporary western doors of Tours Cathedral, a hundred and thirty miles to the east. The larger statues at Nantes' entrances have been destroyed, but in the voussures are many small groups, sometimes with four or five personages in a scene, chiseled with natural attitudes and expressive faces. One of the portals commemorates St. Peter (observe the *Quo Vadis* episode), another, St. Paul, while the place of honor is given to the Saviour. Within the church, under the organ, are XV-century statues, one of which represents the duke patron who began the cathedral, the grandfather of Anne of Brittany.

Through the filial piety of Anne, her birthplace possesses the *canto cygni* of Gothic sculpture, "the most unscathed monument of the Middle Ages," intact because it was taken apart and buried during the Revolution. The tomb of Anne's parents, Francis II, the last duke of Brittany, and his duchess, is the work of a Breton, for an authentic manuscript has proved that Michel Colombe was born in Finistère, within sight of the Kreisker. His genius was fortified by long years passed in the art atmosphere of Tours, and strengthened, too, by the Flemish realism which had come into France by way of the Dijon school that led the first half of the XV century, even as the school of Tours, whose chief master was Colombe, led its latter half. Nor did this Breton, fecundated by Touraine and sturdy Burgundy, ignore the incoming Italian culture, as is shown by his preference for ideal beauty over absolute realism: Celt, Teuton, and Latin—all were needed for the making of the last of the great Gothic masters, one who held loyally to the spiritual essence of the Middle Ages in a day when Renaissance pomp was fast rising to supremacy.

Michel Colombe was seventy years of age when Anne of Brittany, on a visit to Tours shortly after her second marriage, commissioned him to make a mausoleum for her parents, for which she had imported white marble from Genoa, and black from Liège. From 1502 to 1507 Colombe worked on the larger images, in his studio at Tours. His are the recumbent figures of the duke and duchess, and the entrancing little angels who support their headcushion, ministering with the same loving willingness as the XII-century angels of Senlis' lintel. From Colombe's master hand are the four allegorical figures at the corners of the tomb, robust and graceful women, of the local type to be seen in central France to-day. They typify qualities of the defunct, Fortitude, Temperance, Prudence, and Justice—this last image said to be a study from Duchess Anne herself.

Centuries later a similar arrangement of symbolic figures was used by Paul Dubois for his noble tomb of General de Lamoricière (a son of Nantes), which balances, in the north arm of the transept, the ducal tomb to the south. Valor, Faith, Charity, and History, are the four corner statues that commemorate the pioneer of civilization in French Africa, who was so loved by the natives that he went freely among them unarmed, a modern hero who proved himself a true Breton by assuming the leadership of a lost cause.

Lesser masters of the school of Tours worked on the noted ducal tomb of Nantes; Guillaume Regnault made the small images and Jerome of Fiesole the arabesques, the same two masters who composed the tomb of the children of Anne of Brittany and Charles VIII, now in the cathedral at Tours. And when Michel Colombe had finished his statues, Anne had the Lyons master, Jean Perréal, one of the most active agents in popularizing in France the new art standards of Italy, visit Nantes to supervise the erection of the mausoleum whose ordinance he had designed.

THE CATHEDRAL OF QUIMPER[381]

Ce qui me charme en toi, Quimper de Cornouailles,
C'est ton cœur paysan sous tes airs de cité.

—ANATOLE LE BRAZ.

Like the chief church at St. Pol-de-Léon, and that of Tréguier, St. Corentin at Quimper is "widowed of its bishop." Admirably situated, it stands with all the dignity of a cathedral above the pleasant little "river city of gables and fables," which etches itself on the memory. It is a well-cared-for shrine, full of warm Breton piety, seen at its richest during the pardon gatherings of August 15th.

Bishop Rainaud laid the first stone of Quimper Cathedral in 1239. Its ambulatory copied a disposition first used in Soissons Cathedral, but repeated only here and at Bayonne, though across the Rhine it became popular. The vault ribs of each chapel meet in the same keystone as the ribs of that section of the procession path on which the chapel opens. About 1280 a little shrine, which had stood in the rear of the cathedral, separated from it by a lane, was joined to the ambulatory of the new Gothic choir by means of a canted bay. This improvised Lady chapel increased the irregular alignment of the church. The deviation of Quimper's axis is extraordinary. Standing in its central aisle, at the rear of the nave, you cannot see the first of the three bays that usually are apparent at the apse curve, and such

---

[381] R. F. Le Men, *Monographie de la cathédrale de Quimper* (Quimper, 1877); Abbé J. M. Abgrall, "Autour du vieux Quimper," in *Bulletin de la Soc. archéol. du Finistère*, 1901, vol. 28, p. 79; *ibid., L'architecture bretonne, étude des monuments du diocèse de Quimper* (1882); Thomas, *La cathédrale de Quimper* (1892); P. Peyron, "Les églises et chapelles du diocèse de Quimper," in *Bulletin de la Soc. archéol. du Finistère*, vol. 20, pp. 129, 451; vol. 31, pp. 18, 216, 304; vol. 32, p. 183.

is the bend of the choir that its southern aisle possesses one more bay than does the aisle to the north. When the time came to replace the Romanesque nave by the actual one, that new Gothic edifice might have straightened somewhat the axial line by following the false orientation of the choir. But apparently the proximity of the episcopal quarters prevented this being done.

The choir of St. Corentin retains the canopy-image windows of Jamin Sohier (1417), and the nave, those of the Jamin Sohier of a second generation; a western window is dated 1496. The shield and helmet of one of Brittany's dukes of the Montfort line, Anne's immediate forebear, adorn the gable of the main façade. The cathedral works ceased during the first part of the Hundred Years' War; the choir was not roofed in stone till the first quarter of the XV century. In 1424 the nave was begun and the foundations of the west towers laid. Quimper's towers derive directly from the famous one of St. Pierre at Caen. There are the same deep, elongated twin-window recesses serving as buttresses. After another period of inactivity, the cathedral's nave was vaulted. In the latter part of the XIX century the west towers received their crowning of crocketed spires, paid for by a popular collection called "the penny of St. Corentin."

How these dwellers by the sea love their obsolete local saints! How certain they are that to forget them is to lose infinitely precious links with the past. The solidarity of ancestors with descendants is no dead letter in Finistère, that lives not by bread alone. One knows that the white-coiffed women of Quimper—and their daily gathering in their mediæval church makes a brave showing—would not love this shrine of St. Corentin so well had it a name common to western Christendom. But St. Corentin, St. Tugdual, St. Huec, St. Iltud, St. Budoc, St. Jacut, St. Jubel, St. Gulstan, St. Comery—ah, those are the potent ones before the heavenly throne when a true Breton needs assistance!

THE CATHEDRAL OF ST. POL-DE-LÉON[382]

O Dieu qui nous créas ou guerriers ou poètes,
Sur la côte marins, et pâtres dans les champs,
Sous les vils intérêts ne courbe pas nos têtes;
Ne fais pas des Bretons un peuple de marchands.
J'ai vu, par l'avarice ennuyés et vieillis,
Des barbares sans foi, sans cœur, sans espérance,
Et, l'amour m'inspirait, j'ai chanté mon pays.

—A. Brizeux, *L'élégie de la Bretagne.*

The most complete Gothic monument of Brittany is the whilom cathedral of St. Pol-de-Léon, one of the few important churches of the Middle Ages to be entirely carried out, with spired towers, and porches for the different needs of soul and body, one for catechumens, another for lepers. Its choir and nave differ strikingly in color and quality of stone. The nave of yellow sandstone was built first, and is

[382] L. Th. Lecureur, *La cathédrale de St. Pol-de-Léon* (Collection, Petites Monographies), (Paris, H. Laurens); Ch. Chassepied, "Notes sur la cathédrale de St. Pol-de-Léon," in *Bulletin de la Soc. archéol. du Finistère*, 1901, vol. 28, p. 304; Abbé J. M. Abgrall, *Au pays des clochers à jour* (Paris, 1902).

decidedly the most artistic portion of the edifice. The florid Gothic choir is of gray granite.

As the XIII century closed the nave was begun, continuing building up to the dire times of the Hundred Years' War. It has the Norman traits of sculptured bands of academic design below triforium and clearstory, trefoils cut in the spandrels of arches, multiple arch molds, each with its own support, and a circulation passage beneath the upper windows. The triforium was begun elaborately, with much foliate decoration, but economy soon forced the architect to adopt a simpler plan. The nave's south aisle is double beyond the fourth bay where a porch opens, and the stones show that the outer aisle was originally a separate chamber, converted during the XV century into a passageway.

The Flamboyant Gothic choir, that lacks the harmony and elegance of the nave, was built from 1439 to 1472. Chapel has been added to chapel, aisle to aisle, with the profusion loved by the Breton, who would press into God's service every foot of free land around his presbytery. The transept of the XII and XIII centuries was radically reconstructed during the late-Gothic day, retaining vestiges only of its Romanesque and early-Gothic work. It is doubtless to such repeated modelings that some of the buttresses fail to correspond to columns and vault shafts.

During a siege of St. Pol-de-Léon by the English, the church called the Kreisker, "center of the city," was injured. When rebuilt, from 1345 to 1399, there was erected, between its nave and choir, carried merely on open arches, a grandiose tower modeled on Caen's belfry of St. Pierre, as had been the twin towers of St. Pol's cathedral, lesser in height than "the Kreisker." The deeply recessed lancet openings in each face of the giant beacon serve the practical purpose of buttresses. Few cities can show three such brave towers as this little Breton town. "The Kreisker," mantled in golden lichen, is the pride of every Breton. So sure is its poise, so supple and strong, that for centuries all the wild storms of the ocean have swept unheeded through its open stonework spire. The popular songs love to extol it:

> Je suis natif du Finistère,
> A Saint-Pol j'ai reçu le jour,
> Mon clocher est l'plus beau d'la terre,
> Mon pays l'plus beau d'alentour;
> Rendez-moi ma bruyère et mon clocher à jour!

St. Pol received its name from another exile of Britain, and the good man's little bell is rung on the days of Pardon, over the heads of the people, who believe it can cure maladies of the mind. The Revolution tried to change the town's name to Port Pol, but the traditionalists and the independents that are the Bretons soon reverted to their St. Pol-de-Léon.

THE CATHEDRAL OF TRÉGUIER[383]

> Une, deux génerations peuvent oublier la Loi, se rendre coupable de tous les abandons, de toutes les ingratitudes. Mais il faut

---

[383] *Congrès Archéologique*, 1883, on Tréguier; Ch. de la Ronsiere, *Saint Yves* (Collection, Les Saints), (Paris, Lecoffre, 1901); Ernest Renan, *Souvenirs d'enfance* (1883).

bien, à l'heure marquée que la chaine soit reprise et que la petite lampe vacillante brille de nouveau dans la maison.

—Ernest Psichari (1883-1914).

The cathedral of St. Tugdual obtained its name from the founder of a local monastery, a nephew of St. Brieux, who had crossed from Britain with the returning missionary, St. Germain of Auxerre, and in Armorica had established a religious house which eventually gave its name to a Breton city. No church of the region demonstrates more clearly how difficult it is to obtain full Gothic effect with granite. Lacking sculpture, the art is necessarily abortive.

The interior of Tréguier is dark and forbidding. The capitals of the graceless octagonal piers are merely uncut bands. There are Norman balustrades and a Norman interior passage below the clearstory lights. The name of the architect, Goneder, was recently unearthed by M. de la Borderie. From the previous Romanesque cathedral was retained the Tour Hastings which now terminates the northern arm of the transept. Toward the western end of the church the molds of the archivolts die off in the piers.

The nave rose from 1296 to 1333; then came the pause of the Hundred Years' War. Building was resumed—always on the original Rayonnant lines—by Bishop Jean de Coëtquis (1450-61), whose relative, of the same name, was finishing the nave of Tours Cathedral. The charming Flamboyant cloisters of Tréguier were made from 1461 to 1468, and with the Tour Hastings they compose one of the oft-sketched architectural groups of the country. St. Tugdual has suffered by wars and revolutions, being damaged by the English in 1347, by the Spaniards in 1592, the Liguers in 1594, and the Revolution's cyclone passing here as elsewhere.

In the nave of Tréguier Cathedral stands a sumptuous Gothic monument to honor Brittany's patron saint, Yves de Helori, born in 1253, a mile from the town in the manor of Kernartin—modern Minihy. On the nineteenth of every May Tréguier marches in procession to Minihy to commemorate the good man who cleared the region of evil-doers, built a hospital beside his home that he might himself wait on the stricken, rose at midnight to chant matins, preached sometimes five sermons a day, and was the poor man's lawyer, so a popular hymn relates: "An advocate and not a thief, a thing almost beyond belief." The pardon of St. Yves, the Pardon of the Poor, is one of the five chief ones of Brittany. For centuries those who had pending law cases repaired to his primitive tomb. Thus Henry VII, Tudor, crossed from England the year before he won his kingship, to petition the favor of the Breton saint who had supported only just causes in law. Universities selected him as their patron.

St. Yves was the son of a knight who went crusading with St. Louis. When sent, at fourteen, to Paris University, he sat with other young scholars on the rush-strewn floors to listen to the scholastics; even in his student days he visited the sick poor in the hospitals. Before thirty he entered the episcopal magistry, and henceforth his abilities were devoted to the relief of orphans and widows. This good man, after whom myriads of the sons of Brittany have been named, worked assiduously, it is said, to collect funds for the building of the Gothic cathedral of

Tréguier.

In a street near the cloisters of St. Tugdual, Ernest Renan was born in 1828, his name deriving from an Irish anchorite of VI-century Armorica. From his Breton father he derived his gravity, respect, faith, and imagination; from his mother's Gascon stock his irony, gayety, and serenity in skepticism, the result being, as he himself said, a tissue of contradictions. Brittany took his *Vie de Jésus* as a personal affront. That a son of hers, once destined for the priesthood, should call her dear Christ of Calvary a "sorcerer," a "demi-impostor," a *"géant sombre,"* *"un fin et joyeux moralist,"* pierced her to the soul. When, beside the cathedral of Tréguier, partisan politics raised a Renan statue (singularly inartistic), whose inscription was taken as an affront by every believing Christian, two million Bretons donated toward the erection of a monumental protest. The Calvary of Reparation stands at the entrance to Tréguier, voicing the cry attributed to the dying Julian the Apostate, "Thou hast conquered, Galilæan!"

The son of Renan's daughter was that chosen soul, Ernest Psichari, who fell defending Belgium in August, 1914, a death considered by mystic Brittany to be an atonement. He has told of his spiritual anguish, "without defense against evil, without protection against sophistry, wandering without conviction in the poisoned gardens of vice, sick to the soul and ever pursued by obscure remorse, weighed down by the bitter derision of a life ruled by disordered sentiments and thoughts." In his *Appel des Armes* and his *Voyage du Centurion* he has traced his pilgrimage from materialism to Christian belief, taking *"contre son père le parti de ses pères."* His grandfather, of Tréguier, in Armorica, had written many years earlier: "The characteristic trait of the Breton race is idealism—the disinterested pursuit of a moral or intellectual aim. The Celt craves the Infinite. He thirsts for it, seeking it beyond all the prizes of the world."

A SUMMING UP

All our France is in our cathedrals.... Initiation into the beauty of Gothic is initiation into the truth of our race, of our sky, of our landscape.... Gothic art is the sensible, tangible soul of France; it is the religion of the French atmosphere. We are not incredulous; we are merely unfaithful. We have lost at the same time the sense of our race and of our religion. To regain force we must live again in the past, revert to first principles. Taste reigned of yore in our country: we must become French again.

—RODIN, LES CATHÉDRALES DE FRANCE.

With many a gap, with many a lapse, we have followed the earlier stages of Gothic art in the land where it was born. We have seen how, from the efforts of the monks to cover their Romanesque naves with a permanent stone roof, was evolved the intersecting rib vault which was the basis of Gothic architecture, how for a short time churches used the Romanesque and Gothic systems simultaneously as in Morienval and Poissy, and for another short period the churches were Gothic in essentials while retaining a few traits of the earlier phase. By many the imperishable hour that produced Soissons' transept, the choir of St. Remi, Notre Dame at Laon, and Notre Dame at Paris, is beyond all others. When the national art expanded into its full flowering in the XIII century — an era as great in men and the making of history as in art — Gothic science, though ever seeking, ever reaching out, remained disciplined, even as the scholastic builders themselves were disciplined.

While eighty cathedrals in France were rising, and in the same hour some hundreds of lesser churches, the rulers of the nation were capable warriors, compilers of laws, and administrators, the builders were monarchs, crusading bishops, troubadour counts, cloistral ascetics, and arduous sinners. Serf, artisan, burgher, baron, and king built the cathedrals; field laborer, minstrel, maiden, and chatelaine were harnessed to the same cart to drag in the great stones. Little children cleared the church pavement of sand and cement in preparation for the "Day of Benediction" for their city, as the solemn blessing of their church was held to be by those God-fearing generations.

The new school of mediæval archæology, that during three generations has been interpreting the Gothic churches of France, is teaching us to read the stones with sympathy. "Symbol of Faith, the cathedral was also a symbol of Love," says M. Émile Mâle. "All men labored there. The peasants offered their all, the work of their strong arms. They pulled carts and carried stones on their shoulders with the brave good will of the giant-saint, Christopher. The burgess gave his money, the baron his land, the artist his genius. During more than two centuries every vital force in France collaborated on the cathedrals. From that comes the puissant life emanating from these eternal monuments. The dead, too, were associated with the living, for the cathedral was paved with tombstones, and the earlier generations, with hands joined in prayer, continued to worship in their ancient church. Past and present were united in the same feeling of love. The cathedral was the very conscience, the very soul of the city."[384]

After five generations had reared so many and such magnificent churches, their energy, because it was human, passed from plenitude into decline. The death of St. Louis, in 1270, may be taken as the beginning of the change, though even before had been used various cut-and-dried Rayonnant features. Genius flagged when structural perfection was achieved. The divinely restless reaching out of art was stultified by geometric rule. Graceful and stately as is many a XIV-century church, never in them do we find the unexpected entrancing touches of Apogee Gothic. Gothic was fast becoming an art made tongue-tied by authority.

As time went on profiles deteriorated, sharp prismatic molds succeeding to the virile torus, or molds fluid and vague. By the XV century capitals were omitted altogether. The sane marking of the horizontal line had become an offense to the eye. Without capitals the molds died away weakly in the piers. Flamboyant Gothic architecture exhibited all these traits, and, moreover, gave capricious rein to many a redundant detail, yet it was none the less a phase of art far more vigorous <u>and satisfactory</u> than the Rayonnant geometric period, its predecessor. The verve

[384] Émile Mâle, *L'art religieux au XIIIe siècle en France*, p. 442 (Paris, Colin, 1908). (Trans. by Dora Mussey, London, Dent & Sons, New York, Dutton, 1913).

and abundance of Flamboyant Gothic was a rebirth. The inspiration of St. Jeanne d'Arc, the restored political unity, the increase of trade, the love of pageantry, all aided the art renaissance which was in progress before the advent of Italian ideas. No one can say that Gothic architecture ended in decrepitude who knows such masterpieces as the façades of Rouen and Beauvais, the towers at Bordeaux, Rodez, and Chartres, the baldaquin and choir screen of Albi, or statuary as ample in its simplicity as Riom's Virgin of the Bird and "the Saints" at Solesmes. And from end to end of France, as the XVI century opened, such work was in progress.

What, then, killed Gothic art? For it was slain with all this warm blood in its veins. Some say the return to pagan ideals dealt the death blow, the deserting of the celestial man-humble ideal for the terrestrial self-intoxicated pride of the Italian Renaissance: "The Renaissance is man seeking knowledge, happiness, and love, outside of Christianity." A Christian had knelt in prayer on a Gothic tomb, or reposed with serene confidence, awaiting the trumpet call of the archangel, a Book of Hours in his hand. On a Renaissance tomb the deceased reclined like a pagan at a feast. The Italian wars diverted from its natural channels the genius of the northern Latins (who were so strongly Celt and Frank), and in many cases the imported neo-classicism was not that of Italy's supreme masters, but of the lesser artists, their successors.

Others have contended that the printing press and the Protestant Reformation—with its spirit of hostile criticism—proved fatal to the national art, since the very life of Gothic was legend, poetry, and dreams, and symbolism its inspiration. Doubt quickly drained the sources of life. "Its charm had been to retain the candor of childhood, the limpid book of young saints. It was an art whose faith discussed not—it sang."[385] It was an art happy and bold and free of restraint, save the restraint which its own right instinct for discipline imposed—co-ordinating the multitudinous into a symmetrical unity—an art unfettered in its truth telling, daring to sculpture king or bishop marching to Hell, yet giving no offense to authority by so doing.

Alas, one must acknowledge that the Church, so long the guardian of Gothic art, dealt a deadly blow at the sweet naïve gayety of the Middle Ages. To reform Catholic Christendom there gathered at Trent a much-needed Council, impregnated with the critical spirit which Luther had unloosed. Pious churchmen had come to look askance on legends. They were ashamed of the simplicities which the XIII-century man was so certain pleased Our Lady, who accepted them with a friendly smile of comprehension of her fellow creatures. The good fathers at Trent regarded prudishly the spiritual passion of the Canticle of Canticles flaming in cathedral windows; they thought it forwardness to carve mechanics' tools on altar stones. Such manifestations were excessive. What would our critics of Wittem-

---

[385] "Un tel art ne pouvait être effleuré par le doute. L'art et la poésie qui émeuvent sortent du cœur et d'une région obscure où la raison n'a pas accès. L'artiste qui examine, juge, critique, doute, concilie, a déjà perdu la moitié de la force créatrice."—ÉMILE MÂLE, *L'art religieux de la fin du moyen âge en France* (Paris, Colin, 1910).

"Art addresses not pure sense, still less the pure intellect, but the imaginative reason through the senses."—WALTER PATER.

berg and Geneva say? The mystery plays, source of inspiration for the late-Gothic sculptors, now became suspect. Deprived of popular life, the religious themes grew cold. When censured, the creative instinct withered. In 1563 (a year after the iconoclastic outrages in France) the Council of Trent, at its last session, complained that Gothic artists scandalized the faithful by their childish superstitions. The Middle Ages were ended.

Cathedrals are not raised by critics or doubters. When France built her great churches, her faith was humble, her love a mounting flame. Her cathedrals were symbols of the Kingdom of God in her midst, the *pons sæculorum* whereby man passed beyond the bourne of his narrow life. They were solaces in his hours of misery, in his delinquencies; they stood for justice alike to serf and baron; they were the Sermon on the Mount made visible, the *Biblia pauperum* wherein lettered and unlettered read the same lessons; they were the *Credo* chanted by men who believed in Christ, Son of the Living God and Son of the Immaculate Virgin.

Nor should it be forgotten that the generations who raised the great cathedrals believed profoundly in themselves as God's specially loved instruments, his own selected knights-errant. "We are a race that exists to advance in the world the affairs of God," said the old Gallic patrician to Clovis the Frank, and soon a Frankish parchment ran, *"Vivat Christus qui diligit Francos."* When men feel like that they are compelled to express it grandly. When as pagans they feel it, the expression is a cataclysmic war of conquest. When they feel it as Christians, they build cathedrals. The generations whom St. Bernard purified, whom Suger trained, whom St. Louis inspired, founded their church on a firm rock, a living rock, lighted it unto a precious stone, prepared it as a bride adorned for her husband, and ever since sanctity has abided therein; kings have brought hither their honors and glory, and the glory and honor of the people have adorned the walls.

FRANCE

Because for once the sword broke in her hand,
The words she spoke seemed perished for a space;
All wrong was brazen, and in every land
The tyrants walked abroad with naked face.

The waters turned to blood, as rose the Star
Of evil fate, denying all release.
The rulers smote the feeble, crying, "War!"
The usurers robbed the naked, crying, "Peace!"
And her own feet were caught in nets of gold,
And her own soul profaned by sects that squirm,
And little men climbed her high seats and sold
Her honor to the vulture and the worm.

And she seemed broken and they thought her dead,
The Over-Man, so brave against the weak.
Has your last word of sophistry been said,
O cult of slaves? Then it is hers to speak.

Clear the slow mists from her half-darkened eyes,
As slow mists parted over Valmy fell,
And once again her hands in high surprise
Take hold upon the battlements of Hell.

—CECIL CHESTERTON (who died a soldier of the World War).

Regretfully one turns to other interests after spending years in trying to draw closer to the spirit of the Middle Ages—years that have coincided with the apocalyptic struggle that has desolated the classic region of the national art, laying low, one after another, the churches of the first fugitive hour. And watching the giant battle, it has grown clearer how indissoluble is the solidarity of modern Frenchmen with their achieving grandfathers. A nation's bulwark is the unbroken solidarity of Past with Present. And only when *la race lumineuse*, compounded of Celt, Gaul, Latin, and Frank, denies that solidarity will it be conquered.

The peasant-soldier of 1914, starting for the front, who replied with grave dignity to his well-wisher, "Whichever way it turns, I am ready,"[386] would have met death like a paladin at Roncevaux, in 778, holding up his gauntlet to God, his suzerain, certain of the justice of Him who from the grave raised Blessed Lazarus, and Daniel saved from lions.

The young tradesman of 1915 who wrote from the trenches to one who loved him: "I look on this struggle less as a war against an enemy than as a crusade to reinstate God in his place in France," was true to his *race apostolique* that sets the church bells ringing. At Clermont, in 1095, he pressed forward with the cry: "The cross! The cross! God wills it!" The priest-soldier offering sacrifice at an improvised altar within hearing of the guns, his spurs fretting his sacerdotal gown, is Turpin, guarding well the Cross and France.

The stricken lad, flung back, diseased from the prisons beyond the Rhine, weak, broken, in tatters, who cried with vibrant voice, as he and his comrades crossed the Swiss frontier, and friendly strangers gathered round: *"La tête haute! C'est nous la France!"* conquered Jerusalem with Godfrey de Bouillon in the olden days, and related his prowess in a legend-medallion window at Chartres.

Above all, lives the soul of the Past in the generalissimo to whom a righteous destiny granted the freeing of his land from invaders. In churches shattered by shell fire he knelt daily—the weightiest fruit bending lowest—and he begged that the children of Christendom lift up their little white hands to heaven to petition for his endurance. In 1249, with flashing sword and the cry, *"Montjoie-St.-Denis,"* he sprang into the surf beside his saint-king, following the oriflamme as it touched African soil. We have seen them alive again, the cathedral builders, the commune

---

[386] "Hier, pendant son congé de vingt-quatre heures, j'ai rencontré le fils d'une pauvre femme de la campagne, un ouvrier que j'aime bien depuis longtemps. Quand je l'ai quitté, et que je lui ai dit: 'Bonne chance, Marcel,' il m'a regardé de ses yeux sans reproche, et il m'a répondu: 'D'un côté ou de l'autre, je ne crains rien.' Et cela voulait dire: la vie la mort? Qu'importe! je suis prêt. Qu'est ce que tout cela. C'est la chanson de geste qui continue: c'est la croisade qui n'est point finie, c'est Dieu transparaissant à travers la France purifiée."—An episode to the World War, 1914: René Bazin, *Les Preux*.

winners, the crusaders, dying with the farewell sigh, *"Ha! doulce France!"*

And thank God the flame is unquenchable, thank God that in the French race is the underlying sentiment for the Infinite, that peasant, artisan, student, priest, and chief feel the same humility and the same proper pride as those who built Soissons, the lovely stricken virgin; and Laon the intrepid, braving the hammer of Odin and Thor; Amiens the perfect, menaced and shaken but spared to us; and tragic, immortal Rheims, symbol of a people's resurrection. To herald the dawn is the mission of France, to look on her deeds as *Gesta Dei per Francos.* "Hers is the hand that scatters the seed."

THE END.

INDEX

G

I

S

U

V

Lector House believes that a society develops through a two-fold approach of continuous learning and adaptation, which is derived from the study of classic literary works spread across the historic timeline of literature records. Therefore, we aim at reviving, repairing and redeveloping all those inaccessible or damaged but historically as well as culturally important literature across subjects so that the future generations may have an opportunity to study and learn from past works to embark upon a journey of creating a better future.

This book is a result of an effort made by Lector House towards making a contribution to the preservation and repair of original ancient works which might hold historical significance to the approach of continuous learning across subjects.

HAPPY READING & LEARNING!

LECTOR HOUSE LLP
E-MAIL: lectorpublishing@gmail.com